Architectural Reference

INSIDE

C#

Second Edition

Tom Archer
Andrew Whitechapel

Microsoft®
.net™

PUBLISHED BY
Microsoft Press
A Division of Microsoft Corporation
One Microsoft Way
Redmond, Washington 98052-6399

Copyright © 2002 by Microsoft Corporation

All rights reserved. No part of the contents of this book may be reproduced or transmitted in any form or by any means without the written permission of the publisher.

Library of Congress Cataloging-in-Publication Data
Archer, Tom.
    Inside C# / Tom Archer.--2nd ed.
      p. cm.
    Includes index.
    ISBN 0-7356-1648-5
    1. C# (Computer programming language)   I. Title.

  QA76.73.C154   A73   2002
  005 13'3--dc21   2002020763

Printed and bound in the United States of America.

3 4 5 6 7 8 9   QWT   7 6 5 4

Distributed in Canada by H.B. Fenn and Company Ltd.

A CIP catalogue record for this book is available from the British Library.

Microsoft Press books are available through booksellers and distributors worldwide. For further information about international editions, contact your local Microsoft Corporation office or contact Microsoft Press International directly at fax (425) 936-7329. Visit our Web site at www.microsoft.com/mspress. Send comments to *mspinput@microsoft.com*.

Microsoft, Microsoft Press, the .NET logo, Visual Basic, Visual C++, Visual J++, Visual Studio, and Windows are either registered trademarks or trademarks of Microsoft Corporation in the United States and/or other countries. Other product and company names mentioned herein may be the trademarks of their respective owners.

The example companies, organizations, products, domain names, e-mail addresses, logos, people, places, and events depicted herein are fictitious. No association with any real company, organization, product, domain name, e-mail address, logo, person, place, or event is intended or should be inferred.

Acquisitions Editor: Danielle Bird
Project Editor: Devon Musgrave
Technical Editor: Jim Fuchs

Body Part No. X08-68736

To Agatha and Felix.
—Andrew

To one of my very best friends, Doyle Vann. I wouldn't be here today
if it hadn't been for your support and your complete belief in me.
Thank you so much for being the one person
I could always count on.
—Tom

Contents

Foreword

I've spent my entire career at Microsoft working to enhance the developer experience, usually with a focus on increasing developer productivity. My work has spanned a wide variety of products and technologies, but I've never been as excited about the work we've done to enhance the developer experience as I am now. The breadth and depth of the technologies Microsoft .NET delivers is astounding. We're providing a great new language, knocking down the barriers that have traditionally divided developers into separate but unequal language worlds, and enabling Web sites to cooperate to meet users' needs. Any one of these would be interesting on its own, but the combination is truly compelling.

Let's look at the key building blocks of .NET and some related technologies:

- **C#, a new language** C# is the first component-oriented language in the C and C++ family of languages. It's a simple, modern, object-oriented, and type-safe programming language derived from C and C++. C# combines the high productivity of Microsoft Visual Basic and the raw power of C++.

- **Common language runtime** The high-performance common language runtime includes an execution engine, a garbage collector, just-in-time compilation, a security system, and a rich class framework (the .NET Framework). The runtime was designed from the ground up to support multiple languages.

- **Common Language Specification** The Common Language Specification (CLS) describes a common level of language functionality. The relatively high minimum bar of the CLS enables the creation of a club of CLS-compliant languages. Each member of this club enjoys dual benefits: complete access to .NET Framework functionality and rich interoperability with other compliant languages. For example, a Visual Basic class can inherit from a C# class and override its virtual methods.

- **A rich set of languages that target the runtime** Microsoft-provided languages that target the runtime include Visual Basic, Visual C++ with Managed Extensions, Visual C#, and JScript. Third parties are providing many other languages—too many to list here!

- **Web services**   Today's World Wide Web consists primarily of individual sites. While a user might visit multiple sites to accomplish a given task, such as making travel arrangements for a group of people, these Web sites typically do not cooperate. The next generation of the Web will be based on cooperating networks of Web sites. The reason is simple: cooperating Web sites can do a better job of meeting users' needs. Microsoft's Web services technologies foster cooperation among Web sites by enabling communication via standard XML-based protocols that are both language-independent and platform-independent. Many important Web services will be based on C# and the common language runtime running on Windows, but the architecture is truly open.

- **Visual Studio .NET**   Visual Studio .NET ties all of these pieces together and makes it easy to author a wide range of components, applications, and services in a variety of programming languages.

Now that I've touched on some important C#-related technologies, let's take a closer look at C# itself. Developers have a lot invested in their language of choice, and so the onus is on a new language to prove its worth through some combination of simple preservation, incremental improvement, and thoughtful innovation.

Simple Preservation

Hippocrates said, "Make a habit of two things: to help, or at least do no harm." The "do no harm" part played a prominent role in our design of C#. If a C or C++ feature addressed a problem well, we kept it without modification. Most significantly, C# borrows from C and C++ in core areas such as expressions, statements, and overall syntax. Because so much of a typical program consists of these features, C and C++ developers instantly feel comfortable with C#.

Incremental Improvement

Many incremental improvements have been made—too many to mention in this brief foreword—but it's worth calling attention to a few changes that eliminate some common and time-consuming C and C++ errors:

- Variables must be initialized before use, so bugs resulting from uninitialized variables are eliminated.

- Statements like *if* and *while* require Boolean values, so a developer who accidentally uses the assignment operator (=) instead of the equality operator (==) finds the mistake at compilation time.

- Silent fall-through in *switch* statements is disallowed, so a developer who accidentally omits a *break* statement finds the mistake at compilation time.

Thoughtful Innovation

Deeper innovation is found in C#'s type system, which includes the following advances:

- The C# type system employs automatic memory management, thereby freeing developers from time-consuming and bug-prone manual memory management. Unlike most type systems, the C# type system also allows direct manipulation of pointer types and object addresses. (These manual memory management techniques are only permitted in certain security contexts.)

- The C# type system is unified—everything is an object. Through innovative use of concepts such as boxing and unboxing, C# bridges the gap between value types and reference types, allowing any piece of data to be treated as an object.

- Properties, methods, and events are fundamental. Many languages omit intrinsic support for properties and events, creating an unnecessary mismatch between the language and associated frameworks. For instance, if the framework supports properties and the language doesn't, incrementing a property is awkward (for example, *o.Set-Value(o.GetValue( ) + 1)*). If the language also supports properties, the operation is simple (*o.Value++*).

- C# supports attributes, which enable the definition and use of declarative information about components. The ability to define new kinds of declarative information has always been a powerful tool for language designers. Now all C# developers have this capability.

Scott Wiltamuth

Visual C# .NET Group Program Manager

Microsoft Corporation

Inside C#

I claim that forewords are perhaps the most difficult rhetoric to write. Consider for a moment that with a foreword you have a very limited amount of space in which to write a compelling "introduction" that conveys both the breadth and depth of the book and that also speaks to the care with which it was written. To do this successfully, I'm of the firm belief that a foreword needs a theme, a pervasive idea that can be summed up in a single sentence. That sentence for *Inside C#* is, "It's about the details."

Scott has done an awesome job talking about why C# is a great language; now I want to spend a bit of time talking about why reading *Inside C#* is a great way to learn it. I've spent a lot of time programming in many languages over the years, and I have learned two indelible truths: it is impossible to write the "best" code, and it's only possible to write "better" code when you know the details. Let me explain the first statement a bit. As soon as a software project grows over a 100 lines or so, the domain of possible correct implementations—a correct implementation being one that gets the job done—increases to such a large number that it's essentially impossible to find *the* one that solves that domain space in the fastest, most efficient way possible. Even disregarding what people consider the best solution—"mine only has one line of code and is easily maintainable!" and "mine has 300 lines of code but executes 30 times faster!"—it should be obvious that our job as software engineers is to come up with a good solution, not necessarily the best.

Which brings me to my second point: the good solution cannot be found without knowing what bits to twiddle. Don't get me wrong; it's also impossible to write good code without good algorithms. But regardless of what those algorithms are, if they're implemented without knowledge of both the platform and language, I guarantee that taking that code one step closer to the perfect solution would be as easy as changing a class to a struct. And that leads us right back to exactly why *Inside C#* is well worth the read—because Tom delves into the details, and in the end the details lead to better code.

Anson Horton

Visual C# .NET Program Manager

Microsoft Corporation

Introduction

Why I Wrote This Book

After almost 20 years of developing software on everything from System/38s to AS/400s to OS/2 and now Microsoft Windows, I can say without reservation that I was becoming a victim of burnout. The days of looking forward to the evenings and weekends—not because it meant going home but because it meant being able to work all day and all night without interruption—were becoming a distant memory. I had the feeling that everything worth doing had already been done. That feeling changed in the early part of 2000.

Just a few months prior to Microsoft's announcement of .NET at the 2000 PDC in Orlando, Florida, a good friend of mine let me in on a little secret about a "cool" language called C# and a runtime framework (then called NGWS). Despite his obvious enthusiasm, I had a hard time shaking the memories of other ill-fated global architectures such as IBM's SAA and Microsoft's DNA. As a result, I approached it with more than my share of skepticism.

But the more I programmed with this new language and platform, the more my old enthusiasm started to return. Before long I realized that I was waking up not with the dread of writing the same ol' boring applications once again but with the anticipation of learning some new and exciting part of .NET. Well, it's almost two years later and I'm still learning. In fact, it seems that every new item I learn about .NET opens a dimension of topics that I hadn't known existed before!

Some of this might sound corny, but let's face facts" most of us started programming not for the money but for the type of fulfillment and satisfaction that only learning and creating something can bring. For me, C# and the .NET Framework have revived that old enthusiasm that I had started to lose. So, I wrote this book to share in the joy that I've experienced in having fun programming again. Hopefully, when you read this text and start using C#, you'll feel the same way.

What's New About This Edition

If you read the first edition of the book (thanks!), you're probably wondering why this edition is twice the size. Well, for the answer you have to remember

when I wrote the first edition. In the days just after the grand announcement of
.NET and C# almost anyone writing a book on either topic was in a position of
learning the subject matter while writing about it. And, as with any software
project, the more you learn, the more you wish you could start over with your
newfound knowledge. Obviously, it wasn't practical to start the book over, so
I knew at its completion that a second edition would need to be written. Here's
a high-level list of what's new in this edition. I think as you read through the list
you'll see why I was so keen on writing this edition.

■ **Much more material, including new chapters** Readers
responded to the first edition with tons of great feedback, including
their own experiences with different aspects of the language and
opinions on the language features that should have been covered in
more depth. In response to that, we took a hard look at some of the
most asked-for language and framework features and significantly
enhanced the book's coverage of those topics. Many chapters under-
went significant upgrades, and many new chapters cover issues that
the first edition did not broach. As an example, in response to reader
requests, the new "Security" chapter covers a broad array of security
issues, including code access security, role-based security, verifiable
type safety, code signing, crypto/data signing, and isolated storage.
Other new chapters include the following: "String Handling and Regular Expressions," "File I/O with Streams," "Numerical Processing
and the *Math* Class," "Collections and Object Enumeration" (my
favorite new chapter), "Pinning and Memory Management," "Using
COM from C# Applications," and "Using .NET Components in
Unmanaged Code." In addition, the very cool capability of generating XML documentation from C# source code comments is covered
in another new chapter entitled "Documentation with XML."

■ **Truly an "inside" book now** My largest goal with the second edition was to make it much more of an "inside" book. My mistake in
the first edition was that I had made the decision to go into the
Microsoft intermediate language (MSIL) layer only if I thought it
made a difference in how one would code in C#. However, as many
of you were quick to point out, we programmers are curious folks
and sometimes we like to know things simply for the sake of knowing them. To that extent, now in almost every chapter I first explain
the topic and then delve into the compiler-generated MSIL. You'd be
surprised—I know I was—at how some of these features are actually
implemented once you take the time to peek under the hood! In

addition, the chapters are organized in such a way that people who don't care about the underlying MSIL can easily skip over it. Conversely, people who already know the syntax of a given feature and how to use it don't have to muddle through those explanations and can instead jump directly to the section on the underlying MSIL.

■ **"Why" as well as "how"**   Many books detail the syntax needed for a given language feature and then give a series of examples. But you and I can get the syntax from online help. I look to a book to be more of a teaching aid. Therefore, in each chapter I've attempted to explain why a given feature of the language exists in the first place and the problems in your own code it was designed to solve. After all, if you've never used a feature such as interfaces or delegates, the syntax without an explanation of why you would want to use it doesn't do you much good.

■ **Better and more practical examples**   While I personally prefer realistic examples over foo/bar–type examples, only about 10 percent of the first edition's example applications could be called practical. In this book, the number is more like 70 percent. For example, the "Operator Overloading and User-Defined Conversion" chapter has a number of distinct examples. The first two (operator overloading) show how you'd overload the plus (+) operator to aggregate invoice objects, and another demo shows how you'd overload several operators to create an RGB class that can easily be used to generate values for a gradient fill. The conversion demos then show how to convert various temperature scale objects and how to create and use a tristate control. These classes are not meant to be full implementations, but I believe that when we programmers are given practical demos, it serves to give us ideas as to where and how a given feature can be used in our own applications.

Who Should Read This Book

While the content of this book has been considerably upgraded with quite a bit of intermediate-to-advanced information, I've tried to organize the chapters in such a way that each topic is presented without assuming that you're an experienced C# developer. To that extent, each chapter begins by explaining a given feature (of C# or .NET), why that feature exists in the language, and the problems it addresses. From there, I begin with a simple demo application to focus on the subject matter, after which I explain the syntax required. Once the basics of a given subject are covered, the chapter then moves into increasingly advanced demos and material, such as the compiler-generated MSIL. Therefore, this book is for the person looking to get started with C# and .NET development, and it's also for the person that has been programming for a while with the language and would like to learn some of the more advanced uses of the language.

The only assumption this book makes is that you know how to write and build a simple program in C, C++, or Java. The only other prerequisite is the desire to learn and explore new dimensions in writing applications with the C# language. Because you're holding this book in your hands, you obviously have that bit covered!

Organization of This Book

This book has been carefully organized into a three logically sequenced sections; each section consists of a group of chapters addressing a specific category of C# or .NET development.

Part I: C# Class Fundamentals

In Part I, we present the basics of defining and working with classes and basic class members in C#. However, because one of my main goals with this book was to have a very high signal-to-noise ratio, no chapters expound on subjects such as the Microsoft vision or why I think .NET is great. Programmers want to see code, not visions. Chapter 1, "Building C# Applications and Libraries," has you immediately writing applications, building libraries (DLLs) and .NET modules, and creating multifile assemblies. You'll even learn how to view the global assembly cache and use the ILDASM tool to view the compiler's generated assembler code (MSIL). This book hits the ground running. After a brief overview of the common type system in Chapter 2, "The .NET Type System," Chapters 3 and 4 ("Classes and Structs" and "Methods") teach you the basics of C# class and structure definition as well as how to define and call methods. In keeping with the form of the book, these chapters start with the basic, but by the time you're finished you'll know the difference between constants and read-only fields, the purpose of the type initializer, and how to override virtual methods by using the *new* and *override* keywords.

Chapters 5, "Properties, Arrays, and Indexers," combines these three subjects because each of these features shares the common goal of enabling you to write more intuitive class interfaces for your clients. Once the basics have been covered, you'll see lots of the underlying MSIL to understand how these so-called *smart fields* (properties) and *smart arrays* (indexers) are implemented under the hood. Chapter 6, "Attributes," then introduces one of my favorite aspects of C# development. Attributes enable you to define textual annotations for types that can later be reflected to determine certain run-time characteristics of the type. Here we cover everything from how attributes work to querying at run time if a type has a particular attribute and obtaining its value. Also covered are the predefined attributes *Conditional, Obsolete, CLSCompliant, DllImport, StructLayout*, as well as the various assembly attributes. The book's first section then wraps up Chapter 7, "Interfaces," which covers, among other subjects, how to declare and implement interfaces and how to query for interface implementation via the *is* and *as* operators. Also covered are explicit interface member name qualification, the numerous issues regarding interface inheritance, and combining interfaces.

Part II: Writing Code

Part I was dedicated to teaching how to craft classes and structures; Part II is all about programming tasks. After thorough chapters on using expressions and operators (Chapter 8) and controlling program flow (Chapter 9), Chapter 10, "String Handling and Regular Expressions," a new chapter, covers two of the most important aspects of programming in any language. Chapter 11, "File I/O with Streams," another new chapter, then focuses on the subjects of writing and reading data to and from disk by using the streaming and file system classes provided by the .NET Framework. You'll use everything here from String and Binary readers to serializing data by using *BinaryFormatter, SoapFormatter*, and *XMLSerializer*.

I've always felt that no current-day programming book is complete without a chapter on exception handling. This is even truer in the .NET world where exception handling is used to convey error information across language boundaries. Even COM errors are automatically mapped to exceptions. Chapter 12, "Error Handling with Exceptions," illustrates the basics of exception handling syntax, how to use the predefined system exception classes, and how to do define your own.

Personally, I like any aspect of a language that makes my classes more intuitive to use, and operator overloading certainly applies. Therefore, Chapter 13, "Operator Overloading and User-Defined Conversions," not only covers operator overloading syntax and rules but also gives a couple of practical examples of appropriate overloading: aggregating invoices and creating an RGB class whose operators make it easy to generate gradient values in a *for* loop. Next, in the same chapter, we cover something unique to C#: user-defined conversions.

In short, user-defined conversions enable you to declare conversions on structures or classes so that the struct or class can be converted to other structures, classes, or basic C# types.

Next up is Chapter 14, "Delegates and Event Handlers." Along with interfaces and reflection, this topic is one of the most important for someone new to the .NET arena. In this chapter, you'll learn how to define and create delegates and multicast delegates and how to use events to implement the *Publish/Subscribe*, or *Observer*, pattern. Finally, Part II wraps up with yet another cool new chapter, this time on the very C#-specific means of generating XML documentation from C# source code comments! The best part of this feature, of course, is that the XML basis means that it's completely open-ended and customizable, like so many areas of the .NET Framework.

Part III: Advanced C#

Being a geek, I enjoyed writing this section most; it includes some of my favorite topics. After Chapter 16 provides an introduction to numerical processing and the *Math* class, Chapter 17, "Collections and Object Enumeration," illustrates how to use the *IEnumerable* and *IEnumerator* interfaces to allow clients to enumerate your class's data. Included in this chapter are advanced subjects such as creating versioned enumerators, protecting data while allowing enumeration, and implementing the mutator interface. Chapter 18 illustrates how to incorporate multithreading and asynchronous programming into your applications. No single chapter can completely cover the topic of multithreading, but we do cover everything you need to know to get started with threads and a little more. After learning how to create, manage, schedule, and abort threads, you'll learn how communicate data to a thread. After that you'll see several ways to serialize access to a thread method in order to make that method thread-safe. Finally, you'll see how delegates can be used to start an asynchronous method and either block until its return or have that method automatically invoke a callback method upon completion. Chapter 19 covers querying metadata with reflection.

Chapter 20, "Pinning and Memory Management," details quite a bit about memory management and pinning and includes information on the .NET garbage collector (GC), the *Dispose* pattern, the *IDisposable* interface, weak references, and writing unsafe (nonmanaged) code. From there, you'll see that the subject COM interoperation was so extensive that it took two chapters to give it adequate coverage. Chapter 21, "Using COM from C# Applications," looks at how to use classic COM components from .NET (C#) applications, and Chapter 22, "Using .NET Components in Unmanaged Code," delves into using .NET components (written in C#) from both Microsoft Visual C++ and Microsoft Visual Basic clients (using COM). Needless to say, these chapters are far from beginner-level and will require a fair amount of COM experience going in. Part III finishes up with an extremely detailed look at security programming (Chapter 23) that includes sections on code signing, cryptographic services, code access security, role-based security, and isolated storage. Don't miss this chapter!

Appendix: MSIL Instruction Table

Because MSIL listings are such a crucial strategy of this book, the book's appendix includes a complete table detailing every MSIL instruction, its opcode, parameters, description, and even stack transition. The stack transition enables you to see the before-and-after picture of the stack with regards to the instruction being called.

Conventions Used in This Book

Like any programmer, I have my own pet terms and programming style. So, let me define a few terms you'll see throughout the book as well as explain why certain things were done the way they were:

- **"Problem domain"** This is a term I learned years ago while using the Coad/Yourdon Object-Oriented Analysis and Design methodology. A "problem domain" is a generic term that refers to the set of problems to be solved.

- **"Consumers" and "clients"** These terms are used interchangeably to represent any code that uses a class or type.

- **"Server"** This term is used to refer to a piece of code—typically a class—that is used by a client or consumer.

- **"Arguments" and "parameters"** Like most programmers, I use these terms interchangeably when referring to the values passed to a method.

- **"MSIL opcodes" and "MSIL instructions"** Although it's not technically correct to do so, I have used these terms interchangeably in this book.

- **"Method prototype" and "method signature"** These terms are used interchangeably in this book.

- **Semicolons** Sometimes I'll terminate a class definition with a semicolon, and other times I won't. Unlike C++, the C# compiler does not check for this, so you're free to do whichever you choose.

In my consulting practice, I've begun using the semicolon for the simple reason that I believe it creates a visual delimiter between multiple classes defined in the same source code file. However, it's a personal choice and as far as I know no design guideline specifically addresses this issue.

■ **Breaking lines of code**   Unfortunately, there are some times when the format of a book requires some odd line breaking of source code. This is regrettable but unavoidable. Please keep this in mind when you see an oddly formatted line of code.

Building the Demo Applications

One of the goals of this book was that all the demo applications could be built without requiring that the reader use Microsoft Visual Studio .NET. This way anyone with a C# compiler would be able to compile and run the demos. However, because Visual Studio .NET is the prevalent IDE used for writing C# applications, we did use it to create most of the demo projects. The end result is that either you can build the projects by using Visual Studio .NET or you can use the command line compiler as explained in Chapter 1.

As with anything, there are a few notes and exceptions to this.

■ **All Visual Studio projects**   When a C# console application is created using Visual Studio .NET, two source code files are generated. The first, Class1.cs, is the main source code file. You'll learn how to use compile this file into an application in Chapter 1. The second file generated is called AssemblyInfo.cs. This file is typically used to define assembly-level attributes. The subject of assemblies is introduced in Chapter 1, and attributes are covered in Chapter 6. If you're using the command-line compiler and want to compile both the Class1.cs and the AssemblyInfo.cs file into an application, you simply need to use the following C# compiler switches where *appname.exe* is whatever name you want to give the resulting application:

```
csc /out:<appname.exe> class1.cs assemblyinfo.cs
```

■ **Chapter 1**   The HelloWorldVS project is the only project in this chapter that was created with Visual Studio .NET.

- **Chapter 2**   This chapter is a brief overview of the common type system, so it includes no demo applications.

- **Chapter 19**   Visual Studio .NET does not support the creation of C# .NET modules for incorporation into multifile assemblies. Therefore, the CommProtocol demo application can be built from the command line only. To make this easier, I've included a simple make file (buildall.cmd) that builds all of the components necessary for this demo. In addition, for the sake of simplicity, the ILGeneration demo application is also a command-line-only build. This demo also includes a buildall.cmd file to compile its components.

- **Chapter 21**   The subject of this chapter is using classic COM components in C# applications, so several of this chapter's demo applications were built using Visual Basic and Visual C++. You'll need Visual Studio to build these projects. However, I have intentionally used Visual C++ 6 and Visual Basic 6. This way, if you have Visual Studio 6 and have installed the .NET Framework SDK (and not Visual Studio .NET), you can use these demos. Additionally, if you open these projects with Visual Studio .NET, you'll simply get a message asking if you want to convert the projects to the new format. Answer yes, and you're off and running.

- **Chapter 22**   The subject of this chapter is using .NET components from unmanaged code. As with Chapter 21, some demos are written using Visual C++ 6 and Visual Basic 6. The same notes apply here as they do for that chapter.

About the Companion CD

This book contains a companion CD. If you have the AutoRun feature in Windows enabled, you'll see a splash screen when you insert the CD into the CD-ROM drive that will provide you with setup options. To start this screen manually, run StartCD from the root directory of the CD. The StartCD program provides you with links to the eBook contained on the CD, an install program for the book's sample files, and a link to the Microsoft .NET Framework SDK, which is included on the CD.

The sample programs for the book are located in the BookFiles\Code folder. You can view the samples from the CD, or you can install them onto your hard disk by using the installer from StartCD.

> **Note**   If you're unable to browse the files in the Samples folder, you might have an older CD driver that doesn't support long filenames. If this is the case, to browse the files you must install the samples files on your hard disk by running the Setup program.

Sample Code on the Web

The sample code is also available on the book's Web site at *www.microsoft.com/MSPress/books/5861.asp*. You'll find code updates and links to related books on this page.

System Requirements

For you to get the most from this book, I highly recommend working through the sample applications as you read each chapter. Doing so requires the .NET Framework SDK (which includes the C# compiler). Note that if you have Visual Studio .NET, the Framework SDK is part of that package.

Another important requirement is that while .NET code can be executed on Windows 98 and above, only the following operating systems support the Framework SDK:

- Microsoft Windows NT 4.0

- Microsoft Windows 2000 (Service Pack 2 recommended)

- Microsoft Windows XP (Microsoft Windows XP Professional is required to run Microsoft ASP.NET)

Feedback

I'm definitely not one of these "I'm so good because I write books" people. I'm just a regular guy that was lucky enough to get the opportunity to write a book. Therefore, I'm always open to learning from others and, in fact, love doing so. If you have any questions about the book or simply want to talk C# and .NET, I can be reached through my Web site at *www.TheCodeChannel.com*. I also keep a current book erratum on this site, as well as chapter addendums (typically consisting of material that didn't make it into the book because of time constraints) and examples of .NET applications that I've written using C#.

Acknowledgments

Firstly, I want to thank my acquisitions editor, Danielle Bird. Without her belief in me, I wouldn't have had the chance to write the first edition, much less this one. Thanks so much, Danielle! Also from Microsoft Press, special thanks goes to Devon Musgrave and Michelle Goodman for their superior job of editing this text. Devon, who worked with me on the first edition, was once again instrumental in overseeing the editing duties of this book. He and Michelle turned my gibberish into something much more pleasing to read. To Jim, my technical editor, what can I say? You pulled my chestnuts out of the fire on a couple of technical issues! I owe you big time, mate. Thanks so much for a great job that goes well beyond your job description. When I come back to Redmond, you just name the place—the steak and beer is on me.

There were several programmers who contributed to this book that I'd like to thank. Of course, I have to start with my coauthor, Andrew Whitechapel. Andrew, you wrote some incredible chapters in terms of breadth of coverage and in-depth technical information. And your contribution can't be measured solely by the words you penned. With you being a part of this book I was able to spend more time to better my own chapters; your involvement had a very positive effect on the quality of my work as well. Thanks so much, Andrew! I'd also like to thank Aravind Corera, who contributed mightily to both the COM chapters. Your work in this area is unparalleled, Aravind! Additionally, Sachin Nigam (www.dotnetextreme.com) contributed the code and concept for using reflection to model the Abstract Factory. Great idea!

I'd also like to thank Joe Nalewabau (C# Lead Program Manager) and Anson Horton (C# Program Manager). Joe, from the beginning you've always been extremely patient with my questions as I've traversed the learning curve of this exciting new language, and it's much appreciated. Anson, you had immediate answers for some extremely difficult issues that just aren't covered anywhere. Without your help I wouldn't have been able to be so specific about some of the cooler, lower-level material. Thanks to you both! Also, from Andrew: special thanks to Trevor Chapman, for his guidance and support, and his endless patience

Finally, I want to give a shout out to all the people on the DOTNET mailing list (*http://discuss.develop.com*), CodeProject (*www.CodeProject.com*), and CodeGuru (*www.CodeGuru.com*) who so freely give of their time to help others. You make this industry fun to be a part of!

I

C# Class
Fundamentals

1

Building C# Applications and Libraries

In the first edition of *Inside C#* (Microsoft Press, 2001), the first two chapters gave an overview of object-oriented programming and the .NET environment. While this seemed like a good idea at the time, it meant that you, the reader/ programmer, didn't write code until Chapter 3. Since that book was published, I've been fortunate enough to give several talks and teach a few classes on .NET and C# programming. That experience has taught me an important lesson: programmers don't want lectures—they want code! Therefore, I'm taking a slightly different approach with this edition of the book. Instead of starting with "lay of the land" chapters, I'm going to jump right into programming with C#. I'll then explain the different architectural aspects of .NET as I explain the syntax of C# as you work your way through the demo applications. Another major departure from the style of the first edition is that after explaining a given topic or language feature at the C# level, I'll sometimes dive into the nitty-gritty details of how that feature is implemented at the lowest level that we applications programmers can access—the Microsoft intermediate language (MSIL) level.

Let's begin by writing a "Hello, World" application and building and running it from the command line. From there, you'll learn how the .NET version of "Hello, World" works under the covers and how it's executed within the .NET Framework. Once we've gone over that, you'll then write the same application by using Microsoft Visual Studio to see how that development environment can make your programming life much simpler. (You don't need Visual Studio .NET to work through most of the examples in this book. However, all the examples in this book were created with this tool.) From there, I'll go into a bit of depth on the internals of a .NET application, what a just-in-time compiler (JITter) is, and how .NET applications are loaded and executed under Microsoft Windows. Finally, the chapter wraps up with a full section on assemblies—what they are, what benefits they provide, and how to build them—and how to create both .NET modules and dynamic-link libraries (DLLs) for multifile applications.

"Hello, World"—The Command-Line Version

At this point, create a new file in a standard text editor. For purposes of this demo, I'm using the standard Notepad application because it's available on all standard installations of Windows. Once you've created a new file, type in the following code. (Don't worry about what each line does at this point—we'll be covering that soon enough.)

```
namespace InsideCSharp
{
    class HelloWorldConsoleApp
    {
        static void Main()
        {
            System.Console.WriteLine("Hello, World");
        }
    }
}
```

Using the Command-Line Compiler

To see immediately if your environment is set up properly, we'll hold off on explaining the code and first attempt to build and run this application. Therefore, when you've finished typing in the code, save the file as HelloWorldConsole and open a command window. Then run the following command from the command prompt:

```
csc helloworldconsole.cs
```

Here you're simply invoking the C# compiler (csc.exe) and passing it the name of the file to compile. If everything goes well, you should see results that resemble Figure 1-1.

Figure 1-1   When using the command-line compiler, if your application builds correctly, you'll simply see the copyright information of the C# compiler with no errors listed.

If your application compiled, you've not only written your first .NET application in C#, but your system is properly configured to build every demo application in this book! However, if you received the familiar "command not found" error, the command interpreter couldn't locate the csc.exe application. To remedy this, you need make only one slight change to your Windows environment—more specifically, you make the change to a *Path* environment variable.

To do so, open the System Control Panel applet shown in Figure 1-2 and click the Advanced tab.

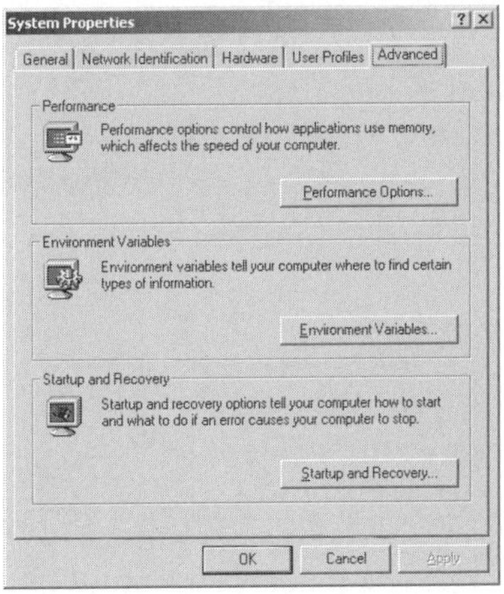

Figure 1-2   Environment variables can be set via the System Control Panel applet so that they're applicable to any newly opened command session.

On the Advanced tab, click the Environment Variables button to open the Environment Variables dialog box shown in Figure 1-3. This dialog box displays both the user environment variables for the currently logged on user as well as the system-level variables—those pertaining to any logged on user.

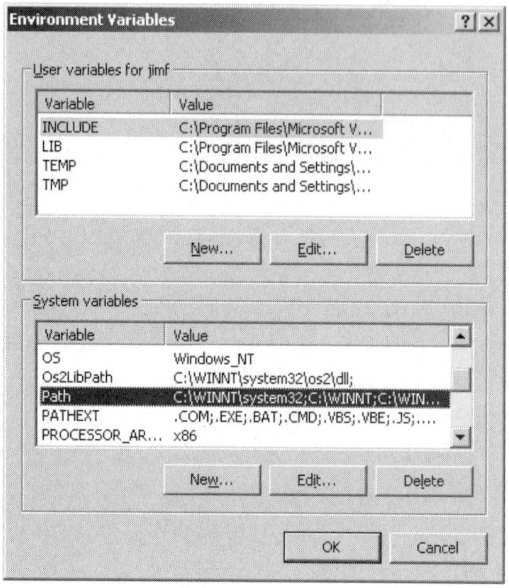

Figure 1-3   Environment variables tell Windows—and its applications—where to find certain types of information.

Now locate the *Path* variable in the System Variables list box, select it, and then click the Edit button to display the Edit System Variable dialog box shown in Figure 1-4. Finally, append the following text to the end of the *Path* variable's value:

```
;C:\Program Files\Microsoft Visual Studio
.NET\FrameworkSDK\Bin;c:\winnt\microsoft.net\framework\v1.0.3705;
C:\Program Files\Microsoft Visual Studio .NET\Vc7\bin;
C:\Program Files\Common Files\Microsoft Shared\VSA\7.0\VsaEnv;
```

Note   The version number in the *Path* is the value that's being used in the build that I'm writing this book with and might be different for your particular installation at the time that you read this book.

Edit System Variable
Variable Name:
Path
Variable Value:
INNT\Microsoft.NET\Framework\v1.0.3621
OK
Cancel

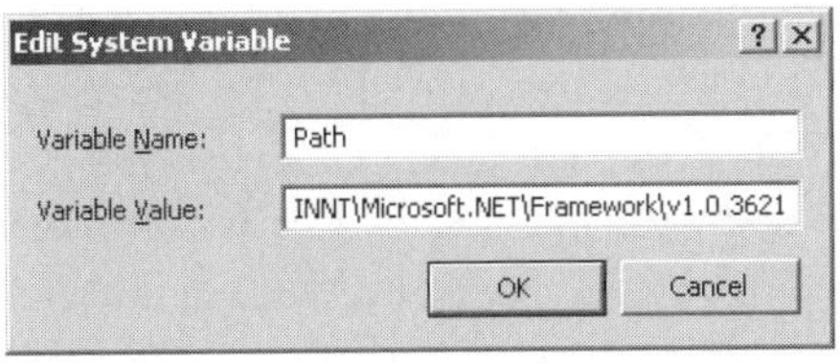

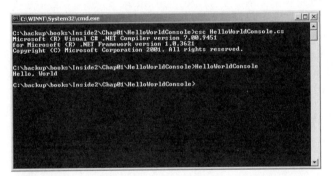

Figure 1-4 The Edit System Variable dialog box.

Once you've set the *Path* variable, you'll need to open a new command prompt and retype the command to compile the HelloWorldConsole application. At this point, everything should build and you should now see that the executable named HelloWorldConsole.exe has been created. Run the program to see the output, shown in Figure 1-5.

C:\WINNT\System32\cmd.exe
C:\backup\books\Inside2\Chap01\HelloWorldConsole>csc HelloWorldConsole.cs
Microsoft (R) Visual C# .NET Compiler version 7.00.9451
for Microsoft (R) .NET Framework version 1.0.3621
Copyright (C) Microsoft Corporation 2001. All rights reserved.
C:\backup\books\Inside2\Chap01\HelloWorldConsole>HelloWorldConsole
Hello, World
C:\backup\books\Inside2\Chap01\HelloWorldConsole>

Figure 1-5 The output of the HelloWorldConsole program.

"Hello, World" Code Walk-Through

Congratulations! While we haven't exactly launched the space shuttle with our little application, you have written your first C# application. Next let's talk a little about the code itself and learn some basic C# syntax and concepts.

One-Stop Programming

The first thing to realize when coding in C# is that when you define a class and its methods, you actually define the methods within the class body itself. If you're background is in C++ programming, you're accustomed to doing this for very small function bodies. However, in the case of C#, all methods are defined within the class definition. The reason for this is simple. The C# language is designed to give you the ability to create "mobile" code.

In other words, when you write a C# class, you end up with a fully encapsulated bundle of functionality that you can easily drop into any other development environment—without worrying how that language processes include files or whether it has a mechanism for including files within files. Using this one-stop programming approach, you can, for instance, take an entire class and drop it into an Active Server Pages (ASP) page. The class will then function as though you were compiling it into a desktop Windows application!

Namespaces

The first line of code that you see in the demo is the definition of a namespace named *InsideCSharp*. For those who are new to namespaces, they are simply a convenient means of semantically grouping elements—such as classes and other namespaces—to avoid name collision. Theoretically, you can nest namespaces to any desired level.

For example, you might want to use namespaces when you know your code will be used in an environment in which the names of your classes might duplicate other classes. Let's say you're writing a grid component and want to either sell it or release it to the general public. You could prepend all your class names with your company name or some special prefix, but with namespaces, you could simply define your classes as follows:

```
namespace MyCompany
{
    class Grid
    {
    }

    class OtherClass
    {
    }
}
```

Now when the user of your grid wants to reference it, his or her code would simply fully qualify the class name with the namespace name—*MyCompany.Grid*.

Namespace declarations consist of the keyword *namespace* followed by the namespace name and a body—and optionally terminated with a semicolon. Here's the syntax for defining a namespace in C#:

```
namespace <namespace_name>
{
    <namespace-body>
}
```

As mentioned, you can nest namespaces, as in the following example:

```
namespace Distrubution
{
    namespace Purchasing
    {
        // Define purchasing classes
    }

    namespace Receiving
    {
        // Define receiving classes
    }

    namespace Inventory
    {
        // Define inventory classes
    }
}
```

An alternative means of defining nested namespaces is to fully qualify each namespace. Besides having to do less typing, you'll benefit from employing this syntax only if you're defining these namespaces across multiple physical files to be compiled into one application:

```
namespace Distrubution.Purchasing
{
    // Define purchasing classes
}

namespace Distrubution.Receiving
{
    // Define receiving classes
}

namespace Distrubution.Inventory
{
    // Define inventory classes
}
```

Although we'll examine the .NET type system and Framework SDK in Chapter 2, "The .NET Type System," it's worth pointing out here that the entire

Framework SDK is represented by classes and types that are grouped into namespaces.

C# Comments

As with C++ and Java, C# supports two types of code comments (textual notes that serve as documentation for source code). In one type the comment is bracketed with /* and */ characters as in the following:

```
/* This is a comment */
class DerivedClass : /* I can place a comment in the middle
 of code */ BaseClass
{
    /* I can preceded code with comments */ int MyField;
    ⋮
}
```

The second type uses the // characters. With this style, there is no ending delimiter and thus everything after the // characters is considered a comment.

```
// This is a comment
class MyClass : BaseClass // The rest of this line is a comment
{
    // This form is typically used when the comment will either
    // be used for the entire line, span multiple lines, or be
    // placed at the end of code
    int MyField;  // Comment to document field's purpose
    ⋮
}
```

In Chapter 15, "Documentation with XML," you'll learn a new way to format your comments that enables you to harness the power of XML and XSL to automatically generate HTML documentation from your C# comments.

Classes and Members

Like any object-oriented language, C# allows you to define classes. In C#, classes can contain members that include constants, fields, methods, properties, events, indexers, operators, instance constructors, destructors, static constructors, and nested type declarations. We'll cover all these members in due time, and we'll define classes themselves in much greater detail in Chapter 2 and Chapter 3, "Classes and Structs." In our little "Hello, World" example, we have a single class named *HelloWorldConsoleApp* that contains a single member—a method named *Main*. Obviously, real-world applications generally consist of dozens to even hundreds of classes.

The *Main* Method

Let's take a look at the only method in our application, *Main*. Every C# application must define a *Main* method in one of its classes. It doesn't matter which class contains the method—you can have as many classes as you want in a given application—as long as one class has a method named *Main*.

The *public* keyword—which is more thoroughly covered in Chapter 3—is an access modifier that tells the C# compiler that any code can call this method. The *static* modifier—also covered in Chapter 3—tells the compiler that the *Main* method is a global method and that the class doesn't need to be instantiated for the method to be called. This restriction makes sense when you think about it because, otherwise, the compiler wouldn't know how or when to instantiate your class. Because the method is static, the compiler stores its address as the entry point so that the .NET common language runtime knows where to begin executing your application.

Note The demonstration programs in this chapter show the *Main* method as returning *void* and not receiving any arguments. However, you can define your *Main* method to return a value and take an array of arguments. Chapter 3 covers these options, as well as how to iterate through the passed arguments to an application's *Main* method.

The *System.Console.WriteLine* Method

As you probably guessed, the *System.Console.WriteLine* method writes the specified string—followed by a line terminator—to the standard output device. In most cases, unless you do something fancy to change the output or use an editor that redirects the output to a window, the string will output in a console window. What isn't so obvious is that the string literal being passed is technically a *managed object*. A managed object can be defined simply as an instance of a CTS-defined type. We'll get into the common type system (CTS) and its supported types in Chapter 2. However, at this point, I'd like to stay at a somewhat higher level. I'll dive into the details of how this application works a bit later in this chapter, in a section entitled "Inside 'Hello, World.'"

Namespaces and the *using* Directive

The .NET Framework SDK is organized into a hierarchical lattice of namespaces. This organization can result in some rather lengthy names when a desired class or type is nested several layers deep. Therefore, to save on typing, C# provides the *using* directive. Let's look at an example of how this directive works. In our "Hello, World" application, we have the following line of code:

```
System.Console.WriteLine("Hello, World");
```

Typing this once isn't such a big deal, but imagine having to fully qualify every type or class in a large application. The *using* directive enables you to list a kind of search path. Thus, if the compiler can't understand something you've typed, it will search the listed namespaces for the definition. When we incorporate the *using* directive, our example program looks like this:

```
using System;

namespace InsideCSharp
{
    class UsingDirectiveApp
    {
        static void Main()
        {
            Console.WriteLine("This an example of the " +
                "using directive.");
        }
    }
}
```

When the compiler parses the *Console.WriteLine* method, it will determine that the method is undefined. However, it will then search through the namespaces specified by the *using* directives and, upon finding the method in the *System* namespace, will compile the code without error.

Note that the *using* directive applies to namespaces and not classes. In our example, *System* is the namespace, *Console* is the class, and *WriteLine* is a static method belonging to *Console*. Therefore, the following code would be invalid:

```
using System.Console; // ERROR Can't use a using
                      // directive with a class.

namespace InsideCSharp
```

```
{
    class UsingErrorApp
    {
        static void Main()
        {
            WriteLine("This application will not compile.");
        }
    }
}
```

Although you can't specify a class in a *using* directive, the following variant of the *using* directive does enable you to create aliases for classes, which can sometimes prove very useful:

```
using alias = class
```

Using this form of the *using* directive, you can write code such as the following:

```
using output = System.Console;

namespace InsideCSharp
{
    class UsingAliasApp
    {
        static void Main()
        {
            output.WriteLine("This an example of the using " +
                "alias directive");
        }
    }
}
```

This gives you the flexibility to apply meaningful aliases to classes nested several layers deep in the .NET hierarchy, thus making your code a little easier to write and maintain.

Skeleton Code

Let's look at skeleton code for most any C# application—code that illustrates a basic outline for a simple, no-frills C# application. (You might want to type this code into a file and save it to use as a template for other programs in this chapter.) The angle brackets denote where you need to supply information.

```
using <namespace>
namespace <your optional namespace>
class <your class>
```

```
    {
        public static void Main()
        {
        }
    }
```

Class Ambiguity

When a type is defined in more than one referenced namespace, the compiler will issue an error denoting the ambiguity. Therefore, the following code won't compile because the class *C* is defined in two namespaces that are referenced with the *using* directive:

```
using A;
using B;

namespace A
{
    class C
    {
        public static void foo()
        {
            System.Console.WriteLine("A.C.foo");
        }
    }
}

namespace B
{
    class C
    {
        public static void foo()
        {
            System.Console.WriteLine("B.C.foo");
        }
    }
}

class MultiplyDefinedClassesApp
{
    public static void Main()
    {
        C.foo();
    }
}
```

Figure 1-6 shows an example of the compiler errors that you'll receive.

Figure 1-6   Compiler errors from a multiply defined class.

Even with namespaces and the *using* directive, you still might run into name collision problems. In these situations, simply fully qualify the type you're addressing. Now let's see how to write our little demo application by using the Visual Studio .NET development environment.

"Hello, World"—The Visual Studio .NET Version

Before we begin with this version of the demo application, I do want to reiterate that you don't need Visual Studio .NET to work through most of the examples in this book. However, all the examples in this book were created with this tool, so I decided to add this section for those of you who are using Visual Studio.

Start Visual Studio, and then select New Project from the File menu. This action will open the New Project dialog box shown in Figure 1-7.

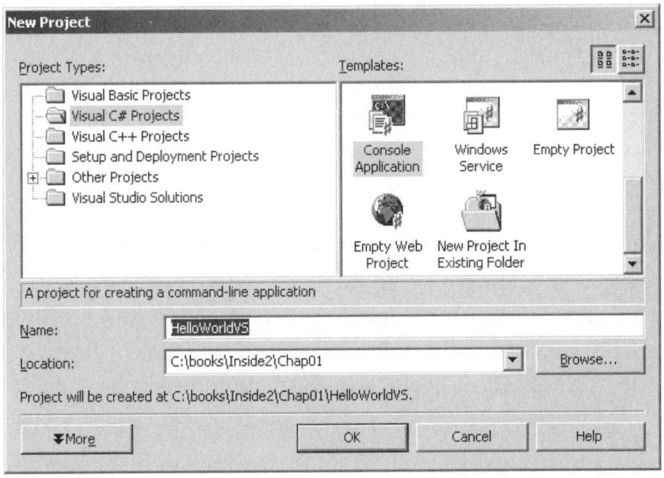

Figure 1-7   The Visual Studio New Project dialog box enables you to create many different types of C# applications from built-in templates.

Select the Visual C# Project icon from the Project Types list, and then select the Console Application template. Then name the project HelloWorldVS, and indicate where you want the new project created. Click OK to continue.

Visual Studio will now create the files needed for the project, open the main class's file (Class1.cs), and place the cursor at the beginning of that file. As Figure 1-8 illustrates, the source code generated by Visual Studio looks very much like the source code that you manually entered in this chapter's first demo.

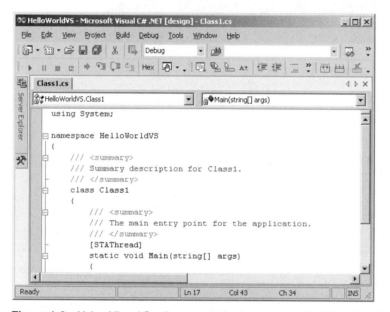

Figure 1-8   Using Visual Studio, you get the beginnings of a C# application with just a couple of clicks of the mouse.

Now move to the cursor inside the *Main* method, and on a blank line, type the following:

```
Console.
```

Visual Studio will automatically pop up a list box containing all the members of the *Console* class, as shown in Figure 1-9. This feature—named IntelliSense—enables you to quickly see which members are available for a defined namespace or class. You can also use the up and down arrow keys to highlight a member, and you can then press Tab to select the highlighted member.

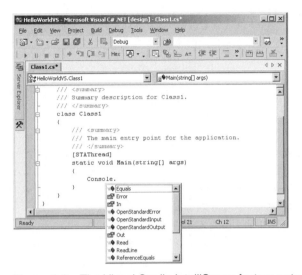

Figure 1-9   The Visual Studio IntelliSense feature automatically displays the members of a namespace or class as you type.

Continue typing the following call to output a "Hello, World" greeting. You'll see that when you type in the left parenthesis, Visual Studio automatically lets you know with a tooltip the number and type of parameters needed for the method call.

```
Console.WriteLine("Hello, World from Visual Studio");
```

Now simply press F5 to run the application. Visual Studio will automatically detect that the code needs to be compiled and will do so before attempting to run the application.

When you run the application, you'll notice that a command prompt opens and shuts immediately after displaying our little message. This behavior isn't very convenient if you really want to read the message. Therefore, add the following line of code after the call to *Console.WriteLine*:

```
String str = Console.ReadLine();
```

The *System.Console.ReadLine* method will cause the application to pause until the user presses the Enter key, thereby giving the user the opportunity to see that the application has printed the expected text.

That's it! This isn't a Visual Studio book, so I won't go into all the different features of the product. However, you can now see from the rapid application development why I use this development environment throughout the book. Now let's take a look at how .NET applications are built and executed within the .NET environment.

Building and Running .NET Applications

As you probably know, a fairly standard process of building applications from source code—and running the resulting binary—has been around for some time now. The first step of that process has typically involved compiling your source code files (compilation units) into a target binary. (In some languages, you link the various compilation units together after the initial compilation step.) This binary image is known in Win32 parlance as a *portable executable*, or PE. After the binary is built, it's installed on the target machine where, upon invocation, the operating system loader loads the binary into memory and "fixes up" any necessary addresses. At this point, the application is executing. However, this entire process is very different in the .NET world.

Two of the most important features of .NET are that all .NET languages have access to the same .NET functionality and that code written in these various languages can interoperate seamlessly. The accomplishment of these goals was, in part, made possible by the introduction of MSIL. A .NET compiler takes source code as input and produces MSIL as output instead of a Windows PE.

I should note here that the .NET Framework SDK ships with an assembler (ILASM) that enables you to write entire applications in MSIL. However, as with assembly language, you'd probably do so only for purely academic reasons or in highly unusual circumstances. Therefore, its inclusion in this book is based on the fact that you can learn a tremendous amount about the C# language—and .NET in general—by looking at your application's underlying MSIL. To that extent, I've listed the supported MSIL opcodes—along with brief descriptions—in the Appendix, "MSIL Opcodes Used in This Book." With MSIL, we know that all .NET applications are being compiled into a standard, common format and will therefore interact with the .NET runtime environment in a consistent manner. Now let's look at what's really happening under the hood when you compile and execute a .NET application:

1.   A programmer writes source code using any .NET language.

2.   The source code is then compiled into what appears to be a standard PE file.

3.   The .NET compiler outputs the MSIL code and a manifest into a read-only part of the EXE that has a standard PE header. (I'll get into exactly what a manifest is in the next section. For now, it's enough to understand that the term *manifest* refers to the information stored in a .NET binary that describes that binary's contents and runtime requirements.)

4. So far, so good. However, here's the important part: when the compiler creates the output, it also imports a function named *_CorExeMain* from the .NET runtime.

5. When the user runs the application, the operating system loads the PE as well as any dependent DLLs, such as the one that exports the *_CorExeMain* function (mscoree.dll), just as it does with any valid PE.

6. The operating system loader then jumps to the entry point inside the PE, which is put there by the .NET compiler. Once again, this process is exactly how any other PE is executed in Windows.

7. Because the operating system obviously can't execute the MSIL code, the entry point is just a small stub that jumps to the *_CorExeMain* function in mscoree.dll.

8. The *_CorExeMain* function starts the execution of the MSIL code that the compiler placed in the PE.

9. MSIL code can't be executed directly because it's not in a machine-executable format. Therefore, the common language runtime compiles the MSIL—by using a just-in-time compiler (or JITter)—into native CPU instructions as it processes the MSIL. JIT compiling occurs only as methods in the program are called. The compiled executable code is cached on the machine and recompiled only if there's some change to the source code.

In addition to the default JITter, two other JITters can be used to convert the MSIL into native code, depending on the circumstances:

■ **Install-time code generation**   This will compile an entire assembly into CPU-specific binary code, just as a C++ compiler does. An assembly is the code package that's sent to the compiler. (I'll talk about assemblies in more detail later in this chapter in the "Assembly Deployment" section.) This compilation is done at install time, when the end user is least likely to notice that the assembly is being JIT-compiled. The advantage of install-time code generation is that it allows you to compile the entire assembly just once before you run it. Because the entire assembly is compiled, you don't have to worry about intermittent performance issues every time a method in your code is executed for the first time. It's like a time-share vacation plan in which you pay for everything up front. Although paying for the vacation plan is painful, the advantage is that you never have to worry about paying for accommodations again. When and whether you use this utility depends on the size of your specific system and your deployment environment. Typically, if you plan to create an installation application for your system, you should go ahead and use this JITter so that the user has a fully optimized version of the system "out of the box."

■   **EconoJit**   Another run-time JITter, the EconoJit, is specifically designed for systems that have limited resources—for example, handheld devices with small amounts of memory. The major difference between this JITter and the regular JITter is the incorporation of something known as code pitching. Code pitching allows the EconoJit to discard the generated, or compiled, code if the system begins to run out of memory. The benefit is that the memory is reclaimed. However, the disadvantage is that if the code being pitched is invoked again, it must be recompiled as though it had never been called.

At this point, I've talked about MSIL and how it enables .NET applications—regardless of their original source code—to be compiled into a consistent format. However, we're still at the 10,000-foot level and haven't really dived into any actual inside information. Let's change that now by peeking under the hood at the HelloWorldConsole demo application presented at the beginning of the chapter and seeing exactly what's going on under the covers.

Inside "Hello, World"

The first thing we'll do is use a utility that Windows programmers have come to rely on for years when spelunking the internals of their binaries—dumpbin. Open a command prompt, change to the folder containing the HelloWorldConsole application, and type the following command:

```
dumpbin /HEADERS /CLRHEADER helloworldconsole.exe
```

Remember that you need to adjust your system's *Path* environment variable as described on page 6. If you attempt to run dumpbin and get an error stating that the executable can't be found, you'll need to include the following folders in your system's *Path* environment variable:

C:\Program Files\Microsoft Visual Studio .NET\Vc7\bin

C:\Program Files\Common Files\Microsoft Shared\VSA\7.0\VsaEnv

Notice in Figure 1-10 that the OPTIONAL HEADER VALUES section contains a "magic #" of 10B, which represents that this file is indeed a valid PE.

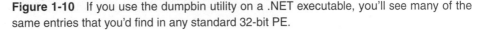

Figure 1-10   If you use the dumpbin utility on a .NET executable, you'll see many of the same entries that you'd find in any standard 32-bit PE.

The next item to note is the relative virtual address (RVA) of the application's "entry point." If we were to actually track down this address in the executable image, we'd see that this entry point contains a single x86 instruction—a jump (*JMP*) to the *_CorExeMain* function mentioned in the previous section. In fact, if you continue looking through the dump of this executable, this application looks fairly normal. However, as you read in the previous section, this application is far from a normal PE because it contains MSIL instructions as well as metadata. So how do we see that information? We need to disassemble the executable image by using an application that understands the .NET elements of this very special file. This application—named ILDASM—ships as part of the Framework SDK and is what I've used to illustrate how the various C# and .NET elements are implemented or function.

To see this information, click the Start menu and type **ILDASM** at the Run prompt. When the ILDASM application runs, open the HelloWorldConsole.exe file via the File menu. You should see a tree view that includes an entry for the assembly's manifest as well as icons for the namespace, class, and method that we defined in our little example application.

At this point, double-click the Manifest entry in the application's tree view, as shown in Figure 1-11. Here you'll see the metadata information that describes the assembly information for this image.

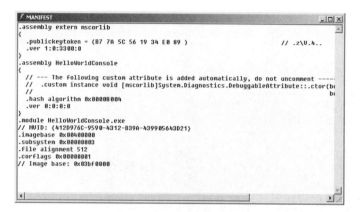

Figure 1-11   The manifest contains the metadata that describes the assembly information for a .NET binary.

As you can see, this particular manifest consists of three blocks of information—known as *records*—that define various elements of the assembly.

The first of those elements is a *.assembly* record that's being used to reference an external assembly. As you know by now, this particular assembly is the system assembly we've been talking about:

```
.assembly extern mscorlib
```

Remember that one of the major benefits of assemblies is versioning. Therefore, note that our *HelloWorldConsole* assembly is using version 1.0.3300.0 of the *MSCORLIB* assembly:

```
.assembly extern mscorlib
{
  .publickeytoken = (B7 7A 5C 56 19 34 E0 89 )   // .z\V.4..
  .ver 1:0:3300:0
}
```

The second record contains information about this assembly. Here our assembly version is 0.0.0.0 because we didn't explicitly state a version number during the build process:

```
.assembly HelloWorldConsole
{
  // --- The following custom attribute is added
  // automatically, do not uncomment -------
  //   .custom instance void
  // [mscorlib]System.Diagnostics.DebuggableAttribute::.ctor(bool,
  //     bool) = ( 01 00 00 01 00 00 )
  .hash algorithm 0x00008004
  .ver 0:0:0:0
}
```

Notice the *DebuggableAttribute* attribute. Although we won't get into attributes until Chapter 6, "Attributes," for now it's enough to know that attributes enable you to attach textual annotations to a piece of code that defines various runtime characteristics for that code. In this case, the *DebuggableAttribute* attribute tells the JITter not to optimize the generated output when compiling the code. The result is that although the code runs a little more slowly, it can be debugged much more easily.

Finally, the last record in the manifest is a *.module* record. This block of information contains items such as the name of the physical file housing the assembly as well as certain offsets into the file where important information can be located.

Next we'll look at the HelloWorldConsoleApp class's constructor, shown in Figure 1-12. Because this is the first MSIL actually seen in this book, let's walk through it briefly. The first line simply denotes a method that is *public* and is also characterized by the *specialname* and *rtspecialname* attributes. Whenever you see these values, the code for the specified method has special significance to the Common Language Infrastructure. The *cil managed* attributes mark the method as a *managed method*. Managed code is code that runs within the .NET Framework.

```
HelloWorldConsoleApp::.ctor : void()                                    _□×
.method public hidebysig specialname rtspecialname
        instance void  .ctor() cil managed
{
  // Code size       7 (0x7)
  .maxstack  1
  IL_0000:  ldarg.0
  IL_0001:  call           instance void [mscorlib]System.Object::.ctor()
  IL_0006:  ret
} // end of method HelloWorldConsoleApp::.ctor
```

Figure 1-12   Peeking at the code's underlying MSIL often can lead to a better understanding of how certain features are implemented in the .NET Framework.

The method first loads a method argument onto the stack via the *ldarg* opcode. The *0* after the *ldarg* opcode signifies that the method's first argument—the *this* value—be used. After that, the *call* opcode is used to invoke the *System.Object* method. Finally, the *ret* opcode simply returns control to the calling method.

More Info   You'll see in Chapter 2 that all types are ultimately derived from this base class type.

The last bit of MSIL that we'll look at in this chapter is the implementation of the *Main* method, as shown in Figure 1-13.

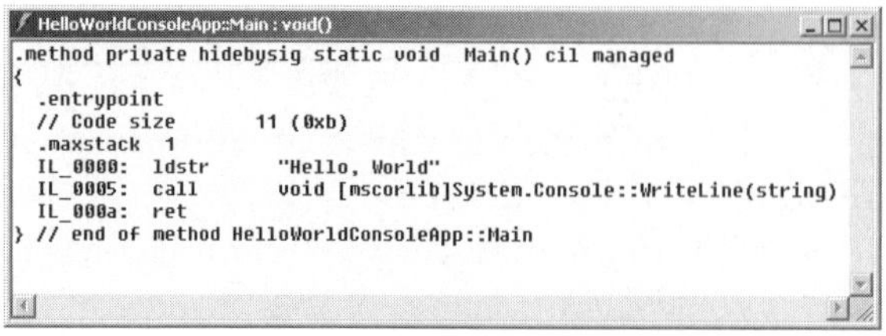


```
.method private hidebysig static void  Main() cil managed
{
  .entrypoint
  // Code size       11 (0xb)
  .maxstack  1
  IL_0000:  ldstr      "Hello, World"
  IL_0005:  call       void [mscorlib]System.Console::WriteLine(string)
  IL_000a:  ret
} // end of method HelloWorldConsoleApp::Main
```

Figure 1-13 Looking at the disassembled MSIL for a "Hello, World" application presents a whole new perspective on the canonical example.

Once again, the *.method* record can be seen as defining a method to .NET, with its attributes further defining how this method will be treated by the runtime. In this case, the method is defined as having *private* scope (the code can't be called by any code except that defined in this specific class) and being *static* (not specific to a given instance of the class).

Other than the *.method* record, the *Main* method contains only three instructions. The first instruction, *ldstr*, pushes the string constant "Hello, World" onto the stack, and the *call* instruction invokes *System.Console::WriteLine*. Note that although we passed a literal string here, this value is actually an instance of the *System.String* class and represents a Unicode-encoded managed object. Finally, the last instruction tells the runtime to return to the calling method.

Obviously, there isn't much to see in an application as simple as "Hello, World." However, now that you see how easy it is to use the ILDASM tool, we'll be using it from time to time to highlight some internal information that should help make you a more productive and knowledgeable C# developer. Now let's talk a little more about assemblies and how you can create libraries and modules using the C# compiler.

Working with Assemblies and Modules

So far, you've seen how to code and build a very basic C# application. Now let's look at the.NET construct named an *assembly*, as well as how to create DLLs and .NET modules.

Assembly Overview

All .NET binaries that use the .NET runtime consist of an assembly or a group of assemblies. When you compile an application by using the C# compiler, you're actually creating an assembly. You might not realize this unless you're specifically attempting to place multiple modules in a single assembly or taking advantage of some assembly-specific feature such as versioning.

However, you need to realize that any time you build an EXE or a DLL by using the */t:library* switch, you're creating an assembly with a manifest that describes the assembly to the .NET runtime. In addition, by using the */t:module* switch, you can create a module that's really a DLL with an extension of .net-module but without a manifest. In other words, although logically the module is still a DLL, it doesn't belong to an assembly and must be added to an assembly either by using the */addmodule* switch when compiling an application or by using the Assembly Generation tool. You'll see how to do this later, in the section "Building Assemblies."

Manifest Data

An assembly's manifest can be stored in different ways. If you compile a standalone application or DLL, the manifest will be incorporated into the resulting PE. This is known as a *single-file assembly*. A *multifile assembly* can also be generated, with the manifest existing as either a standalone entity within the assembly or as an attachment to one of the modules within the assembly.

The definition of an assembly also largely depends on how you're using it. From a client's perspective, an assembly is a named and versioned collection of modules, exported types, and, optionally, resources. From the assembly creator's viewpoint, an assembly is a means of packaging related modules, types, and resources and exporting only what a client should use. Having said that, it's the manifest that provides the level of indirection between the implementation details of the assembly and what the client should use. Here's a breakdown of the information that gets stored in an assembly's manifest:

■ **Assembly name**   The textual name of the assembly.

■ **Versioning information**   This string contains four distinct parts that make up a version number. They include a major and minor version number as well as a revision and build number.

■ **An (optional) shared name and signed assembly hash**   This information pertains to the deployment of assemblies and is covered in "Assembly Deployment" later in this section.

■ **Files** This list includes all files that exist in the assembly.

■ **Referenced assemblies** This is a list of all external assemblies that are directly referenced from the manifest's assembly.

■ **Types** This is the list of all types in the assembly with a mapping to the module containing the type. This data is what helps the reflection example in Chapter 18, "Multithreading and Asynchronous Programming," that iterates through all the types in an assembly execute so quickly.

■ **Security** permissions This is a list of security permissions that are explicitly refused by the assembly.

■ **Custom attributes** As with types, custom attributes are stored in the assembly's manifest for quicker access during reflection.

More Info Chapter 6 describes how to create your own custom attributes.

■ **Product information** This information includes Company, Trademark, Product, and Copyright values.

Benefits of Assemblies

Assemblies afford the developer numerous benefits, including packaging, deployment, and versioning. Let's take a look at each.

Assembly Packaging

One advantage packaging multiple modules in a single physical file is performance improvement. When you create an application and deploy it using a multifile assembly, the .NET runtime needs to load only the required modules. This strategy has the effect of reducing the working set of the application.

Assembly Deployment

The smallest unit of deployment in .NET is the assembly. As I mentioned previously, you can create a .NET module with the */t:module* switch, but you must include that module in an assembly if you want to deploy it. In addition, although it's tempting to say that assemblies are a means of application deployment, this isn't technically true. It's more accurate to view assemblies in .NET as a form of *class deployment*—much like a DLL in Win32—in which a single application can be made up of many assemblies.

Because assemblies are self-describing, the easiest method of deploying them is to copy the assembly to the desired destination folder. Then when you attempt to run an application contained in the assembly, the manifest will instruct the .NET runtime about the modules that are contained in the assembly. In addition, the assembly contains references to any external assemblies that the application needs.

The most common means of deployment is though *private assemblies*— that is, assemblies that are copied to a folder and aren't shared. How do you specify a private assembly? This is the default, and it occurs automatically unless you explicitly make the assembly a *shared assembly*. Sharing assemblies takes a bit more work and will be covered later in this section under "Creating Shared Assemblies."

Assembly Versioning

Another great advantage of using assemblies is built-in versioning—specifically, the end of *DLL hell*. DLL hell refers to the situation in which one application overwrites a DLL needed by another application, usually with an earlier version of the same DLL, breaking the first application. Although the Win32 resource file format does allow for a versioning resource type, the operating system doesn't enforce any versioning rules so that dependant applications will continue to function. This is solely the responsibility of application programmers.

To address this issue, the manifest includes versioning information for the assembly as well as a list of all referenced assemblies and the versioning information for them. Because of this architecture, the .NET runtime can ensure that versioning policies are upheld and that applications will continue to function even when newer, incompatible versions of shared DLLs are installed on the system.

Building Assemblies

If you create a DLL with the */t:library* switch, you won't be able to add it to another assembly. This is because the compiler automatically generates a manifest for the DLL, and therefore, the DLL itself is an assembly. To see this in action, let's build a simple example. Create a file named DllTestServer.cs, and code it as follows:

```
// DllTestServer.cs
// Build with the following command-line switches:
//    csc /t:library DllTestServer.cs
public class DllTestServer
{
    public static void Foo()
```

```
        {
            System.Console.WriteLine("DllTestServer.Foo " +
                "(DllTestServer.DLL)");
        }
}
```

Now build this assembly as a DLL by issuing the following command at the command prompt. The */t* switch tells the compiler that your target is a library (DLL) rather than the default of an application (*/t:exe*):

```
csc /t:library DllTestServer.cs
```

A quick check of your directory will verify that you have indeed created a DLL. Now let's see how easy it is to use a DLL from a C# application. For simplicity's sake, in the same folder, create a new file named DllTestClient.cs and code it as follows:

```
// DllTestClient.cs
// Build with the following command-line switches:
//     csc DllTestClient.cs /r:DllTestServer.dll
using System;
using System.Diagnostics;
using System.Reflection;

class DllTestClientApp
{
    public static void Main()
    {
        Assembly DLLAssembly =
            Assembly.GetAssembly(typeof(DllTestServer));
        Console.WriteLine("\nDllTestServer.dll Assembly " +
            "Information");
        Console.WriteLine("\t" + DLLAssembly);

        Process p = Process.GetCurrentProcess();
        string AssemblyName = p.ProcessName + ".exe";
        Assembly ThisAssembly = Assembly.LoadFrom(AssemblyName);
        Console.WriteLine("DllTestClient.exe Assembly " +
            "Information");
        Console.WriteLine("\t" + ThisAssembly + "\n");

    Console.WriteLine("Calling DllTestServer.Foo...");
    DllTestServer.Foo();
    }
}
```

Now build this client application by issuing the following command at the command prompt. The */r* switch on the command-line compiler simply tells the C# compiler to reference or link to the specified library:

```
csc DllTestClient.cs /r:DllTestServer.dll
```

Don't worry about the specifics of this code for now; it makes use of several topics that we won't discuss until Chapter 19, "Querying Metadata with Reflection," such as reflection and the *Process* object. These are the key points to glean from this example:

- The code loads and displays assembly information from both the DllTestServer.dll and the DllTestClient.exe files to illustrate that they are indeed separate assemblies.

- The code then calls the lone method, *DllTestServer.Foo*, in the DllTestServer.dll to illustrate how incredibly easy it is to separate code into DLLs with .NET and the C# language.

Run the program to see the output shown in Figure 1-14.

Figure 1-14   In .NET, you can build and use DLLs by simply changing a single compiler switch.

Creating Assemblies with Multiple Modules

In the previous example, we had two classes—*DllTestServer* and *DllTest-ClientApp*—in two distinct assemblies. So how was the *DllTestClientApp* class able to access the *DllTestServer* class so easily? This easy access was due to the *public* keyword prefacing the *DllTestServer* class. As you'll learn in Chapter 3, this keyword, known as an *access modifier*, makes the class available to other code—even code outside the current assembly). If you change the access modifier to *internal*, the client code won't compile because, by definition, the *internal* access modifier specifies that the type being modified is accessible only to other code in the same assembly. And we now know that these two classes exist in separate assemblies. So now the question becomes, "How can I create multiple modules but place them in the same assembly so that I can use the *internal* access modifier to prevent outside code from accessing my types?" Well, I'm glad you asked. You perform this task by creating a .NET module (.netmodule) instead of a library (DLL). Let's see how to accomplish this process via a simple demo application.

Create a new file named NetModuleServer.cs, and code it as follows. Notice that you can now use the *internal* access modifier so that the class is accessible only to code within the assembly:

```
// NetModuleTestServer.cs
// Build with the following command-line switches:
//      csc /t:library NetModuleTestServer.cs
public class NetModuleTestServer
{
    public static void Bar()
    {
        System.Console.WriteLine("NetModuleTestServer.Bar " +
            "(NetModuleTestServer.netmodule)");
    }
}
```

Build this module with the following call to the C# compiler:

```
csc /t:module NetModuleServer.cs
```

Now create a new file in the same folder named NetModuleClient:

```
// NetModuleTestClientApp.cs
// Build with the following command-line switches:
//
// csc addmodule:NetModuleServer.netmodule NetModuleTestClientApp.cs
using System;
using System.Diagnostics;
using System.Reflection;

class NetModuleTestClientApp
{
    public static void Main()
    {
        Assembly DLLAssembly = Assembly.GetAssembly(
            typeof(NetModuleTestServer));
        Console.WriteLine("\nNetModuleTestServer.dll Assembly " +
            "Information");
        Console.WriteLine("\t" + DLLAssembly);
```

```
Process p = Process.GetCurrentProcess();
string AssemblyName = p.ProcessName + ".exe";
Assembly ThisAssembly = Assembly.LoadFrom(AssemblyName);
Console.WriteLine("NetModuleTestClient.exe Assembly " +
    "Information");
Console.WriteLine("\t" + ThisAssembly + "\n");

Console.WriteLine("Calling NetModuleTestServer.Bar...");
NetModuleTestServer.Bar();
    }
}
```

Because we're building with a .NET module instead of a DLL, we need to use a different compiler switch. First, you must remove the */r* switch because it's used only to reference external assemblies and now both modules will reside in the same assembly. Then you must insert the */addmodule* switch, which is used to tell the compiler which modules to add to the assembly that's being created:

```
csc /addmodule:NetModuleTestServer.netmodule NetModuleClient.cs
```

Build and run the application to see the results shown in Figure 1-15.

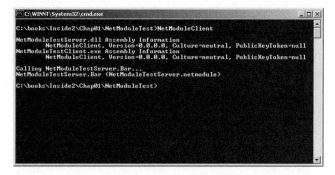

Figure 1-15   By changing a single compiler switch, you can go from a multimodule, multi-assembly application to combining your modules into a single assembly for easier code control.

You can also create an assembly with the Assembly Generation tool. This tool takes as its input one or more files that are either .NET modules—containing MSIL—or resource and image files. The output is a file with an assembly manifest. You use the Assembly Generation tool if you have several DLLs and you want to distribute and version them as a single unit. Assuming that your DLLs are named A.DLL, B.DLL, and C.DLL, you could use the al.exe application to create the composite assembly as follows:

```
al /out:COMPOSITE.DLL A.DLL B.DLL C.DLL
```

Creating Shared Assemblies

You share assemblies when you want to use an assembly with multiple applications and when versioning is important. To share an assembly, you must create a *shared name*—also known as a *strong name*—for the assembly by using the Strong Name tool in the .NET SDK. These are the four main reasons for using a strong name:

■ It's the mechanism in .NET for generating a globally unique name.

■ Because the generated key pair (which I'll explain shortly) includes a signature, you can tell whether an assembly has been tampered with after its original creation.

■ Strong names guarantee that a third party can't release a subsequent version of an assembly you've built. Once again, this is because of signatures—the third party won't have your private key.

■ When .NET loads an assembly, the runtime can verify that the assembly came from the publisher that the caller is expecting.

The first step in creating a strong name is to use the Strong Name tool to create a key file for the assembly. This is done by specifying the –*k* switch with the name of the output file that will contain the key. Here we'll just make something up—InsideCSharp.key—and create the file as follows:

```
sn -k InsideCSharp.key
```

Upon running this, you should get a confirmation message such as that displayed in Figure 1-16.

Figure 1-16 The Strong Name utility enables you to create a key file for an assembly.

The second step is to add the *AssemblyKeyFile* attribute to the client source file. First, create a new file called SharedAssemblyServer.cs, and code it as follows:

```
// SharedAssemblyServer.cs
// Build with the following command-line switches:
//     csc /t:module SharedAssemblyServer.cs
internal class SharedAssemblyServer
{
    public static void Test()
    {
        System.Console.WriteLine("SharedAssemblyServer.Foo " +
            "(SharedAssemblyServer.netmodule)");
    }
}
```

Once you've coded the server, compile it as you have the previous .NET modules:

```
csc /t:module SharedAssemblyServer.cs
```

Now, for the client, create the following SharedAssemblyClient.cs file. Take note of the aforementioned *AssemblyKeyFile* attribute. Although attributes won't be covered until Chapter 6, it's enough for now to understand that they provide a means of defining various run-time characteristics of a class.

```
// SharedAssemblyClient.cs
// Build with the following command-line switches:
//     csc /addmodule:SharedAssemblyServer.netmodule SharedAssemblyClient.cs
using System;
using System.Diagnostics;
using System.Reflection;

[assembly:AssemblyKeyFile("InsideCSharp.key")]

class SharedAssemblyClientApp
{
    public static void Main()
    {
        Assembly DLLAssembly =
            Assembly.GetAssembly(typeof(SharedAssemblyServer));
        Console.WriteLine("SharedAssemblyServer.netmodule " +
            "Assembly Information");
        Console.WriteLine("\t" + DLLAssembly);

        Process p = Process.GetCurrentProcess();
        string AssemblyName = p.ProcessName + ".exe";
        Assembly ThisAssembly = Assembly.LoadFrom(AssemblyName);
```

```
        Console.WriteLine("SharedAssemblyClient.dll " +
            "Assembly Information");
        Console.WriteLine("\t" + ThisAssembly);

        Console.WriteLine("Calling SharedAssemblyClient.Test...");
        SharedAssemblyServer.Test();
    }
}
```

As you can see, the *assembly:AssemblyKeyFile* attribute's constructor takes the name of the key file that was generated with the Strong Name utility. This constructor enables you to specify a key pair you can use to give your assembly a strong name. Another important point is that this attribute is an assembly-level attribute. Therefore, technically it can be placed in any file in the assembly and isn't attached to a specific class. However, it's customary to place this attribute just below the *using* statements and before any class definitions.

When you run the application, take note of the *PublicKeyToken* value of the assembly. This value was *null* in the previous two examples because those assemblies were considered to be private assemblies. However, now we've defined the assembly as a shared assembly, and so it has an associated public key token, as shown in Figure 1-17.

Note that this program fails under Windows 2000 because *ProcessName* truncates the returned string to 15 characters under this operating system.

Figure 1-17   Strong names allow for the sharing of assemblies.

According to the *Assembly* object that we instantiated for this demo, this assembly is shared. But how can we tell which other assemblies in our .NET system are shared? By using the *global assembly cache*. Let's examine this part of .NET and see the role it plays in shared assemblies.

Working with the Global Assembly Cache

Every .NET installation has a code cache known as the global assembly cache. This area serves three primary purposes:

- It's used to store code downloaded from the Internet or other servers—both http and file servers. Note that code downloaded for a particular application is stored in the private portion of the cache, which prevents it from being accessed by others.

- It's a data store for components shared by multiple .NET applications. Assemblies that are installed into the cache by using the Global Assembly Cache tool are stored in the global portion of the cache and are accessible by all applications on the machine.

- One question I hear frequently is, "Where does the JITted code get stored so that my C# code is JITted only the first time it's executed?" Now you know the answer: native code versions of assemblies that have been preJITted are stored in the cache.

Viewing the Cache

Let's take a look at the cache to see the currently installed and shared assemblies. Using Microsoft Explorer, open the c:\winnt\assembly folder. To aid in viewing pertinent information about assemblies, .NET features a shell extension known as the Assembly Cache Viewer (shfusion.dll). This tool enables you to view assembly information, such as the version number, culture, public key token, and even whether the assembly has been preJITted.

Another means of viewing the cache is by using the Global Assembly Cache tool. This tool enables you to perform several basic tasks by specifying any of the following command-line switches, which are mutually exclusive:

- *-i* This flag installs an assembly to the global assembly cache. Here's an example:

```
gacutil -i HelloWorld.DLL
```

- Shortly, you'll see how to add the *SharedAssemblyClient* assembly to the cache by using this switch.

- *-u* This flag uninstalls an assembly, including any version information, from the global assembly cache. If you don't specify the version information, *all* assemblies with the specified name are removed.

Therefore, the first example here uninstalls all *HelloWorld* assemblies, regardless of version number, and the second example uninstalls the specified version:

```
gacutil -u HelloWorld
gacutil -u HelloWorld, ver=1,0,0,0
```

■   *-l*   This flag lists the contents of the global assembly cache, including the assembly name, its version number, its location, and its shared name.

In some of the earlier .NET betas, one problem I noticed was that when exploring the c:\winnt\assembly folder, the shell extension didn't execute. This was caused by the fact that the shfusion.dll extension didn't register properly. If this happens on your system, open a command prompt and enter the following from the c:\winnt\Microsoft.net\framework\v*XXX* folder, where *XXX* represents the version number of the .NET Framework that you're running. Search for the shfusion.dll file, and use that folder. Here I've used the folder representing my current .NET build:

c:\winnt\microsoft.net\framework\v1.0.3705>regsvr32 shfusion.dll

Now that you've created a public key file and assigned it to an assembly, let's add that assembly to the cache. To do that, type the following at the command prompt:

```
gacutil -i SharedAssemblyClient.exe
```

If all goes well, you should receive the following confirmation:

```
Assembly successfully added to the cache
```

At this point, you can use the *gacutil –l* command to view the assemblies listed in the cache and find the *SharedAssemblyClient*, or you can use the Assembly Cache Viewer. Let's use the latter. If you open the cache in Windows Explorer (C:\Winnt\Assembly or C:\Windows\Assembly), you should see the *SharedAssemblyClient* assembly listed along with the other assemblies. Right-click that assembly and select Properties, and you'll see things such as the public key value, version number, and physical location of the assembly on your hard disk. Your public key will be different than mine, but the main point is that it will be the same as that displayed by executing the SharedAssemblyClient application.

Summary

Wow! That was a heck of a lot of work for a first chapter! You started out by writing a simple "Hello, World" application and building and running it from the command line. You then discovered how Visual Studio can help you create the same basic C# application in a fraction of the time. From there, you learned a bit about the internals of a .NET application, what a JITter is, and how .NET applications are loaded and executed under Windows, and you even got your feet wet with some disassembled MSIL. Finally, the chapter wrapped up with a section on assemblies and how to create both .NET modules and DLLs. While it's been fun diving into the code and making things happen, it's now imperative you start to understand some of the underlying bits that make up the .NET Framework. Therefore, in the next chapter, we'll look at the .NET runtime and common type system and how they provide the framework within which managed code is executed.

2

The .NET Type System

In Chapter 1, "Building C# Applications and Libraries," you created several demo applications, most of which used the *System.Console* class and other assorted .NET classes. However, some obvious questions remain: Where do these classes come from? How are they accessed by C#? Can they be extended for your own use? What other types are available to you? These are perfectly valid questions, and they necessitate us taking a short break from coding to look into something known as the *common type system* (CTS). The CTS is responsible for defining all available .NET types as well as the rules that the common language runtime must follow with regard to applications declaring and using these types.

I've intentionally kept this chapter a bit shorter than others for two reasons. First, as mentioned in Chapter 1, I'd rather teach you the .NET underpinnings as you learn to code C#—instead of forcing you to read several dry, technical chapters on the entire .NET infrastructure first. Second, because the CTS is all about the types that .NET supports, I really can't go into too much detail on the idiosyncrasies of how the CTS supports each type because these types aren't covered until subsequent chapters. Therefore, my objective with this chapter is to simply give you an overview of the CTS and the advantages it provides. As you continue with this book and learn about more types, I'll refer you back to this chapter and the CTS in general as needed.

In this chapter, I'll provide a brief overview of this new type system so that you can learn the types available to you as a C# developer. That way, you can begin to understand the ramifications of using the different types in C# programs. We'll begin by exploring the concept that every programming element is an object in .NET. We'll then look at how .NET divides types into two categories— value types and reference types—and we'll discover how a concept known as *boxing* enables a completely object-oriented type system to function efficiently.

Everything Is an Object

Most object-oriented languages have two distinct types: types that are intrinsic to the language (*primitive types*), and types that can be created by users of the language (*classes*). As you might guess, primitive types are usually simple types, such as characters, strings, and numbers. Classes, on the other hand, are more elaborate types whose members are either intrinsic types or other classes. Furthermore, classes are usually either built by the user or provided by a third-party vendor.

Having two discrete sets of types causes a lot of problems. One problem relates to compatibility. For example, let's say you're working in a traditional language—such as C or Pascal—and want to have a collection of both integers and doubles. In most languages, you would need to create two separate classes—one to encapsulate the integers, and one to encapsulate the doubles. This is because these primitive types normally have nothing in common. They aren't real objects, so they don't derive from a common base class. They're more like "magic types"—as Anders Heijlsberg calls them—that you have to deal with individually on their own terms.

A similar compatibility problem surfaces in these traditional systems when you want to specify that a method can take an argument of *any* type supported by the language. Because these primitive types are incompatible, you can't specify a single argument list that enables you to handle any type. In a language such as C++, you have to write a *wrapper class* with an overloaded constructor for each primitive type that you want to support. Here's an example of what that might look like:

```
class COurType
{
public:
    COurType(double d);
    COurType(int i);
    COurType(LPCSTR sz);
    :
    // We need a ctor for every other type we want to support.
};

class CTest
{
    public Foo(COurType& type)
    {
    }
};
```

On top of that, how would you get the value from this magical type? You would have to write an overloaded function to retrieve the value from the special wrapper class. Needless to say, this is too much work. Don't get me wrong—I'm all for writing cool C++ classes to make our lives easier. However, you get to a point of diminishing returns when the amount of work put into a class that was supposed to save you time ends up taking more time to write than that gained! Therefore, the majority of programmers simply accept the fact that they have two categories of types and that the intrinsic types aren't compatible—and they learn to live with that. By the way, this is why most scholars will tell you that C++ isn't an object-oriented language but instead is an *object-based* language.

Thankfully, issues such as these are no longer a problem in the world of .NET and C# programming. Why? Because everything in the CTS is a truly an object! That's right—there aren't any intrinsic data types for the various languages. In fact, not only is everything an object, but more importantly, all objects implicitly derive from a single base class defined as part of the CTS: the *System.Object* type. Let's look at this type now.

The Root of All Types: *System.Object*

As I've mentioned, all types ultimately derive from the *System.Object* type. This derivation happens regardless of whether you explicitly specify it in your class definition. As a result, the following definitions are identical:

```
class DerivedFromObject : System
{
}
```

```
class DerivedFromObject // Implicitly derived from System.Object
{
}
```

Having a single base class from which all other classes are derived is referred to as having a *singly rooted hierarchy*. One of the major benefits of this approach is that all types in the system share the minimum set of abilities. Table 2-1 describes the four public methods that all types inherit from the *System.Object* class.

Table 2-1
Public Methods of the *System.Object* Type

Method Name	Description
bool Equals	Compares two object references at run time to determine whether they're the same object. If the two variables refer to the same object, the return value is *true*. With value types, this method returns *true* if the two types are identical and have the same value.
int GetHashCode	Retrieves the hash code specified for an object. Hash functions are used when the implementer of a class wants to put an object's hash code in a hash table for performance reasons.
Type GetType	Used with the reflection methods (discussed in Chapter 19, "Querying Metadata with Reflection") to retrieve the type information for a given object.
string ToString	Used by default to retrieve the name of the object. This method can be overridden by derived classes to return a more user-friendly string representation of the object.

Table 2-2 describes the protected methods of *System.Object*.

Table 2-2
Protected Methods of the *System.Object* Type

Method Name	Description
void Finalize	Called by the runtime to allow for cleanup prior to garbage collection. Note that this method might or might not be called. Therefore, don't put code that must run into this method. This rule delves into something known as *deterministic finalization*, which I'll cover in detail in Chapter 3, "Classes and Structs."
Object Memberwise-Clone	Represents a *shallow copy* of the object—a copy of the object containing references to other objects that doesn't include copies of the objects referenced. If you need your class to support a *deep copy*, which does include copies of the referenced objects, you must implement the *ICloneable* interface and manually do the cloning, or copying, yourself.

Now that you know that all types are objects in the CTS and that they all ultimately derive from *System.Object*, let's talk about the two main categories of types supported by the CTS: value types and reference types.

Value Types and Reference Types

Creating a language in which everything is an object isn't a new concept. Other languages have tried this, one of the most famous being SmallTalk. The biggest disadvantage of making everything an object has always been poor performance. Let's look at an example that illustrates this point. Suppose you're attempting to add two values in SmallTalk, both of type double.

Because both doubles are actually objects, the result is that the SmallTalk runtime will create a new object on the heap. At the very least, the runtime will need to instantiate whatever class members are defined and then do any necessary background work to keep track of the class for garbage collection purposes. Needless to say, all this work the runtime performs is extremely inefficient when all you want to do is sum two numbers.

Thus, the designers of the CTS were faced with the task of creating a type system in which everything is an object but the type system works efficiently in cases where you really don't care about treating an object like an object, as in our example. Their solution was to separate the CTS types into two categories: *value types* and *reference types*. These terms, as you'll soon see, reflect how variables are allocated and how they function internally and provide the backbone for a more elegant and efficient approach to building an object-oriented development environment.

Value Types

When you have a variable that's a value type, that variable contains actual data. Thus, the first rule of value types is that they can't be *null*. In other words, you can state that a value type variable always has a value. That value might be *0*, but the variable does have a value.

For example, the following statement allocates memory by creating a variable of the CTS type *System.Int32* in C#. This statement allocates a 32-bit space on the stack for the *myInt* variable, and the value *42* is stored in the allocated space:

```
System.Int32 myInt = 42;
```

There are several value types defined in C#, including enumerators, structures, and primitives. (Primitives are now objects internally.) Anytime you declare a variable of one of these types, the compiler allocates the number of bytes associated with that type and you work directly with that allocated memory. In addition, when you pass a variable that's a value type, you're passing that variable's value and not a reference to its underlying object. The subject of passing value types vs. passing reference types is an important one for being able to effectively program .NET applications. Therefore, this subject is covered in great detail in Chapter 4, "Methods."

Reference Types

Reference types are similar to references in C++ because you can view them almost as type-safe pointers. Instead of merely being an address, which might or might not point to what you think it does, a reference—when not *null*—is always guaranteed to point to an object that's of the type specified and that has already been allocated on the heap. Also note that a reference can be *null*, signifying that it currently doesn't refer or point to an object.

In the following example, a *string* reference type is being allocated. But under the covers, the value has been allocated on the heap and a reference to that value has been returned.

```
System.String myString = "Hello, World";
```

Figure 2-1 illustrates the main difference in terms of memory allocation.

```
System.Int32 myInt = 42;
System.String myString = "Hello, World";
```

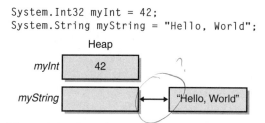

Figure 2-1   One of the key differences between value types and reference types is in how they're allocated and where the value for the variable resides in memory.

Notice that the value for our allocated *System.Int32* variable is in the memory that was allocated for the variable, while the value for the *System.String* value is simply pointed to from the allocated reference type's memory. This means that any time you declare a variable of reference type, you're working with a reference (pointer) to that object instead of working directly with the bits, as with value types. The consequences might not be obvious here, so I'll elaborate a bit. Let's say that you have a variable of type *string* that you allocate in a method named *Foo*. As mentioned already, this means that locally—within the context of the *Foo* method—you have a reference on the heap that points to the real data. If you pass that object to another method—*Bar*—and that method modifies the object before returning, it has modified the one and only datum that both methods' variables are pointing to! Obviously, this isn't always desirable. As I mentioned earlier, I'll discuss how to deal with this type of situation—and many more related issues that come up when passing reference values to methods—in Chapter 4.

Like value types, several types are defined as reference types in C#:

■ Classes

■ Arrays

■ Interfaces

■ Delegates

You already worked a bit with classes in Chapter 1, and I'll cover them in much more detail in Chapter 3. The topics of arrays, interfaces, and delegates are covered in Chapter 5, "Properties, Arrays, and Indexers," Chapter 7, "Interfaces," and Chapter 14, "Delegates and Event Handlers," respectively.

Boxing and Unboxing

The question becomes, "How do these different categories of types make the system more efficient?" The answer lies in understanding the magic of boxing. At its simplest, boxing is the conversion of a value type to a reference type. The reciprocal case—converting a reference type to a value type—is known as *unboxing*. Let's look at some examples of when you would perform boxing and unboxing to bring this concept into focus.

Converting from Value Types to Reference Types

We'll start with a simple example of boxing—or converting a value type instance to a reference type. Take a look at the following code snippet:

```
int foo = 42;        // Value type.
object bar = foo;    // foo is boxed to bar.
```

In the first line of this code, we're creating a variable (*foo*) of type *int*. As you know, *int* is a value type because it's a primitive type. In the second line, the compiler sees the variable *foo* being copied to a reference type, which is represented by the variable *bar*. Let's look at the underlying Microsoft intermediate language (MSIL) by using the ILDASM tool I introduced in Chapter 1.

Notice the *.locals* record where two local variables have been defined in Figure 2-2. Their types are *int32* and *object* and correlate to our *foo* and *bar* variables, respectively. The first instruction of the code is then an *ldc* opcode that loads a numeric constant value (*42*). The *i4.s* part of the instruction refers to the fact that the value is being pushed onto the stack as a 32-bit (4 byte) integer. Because the stack now has our value, that value is popped into our local variable via the *stloc* opcode. Note that the *.0* here refers to the value being popped to the first local variable (*foo*, in this case).

```
Box1::Main : void()                                    _ □ ×

.method public hidebysig static void Main() cil managed  ▲
{
  .entrypoint
  // Code size        11 (0xb)
  .maxstack  1
  .locals init (int32 V_0,
                object V_1)
  IL_0000: ldc.i4.s   42
  IL_0002: stloc.0
  IL_0003: ldloc.0
  IL_0004: box        [mscorlib]System.Int32
  IL_0009: stloc.1
  IL_000a: ret
} // end of method Box1::Main
```

Figure 2-2   Example in MSIL of a value type being boxed.

Once this value has been popped from the stack, it's loaded back onto the stack (*ldloc*) and the CIL *box* instruction is used to convert this value to a reference type. The *stloc.1* instruction then instructs the runtime to pop the value returned from the *box* instruction to the *bar* local variable.

We've seen the C# example and the underlying MSIL code, but what really happens when a value type is boxed? I'm glad you asked:

1. First, memory is allocated on the heap. Obviously, because the value type will ultimately be represented by an object, the amount of memory allocated on the heap must be the size of the value type plus the amount of memory needed to hold the object and its internal structures, such as the virtual method table.

2. The value type's value is then copied to the newly allocated heap memory.

3. The address of the newly allocated object is placed on the stack and now points to a reference type.

Converting from Reference Types to Value Types

Now let's look at the reciprocal side of the equation: unboxing. Here I've added a third variable and will convert the object back to an *int* by casting it:

```
int foo = 42;        // Value type.
object bar = foo;    // foo is boxed to bar.
int baz = (int)bar;  // Unboxed back to int.
```

Notice that when boxing—that is, when converting from a value type to a reference type—there's no explicit cast needed. However, when unboxing—converting from a reference type to a value type—the cast is needed. This requirement exists because, in the case of unboxing, an object can be cast to any type. Therefore, the cast is necessary so that the compiler can verify that the cast is valid for the specified variable type. Casting involves strict rules that are governed by the CTS. We'll take a look at this issue in more detail later in this chapter, in the section, "Casting Between Types."

As we did with the boxing example, let's look at the MSIL of the unboxing code snippet, as shown in Figure 2-3. We'll start by looking at instruction IL__000a because that's where our new code begins. Once again, here the *ldloc* opcode is being used to load (push) a value onto the stack. The *1* indicates the second (relative to 0) local variable—the *bar* object. The *unbox* opcode is then used to convert the value on the stack from a reference type to a value type—to a *System.Int32*, in this case. Finally, the value is popped off the stack (via *stloc.2*) into the *baz* local variable, and the *Main* method returns.

```
Box1::Main : void()                                    _ □ x
.method public hidebysig static void Main() cil managed ▲
{
  .entrypoint
  // Code size       19 (0x13)
  .maxstack  1
  .locals init (int32 V_0,
                object V_1,
                int32 V_2)
  IL_0000: ldc.i4.s   42
  IL_0002: stloc.0
  IL_0003: ldloc.0
  IL_0004: box        [mscorlib]System.Int32
  IL_0009: stloc.1
  IL_000a: ldloc.1
  IL_000b: unbox      [mscorlib]System.Int32
  IL_0010: ldind.i4
  IL_0011: stloc.2
  IL_0012: ret
} // end of method Box1::Main
```

Figure 2-3   Example in MSIL of a reference type being unboxed to a value type.

At the runtime level, the tasks performed to unbox a type are fairly straightforward:

1. Because an object is being converted, the runtime must first determine that the address on the stack points to a valid object and that

the object type can be converted to the value type specified in the MSIL *unbox* instruction call. As mentioned earlier, if either test fails, an exception of type *InvalidCastException* is thrown.

2.   Once it's been determined that the cast is valid, a pointer to the value within the object is returned. Note that while boxing creates a new copy of the type being converted, unboxing doesn't. You might be wondering, "Does that mean that if I convert an object to an *int*, changing the *int* value will alter what the object's pointing at?" The answer is "usually not," but it depends on how the boxing occurred. In the previous code snippet, it wasn't the unbox operation that caused a copy of the bits—it was the fact that we set a third local variable (*baz*) to the unboxed value of the second variable (*bar*).

More Boxing Examples

While conducting research for this book, I was fortunate enough to be invited to Microsoft to work alongside some of the C# and .NET common language runtime team members, one of those being Jeffrey Richter. In our discussion of boxing and unboxing, Jeff brought up some rather interesting examples of when and where boxing is done. Take a look at the following example:

```
using System;

class test
{
    public static void Main()
    {
        int i = 42;   // Simple unboxed value type
        object o = i; // Will cause a boxing operation of i

        Console.WriteLine(i + ", " + (Int32)o);
    }
}
```

Jeff then asked me to tell him how many boxing operations were occurring. You might be surprised to see that there are actually *three* boxing operations happening here. (For the record, I cited two boxing operations and one unboxing operation.) Let's see how that occurs.

The first line of code simply declares a value type variable (*i*) and gives it a hard-coded value of *42*. From what you've already read, you should know what happens in the next line of code. There, a reference type *object* (*o*) is being declared and set to the value of *i*. Because reference types always point to objects on the heap, *i* is boxed and the resulting address is stored as *o*. From there, a call is made to the *Console.WriteLine* method. Although this method has many overloads, the version that's being used here takes a single *String* object as its only parameter. Therefore, if we look at the MSIL for this code, shown in Figure 2-4, we'll see that the static *String.Concat* method is being called to concatenate these values together to produce a single *String* object that's then passed to the *Console.WriteLine* method.

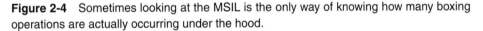

```
test::Main : void() - Notepad
.method public hidebysig static void Main() cil managed
{
  .entrypoint
  // Code size       44 (0x2c)
  .maxstack  3
  .locals init (int32 V_0,
           object V_1)
  IL_0000: ldc.i4.s   42
  IL_0002: stloc.0
  IL_0003: ldloc.0
  IL_0004: box        [mscorlib]System.Int32
  IL_0009: stloc.1
  IL_000a: ldloc.0
  IL_000b: box        [mscorlib]System.Int32
  IL_0010: ldstr      ","
  IL_0015: ldloc.1
  IL_0016: unbox      [mscorlib]System.Int32
  IL_001b: ldind.i4
  IL_001c: box        [mscorlib]System.Int32
  IL_0021: call       string [mscorlib]System.String::Concat(object,
                                                             object,
                                                             object)
  IL_0026: call       void [mscorlib]System.Console::WriteLine(string)
  IL_002b: ret
} // end of method test::Main
```

Figure 2-4   Sometimes looking at the MSIL is the only way of knowing how many boxing operations are actually occurring under the hood.

The *String.Concat* method also has several overloads, but as you can see, the overload of taking parameters of type *object* was the closest matching version that the compiler could locate. Therefore, if you scan down to line IL_000a of the MSIL listing, you'll see that the very first parameter in our *WriteLine* call needs to be boxed from a value type (*i*) to a reference type in accordance with this method signature. The next opcode is a *ldstr* to push the string literal ", " onto the stack. From there, lines IL_0015 and IL_0016 indicate that the *o* object is being pushed onto the stack and then unboxed. This step is necessary because of the explicit cast to an *Int32* type. At this point, we have an unboxed version of the reference type *o*. Therefore, the compiler needs to box this version back into a reference type for the *String.Concat* method. This process is what's happening in lines IL_001b and IL_001c before the call to *String.Concat*. Note that the call to *Console.WriteLine* occurs immediately after the call to *String.Concat*. This arrangement occurs because the *String.Concat* method pushed the concatenated string onto the stack before returning. Therefore, the compiler can simply call *Console.WriteLine* immediately after, because the stack is already set up with the parameter that the *Console.WriteLine* method needs.

Obviously, the explicit cast of the *o* variable to an *Int32* within the *Write-Line* call cost us a rather needless unbox and box operation. However, the point of this exercise was to illustrate that in a system such as .NET, where you have automatic type handling (such as boxing and garbage collection), you have to be very careful how you construct your C# code. Otherwise, you run the risk of unexpected performance penalties.

To get around the issue of gratuitous boxing, you could simply box the value yourself before you call a method that you know will perform implicit boxing. Let's look at an example:

```csharp
using System;
using System.Collections;

struct RGB
{
    public int red;
    public int green;
    public int blue;

    public RGB(int red, int green, int blue)
    {
        this.red = red;
        this.green = green;
        this.blue = blue;
    }

    public override String ToString()
    {
        return red.ToString("X")
            + green.ToString("X")
            + blue.ToString("X");
    }
}

class BoxTest
{
    static ArrayList rgbValues;

    public static void Main()
    {
        RGB rgb = new RGB(255, 255, 255);

        rgbValues = new ArrayList();
        rgbValues.Add(rgb);

        Console.WriteLine("The RGB value is {0}", rgb);
    }
}
```

Although some of the C# in this particular example might be new to you, the points to focus on are the following:

■ A *struct* (*RGB*) is defined. By definition, a *struct* is a value type.

■ This *struct* is passed to two different methods (*ArrayList.Add* and *Console.WriteLine*) that require reference type parameters.

Because of this code, two separate boxing operations are being performed (lines IL_0026 and IL__0037), as you can see in Figure 2-5.

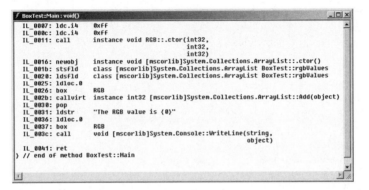

Figure 2-5   Example of a single value type being needlessly boxed twice.

Therefore, if you know that your code will incur a lot of boxing, it might be prudent to make the necessary modifications to limit the amount of boxing code that the compiler will emit. In this example, because we know we'll use the *rgb* value type instance in at least two places where a reference type is needed—thereby causing an implicit boxing operation—we simply need to create a local reference type variable, set it to the *rgb* value, and use the reference type when needed. Here's how that code would look:

```
using System;
using System.Collections;

struct RGB
{
    public int red;
    public int green;
    public int blue;

    public RGB(int red, int green, int blue)
    {
        this.red = red;
        this.green = green;
```

```
            this.blue = blue;
        }

    public override String ToString()
    {
        return red.ToString("X")
            + green.ToString("X")
            + blue.ToString("X");
    }
}

class BoxTest
{
    static ArrayList rgbValues;

    public static void Main()
    {
        RGB rgb = new RGB(255, 255, 255);
        object oRGB = rgb;

        rgbValues = new ArrayList();
        rgbValues.Add(oRGB);

        Console.WriteLine("The RGB value is {0}", oRGB);
    }
}
```

Now check out the MSIL in Figure 2-6. Note that only one boxing operation (when the *oRGB* value is set) occurs (line IL_0017). From then on, this reference type is used when needed (IL_002c and IL_0038), thereby preventing needless boxing operations.

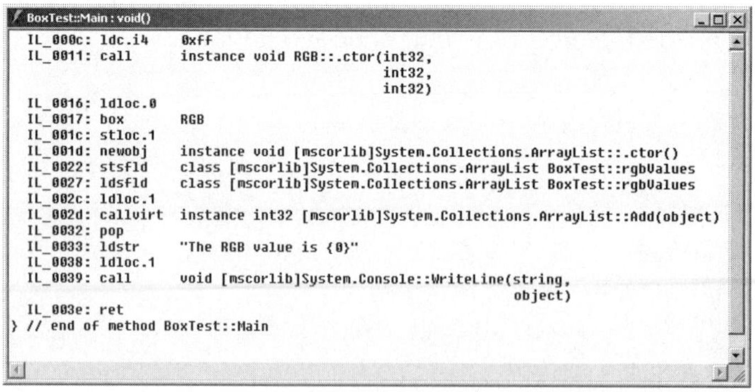

Figure 2-6   Knowing when boxing occurs under the hood can help you to optimize your code considerably with very little effort.

With boxing and unboxing, you can use a primitive type just as efficiently as any primitive type in any language, yet you can convert this primitive type to an object automatically when it needs to be treated like an object. Now let's look at the subject of types and aliases.

Types and Aliases

So far, we haven't written any applications that actually declare and use variables. Therefore, you might be wondering whether you have to use long type names such as *System.Int32* and *System.String* when defining variables in C#. Luckily, you don't have to. While the CTS is responsible for defining the types that you can use across .NET languages, most languages choose to implement *aliases* to those types.

For example, while the *System.Int32* type represents a 4-byte integer value to the CTS, the C# language provides an alias for this type that's simply named *int*. There's no advantage to using one technique over the other; therefore, it simply comes down to personal preference. Table 2-3 lists the different CTS types and their C# aliases.

Table 2-3
CTS Types and Aliases

all should be lower case.

CTS Type Name	C# Alias	Description
System.Object	*Object*	Base class for all CTS types
System.String	*String*	String
System.Sbyte	*Sbyte*	Signed 8-bit byte
System.Byte	*Byte*	Unsigned 8-bit byte
System.Int16	*Short*	Signed 16-bit value
System.UInt16	*Ushort*	Unsigned 16-bit value
System.Int32	*Int*	Signed 32-bit value
System.UInt32	*Uint*	Unsigned 32-bit value
System.Int64	*Long*	Signed 64-bit value
System.UInt64	*Ulong*	Unsigned 64-bit value
System.Char	*Char*	16-bit Unicode character
System.Single	*Float*	IEEE 32-bit float

Table 2-3
CTS Types and Aliases

CTS Type Name	C# Alias	Description
System.Double	*Double*	IEEE 64-bit float
System.Boolean	*Bool*	Boolean value (*true/false*)
System.Decimal	*Decimal*	128-bit data type that is exact to 28 or 29 digits—mainly used for financial applications in which a great degree of accuracy is required

Casting Between Types

Now let's look at one of the most important aspects of types: casting. Assuming we have a base class named *Employee* and a derived class named *ContractEmployee*, the following code works because there's always an implied upcast from a derived class to its base class:

```
class Employee { }

class ContractEmployee : Employee { }

class CastExample1
{
    public static void Main ()
    {
        Employee e = new ContractEmployee();
    }
}
```

However, the following is illegal because the compiler can't provide an implicit downcast:

```
class Employee { }

class ContractEmployee : Employee { }

class CastExample2
{

    public static void Main ()
    {
        ContractEmployee ce = new Employee(); // Won't compile.
    }
}
```

The reason for the different behavior goes back to the object-oriented concept of *substitutability*, which states that you should always be able to use a derived class in place of its base class if the class hierarchy has been defined correctly. Therefore, you should always be able to use an object of type *ContractEmployee* in place of or as an *Employee* object. That's why the first example in this section compiles.

However, you can't implicitly downcast an object of type *Employee* to an object of type *ContractEmployee* because there's no guarantee that the object supports the interface defined by the *ContractEmployee* class. Therefore, in the case of a downcast, an explicit cast is used as follows:

```
class Employee { }

class ContractEmployee : Employee { }

class CastExample3
{
    public static void Main ()
    {
        // Downcast will fail.
        ContractEmployee ce = (ContractEmployee)new Employee();
    }
}
```

But what happens if we try to trick the CTS by explicitly casting a base class to a derived class as follows?

```
class Employee { }

class ContractEmployee : Employee { }

class CastExample4
{
    public static void Main ()
    {
        Employee e = new Employee();
        ContractEmployee c = (ContractEmployee)e;
    }
}
```

The program compiles, but when you execute the program, it generates a run-time exception. There are two things to note here. First, the result isn't a compile-time error because *e* might have been an upcasted *ContractEmployee* object. Therefore, the true nature of the upcasted object can't be known until run time. Second, the common language runtime determines the object types at run time. When the runtime recognizes an invalid cast, it throws a *System.InvalidCastException.*

There's one other way of casting objects: by using the *as* keyword. The advantage to using this keyword instead of a cast is that you don't have to worry about an exception being thrown if the cast is invalid. Instead, the result will be *null.* Here's an example:

```
using System;

class Employee { }

class ContractEmployee : Employee { }

class CastExample5
{
    public static void Main ()
    {
        Employee e = new Employee();
        Console.WriteLine("e = {0}",
                        e == null ? "null" : e.ToString());

        ContractEmployee c  = e as ContractEmployee;
        Console.WriteLine("c = {0}",
                        c == null ? "null" : c.ToString());
    }
}
```

If you run this example, you'll see the following result:

```
c:\>CastExample5
e = Employee
c = null
```

Note that the ability to compare an object to *null* means that you don't run the risk of using a *null* object. In fact, if the example had attempted to call a *System.Object* method on the *c* object, the CTS would have thrown a *System.NullReferenceException.*

CTS Benefits

One of the key features of any language or run-time environment is its support for types. A language that makes available a limited number of types or that limits the programmer's ability to extend the language's built-in types isn't a language with a long life expectancy. However, having a unified type system has many other benefits.

Language Interoperability

The common type system plays an integral role in allowing language interoperability because it defines the set types that a .NET compiler must support to interoperate with other languages. The CTS itself is defined in the Common Language Specification (CLS). The CLS defines a single set of rules for every .NET compiler, ensuring that each compiler will output code that interacts with the common language runtime consistently. One of the CLS requirements is that the compiler must support certain types defined in the CTS. Because all .NET languages use a single type system, you're assured that objects and types created in different languages can interact with one another in a seamless manner. It's this CTS/CLS combination that helps make language interoperability more than just a programmer's dream.

Singly Rooted Object Hierarchy

As I mentioned earlier, an important CTS characteristic is the singly rooted object hierarchy. In the .NET Framework, every type in the system derives from the *System.Object* base class. An important departure from the C++ language, in which there's no implied base class for all classes, this single base class approach is endorsed by object-oriented programming (OOP) theorists and is implemented in most mainstream object-oriented languages. The benefits of a singly rooted hierarchy aren't immediately apparent, but over time you'll come to question how languages were designed before this type of hierarchy was adopted.

A singly rooted object hierarchy is the key to a unified type system because it guarantees that each object in the hierarchy has a common interface and that everything in the hierarchy will ultimately have the same base type. One of the main drawbacks of C++ is its lack of support for such a hierarchy. Let's consider a simple example that illustrates this point.

Suppose you've built an object hierarchy in C++ based on a base class of your own making. We'll call this base class *CFoo*. Now suppose you want to integrate with another object hierarchy whose objects all derive from a base class named *CBar*. In this example, the object hierarchies have incompatible interfaces and it will require a lot of effort to integrate the two hierarchies. You might have to use some sort of wrapper class with aggregation or use multiple inheritance to make this work. However, with a singly rooted object hierarchy, compatibility isn't an issue because each object has the same interface, which is inherited from *System.Object*. As a result, you know that each and every object in your hierarchy—and, crucially, in the hierarchies of third-party .NET code—has a certain minimal set of functionality.

Type Safety

The last benefit of the CTS that I want to mention is type safety. Type safety guarantees that types are what they say they are and that only appropriate operations can be performed on a particular type. Type safety provides a number of advantages and capabilities, most of which stem from the singly rooted object hierarchy:

- Every reference to an object is typed, and the object it's referencing is also typed. The CTS guarantees that a reference always points to what it implies it points to.

- Because the CTS tracks every type in the system, there's no way to trick the system into thinking that one type is actually another. This is obviously a major concern for distributed applications in which security is a priority.

- Each type is responsible for defining the accessibility of its members by specifying an access modifier. This is done on a member-by-member basis and includes allowing any access (by declaring the member *public*), limiting the visibility to inherited classes only (by declaring the member *protected*), denying all access (by declaring the member *private*), and allowing access only to other types in the current compilation unit (by declaring the member *internal*). I'll discuss access modifiers in more detail in Chapter 3.

Summary

The common type system is an important feature of the .NET Framework. The CTS defines the type system rules that applications must follow to run properly in the common language runtime. CTS types are divided into two categories: reference types and value types. The benefits of a common type system include language interoperability, a singly rooted object hierarchy, and type safety. Types can be converted in C# through boxing and unboxing, and compatible types can be made to share characteristics and functionality through casting.

Now let's return to some coding by learning how to define and work with classes and structures in C#.

3

Classes and Structs

Classes lie at the heart of every object-oriented language. A class can be defined as the encapsulation of data and the methods that work on that data. That's true in any object-oriented or object-based language. Beyond that, two major factors set these languages apart: the types of data you can store as members, and the capabilities of each class type. Like a lot of the features of the C# language, C# classes borrow a little from C++ and a little from Java and then add some ingenuity to create elegant solutions to old problems.

In the first part of this chapter, I'll describe the basics of defining classes in C#, including instance members, access modifiers, constructors, and initialization lists. I'll also define static members and the difference between constant and read-only fields, and I'll quickly discuss inheritance and C# classes. The second part of this chapter deals with the concept of *structs*, how they're defined, and how they differ from classes—both from a usage standpoint and internally. Finally, I'll wrap up this chapter with a brief comparison of classes and structs and describe when you'd choose one over the other.

Defining Classes

The syntax used for defining classes in C# is simple, especially if you usually program in C++ or Java:

```
[attributes] [modifiers] class <className> [: baseClassName]
{
    [class-body]
}[;]
```

Many of these items will be explained throughout this chapter, so let's look at a simple class declaration to get started:

```
class Employee
{
    private long employeeId;
}
```

As you can see, this class is as basic as it gets. We have a class named *Employee* that contains a single member named *employeeId*. Notice *private*, which precedes our member. This is called an *access modifier*. You'll recall that the subject of access modifiers came up briefly in Chapter 1, "Building C# Applications and Libraries." In just a minute, I'll explain them in more detail.

If you come from a C++ background, note that it's not necessary to place a terminating semicolon at the end of a class. However, you can do so if you want; in fact, I do this in some of my classes simply out of habit. Having said that, the following two class declarations are identical:

```
class MyClass
{
    // Members
}

class MyClass
{
    // Members
};
```

Now let's look at the various types of members that can be defined with a class.

Class Members

Put simply, classes consist of members. Everything you define within a class is considered to be a member of that class. You already know from Chapter 2, "The .NET Type System," that all the types available to C# programmers originate from the common type system (CTS). Here's a list of the various types that you can define as members of a C# class:

- **Fields**   A field is a member variable used to hold a value. You can apply several modifiers to a field, depending on how you want the field used. These modifiers include *static*, *readonly*, and *const*. We'll discuss what these modifiers signify and how to use them shortly.

- **Methods**   A method is the actual code that acts on the object's data (or field values). In this chapter, we'll focus on defining class data.

> **More Info**   Chapter 4, "Methods," will cover methods in a lot
> more detail.

- **Properties**   Properties are sometimes called *smart fields* because
  they're actually methods that look like fields to the class's clients.
  This allows the client a greater degree of abstraction because it
  doesn't have to know whether it's accessing the field directly or
  whether an accessor method is being called.

> **More Info**   Chapter 5, "Properties, Arrays, and Indexers," covers
> properties in detail.

- **Constants**   As the name suggests, a constant is a field with a value
  that can't be changed. I'll discuss constants and compare them to
  something called *read-only fields* later in this chapter, in the section
  "Constants vs. Read-Only Fields."

- **Indexers**   Just as a property is a *smart field*, an indexer is sometimes referred to as a *smart array*—that is, a member that enables
  you to work with a class that's logically an array of data, as though
  the class itself were an array. For example, although a *ListBox* class
  might have other fields (such as a sort bit) and methods to manipulate and present the control's data, this class will be conceptually
  defined by the array of data elements that it's displaying. However,
  to index the class's data, the class designer typically either allows
  direct access to the class's internal data array or provides a method
  that takes a subscript, or index, value to define which array element
  is being dealt with. Indexers, which are covered in much more detail
  in Chapter 5, enable you to subscript the actual object, thereby giving the client a much more intuitive means of using the class.

- **Events**   An event causes some piece of code to run. Events are an
  integral part of Microsoft Windows programming. For example, an
  event is fired when a user moves the mouse or clicks or resizes a
  window. C# events use the standard publish/subscribe design pattern seen in Microsoft Message Queuing (MSMQ) and the COM+
  asynchronous event model, which gives an application asynchronous event-handling capabilities. But in C#, this design pattern is a
  "first-class" concept—meaning that the language was designed with
  this in mind instead of being bolted on after the fact.

More Info Chapter 14, "Delegates and Event Handlers," describes how to use events.

■ **Operators** C# gives you the ability, via operator overloading, to add the standard mathematical operators to a class so that you can write more intuitive code.

More Info Operator overloading is covered in detail in Chapter 13, "Operator Overloading and User-Defined Conversions."

Access Modifiers

Now that you've briefly read about the different types that can be defined as members of a C# class, let's look at some important modifiers used to specify how visible, or accessible, a given member is to code outside its own class. These modifiers, called *access modifiers*, are listed along with their descriptions in Table 3-1.

Table 3-1
C# Access Modifiers

Access Modifier	Description
Public	Signifies that the member is accessible from outside the class's definition and hierarchy of derived classes.
Protected	The member isn't visible outside the class and can be accessed by derived classes only.
Private	The member can't be accessed outside the scope of the defining class. Therefore, not even derived classes have access to these members.
Internal	The member is visible only within the current compilation unit. The *internal* access modifier creates a hybrid of *public* and *protected* accessibility, depending on where the code resides.

Note that unless you want a member to have the default access modifier of *private*, you must specify an access modifier for it. This is in contrast to C++, in which a member that's not explicitly decorated with an access modifier assumes the visibility characteristics of the previously stated access modifier. For example, in the following C++ code, the members *a*, *b*, and *c* are defined with *public* visibility, and the members *d* and *e* are defined as *protected* members:

```
class CAccessModsInCpp
{
public:
    int a;
    int b;
    int c;
protected:
    int d;
    int e;
};
```

To accomplish the same goal in C#, you would have to change this code to the following:

```
class AccessModsInCSharp
{
    public int a;
    public int b;
    public int c;
    protected int d;
    protected int e;
}
```

The following C# code results in the member *b* being declared as *private* because no access modifier was specified for that member:

```
public MoreAccessModsInCSharp
{
    public int a;
    int b;
}
```

The *Main* Method

Every C# application must define a method named *Main* in one of its classes. This method, which serves as that application's entry point, must be defined as *static*. (We'll discuss what *static* means shortly.) It doesn't matter to the C# compiler which class has the *Main* method defined, and the class you choose doesn't affect the order of compilation. This is unlike C++, in which you must monitor dependencies closely when building an application. The C# compiler is smart enough to go through your source files and locate the *Main* method on its own. However, this all-important method is the entry point to all C# applications.

Although you can place the *Main* method in any class, I recommend creating a class specifically for housing this method. Here's an example of doing that using our—so far—simple *Employee* class:

```
class Employee
{
    private int employeeId;
}


class AppClass
{
    static public void Main()
    {
        Employee emp = new Employee();
    }
}
```

As you can see, the example has two classes. This is a common approach to C# programming even in the simplest applications. The first class (*Employee*) is a problem domain class, and the second class (*AppClass*) contains the needed entry point (*Main*) for the application. In this case, the *Main* method instantiates the *Employee* object. If this were a real application, the *Main* method would use the *Employee* object's members.

Command-Line Arguments

You can access the command-line arguments to an application by declaring the *Main* method as taking a string array type as its only argument. Then you can process the arguments as you would any array. Although we won't cover arrays until Chapter 5, here's some generic code for iterating through the command-line arguments of an application and writing them to the standard output device:

```
using System;

class CommandLine
{
    public static void Main(string[] args)
    {
        Console.WriteLine("\nYou specified {0} arguments",
            args.Length);
        foreach (string arg in args)
        {
            Console.WriteLine("Argument: {0}", arg);
        }
    }
}
```

Figure 3-1 shows an example of calling this application with a couple of randomly selected values.

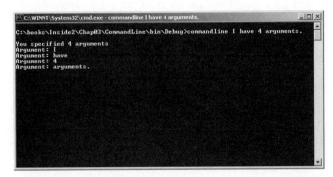

Figure 3-1   Parameters or arguments can easily be passed to a C# application and parsed through the *Main* method.

Note that the command-line arguments are given to you in a string array. Therefore, to process the parameters as flags or switches, you'll need to program that capability yourself.

Now take a look at Figure 3-2 to see how this is implemented in Microsoft intermediate language (MSIL). The *.locals* record declares a local variable (*arg*) that represents the command-line arguments passed to the application. After that, there are two local variables that begin with *CS$*. These are used for the *foreach* statement, which is used to iterate arrays of data, such as the command-line arguments variable—*args*. In fact, as you'll see in Chapter 9, "Program Flow Control," almost all this MSIL is used to handle the *foreach* loop. However, there are a couple of things to note here.

```
CommandLine::Main : void(string[])                                    _ □ X
.method public hidebysig static void  Main(string[] args) cil managed
{
  .entrypoint
  // Code size       56 (0x38)
  .maxstack  2
  .locals init ([0] string arg,
           [1] string[] CS$00000007$00000000,
           [2] int32 CS$00000008$00000001)
  IL_0000:  ldstr        "\nYou specified {0} arguments"
  IL_0005:  ldarg.0
  IL_0006:  ldlen
  IL_0007:  conv.i4
  IL_0008:  box          [mscorlib]System.Int32
  IL_000d:  call         void [mscorlib]System.Console::WriteLine(string,
                                                                  object)
  IL_0012:  ldarg.0
  IL_0013:  stloc.1
  IL_0014:  ldc.i4.0
  IL_0015:  stloc.2
  IL_0016:  br.s         IL_002b
  IL_0018:  ldloc.1
  IL_0019:  ldloc.2
  IL_001a:  ldelem.ref
  IL_001b:  stloc.0
  IL_001c:  ldstr        "Argument: {0}"
  IL_0021:  ldloc.0
  IL_0022:  call         void [mscorlib]System.Console::WriteLine(string,
                                                                  object)
```

Figure 3-2   MSIL generated to iterate through the command-line parameters of a *Main* method by using the *foreach* statement.

The first local variable of an application whose *Main* method defines it as receiving arguments is always the *args* variable. This value is then pushed onto the stack via a call to *ldarg.0* as needed. Notice the lines IL_0005 through IL_000d. Here the array address is first pushed onto the stack. The *ldlen* instruction then examines the array pointed to by the value on the stack and pushes onto the stack that array's length (number of elements). The *conv.i4* instruction converts the length value on the stack to a 4-byte integer value because this value is length-portable across multiple architectures. Finally, the value is boxed into a reference type for the *Console.WriteLine* method call and output to the screen. The *foreach* loop then iterates through the *args* array. As mentioned, I'll discuss the *foreach* loop in more detail in Chapter 9. Now let's look at how to return a value from the *Main* method.

Note Developers using Microsoft Visual C++ are already accustomed to iterating through an array that represents the command-line arguments to an application. However, unlike these Visual C++ arrays, the array of command-line arguments in C# doesn't contain the application name as the first entry in the array.

Returning Values from *Main*

Most examples in this book define *Main* as follows:

```
class SomeClass
{
    // Other members
    public static void Main()
    {
        // Main body
    }
}
```

However, you can also define *Main* to return a value of type *int*. Although not common in GUI applications, this return value can be useful when you're writing console applications to be run in batch. The *return* statement terminates execution of the method, and the returned value is used as an *error level* to the calling application or batch file to indicate user-defined success or failure. To do this, use the following prototype:

```
public static int Main()
{
    // Return some value of type int
    // that represents success or value.
    return 0;
}
```

Multiple *Main* Methods

The designers of C# included a mechanism by which you can define more than
one class with a *Main* method. Why would you want to do this? One reason is
to place test code in your classes. You can then use the */main:<className>*
switch with the C# compiler to specify which class's *Main* method to use.
Here's an example that has two classes containing *Main* methods:

```
using System;

class Main1
{
    public static void Main()
    {
        Console.WriteLine("Main1");
    }
}

class Main2
{
    public static void Main()
    {
        Console.WriteLine("Main2");
    }
}
```

To compile this application so that the *Main1.Main* method is used as the
application's entry point, you'd use this switch:

```
csc MultipleMain.cs /main:Main1
```

Figure 3-3 shows the generated MSIL of the two *Main* methods side by
side. Note that only the *Main1.Main* method has an *.entrypoint* record defined
for it. Changing the switch to */main:Main2* would then cause the application to
use the *Main2.Main* method.

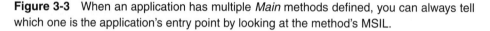

```
/ Main1::Main : void()                                        _ | □ | ×
.method public hidebysig static void  Main() cil managed
{
  .entrypoint
  // Code size       11 (0xb)
  .maxstack  1
  IL_0000:  ldstr       "Main1"
  IL_0005:  call        void [mscorlib]System.Console::WriteLine(string)
  IL_000a:  ret
} // end of method Main1::Main
```

```
/ Main2::Main : void()                                        _ | □ | ×
.method public hidebysig static void  Main() cil managed
{
  // Code size       11 (0xb)
  .maxstack  1
  IL_0000:  ldstr       "Main2"
  IL_0005:  call        void [mscorlib]System.Console::WriteLine(string)
  IL_000a:  ret
} // end of method Main2::Main
```

Figure 3-3 When an application has multiple *Main* methods defined, you can always tell which one is the application's entry point by looking at the method's MSIL.

Obviously, because C# is case-sensitive, you must be careful to use the correct case of the class in the switch. In addition, attempting to compile an application consisting of multiple classes with defined *Main* methods and not specifying the */main* switch will result in a compiler error.

Constructors

One of the biggest advantages of an object-oriented programming (OOP) language such as C# is that you can define special methods that are called whenever an instance of the class is created. These methods are called *constructors*. C# introduces a new type of constructor called a *static constructor*, which you'll see in the next section, "Static Members and Instance Members."

Note While constructors enable the class designer to define methods that will always be called upon an object's initialization, a destructor is the reverse—a method that's called when an object is destroyed or goes out of scope. However, if you come from an exclusive C++ background, you'll probably be surprised to learn that object destruction works much differently in .NET than what you're accustomed to. This new behavior is mostly due to the .NET implementation of garbage collection, so object destruction and cleanup are covered in Chapter 20, "Pinning and Memory Management."

A key benefit of using a constructor is that it guarantees that the object will go through proper initialization before being used. When a user instantiates an object, that object's constructor is called and must return before the user can perform any other work with that object. This guarantee helps ensure the integrity of the object and helps make applications written with object-oriented languages much more reliable.

But how do you name a constructor so that the compiler will know to call it when the object is instantiated? The C# designers followed the lead of the C++ language designer, Bjarne Stroustrup, and dictated that constructors in C# must have the same name as the class itself. Here's a simple class with an equally simple constructor:

```
using System;

class Constructor1App
{
    Constructor1App()
    {
        Console.WriteLine("[Constructor1App.Constructor1App] " +
            "I'm the constructor");
    }

    public static void Main()
    {
        Console.WriteLine("\n[Main] Instantiating a " +
            "Constructor1 object...");
        Constructor1App app = new Constructor1App();
    }
}
```

Constructors don't return values. If you attempt to prefix the constructor with a type, the compiler will issue an error stating that you can't define a member with the same name as the enclosing type.

You should also note the way objects are instantiated in C#. This is done using the *new* keyword with the following syntax:

<class> *<object>* = new *<class>*(*constructor arguments*)

If you come from a C++ background, pay special attention to this. In C++, you can instantiate an object in two ways. You can declare it on the stack, like this:

```
// C++ code. This creates an instance of CMyClass on the stack.
CMyClass myClass;
```

Or you can instantiate the object on the free store (or heap) by using the C++ *new* keyword:

```
// C++ code. This creates an instance of CMyClass on the heap.
CMyClass myClass = new CMyClass();
```

Instantiating objects is different in C# than it is in C++, and this difference is a cause for confusion for new C# developers. The confusion stems from the fact that both languages share a common keyword for creating objects. Although using the *new* keyword in C++ lets you dictate where an object gets created, where an object is created in C# depends upon the type being instantiated. As we saw in Chapter 2, reference types are created on the heap and value types are created on the stack. Therefore, the *new* keyword—which resolves to the *newobj* MSIL instruction—lets you create a new instance of a class, but it doesn't determine where that object is created. Having said that, the following code is valid C# code, but if you're a C++ developer, it might not do what you expect it too:

```
MyClass myClass;
```

In C++, this code would create an instance of *MyClass* on the stack. As mentioned, you can create objects in C# only by using the *new* keyword. Therefore, this line of code in C# merely declares that *myClass* is a variable of type *MyClass*, but it doesn't instantiate the object.

As an example of this, if you compile the following program, the C# compiler will warn you that the variable has been declared but isn't used in the application. You can also use ILDASM and note that although the *Constructor2App* is defined in the *.locals* record as a local variable, the *newobj* instruction is never performed.

```
using System;

class Constructor2App
{
    Constructor2App()
    {
        Console.WriteLine("[Constructor2App.Constructor2App] " +
            "I'm the constructor");
    }

    public static void Main()
    {
        Console.WriteLine("\n[Main] Declaring, but not " +
            "instantiating, a Constructor2 object...");
        Constructor2App app;
    }
}
```

Therefore, if you declare an object type, you need to instantiate it somewhere in your code by using the *new* keyword:

```
Constructor2App app;
app = new Constructor2App();
```

Why would you declare an object without instantiating it? Declaring objects before using them—or "*new*-ing" them—is done in cases in which you declare one class inside another. This nesting of classes is called *containment*, or *aggregation*. For example, I might have an *Invoice* class that has several embedded classes, such as *Customer*, *TermCode*, and *SalesTaxCode*.

Static Members and Instance Members

As with C++, you can define a member of a class as a *static member* or an *instance member*. By default, each member is defined as an instance member, which means that a copy of that member is made for every instance of the class. When you declare a member a static member, only one copy of the member exists. A static member is created when the application containing the class is loaded, and it exists throughout the life of the application. Therefore, you can access the member even before the class has been instantiated. But why would you do this?

One example involves the *Main* method. The common language runtime needs to have a common entry point to your application. You must define a static method called *Main* in one of your classes so that the runtime doesn't have to instantiate one of your objects. You also use static members when you have a method that, from an object-oriented perspective, belongs to a class in terms of semantics but doesn't need an actual object—for example, if you want to keep track of how many instances of a given object are created during the lifetime of an application. Because static members live across object instances, the following code would work:

```
using System;

class InstCount
{
    public InstCount()
    {
        instanceCount++;
    }

    static public int instanceCount;
    // instanceCount = 0;
}
```

```
class AppClass
{
    public static void PrintInstanceCount()
    {
        Console.WriteLine("[PrintInstanceCount] Now there {0} " +
            "{1} instance{2} of the InstCount class",
            InstCount.instanceCount == 1 ? "is" : "are",
            InstCount.instanceCount,
            InstCount.instanceCount == 1 ? "" : "s");
    }

    public static void Main()
    {
        PrintInstanceCount();

        InstCount ic;
        for (int i = 0; i < 2; i++)
        {
            ic = new InstCount();
            Console.WriteLine("[Main] Instantiated a " +
                "{0} object...", ic.GetType());

            PrintInstanceCount();
        }
    }
}
```

Figure 3-4 shows the output this example produces.

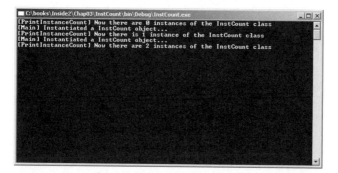

Figure 3-4   A *static field* is a field that exists for all instances of a given class.

If you look at the MSIL for this application, you'll simply see that the *Inst-Count.instanceCount* member is decorated with the *static* attribute. In addition, viewing the MSIL for the *AppClass.PrintInstanceCount* method will reveal that the *ldsfld* opcode is used to push a static field value onto the stack. Other than that, there's not much magic going on here regarding static fields.

Static fields can also be used as a means of producing more efficient code. I'll cover that aspect of their usage later in this chapter in the section "Guidelines to Using Structs."

One last note on static members that are value types: a static member must have a valid value. You can specify this value when you define the member, as follows:

```
static public int instanceCount1 = 10;
```

If you don't initialize the variable, the common language runtime will do so upon application startup by using a default value of *0*. Therefore, the following two lines are equivalent:

```
static public int instanceCount2;
static public int instanceCount2 = 0;
```

Constructor Initializers

All C# object constructors—with the exception of the *System.Object* constructors—include an invocation of the base class's constructor immediately before the execution of the first line of the constructor. These constructor initializers enable you to specify which class and which constructor you want called. These initializers take two forms:

- **base(...)**   Enables you to call the current class's base class constructor—that is, the specific constructor implied by the form of the constructor called.

- this(...)   Enables the current class to call another constructor defined within itself. This is useful when you have overloaded multiple constructors and want to make sure that a default constructor is always called. We'll cover overloaded methods in Chapter 4, but here's a quick and dirty definition in the meantime: overloaded methods are two or more methods with the same name but different argument lists.

To show the order of events in action, the following code executes the constructor for the *BaseClass* class first and then executes the constructor for the *DerivedClass* class:

```
using System;

class BaseClass
{
    public BaseClass()
```

```
        {
            Console.WriteLine("[BaseClass.BaseClass] " +
                "Constructor called");
        }
    }

class DerivedClass : BaseClass
{
    public DerivedClass()
    {
        Console.WriteLine("[DerivedClass.Derived] " +
            "Constructor called");
    }
}

class DefaultInitializer
{
    public static void Main()
    {
        Console.WriteLine("[Main] Instantiating a " +
            "DerivedClass object");
        DerivedClass derived = new DerivedClass();

    }
}
```

If you build and run this application, you'll see the results shown in Figure 3-5.

Figure 3-5   By default, a class's constructor will automatically call the base class's constructor.

However, also look at the MSIL in Figure 3-6. Here you can see more clearly what's going on. In the top window, the *Main* method is using the *newobj* instruction to create a new instance of the *DerivedClass* object and is explicitly calling its constructor. The *DerivedClass* constructor then loads the *this* pointer onto the stack and calls the *BaseClass* constructor to complete the object creation process.

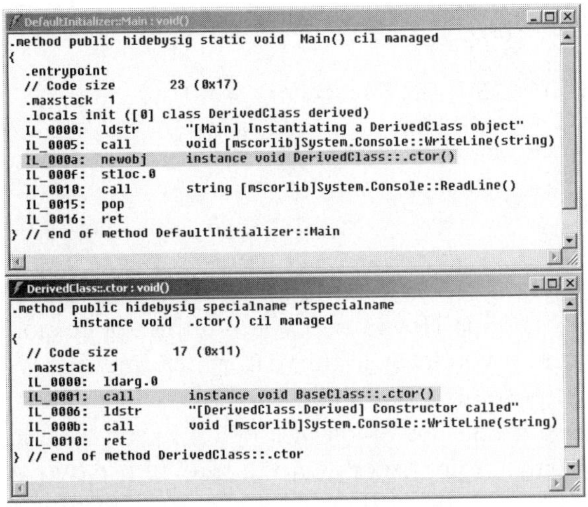

Figure 3-6   Although you don't see the calling of constructors in the C# code, a peek at the MSIL shows exactly how and when this is done.

In the preceding DefaultInitializer1 application, the derived class's constructor automatically calls the base class's constructor. However, as mentioned earlier, constructor initializers enable you to explicitly call a desired base class's constructor, as shown in the following program. This ability can be useful.

```
using System;

class BaseClass
{
    public BaseClass()
    {
        Console.WriteLine("[BaseClass.BaseClass] " +
            "Constructor called");
    }
}

class DerivedClass : BaseClass
{
    public DerivedClass()
        : base()
    {
        Console.WriteLine("[DerivedClass.Derived] " +
            "Constructor called");
```

```
    }
}

class BaseInitializer1
{
    public static void Main()
    {
        Console.WriteLine("[Main] Instantiating a " +
            "DerivedClass object");
        DerivedClass derived = new DerivedClass();

    }
}
```

Here I've changed the *DerivedClass* constructor to explicitly call the base class's (*BaseClass*) constructor. However, if you run this application, the output is exactly the same, and if you look at the MSIL, you'll find that it's exactly the same too. So what purpose does this ability serve?

Well, to understand that, let's look at a better example of a scenario in which constructor initializers are useful. Once again, I'll use two classes: *Base-Class* and *DerivedClass*. This time, *BaseClass* has two constructors: one that takes no arguments, and one that takes an *int*. *DerivedClass* then has a single constructor that takes an *int*. The problem arises in the construction of *Derived-Class*. If I compile the following code, it will result in MSIL that will call the *BaseClass* constructor that takes no arguments, which isn't what I want here:

```
using System;

class BaseClass
{
    public BaseClass()
    {
        Console.WriteLine("[BaseClass.BaseClass()] " +
            "Parameterless constructor called");
    }

    public BaseClass(int foo)
    {
        Console.WriteLine("[BaseClass.BaseClass(int foo)] " +
            "foo = {0}", foo);
    }
}

class DerivedClass : BaseClass
{
    public DerivedClass(int foo)
    {
```

```
            Console.WriteLine("[DerivedClass.DerivedClass] " +
                "foo = {0}", foo);
        }
    }

class BaseInitializer2
{
    public static void Main()
    {
        Console.WriteLine("[Main] Instantiating a " +
            "DerivedClass object...");
        DerivedClass derived = new DerivedClass(42);

    }
}
```

Note   When you run these applications, the base class's constructor
will be called *before* any statements in the derived class's constructor
body is executed. This rule ensures that classes that are based on
(derived from) other classes get properly initialized before their code is
allowed to execute.

However, the main question here is this: "How do I ensure that the
desired *BaseClass* constructor gets called?" By explicitly telling the compiler
which constructor I want called in the initializer list, like this:

```
using System;

class BaseClass
{
    public BaseClass()
    {
        Console.WriteLine("[BaseClass.BaseClass()] " +
            "Parameterless constructor called");
    }

    public BaseClass(int foo)
    {
        Console.WriteLine("[BaseClass.BaseClass(int foo)] " +
            "foo = {0}", foo);
    }
}
```

```
class DerivedClass : BaseClass
{
    public DerivedClass(int foo) : base(foo)
    {
        Console.WriteLine("[DerivedClass.DerivedClass] " +
            "foo = {0}", foo);
    }
}

class BaseInitializer3
{
    public static void Main()
    {
        Console.WriteLine("[Main] Instantiating a " +
            "DerivedClass object...");
        DerivedClass derived = new DerivedClass(42);

    }
}
```

If you execute this code, you'll get the desired result of the correct *Base-Class* constructor (with the *int* parameter) being called.

Specifying Run-Time Information in a Constructor Initializer

The last thing we'll look at in this section is the issue of instance vs. static members in a constructor initializer. The C# language states that only static members can be used when calling base class constructors in the initializer list. Therefore, the following code won't compile:

```
class MyBase
{
    protected MyBase(int i) { }
};

class MyDerived : MyBase
{
    int i;

 // ERROR: The compiler states that the following will not
 // compile because an object reference is needed for
 // nonstatic fields. However, if you qualify the i parameter
 // with the this value--base(this.i)--you will still receive
 // an error, this time indicating that the this keyword cannot
 // be used in this context (constructor initializer).
    MyDerived() : base(i) { }
};
```

However, in some scenarios, you'll need to pass information to a base class constructor that you won't know until run time. Your first response might be to pass that run-time piece of information to the derived class's constructor, as we did in the previous examples. But what if the derived class's constructor doesn't have the information in its parameter list?

As an example, let's say that we've defined a generic class for dealing with comma-delimited formatted files (CSV files). This class would probably take a *string* object representing a filename as a parameter to its constructor:

```
class CommaDelimitedFile
{
    public CommaDelimitedFile(string fileName)
    {
      ⋮
    }
    ⋮
}
```

Let's further suppose that we have a set of database files that are all in this CSV format. These files represent problem domain entities such as customers, suppliers, and vendors. Because the *CommaDelimitedFile* class dynamically determines the file's structure and data and stores it in collections, we don't need separate classes for each entity. Therefore, we simply need one derived class (*DbTable*) whose constructor takes a parameter that indicates the file to be opened. Because we don't want the class's user specifying the actual filename (to ensure that a valid filename is always used), we could create an *enum* of table IDs, where one of those IDs is passed to the *DbTable* constructor that represents the table being accessed.

```
enum TableId
{
    Customers,
    Suppliers,
    Vendors
};

class DbTable : CommaDelimitedFile
{
    public DbTable(TableId tableId)
    {
      ⋮
    }
    ⋮
}
```

However, there's a problem. If you attempt to compile this code, the compiler will tell you that there's no overload for the *CommaDelimitedFile* method that takes 0 parameters. The compiler had to assume that you wanted the default (parameterless) *CommaDelimitedFile* constructor called because you didn't specify otherwise. Therefore, the question becomes, "How do we pass the value that won't be known until run time to the *CommaDelimitedFile* constructor?" The answer, of course, is to use a static method. Simply code a static method and use it along with the *base* keyword in the initializer list, as in the following example:

```
using System;

class CommaDelimitedFile
{
    public CommaDelimitedFile(string fileName)
    {
        Console.WriteLine("[CommaDelimitedFile." +
            "CommaDelimitedFile] file name = {0}", fileName);
    }
}


enum TableId
{
    Customers,
    Suppliers,
    Vendors
};


class DbTable : CommaDelimitedFile
{
    static string GetFileName(TableId tableId)
    {
        string fileName;

        switch(tableId)
        {
            case TableId.Customers:
                fileName = "customers.txt";
                break;

            case TableId.Suppliers:
                fileName = "suppliers.txt";
                break;

            case TableId.Vendors:
                fileName = "venders.txt";
                break;
```

```
                default:
                    throw new ArgumentException("[DbTable." +
                        "GetFileName] Could not resolve table name");
            }

            return fileName;
        }

        public DbTable(TableId tableId) : base(GetFileName(tableId))
        {
            Console.WriteLine("[DbTable.DbTable] tableId = {0}", " +
                tableId.ToString());
        }
    }

    class BaseInitializer4
    {
        public static void Main()
        {
            Console.WriteLine("[Main] Instantiating a " +
                "Customer Table object...");
            DbTable derived = new DbTable(TableId.Customers);

        }
    }
```

Now let's move on to a topic that's a source of confusion for many programmers new to C#—the issue of constants and read-only fields and how they
compare to each other.

Constants vs. Read-Only Fields

There will certainly be times when you have fields that you don't want altered
during the execution of the application. Examples of fields you might want to
protect include the names of data files your application depends on, certain
unchanging values for a math class such as *pi*, or even server names and IP
addresses that your computer connects to. Obviously, this list could go on ad
infinitum. To address these situations, C# allows for the definition of two closely
related member types: constants and read-only fields, which I'll cover in this
section.

Constants

As you can guess from the name, constants—represented by the *const* keyword—are fields that remain constant for the life of the application. There are only three rules to keep in mind when defining something as a *const*:

■ A constant is a member whose value is set at compile time.

■ A constant member's value must be written as a literal.

■ To define a field as a constant, simply specify the *const* keyword before the member being defined, as follows:

```
using System;

class MagicNumbers
{
    public const double pi = 3.1415;
    public const int answerToAllLifesQuestions = 42;
}

class ConstApp
{
    public static void Main()
    {
        Console.WriteLine("CONSTANTS: pi = {0},"
            "everything else = {1}",
            MagicNumbers.pi,
            MagicNumbers.answerToAllLifesQuestions);
    }
}
```

Notice that there's no need for the client to instantiate the *MagicNumbers* class because, by default, *const* members are static. To get a better idea of this, take a look at Figure 3-7 to see the MSIL generated for these two members.

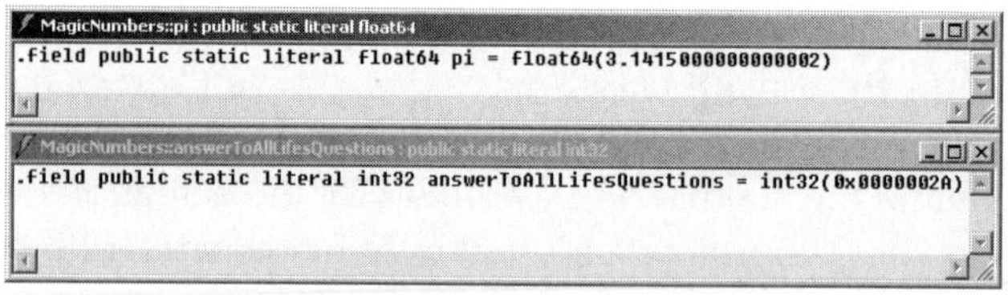

Figure 3-7   ILDASM shows that *const* values are created as static literals by the C# compiler.

A quick peek at the *Main* method depicted in Figure 3-8 shows that the compiler uses the *ldc* (load constant) opcode to push these constant values onto the stack. Although we don't do this here, if we had stored any of these values into local variables, the *stc* (store constant) opcodes would've been used for that purpose.

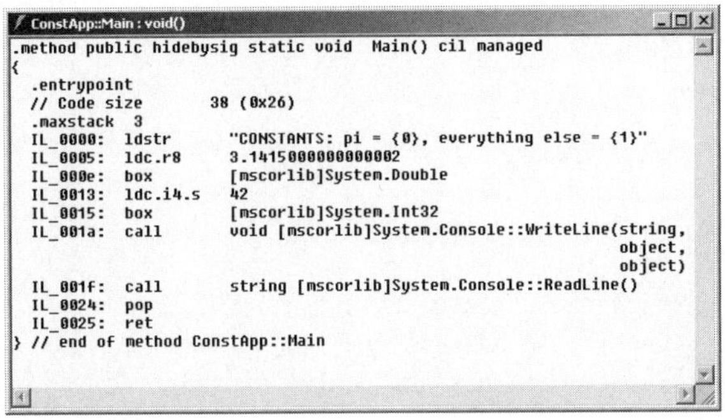

Figure 3-8   The compiler uses the *ldc* opcode to push constant values onto the stack.

Read-Only Fields

A field defined as a *const* is useful because it clearly documents the programmer's intention that the field contains an immutable value. However, that works only if you know the value at compile time. So what does a programmer do when the need arises for a field with a value that won't be known until run time and shouldn't be changed once it's been initialized? This issue—typically not addressed in other languages—was resolved by the designers of the C# language with what's called a *read-only field*.

When you define a field with the *readonly* keyword, you have the ability to set that field's value in one place: the constructor. After that point, the field can't be changed by the class itself or the class's clients. Let's say that your application needs to keep track of the current workstation's IP address. You wouldn't want to address this problem with a *const* because that would entail hard-coding the value—and even that technique wouldn't work if the workstation obtains its IP address dynamically. However, a run-time field would do just the trick:

```
using System;
using System.Net;

class Workstation
{
    public Workstation()
    {
        IPAddress ipAddress =
            Dns.Resolve(HostName).AddressList[0];
```

```
            IPAddressString = ipAddress.ToString();
    }

    public const string HostName = "cosette";
    public readonly string IPAddressString;
}

class GetIpAddress
{
    public static void Main()
    {
        Workstation workstation = new Workstation();
        Console.WriteLine("The IP address for '{0}' is {1}",
            Workstation.HostName, workstation.IPAddressString);

    }
}
```

Running this application will result in the display of the IP address associated with the supplied host name (*cosette*), as shown in Figure 3-9. Obviously,
this program won't work correctly if you aren't connected to a machine with a
host name of *cosette*. To specify the name of the machine to which you're connected, simply modify the *WorkStation* class's const field (*HostName*) to the
name of the machine whose IP address you're attempting to determine. Supply
your PC's machine name for your own workstation IP address.

Figure 3-9   Read-only fields are very similar to constants except that they can be initialized in their encasing class's constructor.

Because the *Workstation* class contains both a const field example (*Host-
Name*) and a read-only field example (*IPAddressString*), it's easy to compare
how each is declared in MSIL, as Figure 3-10 illustrates. As you can see, while
the *HostName* const field is defined as a *static literal*, the *IPAddressString* read-
only field is defined with the *initonly* attribute.

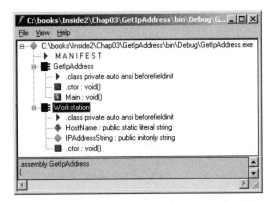

Figure 3-10 A read-only field is marked with a special *initonly* attribute indicating that once the field is initialized, it can't be modified.

At first glance, this code seems to be just what you need. However, there's one small issue: the *IPAddressString* read-only field that I defined is an instance field, meaning that the client is forced to instantiate the class to use this field. This situation might not be a problem and might even be what you want in cases in which the way the class is instantiated determines the read-only field's value. But what if you want a constant—which is static by definition—that you can initialize at run time? In that case, you'd define the field with both the *static* and the *readonly* modifiers. Then you'd create a special type of constructor called a *static constructor*. Static constructors are used to initialize static fields, read-only or otherwise. Here I've modified the previous example to make the *IPAddressString* field static and read-only, and I've added a static constructor. Note the addition of the *static* keyword to the constructor's definition as well as the removal of the access modifier. These changes were made because static constructors are, by definition, always public.

```
using System;
using System.Net;

class Workstation
{
    static Workstation()
    {
        IPAddress ipAddress =
            Dns.Resolve(HostName).AddressList[0];
        IPAddressString = ipAddress.ToString();
    }
```

```
        public const string HostName = "cosette";
        public static readonly string IPAddressString;
}

class GetIpAddress2
{
        public static void Main()
        {
            Workstation workstation = new Workstation();
            Console.WriteLine("The IP address for '{0}' is {1}",
                Workstation.HostName, Workstation.IPAddressString);


        }
}
```

If you run this application, you'll get the same results yielded by the Get-IpAddress demo. The main difference is in the underlying code: now the client doesn't have to needlessly instantiate the *Workstation* class. Now take a look at Figure 3-11 to see a very special type of method—the *type initializer*. Type initializers are methods that are defined in the class that contains the type and enables the type to initialize itself. The rules of this method are that it be static, take no parameters, return no value, be decorated with the with *rtspecialname* and *specialname* attributes, and be named *.cctor*. In this case, any time a field is marked as *initonly* and *static*, it can be modified only inside a type initializer.

```
Workstation::.cctor : void()                                    _ □ x
.method private hidebysig specialname rtspecialname static
        void .cctor() cil managed
{
  // Code size        30 (0x1e)
  .maxstack  2
  .locals init ([0] class [System]System.Net.IPAddress ipAddress)
  IL_0000:  ldstr         "cosette"
  IL_0005:  call          class [System]System.Net.IPHostEntry [Syste
  IL_000a:  callvirt      instance class [System]System.Net.IPAddress
  IL_000f:  ldc.i4.0
  IL_0010:  ldelem.ref
  IL_0011:  stloc.0
  IL_0012:  ldloc.0
  IL_0013:  callvirt      instance string [System]System.Net.IPAddres
  IL_0018:  stsfld        string Workstation::IPAddressString
  IL_001d:  ret
} // end of method Workstation::.cctor
```

Figure 3-11   Only a type initializer can modify a field marked as both *initonly* and *static*.

Now that we've covered classes and the member types that can be defined for them, let's look at the all-important issue of inheritance.

Inheritance

Inheritance is used when a class is built upon another class, in terms of data or behavior. For example, suppose you were writing a hierarchy of database classes. Let's say you want a class for handling Microsoft SQL Server databases and Oracle databases. Because these databases differ in some respects, you'd want to have a class for each. However, both databases do share enough functionality that you'd want to put common functionality into a base class, derive the other two classes from that base class, and override or modify the inherited base class behavior at times. This, in a nutshell, is what inheritance is all about.

Note   Although I'm introducing the concept of class inheritance here, I'm doing so only as it applies to the basic concepts and syntax. Therefore, this discussion will continue in much greater detail in Chapter 4, where I cover virtual methods, method overriding, and several keywords used to control how one class inherits methods from another.

To inherit one class from another, use the following syntax:

class *<derivedClass>* : *<baseClass>*

Here's what this database example would look like:

```
using System;

class Database
{
    public Database()
    {
        CommonField = 42;
    }

    public int CommonField;

    public void CommonMethod()
    {
        Console.WriteLine("[Database.CommonMethod] " +
            "Method called");
    }
}
```

```csharp
class SQLServer : Database
{
    public void SomeMethodSpecificToSQLServer()
    {
        Console.WriteLine("[SQLServer.SomeMethodSpecific" +
            "ToSQLServer] Method called");
    }
}

class Oracle : Database
{
    public void SomeMethodSpecificToOracle()
    {
        Console.WriteLine("[Oracle.SomeMethodSpecific" +
            "ToOracle] Method called");
    }
}

class InheritanceApp
{
    public static void Main()
    {
        Console.WriteLine("[Main] Instantiating a " +
            "SQLServer object");
        SQLServer sqlserver = new SQLServer();

        Console.WriteLine("[Main] Calling Sqlserver." +
            "SomeMethodSpecificToSQLServer");
        sqlserver.SomeMethodSpecificToSQLServer();

        Console.WriteLine("[Main] Calling Sqlserver." +
            "CommonMethod");
        sqlserver.CommonMethod();

        Console.WriteLine("[Main] Accessing inherited " +
            "Sqlserver.CommonField, value = {0}",
            sqlserver.CommonField);

    }
}
```

Compiling and executing this application results in the output shown in Figure 3-12.

Figure 3-12   Simple example of class inheritance.

Notice that the *Database.CommonMethod* and *Database.CommonField* methods are now a part of the *SQLServer* class's definition. Because the *SQLServer* and *Oracle* classes are derived from the base *Database* class, they both inherit almost all its members that are defined as *public*, *protected*, or *internal*. The only exception to this is the constructor, which can't be inherited. Each class must implement its own constructor, irrespective of its base class. Figure 3-13 shows how this looks in MSIL.

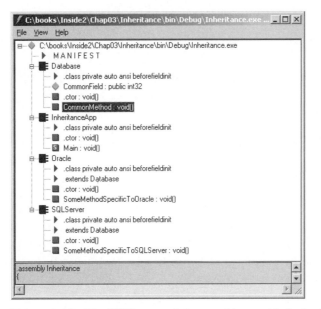

Figure 3-13   The MSIL *extends* keyword is used to indicate the derivation of one class from another.

First, notice that both the *Oracle* and *SQLServer* classes are defined as *extends Database*. The term *extends* is simply the MSIL equivalent of *derives from*. The second thing to notice is that the *Database.Common* method isn't present under either derived class. So how does a call to the *SQLServer.CommonMethod* ultimately resolve to a call to the *Database.Common* method? Actually, this question gets into the meat of inheritance—inheriting and overriding default behavior—which I'll discuss that in great detail in Chapter 4.

Multiple Interfaces

Because multiple inheritance has become a controversial subject on many newsgroups and mailing lists, I need to make this point clear: C# *does not* support multiple inheritance through derivation. You can, however, aggregate the behavioral characteristics of multiple programmatic entities by implementing multiple interfaces. You'll learn about interfaces and how to work with them in Chapter 7, "Interfaces." For now, think of C# interfaces as you would COM interfaces.

Having said that, the following code is invalid and won't compile:

```
class Foo
{
}

class Bar
{
}

class MITest : Foo, Bar
{
    public static void Main ()
    {
    }
}
```

The error that you'll get in this example has to do with how you implement interfaces. The interfaces you choose to implement are listed after the class's base class. Therefore, in this example, the C# compiler thinks that *Bar* should be an interface type. That's why the C# compiler will give you the following error message:

```
'Bar' : type in interface list is not an interface
```

The following example, which is more realistic, is perfectly valid because the *MyFancyGrid* class is derived from *Control* and implements the *ISerializable* and *IDataBound* interfaces:

```
class Control
{
}

interface ISerializable
{
}


interface IDataBound
{
}

class MyFancyGrid : Control, ISerializable, IDataBound
{
}
```

The point here is that the only way you can implement something like multiple inheritance in C# is through the use of interfaces.

Sealed Classes

If you want to make sure that a class can never be used as a base class, use the *sealed* modifier when defining the class. The only restriction is that an abstract class can't be used as a sealed class because, by their nature, abstract classes are meant to be used as base classes. Although the purpose of a sealed class is to prevent unintended derivation, certain run-time optimizations are enabled as a result of defining a class as sealed. Specifically, because the compiler guarantees that the class can never have any derived classes, it's possible to transform virtual function member invocations on sealed class instances into nonvirtual invocations. Here's an example of sealing a class:

```
using System;

sealed class Point
{
    public Point(int x, int y)
    {
        X = x;
        Y = y;
    }

    public int X;
    public int Y;
}
```

```
/*
Uncommenting this class and attempting to build the application
will result in a compiler error, as sealed classes cannot be
derived from.

class MyPoint : Point
{
}
*/

class SealedApp
{
    public static void Main()
    {
        Point pt = new Point(6,16);
        Console.WriteLine("x = {0}, y = {1}", pt.X, pt.Y);

    }
}
```

Note that if you use the *protected* modifier on a sealed class member, you'll receive a warning when you attempt to build the code. This is because protected members are visible to derived classes and, as you now know, sealed classes don't have any derived classes.

Defining Structs in C#

So far in this chapter, I've confined the conversation to classes. Now we'll take a look at a closely associated language feature—the C# struct. Like a class, a struct can contain other types and is sometimes referred to as a lightweight version of a class because internally a struct is a value type. For this reason, structs don't incur the overhead associated with reference objects—such as classes—except when boxed. However, structs have some severe limitations that restrict their usage to very specialized situations. In this section, I'll introduce the syntax of defining structs, talk about their limitations and benefits, and compare their usage to that of classes.

Struct Usage

Defining a struct takes an almost identical form to that of defining a class:

```
[attributes] [modifiers] struct <structName> [: interfaces]
{
    [struct-body]
}[;]
```

For example, here I'll define the standard *RGB* struct with fields to hold the red, green, and blue values:

```
struct RGB
{
    public int Red;
    public int Green;
    public int Blue;
}
```

So far, this declaration looks just like a class. However, you'll soon see the many limitations to using structs that I mentioned earlier. Now let's quickly look at how a client would use this struct:

```
RGB rgb;
rgb.Red = 0xFF;
rgb.Green = 0xFF;
rgb.Blue = 0xFF;
```

Notice that the client didn't have to instantiate the struct (via the *new* keyword). This reason for this behavior is that, as a value type, a struct is allocated once it's declared. This usage is obviously in contrast to a reference type that needs to be instantiated before use. However, keep in mind that because of that usage, the fields won't be initialized until you either *new* the struct or explicitly initialize the members yourself. As a result, the following code won't compile because it's attempting to use an uninitialized value:

```
RGB rgb; // ERROR: Use of unassigned field
Console.WriteLine(rgb.Red);
```

The following code fixes this problem. Note that because *RGB.Red* is a value type, it initializes to *0*.

```
RGB rgb = new RGB();
Console.WriteLine(rgb.Red);
```

Although my *RGB* struct contains only fields thus far, struct members can be constructors, constants, fields, methods, properties, indexers, operators, and nested types. However, a very important limitation of structs deals with constructors: it's an error to create a parameterless constructor for a struct. Therefore, the following will result in a compile-time error:

```
struct RGB
{
    // ERROR: Structs cannot contain explicit
    // parameterless constructors
    public RGB();
```

```
    public int Red;
    public int Green;
    public int Blue;
}
```

Although you can't define an explicit parameterless constructor for a struct, the following definition—in which the constructor signature includes parameters—is valid:

```
struct RGB
{
    public RGB(int red, int green, int blue)
    {
        Red = red;
        Green = green;
        Blue = blue;
    }

    public int Red;
    public int Green;
    public int Blue;
}
```

If you look back at the syntax for defining structs, you'll notice the omission of the base class list. This is because structs can't be based on other structs or classes, and they can't be a base for other structs or classes. Let's look at the following example, in which I define the same fields for both a class and a struct:

```
class cRGB
{
    public int Red;
    public int Green;
    public int Blue;
}

struct sRGB
{
    public int Red;
    public int Green;
    public int Blue;
}
```

Now let's look at the MSIL emitted by the compiler, as shown in Figure 3-14. Surprise! A struct is actually defined internally as a class with only three key differences. First, the struct is defined as sealed, which as you know, means that it can't serve as a base class. Second, the struct is implicitly derived from *System.ValueType*—the supertype, or ultimate base class, of all value types. Finally, as mentioned before, there's no default constructor for a struct.

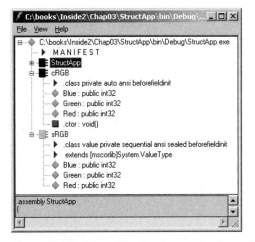

Figure 3-14   Internally structs are simply sealed classes that derive from *System.Value-Type*.

Guidelines to Using Structs

Although structs are certainly more efficient than classes—because of their underlying value type structure—their limitations restrict their usage. As a general rule of thumb, you should use structs when:

■ The data being contained is very small. Examples of this are structs that hold *Point* values (*x* and *y*), RGB values, or simple application or object state information.

■ The struct will contain few or even no methods to access or modify the contained data. Remember that a class is an encapsulation of data and the methods that work on that data. Structs can be viewed as simply data.

At this point, I'll give a practical example of a struct that combines the benefits of a struct and static fields to create a very efficient construct. Let's say that in our little *RGB* struct we want to define certain frequently used colors so that the struct's client doesn't have to remember each color's exact RGB values. We can easily do so by defining a constant or an enum that the client will pass to a constructor. The constructor will then instantiate the struct's red, green, and blue values accordingly. However, there's a much better way. How about defining these frequently used instances of the RGB struct as static members? The code would look like this:

```csharp
using System;

struct RGB
{
    public static readonly RGB RED = new RGB(255, 0, 0);
    public static readonly RGB GREEN = new RGB(0, 255, 0);
    public static readonly RGB BLUE = new RGB(0, 0, 255);
    public static readonly RGB WHITE= new RGB(255, 255, 255);
    public static readonly RGB BLACK= new RGB(0, 0, 0);

    public RGB(int red, int green, int blue)
    {
        Red = red;
        Green = green;
        Blue = blue;
    }

    public int Red;
    public int Green;
    public int Blue;

    public override string ToString()
    {
        return
          (Red.ToString("X2")
          + Green.ToString("X2")
          + Blue.ToString("X2"));
    }
}

class StructApp
{
    static void PrintRGBValue(string color, RGB rgb)
    {
        Console.WriteLine("The value for {0} is {1}",
            color, rgb);
    }

    static void Main(string[] args)
    {
        PrintRGBValue("red", RGB.RED);
        PrintRGBValue("green", RGB.GREEN);
        PrintRGBValue("blue", RGB.BLUE);
        PrintRGBValue("white", RGB.WHITE);
        PrintRGBValue("black", RGB.BLACK);

    }
}
```

Building and running this application would yield the results shown in Figure 3-15.

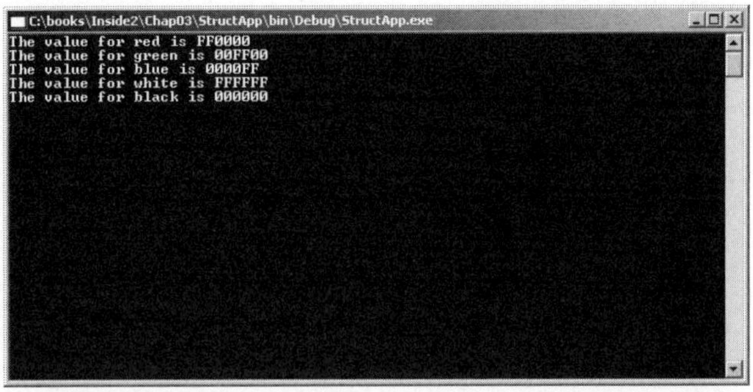

Figure 3-15   The combination of the struct and static semantics enable you to create very efficient constructs for cases in which you have a small amount of data that's frequently instantiated with common values.

Now our little struct offers the following benefits:

■ Because a small amount of data is being stored (three fields), a struct is being used, which is more efficient than a class.

■ The client can easily access key values without having to remember their respective RGB values.

■ Each key RGB value (*RGB.RED*, *RGB.BLUE*, and so on) is now defined only once for the entire system, which is obviously more efficient than allocating a new struct each time one of these colors is needed.

Summary

In the first part of this chapter, you learned how to define and use classes in C#. That discussion included how to define members for a class and how to set access modifiers to limit class visibility—and access—to code outside the class. After that, we covered the various class member types—the all-important *Main* method, class constructors, constants, and read-only fields. Finally, we wrapped up the discussion of classes with a brief introduction to the semantics of class inheritance. Once we were done with classes, we discussed their close cousins—structs. You learned about the syntax of structs, why they're more efficient than classes, and the limitations of structs, and you saw a practical example in which using a struct was much more efficient than using a class. In Chapter 4, we'll build on what you learned here by exploring the topic of class methods.

Methods

In most programming languages used today, there's a clear distinction between data and processing and between variables and functions. As you learned in Chapter 3, "Classes and Structs," C# classes are encapsulated bundles of data and the methods that work on that data. The terms *function* and *method* are synonymous in C#, and all methods are encapsulated in some class or struct— the language doesn't support global methods. Therefore, in terms of encapsulation, C# has the same object-oriented pedigree as Java and a better pedigree than C++.

Methods give classes their behavioral characteristics, and you name methods after the actions you want the classes to carry out on your behalf. So far, we haven't gotten into the more specific issues of defining and calling methods in C#. That's where this chapter comes in. We'll first consider the two primary mechanisms for passing parameters: passing them by *value,* and passing them by *reference.* Then we'll see how the *ref* and *out* keywords affect these basic mechanisms and how these keywords enable you to define a method that can return more than a single value to the caller. You'll also learn how to define overloaded methods so that multiple methods with the same name can function differently depending on the type and number of arguments passed to them. Then you'll learn how to handle situations in which you don't know the exact number of arguments a method has until run time.

We'll then turn our attention to a very powerful feature, *polymorphism,* and we'll see how virtual and override methods can make our code open ended. Finally, we'll wrap up the chapter with a discussion of static methods.

Value and Reference Parameters

First, let's revisit the concept of value and reference types. This section should serve merely as a reminder because the way that value and reference types behave when used as parameters to methods is intuitive. You pass value-type method parameters by value—that is, you pass a copy of the value to the method. Therefore, what the called method does with the incoming parameter doesn't affect the variable passed down from the calling method. Consider the following simple example:

```
class SomeClass
{
    public int ChangeInt(int val)
    {
        return val*2;
    }
}

class ValRefTest
{
    static void Main(string[] args)
    {
        SomeClass sc = new SomeClass();
        int val1 = 3;
        int val2 = sc.ChangeInt(val1);
        Console.WriteLine("val1 = {0}, val2 = {1}",
            val1, val2);
    }
}
```

The output from this code will be:

```
val1 = 3, val2 = 6
```

The behavior with reference-type parameters is different because what gets passed is a copy of the reference (another reference to the same data). Therefore, if the called method makes changes to the data through the reference, the changes are made to the original data. The reference held by the calling method is a reference to the same data, so the changes will be available to the calling method when the called method returns:

```
class AnotherClass
{
    public int ID;
}
class SomeClass
{
```

```
    public AnotherClass ChangeObject(AnotherClass ref1)
    {
        ref1.ID = ref1.ID*2;
        return ref1;
    }
}
class ValRefTest
{
    static void Main(string[] args)
    {
        AnotherClass ref1 = new AnotherClass();
        ref1.ID = 3;
        AnotherClass ref2 = sc.ChangeObject(ref1);
        Console.WriteLine("ref1.ID = {0}, ref2.ID = {1}",
            ref1.ID, ref2.ID);
    }
}
```

The output from this code will be:

```
ref1.ID = 6, ref2.ID = 6
```

Let's be clear about this process: in both cases, a copy of the parameter passes from caller to called method. If you pass a copy of a value type, you get a copy of the data. But if you pass a copy of a reference type, you get a copy of the reference. When accessing the original data, a copy of a reference is indistinguishable from the original reference.

ref Method Parameters

When you attempt to retrieve information by using a method in C#, you receive only a return value. Therefore, at first glance, it appears that you can retrieve only one value per method call. Obviously, calling one method for every piece of necessary data can be cumbersome. For example, let's say you have a *Color* class that represents a given color with three values, which you describe using the standard RGB (red, green, blue) model. Using only return values, you'd be forced to write code like this to retrieve all three values:

```
Color c = new Color();
int red = c.GetRed();
int green = c.GetGreen();
int blue = c.GetBlue();
```

But what you want is something similar to this:

```
int red;
int green;
int blue;
c.GetRGB(red, green, blue);
```

There's a problem here. When you call the *c.GetRGB* method, the code copies the values for the red, green, and blue arguments into the method's local stack, and any changes that the method makes aren't made to the caller's variables.

In C++, we circumvent this problem by having the calling method pass pointers (or references) to the variables so that the method works on the caller's data. The solution in C# is similar. Actually, C# offers two solutions. The first involves the keyword *ref*. This keyword tells the C# compiler that the arguments being passed point to the same memory as the variables in the calling code. That way, if the called method modifies the values and then returns, the calling code's variables are modified. The following code illustrates how to use the *ref* keyword with the *Color* class example:

```
class Color
{
    public Color()
    {
        this.red = 0;
        this.green = 127;
        this.blue = 255;
    }

    protected int red;
    protected int green;
    protected int blue;

    public void GetRGB(
        ref int red, ref int green, ref int blue)
    {
        red = this.red;
        green = this.green;
        blue = this.blue;
    }

}

class Class1
{
    static void Main(string[] args)
    {
        Color c = new Color();
        int red;
        int green;
        int blue;
        c.GetRGB(ref red, ref green, ref blue);
```

```
        Console.WriteLine("R={0}, G={1}, B={2}",
            red, green, blue);
    }
}
```

Using the *ref* keyword has a limitation that, in fact, prevents the previous code from compiling. In the interest of robustness, the compiler will insist that when you use the *ref* keyword, you initialize the passed arguments before calling the method. Therefore, for this code to work, you must modify it like this:

```
class Color
{
    public Color()
    {
        this.red = 0;
        this.green = 127;
        this.blue = 255;
    }

    protected int red;
    protected int green;
    protected int blue;

    public void GetRGB(
        ref int red, ref int green, ref int blue)
    {
        red = this.red;
        green = this.green;
        blue = this.blue;
    }

}

class Class1
{
    static void Main(string[] args)
    {
        Color c = new Color();
        int red = 0;
        int green = 0;
        int blue = 0;
        c.GetRGB(ref red, ref green, ref blue);

        Console.WriteLine("R={0}, G={1}, B={2}",
            red, green, blue);
    }
}
```

The output from this code will be:

```
R=0, G=127, B=255
```

Look briefly at the Microsoft intermediate language (MSIL) shown in Figure 4-1. As you can see, the *ref* parameters are prefixed with an ampersand (&), which clearly is based on the reference/address type in C++. Also, note the *stind* instruction—this is for popping indirect values off the stack (via addresses).

```
Color::GetRGB : void(int32&,int32&,int32&)                          _ □ ×
.method public hidebysig instance void  GetRGB(int32& red,
                                                int32& green,
                                                int32& blue) cil managed
{
  // Code size       25 (0x19)
  .maxstack  2
  IL_0000:  ldarg.1
  IL_0001:  ldarg.0
  IL_0002:  ldfld      int32 ColorByRef.Color::red
  IL_0007:  stind.i4
  IL_0008:  ldarg.2
  IL_0009:  ldarg.0
  IL_000a:  ldfld      int32 ColorByRef.Color::green
  IL_000f:  stind.i4
  IL_0010:  ldarg.3
  IL_0011:  ldarg.0
  IL_0012:  ldfld      int32 ColorByRef.Color::blue
  IL_0017:  stind.i4
  IL_0018:  ret
} // end of method Color::GetRGB
```

Figure 4-1   MSIL for *ref* parameters.

Figure 4-2 shows how the MSIL looks if we don't use the *ref* keyword. Note the use of *starg*—which simply pops a value off the stack—instead of *stind*.

```
Color::GetRGB : void(int32,int32,int32)                             _ □ ×
.method public hidebysig instance void  GetRGB(int32 red,
                                                int32 green,
                                                int32 blue) cil managed
{
  // Code size       25 (0x19)
  .maxstack  1
  IL_0000:  ldarg.0
  IL_0001:  ldfld      int32 ColorByRef.Color::red
  IL_0006:  starg.s    red
  IL_0008:  ldarg.0
  IL_0009:  ldfld      int32 ColorByRef.Color::green
  IL_000e:  starg.s    green
  IL_0010:  ldarg.0
  IL_0011:  ldfld      int32 ColorByRef.Color::blue
  IL_0016:  starg.s    blue
  IL_0018:  ret
} // end of method Color::GetRGB
```

Figure 4-2   MSIL for value parameters.

out Method Parameters

In the previous example, initializing the variables to be overwritten seemed pointless, didn't it? Fortunately, C# provides an alternate means of passing an argument whose changed value must be seen by the calling code: the *out* keyword. Here's the same *Color* class example using the *out* keyword:

```
class Color
{
    public Color()
    {
        this.red = 0;
        this.green = 127;
        this.blue = 255;
    }

    protected int red;
    protected int green;
    protected int blue;

    public void GetRGB(out int red, out int green,
        out int blue)
    {
        red = this.red;
        green = this.green;
        blue = this.blue;
    }

}

class Class1
{
    static void Main(string[] args)
    {
        Color c = new Color();
        int red;
        int green;
        int blue;
        c.GetRGB(out red, out green, out blue);

        Console.WriteLine("R={0}, G={1}, B={2}",
            red, green, blue);
    }
}
```

The significant difference between the *ref* keyword and the *out* keyword is that the *out* keyword doesn't require the calling code to initialize the passed arguments first. When do you use the *ref* keyword? You should use it when you need assurance that the calling method has initialized the argument. In the previous examples, you could use *out* because the method being called wasn't dependent on the value of the variable being passed. But what if the called method uses a parameter value? Take a look at this code:

```
using System;

class Window
{
    public Window(int x, int y)
    {
        this.x = x;
        this.y = y;
    }

    protected int x;
    protected int y;

    public void Move(int x, int y)
    {
        this.x = x;
        this.y = y;
    }

    public void ChangePos(ref int x, ref int y)
    {
        this.x += x;;
        this.y += y;

        x = this.x;
        y = this.y;
    }
}

class TestWindowByRef
{
    public static void Main()
    {
        Window wnd = new Window(5, 5);
        int x = 5;
        int y = 5;

        wnd.ChangePos(ref x, ref y);
        Console.WriteLine("{0}, {1}", x, y);
```

```
        x = -1;
        y = -1;
        wnd.ChangePos(ref x, ref y);
        Console.WriteLine("{0}, {1}", x, y);
    }
}
```

As you can see, the method being called—*Window.ChangePos*—bases its work on the parameters being passed in. In fact, this method relies entirely on the parameters having acceptable values. In this case, the *ref* keyword forces the caller to initialize the value so that the method will function properly.

A more subtle difference between *ref* and *out* is that *out* parameters must be modified in the called method, whereas *ref* parameters can be but don't have to be modified. Let's revisit our *Color* class example. The following code would work fine, and the output would be the initial values of red, green, and blue:

```
class Color
{
    public Color()
    {
        this.red = 0;
        this.green = 127;
        this.blue = 255;
    }

    protected int red;
    protected int green;
    protected int blue;

    public void GetRGB(ref int red, ref int green,
        ref int blue)
    {
//      red = this.red;
//      green = this.green;
//      blue = this.blue;
    }

}

class Class1
{
    static void Main(string[] args)
    {
        Color c = new Color();
        int red = 0;
        int green = 0;
        int blue = 0;
        c.GetRGB(ref red, ref green, ref blue);
```

```
            Console.WriteLine("R={0}, G={1}, B={2}",
                red, green, blue);
        }
    }
```

However, this code won't compile because the *red*, *green*, and *blue* parameters must be assigned in the *GetRGB* method:

```
class Color
{
    public Color()
    {
        this.red = 0;
        this.green = 127;
        this.blue = 255;
    }

    protected int red;
    protected int green;
    protected int blue;

    public void GetRGB(out int red, out int green,
        out int blue)
    {
//      red = this.red;
//      green = this.green;
//      blue = this.blue;
    }

}

class Class1
{
    static void Main(string[] args)
    {
        Color c = new Color();
        int red;
        int green;
        int blue;
        c.GetRGB(out red, out green, out blue);

        Console.WriteLine("R={0}, G={1}, B={2}",
            red, green, blue);
    }
}
```

Value and Reference Parameters (Again)

Recall that in the simplest case, when you pass a parameter to a method, you're passing a copy of the parameter. If the parameter is a value type, you get a copy of the data. If the parameter is a reference type, you get a copy of the reference. How does this relate to the *ref* and *out* keywords? In the earlier examples, we passed value types (integers) by reference using the *ref* or *out* keywords. But can we pass a reference type by reference? The answer is yes, and the result is interesting.

If all we do is pass a reference type parameter by reference, the result is no different than passing a reference type parameter by value:

```
class AnotherClass
{
    public int ID;
}
class SomeClass
{
//      public AnotherClass ChangeObject(AnotherClass ref1)
    public AnotherClass ChangeObject(ref AnotherClass ref1)
    {
        ref1.ID = ref1.ID*2;
        return ref1;
    }
}

class ValRefTest
{
    static void Main(string[] args)
    {
        SomeClass sc = new SomeClass();
        AnotherClass ref1 = new AnotherClass();
        ref1.ID = 3;
//          AnotherClass ref2 = sc.ChangeObject(ref1);
        AnotherClass ref2 = sc.ChangeObject(ref ref1);
        Console.WriteLine("ref1.ID = {0}, ref2.ID = {1}",
            ref1.ID, ref2.ID);
    }
}
```

In both cases, the output will be:

```
ref1.ID = 6, ref2.ID = 6
```

Figures 4-3 and 4-4 show the difference in the MSIL.

SomeClass::ChangeObject : class AnotherClass(class AnotherClass)

```
.method public hidebysig instance class AnotherClass
        ChangeObject(class AnotherClass ref1) cil managed
{
  // Code size       20 (0x14)
  .maxstack  3
  .locals init ([0] class AnotherClass CS$00000003$00000000)
  IL_0000:  ldarg.1
  IL_0001:  ldarg.1
  IL_0002:  ldfld      int32 AnotherClass::ID
  IL_0007:  ldc.i4.2
  IL_0008:  mul
  IL_0009:  stfld      int32 AnotherClass::ID
  IL_000e:  ldarg.1
  IL_000f:  stloc.0
  IL_0010:  br.s       IL_0012
  IL_0012:  ldloc.0
  IL_0013:  ret
} // end of method SomeClass::ChangeObject
```

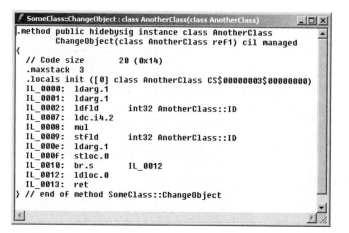

Figure 4-3 Reference parameter passed by value.

SomeClass::ChangeObject : class AnotherClass(class AnotherClass&)

```
.method public hidebysig instance class AnotherClass
        ChangeObject(class AnotherClass& ref1) cil managed
{
  // Code size       23 (0x17)
  .maxstack  3
  .locals init ([0] class AnotherClass CS$00000003$00000000)
  IL_0000:  ldarg.1
  IL_0001:  ldind.ref
  IL_0002:  ldarg.1
  IL_0003:  ldind.ref
  IL_0004:  ldfld      int32 AnotherClass::ID
  IL_0009:  ldc.i4.2
  IL_000a:  mul
  IL_000b:  stfld      int32 AnotherClass::ID
  IL_0010:  ldarg.1
  IL_0011:  ldind.ref
  IL_0012:  stloc.0
  IL_0013:  br.s       IL_0015
  IL_0015:  ldloc.0
  IL_0016:  ret
} // end of method SomeClass::ChangeObject
```

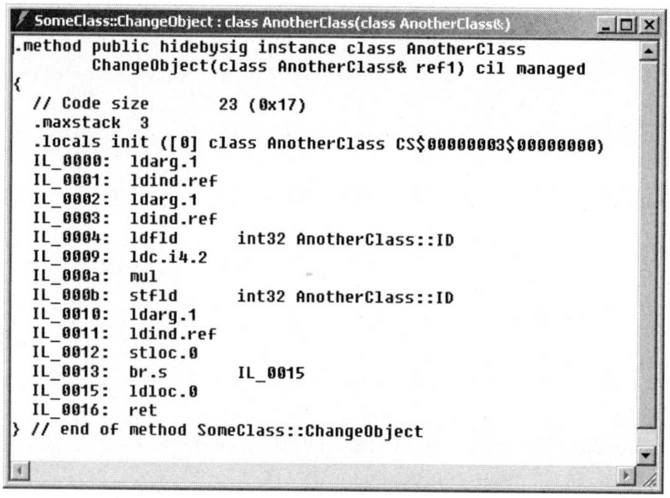

Figure 4-4 Reference parameter passed by reference.

Note that a method that takes an *out* parameter must assign a value to the parameter. In the case of value types, this assignment is easy because the value type is by definition a simple, discrete type. However, in the case of reference types, the restriction is more obvious: you must assign to the parameter, not just to some field within the parameter and not just via some modification. In fact, you can't use the *out* parameter until you've assigned a value to it, and you must assign to it before returning from the method:

```
class AnotherClass
{
    public int ID;
}
class SomeClass
{
    // This won't compile
    public AnotherClass ChangeObject(out AnotherClass ref1)
    {
        ref1.ID = ref1.ID*2;
        return ref1;
    }
    // This won't compile
    public AnotherClass ChangeObject(out AnotherClass ref1)
    {
        ref1.ID = 4;
        return ref1;
    }
    // This won't compile
    public AnotherClass ChangeObject(out AnotherClass ref1)
    {
        int x = ref1.ID;
        ref1 = new AnotherClass();
        ref1.ID = x * 2;
        return ref1;
    }

    // This WILL compile
    public AnotherClass ChangeObject(out AnotherClass ref1)
    {
        ref1 = new AnotherClass();
        ref1.ID = 99;
        return ref1;
    }
}

class RefByOutTest
{
    static void Main(string[] args)
    {
        SomeClass sc = new SomeClass();
        AnotherClass ref1 = new AnotherClass();
        ref1.ID = 3;

        AnotherClass ref2 = sc.ChangeObject(out ref1);
        Console.WriteLine("ref1.ID = {0}, ref2.ID = {1}",
            ref1.ID, ref2.ID);

    }
}
```

The output from this code will be:

```
ref1.ID = 99, ref2.ID = 99
```

There's also a more subtle significance in passing a reference type by reference. Consider the code listed here.

```
class AnotherClass
{
    public int ID;
}
class SomeClass
{
    public AnotherClass ChangeObject(ref AnotherClass ref1)
    {
        ref1.ID = ref1.ID*2;
        return ref1;
    }
    public void SubtleChange(
        ref AnotherClass ref1, AnotherClass ref2)
    {
        ref1 = new AnotherClass();
        ref1.ID = 999;

        ref2 = new AnotherClass();
        ref2.ID = 999;
    }
}

class ValRefTest
{
    static void Main(string[] args)
    {
        SomeClass sc = new SomeClass();
        AnotherClass ref1 = new AnotherClass();
        ref1.ID = 3;
        AnotherClass ref2 = sc.ChangeObject(ref ref1);
        Console.WriteLine("ref1.ID = {0}, ref2.ID = {1}",
            ref1.ID, ref2.ID);

        sc.SubtleChange(ref ref1, ref2);
        Console.WriteLine("ref1.ID = {0}, ref2.ID = {1}",
            ref1.ID, ref2.ID);
    }
}
```

The output this time will be:

```
ref1.ID = 999, ref2.ID = 6
```

who taught to? that proph rits?

Are you following this? If we pass a reference by value, we're passing a copy of the reference, which means we can access the original data that the reference refers to. However, the incoming reference is only a copy. Therefore, assigning a new value to this copy won't affect the original reference. On the other hand, if we pass a reference by reference, we're actually passing the original reference. If we then reassign the reference, we not only have the same access to the data that's referred to, we also reassign the original reference.

Method Overloading

Method overloading enables the C# programmer to use the same method name multiple times with only the passed arguments changed. This ability is extremely useful in at least two scenarios. The first allows you to use a single method name for situations where the behavior of the method differs slightly depending on the value types passed. (We'll examine the second scenario a bit later in this section.) For example, let's say you have a logging class that enables your application to write diagnostic information to disk. To make the class a bit more flexible, you might use several forms of the *Write* method to specify the information to be written. Besides accepting the string that will be written, the method could also accept a string resource ID. Without the ability to overload methods, you'd have to implement a method for each of these situations, such as *WriteString* and *WriteFromResourceId*. However, using method overloading, you could implement the following two *WriteEntry* methods, which differ only in parameter type:

```
class Log
{
    public Log(string fileName)
    {
        // Open fileName and seek to end.
    }

    public void WriteEntry(string entry)
    {
        Console.WriteLine(entry);
    }

    public void WriteEntry(int resourceId)
    {
        Console.WriteLine(
        "Retrieve string using resource id and write to log");
    }
}
```

```
class Class1
{
    static void Main(string[] args)
    {
        Log log = new Log("My File");
        log.WriteEntry("Entry one");
        log.WriteEntry(42);
    }
}
```

The following methods are considered legal overloads—after all, the parameter list *is* different:

```
public void WriteEntry(string entry, int resourceId)
{
    Console.WriteLine(entry + " " + resourceId);
}

public void WriteEntry(int resourceId, string entry)
{
    Console.WriteLine(resourceId + " " + entry);
}
```

The important point to remember about method overloading is that each method's *parameter list* must be different; it doesn't count if a method's return type and access modifier are different. Therefore, the following code won't compile because we have three versions of the *WriteEntry* method, two of which differ only in return type, not in parameter list:

```
class Log
{
    public Log(string fileName)
    {
        // Open fileName and seek to end.
    }

    public void WriteEntry(string entry)
    {
        Console.WriteLine(entry);
    }

    // This won't compile: return type doesn't count
    public int WriteEntry(string entry)
    {
        Console.WriteLine(entry);
        return entry.Length;
    }
```

```
public void WriteEntry(int resourceId)
{
    Console.WriteLine(
    "Retrieve string using resource id and write to log");
}
}
```

The access modifier also doesn't count when differentiating method overloads:

```
// This won't compile: access modifier doesn't count
protected void WriteEntry(string entry)
{
    Console.WriteLine(entry);
}
```

The bottom line is that there must be a difference in the parameter list. Thus, this overload is acceptable:

```
public void WriteEntry(ref string entry)
{
    Console.WriteLine(entry);
}
```

While the *ref* and *out* modifiers are sufficient to differentiate from other versions of the method, the compiler considers *ref* and *out* equivalent to each other. This means you can provide an overload by modifying a specific parameter with either *ref* or *out*, but not both:

```
// Either of these is OK, but not both:
public void WriteEntry(ref string entry)
{
    Console.WriteLine(entry);
}

public void WriteEntry(out string entry)
{
    entry = "Foo";
    Console.WriteLine(entry);
}
```

Overloading Constructors

The second scenario in which method overloading is helpful occurs when you use *constructors*, which are essentially methods called when you instantiate an object. Let's say you want to create a class that can be constructed in more than one way—for example, by requiring either a file handle (an *int*) or a filename (a *string*) to open a file. Because C# rules dictate that a class's constructor must have the same name as the class itself, you can't simply create different method names for each variable type. Instead, you need to overload the constructor:

```
class File
{
}

class CommaDelimitedFile
{
    public CommaDelimitedFile(String fileName)
    {
        Console.WriteLine("Constructed with a file name");
    }

    public CommaDelimitedFile(File file)
    {
        Console.WriteLine("Constructed with a file object");
    }
}

class Class1
{
    static void Main(string[] args)
    {
        File file = new File();
        CommaDelimitedFile file2 =
            new CommaDelimitedFile(file);
        CommaDelimitedFile file3 =
            new CommaDelimitedFile("Some file name");
    }
}
```

Given the previous listing, you can't declare a *CommaDelimitedFile* like this:

```
CommaDelimitedFile file4 =
    new CommaDelimitedFile();
```

But suppose we remove the constructors we've written. You'll find that the statement just shown *does* work now. How can this be?

```
class File
{
}

class CommaDelimitedFile
{
```

```
/*      public CommaDelimitedFile(String fileName)
    {
        Console.WriteLine("Constructed with a file name");
    }

    public CommaDelimitedFile(File file)
    {
        Console.WriteLine("Constructed with a file object");
    }
*/
}

class Class1
{
    static void Main(string[] args)
    {
        File file = new File();
//          CommaDelimitedFile file2 =
//              new CommaDelimitedFile(file);
//          CommaDelimitedFile file3 =
//              new CommaDelimitedFile("Some file name");

        CommaDelimitedFile file4 =
            new CommaDelimitedFile();
    }
}
```

Clearly, if we don't write any constructors of our own, we can instantiate the class without passing parameters—using the so-called *default constructor*. But as soon as we write any nondefault constructor, we can't instantiate the class without passing parameters. The logic behind this arrangement is that this code:

```
public CommaDelimitedFile(String fileName)
{
}
```

is implicitly compiled as though it were written:

```
public CommaDelimitedFile(String fileName) : this()
```

and the expression *this()* resolves to a call to:

```
public CommaDelimitedFile()
{
}
```

which must therefore be available. This behavior becomes obvious if we look at the MSIL, as shown in Figure 4-5.

```
CommaDelimitedFile::.ctor : void(class DefaultCtors.File)                    _□×
.method public hidebysig specialname rtspecialname
        instance void   .ctor(class DefaultCtors.File file) cil managed
{
  // Code size       17 (0x11)
  .maxstack  1
  IL_0000:  ldarg.0
  IL_0001:  call       instance void [mscorlib]System.Object::.ctor()
  IL_0006:  ldstr      "Constructed with a file object"
  IL_000b:  call       void [mscorlib]System.Console::WriteLine(string)
  IL_0010:  ret
} // end of method CommaDelimitedFile::.ctor
```

Figure 4-5   Implicit call to default constructor.

It boils down to this: every instantiation of a class must have a matching constructor if the code is to compile, even if the constructor doesn't do anything.

You can also use a constructor initializer list to explicitly call one constructor from another, as shown here and in Figure 4-6:

```
public CommaDelimitedFile() : this("Default string")
{
}
```

```
CommaDelimitedFile::.ctor : void()                                          _□×
.method public hidebysig specialname rtspecialname
        instance void   .ctor() cil managed
{
  // Code size       12 (0xc)
  .maxstack  2
  IL_0000:  ldarg.0
  IL_0001:  ldstr      "Default string"
  IL_0006:  call       instance void DefaultCtors.CommaDelimitedFile::.ctor(string)
  IL_000b:  ret
} // end of method CommaDelimitedFile::.ctor
```

Figure 4-6   Explicit call to overloaded constructor.

Inheritance and Overloading

When it comes to the combination of inheritance and overloading, C# behaves like Java, not like C++. That is, an overloaded method is considered an overload even if the other overloaded versions of the function exist in a base class rather than the current class.

```
class Log
{
    public Log(string fileName) {}
    public Log() {}

    public void WriteEntry(string entry)
    {
        Console.WriteLine(entry);
    }
}
```

```
class LogEx : Log
{
    public LogEx(string fileName) {}

    public void WriteEntry(int resourceId)
    {
        Console.WriteLine(
            "Retrieve resource id and write to log");
    }
}

class Class1
{
    static void Main(string[] args)
    {
        LogEx log = new LogEx("My File");
        log.WriteEntry("Entry one");
        log.WriteEntry(42);
    }
}
```

The output from this application will be:

```
Entry one
Retrieve resource id and write to log
```

Variable Method Parameters

Sometimes you won't know the number of arguments that you pass to a method until run time. For example, suppose you want a class that plots a line on a graph according to a series of *x* and *y* coordinates. You could have the class use a method that takes as its only argument a single *Point* object representing both an *x* value and a *y* value. This method will then store each *Point* object in a linked list or array member until the caller wants to print out the entire sequence of points. However, this is a poor design decision for a couple of reasons. First, it requires the user to perform the unnecessary work of calling one method for each point of the line to draw (which is very tedious if the line is long) and then calling another method to draw the line. The technique's second drawback is that it requires the class to somehow store these points even though they're needed only for a single method, *DrawLine*.

Variable arguments work well to solve these problems. You can specify a variable number of method parameters by using the *params* keyword and by specifying an array in the method's argument list. This example of the *Draw* class in C# allows the user to make a single call that takes a variable number of *Point* objects and prints each one:

```
class Point
{
    public Point(int x, int y)
    {
        this.x = x;
        this.y = y;
    }

    public int x;
    public int y;
}

class Chart
{
    public void DrawLine(params Point[] p)
    {
        Console.WriteLine("\nThis method would print a line "
            + "along the following points:");
        for (int i = 0; i < p.GetLength(0); i++)
        {
            Console.WriteLine("{0}, {1}", p[i].x, p[i].y);
        }
    }
}

class TestVarArgs
{
    static void Main(string[] args)
    {
        Point p1 = new Point(5,10);
        Point p2 = new Point(5, 15);
        Point p3 = new Point(5, 20);

        Chart chart = new Chart();
        chart.DrawLine(p1, p2, p3);
    }
}
```

The output from this code will be:

```
This method would print a line along the following points:
5, 10
5, 15
5, 20
```

The *DrawLine* method tells the C# compiler that it can take a variable number of *Point* objects. At run time, the method uses a simple *for* loop to iterate through the *Point* objects that are passed, printing each one.

The *params* parameter can be a variable number of parameters of the correct type, as just shown, or it can be a single array of that type. For example:

```
Point[] pts = { new Point(1,2),
    new Point(3,4),
    new Point(5,6) };
chart.DrawLine(pts);
```

The output from this code will be:

```
This method would print a line along the following points:
1, 2
3, 4
5, 6
```

More Info   In a real application, it's much better to use properties to access an object's data members than to make the members public. In addition, it's also better to use the *foreach* statement instead of a *for* loop to iterate through an array. Although it's worth making this point about arrays here, we won't examine arrays in any detail until we reach Chapter 5, "Properties, Arrays, and Indexers." We'll cover the *foreach* statement in Chapter 9, "Program Flow Control."

As you've seen from your examination of the common type system (CTS) in Chapter 3, you can treat all types as objects. By logical extension, you can write a method to take a *params* parameter of type *object*, which you can then use to take in any number of parameters of *any* type:

```
class OpenEnded
{
    public void Foo(params object[] pp)
    {
        for (int i = 0; i < pp.GetLength(0); i++)
        {
            Console.WriteLine(pp[i]);
        }
    }
}

class TestVarArgs
{
    static void Main(string[] args)
    {
        OpenEnded oe = new OpenEnded();
```

```
        oe.Foo(123, 456, "Hello", new Point(7,8),
            9.0m, true, 'X');
    }
}
```

The output from this code will be:

```
123
456
Hello
VarArgs.Point
9
True
X
```

Given this feature, you could argue that there's no need to dwell on multiple method overloads—instead, you could routinely write just one method in a class that takes a *params object[]* parameter. But consider the disadvantages: you gain the simplicity of treating all types as objects but pay a performance penalty when you need to treat those same parameters as specific types rather than generic objects. Suppose, for instance, that you want the *x,y* coordinate values from the *Point object*, not just a string representation of its type. That is, suppose you want this output from the same application:

```
123
456
Hello
7, 8
9
True
X
```

You actually have two choices (or three, if you're picky). The simplest choice is to use virtual method overriding, which we'll take at look at in the next section. The other choice is to use the *is* or *as* operator.

More Info   The *is* and *as* operators are covered in Chapter 7, "Interfaces."

Virtual Methods

As you saw in Chapter 3, you can derive one class from another—that is, one class can inherit and build on the capabilities of an existing class. Because we hadn't discussed methods yet, that discussion only touched on the inheritance of fields and methods. In other words, we didn't look at the ability to modify the base class's behavior in the derived class. You perform this modification by using virtual methods, which we'll discuss in this section.

Method Overriding

Let's first look at how to override the base class functionality of an inherited method. We'll begin with a base class that represents an employee. To keep the example as simple as possible, we'll give this base class a single method named *CalculatePay, shown in the following code.* The body of this method will simply let us know the name of the method called. This will help us determine which methods in the inheritance tree are being called later.

```
class Employee
{
    public void CalculatePay()
    {
        Console.WriteLine("Employee.CalculatePay()");
    }
}
```

Now let's say that you want to derive a class from *Employee* and you want to override the *CalculatePay* method so that it does something specific to the derived class. To do this, you need to use the *new* keyword with the derived class's method definition. This code shows how easy it is:

```
class SalariedEmployee : Employee
{
    new public void CalculatePay()
    {
        Console.WriteLine("SalariedEmployee.CalculatePay()");
    }
}

class TestNewMethods
{
    static void Main(string[] args)
    {
        Employee e = new Employee();
        e.CalculatePay();

        SalariedEmployee s = new SalariedEmployee();
        s.CalculatePay();
    }
}
```

Compiling and executing this code generates the following output:

```
Employee.CalculatePay()
SalariedEmployee.CalculatePay()
```

Look what happens if we omit the *new* keyword:

```
//new public void CalculatePay()
public void CalculatePay()
{
    Console.WriteLine("SalariedEmployee.CalculatePay()");
}
```

As you can see in Figure 4-7, the code compiles just fine and the runtime behavior is identical. In this situation, *new* is the implicit default. Note that the compiler indicates its reservations about the *new* method with its customary blue squiggly underscore and the IntelliSense comment: The *new* keyword is required on *'NewMethods.SalariedEmployee.CalculatePay()'* because it hides inherited member *'NewMethods.Employee.CalculatePay()'*.

```
public void CalculatePay()
{
    Console.Wri │ The keyword new is required on 'NewMethods.SalariedEmployee.CalculatePay()'
}              │ because it hides inherited member 'NewMethods.Employee.CalculatePay()'
```

Figure 4-7   Compiler diagnostic on implicit *new* method.

The subtle message here is that whether we specify it implicitly or explicitly, a *new* method is in no way associated with a method in the base class—regardless of the name, signature, return type, and access modifiers. In the *CalculatePay* example, the two methods—one in the base *Employee* class, the other in the derived *SalariedEmployee* class—are in no way related. The fact that they have identical signatures is pure coincidence and of no consequence.

Polymorphism

Method overriding with the *new* keyword works fine if you have a reference to the derived object. But what happens if you have an upcasted reference to a base class and want the compiler to call the derived class's implementation of a method? This situation is where polymorphism comes in. Polymorphism enables you to define a method multiple times throughout your class hierarchy so that the runtime calls the appropriate version of the method for the specific object being used.

Let's look at our employee example to see this idea in action. The previous sample code runs correctly because we have two objects: an *Employee* object, and a *SalariedEmployee* object. In a more practical application, we'd probably read all the employee records from a database and populate an array.

Although some of these employees would be contractors and some would be salaried employees, we'd need to place them all in our array as the same type—the base class type, *Employee*. However, when we iterate through this array, retrieving and calling each object's *CalculatePay* method, we want the compiler to call the correct object's implementation of the *CalculatePay* method.

In the following example, I've added a new class, *ContractEmployee*. The main application class now contains an array of type *Employee* and two additional methods. *LoadEmployees* loads the *Employee* objects into the array, and *DoPayroll* iterates through the array, calling each object's *CalculatePay* method.

```
class Employee
{
    public string name;

    public Employee(string name)
    {
        this.name = name;
    }

    public void CalculatePay()
    {
        Console.WriteLine(
            "Employee.CalculatePay called for {0}",
            name);
    }
}

class ContractEmployee : Employee
{
    public ContractEmployee(string name) : base(name)
    {
    }

    public new void CalculatePay()
    {
        Console.WriteLine(
            "ContractEmployee.CalculatePay called for {0}",
                name);
    }
}

class SalariedEmployee : Employee
{
    public SalariedEmployee (string name) : base(name)
    {
    }
```

```
    public new void CalculatePay()
    {
        Console.WriteLine(
            "SalariedEmployee.CalculatePay called for {0}",
                name);
    }
}


class TestNotPolymorphic
{
    protected Employee[] employees;

    public void LoadEmployees()
    {
        // Simulating loading from a database.
        employees = new Employee[2];
        employees[0] = new ContractEmployee(
            "Adam Barr");
        employees[1] = new SalariedEmployee(
            "Max Benson");
    }

    public void DoPayroll()
    {
        for (int i = 0; i < employees.GetLength(0); i++)
        {
            employees[i].CalculatePay();
        }
    }

    static void Main(string[] args)
    {
        TestNotPolymorphic t = new TestNotPolymorphic();
        t.LoadEmployees();
        t.DoPayroll();
    }
}
```

However, running this application results in the following output:

```
Employee.CalculatePay called for Adam Barr
Employee.CalculatePay called for Max Benson
```

Obviously, this isn't what we wanted—the base class's implementation of *CalculatePay* is called for each object. This is an example of a phenomenon called *early binding*. When the code compiles, the C# compiler looks at the call to *CalculatePay* and determines the address in memory needed to jump to when the call is made. In this case, that's the memory location of the *Employee.CalculatePay* method.

The call to the *Employee.CalculatePay* method is the problem. Instead, we want late binding to occur. *Late binding* means that the compiler doesn't select the method to execute until run time. To force the compiler to call the correct version of an upcasted object's method, we use two keywords: *virtual* and *override*. You must use the *virtual* keyword on the base class's method, and you use the *override* keyword on the derived class's implementation of that method. Here's the example again, this time functioning polymorphically:

```
class Employee
{
    public string name;

    public Employee(string name)
    {
        this.name = name;
    }

    public virtual void CalculatePay()
    {
        Console.WriteLine(
            "Employee.CalculatePay called for {0}",
            name);
    }
}

class ContractEmployee : Employee
{
    public ContractEmployee(string name) : base(name)
    {
    }

    public override void CalculatePay()
    {
        Console.WriteLine(
            "ContractEmployee.CalculatePay called for {0}",
            name);
    }
}

class SalariedEmployee : Employee
{
    public SalariedEmployee (string name) : base(name)
```

```
        {
        }

        public override void CalculatePay()
        {
            Console.WriteLine(
                "SalariedEmployee.CalculatePay called for {0}",
                name);
        }
    }

    class TestPolymorphic
    {
        protected Employee[] employees;

        public void LoadEmployees()
        {
            // Simulating loading from a database.
            employees = new Employee[2];
            employees[0] = new ContractEmployee(
                "Adam Barr");
            employees[1] = new SalariedEmployee(
                "Max Benson");
        }

        public void DoPayroll()
        {
            for (int i = 0; i < employees.GetLength(0); i++)
            {
                employees[i].CalculatePay();
            }
        }

        static void Main(string[] args)
        {
            TestPolymorphic t = new TestPolymorphic();
            t.LoadEmployees();
            t.DoPayroll();
        }
    }
```

Running the code at this point should yield the following results:

```
ContractEmployee.CalculatePay called for Adam Barr
SalariedEmployee.CalculatePay called for Max Benson
```

If we examine the MSIL, there's no apparent difference between the non-polymorphic classes (using *new* methods) and the polymorphic classes (using *virtual* and *override* methods). This is because both cases use the MSIL instruction *callvirt*, as Figure 4-8 shows.

```
TestNotPolymorphic::DoPayroll : void()
.method public hidebysig instance void  DoPayroll() cil managed
{
  // Code size       37 (0x25)
  .maxstack  3
  .locals init ([0] int32 i)
  IL_0000:  ldc.i4.0
  IL_0001:  stloc.0
  IL_0002:  br.s       IL_0015
  IL_0004:  ldarg.0
  IL_0005:  ldfld      class NotPolymorphic.Employee[] NotPolymorphic.TestNotPo
  IL_000a:  ldloc.0
  IL_000b:  ldelem.ref
  IL_000c:  callvirt   instance void NotPolymorphic.Employee::CalculatePay()
  IL_0011:  ldloc.0
  IL_0012:  ldc.i4.1
  IL_0013:  add
  IL_0014:  stloc.0
  IL_0015:  ldloc.0
  IL_0016:  ldarg.0
  IL_0017:  ldfld      class NotPolymorphic.Employee[] NotPolymorphic.TestNotPo
  IL_001c:  ldc.i4.0
  IL_001d:  callvirt   instance int32 [mscorlib]System.Array::GetLength(int32)
  IL_0022:  blt.s      IL_0004
  IL_0024:  ret
} // end of method TestNotPolymorphic::DoPayroll
```

Figure 4-8 The MSIL instruction *callvirt* calls virtual and nonvirtual methods.

The true difference lies in the setup of the virtual function table (VTBL). We need to examine four sets of MSIL: the base class *Employee.CalculatePay* in both nonvirtual and virtual forms (Figures 4-9 and 4-10), and the derived class *SalariedEmployee.CalculatePay* in both nonvirtual and virtual forms (Figures 4-11 and 4-12).

```
Employee::CalculatePay : void()
.method public hidebysig instance void  CalculatePay() cil managed
{
  // Code size       17 (0x11)
  .maxstack  2
  IL_0000:  ldstr      "Employee.CalculatePay called for {0}"
  IL_0005:  ldarg.0
  IL_0006:  ldfld      string NotPolymorphic.Employee::name
  IL_000b:  call       void [mscorlib]System.Console::WriteLine(string,
                                                                object)
  IL_0010:  ret
} // end of method Employee::CalculatePay
```

Figure 4-9 Nonvirtual base class method.

```
Employee::CalculatePay : void()
.method public hidebysig newslot virtual
        instance void  CalculatePay() cil managed
{
  // Code size       17 (0x11)
  .maxstack  2
  IL_0000:  ldstr      "Employee.CalculatePay called for {0}"
  IL_0005:  ldarg.0
  IL_0006:  ldfld      string PolyMorphic.Employee::name
  IL_000b:  call       void [mscorlib]System.Console::WriteLine(string,
                                                                object)
  IL_0010:  ret
} // end of method Employee::CalculatePay
```

Figure 4-10 Virtual base class method.

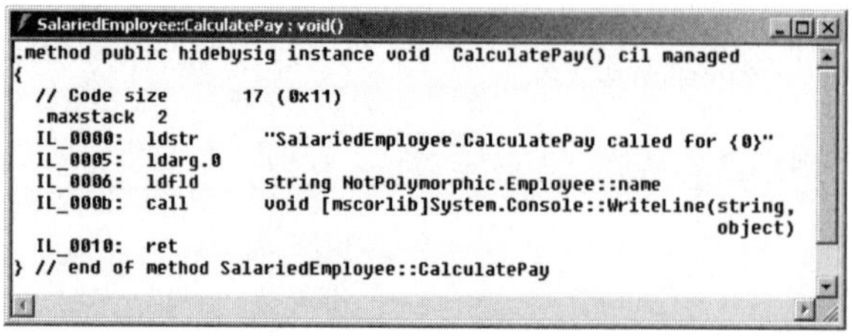

```
.method public hidebysig instance void  CalculatePay() cil managed
{
  // Code size       17 (0x11)
  .maxstack  2
  IL_0000:  ldstr      "SalariedEmployee.CalculatePay called for {0}"
  IL_0005:  ldarg.0
  IL_0006:  ldfld      string NotPolymorphic.Employee::name
  IL_000b:  call       void [mscorlib]System.Console::WriteLine(string,
                                                                 object)
  IL_0010:  ret
} // end of method SalariedEmployee::CalculatePay
```

Figure 4-11 Nonvirtual derived class method.

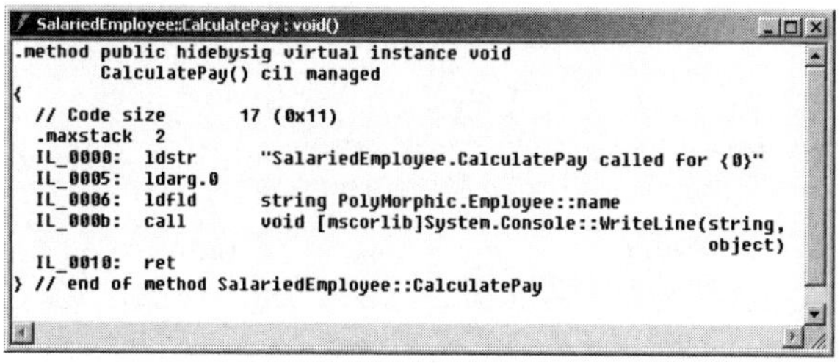

```
.method public hidebysig virtual instance void
        CalculatePay() cil managed
{
  // Code size       17 (0x11)
  .maxstack  2
  IL_0000:  ldstr      "SalariedEmployee.CalculatePay called for {0}"
  IL_0005:  ldarg.0
  IL_0006:  ldfld      string PolyMorphic.Employee::name
  IL_000b:  call       void [mscorlib]System.Console::WriteLine(string,
                                                                 object)
  IL_0010:  ret
} // end of method SalariedEmployee::CalculatePay
```

Figure 4-12 Virtual derived class method.

The crucial attributes are *newslot* and *virtual*, which are used in the polymorphic version of the class hierarchy. Together these attributes indicate that the base class *Employee.CalculatePay* method must have a new slot in the object's VTBL and that the derived class *SalariedEmployee.CalculatePay* is a virtual method that will end up in the same VTBL because it doesn't specify *newslot*. By comparison, in the nonpolymorphic version, both the base and the derived versions are *not* virtual.

Note that an *override* function must have the same access level (*private*, *protected*, *public*, and so on) as the *virtual* function it overrides. Also, a *virtual* member can't be declared *private* because the member would then be impossible to override. You can declare a member *protected*, but the usefulness of a virtual function is questionable if you can't access it outside the hierarchy. The following code illustrates:

```
class Employee
{
⋮
//      private virtual void CalculatePay()   // Illegal
//      protected virtual void CalculatePay() // Legal but dumb
    public virtual void CalculatePay()
    {
        Console.WriteLine(
            "Employee.CalculatePay called for {0}",
            name);
    }
}
```

```
class SalariedEmployee : Employee
{
// Legal if base class CalculatePay is protected
//      protected override void CalculatePay()
public override void CalculatePay()
    {
        Console.WriteLine(
            "SalariedEmployee.CalculatePay called for {0}",
            name);
    }
}
```

Note   Although this might be obvious, you can't declare a constructor
to be virtual because doing so doesn't make any sense:

```
//virtual public Employee(string name) // Illegal
public Employee(string name)
{
    this.name = name;
}
```

---

new and *virtual* Methods

Although it might be surprising, you can combine *new* and *virtual* when declaring a class function. Because the function is *new*, it will behave like any other *new* function, hiding any inherited function with the same signature. Because the function is also *virtual*, you can then further override it in derived classes so that it forms a new base level for this *virtual* function. For example, suppose we change the hierarchy so that *ContractEmployee* derives from *SalariedEmployee*:

```
class Employee
{
    public string name;

    public Employee(string name)
    {
        this.name = name;
    }

    public virtual void CalculatePay()
    {
        Console.WriteLine(
```

```
                        "Employee.CalculatePay called for {0}",
                        name);
        }
    }

    class SalariedEmployee : Employee
    {
        public SalariedEmployee (string name) : base(name)
        {
        }

        public new virtual void CalculatePay()
        {
            Console.WriteLine(
                "SalariedEmployee.CalculatePay called for {0}",
                name);
        }
    }

    class ContractEmployee : SalariedEmployee
    {
        public ContractEmployee(string name) : base(name)
        {
        }

        public override void CalculatePay()
        {
            Console.WriteLine(
                "ContractEmployee.CalculatePay called for {0}",
                name);
        }
    }

    class TestNewVirtuals
    {
        protected Employee[] employees;

        public void LoadEmployees()
        {
            employees = new Employee[2];
            employees[0] = new ContractEmployee(
                "Adam Barr");
            employees[1] = new SalariedEmployee(
                "Max Benson");
        }

        public void DoPayroll()
```

```
    {
        for (int i = 0; i < employees.GetLength(0); i++)
        {
            employees[i].CalculatePay();
        }
    }

    static void Main(string[] args)
    {
        TestNewVirtuals t = new TestNewVirtuals();
        t.LoadEmployees();
        t.DoPayroll();
    }
}
```

The output from this code will be:

```
Employee.CalculatePay called for Adam Barr
Employee.CalculatePay called for Max Benson
```

As you can see, adding the *new* keyword to the declaration of *Salaried-Employee.CalculatePay* means that the method is no longer considered when we iterate the *Employee* object references in the *DoPayroll* method. Also, because it's *virtual*, the override in the further derived class *ContractEmployee* is now an override for the virtual in *SalariedEmployee* rather than for the virtual in *Employee*. Therefore, the *ContractEmployee.CalculatePay* method isn't considered either.

Declaring a function *virtual* is the same as declaring it *new virtual* because *new* is still the default. Therefore, these statements are identical:

```
public new virtual void CalculatePay()
//public virtual void CalculatePay()
```

What's the point of new virtuals? Suppose we want to sort our employees based on a subset containing all *SalariedEmployees*:

```
public void ProcessSalariedEmployees()
{
    SalariedEmployee[] se = new SalariedEmployee[2];
    se[0] = new ContractEmployee("Adam Barr");
    se[1] = new SalariedEmployee("Max Benson");
    for (int i = 0; i < se.GetLength(0); i++)
    {
        se[i].CalculatePay();
    }
}
```

```
static void Main(string[] args)
{
    t.ProcessSalariedEmployees();
}
```

The output from this code will be:

```
ContractEmployee.CalculatePay called for Adam Barr
SalariedEmployee.CalculatePay called for Max Benson
```

We're basically establishing a level partition in the hierarchy. In a large hierarchy, this might become useful. For example, consider the inheritance for the *System.Windows.Form* class shown in Figure 4-13.

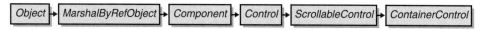

Figure 4-13   The inheritance for the *System.Windows.Form* class.

It's easy to imagine a situation in which you'd want to treat a collection of derived forms as forms instead of objects.

Calling Virtual Methods from Constructors

As a final point, consider what happens if you call virtual functions from constructors. The behavior is similar to that of Java, not that of C++—the most derived override is called, not the version at the level currently executing in the inheritance. However, the derived object itself might not be fully constructed when its derived override is called.

For instance, when we instantiate a derived *SalariedEmployee* object, the first constructor to run is the base *Employee* constructor, which calls the derived *SalariedEmployee.CalculatePay* method. However, this call happens before the derived *SalariedEmployee* constructor. Therefore, the additional *Salaried-Employee* field hasn't yet been initialized:

```
class Employee
{
    public string name;
    public Employee(string name)
    {
        this.name = name;
        Console.Write("Employee.CalculatePay:\n\t");
        CalculatePay();
    }

    public virtual void CalculatePay()
```

```
    {
        Console.WriteLine(
            "Employee.CalculatePay called for {0}",
            name);
    }
}

class SalariedEmployee : Employee
{
    public decimal salary;
    public SalariedEmployee (string name, decimal salary)
        : base(name)
    {
        this.salary = salary;
        Console.Write("SalariedEmployee.CalculatePay:\n\t");
        CalculatePay();
    }
    public override void CalculatePay()
    {
        Console.WriteLine(
            "{0}, SalariedEmployee, salary={1:C}",
            name, salary);
    }
}

class ContractEmployee : Employee
{
    public double rate;
    public ContractEmployee(string name, double rate)
        : base(name)
    {
        this.rate = rate;
        Console.Write("ContractEmployee.CalculatePay:\n\t");
        CalculatePay();
    }

    public override void CalculatePay()
    {
        Console.WriteLine(
            "{0}, ContractEmployee, rate={1:C}",
            name, rate);
    }
}

class Test
{
    protected Employee[] employees;
```

```
static void Main(string[] args)
{
    Employee[] employees = new Employee[2];
    employees[0] = new ContractEmployee(
        "Adam Barr", 123.45);
    employees[1] = new SalariedEmployee(
        "Max Benson", 67890m);
}
}
```

The output from this code will be:

```
Employee.CalculatePay:
        Adam Barr, ContractEmployee, rate=$0.00
ContractEmployee.CalculatePay:
        Adam Barr, ContractEmployee, rate=$123.45
Employee.CalculatePay:
        Max Benson, SalariedEmployee, salary=$0.00
SalariedEmployee.CalculatePay:
        Max Benson, SalariedEmployee, salary=$67,890.00
```

Static Methods

A *static method* is a method that exists in a class as a whole, rather than in a specific instance of the class. As with other static members, the key benefit of static methods is that they reside apart from a particular instance of a class without polluting the application's global space and without going against the object-oriented grain by not being associated with a class.

An example of a static member is a database API I wrote in C#. Within my class hierarchy, I had a class named *SQLServerDb*. Along with the basic new, update, read, and delete (NURD) capabilities, the class also contained a method to repair the database. In the class's *Repair* method, I had no need to open the database itself. In fact, the open database connectivity (ODBC) function I used (*SQLConfigDataSource*) mandated that the database be closed for the operation. However, the *SQLServerDb* constructor opened a database specified in a database name passed to it. Therefore, a static method was perfect. The static method allowed me to place a method in the *SQLServerDb* class where it belonged, without going through my class's constructor. Obviously, on the client side, the benefit was that the client didn't have to instantiate the *SQLServerDb* class either. In the next example, you'll see a static method (*RepairDatabase*) being called from within the *Main* method. Notice that we don't create an instance of *SQLServerDb* to do this:

```
class SQLServerDb
{
    // Bunch of other nonsalient members
    public static void RepairDatabase()
    {
        Console.WriteLine("repairing database...");
    }
}

class StaticMethod1App
{
    static void Main(string[] args)
    {
        SQLServerDb.RepairDatabase();
    }
}
```

Defining a method as static involves using the *static* keyword. The user then employs the *Class.Method* syntax to call the method. This syntax is necessary even if the user has a reference to an instance of the class. For example, the following code would fail to compile:

```
static void Main(string[] args)
{
    SQLServerDb.RepairDatabase();
    SQLServerDb db = new SQLServerDb();
    db.RepairDatabase();
}
```

Access to Class Members

The last point I'll make about static methods is the rule governing which class members you can access from a static method. As you might imagine, a static method can access any static member within the class, but it can't access an instance member. This situation is illustrated in the following code:

```
class SQLServerDb
{
    static string progressString1 = "starting repair...";
    string progressString2 = "...repair finished";

    public static void RepairWithStrings()
    {
        Console.WriteLine(progressString1); // OK
//          Console.WriteLine(progressString2); // Illegal
    }
}
```

```
class Test
{
    static void Main(string[] args)
    {
        SQLServerDb.RepairWithStrings();
    }
}
```

On the other hand, a nonstatic method can access both static and non-static members:

```
class SQLServerDb
{
    static string progressString1 = "starting repair...";
    string progressString2 = "...repair finished";

    public void InstanceRepair()
    {
        Console.WriteLine(progressString1); // OK
        Console.WriteLine(progressString2); // OK
    }
}

class Test
{
    static void Main(string[] args)
    {
        SQLServerDb db = new SQLServerDb();
        db.InstanceRepair();
    }
}
```

This behavior carries through to constructors, where it becomes clear that you can use the *this* keyword only with nonstatic members:

```
public SQLServerDb(string s1, string s2)
{
//      this.progressString1 = s1; // Illegal
    this.progressString2 = s2;
}
```

Static Constructors

If you want, you can declare *static constructors* for your class. A static constructor is handled in a special way: you can have only one static constructor, it can't take parameters, and it of course can't access instance members—including the *this* pointer. A static constructor is executed before the first instance of a class is created, as shown next. Note that access modifiers such as *public* and *private* aren't allowed on static constructors.

```
class SomeClass
{
    public static int x;
    public int y;

//      static public SomeClass()      // Access modifiers illegal
//      static SomeClass(int i, int j) // Parameters illegal
    static SomeClass()
    {
        x = 1;
//          this.y = 2; // this illegal in static method
        Console.WriteLine("SomeClass initialized");
    }
}

class Test
{
    static void Main(string[] args)
    {
        SomeClass sc = new SomeClass();
    }
}
```

The output from this code will be:

```
SomeClass initialized
```

Contrary to normal overloading rules, you can provide a nonstatic constructor with the same signature as the static constructor. If you do this, *both* constructors will be called before the first instance of a class is created, with the static version being called first:

```
public SomeClass()
{
    Console.WriteLine("Non-static ctor");
}
```

The output from this revised code will be:

```
SomeClass initialized
Non-static ctor
```

A static constructor is executed before any static member—either data or function—of the class is accessed:

```
class SomeClass
{
    public static int x;

    static SomeClass()
    {
        x = 1;
        Console.WriteLine("SomeClass initialized");
    }

    public SomeClass()
    {
        Console.WriteLine("Non-static ctor");
    }

    public static void Foo()
    {
        Console.WriteLine("Foo");
    }
}

class Test
{
    static void Main(string[] args)
    {
        // Any of these 3 lines will invoke the static ctor
        SomeClass sc = new SomeClass();
        SomeClass.Foo();
        Console.WriteLine(SomeClass.x);
    }
}
```

Summary

Methods give classes their behavioral characteristics and carry out actions on our behalf. Methods in C# are fully encapsulated and flexible, allowing for the return of multiple values, overloading, and variable parameters. The *ref* and *out* keywords allow a method to return more than a single value to the caller and are used in slightly different scenarios. Overloading allows multiple methods with the same name to function differently, depending on the type and number of arguments passed to them. Methods can take variable parameters: the *params* keyword allows you to deal with methods for which the number of arguments isn't known until run time. Virtual methods used in conjunction with inheritance allow you to set up open-ended polymorphic systems. Finally, the *static* keyword allows for methods that exist as part of a class rather than as part of an object.

5

Properties, Arrays, and Indexers

I'm frequently asked what the most significant improvement introduced by the C# language is. To answer that, I refer to the law of complex systems, which states that an inherently complex system such as a programming language can be simplified only so much. As a result, once a complex system has been made as simple as it can be and still perform its originally designed functions, the only way you can further simplify the system is to shift the complexity from one part of the system to another so that the more taxing work is performed by the part of the system best equipped to handle it.

Let's see how that law would apply to a programming language. Think of the programmers who design and write classes in an object-oriented language such as C# as *providers*. The programmers that use those classes can then be termed *consumers*. Now think of any object-oriented system you've designed. Where has the majority of the difficult, or complex, code existed—in the classes that address the problem domain, or in the code that uses those classes (such as user interface and printer-type functions)? The answer, of course, is the former. In any well-designed system, the majority of the problem domain–specific code should be localized in your class library, or framework. For this reason, the better, more experienced, and more knowledgeable programmers are generally assigned the task of writing the class lattice upon which the entire system is based.

Having said that, the challenge facing any object-oriented language designer is how to shift the more difficult work to the class provider's side of the equation while making the class consumer's job easier. This is where C# makes a substantive leap ahead of current object-oriented languages. In this chapter, you'll learn about three separate field types—properties, arrays, and indexers. You'll also see how their implementation by the C# compiler team enables you, the C# developer, to expose a more robust, intuitive, and natural interface to your class's data—thereby easing the burden on the consumer using your classes.

Properties as Smart Fields

A desirable goal of any system developer is to design classes that not only hide the implementation of their methods but also disallow any direct member access to their fields. By providing *accessors* that retrieve and set the values of these fields, you can be assured that a field is treated correctly—that is, according to the rules of your specific problem domain—and that any additional processing that's needed is performed. To illustrate this point, let's look at an example that has a class containing two logically associated fields. In this example, we'll want to ensure that the setting of one field correctly affects the other.

Our example contains a class named *Address* that includes a *ZipCode* field and a *City* field, among others. When the client (consumer) modifies the *Address.ZipCode* field, the rules of *Address* class dictate that the ZIP code value be validated and the *Address.City* field value be set based on that ZIP code. If the client had direct access to a *public Address.ZipCode* member, there would be no way to guarantee that the *Address.ZipCode* was validated or that the *Address.City* field was set. Therefore, instead of granting direct access to the *Address.ZipCode* field, you define the *Address.ZipCode* and *Address.City* fields as *protected* and provide accessors for getting and setting the *Address.ZipCode* field. This way, you can attach code to the change that performs any additional work that needs to be done.

You'd program this ZIP code example in C# as follows. Notice that the actual *ZipCode* field is defined as *protected* and, therefore, not accessible from the client. Also, notice that the accessors, *GetZipCode* and *SetZipCode*, are defined as *public*.

```
// Address class example using standard accessors
class Address
{
    protected string City;

    protected string ZipCode;
    public string GetZipCode()
    {
        return this.ZipCode;
    }
```

```
public void SetZipCode(string ZipCode)
{
    // Validate ZipCode against some data store.
    this.ZipCode = ZipCode;
    // Update this.City based on validated ZIP code.
}
```
}

The client would then access the *Address.ZipCode* value like this:

```
Address addr = new Address();
addr.SetZipCode("30338");
string zip = addr.GetZipCode();
```

As you can see, this code ensures that the problem domain rules associated with the *Address* class are carried out. Next you'll see how C# takes the concept of accessors a step further, as you'll see next.

Defining and Using Properties

Using accessors works well and is a technique used by programmers of several object-oriented languages, including C++ and Java. However, C# provides an even richer mechanism: properties. Sometimes referred to as *smart fields*, properties have the same capabilities as accessors and is much more elegant on the client side.

A C# property consists of a field declaration and accessors used to modify that field's value. These accessors are referred to as *getter* and *setter* methods. They're used to modify and retrieve a field's values, respectively, and they take the following form:

```
[attributes] [modifers] <type> <property-name>
{
    [ set { <accessor-body> } ]
    [ get { <accessor-body >} ]
}
```

Here are some things to keep in mind about property syntax:

■ Although you don't have to have both a getter and a setter, you must have one of the two.

■ A property defined with both a getter and a setter is called a *read-write* property.

■ A property defined with only a getter is called a *read-only* property.

■ A property defined with only a setter is called a *write-only* property.

■   Properties can't be used as parameters to methods because although they appear to be fields from the client's perspective, they're not fields and are used only to contain accessors (getters and setters). When we discuss the underlying Microsoft intermediate language (MSIL) of properties, you'll understand this point better.

■   Although properties can be defined with the *static* modifier, you can't combine that modifier with the *virtual, abstract,* or *override* modifiers because these modifiers are used only for instance members.

Here's the earlier *Address* class example rewritten using C# properties:

```
// Example Address class using C# properties
class Address
{
    protected string city;
    protected string zipCode;

    public string ZipCode
    {
        get { return zipCode; }
        set
        {
            // Validate value against some data store.
            zipCode = value;
            // Update city based on validated zipCode.
        }
    }
}
```

The definition of two ZIP *code* members can be confusing to developers new to C#. However, if you look closely at the case of each member, you'll see that the *zipCode* member is the field and the *ZipCode* member is the property. It's become something of a standard among C# programmers that when creating a property with the same name as a field, the first letter of the *protected* (or *private*) field name is a lowercase letter and the first letter of the property name (the member the client will see) is uppercase. Regardless of the naming convention employed, you can easily tell which member is the field and which is the property because property definitions—like all methods—are enclosed in braces.

Note that if I omit the *Address.zipCode* field and change the statement in the setter (*Address.ZipCode*) from *zipCode = value* to *ZipCode = value*, I'll cause the setter method to call itself infinitely, which will eventually result in a stack overflow.

Notice also that the setter doesn't take any arguments. Yet when the class's client codes something such as *ZipCode = "30338"*, the *rvalue* is somehow accessible from within the setter via a local variable named *value*. (You'll soon see how this bit of magic happens in MSIL.)

Now that we've written the *Address.ZipCode* property, let's look at the changes needed for the client code:

```
Address addr = new Address();
addr.ZipCode = "30338";
string zip = addr.ZipCode;
```

As you can see, the client accesses the fields intuitively: there's no more guessing or looking through documentation—in other words, the source code—to determine whether a field is *accessible* and, if it isn't, to determine the name of the accessor.

In addition, using properties affords us another advantage over using accessors. Let's say you're using the standard method of accessors presented earlier. When you design a given class, you need to decide which fields will have accessors and which will allow direct member (public) access. If after writing the client code to use this class you decide to replace a public field with an accessor, you'll need to modify all client code accessing that member. However, because the syntax used to access properties is the same as that used to access fields, the class provider can go back and change the class member from a field to a property without any impact on the client source code. The only thing you'd have to do is recompile the client source code. You'd need to recompile because, as you'll see next, while the client code looks the same whether it's accessing a field or a property, the underlying MSIL generated by the compiler is different.

Inside Properties

How does the compiler enable a call to a method when the client code appears to be simply setting a field's value? Within a setter method, where does the *value* variable come from when there's no argument list? To answer these questions, we need to look at the MSIL being produced by the compiler. At this point, we'll look at the complete example so that we have something to compile:

```
using System;

class Address
{
    protected string city;
    public string City
    {
      get { return city; }
    }
```

```
    protected string zipCode;
    public string ZipCode
    {
        get { return zipCode; }
        set
        {
            zipCode = value;
            city = "Atlanta";
        }
    }
}

class PropertyApp
{
    public static void Main()
    {
        Address addr = new Address();
        addr.ZipCode = "30338";
        string zip = addr.ZipCode;

        Console.WriteLine("The city for ZIP code {0} is {1}",
                            addr.ZipCode,
                            addr.City);
    }
}
```

If you compile this application and then look at the generated MSIL shown
in Figure 5-1, you'll see that along with the *zipCode* string field, the compiler
has created a property member named *ZipCode* as well as two methods:
get_ZipCode and set_ZipCode. A *City* property, *get_City* method, and *city* field
have also been defined, but I'll get to those toward the end of this section.

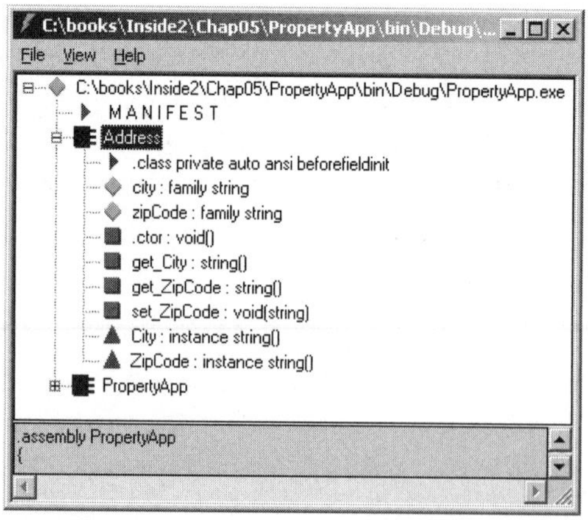

Figure 5-1   When a property is defined in C#, the generated MSIL will contain the property definition as well as method definitions for both the getter and setter, if defined.

Let's talk now about the *get_ZipCode* method. First, you can always tell the name of a getter and setter method for a property because these methods are prefixed with *get_* or *set_*, respectively. In addition, because you now know the name of the setter method, it might be tempting to try the following explicit call to the accessor:

```
String str = addr.get_ZipCode; // **ERROR - Won't compile
```

However, in this case, the code won't compile because it's illegal to explicitly call an internal MSIL method. Now let's look at the *get_ZipCode* method in more detail, as shown in Figure 5-2.

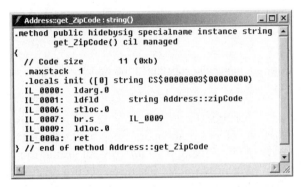

Figure 5-2 The MSIL for the *Address.ZipCode* property's getter method indicates your basic assembly for acquiring and returning an instance field's value.

The getter method might look like a lot of code (everything does in assembler), but it breaks down simply, as follows:

1. The *ldarg.0* instruction loads the method's first argument (the hidden *this* pointer) onto the stack.

2. The *ldfld* instruction first determines the object that's on the stack (loaded in step 1) and then loads onto the stack the value for that object's specified field (*Address.zipCode*).

3. The *stloc.0* instruction stores the *ldfld*-returned value into the first locally defined object.

4. The *ldloc.0* instruction loads that value back onto the stack.

5. The getter method then returns to its caller (via the *ret* instruction).

So we have your basic accessor. Now let's look at the client side of the equation, as shown in Figure 5-3.

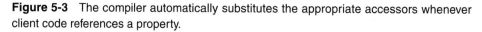

```
PropertyApp::Main : void()                                          _|□|x|
.method public hidebysig static void  Main() cil managed
{
  .entrypoint
  // Code size       53 (0x35)
  .maxstack  4
  .locals init ([0] class Address addr,
           [1] string zip)
  IL_0000:  newobj     instance void Address::.ctor()
  IL_0005:  stloc.0
  IL_0006:  ldloc.0
  IL_0007:  ldstr      "30338"
  IL_000c:  callvirt   instance void Address::set_ZipCode(string)
  IL_0011:  ldloc.0
  IL_0012:  callvirt   instance string Address::get_ZipCode()
  IL_0017:  stloc.1
  IL_0018:  ldstr      "The city for ZIP code {0} is {1}"
  IL_001d:  ldloc.0
  IL_001e:  callvirt   instance string Address::get_ZipCode()
  IL_0023:  ldloc.0
  IL_0024:  callvirt   instance string Address::get_City()
  IL_0029:  call       void [mscorlib]System.Console::WriteLine(string,
                                                                object,
                                                                object)
  IL_002e:  call       string [mscorlib]System.Console::ReadLine()
  IL_0033:  pop
  IL_0034:  ret
} // end of method PropertyApp::Main
```

Figure 5-3   The compiler automatically substitutes the appropriate accessors whenever client code references a property.

Looking at the MSIL for the *Main* method, you can easily discern that the code is loading the *Address* object pointer onto the stack (IL_0011) and calling the *Address.get_ZipCode* method using the *callvirt* (call virtual method) instruction (IL_0012). Therefore, we now know that upon seeing an attempted access to a property, the compiler simply substitutes that property's *get_* method. That's all there is to it!

Now take a look at the call to set the property (IL_0007 through IL_000c). Even though the C# code implies simple fieldlike access, the compiler has taken the *rvalue* of the property assignment, loaded it onto the stack, and then called the property's *set_ZipCode* method. Remember that the setter method seemed to magically have access to a variable named *value* even though we didn't define that variable anywhere (neither locally in the setter nor in the setter's parameter list). Now that you're seeing how the compiler substitutes methods and parameters, it should be pretty easy to see where I'm going with this. When the C# compiler generates the MSIL for a setter method, it injects this variable as an argument in a method named *set_ZipCode*, as Figure 5-4 shows.

As you can see, the *set_ZipCode* method simply does the following:

1.   Sets up the stack—pushing the *this* pointer and the *value* variable's address

2.   Calls the *stfld* instruction to store the *value* variable's value in the *Address.zipCode* instance field

3.   Sets up the stack—pushing the *this* pointer and the string literal "Atlanta"

4.   Calls the *stfld* instruction to store the string literal "Atlanta" in the

Address.City instance field

```
Address::set_ZipCode : void(string)
.method public hidebysig specialname instance void
        set_ZipCode(string 'value') cil managed
{
  // Code size       19 (0x13)
  .maxstack  2
  IL_0000:  ldarg.0
  IL_0001:  ldarg.1
  IL_0002:  stfld      string Address::zipCode
  IL_0007:  ldarg.0
  IL_0008:  ldstr      "Atlanta"
  IL_000d:  stfld      string Address::city
  IL_0012:  ret
} // end of method Address::set_ZipCode
```

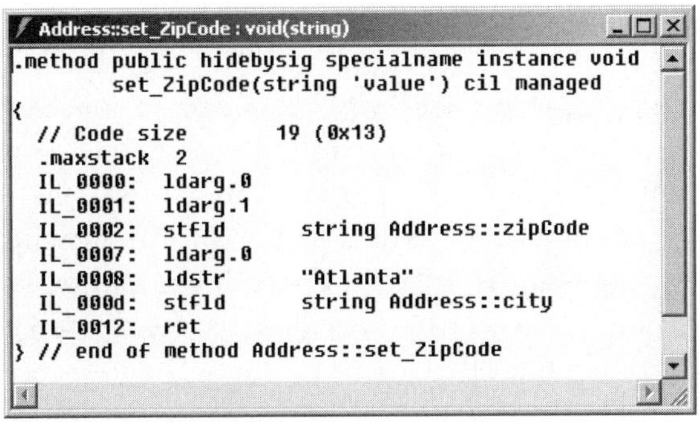

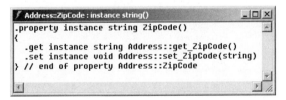

Figure 5-4 Although the setter doesn't define any arguments that can be seen in the C# code, the compiler generates MSIL that will pass the *rvalue* specified by the client as a parameter (named *value*).

And that's how it appears in C#—as though you're accessing a variable that has never been declared. As with the *get_ZipCode* method, attempting to call the *set_zipCode* method directly in C# generates an error.

The last thing I want to call to your attention is the MSIL definition for the *ZipCode* property. As you can see in Figure 5-5, a property is defined with the special *.property* directive and includes information such as the calling convention (*instance*, in this case), type (*string*), and ID (*ZipCode*). However, what's interesting here is the body of the property definition.

```
Address::ZipCode : instance string()
.property instance string ZipCode()
{
  .get instance string Address::get_ZipCode()
  .set instance void Address::set_ZipCode(string)
} // end of property Address::ZipCode
```

Figure 5-5 The property definition is used for reflection—or run-time type information querying.

Note that both the getter and setter methods are defined here. At first, you might wonder why these methods are here when the compiler has already resolved client usages of this property to the appropriate getter or setter method. In fact, the runtime doesn't know anything about the C# concept of properties—because the MSIL produced is comprised of plain old method calls. The answer is that this information is here for *reflection*. Reflection enables client code to obtain information about loaded objects and types at run time and is the subject of Chapter 19, "Querying Metadata with Reflection."

Inheriting Properties

As you learned in Chapter 4, "Methods," members can be inherited from base classes in which the modifiers *virtual*, *override*, *abstract*, and *new* are used to define the terms of that inheritance. Properties can also be inherited through derivation. However, there are some issues to keep in mind when inheriting properties. The first issue is that the inheritance modifiers can be specified only at the property level. Therefore, you can't stipulate that for a given property one accessor will be virtual while the other won't.

Let's look at two common scenarios involving property inheritance:

- Overriding inherited properties
- Enforcing property implementation via abstract properties

Overriding Inherited Properties

The syntax for overriding inherited properties is easy enough. In the base class, you specify the *virtual* modifier for any properties that can be overridden. Then, in the derived class, you specify the *override* modifier on the derived class's implementation the inherited property.

For example, let's say that you've created a base class for handling comma-delimited files (*CSVFile*) and that your customer table class (*CustomerTable*) is then derived from that base class. We'll stipulate that while the *CSVFile* has a property to return the associated physical file, the *CustomerTable* will instead override that inherited property and return a short description of the file.

```
using System;

class CSVFile
{
    public CSVFile(string fileName)
    {
        this.fileName = fileName;
    }

    protected string fileName;
    public virtual string FileName
    {
        get { return fileName; }
    }
}

class CustomerTable : CSVFile
{
```

```
    public const string FILENAME = "customers.txt";

    public CustomerTable() : base(FILENAME) {}

    public override string FileName
    {
        get { return "Customers table"; }
    }
}

class OverrideProperties
{
    public static void Main()
    {
        Console.WriteLine("\nInstantiating a CSV object for " +
            "the Customer file...");
        CSVFile customerFile =
            new CSVFile(CustomerTable.FILENAME);
        Console.WriteLine("Customer file name = {0}",
            customerFile.FileName);

        Console.WriteLine("\nInstantiating a Customer " +
            "Table object...");
        CustomerTable customerTable = new CustomerTable();
        Console.WriteLine("Customer file name = {0}",
            customerTable.FileName);

        Console.ReadLine();
    }
}
```

Now when you run this application, as shown in Figure 5-6, the value returned depends on whether you have the base class reference or the derived class reference.

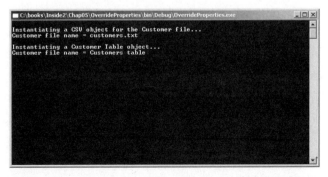

Figure 5-6   Virtual properties enable you to implement the same polymorphic behavior as you can with methods.

Enforcing Property Implementation via Abstract Properties

The next property inheritance issue that we'll look at involves abstract classes and properties. An *abstract class* is a class that won't be instantiated but serves as a class definition for derivation. Members that are defined as *abstract* within an abstract class must be implemented by any derived classes. The concept of abstract classes helps class designers ensure that derived classes are properly defined.

To define a class (or class member) as abstract, you simply place the keyword *abstract* in front of the identifier. In addition, the desired accessors must be specified with only their name followed by a semicolon:

```
abstract class AbstractBaseClass
{
    public abstract double AbstractProperty
    {
        get;
        set;
    }
}
```

Now let's look at an example of defining and implementing abstract properties. In this example, I have a classic employee payroll scenario in which I've defined a base *Employee* class and two derived classes: *ContractEmployee* and *SalariedEmployee*. Because the *Employee* class can't be instantiated, it's defined as abstract. In addition, I have a property that I want all derivations of the *Employee* class to implement. This property (*HourlyCost*) is used to determine how much a given employee is costing me per hour. The following shows how this simple example would be coded. Note that the derived class must use the *override* modifier when implementing a base class abstract member.

```
using System;
using System.Collections;

abstract class Employee
{
    protected Employee(int employeeId, int hoursWorked)
    {
        this.employeeId = employeeId;
        HoursWorked = hoursWorked;
    }

    protected int employeeId;
    public int EmployeeId
    {
        get { return employeeId; }
    }
```

```
    protected int HoursWorked;

    protected double hourlyCost = -1; // dummy init value
    public abstract double HourlyCost
    {
        get;
    }
}

class ContractEmployee : Employee
{
    public ContractEmployee(int employeeId, double hourlyWage,
        int hoursWorked)
        : base(employeeId, hoursWorked)
    {
        HourlyWage = hourlyWage;
    }

    protected double HourlyWage;
    public override double HourlyCost
    {
        get
        { return HourlyWage; }
    }
}

class SalariedEmployee : Employee
{
    public SalariedEmployee(int employeeId, double salary,
        int hoursWorked)
        : base(employeeId, hoursWorked)
    {
        Salary = salary;
    }

    protected double Salary;
    public override double HourlyCost
    {
        get
        {
            return (Salary / 52) / HoursWorked;
        }
    }
}

class OverrideProperties
{
    public static ArrayList employees = new ArrayList();
```

```
public static void PrintEmployeesHourlyCostToCompany()
{
    foreach (Employee employee in employees)
    {
        Console.WriteLine("{0} employee (id={1}) costs {2}" +
            " per hour",
            employee,
            employee.EmployeeId,
            employee.HourlyCost);
    }
}

public static void Main()
{
    ContractEmployee c  = new ContractEmployee(1, 50, 40);
    employees.Add(c);

    SalariedEmployee s =
        new SalariedEmployee(2, 100000, 65);
    employees.Add(s);

    PrintEmployeesHourlyCostToCompany();

    Console.ReadLine();
}
}
```

Now that the *abstract* modifier forces any derived classes of *Employee* to implement the *HourlyCost* property, I'm assured that my *PrintEmployeesHourlyCostToCompany* method will always function properly when upcasting the derived objects, as shown in Figure 5-7.

Figure 5-7 The concept of abstract classes helps class designers to ensure that derived classes are properly defined.

Advanced Use of Properties

So far, I've talked about properties being useful for the following reasons:

- They provide a level of abstraction to clients so that the client doesn't need to know if an accessor exists for the member being accessed.

- They provide a generic means of accessing class members by using the standard *object.field* syntax.

- They enable a class to guarantee that any additional processing can be done when a particular field is modified or accessed.

The third reason points us to another helpful use for properties: the implementation of something referred to as *lazy initialization*. This is an optimization technique in which some of a class's members aren't initialized until they're needed.

Lazy initialization is beneficial when you have a class that contains seldom-referenced members whose initialization consumes a good deal of time or resources. An example of this is a situation in which data must be read from a database or across a congested network. Because you know that these members aren't referenced often and that their initialization is expensive, you can delay their initialization until their getter methods are called.

To better understand this benefit, suppose you have an inventory application that sales representatives run on their laptop computers to place customer orders and that they occasionally use to check inventory levels. If you know that the inventory level isn't used very often, you can allow the relevant members of the class to be instantiated without the inventory records having to be read. Therefore, if a sales representative does want to access the inventory count for an item, the getter method will access the remote database at that time. The following code depicts lazy initialization in action:

```
class Sku
{
    protected double onHand;

    public string OnHand
    {
        get
        {
            // Read from central database and set onHand value.
            return onHand;
        }
    }
}
```

As you've seen so far in this chapter, properties enable you to provide accessors to fields and a generic and intuitive interface for the client. Because of this, properties are sometimes referred to as *smart fields,* as mentioned earlier in the section. Now let's take this a step further and look at how arrays are defined and used in C#. We'll also see how properties are used with arrays in the form of indexers.

Arrays

So far, most of the examples in this book have shown how to define variables in finite, predetermined numbers. However, in most practical applications, you don't know the exact number of objects you need until run time. For example, if you're developing an editor and you want to keep track of the controls that are added to a dialog box, the exact number of controls the editor will display can't be known until run time. You can, however, use an array to store and keep track of a dynamically allocated grouping of objects—in this case, the controls on the editor.

In C#, arrays are objects that have the *System.Array* class defined as their base class. Therefore, although the syntax for defining an array looks similar to that in C++ or Java, you're actually instantiating a .NET class, which means that every declared array contains the same members inherited from *System.Array.* In this section, I'll cover how to declare and instantiate arrays, work with the different array types, and iterate through the elements of an array. I'll also look at some of the more commonly used properties and methods of the *System.Array* class.

Declaring Arrays

You declare an array in C# by placing empty square brackets between the type and the variable name, like this:

```
int[] numbers;
```

Note that this syntax differs slightly from C++, in which the brackets are specified after the variable name. Because arrays are class based, many of the same rules that apply to declaring a class also pertain to arrays. For example, you must instantiate the array before it can be used. In the following example, I declare and instantiate an array at the same time:

```
// Declares and instantiates a single-
// dimensional array of six integers.
int[] numbers = new int[6];
```

However, when declaring the array as a member of a class, you can declare and instantiate the array in one of two ways: in one step at the point of declaration, or in two distinct steps, depending on your application needs. As the following code shows, the *numbers2* member won't be initialized until the *SomeInitMethod* is called:

```
class YourClass
{
    int[] numbers1 = new int[6];
    int[] numbers2;

    void SomeInitMethod()
    {
        // This will cause the initialization to occur
        // when this method is called.
        numbers2 = new int[6];
    }
}
```

Single-Dimensional Array Example

Here's a simple example of declaring a single-dimensional array as a class member, instantiating and filling the array in the constructor, and then using a *for* loop to iterate through the array, printing out each element:

```
using System;

class SingleDimArrayApp
{
    protected int[] numbers;

    SingleDimArrayApp()
    {
        numbers = new int[6];
        for (int i = 0; i < 6; i++)
        {
            numbers[i] = i * i;
        }
    }

    protected void PrintArray()
    {
        Console.WriteLine("Printing a single-dimensional " +
                        "array of numbers...\n");
        for (int i = 0; i < numbers.Length; i++)
        {
            Console.WriteLine("numbers[{0}]={1}",
```

```
                                        i, numbers[i]);
        }
    }


    public static void Main()
    {
        SingleDimArrayApp app = new SingleDimArrayApp();
        app.PrintArray();
    }
}
```

Running this example produces the output shown in Figure 5-8.

Figure 5-8   Arrays are incredibly easy to define and initialize with C#.

In this example, the *SingleDimArray.PrintArray* method uses the *System.Array Length* property to determine the number of elements in the array. It's not obvious here because we have only a single-dimensional array, but the *Length* property actually returns the number of *all* the elements in all the dimensions of an array. Therefore, in the case of a two-dimensional array of 5 by 4, the *Length* property would return 20 because the array contains 20 elements. Next we'll look at multidimensional arrays and how to determine the upper bound of a specific array dimension.

Multidimensional Arrays

In addition to single-dimensional arrays, C# supports the declaration of multidimensional arrays, in which each dimension of the array is separated by a comma. Here I'm declaring a three-dimensional array of doubles:

```
double[,,] numbers;
```

To quickly determine the number of dimensions in a declared C# array, count the number of commas and add one to that total.

The following example contains a two-dimensional array of sales figures that represent this year's year-to-date figures and last year's totals for the same time frame. Take special note of the syntax used to instantiate the array in the *MultiDimArrayApp* constructor:

```
using System;

class MultiDimArrayApp
{
    protected int currentMonth;
    protected double[,] sales;

    MultiDimArrayApp()

    {
        currentMonth=10;

        sales = new double[2, currentMonth];
        for (int i = 0; i < sales.GetLength(0); i++)
        {
            for (int j=0; j < 10; j++)
            {
                sales[i,j] = (i * 100) + j;
            }
        }
    }

    protected void PrintSales()
    {
        Console.WriteLine("Printing a multi-dimensional " +
                          "array of numbers...\n");
        for (int i = 0; i < sales.GetLength(0); i++)
        {
            for (int j=0; j < sales.GetLength(1); j++)
            {
                Console.WriteLine("[{0}][{1}]={2}", i,
                    j, sales[i,j]);
            }
        }
    }

    public static void Main()
    {
        MultiDimArrayApp app = new MultiDimArrayApp();
        app.PrintSales();
    }
}
```

Running the *MultiDimArrayApp* example results in the output shown in Figure 5-9.

Figure 5-9   Because arrays are objects in C#, it's very easy to dynamically determine array properties such as the number of elements and then iterate through the array retrieving each element's value.

Remember that in the single-dimensional array example I said that the *Length* property will return the total number of items in the array. Therefore, in this example, that return value would be 20. In the *MultiDimArray.PrintSales* method, I used the *Array.GetLength* method to determine the length, or upper bound, of each dimension of the array. I was then able to use each specific value in the *PrintSales* method.

Querying for Rank

Now that you've seen how easy it is to dynamically iterate through a single-dimensional or multidimensional array, you might be wondering how to determine the number of dimensions in an array programmatically. The number of dimensions in an array is known as an array's *rank*, and rank is retrieved using the *Array.Rank* property. Here's an example of performing this task on several arrays:

```
using System;

class RankArrayApp
{
    int[] singleD;
    int[,] doubleD;
    int[,,] tripleD;

    protected RankArrayApp()
    {
        Console.WriteLine("singleD is being defined a single- " +
```

```
                              "dimensional array");
        singleD = new int[6];

        Console.WriteLine("singleD is being defined as having " +
                          "two dimensions");
        doubleD = new int[6,7];

        Console.WriteLine("singleD is being defined as having " +
                          "three dimensions");
        tripleD = new int[6,7,8];
    }

    protected void PrintRanks()
    {
        Console.WriteLine("\nPrinting the ranks of three " +
                          "different arrays...\n");
        Console.WriteLine("singleD Rank = {0}", singleD.Rank);
        Console.WriteLine("doubleD Rank = {0}", doubleD.Rank);
        Console.WriteLine("tripleD Rank = {0}", tripleD.Rank);
    }

    public static void Main()
    {
        RankArrayApp app = new RankArrayApp();
        app.PrintRanks();
    }
}
```

As expected, the *RankArrayApp* application outputs the code shown in Figure 5-10.

Figure 5-10 The *Array.Rank* property enables you to determine the number of dimensions to an array.

Jagged Arrays

The last thing we'll look at with regard to arrays is the *jagged array*. A jagged array is simply an array of arrays. Here's an example of defining an array containing integer arrays:

```
int[][] jaggedArray;
```

For example, you might use a jagged array if you're developing an editor. In this editor, you might want to store the object representing each user-created control in an array. To keep this example manageable, let's suppose you have an array of buttons and combo boxes, with three buttons stored in one array and two combo boxes stored in another array. Declaring a jagged array enables you to have a parent array for those arrays so that you can easily and programmatically iterate through the controls when you need to, as shown here:

```
using System;

class Control
{
    virtual public void SayHi()
    {
        Console.WriteLine("base control class");
    }
}

class Button : Control
{
    override public void SayHi()
    {
        Console.WriteLine("button control");
    }
}

class Combo : Control
{
    override public void SayHi()
    {
        Console.WriteLine("combobox control");
    }
}

class JaggedArrayApp
{
    public static void Main()
    {
    // Define a two-dimensional array as a "parent" array.
    // The first dimension represents how many arrays
    // this parent array will contain.
    Control[][] controls;
```

```
controls = new Control[2][];

// The first dimension will contain three controls...
controls[0] = new Control[3];
for (int i = 0; i < controls[0].Length; i++)
{
    controls[0][i] = new Button();
}

// The second dimension will contain two controls...
controls[1] = new Control[2];
for (int i = 0; i < controls[1].Length; i++)
{
    controls[1][i] = new Combo();
}

// Now I can simply iterate through a nested for loop
// and using polymorphism access all my controls'
// members!
for (int i = 0; i < controls.Length;i++)
{
    for (int j=0;j< controls[i].Length;j++)
    {
        Control control = controls[i][j];
        control.SayHi();
    }
}
}
```

As you can see, I've defined a base class (*Control*) and two derived classes (*Button* and *Combo*), and I've declared the jagged array as an array of arrays that contain *Controls* objects. This way, I can store the specific types in the array and—through the magic of polymorphism—know that when it's time to extract the objects from the array (via an *upcasted* object), I'll get the behavior I expect. Figure 5-11 shows the output from running this application.

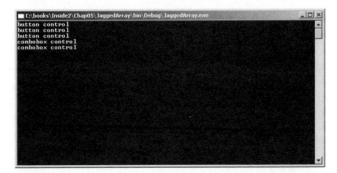

Figure 5-11   Jagged arrays are especially useful when storing multiple arrays within an array.

Treating Objects Like Arrays by Using Indexers

In the "Arrays" section, you learned how to declare and instantiate arrays, work with the different array types, and iterate through the elements of an array. You also learned how to take advantage of some of the more commonly used properties and methods of the array types underlying the *System.Array* class. Let's continue working with arrays by looking at how a C#-specific feature named *indexers* enables you to programmatically treat objects as though they were arrays.

Why would you want to treat an object like an array? As with most features of a programming language, the benefit of indexers comes down to making your applications more intuitive to write. In the first section of this chapter, "Properties as Smart Fields," you saw how C# properties give you the ability to reference class fields by using the standard *class.field* syntax yet ultimately resolve to getter and setter methods. This abstraction frees the programmer writing a client for the class from having to determine whether getter and setter methods exist for the field and from having to know the exact format of these methods. Similarly, indexers enable a class's client to index into an object as though the object itself were an array.

Consider the following example: You have a list box class that needs to expose a way in which its users can insert strings. If you're familiar with the Win32 SDK, you know that to insert a string into a list box window you send it an *LB_ADDSTRING* or *LB_INSERTSTRING* message. When this mechanism appeared in the late 1980s, we thought we really were object-oriented programmers. After all, weren't we sending messages to an object the same way those fancy object-oriented analysis and design books told us to? But as object-oriented and object-based languages such as C++ and Object Pascal began to proliferate, we learned that objects could be used to create more intuitive programming interfaces for such tasks. Using C++ and Microsoft Foundation Classes (MFC), we were given an entire lattice of classes that enabled us to treat windows such as list boxes as objects, with these classes exposing member functions that basically provided a thin wrapper for sending and receiving messages to and from the underlying Microsoft Windows control. For the *CListBox* class—that is, the MFC wrapper for the Windows list box control—we were given the *AddString* and *InsertString* member functions for the tasks previously accomplished by sending the *LB_ADDSTRING* or *LB_INSERTSTRING* message.

To help class writers make their code more intuitive for other programmers, the C# language design team looked at this issue and wondered, "Why not have the ability to treat like an array an object that at its heart *is* an array?" Isn't a list box just an array of strings with the additional functionality of displaying and sorting? From this idea, the concept of indexers was born.

Defining Indexers

Because properties are sometimes referred to as *smart fields* and indexers are known as *smart arrays*, it makes sense that properties and indexers would share the same syntax. Indeed, defining indexers is similar to defining properties; however, two major differences exist. First, the indexer takes an *index* argument. Second, because the class itself is being used as an array, the *this* keyword is used as the name of the indexer. You'll see a more complete example shortly, but for now, take a look at this sample indexer:

```
class MyClass
{
    public object this [int idx]
    {
        get
        {
            // Return desired data.
        }
        set
        {
            // Set desired data.
        }
    }
}
```

I haven't shown you a full example that illustrates the syntax of indexers because the actual internal implementation of how you define your data and how you get and set that data isn't relevant to indexers. Keep in mind that regardless of how you store your data internally—that is, as an array, a collection, and so on—indexers are simply a means for the programmer instantiating the class to write code such as this:

```
MyClass cls = new MyClass();
cls[0] = someObject;
Console.WriteLine("{0}", cls[0]);
```

What you do within the indexer is your own business, as long as the class's client gets the expected results from accessing the object as an array.

Indexer Example

Let's look at some situations in which indexers make the most sense. I'll start with the list box example discussed earlier. As mentioned, from a conceptual standpoint, a list box is simply a list, or an array of strings to be displayed. In the following example, I've declared a class named *MyListBox* that contains an indexer to set and retrieve strings through an *ArrayList* object. (The *ArrayList* class is a .NET Framework class used to store a collection of objects.)

```
using System;
using System.Collections;

class MyListBox

{
    protected ArrayList data = new ArrayList();

    public object this[int idx]
    {
        get
        {
            if (idx > -1 && idx < data.Count)
            {
                return (data[idx]);
            }
            else
            {
                throw new InvalidOperationException("[MyListBox.set_Item]" +
                    " Index out of range");
            }
        }
        set
        {
            if (idx > -1 && idx < data.Count)
            {
                data[idx] = value;
            }
            else if (idx == data.Count)
            {
                data.Add(value);
            }
            else
            {
                throw new InvalidOperationException(
                    "[MyListBox.get_Item] Index out of range");
            }
        }
    }
}

class IndexersApp
{
    public static void Main()
    {
        MyListBox lbx = new MyListBox();
        lbx[0] = "foo";
        lbx[1] = "bar";
```

```
        lbx[2] = "baz";
        Console.WriteLine("{0} {1} {2}",
            lbx[0], lbx[1], lbx[2]);
    }
}
```

If you compile and execute this code, you'll see the output shown in Figure 5-12.

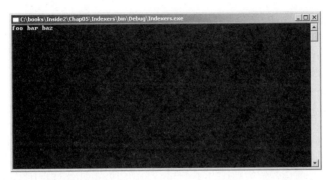

Figure 5-12   Indexers enable you to access an object as though it were an array, allowing you to treat certain objects in a manner consistent with their intended use.

Notice in this example that I check for out-of-bounds errors in the indexing of the data. This isn't technically tied to indexers because, as I mentioned, indexers pertain only to how the class's client can use the object as an array, and they have nothing to do with the internal representation of the data. However, when learning a new language feature, it helps to see its practical usage rather than only its syntax. Thus, in both the indexer's getter and setter methods, I validate the index value being passed with the data being stored in the class's *ArrayList* member. I'd probably choose to throw exceptions in the cases where the index value being passed can't be resolved. However, that's a personal choice—your error handling might differ. The point is that you need to indicate failure to the client in cases where an invalid index has been passed.

Inside Indexers

Now let's take a quick look at how indexers work internally. This section will be brief because the implementation of indexers is built on the concepts of properties that you've already learned about. When the C# compiler comes across the syntax for an indexer, it automatically defines a property named *Item* and the accessors for that property that correlate to the defined getter and setter. Take a look at Figure 5-13 to see what I mean.

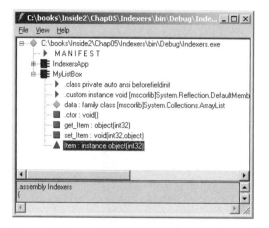

Figure 5-13   In MSIL, indexers resolve to an *Item* property and the specified accessors.

As you can see, the last entry in the ILDASM tree view is named Item. If you double-click this entry, you'll see the standard *.property* directive and accessor names in the property body that you saw earlier, in the "Inside Properties" section. In addition, note the *get_Item* and *set_Item* accessors. Once again, these members are the standard property accessors you saw earlier—the only difference being that these accessors were created with a built-in name (*Item*), which does lead to one interesting tidbit of information. If you attempt to define a member in your class named *get_Item* or *set_Item*, the compiler will bark because, of course, those names conflict with the method names for the indexer accessors. The MSIL for the application's *Main* method—shown in Figure 5-14—confirms that the client's accessing of the class's indexers is resolved to the *get_Item* and *set_Item* method calls.

```
IL_0012:  ldloc.0
IL_0013:  ldc.i4.1
IL_0014:  ldstr      "bar"
IL_0019:  callvirt   instance void MyListBox::set_Item(int32,
                                                        object)

IL_001e:  ldloc.0
IL_001f:  ldc.i4.2
IL_0020:  ldstr      "baz"
IL_0025:  callvirt   instance void MyListBox::set_Item(int32,
                                                        object)

IL_002a:  ldstr      "{0} {1} {2}"
IL_002f:  ldloc.0
IL_0030:  ldc.i4.0
IL_0031:  callvirt   instance object MyListBox::get_Item(int32)
```

Figure 5-14   As with properties, client access to indexers resolves to accessor method calls at the MSIL level.

Also note that the *set_Item* method takes as its second argument an *Object* reference. This arrangement obviously allows you to use indexers with any type you choose—yet another benefit of a singly rooted class hierarchy.

Because an indexer can make an array look like a class to the client, you might be tempted to write code like this:

```
MyListBox lbx = new MyListBox();
lbx[0] = "foo";
lbx[1] = "bar";
lbx[2] = "baz";

foreach (object obj in lbx)
{
  ⋮
}
```

Alas, indexers aren't designed to allow you to completely treat a class as an array. However, the combination of the *IEnumerable* interface and *IEnumerate* class do enable you to publish a way for your class's clients to enumerate your defined collections. I'll get into this ability in more detail in Chapter 17, "Collections and Object Enumeration."

Design Guidelines

Indexers are yet another example of how the C# design team added subtle yet powerful features to the language to help us become more productive in our development endeavors. However, as any feature of any language, indexers have their place. They should be used only in situations in which it would be intuitive to treat an object like an array. Let's look at an example that involves invoicing. It's reasonable that an invoicing application has an *Invoice* class that defines a member array of *InvoiceDetail* objects. In such a case, it would be perfectly intuitive for the user to access these detail lines with the following syntax:

```
InvoiceDetail detail = invoice[2]; // Retrieves the
                                   // third detail line.
```

However, it wouldn't be intuitive for the user if you took that a step further and tried to turn all the *InvoiceDetail* members into an array to be accessed via an indexer. As you can see here, the first line is much more readily understood than the second:

```
TermCode terms = invoice.Terms; // Property accessor
                                // to Terms member.
TermCode terms = invoice[3];    // A solution in search
                                // of a problem.
```

In this case, the maxim "just because you can do something, doesn't mean you should" holds true. In more concrete terms, think of how implementing any new feature will affect your class's clients, and let that thinking guide you when deciding whether implementing the feature will make using your class easier.

Summary

In this chapter, you learned that C# properties consist of field declaration and accessors. Properties enable smart access to class fields so that consumers for a given class don't have to know whether—and how—an accessor for the field was created. You declare arrays in C# by placing an empty square bracket *between* the type and the variable name, a syntax slightly different than the one used in C++. C# arrays can be single-dimensional, multidimensional, or jagged. Objects in C# can be treated like arrays through the use of indexers. Indexers allow programmers to easily work with and track many objects of the same type. In Chapter 6, "Attributes," we'll look at the concept of attributes and how they provide a mechanism for annotating types and members at design time with information that can later be retrieved at run time through reflection.

6

Attributes

Programming languages before the .NET era were essentially static: they consisted of a predefined set of keywords and operators, and the compiler applied rules in a predefined manner. Such programming languages were designed with a finite set of abilities in mind. For example, when you set out to design a compiler, you think about how an application written in the new language will be structured, how code will call other code, how functionality will be packaged, and many other issues that make the language a productive medium for developing software. Most of what a compiler designer comes up with is static. For example, in C#, you define a class by placing the keyword *class* before the class name. You then signify derivation by inserting a colon after the class name, followed by the name of the base class. This is an example of a decision that, once made by the language designer, can't be changed.

The people who write compilers are darn good at what they do. However, even they can't anticipate all the developments in the programming industry and how those developments will alter the way programmers want to express their types in a given language. For example, how do you create the relationship between a class in C++ and a documentation URL for that class? And how do you associate the specific members of a C++ class with the XML fields for your company's new business-to-business solution? Because C++ was designed many years before the advent of the Internet and protocols such as XML, it's not easy to perform either of these tasks.

Until now, the solutions to problems such as these involved storing extra information in a separate file (DEF, IDL, and so on) that was then loosely associated with the type or member in question. Because the compiler has no knowledge of the separate file or the code-generated relationship between your class and the file, this approach is usually called a *disconnected solution*. For example, standard C++ doesn't provide any mechanism for binding a COM

GUID with the class that represents it. IDL, of course, does allow you to anno-tate an interface or a coclass with attributes including GUIDs, which is why it's common to develop COM code with both IDL and C++. On its own, neither lan-guage covers all the bases. The main problem with such disconnected solutions is that the class is no longer *self-describing*—that is, a user can no longer look at the class definition by itself and know everything about that class. One advantage of a self-describing component is that the compiler and common lan-guage runtime can ensure that the rules associated with the component are adhered to. Additionally, a self-describing component is easier to maintain because the developer can see all the information related to the component in one place.

This has been the way of the world for many decades of compiler evolu-tion. The language designers try to determine what developers need the lan-guage to do, they give the compiler those capabilities, and, for better or worse, those are the capabilities developers have until another compiler comes along. However, C# offers a different paradigm, one which stems from the introduc-tion of a feature called *attributes*.

Introducing Attributes

What attributes allow you to do is nothing short of groundbreaking. They pro-vide you with a generic means of associating information—as annotations—with your defined C# types. Such information is arbitrary—that is, it's not stati-cally fixed by the language itself, and you're free to invent and associate any information of any kind. You can use attributes to define design-time informa-tion (such as documentation), run-time information (such as the name of a database column for a field), or even run-time behavioral characteristics (such as whether a given member is *transactionable*, or capable of participating in a transaction). The possibilities are endless, which is the point. In a sense, this association of information follows the same principles used in the development of XML. Because you can create an attribute based on any information you want, a standard mechanism exists for defining the attributes themselves and for querying the member or type at run time about its attached attributes.

An example will better illustrate how to use this powerful feature. Let's say you have an application that stores some of its information in the Microsoft Windows Registry. One design issue would be deciding where in the applica-tion to store this Registry key information. In most development environments, this information is stored in a resource file or in constants, or it's even hard-coded in the calls to the Registry APIs. However, once again, an integral part of a class is being stored apart from the rest of the class's definition. Using attributes, we can attach this information to the class members so that we have a completely self-describing component. Here's an example of how this looks, assuming that we've already defined the *RegKey* attribute elsewhere:

```
class SomeClass
{
    [RegKey(RegHives.HKEY_CURRENT_USER, "Foo")]
    public int Foo;
}
```

To attach a defined attribute to a C# type or member, you simply specify the attribute data in brackets before the target type or member. Here we attached an attribute named *RegKey* to the *SomeClass.Foo* field. At run time—which you'll see shortly—all we have to do is query the field for its Registry key and then use that value to save the date into the Registry.

Defining Attributes

In the previous example, note that the syntax used to attach an attribute to a type or member looks a little like the instantiation of a class. This is because an attribute is actually a class derived from the *System.Attribute* base class. The *System.Attribute* class contains a few useful methods designed for accessing and testing custom attributes. Although you're at liberty to define any class you like as an attribute, it makes sense to stick with the norm in this situation by deriving your class from *System.Attribute*.

Now let's flesh out the *RegKey* attribute a little:

```
using System;
using System.Reflection;

    public enum RegHives
    {
        HKEY_CLASSES_ROOT,
        HKEY_CURRENT_USER,
        HKEY_LOCAL_MACHINE,
        HKEY_USERS,
        HKEY_CURRENT_CONFIG
    }

    public class RegKeyAttribute : Attribute
    {
        public RegKeyAttribute(RegHives Hive, String ValueName)
        {
            this.Hive = Hive;
            this.ValueName = ValueName;
        }
```

```
    protected RegHives hive;
    public RegHives Hive
    {
        get { return hive; }
        set { hive = value; }
    }

    protected String valueName;
    public String ValueName
    {
        get { return valueName; }
        set { valueName = value; }
    }
}
```

What we've done here is add an enum for the different Registry types, a constructor for the attribute class (which takes a Registry type and a value name), and two properties for the Registry hive and value name. You can do much more when defining attributes, but because we now know the basics of defining and attaching attributes, let's go ahead and learn how to query for attributes at run time. That way, we'll have a fully working example to play with. Once we've done that, we'll move on to some of the more advanced issues of defining and attaching attributes.

Note that in the examples the attribute class names are appended with the word *Attribute*. However, when we attach the attribute to a type or member, we don't include the *Attribute* suffix. This is a shortcut thrown in for free by the C# language designers. When the compiler sees that an attribute is being attached to a type or member, it searches for a *System.Attribute* derived class with the name of the attribute specified. If it can't locate a class, the compiler appends *Attribute* to the specified attribute name and searches for that. Therefore, it's common practice to define attribute class names as ending in *Attribute* and then to omit that part of the name.

Let's examine the Microsoft intermediate language (MSIL) briefly. Compare, for instance, the MSIL for the nonattributed *Bar* method with that of the attributed *Foo* method, as shown in Figures 6-1 and 6-2.

Figure 6-1 MSIL for nonattributed *Bar* method.

Figure 6-2   MSIL for attributed *Foo* method.

Of course, the string shown in the MSIL as *(01 00 01 00 00 00 03 46 6F 6F 00 00)* is a length-prefixed (for example, 3) representation of *Foo*—for example, 0x46, 0x6F 0x6F. This is more obvious if we look at the metadata for these methods, as shown in Figure 6-3.

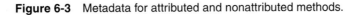

Figure 6-3   Metadata for attributed and nonattributed methods.

Now suppose we want to attach an attribute to a class as a whole:

```
[RegKey(RegHives.HKEY_CURRENT_USER, "SomeClass")]
class SomeClass
{
    public int Foo;
    public int Bar;
}
```

As you can see from the metadata in Figure 6-4, the attribute MSIL is now associated with the class as a whole instead of with just one field.

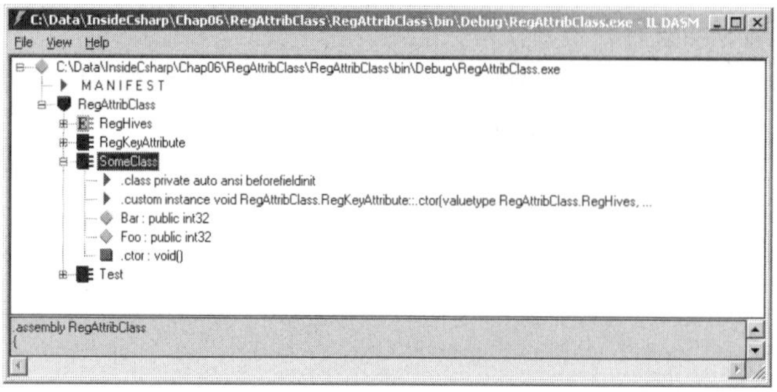

Figure 6-4   Metadata for attributed class.

> **Note**   This example nicely illustrates the basic nature of attributes. However, it's a little artificial because if you really want to work with the Windows Registry, you'll likely use the *Microsoft.Win32.Registry* and *Microsoft.Win32.RegistryKey* classes.

At this point, it's worth mentioning that regular wizard-generated code for the *Main* method generally includes an attribute:

```
class Class1
{
    [STAThread]
    static void Main(string[] args)
    {
    }
}
```

As you can see from the metadata in Figure 6-5, this is also a custom attribute—it's part of the .NET Framework classes, not the language itself.

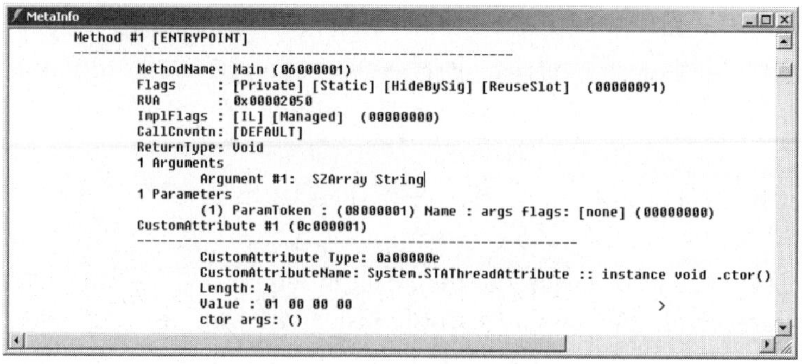

Figure 6-5   Metadata for wizard-generated *Main*.

You use the *STAThread* attribute to specify that the default threading model for an application is single-threaded apartment (STA). Note that threading models pertain only to applications that use COM interop and that applying this attribute to an application that doesn't use COM interop has no effect.

More Info   We'll look at the whole .NET/COM interop issue in Chapter 21, "Using COM from C# Applications."

Querying for Attributes

OK, we now know how to define an attribute by deriving it from *System.Attribute* and how to attach it to a type or member. So what's next? How can we use attributes in code? In other words, how can we query a type or member about the attributes (and parameters) that have been attached?

To query a type or member about its attached attributes, we must use *reflection*. Reflection is an advanced topic that's covered in Chapter 19, "Querying Metadata with Reflection." We'll discuss only enough about reflection here to illustrate what's needed to retrieve attribute information at run time.

More Info   For a detailed discussion of reflection, see Chapter 19.

Reflection allows you to dynamically determine at run time the type characteristics of an application. For example, you can use the .NET Framework Reflection APIs to iterate through the metadata for an entire assembly and produce a list of all classes, types, and methods defined for that assembly. Let's look at some examples of attributes and how to query them using reflection.

Class Attributes

How you retrieve an attribute depends on the member type you're querying. Let's say you want to define an attribute that will define the remote server on which an object will be created. Without attributes, you'd save this information in a constant or in the application's resource file. Using attributes, you can simply annotate the class with its remote server in this way:

```
public enum RemoteServers
{
    JEANVALJEAN,
    JAVERT,
    COSETTE
}
```

```
public class RemoteObjectAttribute : Attribute
{
    public RemoteObjectAttribute(RemoteServers Server)
    {
        this.server = Server;
    }

    protected RemoteServers server;
    public string Server
    {
        get
        {
            return RemoteServers.GetName(
                typeof(RemoteServers), this.server);
        }
    }
}


[RemoteObject(RemoteServers.COSETTE)]
class MyRemotableClass
{
}
```

To determine the server on which to create the object, use code such as the following:

```
class Test
{
    [STAThread]
    static void Main(string[] args)
    {
        Type type = typeof(MyRemotableClass);
        foreach (Attribute attr in
            type.GetCustomAttributes(true))
        {
            RemoteObjectAttribute remoteAttr =
                attr as RemoteObjectAttribute;
            if (null != remoteAttr)
            {
                Console.WriteLine(
                    "Create this object on {0}.",
                    remoteAttr.Server);
            }
        }
    }
}
```

As you might expect, this is the output from the application:

```
Create this object on COSETTE.
```

Because all variations of this example use some common code, let's examine what reflection does here and how it returns the attribute's value at run time.

The first line you'll notice in the *Main* method is the use of the *typeof* operator:

```
Type type = typeof(MyRemotableClass);
```

This operator returns the *System.Type* object associated with the type that's passed as its only argument. Once you have that object, you can start to query it.

The next line of code raises two issues:

```
foreach (Attribute attr in
    type.GetCustomAttributes(true))
{
```

The first issue is the call to the *Type.GetCustomAttributes* method. This method returns an array of type *Attribute* that, in this case, contains all the attributes attached to the class named *MyRemotableClass*. The Boolean parameter specifies whether to search this member's inheritance chain to find the attributes: in these example classes, the *true/false* value won't make any difference because we have no inheritance. *Type.GetCustomAttributes* will return an array of objects. The second issue is the *foreach* statement, which iterates the return array, putting each successive value into a variable (*attr*) of type *Attribute*.

Thus, for each *Attribute* variable in the array, we use the *as* operator to attempt to convert the current variable to one of type *RemoteObjectAttribute*, *which is* our custom attribute. Note that in this context we must use the full class name because the truncated form (*RemoteObject*) is legal only when used to associate the attribute (within square brackets):

```
RemoteObjectAttribute remoteAttr =
    attr as RemoteObjectAttribute;
```

The *as* operator will return a *null* reference if the current variable can't in fact be converted into a *RemoteObjectAttribute*. Therefore, we must test for a *null* value at this point. If the value isn't *null*—meaning that the *remoteAttr* variable holds a valid attribute attached to the *MyRemotableClass* type—we can access the *RemoteObjectAttribute* properties to print the remote server name. Note that there's only one *RemoteObjectAttribute* property in this example:

```
if (null != remoteAttr)
{
    Console.WriteLine(
        "Create this object on {0}.",
        remoteAttr.Server);
}
```

Method Attributes

Now that we've seen how to work with class attributes, let's look at how to use method attributes. This discussion warrants a separate section because the reflection code needed to query a method attribute is different from that needed to query a class attribute. In this example, we'll use an attribute that defines a method as transactionable:

```
namespace MethodAttribs
{
    public class TransactionableAttribute : Attribute
    {
        public TransactionableAttribute()
        {
        }
    }

    class SomeClass
    {
        [Transactionable]
        public void Foo()
        {}

        public void Bar()
        {}

        [Transactionable]
        public void Goo()
        {}
    }

    class Test
    {
        [STAThread]
        static void Main(string[] args)
        {
            Type type = Type.GetType("MethodAttribs.SomeClass");
            foreach (MethodInfo method in type.GetMethods())
            {
                foreach (Attribute attr in
                    method.GetCustomAttributes(true))
                {
                    if (attr is TransactionableAttribute)
                    {
                        Console.WriteLine(
                            "{0} is transactionable.",
```

```
                              method.Name);
                }
              }
            }
          }
        }
    }
}
```

The code outputs the following:

```
Foo is transactionable.
Goo is transactionable.
```

In this particular example, the mere presence of the *Transactionable-Attribute* tells the code that the method decorated with this attribute can belong in a transaction. That's why it's defined with only a bare-bones, parameterless constructor and no other members.

SomeClass is then defined with three methods, *Foo*, *Bar*, and *Goo*—with *Foo* and *Goo* defined as transactionable. Notice that when attaching an attribute with a constructor that takes no parameters, you don't need to include any parentheses.

Now for the fun stuff. Let's look more closely at how we can query a class's methods about the methods' attributes. We start off by using the static *Type* method *GetType* to obtain a *System.Type* object for the *SomeClass* class. Note that if the class is in a namespace (even the current namespace), it must be fully qualified:

```
Type type = Type.GetType("MethodAttribs.SomeClass");
```

Then we use the *Type.GetMethods* method to retrieve an array of *Method-Info* objects. Each of these objects contains the information about a method in the *SomeClass* class. Using a *foreach* statement, we iterate through every method:

```
foreach (MethodInfo method in type.GetMethods())
{
```

Now that we have a *MethodInfo* object, we can use the *MethodInfo.Get-CustomAttributes* method to retrieve all the user-created attributes for the method. Once again, we use a *foreach* statement to iterate through the returned array of objects:

```
foreach (Attribute attr in
    method.GetCustomAttributes(true))
{
```

At this point in the code, we have an attribute for a method. Now, using the *is* operator, we query whether it's a *TransactionableAttribute* attribute. If it is, we print the name of the method:

```
if (attr is TransactionableAttribute)
{
    Console.WriteLine(
        "{0} is transactionable.",
        method.Name);
}
```

Field Attributes

In the last example of querying members for their attached attributes, we'll look at how to query a class's fields. Let's say you have a class that contains some fields whose values you want to save in the Registry. To do so, you could define an attribute with a constructor that takes as its parameters an enum representing the correct Registry hive and a string representing the Registry value name. You could then query the field at run time for its Registry key:

```
using System;
using System.Reflection;

namespace FieldAttribs
{
    public enum RegHives
    {
        HKEY_CLASSES_ROOT,
        HKEY_CURRENT_USER,
        HKEY_LOCAL_MACHINE,
        HKEY_USERS,
        HKEY_CURRENT_CONFIG
    }

    public class RegKeyAttribute : Attribute
    {
        public RegKeyAttribute(RegHives Hive, String ValueName)
        {
            this.Hive = Hive;
            this.ValueName = ValueName;
        }

        protected RegHives hive;
        public RegHives Hive
        {
            get { return hive; }
            set { hive = value; }
        }

        protected String valueName;
        public String ValueName
```

```
        {
            get { return valueName; }
            set { valueName = value; }
        }
    }

class SomeClass
{
    [RegKey(RegHives.HKEY_CURRENT_USER, "Foo")]
    public int Foo;

    public int Bar;
}

class Test
{
    [STAThread]
    static void Main(string[] args)
    {
        Type type = Type.GetType("FieldAttribs.SomeClass");
        foreach (FieldInfo field in type.GetFields())
        {
            foreach (Attribute attr in
                field.GetCustomAttributes(true))
            {
                RegKeyAttribute rka =
                    attr as RegKeyAttribute;
                if (null != rka)
                {
                    Console.WriteLine(
                        "{0} will be saved in"
                        + " {1}\\\\{2}",
                        field.Name,
                        rka.Hive,
                        rka.ValueName);
                }
            }
        }
    }
}
}
```

We won't walk through all this code because some of it is duplicated from the previous example. However, a couple of details are important. First, just as a *MethodInfo* object retrieves method information from a type object, a *FieldInfo* object provides the same functionality for obtaining field information from a type object. As in the previous example, we start by obtaining the type object associated with our test class. We then iterate through the *FieldInfo* array, and for each *FieldInfo* object, we iterate through its attributes until we find the one we're looking for: *RegKeyAttribute*. If and when we locate that attribute, we print the name of the field and retrieve from the attribute its *Hive* and *Value-Name* fields.

Attribute Parameters

In the earlier examples, we examined attaching attributes via their constructors. Now we'll look at some issues of attribute constructors that we didn't cover earlier.

Positional Parameters and Named Parameters

In the *FieldAttribs* example in the previous section, you saw an attribute named *RegKeyAttribute*. Its constructor looked like the following:

```
public RegKeyAttribute(RegHives Hive, String ValueName)
```

Based on that constructor signature, we then attached the attribute to a field like this:

```
[RegKey(RegHives.HKEY_CURRENT_USER, "Foo")]
public int Foo;
```

So far, this is straightforward. The constructor has two parameters, and we used two parameters to attach that attribute to a field. However, we can make this easier to program. If the parameter will remain the same in the majority of cases, why make the class's user type it in each time? We can set default values by using *positional parameters* and *named parameters*.

Positional parameters are parameters to the attribute's constructor. They are mandatory and must be specified every time you use the attribute. In the *RegKeyAttribute* example you just saw, *Hive* and *ValueName* are both positional parameters. Named parameters actually aren't defined in the attribute's constructor—rather, they're nonstatic fields and properties. Therefore, named parameters enable the client to set an attribute's fields and properties when the attribute is instantiated, without you having to create a constructor for every possible combination of fields and properties that the client might want to set.

Each public constructor can define a sequence of positional parameters. This sequence is the same as any type of class. However, with attributes, once you've stated the positional parameters, the user can then reference certain fields or properties with the syntax *FieldOrPropertyName=Value*. Let's modify the attribute *RegKeyAttribute* to illustrate this process. In this example, we'll make *RegKeyAttribute.ValueName* the only positional parameter, and *RegKey-Attribute.Hive* will become an optional named parameter. So, the question is, "How do you define something as a named parameter?" Because only positional—and therefore, mandatory—parameters are included in the constructor's definition, you simply remove the parameter from the constructor's definition. The user can then reference as a named parameter any field that isn't *readonly*, *static*, or *const* or any property that includes a set accessor method—or setter—that isn't static. Therefore, to make the *RegKeyAttribute.Hive* a named parameter, you remove it from the constructor's definition because it already exists as a public read/write property:

```
//public RegKeyAttribute(RegHives Hive, String ValueName)
public RegKeyAttribute(String ValueName)
{
//     this.Hive = Hive;
    this.ValueName = ValueName;
}
```

The user can now attach the attribute in one of two ways. Either like this:

```
// either
[RegKey("Foo")]
public int Foo;
```

in which case the application produces this output:

```
Foo will be saved in HKEY_CLASSES_ROOT\\Foo
```

or like this:

```
// or
[RegKey("Foo", Hive = RegHives.HKEY_LOCAL_MACHINE)]
public int Foo;
```

in which case the application uses the parameter value supplied and produces this output:

```
Foo will be saved in HKEY_LOCAL_MACHINE\\Foo
```

This arrangement gives you the flexibility of having a default value for a field while enabling the user to override that value if needed. But hold on! If the user doesn't set the value of the *RegKeyAttribute.Hive* field, how do you default it? You might be thinking, "Well, we check to see whether it's been set in the constructor." However, the *RegKeyAttribute.Hive* is an enum with an underlying type of *int*—it's a value type that the compiler, by definition, has initialized to *0*! If we examine the *RegKeyAttribute.Hive* value in the constructor and find it equal to *0*, we won't know whether the caller placed that value there via a named parameter or the compiler initialized the value because it's a value type.

If this distinction matters to you, or if for some other reason you don't like a default value of *0*, the only way to get around this problem is to change the code so that the value *0* isn't valid. You can make this change by altering the *RegHives* enum as follows:

```
public enum RegHives
{
    HKEY_CLASSES_ROOT = 1,
    HKEY_CURRENT_USER,
    HKEY_LOCAL_MACHINE,
    HKEY_USERS,
    HKEY_CURRENT_CONFIG
}
```

Now we know that the only way *RegKeyAttribute.Hive* can be *0* is if the compiler initializes it to *0* and the user doesn't override that value via a named parameter. We can now write code like this to initialize the value:

```
public RegKeyAttribute(String ValueName)
{
    if (this.Hive == 0)
        this.Hive = RegHives.HKEY_CURRENT_USER;
    this.ValueName = ValueName;
}
```

Common Mistakes with Named Parameters

When using named parameters, you must specify the positional parameters first. After that, the named parameters can exist in any order because they're preceded by the name of the field or property. For example, the following code will result in a compiler error:

```
// Error: positional parameters cannot follow
// named parameters.
[RegKey(Hive=RegHives.HKEY_LOCAL_MACHINE, "Foo")]
public int Foo;
```

In addition, you can't name positional parameters. When the compiler is compiling an attribute's usage, it will attempt to resolve the named parameters first. Then it will attempt to resolve what's left—the positional parameters—with the method signature. The following code won't compile because the compiler resolves each named parameter but, when finished with them, can't find any positional parameters. Thus, the compiler states, *No overload for method 'RegKeyAttribute' takes '0' arguments*:

```
// Error: no positional parameters supplied
[RegKey(ValueName="Foo", Hive=RegHives.HKEY_LOCAL_MACHINE)]
public int Foo;
```

Finally, named parameters can be any publicly accessible field or property—including a setter method—that isn't static or constant.

Valid Attribute Parameter Types

The types of positional parameters and named parameters for an attribute class are limited to the attribute parameter types, which are listed here:

■ *bool, byte, char, double, float, int, long, short, string*

■ System.Type

■ object

■ An *enum* type, provided that it and any types in which it's nested are publicly accessible—as in the example used with the *RegHives* enumeration

■ A one-dimensional array involving any of the types just listed

Because the parameter types are limited to the types in this list, you can't pass data structures such as classes to the attribute constructor. This restriction makes sense because attributes are attached at design time and you don't have the instantiated instance of the class (an object) at that point. You can hardcode the values of the valid types in this list at design time, which is why you use these types.

The *AttributeUsage* Attribute

In addition to the custom attributes that you use to annotate regular C# types, you can use the *AttributeUsage* attribute to define how you want these attributes to be used. The *AttributeUsage* attribute has the following documented calling conventions:

```
[AttributeUsage(
    validon,
    AllowMultiple = allowmultiple,
    Inherited = inherited
)]
```

As you can see, it's easy to discern positional parameters from named parameters. We strongly recommend that you document your attributes in this fashion so that users of your attributes don't need to look through your attribute classes' source code to find the public read and write fields and properties that can be used as named attributes.

Defining an Attribute Target

Looking again at the *AttributeUsage* attribute, notice that the *validon* parameter is a positional parameter—and therefore, mandatory. This parameter enables you to specify the types on which your attribute can be attached. Actually, the *validon* parameter in the *AttributeUsage* attribute is of the type *AttributeTargets*, which is an enumeration defined as follows:

```
public enum AttributeTargets
{
    Assembly    = 0x0001,
    Module      = 0x0002,
    Class       = 0x0004,
    Struct      = 0x0008,
    Enum        = 0x0010,
    Constructor = 0x0020,
    Method      = 0x0040,
    Property    = 0x0080,
    Field       = 0x0100,
    Event       = 0x0200,
    Interface   = 0x0400,
    Parameter   = 0x0800,
    Delegate    = 0x1000,
    All = Assembly | Module | Class | Struct | Enum | Constructor |
        Method | Property | Field | Event | Interface | Parameter |
        Delegate,

    ClassMembers  =  Class | Struct | Enum | Constructor | Method |
        Property | Field | Event | Delegate | Interface,
}
```

Notice when using the *AttributeUsage* attribute that you can specify *AttributeTargets.All* so that the attribute can be attached to any of the types listed in the *AttributeTargets* enumeration. If you don't specify the *Attribute-Usage* attribute, *AttributeTargets.All* is the default. Given this default, you might be wondering why you'd ever use the *validon* value. The answer is that you can use named parameters on this attribute and you might want to change one of them. Remember that if you use a named parameter, you must precede it with all the positional parameters. This gives you an easy way to specify that you want the default attribute usage of *AttributeTargets.All*, and it still lets you set the named parameters.

When would you specify the *validon* (*AttributeTargets*) parameter and why? You use it when you want to control exactly how an attribute is used. In the earlier examples, we created a *RemoteObjectAttribute* attribute that's applicable to classes only, a *TransactionableAttribute* attribute that applies only to methods, and a *RegKeyAttribute* attribute that makes sense only with fields. If we want to make sure that these attributes are used to annotate only the types for which they were designed, we can define them as follows (attribute bodies left out for brevity):

```
[AttributeUsage(AttributeTargets.Class)]
public class RemoteObjectAttribute : Attribute
{
...
}

[AttributeUsage(AttributeTargets.Method)]
public class TransactionableAttribute : Attribute
{
    :
}

[AttributeUsage(AttributeTargets.Field)]
public class RegKeyAttribute : Attribute
{
    :
}

[RemoteObject(RemoteServers.COSETTE)]
class SomeClass
{
    [Transactionable]
    public void Foo() {}

    [RegKey(RegHives.HKEY_CURRENT_USER, "Bar")]
    public int Bar;
}
```

We can then use reflection to report on these various custom attributes:

```
Create this object on COSETTE.
Foo is transactionable.
Bar will be saved in HKEY_CURRENT_USER\\Bar
```

One last point regarding the *AttributeTargets* enumeration: you can combine members by using the OR (|) operator. If you have an attribute that applies to both fields and properties, you can attach the *AttributeUsage* attribute to it as follows:

```
[AttributeUsage(AttributeTargets.Field
    | AttributeTargets.Property)]
```

Single-Use and Multiuse Attributes

You can use *AttributeUsage* to define attributes as either single-use or multiuse. This decision pertains to how many times you can use a single attribute on a single field. By default, all attributes are single-use, meaning that compiling the following will result in a compiler error:

```
public class SomethingAttribute : Attribute
{
    public SomethingAttribute(String str)
    {
    }
}

// Error: "Duplicate single-use Something attribute"
[Something("abc")]
[Something("def")]
class MyClass
{
}
```

To fix this problem, specify on the *AttributeUsage* line that you want to allow the attribute to be attached to a given type multiple times. This code would work:

```
[AttributeUsage(AttributeTargets.All, AllowMultiple=true)]
public class SomethingAttribute : Attribute
{
    public SomethingAttribute(String str)
    {
    }
}

[Something("abc")]
[Something("def")]
class MyClass
{
}
```

For example, you might want to use this approach with the *RegKey-Attribute* attribute presented in the "Defining Attributes" section earlier in this chapter. Because it's conceivable that a field might be saved in multiple places in the Registry, you could attach the *AttributeUsage* attribute with the *Allow-Multiple* named parameter, as in the preceding code.

Specifying Inheritance Attribute Rules

The last parameter for the *AttributeUsageAttribute* attribute is the inherited flag, which dictates whether the attribute can be inherited. The default for this value is *false*. However, if the inherited flag is set to *true*, its meaning depends on the value of the *AllowMultiple* flag. If the inherited flag is set to *true* and the *Allow-Multiple* flag is *false*, the attribute will override the inherited attribute. However, if the inherited flag is set to *true* and the *AllowMultiple* flag is also set to *true*, the attribute accumulates on the member. Table 6-1 summarizes these permutations.

Table 6-1 Inherited and *AllowMultiple* Permutations

Inherited	***AllowMultiple***	**Result**
true	false	Derived attribute overrides base.
true	*true*	Derived and base attributes are combined.

For example:

```
using System;
using System.Reflection;

namespace AttribInheritance
{
    [AttributeUsage(
        AttributeTargets.All,
//        AllowMultiple=true,
        AllowMultiple=false,
        Inherited=true
    )]
    public class SomethingAttribute : Attribute
    {
        private string name;
        public string Name
        {
            get { return name; }
            set { name = value; }
        }

        public SomethingAttribute(string str)
        {
            this.name = str;
        }
    }
```

```
    [Something("abc")]
    class MyClass
    {
    }

    [Something("def")]
    class Another : MyClass
    {
    }

    class Test
    {
        [STAThread]
        static void Main(string[] args)
        {
            Type type =
                Type.GetType("AttribInheritance.Another");
            foreach (Attribute attr in
                type.GetCustomAttributes(true))
//                  type.GetCustomAttributes(false))
            {
            SomethingAttribute sa =
                attr as SomethingAttribute;
            if (null != sa)
            {
                Console.WriteLine(
                    "Custom Attribute: {0}",
                    sa.Name);
            }
            }

        }
    }
}
```

With *AllowMultiple* set to *false*, the result is:

```
Custom Attribute: def
```

whereas with *AllowMultiple* set to *true*, the result is:

```
Custom Attribute: def
Custom Attribute: abc
```

Note that if you pass *false* to *GetCustomAttributes*, it won't walk the inheritance tree, so you'll still get only the derived class attributes.

Attribute Identifiers

Look at the following line of code, and try to figure out whether the attribute annotates the return value or the method:

```
class SomeClass
{
    [HRESULT]
    public long Foo() { return 0; }
}
```

If you have some COM experience, you know that an *HRESULT* is the standard return type for all methods not named *AddRef* or *Release*. We might define such an *HRESULT* attribute like this:

```
public class HRESULTAttribute : Attribute
{
    public HRESULTAttribute()
    {
    }
}
```

However, it's easy to see that if the attribute name applies to both the return value and the method name, it's impossible for the compiler to know what your intention is. Here are some other scenarios in which the compiler won't recognize your intention from the context:

■ Method vs. return type

■ Event vs. field vs. property

■ Delegate vs. return type

■ Property vs. accessor vs. return value of getter method vs. value parameter of setter method

In each of these cases, the compiler makes a determination based on what's considered most common. To override this determination, you use an attribute identifier, all of which are listed here:

■ assembly

■ module

■ type

■ method

- property

- event

- field

- param

- *return*

To use an attribute identifier, preface the attribute name with the identifier and a colon. In the *SomeClass* example, if you want to ensure that the compiler can determine that the *HRESULT* attribute is meant to annotate the return value and not the method, you specify the class as follows:

```
class SomeClass
{
    [HRESULT]
    public long Foo() { return 0; }

    [return: HRESULT]
    public long Bar() { return 0; }
}
```

As a result, you can specify *method* as a method attribute identifier—although this is the default assumed by the compiler—or you can specify *property* or some other element:

```
class SomeClass
{
    [method: HRESULT]
    public long Foo() { return 0; }

    [return: HRESULT]
    public long Bar() { return 0; }

    [property: HRESULT]
    public long Goo { get { return 12345; } }
}
```

Just as we used slightly different reflection techniques to iterate method attributes, rather than field or class attributes, we need to use slightly different reflection techniques to determine attribute identifiers. For example:

```
static void Main(string[] args)
{
    Type type =
        Type.GetType("AttribIdentifiers.SomeClass");
    foreach (MethodInfo m in type.GetMethods())
    {
```

```csharp
            foreach (Attribute a in
                m.GetCustomAttributes(true))
            {
                if (a is HRESULTAttribute)
                {
                    Console.WriteLine(
                        "method: {0}, "
                        + "CustomAttributes: {1}",
                        m.Name, a);
                }
            }
            ICustomAttributeProvider icap =
                m.ReturnTypeCustomAttributes;
            foreach (Attribute a in
                icap.GetCustomAttributes(true))
            {
                Console.WriteLine(
                    "method: {0}, "
                    + "ReturnTypeCustomAttribs: {1}",
                    m.Name, a);
            }
        }
        foreach (MemberInfo m in type.GetProperties())
        {
            foreach (Attribute a in
                m.GetCustomAttributes(true))
            {
                Console.WriteLine(
                    "property: {0}, "
                    + "CustomAttributes: {1}",
                    m.Name, a);
            }
        }
    }
```

This code results in the following output:

```
method: Foo, CustomAttributes: AttribIdentifiers.HRESULTAttribute
method: Bar, ReturnTypeCustomAttribs:
AttribIdentifiers.HRESULTAttribute
property: Goo, CustomAttributes: AttribIdentifiers.HRESULTAttribute
```

Predefined Attributes

The .NET Framework classes offer a comprehensive set of predefined attribute classes, including those listed in Table 6-2, some of which we've already come across.

Table 6-2 Common Predefined Attributes

Predefined .NET Attribute	Valid Targets	Description
AttributeUsage	Class	Specifies the valid usage of another attribute class.
CLSCompliant	All	Indicates whether a program element is compliant with the Common Language Specification (CLS).
Conditional	Method	Indicates that the compiler can ignore any calls to this method if the associated string is defined.
DllImport	Method	Specifies the DLL location that contains the implementation of an external method.
MTAThread	Method (*Main*)	Indicates that the default threading model for an application is multithreaded apartment (MTA).
NonSerialized	Field	Applies to fields of a class flagged as *Serializable*; specifies that these fields won't be serialized.
Obsolete	All except *Assembly*, *Module*, *Parameter*, and *Return*	Marks an element obsolete—in other words, it informs the user that the element will be removed in future versions of the product.
ParamArray	Parameter	Allows a single parameter to be implicitly treated as a *params* (*array*) parameter.
Serializable	Class, struct, enum, delegate	Specifies that all public and private fields of this type can be serialized.
STAThread	Method (*Main*)	Indicates that the default threading model for an application is STA.
StructLayout	Class, struct	Specifies the nature of the data layout of a class or struct, such as *Auto*, *Explicit*, or *Sequential*.
ThreadStatic	Field (static)	Implements thread-local storage (TLS)—in other words, the given static field isn't shared across multiple threads and each thread has its own copy of the static field.

Conditional **Attribute**

Let's try out some of these predefined attributes. First, let's try *Conditional*. You can attach this attribute to a method so that when the compiler encounters a call to the method, it ignores the call unless the corresponding string value is defined. For example, the following method is compiled depending upon whether the string *"DEBUG"* is defined:

```
[Conditional("DEBUG")]
public void SomeDebugFunc()
    { Console.WriteLine("SomeDebugFunc"); }
```

Let's see how this works in an example. In the following code, if tested with the default settings, *"DEBUG"* will be defined. Therefore, *SomeDebugFunc* is called, as well as the nonconditional *SomeFunc* method. The *Conditional* attribute specifies that *SomeDebugFunc* will be compiled into the code only if the preprocessor directive *"DEBUG"* is defined:

```
using System;
using System.Diagnostics;

namespace CondAttrib
{
    class Thing
    {
        private string name;
        public Thing(string name)
        {
            this.name = name;
            SomeDebugFunc();
            SomeFunc();
        }
        public void SomeFunc()
            { Console.WriteLine("SomeFunc"); }

        [Conditional("DEBUG")]
        public void SomeDebugFunc()
            { Console.WriteLine("SomeDebugFunc"); }
    }

    public class Class1
    {
        [STAThread]
        static void Main(string[] args)
        {
            Thing t = new Thing("T1");
        }
    }
}
```

The output from this application will be:

```
SomeDebugFunc
SomeFunc
```

To test this code properly, we need to switch configurations: right-click in the Solution Explorer on the project name, select Properties, and then click the Configuration Properties node. The default configuration is Debug, and as you can see in Figure 6-6, the conditional compilation constants are DEBUG and TRACE.

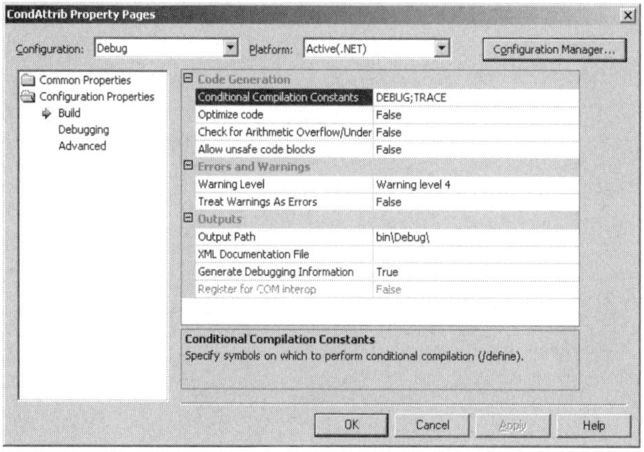

Figure 6-6   Debug configuration properties.

To switch to a release build, click the Configuration Manager button shown in Figure 6-7 and change the active solution configuration.

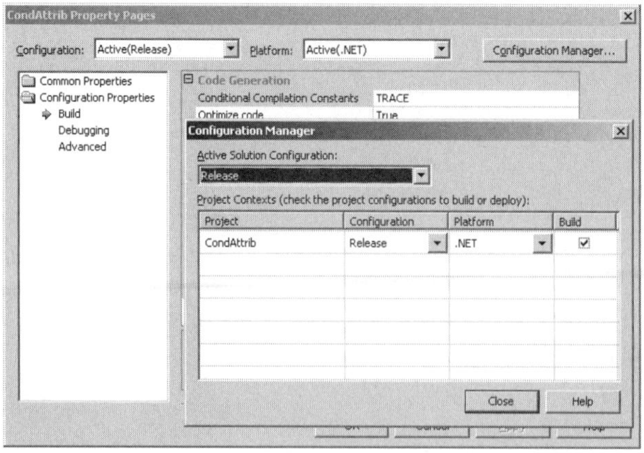

Figure 6-7   Configuration manager.

This time, only *SomeFunc* is called because the compiler has removed the call to *SomeDebugFunc* that was conditional upon the *"DEBUG"* string being defined. Note that the compiler will generate the MSIL for both methods but not for the *call* to the conditional method. The new output will be:

```
SomeFunc
```

You could combine the *Conditional* attribute with conditional preprocessor directives like this:

```
#if DEBUG
    SomeDebugFunc();
#else
    SomeFunc();
#endif
```

in which case, if *"DEBUG"* is defined, only *SomeDebugFunc* is called, instead of both methods as before. If *"DEBUG"* isn't defined, only *SomeFunc* is called.

> **Note**   *Conditional* is a multiuse attribute, so the following code construct is also legal:
>
> ```
> [Conditional("DEBUG")]
> [Conditional("ANDREW")]
> public void SomeDebugFunc()
>     { Console.WriteLine("SomeDebugFunc"); }
> ```

Obsolete Attribute

As a code base evolves over time, inevitably you'll be left with some obsolete methods. You could remove them altogether, but sometimes the presence of a piece of suitably annotated code is better than its absence. A simple example should make this clear:

```
namespace ObsAttrib
{
    class SomeClass
    {
        [Obsolete("Don't use OldFunc, use NewFunc instead", true)]
        public void OldFunc( ) { Console.WriteLine("Oops"); }

        public void NewFunc( ) { Console.WriteLine("Cool"); }
    }
```

```
class Class1
{
    [STAThread]
    static void Main(string[] args)
    {
        SomeClass sc = new SomeClass();
        sc.NewFunc();
        sc.OldFunc();
    }
}
}
```

We've carefully set the second (*Boolean*) parameter of the *Obsolete* attribute to *true*: this forces the compiler to produce an error if we attempt to call the method. If you set this to *false*, the code compiles with no warnings or errors. If you do generate an error, the first (*string*) parameter is used as part of the compiler diagnostic:

```
C:\InsideCsharp\Chap06\ObsAttrib\ObsAttrib\Class1.cs(19):
 'ObsAttrib.SomeClass.OldFunc()' is obsolete: 'Don't use OldFunc,
 use NewFunc instead'
```

CLSCompliant Attribute

This is an attribute that you can apply to assemblies or modules: all such attributes must occur after the *using* clauses and before the code. If an assembly is marked as *CLSCompliant*, any publicly exposed type in the assembly that's not CLS-compliant must be marked with *CLSCompliant(false)*. Similarly, if a class is marked as CLS-compliant, you must individually mark all members that aren't CLS-compliant. For example:

```
[assembly: CLSCompliant(true)]

namespace Compliance
{
    public class SomeClass
    {
//        public ulong b;
        private ulong b;
        public long B
        {
            get { return (long)b; }
            set { b = (ulong)value; }
        }

        [field: CLSCompliant(false)]
        public int c;
```

```
        [field: CLSCompliant(false)]
        public int C;

        public int c1;
        public int c2;
    }
    class Test
    {
        [STAThread]
        static void Main(string[] args)
        {
        }
    }
}
```

The public *ulong* field named *b* wouldn't be CLS-compliant, so here we've decided to change the field to a private property and instead use a public, CLS-compliant, long property called *B*. The public *int* fields named *c* and *C* aren't CLS-compliant because their names are distinguished only by case. Here, the strategy we choose is to flag these fields as not CLS-compliant with the appropriate attribute and to provide an alternative by using the fields *c1* and *c2*.

Note   You can place more than one attribute on a declaration, either separately or within the same set of brackets, as in:

```
[Serializable, Obsolete, CLSCompliant(true)]
public class Foo
{
}

[Serializable] [Obsolete] [CLSCompliant(true)]
public class Bar
{
}
```

DllImport and *StructLayout* Attributes

C# code can call functions in native code—that is, code native to the operating system the application is currently running on—residing in DLLs through a runtime feature called *platform invoke*. You simply import the DLL with the *DllImport* attribute. In the following example, we have a simple console application that imports a Windows DLL to use the native Win32 API function *MessageBoxA*:

```
public class Test
{
    [DllImport ("user32.dll")]
    public static extern int MessageBoxA (
        int h, string m, string c, int type);

    [STAThread]
    public static void Main(string[] args)
    {
        MessageBoxA(0, "Hello World", "nativeDLL", 0);
    }
}
```

This will produce the familiar output shown in Figure 6-8.

Figure 6-8   Win32 *MessageBoxA* and *DllImport.*

Notice that the .NET runtime silently marshals the parameters from the managed C# code to the native DLL function. Also note that we must use a real function such as *MessageBoxA* or *MessageBoxW*, not macros such as *Message-Box*. Finally, the *DllImport* attribute has additional parameters that you can use if you want:

```
[DllImport("user32", EntryPoint="MessageBoxA",
    SetLastError=true,
    CharSet=CharSet.Ansi, ExactSpelling=true,
    CallingConvention=CallingConvention.StdCall)]
public static extern int MessageBoxA (
    int h, string m, string c, int type);
```

If you want the runtime to correctly marshal structs from managed to unmanaged code (or vice versa), you need to declare additional attributes for the struct declaration. For example, consider the native Win32 API function *Get-LocalTime*, which takes a *SystemTime* struct as its parameter:

```
[DllImport ("kernel32.dll")]
public static extern void GetLocalTime(SystemTime st);
```

For the struct parameter to be correctly marshaled, you must declare it with the *StructLayout* attribute, specifying that the data should be laid out exactly as listed in the declaration (*Sequential*). If you don't do it this way, the data won't be correctly marshaled and the application will likely crash:

```
[StructLayout(LayoutKind.Sequential)]
public class SystemTime {
    public ushort wYear;
    public ushort wMonth;
    public ushort wDayOfWeek;
    public ushort wDay;
    public ushort wHour;
    public ushort wMinute;
    public ushort wSecond;
    public ushort wMilliseconds;
}
```

You can then call the function like this:

```
public static void Main(string[] args)
{
    SystemTime st = new SystemTime();
    GetLocalTime(st);
    string s = String.Format("date: {0}-{1}-{2}",
        st.wMonth, st.wDay, st.wYear);
    string t = String.Format("time: {0}:{1}:{2}",
        st.wHour, st.wMinute, st.wSecond);
    string u = s + ", " + t;

    MessageBoxA(0, u, "Now", 0);
}
```

Figure 6-9 shows the dialog box produced by this code.

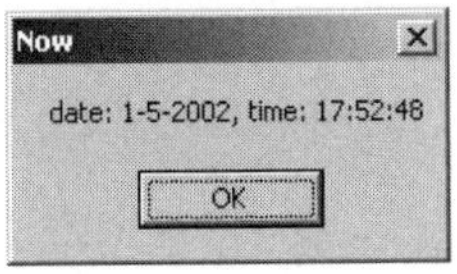

Figure 6-9   Using *DllImport* and *StructLayout* attributes.

Assembly Attributes

When you use Microsoft Visual Studio .NET to generate any kind of C# project, it automatically generates an AssemblyInfo.cs source file in addition to the application source files. The AssemblyInfo file contains code that's built into the assembly (the EXE or DLL). Some of the information is purely for informational purposes, while some allows the runtime to guarantee unique naming and versioning for client code that wants to reuse your assembly.

If you examine the contents of this file, you'll see lots of comments explaining the entries and a few entries. For now, we can make some minor changes to the informational attributes. For example, consider this sequence of entries:

```
[assembly: AssemblyTitle("")]
[assembly: AssemblyDescription("")]
[assembly: AssemblyConfiguration("")]
[assembly: AssemblyCompany("")]
[assembly: AssemblyProduct("")]
[assembly: AssemblyCopyright("")]
[assembly: AssemblyTrademark("")]
[assembly: AssemblyCulture("")]
```

We could change this to, say, the following:

```
[assembly: AssemblyTitle("Whizzo")]
[assembly: AssemblyDescription("The Whizzo Application")]
[assembly: AssemblyConfiguration("Retail")]
[assembly: AssemblyCompany("Acme Engineering Inc")]
[assembly: AssemblyProduct("Super Whizzo Pro")]
[assembly: AssemblyCopyright("2001 Andrew Whitechapel")]
[assembly: AssemblyTrademark("Acme")]
[assembly: AssemblyCulture("it")]
```

Note   The *AssemblyCulture* attribute applies to library assemblies only and must be blank for EXEs.

If you then build and test again, you'll find that these changes don't make any difference in how the application executes. However, if you use Windows Explorer to navigate to the EXE, right-click the file, select Properties, and then click the Version tab, you should see the assembly information listed, as shown in Figure 6-10. Note that you have to select each item individually to see its value.

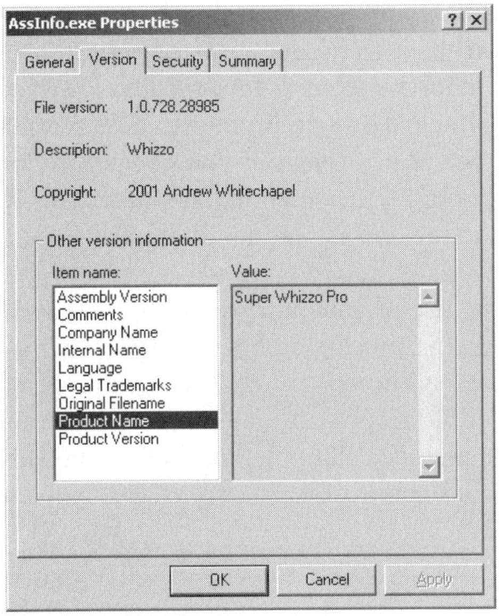

Figure 6-10   AssemblyInfo.

Context Attributes

The .NET Framework offers another kind of attribute: the *context attribute*. Context attributes provide an interception mechanism that can preprocess and postprocess class instantiation and method calls. This feature is intended for use in object remoting and has evolved from the use of COM+ component services and Microsoft Transaction Services (MTS) interception services for COM-based systems.

In its simplest form, the feature works like this: suppose you have a method on a class that's part of a transaction and the transaction spans multiple objects. We don't want to write a lot of plumbing code to manage this multi-object transaction, so we rely on the runtime to do the drudge work for us. If we derive that class from *System.ContextBoundObject*, the system will enforce the rules regarding the transactions associated with that object and its methods.

The term *context-bound* has evolved from COM+ contexts. A *context* is a subdivision of an application domain that provides external run-time support of some kind—for example, transaction support—for the objects that live in that subdivision. Every application domain has a default context, and most managed code creates objects and calls members directly using that domain's default context, completely oblivious to any context-related issues.

The namespace *System.Runtime.Remoting.Contexts* also offers the *ContextAttribute* class. If you want to invent a custom context attribute, you derive from this class rather than the regular *Attribute* class. As you might suspect, to get access to this namespace, you'll need to add a reference to the *System.Runtime.Remoting.dll* in your project. If you check the documentation for the *ContextAttribute* class, you'll see something like this: "This type supports the .NET Framework infrastructure and is not intended to be used directly from your code."

A realistic example of the use of context attributes requires a discussion of .NET object remoting. However, a much-simplified example is presented next. Although we're not actually using the context in any significant manner, we're setting up an attribute-based interception mechanism. The essence of this example is that whenever we make a call to the methods of the attributed class, the *Attribute* class itself provides some additional functionality—in this case, by simply incrementing a count:

```
using System;
using System.Runtime.Remoting.Contexts;

namespace ContextAttribs
{
    [AttributeUsage(AttributeTargets.All)]
    public class FooAttribute : ContextAttribute
    {
        public FooAttribute() : base("Foo")
        {
            Console.WriteLine("FooAttribute instance ctor");
        }
        static FooAttribute()
        {
            count = 1;
            Console.WriteLine("FooAttribute static ctor");
        }
        public static int Count
        {
            get { return count++; }
        }
        private static int count;
    }

    [Foo]
    public class SomeClass : ContextBoundObject
    {
        public string name;
        public SomeClass(string s)
```

```
        {
            name = s;
            Console.WriteLine("{0} created", name);
        }
        public void SomeFunc()
        {
            Console.WriteLine("{0}, SomeFunc: {1}",
                name, FooAttribute.Count);
        }
    }

    class Test1
    {
        [STAThread]
        static void Main(string[] args)
        {
            SomeClass sc = new SomeClass("Bill");
            sc.SomeFunc();

            SomeClass sc2 = new SomeClass("Mary");
            sc2.SomeFunc();

            sc.SomeFunc();
        }
    }
}
```

The run-time output from this application is shown here:

```
FooAttribute static ctor
FooAttribute instance ctor
Bill created
Bill, SomeFunc: 1
FooAttribute instance ctor
Mary created
Mary, SomeFunc: 2
Bill, SomeFunc: 3
```

If you're up to thinking about a realistic example of a context attribute, consider the enhanced version of this code, listed next. Note that in the following example we use some .NET Framework class interfaces, specifically *IMessageSink, IConstructionCallMessage, IContextProperty, IContributeObjectSink,* and *IMessage.*

More Info   We'll discuss interfaces in detail in Chapter 7, "Interfaces."

For now, just know that implementing an interface is superficially similar to deriving from an abstract class, where the derived class must implement (override) the methods in the interface. The point is that the runtime system uses certain specific interfaces in an object remoting scenario, so if we want to play this game, we must implement these interfaces.

```
using System;
using System.Runtime.Remoting.Contexts;
using System.Threading;

// for IMessageSink
using System.Runtime.Remoting.Messaging;

// for IConstructionCallMessage
using System.Runtime.Remoting.Activation;

namespace ContextAttribs
{
    public class FooObjectSink : IMessageSink
    {
        private IMessageSink next;
        public FooObjectSink (IMessageSink ims) { next = ims; }
        public IMessage SyncProcessMessage (IMessage imCall)
        {
            Console.WriteLine("\nPreprocessing...");
            IMessage imReturn = next.SyncProcessMessage(imCall);
            Console.WriteLine("...Postprocessing\n");
            return imReturn;
        }
        public IMessageCtrl AsyncProcessMessage (
            IMessage imCall, IMessageSink ims) { return null; }
        public IMessageSink NextSink { get { return next; } }
    }

    public class FooProperty :
        IContextProperty, IContributeObjectSink
    {
        public IMessageSink GetObjectSink(
            MarshalByRefObject o, IMessageSink next)
        {
            return new FooObjectSink(next);
        }
        public bool IsNewContextOK(Context c) { return true; }
        public void Freeze(Context c) { return; }
        public string Name { get { return "Foo"; } }
    }
```

```
[AttributeUsage(AttributeTargets.All)]
public class FooAttribute : ContextAttribute
{
    public FooAttribute() : base("Foo")
    {
        Console.WriteLine("FooAttribute instance ctor");
    }
    static FooAttribute()
    {
        count = 1;
        Console.WriteLine("FooAttribute static ctor");
    }
    public static int Count
    {
        get { return count++; }
    }
    private static int count;

    public override bool IsContextOK(Context c,
        IConstructionCallMessage ctor)
    {
        return false;
    }
    public override void GetPropertiesForNewContext(
        IConstructionCallMessage ctor)
    {
        ctor.ContextProperties.Add(new FooProperty());
    }
}

[Foo]
public class SomeClass : ContextBoundObject
{
    public string name;
    public SomeClass(string s)
    {
        name = s;
        Console.WriteLine("{0} created", name);
    }
    public void SomeFunc()
    {
        Console.WriteLine("{0}, SomeFunc: {1}",
            name, FooAttribute.Count);
    }
}
```

```
class Test1
{
    [STAThread]
    static void Main(string[] args)
    {
        SomeClass sc = new SomeClass("Bill");
        sc.SomeFunc();

        SomeClass sc2 = new SomeClass("Mary");
        sc2.SomeFunc();

        sc.SomeFunc();
    }
}
}
```

This is the run-time output:

```
FooAttribute static ctor
FooAttribute instance ctor
Bill created

Preprocessing...
Bill, SomeFunc: 1
...Postprocessing

FooAttribute instance ctor
Mary created

Preprocessing...
Mary, SomeFunc: 2
...Postprocessing

Preprocessing...
Bill, SomeFunc: 3
...Postprocessing
```

Figure 6-11 summarizes the relationships between these classes.

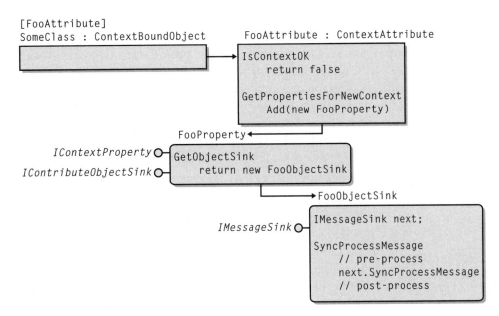

Figure 6-11   Context and context attribute classes.

This is how the code works: Recall that context attributes are intended for use in a .NET object remoting scenario. At the beginning of the chain, we have some innocent class that we attach the *Foo* attribute to, with the aim that whenever the methods of this class are called, we can provide enhanced runtime functionality. When the application creates an instance of the *SomeClass* class and before the thread returns to the application code, the system sends an *IConstructionCallMessage* to the remote object server application. This construction message includes a list of context properties that define the context in which the object will be created—and we add a new *FooProperty* to this list. We also make sure that our override of *ContextAttribute.IsContextOK* returns *false*—this indicates that we're not happy with the current calling context and we want the system to generate a new context for this object. This strategy ensures that our object is isolated in a separate context, allowing us to take maximum advantage of the system's cross-context interception.

Our *FooProperty* class implements two interfaces: *IContextProperty* and *IContributeObjectSink*. In this example, the *IContextProperty* isn't significant. On the other hand, we implement *IContributeObjectSink.GetObjectSink* to instantiate and return a new object of our *FooObjectSink* class. In this final class, we implement *IMessageSink*. In an object remoting scenario, a remote method call is a message that travels from the client end to the server end—and possibly back again. As it crosses remoting boundaries along the way, the remote method call passes through a chain of *IMessageSink* objects. Each sink in the chain receives the message object, performs a specific operation, and delegates to the next sink in the chain. In our example, we focus on synchronous messages, such as regular synchronous method calls, and it's here that we provide our interception preprocessing and postprocessing.

Summary

The .NET Framework supports two types of attribute. Metadata attributes provide a mechanism for annotating types and members at design time with information that can later be retrieved at run time through reflection. This gives you the ability to create truly self-contained, self-describing components without having to resort to stuffing necessary parts into resource files and constants, or switching between IDL and C++, or maintaining REG files, and so on. The advantage is a more mobile component that's both easier to write and easier to maintain. Through attributes, .NET allows you to extend the metadata of your code in a completely arbitrary, open-ended fashion. In this way, attributes are like a breath of fresh air—in one fell swoop releasing the shackles that have bound developers for so many years. Context attributes represent a sophisticated evolution of COM+ interception services for COM-based component systems, allowing you to enhance the runtime support for your objects in a way that's just as open-ended as that of metadata attributes.

7

Interfaces

The key to understanding interfaces might be to compare them with classes. As you learned in Chapter 3, "Classes and Structs," classes consist of data (fields) and the methods that act on that data. Although the existence of class methods does imply the concept of behavioral characteristics, classes are more accurately classified as *things* as opposed to *behaviors*—and that's where interfaces come in. Interfaces enable you to define behavioral characteristics, or abilities, and apply those behaviors to classes, irrespective of the class hierarchy.

For example, suppose that you have a distribution application in which some of the entities can be serialized. These might include the *Customer*, *Supplier*, and *Invoice* classes. Some other classes, such as *MaintenanceView* and *Document*, might not be defined as serializable. How would you make only the classes you choose serializable? One obvious way is to create a base class, perhaps named *Serializable*. However, that approach has a major drawback. A single inheritance path won't work because we don't want all the behaviors of the class to be shared. C# doesn't support multiple inheritance, so there's no way to have a given class selectively derive from multiple classes. The solution is to use interfaces. Interfaces give you the ability to define a set of semantically related methods and properties that selected classes can implement, regardless of the class hierarchy.

From a conceptual standpoint, interfaces are contracts between two disparate pieces of code. That is, once an interface is defined and a class is defined as implementing that interface, clients of the class are guaranteed that the class has implemented all methods defined in the interface. You'll see this soon in some examples, when we get to this chapter's "Implementing Interfaces" section.

In this chapter, we'll look at why interfaces are such an important part of C# and component-based programming in general. Then we'll take a look at how to declare and implement interfaces in a C# application. Finally, we'll delve into more of the specifics of using interfaces and overcoming the inherent problems with multiple inheritance and name collision.

Note   When you define an interface and specify that a class will make use of that interface in its definition, the class is said to be *implementing the interface* or *inheriting from the interface*. You can use both phrases, and you'll see them used interchangeably in other texts. Personally, I believe that *implement* is the more semantically correct term; interfaces are defined behaviors, and a class is defined as implementing that behavior, as opposed to inheriting from another class. However, both terms are correct.

Interface Use

To understand where interfaces are useful, let's first look at a traditional programming problem in Microsoft Windows development that doesn't use an interface but has two pieces of disparate code that need to communicate in a generic fashion. Imagine that you work for Microsoft and are the lead programmer for the Control Panel team. You need to provide a generic means for any client applet to bolt into Control Panel so that the applet's icon appears in Control Panel and the end user can execute the program. Keep in mind that this functionality actually was designed before COM was introduced, and ask yourself this: "How would I provide a means for any future application to be integrated into Control Panel?" The solution that Microsoft conceived has been a standard part of Windows development for years.

You, as lead programmer for the Control Panel team, design and document the function or functions that you need the client application to implement, along with a few rules. In the case of Control Panel applets, Microsoft determined that to write a Control Panel applet, you need to create a DLL that implements and exports a function named *CPlApplet*. You also need to append this DLL's name with an extension of .cpl and place the DLL in the Windows System32 folder. (On Windows ME, Windows 98 or Windows XP, this will be Windows\System32, and on Windows 2000, this will be WINNT\System32.) Once Control Panel loads, it loads all DLLs in the System32 folder with the .cpl extension—by using the *LoadLibrary* Win32 API function—and then uses the

GetProcAddress function to load the *CPlApplet* function, thus verifying that you've followed the rules and can properly communicate with Control Panel.

As I mentioned, this is a standard Windows programming model for handling situations in which you have a piece of code that you'll want future code to communicate with in a generic manner. However, this isn't the most elegant solution in the world, and it definitely has its problems. The biggest disadvantage to this technique is that it forces the server—the Control Panel code, in this case—to include a lot of validation code to ensure proper usage. For example, Control Panel can't just assume that any .cpl file in the folder is a Windows DLL. Also, Control Panel needs to verify that the correct functions are in that DLL and that those functions do what the documentation specifies.

This is where interfaces come in. Interfaces enable you create the same contractual arrangement between disparate pieces of code, but in a more object-oriented and flexible manner. In addition, because interfaces are a part of the C# language, the compiler ensures that when a class is defined as implementing a given interface, the class does what it says it does.

In C#, an interface is a first-class concept that declares a reference type that includes method declarations only. What do I mean by *first-class concept?* This term indicates that the feature in question is a built-in, integral part of the language. In other words, it's not something that was bolted on after the language was designed. Now let's take a closer look at what interfaces are and how to declare them.

Note   To the C++ developers in attendance, an interface is basically an abstract class with only pure virtual methods declared in addition to other C# class member types, such as properties, events, and indexers. In fact, if you were to define an interface named *IInterfaceName*, you'd see the following Microsoft intermediate language (MSIL) generated by the C# compiler:

```
.class interface private abstract auto ansi IInterfaceName
{
} // End of class IInterfaceName
```

Declaring Interfaces

Interfaces can contain methods, properties, indexers, and events—none of which are implemented in the interface itself. Let's look at an example to see how to use this feature. Suppose you're designing an editor for your company that hosts different Windows controls. You're writing the editor and the routines that validate the controls that users can place on the editor's form. The rest of the team is writing the controls that the forms will host. You almost certainly need to provide some sort of form-level and field-level validation. However, not all fields need to be validated. For example, if you have input fields such as social security number (SSN) and vehicle identification number (VIN), these fields will almost certainly need to be validated. But other fields such as address information probably wouldn't be validated. Therefore, we need to define our classes so that the classes that validate information can publish, or make known, the fact that they implement that behavior. Then, when appropriate—such as when the user explicitly tells the form to validate all controls during form processing—the form can iterate through all its attached controls and tell each control that implements validation to validate itself.

How would you provide this control validation capability? This is where interfaces excel. Here's a simple interface example containing a single method named *Validate*. This code lets you document the fact that each control that can be validated must implement the *IValidate* interface.

```
interface IValidate
{
    bool Validate();
}
```

Let's examine a couple of aspects of this code snippet. First, you don't need to specify an access modifier such as *public* on an interface method. In fact, prepending the method declaration with an access modifier results in a compile-time error. This is because all interface methods are public by definition. (C++ developers might also notice that because interfaces, by definition, are abstract classes, you don't need to explicitly declare the method as being *pure virtual* by appending *=0* to the method declarations.)

In addition to methods, interfaces can define properties, indexers, and events, as shown here:

```
interface IExampleInterface
{
    // Example property declaration
    int testProperty { get; }

    // Example event declaration
    event testEvent Changed;

    // Example indexer declaration
```

```
    string this[int index] { get; set; }
}
```

Now let's look at how to implement an interface from a class writer's perspective.

Implementing Interfaces

Because an interface defines a contract, any class that implements an interface *must define each and every member of that interface*—otherwise, the code won't compile. Using the *IValidate* example from the previous section, a client class would need to implement only the interface's methods. In the following example, I have a base class named *Control* and an interface named *IValidate*. I also have a class named *SSN* that derives from *Control* and implements *IValidate*. Note the syntax and how the *SSN* object can be cast to the *IValidate* interface to reference its members:

```
using System;

public class Control
{
    public Control(string data) { Data = data; }

    protected string data;
    public string Data
    {
        get { return data; }
        set { data = value; }
    }
}

interface IValidate
{
    bool Validate();
}

class SSN : Control, IValidate
{
    const char DELIMITER = '-';

    public SSN(string val) : base(val) {}

    public bool Validate()
    {
        Console.WriteLine("[SSN.Validate] : Validating '{0}'",
            data);
```

```
        return (11 == data.Length) && (CorrectFormat());
    }

    protected bool CorrectFormat()
    {
        bool correctFormat = true;

        for (int i = 0; (correctFormat && i < data.Length); i++)
        {
            correctFormat =
                ((IsDelimiterPosition(i)
                && data[i] == DELIMITER)
                || (IsNumberPosition(i)
                && char.IsNumber(data[i])));
        }

        return correctFormat;
    }

    protected bool IsDelimiterPosition(int i)
    { return (i == 3 | i == 6); }

    protected bool IsNumberPosition(int i)
    { return (i != 3 && i != 6); }
}

class InterfacesApp
{
    public static void Main(string[] args)
    {
        string data = "";

        if (0 < args.GetLength(0))
            data = args[0];

        SSN ssn = new SSN(data);

        // ...

        // When the editor needs to
        // validate the control, it can do
        // the following:

        IValidate val = (IValidate)ssn;

        Console.WriteLine("[Main] Calling SSN.Validate");
        bool success = val.Validate();
```

```
Console.WriteLine("[Main] The validation of " +
    "SSN '{0}' was {1}successful",
    ssn.Data,
    (true == success ? "" : "NOT "));
    }
}
```

Note that this simple validation assumes that the SSN will contain a dash-delimited value containing dashes at positions 3 and 6 (both positions relative to 0) and numbers in the other positions. Figure 7-1 shows where I've run the application several times in order to illustrate that the *Validate* method is being called and is properly validating the value passed on the command line.

Figure 7-1   Properties enable you to write accessor methods for fields while insulating clients from having to know of their existence.

Using the preceding class and interface definition, the editor can query the control as to whether the control implements the *IValidate* interface. If the class does implement the *IValidate* interface, the editor can then call the implemented interface methods knowing that the compiler has already guaranteed that these methods have been implemented by the class. Let's see how that's done in C# by using both the *is* operator and the *as* operator.

Querying for Implementation by Using *is*

In the *InterfacesApp* example, you saw the following code, which was used to cast an object (*SSN*) to one of its implemented interfaces (*IValidate*) and then call one of those interface members (*Validate*):

```
SSN ssn = new SSN(data);

IValidate val = (IValidate)ssn;
bool success = val.Validate();
```

However, what would happen if a client attempted to use a class as though the class had implemented a method that it hadn't? You can test this process with the *InterfacesApp* application by simply removing, or commenting out (as I've done here), the interface from the *SSN* class's definition:

```
class SSN : Control /* , IValidate */
```

Now, if you build and execute the application, the common language runtime will raise a *System.InvalidCastException* and the application will abort unless this exception was explicitly caught. However, as you'll see in Chapter 12, "Error Handling with Exceptions," exceptions should be used only when an error would cause the normal flow of a code path—that is, a series of method calls on the call stack—to be impractical or imprudent. In our case, we're expecting that some controls won't support validation. Therefore, we need a mechanism that simply gives us a way to query an object as to whether it implements an interface *before* we attempt to cast it. As you'll now see, one way of doing this is by using the *is* operator.

The *is* operator enables you to check at run time whether one type is compatible with another type. It takes the following form, in which *expression* is a reference type:

expression is type

In the following example, I've modified the original *InterfacesApp* to include a second class (*Address*) that doesn't implement the *IValidate* interface. The *Main* method instantiates both an *SSN* and an *Address* object, adds them to an array of controls, and then iterates through the array by using the *is* operator to determine which controls implement *IValidate*.

```
using System;
using System.Collections;

public class Control
{
    public Control(string data) { Data = data; }

    protected string data;
    public string Data
    {
        get { return data; }
        set { data = value; }
    }
}


interface IValidate
{
```

```
        bool Validate();
}

class SSN : Control , IValidate
{
    const char DELIMITER = '-';

    public SSN(string val) : base(val) {}

    public bool Validate()
    {
        Console.WriteLine("[SSN.Validate] : Validating '{0}'",
            data);
        return (11 == data.Length) && (CorrectFormat());
    }

    protected bool CorrectFormat()
    {
        bool correctFormat = true;

        for (int i = 0; (correctFormat && i < data.Length); i++)
        {
            correctFormat =
                ((IsDelimiterPosition(i)
                && data[i] == DELIMITER)
                || (IsNumberPosition(i)
                && char.IsNumber(data[i])));
        }

        return correctFormat;
    }

    protected bool IsDelimiterPosition(int i)
    { return (i == 3 | i == 6); }

    protected bool IsNumberPosition(int i)
    { return (i != 3 && i != 6); }
}

class Address : Control
{
    public Address(string data) : base(data) {}
}

class IsOperatorApp
{
    public static void Main()
    {
```

```
ArrayList controls = new ArrayList();

Console.WriteLine("Adding an SSN to the " +
    "controls array");
SSN ssn = new SSN("555-55-5555");
controls.Add(ssn);

Console.WriteLine("Adding an Address to the " +
    "controls array");
Address addr = new Address("1 Microsoft Way");
controls.Add(addr);

Console.WriteLine("\nIterating through array...");
foreach (Control control in controls)
{
    if (control is IValidate)
    {
        Console.WriteLine("\n\t{0} implements IValidate",
            control);
        Console.Write("\t");
        bool b = ((IValidate)control).Validate();
        Console.WriteLine("\tValidation {0}",
            (b == true ? "succeded" : "failed"));
    }
    else
    {
        Console.WriteLine("\t{0} does NOT implement " +
            "IValidate", control);
    }
}
```

Now if you execute this application, you'll see the output shown in Figure 7-2, proving that the *is* operator has indeed enabled us to determine which object implements the *IValidate* interface.

Figure 7-2   The *is* operator can be used to determine whether a class implements a given interface.

Although the *is* operator certainly seems to do the job we wanted, it's not the most efficient technique in our particular situation. To see what I mean, look at the generated MSIL shown in Figure 7-3.

```
IsOperatorApp::Main : void()
.try
{
    IL_0052:  br.s        IL_00b2
    IL_0054:  ldloc.s     CS$00000006$00000000
    IL_0056:  callvirt    instance object [mscorlib]System.Collections.IEnumer
    IL_005b:  castclass   Control
    IL_0060:  stloc.3
    IL_0061:  ldloc.3
    IL_0062:  isinst      IValidate
    IL_0067:  brfalse.s   IL_00a7
    IL_0069:  ldstr       "\n\t{0} implements IValidate"
    IL_006e:  ldloc.3
    IL_006f:  call        void [mscorlib]System.Console::WriteLine(string,
                                                                   object)
    IL_0074:  ldstr       "\t"
    IL_0079:  call        void [mscorlib]System.Console::Write(string)
    IL_007e:  ldloc.3
    IL_007f:  castclass   IValidate
    IL_0084:  callvirt    instance bool IValidate::Validate()
    IL_0089:  stloc.s     b
    IL_008b:  ldstr       "\tValidation {0}"
    IL_0090:  ldloc.s     b
    IL_0092:  brtrue.s    IL_009b
```

Figure 7-3   The *is* operator resolves to a call to the *isinst* instruction.

As you can see, the *is* operator generated an *isinst* instruction (IL_0062). The *isinst* instruction checks that the class of the object on the stack (pushed at IL_0061) either implements the specified interface or derives from the specified class. If the result of this verification is *true*, the object is cast to the specified type and pushed onto the stack. Otherwise, a *null* is pushed onto the stack.

In our case, once the *isinst* instruction returns, a test is performed (using the *brfalse.s* instruction) that branches control to IL_00a7 if what's on the stack is *null* (indicating that the *isinst* instruction failed). If what's on the stack is anything other than *null*, the code attempts to call the object's *Validate* method.

Now take a look at instruction IL_007f, a *castclass* instruction. This instruction is here because once the code determines that an object implements the *IValidate* interface, the code explicitly casts the object to *IValidate* and calls the object's *Validate* method. The problem with that arrangement is that the *castclass* instruction does its own validation to determine whether the cast is correct (basically the same checking that the *isinst* already performed).

Therefore, in our example, the code would be performing the same verification twice for every control in the *controls* array—once in the conditional *if* statement, and again when casting the object. What we need is a statement that will perform the verification and the cast in single step. This situation is where the *as* operator comes in.

Querying for Implementation by Using *as*

In our particular application, the code can be made much more efficient by using the *as* operator. The *as* operator converts between compatible types and takes the following form, in which *expression* is any reference type:

object = expression as type

While the *is* operator is used to branch based on whether the *isinst* instruction pushed a valid object onto the stack, the *as* operator results in that value being stored in a local variable. Once that's done, your code can verify whether that variable has a valid value. Our example can now be rewritten in a more efficient manner:

```
using System;
using System.Collections;

public class Control
{
    public Control(string data) { Data = data; }

    protected string data;
    public string Data
    {
        get { return data; }
        set { data = value; }
    }
}

interface IValidate
{
    bool Validate();
}
```

```
class SSN : Control , IValidate
{
    const char DELIMITER = '-';

    public SSN(string val) : base(val) {}

    public bool Validate()
    {
        Console.WriteLine("[SSN.Validate] : Validating '{0}'",
            data);
        return (11 == data.Length) && (CorrectFormat());
    }

    protected bool CorrectFormat()
    {
        bool correctFormat = true;

        for (int i = 0; (correctFormat && i < data.Length); i++)
        {
            correctFormat =
                ((IsDelimiterPosition(i)
                && data[i] == DELIMITER)
                || (IsNumberPosition(i)
                && char.IsNumber(data[i]))));
        }

        return correctFormat;
    }

    protected bool IsDelimiterPosition(int i)
    { return (i == 3 | i == 6); }

    protected bool IsNumberPosition(int i)
    { return (i != 3 && i != 6); }
}

class Address : Control
{
    public Address(string data) : base(data) {}
}

class AsOperatorApp
{
    public static void Main()
    {
        ArrayList controls = new ArrayList();
```

```
Console.WriteLine("Adding an SSN to the " +
    "controls array");
SSN ssn = new SSN("555-55-5555");
controls.Add(ssn);

Console.WriteLine("Adding an Address to the " +
    "controls array");
Address addr = new Address("1 Microsoft Way");
controls.Add(addr);

Console.WriteLine("\nIterating through array...");
IValidate iValidate;
foreach (Control control in controls)
{
    iValidate = control as IValidate;
    if (null != iValidate)
    {
        Console.WriteLine("\n\t{0} implements IValidate",
            control);
        Console.Write("\t");
        bool b = iValidate.Validate();
        Console.WriteLine("\tValidation {0}",
            (b == true ? "succeded" : "failed"));
    }
    else
    {
        Console.WriteLine("\n\t{0} does NOT " +
            "implement IValidate", control);
    }
}
    }
}
```

Now the verification ensuring a valid cast is done only once, which is obviously much more efficient. Figure 7-4 shows the resulting MSIL of using the *as* operator—to cast a local variable to the desired type—and then checking that the local variable has a valid value.

```
AsOperatorApp::Main : void()                                          _ □ ×
.try
{
    IL_0052:  br.s        IL_00b3
    IL_0054:  ldloc.s     CS$00000006$00000000
    IL_0056:  callvirt    instance object [mscorlib]System.Collections.IEnumer
    IL_005b:  castclass   Control
    IL_0060:  stloc.s     control
    IL_0062:  ldloc.s     control
    IL_0064:  isinst      IValidate
    IL_0069:  stloc.3
    IL_006a:  ldloc.3
    IL_006b:  brfalse.s   IL_00a7
    IL_006d:  ldstr       "\n\t{0} implements IValidate"
    IL_0072:  ldloc.s     control
    IL_0074:  call        void [mscorlib]System.Console::WriteLine(string,
                                                                   object)
    IL_0079:  ldstr       "\t"
    IL_007e:  call        void [mscorlib]System.Console::Write(string)
    IL_0083:  ldloc.3
    IL_0084:  callvirt    instance bool IValidate::Validate()
    IL_0089:  stloc.s     b
    IL_008b:  ldstr       "\tValidation {0}"
    IL_0090:  ldloc.s     b
    IL_0092:  brtrue.s    IL_009b
    IL_0094:  ldstr       "failed"
    IL_0099:  br.s        IL_00a0
    IL_009b:  ldstr       "succeded"
```

Figure 7-4 The *as* operator enables you to verify that an object can be cast to another type, and it performs that cast to a local variable in one step.

Now that you've seen the semantics of defining, implementing, and querying for the support of interfaces, let's look briefly at how interfaces differ from the alternative techniques.

Interfaces vs. the Alternatives

Let's look at some alternatives to using interfaces. Continuing with the editor example, you might be prompted to ask, "Why don't I just define a base class to use with this editor that has a pure virtual function named *Validate*? The editor would then accept only controls that are derived from this base class, right?" To answer that, look at Figure 7-5.

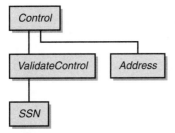

Figure 7-5 Injecting interfaces into the class hierarchy as abstract base classes mixes the concepts of things (classes) and behaviors (interfaces).

Here I've defined a *Control* base class, and from that class, I've derived the *ValidateControl* class (because some controls don't validate their data). Now the *Address* class can derive directly from *Control*, and the *SSN* class can derive directly from *ValidateControl*. The result would be that the previous code for reading from a collection of controls, querying a control as to its type, and then calling a method based on whether it supports the *Validate* method will still work. The only difference is that we'd be passing a class name to the *is* (or *as*) operator instead of an interface name.

At first glance, this scheme seems to work. However, there are some logical problems here. First, to inject a behavior such as *Validate* into the control's inheritance lineage obviously implies that *Validate* is somehow meant to extend *Control*. This implication obviously isn't the case. Second, what if you want to use a class that isn't defined in this hierarchy? For example, you might purchase a third-party *VIN* (vehicle identification number) control that's derived from another class. Without multiple inheritance, what would you do? The answer in this particular case is to use a combination of abstract classes and *containment* (shown in Figure 7-6).

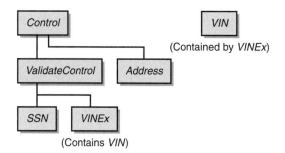

(Contained by *VINEx*)

(Contains *VIN*)

Figure 7-6   Containment is the most obvious alternative to not having multiple inheritance.

Using containment, you could define your own *ValidateControl*-derived *VIN* class and have it contain, as a member, an instance of the *VIN* class. The only drawback here would be that clients wanting to access the "inner *VIN*" would have to go through another layer to do so:

```
VINEx vin = new VINEx();
vin.innerVin.GetMake();
vin.innerVin.GetModel();
```

Although both of these solutions seem to work, they begin to break down when the example moves from the simplicity of a single behavior being applied to a single branch of an inheritance tree to a more practical example. As an example, look at the classes depicted in Figure 7-7.

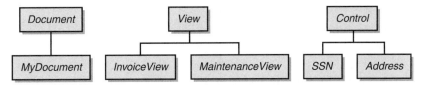

Figure 7-7   Without interfaces, having to define multiple dissimilar behaviors to be implemented across a class framework can be quite difficult.

In this example, I have three base classes (*Document*, *View*, and *Control*), and I want two classes (*MaintenanceView* and *SSN*) to support the validation of data. In the controls example, I was able to define an abstract class (*ValidateControl*), and although it logically didn't extend the *Control* class, it could define a constructor that matched its base class's constructor and it could act as the base class for the *SSN* class.

```
public class Control
{
    public Control(string data) { Data = data; }
    ⋮
}
abstract class ValidateControl : Control
{
    public Validate(string data) : base(data) {}
    public abstract bool Validate();
}
```

However, if *MaintenanceView* and *SSN* have different nondefault constructors (and they almost certainly will), I'll have to define two separate abstract classes even though they're meant to define the same behavior (data validation) so that I can use abstract classes with the scenario presented in Figure 7-7.

I have yet another problem—the problem of implementing multiple dissimilar behaviors. What if in addition to *MaintenanceView* and *Control* supporting validation, I also want *Document* and *Control* to support a new behavior—serialization? As you should see by now, the more complex the scenarios get, the more hoops you'll have to jump through when using other techniques. Using C# interfaces, I can address this scenario very easily:

```
interface ISerializable
⋮⋮
interface IValidate
⋮
public class Control
⋮
public class Address : Control
```

```
      ⋮
public class Address : Control, IValidate, ISerializable
      ⋮


public class Document : ISerializable
      ⋮


public class MaintenanceView : View
      ⋮
public class MaintenanceView : View, IValidate
      ⋮
```

The point is that there are always ways to get around any problem. However, interfaces are a built-in mechanism that enables you to easily define as many behaviors as you want and then specify that any number of classes implement those behaviors in any desired combination—without respect to the class hierarchy.

Explicit Interface Member Name Qualification

So far, you've seen classes implement interfaces by specifying the access modifier *public*, followed by the interface method's signature. However, sometimes you'll want—or need—to explicitly qualify the member name with the name of the interface. In this section, we'll examine two common reasons for doing this.

Name Hiding with Interfaces

The most common way to call a method implemented from an interface is to cast an instance of that class to the interface type and then call the desired method. Although this is valid and many people use this technique (including me), technically you don't have to cast the object to its implemented interface to call that interface's methods. This is because when a class implements an interface's methods, those methods are also public methods of the class. Take a look at this C# code—especially the *Main* method—to see what I mean:

```csharp
using System;

public interface IDataBound
{
    void Bind();
}

public class EditBox : IDataBound
```

```
{
    // IDataBound implementation
    public void Bind()
    {
        Console.WriteLine("Binding to data store...");
    }
}

class NameHiding1App
{
    // Main entry point
    public static void Main()
    {
        Console.WriteLine();

        EditBox edit = new EditBox();
        Console.WriteLine("Calling EditBox.Bind()...");
        edit.Bind();

        Console.WriteLine();

        IDataBound bound = (IDataBound)edit;
        Console.WriteLine("Calling (IDataBound)" +
            "EditBox.Bind()...");
        bound.Bind();
    }
}
```

Although this application calls the implemented *Bind* method two different ways—one with a cast and one without—both calls function correctly in that the *Bind* method is processed. Although at first blush the ability to directly call the implemented method without casting the object to an interface might seem like a good idea, sometimes this is less than desirable. The most obvious reason is that the implementation of several interfaces—each of which might contain numerous members—could quickly pollute your class's public namespace with members that have no meaning outside the scope of the implementing class. You can prevent the implemented members of interfaces from becoming public members of the class by using a technique known as *name hiding*.

At its simplest, name hiding gives you the ability to hide an inherited member name from any code outside the derived or implementing class. Let's use the same example that we used earlier, in which an *EditBox* class needs to implement the *IDataBound* interface. However, this time, the *EditBox* class doesn't want to expose the *IDataBound* methods to the outside world. Instead, the class needs this interface for its own purposes, or perhaps the programmer simply doesn't want to clutter the class's namespace with a large number of methods that a typical client won't use. To hide an implemented interface member, you need only remove the member's *public* access modifier and qualify the member name with the interface name, as shown here:

```
using System;

public interface IDataBound
{
    void Bind();
}

public class EditBox : IDataBound
{
    // IDataBound implementation
    void IDataBound.Bind()
    {
        Console.WriteLine("Binding to data store...");
    }
}

class NameHiding2App
{
    public static void Main()
    {
        Console.WriteLine();


        EditBox edit = new EditBox();
        Console.WriteLine("Calling EditBox.Bind()...");

        // ERROR: This line won't compile because
        // the Bind method no longer exists in the
        // EditBox class's namespace.
        edit.Bind();

        Console.WriteLine();

        IDataBound bound = (IDataBound)edit;
        Console.WriteLine("Calling (IDataBound)" +
            "EditBox.Bind()...");

        // This is OK because the object was cast to
        // IDataBound first.
        bound.Bind();
    }
}
```

The preceding code won't compile because the member name *Bind* is no longer a part of the *EditBox* class. Therefore, this technique enables you to remove the member from the class's namespace while still allowing explicit access by using a cast operation.

I want to reiterate one point: when you're hiding a member, you can't use an access modifier. You'll receive a compile-time error if you try to use an access modifier on an implemented interface member. You might find this odd, but remember that the reason for hiding something is to prevent it from being visible outside the current class. Because access modifiers exist only to define the level of visibility outside the base class, you can see that they don't make sense when you use name hiding.

Avoiding Name Ambiguity

While C# doesn't support multiple inheritance, it does support inheritance from one class and the additional implementation of multiple interfaces. However, with this power comes a price: name collision.

In the following example, we have two interfaces, *ISerializable* and *IDataStore*, which support the reading and storing of data in two different formats—one as an object to disk in binary form, and the other to a database. The problem is that they both contain methods named *SaveData*:

```
using System;

interface ISerializable
{
    void SaveData();
}

interface IDataStore
{
    void SaveData();
}

class Test : ISerializable, IDataStore
{
    public void SaveData()
    {
        Console.WriteLine("Test.SaveData called");
    }
}

class NameCollisions1App
{
    public static void Main()
```

```
    {
        Test test = new Test();

        Console.WriteLine("Calling Test.SaveData()");
        test.SaveData();
    }
}
```

When I wrote the first edition of this book, I was told that although this code would compile, it wouldn't do so in future builds of C#. However, the code still compiles on version 1 of the released C# compiler. Regardless of whether the code compiles in the version of the compiler you're working with, the main problem here is that the client of the *Test* class can't tell which interface's *SaveData* is being implemented.

The following code is even more ambiguous:

```
using System;

interface ISerializable
{
    void SaveData();
}

interface IDataStore
{
    void SaveData();
}

class Test : ISerializable, IDataStore
{
    public void SaveData()
    {
        Console.WriteLine("Test.SaveData called");
    }
}

class NameCollisions2App
{
    public static void Main()
    {
        Test test = new Test();

        Console.WriteLine("Testing to see if Test " +
            "implements ISerializable...");
        Console.WriteLine("ISerializable is {0}implemented\n",
            test is ISerializable ? "" : "NOT ");
```

```
        Console.WriteLine("Testing to see if Test " +
            "implements IDataStore...");
        Console.WriteLine("IDataStore is {0}implemented\n",
            test is IDataStore ? "" : "NOT ");
    }
}
```

When you compile this code, take a look at the warning messages because they indicate that both the *ISerializable* and *IDataStore* interfaces are implemented—something we know isn't true from a logical point of view.

```
NameCollisions2.cs(29,21): warning CS0183: The given
 expression is always of the provided ('ISerializable') type
NameCollisions2.cs(33,21): warning CS0183: The given
 expression is always of the provided ('IDataStore') type
```

Let's look at the MSIL at this point. As you can see from Figure 7-8, the Test class is defined with the *implements* keyword for both *ISerializable* and *IDataStore*. The C# compiler generated this MSIL because it simply saw that all the members of the two interfaces that *Test* indicated it was implementing do, in fact, have definitions.

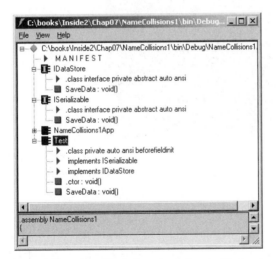

Figure 7-8 The Test class is defined with the *implements* keyword for both *ISerializable* and *IDataStore*.

It gets worse: take a look at the *Main* method's MSIL, and you'll see what the warning message "the given expression is always of the provided type" means (shown in Figure 7-9).

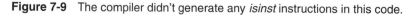

```
NameCollisions1App::Main : void()                                    _ □ X
.method public hidebysig static void  Main() cil managed
{
  .entrypoint
  // Code size       29 (0x1d)
  .maxstack  1
  .locals init ([0] class Test test)
  IL_0000:  newobj      instance void Test::.ctor()
  IL_0005:  stloc.0
  IL_0006:  ldstr       "Calling Test.SaveData()"
  IL_000b:  call        void [mscorlib]System.Console::WriteLine(string)
  IL_0010:  ldloc.0
  IL_0011:  callvirt    instance void Test::SaveData()
  IL_0016:  call        string [mscorlib]System.Console::ReadLine()
  IL_001b:  pop
  IL_001c:  ret
} // end of method NameCollisions1App::Main
```

Figure 7-9   The compiler didn't generate any *isinst* instructions in this code.

Notice something missing here? There are no *isinst* instructions! The compiler is so sure that the interfaces are implemented that it optimized our conditional statements and isn't going to perform the run-time check (which would return *true* anyway). Figure 7-10 confirms that this optimization was correct—the application prints out that both interfaces are implemented.

Figure 7-10   Implementing multiple interfaces that contain the same member names can result in a confusing situation in which you're not sure which interface is actually implemented.

The problem is that the class has implemented either a serialized version or a database version of the *SaveData* method, but not both. However, if the client checks for the implementation of one of the interfaces—both will succeed—and tries to use the one that wasn't truly implemented, unexpected results will occur.

One means of circumventing this problem is to use explicit member name qualification. This qualification is done by simply removing the access modifier and prepending the member name—*SaveData*, in this case—with the interface name. Here's an example of that modification:

```
using System;

interface ISerializable
{
    void SaveData();
}

interface IDataStore
{
    void SaveData();
}

class Test : ISerializable, IDataStore
{
    void IDataStore.SaveData()
    {
        Console.WriteLine("[Test.SaveData] IDataStore " +
            "implementation called");
    }

    void ISerializable.SaveData()
    {
        Console.WriteLine("[Test.SaveData] ISerializable " +
            "implementation called");
    }
}

class NameCollisions3App
{
    public static void Main()
    {
        Test test = new Test();

        Console.WriteLine("[Main] " +
            "Testing to see if Test implements " +
            "ISerializable...");
        Console.WriteLine("[Main] " +
            "ISerializable is {0}implemented",
            test is ISerializable ? "" : "NOT ");
        ((ISerializable)test).SaveData();

        Console.WriteLine();

        Console.WriteLine("[Main] " +
            "Testing to see if Test implements " +             "IDataStore...");
        Console.WriteLine("[Main] " +
            "IDataStore is {0}implemented",
            test is IDataStore ? "" : "NOT ");
```

```
        ((IDataStore)test).SaveData();
    }
}
```

There are a couple of things to note here. First, the code is explicitly telling the compiler which interface's *SaveData* method is being implemented. If you specify that both interfaces are being implemented but define only one of the *SaveData* methods, this specification will result in a compile-time error. Second, the client code (*NameCollisions3App.Main*) needs to cast to the appropriate interface to ensure that the appropriate method is being called. Although this is a bit of extra work, there won't be any ambiguity about which method will be called. Both methods are implemented with their fully qualified names, and the resulting output from this application is what you'd expect, as shown in Figure 7-11.

Figure 7-11   Explicit member name qualification is the best way to get around name collisions resulting from implementing multiple interfaces with members that have the same name.

Interfaces and Inheritance

Two problems commonly are associated with interfaces and inheritance. The first problem, illustrated here with a code example, deals with the issue of deriving from a base class that contains a method name identical to the name of an interface method that the class needs to implement:

```
using System;

public class Control
{
    public void Serialize()
    {
        Console.WriteLine("Control.Serialize called");
```

```
    }
}

public interface IDataBound
{
    // EditBox never implements this, but it still compiles!!!
    void Serialize();
}

public class EditBox : Control, IDataBound
{
}

class InterfaceInhlApp
{
    public static void Main()
    {
        EditBox edit = new EditBox();
        edit.Serialize();
    }
}
```

As you know, to implement an interface, you must provide a definition for every member in that interface's declaration. However, in the preceding example, we don't do that, and the code still compiles! In fact, if you build this example, the output will show that the *Control.Serialize* method is being called.

The reason the code compiles is that the C# compiler looks for an implemented *Serialize* method in the *EditBox* class and finds one. However, the compiler is incorrect in determining that this is the implemented method. The *Serialize* method found by the compiler is the *Serialize* method inherited from the *Control* class and not an actual implementation of the *IDataBound.Serialize* method. Therefore, although the code compiles, it won't function as expected, as we'll see next.

Now let's make things even more interesting. Notice that the following code first checks—via the *as* operator—that the interface is implemented and then attempts to call an implemented *Serialize* method. The code compiles and works. However, as we know, the *EditBox* class doesn't really implement a *Serialize* method as a result of the *IDataBound* inheritance. The *EditBox* already had a *Serialize* method—which it inherited—from the *Control* class. This means that, in all likelihood, the client won't get the expected results.

```
using System;

public class Control
{
```

```
    public void Serialize()
    {
        Console.WriteLine("Control.Serialize called");
    }
}

public interface IDataBound
{
    void Serialize();
}

public class EditBox : Control, IDataBound
{
}

class InterfaceInh2App
{
    public static void Main()
    {
        EditBox edit = new EditBox();

        IDataBound bound = edit as IDataBound;
        if (bound != null)
        {
            Console.WriteLine("IDataBound is supported...");
            bound.Serialize();
        }

        else
        {
            Console.WriteLine("IDataBound is NOT supported...");
        }
    }
}
```

Another potential problem to watch for occurs when a derived class has a method with the same name as the base class implementation of an interface method. Let's look at that in code now:

```
using System;

interface ITest
{
    void Foo();
}

// Base implements ITest.
class Base : ITest
```

```
{
    public void Foo()
    {
        Console.WriteLine("Base.Foo (ITest implementation)");
    }
}

class MyDerived : Base
{
    public new void Foo()
    {
        Console.WriteLine("MyDerived.Foo");
    }
}

public class InterfaceInh3App
{
    public static void Main()
    {
        Console.WriteLine("InterfaceInh3App.Main : " +
            "Instantiating a MyDerived class");
        MyDerived myDerived = new MyDerived();
        Console.WriteLine();

        Console.WriteLine("InterfaceInh3App.Main : " +
            "Calling MyDerived.Foo - Which method will be " +
            "called?");
        myDerived.Foo();
        Console.WriteLine();

        Console.WriteLine("InterfaceInh3App.Main : " +
            "Calling MyDerived.Foo - Casting to ITest " +
            "interface...");
        ((ITest)myDerived).Foo();
    }
}
```

This code results in the output shown in Figure 7-12.

Figure 7-12 With interface inheritance, name collisions can cause all sorts of ambiguity problems.

In this situation, the *Base* class implements the *ITest* interface and its *Foo* method. However, the *MyDerived* class derives from *Base* with a new class and implements a new *Foo* method for that class. Which *Foo* gets called? That depends on which reference you have. If you have a reference to the *MyDerived* object, its *Foo* method will be called. Although the *myDerived* object has an inherited implementation of *ITest.Foo*, the run time will execute *MyDerived.Foo* because the *new* keyword specifies an override of the inherited method.

However, when you explicitly cast the *myDerived* object to the *ITest* interface, the compiler resolves to the interface implementation. The *MyDerived* class has a method of the same name, but that's not what the compiler is looking for. When you cast an object to an interface, the compiler traverses the inheritance tree until a class is found that contains the interface in its base list. This is why the last two lines of code in the *Main* method result in the implementation of *ITest.Foo* being called.

Hopefully, some of these pitfalls of name collisions and interface inheritance have convinced you to follow my strong recommendation: always cast the object to the interface whose member you're attempting to use.

Combining Interfaces

Another powerful feature of C# is the ability to combine two or more interfaces so that a class need only implement the combined result. For example, let's say you want to create a new *TreeView* class that implements both the *IDragDrop* and *ISortable* interfaces. Because it's reasonable to assume that other controls, such as *ListView* and *ListBox*, would also want to combine these features, you might want to combine the *IDragDrop* and *ISortable* interfaces into a single interface:

```
using System;

public class Control
{
}

public interface IDragDrop
{
    void Drag();
    void Drop();
}


public interface ISerializable
{
    void Serialize();
}

public interface ICombo : IDragDrop, ISerializable
{
    // This interface doesn't add anything new in
    // terms of behavior as its only purpose is
    // to combine the IDragDrop and ISerializable
    // interfaces into one interface.
}

public class MyTreeView : Control, ICombo
{
    public void Drag()
    {
        Console.WriteLine("MyTreeView.Drag called");
    }

    public void Drop()
    {
        Console.WriteLine("MyTreeView.Drop called");
    }

    public void Serialize()
    {
        Console.WriteLine("MyTreeView.Serialize called");
    }
}

class CombiningInterfacesApp
```

```
{
    public static void Main()
    {
        Console.WriteLine("CombiningInterfacesApp.Main " +
            ": Instantiating a MyTreeView class\n");
        MyTreeView tree = new MyTreeView();

        Console.WriteLine("Calling MyTreeView.Drag");
        tree.Drag();
        Console.WriteLine();

        Console.WriteLine("Calling MyTreeView.Drop");
        tree.Drop();
        Console.WriteLine();

        Console.WriteLine("Calling MyTreeView.Serialize");
        tree.Serialize();
        Console.WriteLine();
    }
}
```

Running this application results in the expected output, shown in Figure 7-13. With the ability to combine interfaces, not only can you simplify the ability to aggregate semantically related interfaces into a single interface, you also can add methods to the new composite interface, if needed.

Figure 7-13   C# enables you to easily aggregate multiple interfaces into one composite interface for easier use and maintenance.

Summary

Interfaces in C# allow the development of classes that can share features but aren't part of the same class hierarchy. Interfaces play a special role in C# development because C# doesn't support multiple inheritance. To share semantically related methods and properties, classes can implement multiple interfaces. Also, the *is* and *as* operators can be used to determine whether a particular interface is implemented by an object, which can help prevent errors associated with using interface members. Finally, explicit member naming and name hiding can be used to control interface implementation and to help prevent errors.

II

Writing Code

8

Expressions and Operators

In this chapter, we'll take a look at the most basic part of any programming language: its ability to express assignments and comparisons through the use of operators. We'll look at what operators are and how operator precedence is determined in C#, and then we'll delve into specific categories of expressions for performing math, assigning values, making comparisons between operands, and operating on the individual bits of a value.

Operators Defined

An operator is a symbol that indicates an operation to be performed on one or more arguments. This operation produces a result. The syntax used with operators is a bit different than that used with method calls, but the C# format of an expression using operators should be second nature to you. Like operators in most other programming languages, C# operator semantics follow the basic rules and notations we learned as children in mathematics classes. The most basic C# operators include multiplication (*), division (/), addition and unary plus (+), subtraction and unary minus (−), modulus (%), and assignment (=).

Operators are specifically designed to produce a new value from the values that are being operated on. The values being operated on are called *operands*. When applied to an operator, the terms *unary*, *binary*, and *ternary* refer to the number of operands that the operator is used with. For instance, we have the unary minus, which takes one operand (for example, −3), as opposed to the binary (arithmetic) minus, which takes two operands (for example, 4−3). Although the same lexical symbol is used (−), these are different operators. There's only one ternary operator—the conditional ?: operator, which is often called the *ternary operator*.

The result of an operation must be stored somewhere in memory. In some cases, the value produced by an operation is stored in the variable containing one of the original operands. The C# compiler generates an error message if you use an operator and no new value can be determined or stored. In the following example, the code results in nothing being changed. The compiler generates an error message because writing an arithmetic expression that doesn't result in a change to at least one value is generally a mistake on the part of the developer:

```
class NoResultApp
{
    static void Main(string[] args)
    {
        int i;
        int j;

        i + j; // Error
    }
}
```

Most operators work only with numeric data types, such as *Byte, Short, Long, Integer, Single, Double,* and *Decimal.* Exceptions include the comparison operators (==" and "!=) and the assignment operator (=), which can also work on objects. In addition, C# defines the + and += operators for the *String* class and even allows for the use of increment operators (++ and −−) on unique language constructs such as delegates. We'll examine that last example in Chapter 14, "Delegates and Event Handlers."

Operator Precedence

When a single expression or statement contains multiple operators, the compiler must determine the order in which the operators will be evaluated. The rules that govern how the complier makes this determination are called *operator precedence.* Understanding operator precedence can mean the difference between writing your expressions with confidence and staring at a single line of code as you wonder why the result isn't what you want.

Take a look at the following expression: 42 + 6 * 10. If you add 42 and 6 and then multiply the sum by 10, the product is 480. If you multiply 6 and 10 and then add that product to 42, the result is 102. When code is compiled, a special part of the compiler called the *lexical analyzer* is responsible for determining how to read this code. It's the lexical analyzer that determines the relative precedence of operators when more than one kind of operator is present in an expression. The analyzer does this by specifying a value (or precedence) for each supported operator. The higher precedence operators are resolved first. In our example, the * operator has a higher precedence than the + operator because * takes its operands before + does. (We'll take a closer look at precedence in a moment.) The reason for this stems from the basic rules of arithmetic: multiplication and division always take higher precedence than addition and subtraction. With that said, let's get back to our example: 6 is taken by the * in both 42 + 6 * 10 and 42 * 6 + 10, making expressions the equivalent of 42 + (6 * 10) and (42 * 6) + 10.

How C# Determines Precedence

Let's look specifically at how C# assigns precedence to operators. Table 8-1 illustrates C# operator precedence from highest precedence to lowest. After this section, we'll go into more detail on the categories of operators that are supported in C#.

Table 8-1
C# Operator Precedence

Category of Operator	Operators
Primary	(x), x.y, f(x), a[x], x++, x−−, *new, typeof, sizeof, checked, unchecked*
Unary	+, -, !, ~, ++x, −−x , (T)x
Multiplicative	*, /, %
Additive	+, −
Shift	<<, >>
Relational	<, >, <=, >=, is
Equality	==
Logical AND	&
Logical XOR	^
Logical OR	|
Conditional AND	&&
Conditional OR	||
Conditional	?:
Assignment	=, *=, /=, %=, +=, −= , <<=, >>=, &=, ^=, |=

Left and Right Associativity

Associativity determines which side of an expression should be evaluated first. For example, the following expression could result in a sum of either 21 or 33, depending on the left or right associativity of the – operator:

```
42–15–6
```

The – operator is defined as *left-associative*, meaning that 42–15 is evaluated and then 6 is subtracted from the result. If the – operator were defined as *right-associative*, the expression to the right of the operator would be evaluated first: 15–6 would be evaluated and then subtracted from 42.

All binary operators—that is, operators that take two operands—except assignment operators are left-associative, meaning that the expression is evaluated from left to right. Therefore, a + b + c is the same as (a + b) + c, in which a + b is evaluated first and c is added to the resulting sum. Assignment operators and the conditional operator are right-associative—the expression is evaluated from right to left. In other words, a = b = c is equivalent to a = (b = c). This trips up some people who want to place multiple assignment operations on the same line, so let's look at some code:

```
class RightAssocApp
{
    static void Main(string[] args)
    {
        int a = 1;
        int b = 2;
        int c = 3;

        Console.WriteLine(
            "a={0} b={1} c={2}", a, b, c);
        a = b = c;
        Console.WriteLine(
            "After 'a=b=c': a={0} b={1} c={2}", a, b, c);
    }
}
```

Here are the results of running this example:

```
a=1 b=2 c=3
After 'a=b=c': a=3 b=3 c=3
```

Seeing an expression evaluated from the right might be confusing at first, but think of it like this: If the assignment operator were left-associative, the compiler would first evaluate a = b, which would give a value of *2* to a, and then it would evaluate b = c, which would give a value of *3* to b. The end result would be a=2 b=3 c=3. Needless to say, that wouldn't be the expected result for a = b = c, which is why the assignment and conditional operator are both right-associative.

Practical Usage

Nothing is more insidious than tracking down a bug for a long period of time only to find that it resulted from a developer not knowing the rules of precedence or associativity. We've all seen posts on mailing lists in which intelligent people have suggested a programming convention that uses spaces to indicate which operators they think will have precedence—a kind of self-documenting mechanism. For example, because we know that the multiplication operator has precedence over the addition operator, we could write code like this where white space indicates the order of intended precedence:

```
a = b*c + d;
```

However, this approach is severely flawed—the compiler doesn't parse code properly without specific syntax. The compiler parses expressions based on the rules determined by the people that developed it. To that end, a symbol exists that allows you to set precedence and associativity: the parenthesis. For example, you could rewrite the expression a = b * c + d as either a = (b * c) + d or a = b * (c + d), and the compiler will evaluate what's in the parentheses first. If two or more pairs of parentheses exist, the compiler evaluates the value in each pair and then the entire statement by using the precedence and associativity rules we've described.

Our firm opinion is that you should always use parentheses when using multiple operators in a single expression. We recommend this even if you know the order of precedence because the folks who maintain your code might not be as well informed.

C# Operators

It's helpful to think of operators according to their precedence. In this section, we'll describe the most commonly used operators in the order presented earlier in Table 8-1.

Primary Expression Operators

The first category of operators that we'll look at is the primary expression operators. Because most of these operators are fairly basic, we'll just list them and give a short blurb about their function. We'll then explain the other less obvious operators a bit more thoroughly.

- **(x)** This form of the parenthesis operator is used to control precedence, either in mathematical operations or in method calls.

- **x.y** The dot operator is used to specify a member of a class or structure where *x* represents the containing entity and *y* represents the member.

- **f(x)** This form of the parenthesis operator is used to list the arguments to a method.

- **a[x]** Square brackets are used to index into an array. They are also used in conjunction with indexers where objects can be treated as arrays.

More Info   For more information on indexers, refer to Chapter 5, "Properties, Arrays, and Indexers."

- **x++** Because there's a lot to talk about here, the increment operator is covered later in this section in "Increment Operators and Decrement Operators."

- **x––** The decrement operator is also covered later in this section.

- **new** The *new* operator is used to instantiate objects from class definitions.

typeof

Reflection is the ability to retrieve type information at run time. This information includes type names, class names, and structure members. A class named *System.Type* is integral to this ability in the .NET Framework. This class is the root of all reflection operators, and it can be obtained by using the *typeof* operator. We won't go into reflection in great detail here—that's a task reserved for Chapter 19, "Querying Metadata with Reflection." However, here's a simple example to illustrate how easy it is to use the *typeof* operator to retrieve almost any information you want about a type or an object at run time:

```
using System;
using System.Reflection;

public class Apple
{
    public int nSeeds;
    public void Ripen()
    {
    }
}
```

```
public class TypeOfApp
{
    static void Main(string[] args)
    {
        Type t = typeof(Apple);
        string className = t.ToString();

        Console.WriteLine("\nInformation on the class {0}",
            className);

        Console.WriteLine("\n{0} methods", className);
        Console.WriteLine("---------------------------");
        MethodInfo[] methods = t.GetMethods();
        foreach (MethodInfo method in methods)
        {
            Console.WriteLine(method.ToString());
        }

        Console.WriteLine("\nAll {0} members", className);
        Console.WriteLine("---------------------------");
        MemberInfo[] allMembers = t.GetMembers();
        foreach (MemberInfo member in allMembers)
        {
            Console.WriteLine(member.ToString());
        }
    }
}
```

The program contains a class named *Apple* that has only two members: a field named *nSeeds* and a method named *Ripen*. The first thing we do is use the *typeof* operator and the class name to yield a *System.Type* object, which we then store in a variable named *t*. From that point on, we can use the *System.Type* methods to obtain all the *Apple* class methods and members. These tasks are performed using the *GetMethods* and *GetMembers* methods, respectively. The results of these method calls are printed to standard output, as shown here:

```
Information on the class Apple

Apple methods
---------------------------
Int32 GetHashCode()
Boolean Equals(System.Object)
System.String ToString()
Void Ripen()
System.Type GetType()

All Apple members
---------------------------
```

```
Int32 nSeeds
Int32 GetHashCode()
Boolean Equals(System.Object)
System.String ToString()
Void Ripen()
System.Type GetType()
Void .ctor()
```

Before we move on, there are two more points we must make. First, notice that the class's inherited members are also listed in the output. Because we didn't explicitly derive the class from another class, we know that all the members not defined in the *Apple* class are inherited from the implicit base class, *System.Object*. Second, note that you can use the *GetType* method to retrieve the *System.Type* object. *GetType* is inherited from *System.Object* and enables you to work with objects, as opposed to classes. The following two code snippets can be used interchangeably to retrieve a *System.Type* object:

```
// Retrieve the System.Type object from the class definition.
Type t = typeof(Apple);

// Retrieve the System.Type object from the object.
Apple apple = new Apple();
Type t2 = apple.GetType();
```

sizeof

The *sizeof* operator is used to obtain the size, in bytes, of a given type. You should keep in mind two extremely important factors when using this operator. First, you can use the *sizeof* operator with value types only. Therefore, although this operator can be used on class members, it can't be used on the class type itself. Second, this operator can be used only in a method or code block marked as unsafe.

More Info We'll discuss unsafe code in Chapter 20, "Pinning and Memory Management."

Here's an example of using the *sizeof* operator from a class method marked as unsafe:

```
class SomeClass
{
    // NOTE: You must declare that code that uses the
    // sizeof operator as unsafe.
    static unsafe public void ShowSizes()
    {
        Console.WriteLine("\nBasic type sizes");
```

```
        Console.WriteLine("sizeof short = {0}", sizeof(short));
        Console.WriteLine("sizeof int = {0}", sizeof(int));
        Console.WriteLine("sizeof long = {0}", sizeof(long));
        Console.WriteLine("sizeof bool = {0}", sizeof(bool));
    }
}

class SizeofBasicTypesApp
{
    unsafe public static void Main(string[] args)
    {
        SomeClass.ShowSizes();
    }
}
```

To get this code to compile, you must compile with the */unsafe* compiler switch. To do this from Microsoft Visual Studio .NET, right-click the project in the Solution Explorer window, select Properties, and then select Configuration Properties. Change the Allow Unsafe Code Blocks entry to True, as shown in Figure 8-1.

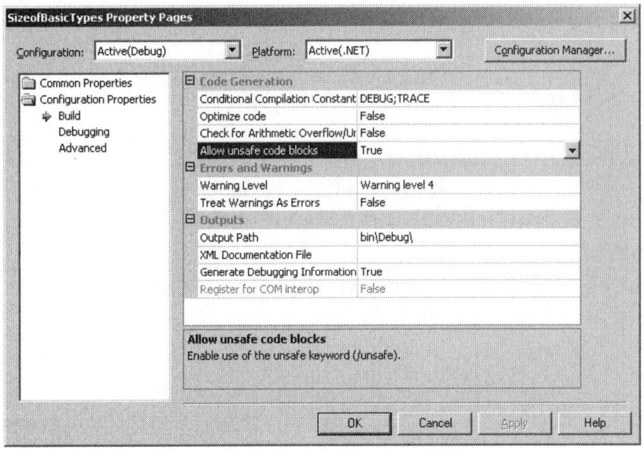

Figure 8-1   Allow unsafe code blocks.

These are the results of running this application:

```
Basic type sizes
sizeof short = 2
sizeof int = 4
sizeof long = 8
sizeof bool = 1
```

Aside from simple built-in types, the *sizeof* operator can also be used to determine the sizes of other user-created value types, such as structs. However, the results of the *sizeof* operator can sometimes be less than obvious, as in the following example:

```
struct StructWithNoMembers
{
}

struct StructWithMembers
{
    short s;
    int i;
    long l;
    bool b;
}

struct CompositeStruct
{
    StructWithNoMembers a;
    StructWithMembers b;
    StructWithNoMembers c;
}

class SizeofCustomTypesApp
{
    unsafe public static void Main(string[] args)
    {
        Console.WriteLine(
            "sizeof StructWithNoMembers structure = {0}",
            sizeof(StructWithNoMembers));
        Console.WriteLine(
            "sizeof StructWithMembers structure = {0}",
            sizeof(StructWithMembers));
        Console.WriteLine(
            "sizeof CompositeStruct structure = {0}",
            sizeof(CompositeStruct));
    }
}
```

While you might expect this application to print a value of *0* for the structure with no members (*StructWithNoMembers*), the value *15* for the structure with four of the basic members (*StructWithMembers*), and the value *15* for the structure that aggregates the two (*CompositeStruct*), the actual result follows:

```
sizeof StructWithNoMembers structure = 1
sizeof StructWithMembers structure = 16
sizeof CompositeStruct structure = 24
```

The reason for this is padding and structure alignment, which relates to how the compiler lays out a struct in the output file's image. For example, if a struct were 3 bytes long and the byte alignment was set at 4 bytes, the compiler would automatically pad it with an extra byte and the *sizeof* operator would report that the struct is 4 bytes in length. Therefore, you must take this into consideration when determining the size of a structure in C#.

checked and *unchecked*

These two operators control overflow checking for mathematical operations. I'll cover them later in this chapter in the "*checked* and *unchecked* Context" section.

Mathematical Operators

The C# language supports the basic mathematical operators that almost all programming languages support: multiplication (*), division (/), addition (+), subtraction (−) , and modulus (%). The first four operators are obvious in their meaning; the modulus operator produces the remainder from integer division. The following code illustrates these mathematical operators in use:

```
class MathOpsApp
{
    static void Main(string[] args)
    {
        // The System.Random class is part of the .NET
        // Framework class library. Its default constructor
        // seeds the Next method using the current date/time.
        Random rand = new Random();
        int a, b, c;

        a = rand.Next() % 100; // Limit max to 99.
        b = rand.Next() % 100; // Limit max to 99.

        Console.WriteLine("a={0} b={1}", a, b);

        c = a * b;
        Console.WriteLine("a * b = {0}", c);

        // Note the following code uses integers. Therefore,
        // if a is less than b, the result will always
        // be 0. To get a more accurate result, you would
        // need to use variables of type double or float.
        c = a / b;
        Console.WriteLine("a / b = {0}", c);
```

```
        c = a + b;
        Console.WriteLine("a + b = {0}", c);

        c = a - b;
        Console.WriteLine("a - b = {0}", c);

        c = a % b;
        Console.WriteLine("a % b = {0}", c);
    }
}
```

Because we're using *Random*, we should get different results every time we run this code, but this is a sample of what to expect:

```
a=65 b=70
a * b = 4550
a / b = 0
a + b = 135
a - b = -5
a % b = 65
```

Unary Operators

There are two unary arithmetic operators: plus and minus. The unary minus operator indicates to the compiler that the operand should be made negative. Therefore, the following would result in the variable *a* being equal to −42:

```
class UnaryOpsApp
{
    static void Main(string[] args)
    {
        int a;
        a = -42;
        Console.WriteLine("{0}", a);
    }
}
```

However, ambiguity creeps in when you do something like this:

```
static void Main(string[] args)
{
    int a;
    a = -42;
    Console.WriteLine("{0}", a);

    int b = 2;
    int c = 42;
    a = b * -c;
    Console.WriteLine("{0}", a);
}
```

The output from the second *WriteLine* is −84, but the a = b * −c can be a bit confusing. Once again, the use of parentheses helps to make this line of code much clearer:

```
// With parentheses, it's obvious that you're
// multiplying b by the negative of c.
a = b * (-c);
```

If the unary minus returns the negative value of an operand, you'd think that the unary plus would return the operand's positive value. However, the unary plus does nothing but return the operand in its original form, thereby having no effect on the operand. For example, the following code will also result in the output of −84:

```
static void Main(string[] args)
{
    int a;
    a = -42;
    Console.WriteLine("{0}", a);

    int b = 2;
    int c = 42;

    a = b * (-c);
    Console.WriteLine("{0}", a);

    c = -42;
    a = b * (+c);
    Console.WriteLine("{0}", a);
}
```

Why is this? If you think about it a bit, you'll realize that the statement

```
a = b * (+c);
```

really evaluates to

```
a = b * (+-42);
```

which is arithmetically the same as

```
a = b * (0+-42);
```

so the subexpression in parentheses evaluates to −42, and everything makes sense again.

If you really want to retrieve the positive form of an operand, use the *Math.Abs* method. The following will produce a result of 84:

```
class TestAbsApp
{
    static void Main(string[] args)
```

```
    {
        int a;
        int b = 2;
        int c = -42;
        a = b * Math.Abs(c);
        Console.WriteLine("{0}", a);
    }
}
```

One last unary operator that we'll mention briefly is the (T)x operator. This is a form of the parenthesis operator that enables a cast of one type to another type. Because this operator can be overloaded by virtue of creating a user-defined conversion, it's covered in Chapter 13, "Operator Overloading and User-Defined Conversions."

Compound Assignment Operators

A compound assignment operator is a combination of a binary operator and the assignment (=) operator. Its syntax is

```
x op= y
```

where *op* represents the operator. Note that instead of the *rvalue*—the value on the assignment operator's right side—being replaced by the *lvalue*—the value on the assignment operator's left side—the compound operator has the effect of writing

```
x = x op y
```

using the lvalue as the base for the result of the operation. For example:

```
public class CompoundAssApp
{
    public static void Main(string[] args)
    {
        int nCalc = 10;
        nCalc += 5;
        Console.WriteLine(nCalc);

        nCalc -= 3;
        Console.WriteLine(nCalc);

        nCalc *= 2;
        Console.WriteLine(nCalc);

        nCalc /= 4;
        Console.WriteLine(nCalc);

        nCalc %= 4;
        Console.WriteLine(nCalc);
    }
}
```

This code will produce this output:

```
15
12
24
6
2
```

Note that we use the words *has the effect*. The compiler doesn't literally translate an expression such as x += 5 into x = x + 5. It just works that way logically. For example, would you consider the following statements equivalent?

```
int x;
x = 5;
x = x * 3 + 4;
Console.WriteLine("{0}", x);


x = 5;
x *= 3 + 4;
Console.WriteLine("{0}", x);
```

The first *WriteLine* will output 19, the second 35. Why? It comes back to precedence. In the first expression, we have an assignment operator, a multiplication operator, and an addition operator. These three operators have different levels of precedence, in order: *, +, =. In the second expression, we have only two operators, a compound assignment operator and an addition operator. The precedence of these two operators is, in order: +, *=. Bear in mind that although multiplication has a higher level of precedence than addition and a much higher level of precedence than assignment, the compound *= operator is a compound *assignment* operator. This means the compound *= operator has the same level of precedence as all assignment operators—and this is the lowest of all precedence.

There's another issue to worry about when you're considering whether to use a single compound assignment operation or two separate operations—assignment and another operation. This caveat applies to using an operation when the lvalue is a method or property. Let's examine it now:

```
public class SomeClass
{
    private int num;
    public SomeClass(int i)
    {
        num = i;
    }
    public int Num
    {
        get { return num; }
```

```
            set { num = value; }
        }
    }

public class CompoundAssPropApp
{
    public static void Main(string[] args)
    {
        SomeClass sc = new SomeClass(42);
        Console.WriteLine("{0}", sc.Num);

        sc.Num = sc.Num + 5;
        Console.WriteLine("{0}", sc.Num);
    }
}
```

The result of this code is:

```
42
47
```

Notice in the call to the *SomeClass.Num* property and the subsequent modification of its field that we use this assignment syntax:

```
x = x op y
```

The generated Microsoft intermediate language (MSIL) code is shown in Figure 8-2.

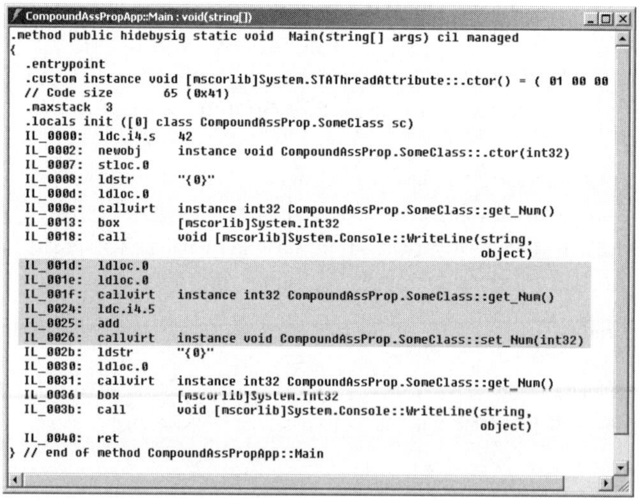

Figure 8-2 Using assignment and addition with a property.

You can see that the single x = x op y expression results in calls to two methods: the *get* and *set* methods for the *Num* property. In a best-case scenario, this is inefficient. In the worst case, it could be disastrous, depending on what other tasks the *get* and *set* property methods need to perform.

Let's tack on a little extra code, to use the alternative mechanism of the compound assignment operator:

```
sc.Num += 5;
Console.WriteLine("{0}", sc.Num);
```

Examine the relevant MSIL, shown in Figure 8-3.

```
IL_0040:  ldloc.0
IL_0041:  dup
IL_0042:  callvirt    instance int32 CompoundAssProp.SomeClass::get_Num()
IL_0047:  ldc.i4.5
IL_0048:  add
IL_0049:  callvirt    instance void CompoundAssProp.SomeClass::set_Num(int32)
```

Figure 8-3   Using compound assignment with a property.

As you can see, the only difference is that when we used two separate operators (the + and the =), the MSIL used *ldloc* twice. On the other hand, when we used the compound assignment operator, the MSIL used *ldloc* once, followed by *dup*. The *ldloc* opcode loads a local variable onto the evaluation stack—in this case, the first local variable, variable *0*. The *dup* opcode duplicates the top element on the stack, thereby making a copy of the value retrieved from the call to the *get_Num* method. In performance terms, there's no difference between these two approaches, but then we're using a property and we know that expressions involving properties always evaluate to *get* and *set* method calls. Also, in this example, the field we're ultimately working with is a value type field. How do the two alternative operator strategies compare when we access a reference type field?

```
public class SomeClass
{
    private int[] nums;
    public SomeClass(int i)
    {
        nums = new int[10];
        nums[0] = i;
    }
    public int[] Nums
    {
        get { return nums; }
        set { nums = value; }
    }
}
```

```
public class CompoundAssRefApp
{
    public static void Main(string[] args)
    {
        SomeClass sc = new SomeClass(42);
        Console.WriteLine("{0}", sc.Nums[0]);

        sc.Nums[0] = sc.Nums[0] + 5;
        Console.WriteLine("{0}", sc.Nums[0]);
    }
}
```

The MSIL is shown in Figure 8-4.

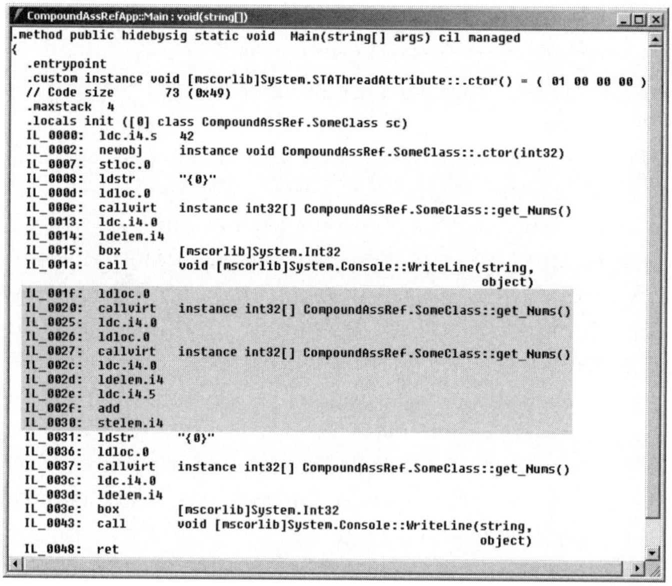

Figure 8-4 Using assignment and addition with a reference property.

As you can see, the x = x op y expression results in the *get* method being called twice. Let's tack the same two lines of code on again, to see how the compound assignment operation compares:

```
sc.Nums[0] += 5;
Console.WriteLine("{0}", sc.Nums[0]);
```

The relevant part of the MSIL is shown in Figure 8-5.

```
IL_0048:  ldloc.0
IL_0049:  callvirt   instance int32[] CompoundAssRef.SomeClass::get_Nums()
IL_004e:  dup
IL_004f:  stloc.1
IL_0050:  ldc.i4.0
IL_0051:  ldloc.1
IL_0052:  ldc.i4.0
IL_0053:  ldelem.i4
IL_0054:  ldc.i4.5
IL_0055:  add
IL_0056:  stelem.i4
```

Figure 8-5   Using compound assignment with a reference property.

As you can see, there's now only one call to the *get* method, and the *ldloc* opcode is again replaced with *dup*. This exercise has illustrated that although conceptually x += y is equivalent to x = x + y, subtle differences appear in the generated MSIL. Because of these differences, you need to think carefully about which syntax to use in each circumstance. A basic rule of thumb—and our recommendation—is to use compound assignment operators whenever and wherever possible.

Increment Operators and Decrement Operators

As holdovers from shortcuts first introduced in the C language and carried forward in both C++ and Java, increment operators and decrement operators allow you to more concisely state that you want to increment or decrement a variable representing a numeric value by 1. Therefore, *i*++ is the equivalent of adding 1 to the current value of *i*.

Two versions of both the increment and decrement operators exist and thus are often a source of confusion. Typically referred to as *prefix* and *postfix*, the type of operator indicates when the variable is modified. With the prefix versions of the increment operator and decrement operator—that is, ++*a* and −−*a*, respectively—the operation is performed and then the value is produced. With the postfix versions of the increment operator and decrement operator—*a*++ and *a*−−, respectively—the value is produced and then the operation is performed. Take a look at the following example:

```
class IncDecApp
{
    public static void Foo(int j)
    {
        Console.WriteLine("IncDecApp.Foo j = {0}", j);
    }

    static void Main(string[] args)
    {
        int i = 1;
```

```
        Console.WriteLine("Before Foo(i++) = {0}", i);
        Foo(i++);
        Console.WriteLine("After Foo(i++) = {0}", i);

        Console.WriteLine();

        Console.WriteLine("Before Foo(++i) = {0}", i);
        Foo(++i);
        Console.WriteLine("After Foo(++i) = {0}", i);
    }
}
```

This application produces this result:

```
Before Foo(i++) = 1
IncDecApp.Foo j = 1
After Foo(i++) = 2

Before Foo(++i) = 2
IncDecApp.Foo j = 3
After Foo(++i) = 3
```

The difference here lies in when the value is produced and the operand is modified. In the call to *Foo(++i)*, the value *i* is passed—unchanged—to *Foo*, and after the *Foo* method returns, *i* is incremented. You can see this in the following MSIL excerpt. Notice that the MSIL *add* opcode isn't called until after the value has been placed on the stack, as shown in Figure 8-6.

```
IL_0012:  ldloc.0
IL_0013:  dup
IL_0014:  ldc.i4.1
IL_0015:  add
IL_0016:  stloc.0
IL_0017:  call        void IncDec.IncDecApp::Foo(int32)
```

Figure 8-6   MSIL for the postincrement operator.

Now let's look at the preincrement operator used in the call to *Foo(++a)*. In this case, the MSIL generated looks like the code shown in Figure 8-7. Notice that the MSIL *add* opcode is called before the value is placed on the stack for the subsequent call to the *Foo* method.

```
IL_0046:  ldloc.0
IL_0047:  ldc.i4.1
IL_0048:  add
IL_0049:  dup
IL_004a:  stloc.0
IL_004b:  call        void IncDec.IncDecApp::Foo(int32)
```

Figure 8-7   MSIL for the preincrement operator.

Numeric Conversions

While we're looking at operators, we should bear in mind that some operations will have side effects. These side effects are predictable, but you must be aware of their nature. Even a simple numeric assignment operation could produce an unexpected result if you don't take the side effect into account. First, consider the *operator promotion* side effect, shown in the following code, which contains an error:

```
public class NumConvertApp
{
    public static void Main(string[] args)
    {
        short s1 = 123;
        short s2 = 456;
        short ssum = (s1 + s2);              // Build error
        Console.WriteLine("sum = {0}", ssum);
    }
}
```

The problem arises from the fact that the C# language has built-in operations for the *int, uint, long, ulong, float, double,* and *decimal* types but not for *short*. Therefore, when you do arithmetic on types for which there's no built-in operation, the compiler implicitly modifies the expression to promote it to one of the types that does have a built-in operation. In this case, the expression *s1+s2* is promoted to an *int*, which then can't be assigned to the *ssum short*. In C++, of course, this code would build (and possibly lose data), but in C#, the compiler won't build it. If you're clear on what you're trying to do here, you can resolve this problem by casting the type of the expression to a *short*:

```
//short ssum = (s1 + s2);          // Build error
short ssum = (short)(s1 + s2);
```

Here's the output:

```
sum = 579
```

A related problem arises if the result of an arithmetic expression exceeds the allowable size of the target assignment. For example, the maximum value that can be represented as a *signed short* is *32767* (and a *short* is implicitly a *signed short*). Thus, if a variable currently holds the maximum value for its type, what happens if you then try to increase this value? The code that follows illustrates this situation:

```
Console.WriteLine(
    "Max int = {0}", short.MaxValue);  // 32767
short s3 = 32767;
short s4 = 1;
```

```
short ssum2 = (short)(s3 + s4);
Console.WriteLine("sum2 = {0}", ssum2);
```

Here's the output:

```
Max int = 32767
sum2 = -32768
```

The result of −32768 arises because the addition exceeds the storage for the type of the variable and flips the interpretation of the bit values to a negative. Recall that a signed numeric type reserves the topmost bit for the sign—positive if not set, negative if set. Therefore, a signed short has only 31 of the 32 bits to use for the value. If you're already on the maximum, it means you've already used all 31 bits. Increasing the value will have to use the topmost bit, which means that the whole number is now interpreted as a negative value. If this isn't the intended design, the problematic expression should be executed in a *checked* context—which will cause a runtime error and a debug break, instead of an unexpected data value:

```
checked
{
    short ssum2 = (short)(s3 + s4); // OverflowException
    Console.WriteLine("sum2 = {0}", ssum2);
}
```

C# supports two types of conversion between types:

- **Implicit conversions**   Always succeed without loss of data.

- **Explicit conversions**   Require casts, which might lose data.

```
// Implicit conversions smaller --> larger
sbyte a = 12;
byte b = 34;
short c = 56;
int d = 78;
long e = 90;

// Explicit larger --> smaller
d = (int)e;
c = (short)d;
b = (byte)c;
a = (sbyte)b;
```

Bear in mind that explicit conversions might lose data:

```
e = 4294967295;
Console.WriteLine("(int)4294967295 = {0}", (int)e);
c = 321;
Console.WriteLine("(byte)321 = {0}", (byte)c);
```

Here's the output:

```
(int)4294967295 = -1
(byte)321 = 65
```

Also note that in contrast with C/C++, there's no implicit conversion from numeric data to character data, but as with C/C++, you can cast (explicitly convert) to your heart's content:

```
//char x = 65;          // Error: no conversion
Console.WriteLine("(char)(byte)321 = {0}", (char)(byte)c);
```

The output follows:

```
(char)(byte)321 = A
```

checked and *unchecked* Context

C# statements can execute in either *checked* or *unchecked* context. In a *checked* context, arithmetic overflow raises an exception. In an *unchecked* context, arithmetic overflow is ignored and the result is truncated. If *checked* and *unchecked* aren't specified in the code, the default context depends on the / *checked* compiler switch. The following operations are affected by the overflow checking:

- Expressions using the following predefined operators on integral types: ++, --, -(unary), +, -, *, /

- Explicit numeric conversions between integral types

The */checked* compiler option lets you specify *checked* (*/checked* or / *checked+*) or *unchecked* (*/checked-*) context for all integer arithmetic statements that aren't explicitly in the scope of a *checked* or *unchecked* keyword. Consider this code:

```
try
{
    checked
    {
        short f = 321;
        byte g = (byte)f;
        Console.WriteLine("(byte)321 = {0}", g);
    }
}
catch (Exception z)
{
        Console.WriteLine("{0}", z.Message);
}
```

Here's the output:

```
An exception of type System.OverflowException was thrown.
```

Now consider this code:

```
//checked
unchecked
{
    short f = 321;
    byte g = (byte)f;
    Console.WriteLine("(byte)321 = {0}", g);
}
```

The output follows:

```
(byte)321 = 65
```

Also consider the permutations of using the *checked/unchecked* statements in combination with the */checked* compiler option:

```
short h = 321;
byte i = (byte)h;           // Checked if /checked
i = unchecked((byte)h);     // Always unchecked
i = checked((byte)h);       // Always checked
```

Note   To set the */checked* compiler switch in Visual Studio .NET, open the project's Property Pages dialog box, click the Configuration Properties folder and the Build properties, and set the Check For Overflow Underflow property to True or False.

Bitwise Operators

The bitwise operators are a loose group that include the shift operators << and >>, the logical operators &, ∧, and |, and five of the compound assignment operators <<=, >>=, &=, ∧=, and |=. They're called the bitwise operators because they operate on individual bits within a value. To take the simplest of these, consider first the bitwise left-shift operator:

```
class BitOpsApp
{
    static void Main(string[] args)
    {
        int i = 1;
        for (int j = 0; j < 8; j++)
        {
```

```
        Console.WriteLine(
            "{0} << {1} = {2}", i, j, i << j);
    }
  }
}
```

The output from this code will be:

```
1 << 1 = 2
1 << 2 = 4
1 << 3 = 8
1 << 4 = 16
1 << 5 = 32
1 << 6 = 64
1 << 7 = 128
```

Let's modify the output a little to use the *System.Convert* class to make this easier to follow:

```
for (int j = 0; j < 8; j++)
{
    Console.WriteLine(
        "{0:D8} << {1} = {2,8} = {3,3}",
        i, j,
        Convert.ToString((i << j), 2),
        i << j);
}
```

The output from this code will be:

```
00000001 << 1 =       10 =   2
00000001 << 2 =      100 =   4
00000001 << 3 =     1000 =   8
00000001 << 4 =    10000 =  16
00000001 << 5 =   100000 =  32
00000001 << 6 =  1000000 =  64
00000001 << 7 = 10000000 = 128
```

By the same token, the use of the right-shift operator should be fairly obvious:

```
int k = 128;
for (int n = 0; n < 8; n++)
{
    Console.WriteLine(
        "{0:D8} >> {1} = {2,8} = {3,3}",
        Convert.ToString(k, 2),
        n,
        Convert.ToString((k >> n), 2),
        k >> n);
}
```

This code will produce the following output:

```
10000000 >> 0 = 10000000 = 128
10000000 >> 1 =  1000000 =  64
10000000 >> 2 =   100000 =  32
10000000 >> 3 =    10000 =  16
10000000 >> 4 =     1000 =   8
10000000 >> 5 =      100 =   4
10000000 >> 6 =       10 =   2
10000000 >> 7 =        1 =   1
```

While we're here, let's look at the logical bitwise operators. This should take you back to Computer Science 101—no pun intended. When you bitwise AND (&) two bits, the result is set if both operands are set. When you bitwise OR (|) two bits, the result is set if one or both operands are set. When you bitwise XOR (∧) two bits, the result is set if only one operand is set. When you bitwise NOT (~), you simply toggle the bit. The following code illustrates:

```
class LogOpsApp
{
    public static void display(
        byte left, byte right, byte ans, string op)
    {
        string Lstr = null;
        string Rstr = null;
        string Astr = null;
        Lstr = Convert.ToString(left, 2);
        if (0 != right)
            Rstr = Convert.ToString(right, 2);
        else
            Rstr = "--------";
        Astr = Convert.ToString(ans, 2);

        Console.WriteLine(
            "\t{0,8}\n{1}\t{2,8}\n\t{3,8}\n",
            Lstr, op, Rstr, Astr);
    }

    static void Main(string[] args)
    {
        byte a, b, c, d, e, f, g;
        a = 255;
        b = 132;
        c = 85;
        byte OneOperand = 0;

        d = (byte)(a & b);
        display (a, b, d, "&");
```

```
        e = (byte)(d | c);
        display (d, c, e, "|");
        f = (byte)(e ^ a);
        display (e, a, f, "^");
        g = (byte)~f;
        display (f, OneOperand, g, "~");
    }
}
```

This code will produce the following output:

```
       11111111
&      10000100
       10000100

       10000100
|       1010101
       11010101

       11010101
^      11111111
         101010

         101010
~      --------
       11010101
```

The bitwise compound assignment operators are also fairly easy to follow:

```
class CompoundBitOpsApp
{
    static void Main(string[] args)
    {
        for (byte j = 0; j < 8; j++)
        {
            byte k = 1;
            Console.WriteLine(
                "1 <<= {0,3} ({1}) = {2,8} ({3,3})",
                Convert.ToString(j, 2), j,
                Convert.ToString((k <<= j), 2), k);
        }
    }
}
```

This code will produce the following output:

```
1 <<=   0 (0) =        1 (  1)
1 <<=   1 (1) =       10 (  2)
1 <<=  10 (2) =      100 (  4)
1 <<=  11 (3) =     1000 (  8)
1 <<= 100 (4) =    10000 ( 16)
```

```
1 <<= 101 (5) =   100000 ( 32)
1 <<= 110 (6) =  1000000 ( 64)
1 <<= 111 (7) = 10000000 (128)
```

Relational Operators

Most operators return a numeric result. Relational operators, however, are a bit different: they generate a Boolean result. Instead of performing some mathematical operation on a set of operands, a relational operator compares the relationship between the operands and returns a value of *true* if the relationship is true and a value of *false* if the relationship is untrue.

Comparison Operators

The set of relational operators referred to as comparison operators are less than (<), less than or equal to (<=), greater than (>), greater than or equal to (>=), equal to (==), and not equal to (!=). The meaning of each of these operators is obvious when working with numbers, but the way each operator works on objects isn't so obvious. Here's an example:

```
class NumericTest
{
    protected int i;
    public NumericTest(int i)
    {
        this.i = i;
    }
}
class RelOpRefsApp
{
    static void Main(string[] args)
    {
        NumericTest test1 = new NumericTest(42);
        NumericTest test2 = new NumericTest(42);
        Console.WriteLine("{0}", test1 == test2);
    }
}
```

If you're a Java programmer, you know what's going to happen here. However, C++ developers might be surprised to see that this example prints a value of *false*. Remember that when you instantiate an object, you get a reference to a heap-allocated object. Therefore, when you use a relational operator to compare two objects, the C# compiler doesn't compare the contents of the objects. Instead, it compares the addresses of these two objects. Once again, to fully understand what's going on here, we'll look at the MSIL for this code, shown in Figure 8-8.

```
┌─────────────────────────────────────────────────────────────────────┐
│ ▓ RelOpRefsApp::Main : void(string[])                      _ □ x      │
├─────────────────────────────────────────────────────────────────────┤
│.method private hidebysig static void  Main(string[] args) cil managed │
│{                                                                       │
│  .entrypoint                                                           │
│  .custom instance void [mscorlib]System.STAThreadAttribute::.ctor() = ( 01 00 00 00 )│
│  // Code size       36 (0x24)                                          │
│  .maxstack  3                                                          │
│  .locals init ([0] class RelOpRefs.NumericTest test1,                  │
│           [1] class RelOpRefs.NumericTest test2)                       │
│  IL_0000:  ldc.i4.s    42                                              │
│  IL_0002:  newobj      instance void RelOpRefs.NumericTest::.ctor(int32)│
│  IL_0007:  stloc.0                                                     │
│  IL_0008:  ldc.i4.s    42                                              │
│  IL_000a:  newobj      instance void RelOpRefs.NumericTest::.ctor(int32)│
│  IL_000f:  stloc.1                                                     │
│  IL_0010:  ldstr       "{0}"                                           │
│  IL_0015:  ldloc.0                                                     │
│  IL_0016:  ldloc.1                                                     │
│  IL_0017:  ceq                                                         │
│  IL_0019:  box         [mscorlib]System.Boolean                        │
│  IL_001e:  call        void [mscorlib]System.Console::WriteLine(string, │
│                                                               object)   │
│                                                                        │
│  IL_0023:  ret                                                         │
│} // end of method RelOpRefsApp::Main                                   │
│◄                                                                    ►  │
└─────────────────────────────────────────────────────────────────────┘
```

Figure 8-8 Relational operators with reference types.

Take a look at the .locals line. The compiler is declaring that this *Main* method will have two local variables, both of them *NumericTest* objects. Now skip down to lines IL_0002 and IL_0007. It's here that the MSIL instantiates the *test1* object and, with the *stloc* opcode, stores the returned reference to the first local variable. However, the key point here is that the MSIL stores the address of the newly created object. Then, in lines IL_000a and IL_000f, you can see the MSIL opcodes to create the *test2* object and store the returned reference in the second local variable. Finally, lines IL_0015 and IL_0016 simply load the local variables on the stack via a call to *ldloc*, and then line IL_0017 calls the *ceq* opcode, which compares the top two values on the stack—that is, the references to the *test1* and *test2* objects. The Boolean result of the test is boxed and then printed via the call to *WriteLine*.

How can you produce a member-by-member comparison of two objects? In the implicit base class of all .NET Framework objects. The *System.Object* class has a method named *Equals* that's designed for just this purpose. For example, the following code performs a comparison of the object contents as you'd expect and returns a value of *true*:

```
Decimal d1 = new Decimal(42);
Decimal d2 = new Decimal(42);
Console.WriteLine("{0}", d1.Equals(d2));
```

Note that the earlier example employed a user-defined class (*NumericTest*), and the second example used a .NET class (*Decimal*). This is because the *System.Object.Equals* method must be overridden to do the actual member-by-member comparison. Therefore, using the *Equals* method on the *NumericTest* class won't work because we haven't overridden the method. However, because the *Decimal* class does override the inherited *Equals* method, it works as you'd expect.

More Info   In Chapter 13, we'll consider in detail how to override the *Equals* method as well as other related strategies.

Another way to handle an object comparison is through operator overloading. Overloading an operator defines the operations that take place between objects of a specific type. For example, with string objects, the + operator concatenates the strings rather than performing an add operation.

More Info   We'll get into operator overloading in Chapter 13.

Simple Assignment Operators

As you'll recall, the value on the left side of an assignment operator is the lvalue, and the value on the right side is the rvalue. The rvalue can be any constant, variable, number, or expression that can be resolved to a value compatible with the lvalue. However, the lvalue must be a variable of a defined type. This is because a value is copied from the right to the left. Therefore, you must allocate physical space in memory, which is the ultimate destination of the new value. For example, you can state $i = 4$ because i represents a physical location in memory, either on the stack or on the heap, depending on the actual type of the i variable. However, you can't execute the statement $4 = i$ because 4 is a value, not a variable in memory—the contents of which can be changed.

Note   Technically the rule in C# is that the lvalue can be a variable, property, or indexer. For more on properties and indexers, refer back to Chapter 5. To keep things simple, we'll stick to examples using variables found in this chapter.

Although numeric assignment is fairly straightforward, assignment operations involving objects is a much trickier proposition. Remember that when you're dealing with objects, you're not dealing with simple stack-allocated elements that are easily copied and moved around. When manipulating objects, you really have only a reference to a heap-allocated entity. Therefore, when you attempt to assign an object—or any reference type—to a variable, you're not copying data as you are with value types. You're simply copying a reference from one place to another.

Let's say you have two objects: *test1* and *test2*. If you state that test1 = test2, *test1* is not a copy of *test2*. It's the same thing! The *test1* object points to the same memory as *test2*. Therefore, any changes on the *test1* object are also changes on the *test2* object. The key concept here is that when you declare a variable of a reference type using *new*, that variable is a reference to some heap memory—it's not the heap memory itself. Here's a program that illustrates this concept:

```
public class Foo
{
    public int i;
}

class RefTest1App
{
    static void Main(string[] args)
    {
        Foo test1 = new Foo();
        test1.i = 1;

        Foo test2 = new Foo();
        test2.i = 2;

        Console.WriteLine(
            "BEFORE OBJECT ASSIGNMENT");
        Console.WriteLine("test1.i={0}", test1.i);
        Console.WriteLine("test2.i={0}", test2.i);
        Console.WriteLine();

        test1 = test2;

        Console.WriteLine(
            "AFTER OBJECT ASSIGNMENT");
        Console.WriteLine("test1.i={0}", test1.i);
        Console.WriteLine("test2.i={0}", test2.i);
        Console.WriteLine();

        test1.i = 42;

        Console.WriteLine(
            "AFTER CHANGE TO ONLY TEST1 MEMBER");
        Console.WriteLine("test1.i={0}", test1.i);
        Console.WriteLine("test2.i={0}", test2.i);
    }
}
```

Run this code, and you'll see the following output:

```
BEFORE OBJECT ASSIGNMENT
test1.i=1
test2.i=2

AFTER OBJECT ASSIGNMENT
test1.i=2
test2.i=2

AFTER CHANGE TO ONLY TEST1 MEMBER
test1.i=42
test2.i=42
```

Let's walk through this example to see what happens each step of the way. *Foo* is a simple class that defines a single member named *i*. Two instances of this class—*test1* and *test2*—are created in the *Main* method and, in each case, the new object's *i* member is set—to the values of *1* and *2*, respectively. At this point, we print the values, and they look like you'd expect, with *test1.i* being *1* and *test2.i* having a value of *2*. Here's where the fun begins. The next line assigns the *test2* object to *test1*. The Java programmers in attendance know what's coming next. However, most C++ developers would expect that the *test1* object's *i* member will now be equal to the *test2* object's members—assuming that because the application compiled, there must be some kind of implicit member-wise copy operator being performed. In fact, that's the appearance given by printing the value of both object members. However, the new relationship between these objects goes much deeper than that.

The code assigns 42 to *test1.i* and once again prints the values of both object's *i* members. That's right—changing the *test1* object changed the *test2* object as well! This is because the object formerly known as *test1* no longer exists. By assigning *test1* to *test2*, we basically lose the *test1* object because it's no longer referenced in the application and is eventually collected by the garbage collector (GC). The *test1* and *test2* objects now point to the same memory on the heap. Therefore, a change made to either variable will be seen by the user of the other variable.

Notice in the last two lines of output that even though the code sets the *test1.i* value only, the *test2.i* value also is affected. Once again, this is because both variables now point to the same place in memory, the behavior you'd expect if you're a Java programmer. However, this behavior is in stark contrast to what C++ developers would expect because in C++, the act of copying objects means just that—each variable has its own unique copy of the members so that modification of one object has no impact on the other. Because this is key to understanding how to work with objects in C#, let's take a quick detour and see what happens if you pass an object to a method:

```
public class Foo
{
    public int i;
}

class RefTest2App
{
    public static void ChangeValue(Foo f)
    {
        f.i = 42;
    }

    static void Main(string[] args)
    {
        Foo test = new Foo();
        test.i = 6;

        Console.WriteLine("BEFORE METHOD CALL");
        Console.WriteLine("test.i={0}", test.i);
        Console.WriteLine();

        ChangeValue(test);

        Console.WriteLine("AFTER METHOD CALL");
        Console.WriteLine("test.i={0}", test.i);
    }
}
```

In most languages—Java excluded—this code would result in a copy of the test object being created on the local stack of the *RefTest2App.ChangeValue* method. If that were the case, the test object created in the *Main* method would never see any changes made to the *f* object within the *ChangeValue* method. However, once again, the *Main* method has passed a reference to the heap-allocated test object. When the *ChangeValue* method manipulates its local *f.i* variable, it also directly manipulates the *Main* method's *test* object:

```
BEFORE METHOD CALL
test.i=6

AFTER METHOD CALL
test.i=42
```

The Conditional Operator

Also called the ternary operator because it's the only operator in the language that takes three operands, the conditional operator can be used in place of an *if* statement in some circumstances. This operator is equivalent to the *=IF()* function offered by database systems and Microsoft Excel, for example. Lexically, the conditional operator has two parts: a question mark (?) and a colon (:), delimiting the three operands. A conditional expression of the form b? x: y first evaluates the condition *b*. Then, if *b* evaluates to *true*, *x* is evaluated and becomes the result of the operation. Otherwise, *y* is evaluated and becomes the result of the operation. A conditional expression never evaluates both *x* and *y*. The conditional operator is right-associative, meaning that operations are grouped from right to left. For example, an expression of the form a? b: c? d: e is evaluated as a? b: (c? d: e). The first operand of the ?: operator must be a Boolean expression, while the other two operands can be of any type, although one of the two must be implicitly convertible to the other. The following code illustrates:

```
class CondOpApp
{
    [STAThread]
    static void Main(string[] args)
    {
        Random rand = new Random();
        int a = 0, b = 0;

        for (int i = 0; i < 5; i++)
        {
            a = rand.Next() % 100;
            b = rand.Next() % 100;

            Console.WriteLine(
                "a={0}, b={1}, so the winner is: {2}",
                a, b,
                a > b ? 'a' : 'b');
        }
    }
}
```

This application will produce the following output—or something similar, given that we're using *Random* again:

```
a=33, b=90, so the winner is: b
a=81, b=48, so the winner is: a
a=69, b=55, so the winner is: a
a=65, b=77, so the winner is: b
a=63, b=53, so the winner is: a
```

It's interesting to see how the MSIL for the conditional operator compares with the MSIL generated for the equivalent *if* statement. Compare these equivalent C# statements:

```
char c = ' ';
c = (a > b) ? 'a' : 'b';
Console.WriteLine("{0} is bigger", c);

if (a > b)
    c = 'a';
else
    c = 'b';
Console.WriteLine("{0} is bigger", c);
```

The MSIL for this code is shown in Figure 8-9.

```
CondOpApp::Main : void(string[])
  IL_004f:  ldc.i4.s    32
  IL_0051:  stloc.s     c
  IL_0053:  ldloc.1
  IL_0054:  ldloc.2
  IL_0055:  bgt.s       IL_005b
  IL_0057:  ldc.i4.s    98
  IL_0059:  br.s        IL_005d
  IL_005b:  ldc.i4.s    97
  IL_005d:  stloc.s     c
  IL_005f:  ldstr       "{0} is bigger"
  IL_0064:  ldloc.s     c
  IL_0066:  box         [mscorlib]System.Char
  IL_006b:  call        void [mscorlib]System.Console::WriteLine(string,
                                                                 object)

  IL_0070:  ldloc.1
  IL_0071:  ldloc.2
  IL_0072:  ble.s       IL_007a
  IL_0074:  ldc.i4.s    97
  IL_0076:  stloc.s     c
  IL_0078:  br.s        IL_007e
  IL_007a:  ldc.i4.s    98
  IL_007c:  stloc.s     c
  IL_007e:  ldstr       "{0} is bigger"
  IL_0083:  ldloc.s     c
  IL_0085:  box         [mscorlib]System.Char
  IL_008a:  call        void [mscorlib]System.Console::WriteLine(string,
                                                                 object)

  IL_008f:  ret
} // end of method CondOpApp::Main
```

Figure 8-9   MSIL for conditional operator vs. *if* statement.

As you can see, using the conditional operator, the system loads the two variables onto the evaluation stack and performs the comparison, using the opcode *bgt* (branch greater than). That is, if the first variable is greater than the second, execution branches to IL_005b, where the value *97* ('a') is pushed onto the stack. This bypasses the instruction at IL_0057, where the value *98* ('b') is pushed onto the stack—and this instruction is executed only if the *bgt* isn't performed. Using the *if* statement instead, you can see that the MSIL uses the *ble* opcode (branch on less than or equal), and one more *stloc.s* opcode (pop the value off the top of the evaluation stack and store it in the variable—*c*, in this case).

It seems that the conditional operator will result in marginally smaller—though no more efficient—MSIL. Is that a good enough reason to use it? The counterargument is to consider the ease with which you can maintain code that makes heavy use of the conditional operator. Compare the following:

```
int d = 10, e = 100;
if (a > b)
    if (a > d)
        if (a > e)
            Console.WriteLine("a");
        else
            Console.WriteLine("e");
    else
        Console.WriteLine("d");
else
    Console.WriteLine("b");

Console.WriteLine(
    (a > b) ? ((a > d) ?
    ((a > e) ? "a" : "e") : "d") : "b");
```

The two blocks are equivalent: again, one uses nested *if..else* statements, while the other uses nested conditional operators. The first takes longer to type in, but the second will to be a serious pain in the neck to maintain.

Summary

A key part of any programming language is the way that it handles assignment, mathematical, relational, and logical operations to perform the basic work required by any real-world application. These operations are controlled in code through operators. Factors that determine the effects that operators have in code include precedence and left and right associativity. In addition to providing a powerful set of predefined operators, C# extends these operators through user-defined implementations, which we'll discuss in Chapter 13.

9

Program Flow Control

Most programming languages provide *program flow statements*—also known as *execution control statements*—that enable you to control the order of statement execution within an application. In the C# language, these statements can be split into three distinct categories—selection, iteration, and branching. The statements include keywords that are probably familiar to you, such as *if*, *switch*, *while*, *for*, *goto*, and *return*—all of which we'll cover in this chapter, along with a few others. As you'll see in this chapter, the majority of these statements evaluate an expression that results in a Boolean value. This value is then used to determine which statement to execute next. As we discuss each program flow statement, not only will I try to teach you the semantics of it, I'll also illustrate when and why the statement should be used so that you can achieve the desired results in your code.

Selection Statements

Selection statements are used to determine what code should be executed and when. C# features two selection statements: the *switch* statement, used to run code based on a value, and the *if* statement, which runs code based on a Boolean condition. The most commonly used selection statement is the *if* statement.

The *if* Statement

The *if* statement executes one or more statements if the expression being evaluated is *true*. The *if* statement's syntax follows. The square brackets denote the optional use of the *else* statement, which we'll cover shortly.

```
if (expression)
    statement1
[else
    statement2]
```

Here, *expression* is any test that produces a Boolean result. If *expression* results in *true*, control is passed to *statement1*. If the result is *false* and an *else* clause exists, control is passed to *statement2*. Also note that *statement1* and *statement2* can consist of a single statement terminated by a semicolon—known as a *simple statement*—or of multiple statements enclosed in braces—known as a *compound statement*. The following illustrates a compound statement being used if *expression1* resolves to *true*:

```
if (expression1)
{
    statement1
    statement2
}
```

In the following example, the application requests that the user type in a number between 1 and 10. A random number is then generated, and the user is told whether the number he or she picked matches the random number. This simple example illustrates how to use the *if* statement in C#:

```csharp
using System;

class IfTest
{
    const int MAX = 10;

    public static void Main()
    {
        Console.WriteLine("This is a simple demo of the " +
            "if statement usage.\n");
        Console.Write("Guess a number between 1 and {0}...",
            MAX);
        string inputString = Console.ReadLine();

        int userGuess = Convert.ToInt32(inputString);

        Random rnd = new Random();
        double correctNumber = rnd.NextDouble() * MAX;
        correctNumber = Math.Round(correctNumber);

        Console.Write("The correct number was {0} and " +
            "you guessed {1}...",
        correctNumber, userGuess);
```

```
if (userGuess == correctNumber) // They got it right!
{
    Console.WriteLine("Congratulations!");
}
else // Wrong answer!
{
    Console.WriteLine("maybe next time!");
}
    }
}
```

Figure 9-1 shows the output from this simple demo application.

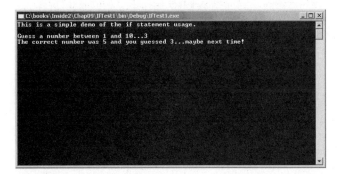

Figure 9-1   The *if* statement enables you to specify execution flow based on run-time decisions.

Multiple *else* Clauses

The *if* statement's *else* clause enables you to specify an alternative course of action should the *if* statement resolve to *false*. In the number-guessing example, the application performed a simple comparison between the number the user guessed and the randomly generated number. Only two possibilities existed: the user was either correct or incorrect. You can also combine *if* and *else* to handle situations in which you want to test more than two conditions. In the example that follows, I ask the user which language he or she is currently using, excluding C#. I've included the ability to select from three languages; therefore, the *if* statement must be able to deal with four possible answers: the three languages I've specified, and the possibility that the user selects an unknown language. Here's one way of programming this with an *if/else* statement:

```csharp
using System;

class IfTest2
{
    const string CPlusPlus = "C++";
    const string VisualBasic = "Visual Basic";
    const string Java = "Java";

    public static void Main()
    {
        Console.Write("What is your current language of choice " +
                "(excluding C#)?");
        string inputString = Console.ReadLine();

        if (0 == String.Compare(inputString, CPlusPlus, true))
        {
            Console.WriteLine("\nYou'll have no problem " +
                "picking up C# !");
        }
        else if (0 == String.Compare(inputString, VisualBasic,
            true))
        {
            Console.WriteLine("\nYou'll find lots of cool " +
                "VB features in C# !");
        }
        else if (0 == String.Compare(inputString,
            Java, true))
        {
            Console.WriteLine("\nYou'll have an easier time " +
                "picking up C# <G> !!");
        }
        else
        {
            Console.WriteLine("\nSorry - doesn't compute.");
        }
    }
}
```

Figure 9-2 shows the output from this application.

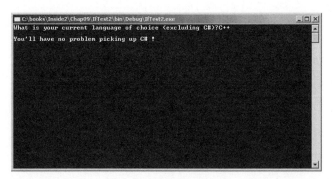

Figure 9-2 The *else* statement enables you to specify an alternative course of action should the *if* statement resolve to *false*.

Looking back at the *IfTest2* code, notice the use of the == operator to compare 0 to the returned value of *String.Compare*. We do this because *String.Compare* will return −1 if the first string is less than the second string, 1 if the first string is greater than the second, and 0 if the two are identical. However, this example illustrates some interesting details, described next, about how C# enforces use of the *if* statement.

How C# Enforces *if* Rules

One aspect of the *if* statement that catches new C# programmers off guard is that the expression evaluated must result in a Boolean value. This is in contrast with languages such as C++, in which you're allowed to use the *if* statement to test for any variable that has a value other than 0. The following example illustrates several common errors that C++ developers make when attempting to use the *if* statement in C# for the first time:

```
using System;

interface ITest
{
}

class TestClass : ITest
{
}

class InvalidIf
{
    protected static TestClass GetTestClass()
    {
        return new TestClass();
    }
```

```
public static void Main()
{
    int foo = 1;
    if (foo) // ERROR: attempting to convert int to bool
    {
    }

    TestClass t = GetTestClass();
    if (t) // ERROR: attempting to convert TestClass to bool
    {
        Console.WriteLine("{0}", t);

        ITest i = t as ITest;
        if (i) // ERROR: attempting to convert ITest to bool
        {
            // ITest methods
        }
    }
}
}
```

If you attempt to compile this code, you'll receive compile-time errors indicating that the conversion from the types used in the *if* statement to the Boolean type required by an *if* statement couldn't be made. These errors are shown in the Microsoft Visual Studio Build window in Figure 9-3.

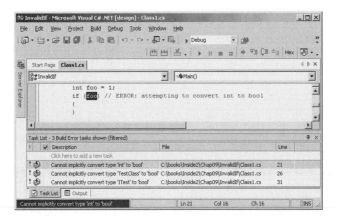

Figure 9-3   In contrast with languages such as C and C++, the expression being evaluated in a C# *if* statement must evaluate to a Boolean type.

As you can see, the compiler barks three times in response to three attempts to use the *if* statement with an operation that doesn't yield a Boolean value. The reason for this response is that the C# designers want to help you avoid ambiguous code and believe that the compiler should enforce the original purpose of the *if* statement—that is, to control the flow of execution based on the result of a Boolean test. The previous example is rewritten next to compile without error. Each line that caused the compiler error in the previous program has been modified to contain an expression that returns a Boolean result, thereby appeasing the compiler.

```
using System;

interface ITest
{

}

class TestClass : ITest
{
}

class ValidIf
{
    protected static TestClass GetTestClass()
    {
        return new TestClass();
    }

    public static void Main()
    {
        Console.WriteLine("This  code snippet " +
            "illustrates simple usage " +
            "of the if statement.\n");

        int foo = 1;
        if (foo > 0)
        {
            Console.WriteLine("foo is greater than 0");
        }

        TestClass t = GetTestClass();
        if (t != null)
        {
            Console.WriteLine("t is an object of type {0}", t);

            ITest i = t as ITest;
            if (i != null)
            {
                Console.WriteLine("i is an object of type {0}",
                    i);
```

```
            }
        }
        Console.ReadLine();
    }
}
```

The output of this program is shown in Figure 9-4.

Figure 9-4 To test non-Boolean expressions within an *if* statement, you must use one of the comparison operators so that the result of that comparison is the basis for the *if* statement.

The *switch* Statement

Using the *switch* statement, you can specify an expression that returns an integral value and one or more pieces of code that will be run, depending on the result of the expression. Using the *switch* statement is similar to using multiple *if/else* statements, but with one caveat: although you can specify multiple—possibly unrelated—conditional statements with multiple *if/else* statements, a *switch* statement consists of only one conditional statement followed by all the results that your code is prepared to handle. Here's the syntax:

```
switch (switch_expression)
{
    case constant-expression:
        statement
        jump-statement

    case constant-expressionN:
        statementN
    [default]
}
```

There are two main rules to keep in mind here. First, the *switch_expression* must be of the type—or implicitly convertible to—*sbyte, byte, short, ushort, int, uint, long, ulong, char, string*, or an enum based on one of these types. Second, you must provide a *jump-statement* (such as a *break* statement) for each *case* statement—unless a *case* statement is the last one in the switch. Because this behavior differs from that of several other languages, I'll explain it more thoroughly later in this section, in the discussion "No Fall-Through in *switch* Statements."

Conceptually, the *switch* statement works the same way as the *if* statement does. First, the *switch_expression* is evaluated, and then the result is compared to each of the *constant-expressions* or *case labels*, defined in the different *case* statements. Once a match is made, control is passed to the first line of code in that *case* statement.

In addition to letting you specify different *case* statements, the *switch* statement allows for the definition of a *default* statement. This *default* clause is similar to the *else* clause of an *if* statement. Note that there can be only one default label for each *switch* statement and that if no appropriate case label is found for the *switch_expression*, control is passed to the first line of code after the *switch* statement's ending brace. Here's an example—a *Payment* class that uses the *switch* statement to determine which tender has been selected:

```
using System;

enum Tenders : int
{
    Cash = 1,
    Visa,
    MasterCard,
    AmericanExpress
};

class Payment
{
    public Payment(Tenders tender)
    {
        this.Tender = tender;
    }

    protected Tenders tender;
    public Tenders Tender
    {
        get
        {
            return this.tender;
        }
        set
        {
```

```
                this.tender = value;
            }
        }


        public void ProcessPayment()
        {
            switch ((int)(this.tender))
            {
                case (int)Tenders.Cash:
                    Console.WriteLine("\nCash - Always good");
                    break;

                case (int)Tenders.Visa:
                    Console.WriteLine("\nVisa - Accepted");
                    break;

                case (int)Tenders.MasterCard:
                    Console.WriteLine("\nMasterCard - Accepted");
                    break;

                case (int)Tenders.AmericanExpress:
                    Console.WriteLine("\nAmerican Express - " +
                        "Accepted");
                    break;

                default:
                    Console.WriteLine("\nSorry - Invalid tender");
                    break;
            }
        }
    }

    class Switch
    {
        public static void DisplayMenu()
        {
            Console.WriteLine("Which form of payment is " +
                "being used:");
            Console.WriteLine("\t1 = Cash");
            Console.WriteLine("\t2 = Visa");
            Console.WriteLine("\t3 = MasterCard");
            Console.WriteLine("\t4 = American Express");
            Console.Write("===>");
        }


        public static int GetTender()
        {
            int tenderChoice = -1;
```

```
        DisplayMenu();

        bool validTender = false;
        while (!validTender)
        {
            string str = Console.ReadLine();
            tenderChoice = Convert.ToInt32(str);

            if (tenderChoice >= 0
                && tenderChoice <= 4)
                validTender = true;
            else
                Console.WriteLine("Invalid choice - try again");
        }

        return tenderChoice;
    }

    public static void Main()
    {
        Tenders tenderChoice = (Tenders)GetTender();
        Payment payment = new Payment(tenderChoice);
        payment.ProcessPayment();

        Console.ReadLine();
    }
}
```

Figure 9-5 illustrates an example of running this application in which I selected the cash payment—thus causing the *Payment* class to be instantiated with a value of *Tenders.Cash*.

Figure 9-5   *Switch* statements provide a more elegant and readable approach than *if/else* statements.

Combining Case Labels

In the *Payment* example, we used a different case label for each possible evaluation of the *Payment.tender* field. But what if you want to combine case labels? For example, you might want to display a credit card authorization dialog box for any of the three credit card types deemed valid in the *Tenders* enum. In that case, you could place the case labels one right after the other. In the following example, a menu is presented and the user can select from four tenders (cash, or one of the three types of credit card). Based on the tender selected, a text message is displayed. Because three of the four accepted tenders would involve displaying an authorization dialog box, I've combined those three case labels.

```
using System;

enum Tenders : int
{
    Cash = 1,
    Visa,
    MasterCard,
    AmericanExpress
};

class Payment
{
    public Payment(Tenders tender)
    {
        this.Tender = tender;
    }

    protected Tenders tender;
    public Tenders Tender
    {
        get
        {
            return this.tender;
        }
        set
        {
            this.tender = value;
        }
    }

    public void ProcessPayment()
    {
        switch ((int)(this.tender))
        {
```

```csharp
            case (int)Tenders.Cash:
                Console.WriteLine("\nCash - Everyone's " +
                    "favorite tender.");
                break;

            case (int)Tenders.Visa:
            case (int)Tenders.MasterCard:
            case (int)Tenders.AmericanExpress:
                Console.WriteLine("\nDisplay Credit " +
                    "Card Authorization Dialog.");
                break;

            default:
                Console.WriteLine("\nSorry - Invalid tender.");
                break;
        }
    }
}

class CombiningCaseLabels
{
    public static void DisplayMenu()
    {
        Console.WriteLine("Which form of payment is " +
            "being used:");
        Console.WriteLine("\t1 = Cash");
        Console.WriteLine("\t2 = Visa");
        Console.WriteLine("\t3 = MasterCard");
        Console.WriteLine("\t4 = American Express");
        Console.Write("===>");
    }

    public static int GetTender()
    {
        int tenderChoice = -1;

        DisplayMenu();

        bool validTender = false;
        while (!validTender)
        {
            string str = Console.ReadLine();
            tenderChoice = Convert.ToInt32(str);

            if (tenderChoice >= 0
                && tenderChoice <= 4)
                validTender = true;
            else
```

```
            Console.WriteLine("Invalid choice - try again");
        }

        return tenderChoice;
    }

    static void Main(string[] args)
    {
        Tenders tenderChoice = (Tenders)GetTender();
        Payment payment = new Payment(tenderChoice);
        payment.ProcessPayment();
    }
}
}
```

If you now run the application and select the Visa, MasterCard, or American Express menu option, you'll see the output shown in Figure 9-6.

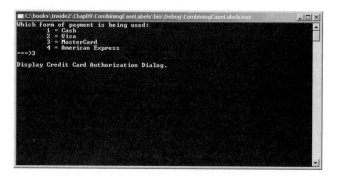

Figure 9-6 *Case* statements can be grouped when appropriate to realize code that's more readable and therefore, easier to maintain.

No Fall-Through in *switch* Statements

Throughout the design phase of C#, the designers were cognizant of applying a risk/reward test when deciding whether a feature should be included in the language. The fall-through feature is one that didn't pass the test. Normally in C++, a *case* statement runs when its *constant-expression* matches the *switch_expression*. The *switch* statement is then exited with a *break* statement. Fall-through causes the next *case* statement in the *switch* statement to execute in the absence of a *break* statement.

Though not supported in C#, fall-through is typically used in situations in which you have two case labels and the second label represents an operation that will be performed in either case. For example, I once wrote a database editor in C++ that allowed end users to create their tables and fields graphically. Each of these tables was displayed in a tree view in a Microsoft Windows

Explorer–like user interface. In the event that the end user right-clicked the tree view, I wanted to display a menu with options such as Print All Tables and Create New Table. In the event that the end user right-clicked a specific table, I wanted to display a context menu for that table. However, that context menu also needed to include all the tree view options. Conceptually my code was similar to the following:

```
// Dynamically create menu in C++.
switch (itemSelected)
{

    case TABLE:
        // Add menu options based on current table;
        // break left out intentionally.

    case TREE_VIEW:
        // Add menu options for tree view.
        break;
}
// Display menu.
```

The first case label amounts to a combination of the two labels without having to duplicate code or insert two calls to the same method. However, the C# language designers decided that although this feature can be handy, its reward wasn't worth the risk involved. This is because the majority of the time, a *break* statement is left out unintentionally, which results in bugs that are difficult to track down.

To accomplish this task in C#, you have two options. The first option is to simply use an *if* statement as in the following example. Notice that if the item selected is a table, the user will see both table and tree view menu items. But if the selected item isn't a table, the user will see only tree view menu items.

```
// Dynamically create menu.
if (itemSelected == TABLE)
{
    // Add menu options based on current table.
}
// Add menu options for tree view.
// Display menu.
```

The second way to solve this lack of switch fall-through syntax is by using the *goto* statement. I'll cover the *goto* statement in more detail later in this chapter in the "Branching with Jump Statements" section, but its usage should be clear here—a *goto* statement simply allows you to specify a jump from one point of execution to another. Using the *goto* statement, we can now code our example as follows:

```
// Dynamically create menu.
switch(itemSelected)
{

    case TABLE:
        // Add menu options based on current table;
        // break left out intentionally.
        goto case TREE_VIEW;

    case TREE_VIEW:
        // Add menu options for tree view.
        break;
}
// Display menu.
```

Although I'll admit that I wasn't too fond of this change at first, I now realize that the one extra line of code required to explicitly specify my intentions is more than offset by the risks involved in unintentionally omitting a *break* statement. In addition, the explicit branching makes it easier to write *switch* statements in which I need to jump over other blocks instead of simply falling through to the next statement block:

```
// Dynamically create menu.
switch(itemSelected)
{

    case TABLE:
        // Add menu options based on current table;
        // break left out intentionally.
        goto case TREE_VIEW;

    case FIELD:
        // Add menu options based on current table;
        // break left out intentionally.
        goto case TREE_VIEW;

    case TREE_VIEW:
        // Add menu options for tree view.
        break;
}
// Display menu.
```

Iteration Statements

In C#, the *while*, *do/while*, *for*, and *foreach* statements enable you to perform controlled iteration, or looping. In each case, a specified simple or compound statement is executed until a Boolean expression resolves to *true*, except for the case of the *foreach* statement, which is used to iterate through a list of objects.

The *while* Statement

The *while* statement takes the following form:

while (*Boolean-expression*)

   embedded-statement

Using the number-guessing example from earlier in the chapter in "The *if* Statement" section, we could rewrite the example with a *while* statement so that you could continue the game until you either guessed the correct number or decided to quit:

```
using System;

class While
{
    const int MIN = 1;
    const int MAX = 10;
    const string QUIT_CHAR = "Q";

    public static void Main()
    {
        Random rnd = new Random();
        double correctNumber;

        string inputString;
        int userGuess;

        bool correctGuess = false;
        bool userQuit = false;

        while (!correctGuess && !userQuit)
        {
            correctNumber = rnd.NextDouble() * MAX;
            correctNumber = Math.Round(correctNumber);

            Console.Write("Guess a number between {0} and " +
                "{1}...({2} to quit)",
                MIN, MAX, QUIT_CHAR);
```

```
            inputString = Console.ReadLine();

            if (0 == string.Compare(inputString,
                QUIT_CHAR, true))
                userQuit = true;
            else
            {
                userGuess = Convert.ToInt32(inputString);
                correctGuess = (userGuess == correctNumber);

                Console.WriteLine("The correct number " +
                    "was {0}\n", correctNumber);
            }
        }

        if (correctGuess && !userQuit)
        {
            Console.WriteLine("Congratulations!");
        }
        else
        {
            Console.WriteLine("Maybe next time!");
        }
    }
}
```

Coding and running this application will result in output similar to that shown in Figure 9-7.

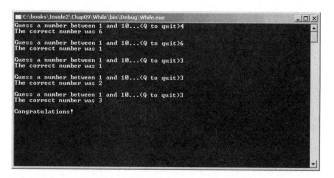

Figure 9-7   The *while* statement enables you to loop, or cycle, through code until a specified criteria is met.

The *do/while* Statement

Looking back at the syntax for the *while* statement, you can see the possibility for one problem. The *Boolean-expression* is evaluated before the *embedded-*

statement is executed. For this reason, the previous application initialized the *correctGuess* and *userQuit* variables to *false* to guarantee that the *while* loop would be entered. From there, those values are controlled by whether the user correctly guesses the number or quits. But what if we want to make sure that the *embedded-statement* always executes at least once without having to set the variables artificially? This is what we use the *do/while* statement for.

The *do/while* statement takes the following form:

do

    embedded-statement

while (*Boolean-expression*)

Because the evaluation of the *while* statement's *Boolean-expression* occurs after the *embedded-statement*, you're guaranteed that the *embedded-statement* will be executed at least one time. The number-guessing application rewritten to use the *do/while* statement appears as follows:

```
using System;

class DoWhile
{
    const int MIN = 1;
    const int MAX = 10;
    const string QUIT_CHAR = "Q";

    public static void Main()
    {
        Random rnd = new Random();
        double correctNumber;

        string inputString;
        int userGuess = -1;

        bool userHasNotQuit = true;

        Console.WriteLine("This is a number guessing game " +
            "that shows the " +
            "use of the do/while statement.\n");
        do
        {
            correctNumber = rnd.NextDouble() * MAX;
            correctNumber = Math.Round(correctNumber);

            Console.Write("Guess a number between {0} and " +
                "{1}...({2} to quit)",
                MIN, MAX, QUIT_CHAR);
```

```
        inputString = Console.ReadLine();

        if (0 == string.Compare(inputString,
            QUIT_CHAR, true))
            userHasNotQuit = false;
        else
        {
            userGuess = Convert.ToInt32(inputString);
            Console.WriteLine("The correct number " +
                "was {0}\n", correctNumber);
        }
    } while (userGuess != correctNumber
        && userHasNotQuit);

    if (userHasNotQuit
        && userGuess == correctNumber)
    {
        Console.WriteLine("Congratulations!");
    }
    else // Wrong answer!
    {
        Console.WriteLine("Maybe next time!");
    }
  }
}
```

Building and executing the DoWhile application, which is shown in Figure 9-8, should yield the same type of output you saw with the While application.

Figure 9-8   The *do/while* statement functions almost identically to the *while* statement by enabling you to loop, or cycle, through code until a specified criteria is met.

The only difference between the two applications is how the loop is controlled. In practice, you'll find that the *while* statement is used more often than the *do/while* statement. However, because you can easily control entry into the loop with the initialization of a Boolean variable, choosing one statement over the other is a matter of personal preference.

The *for* Statement

By far, the most common iteration statement that you'll see and use is the *for* statement. The *for* statement is made up of three parts. One part is used to perform initialization at the beginning of the loop—this part is carried out only once. The second part is the conditional test that determines whether the loop will be run again. And the last part, known as *stepping*, is typically (but not necessarily) used to increment the counter that controls the loop's continuation—this counter is what's usually tested in the second part. The *for* statement takes the following form:

for (*initialization; Boolean-expression; step*)
   embedded-statement

Note that any of the three parts—*initialization, Boolean-expression, step*—can be empty. When *Boolean-expression* evaluates to *false*, control is passed from the top of the loop to the next line following the *embedded-statement*. Therefore, the *for* statement works the same way as a *while* statement except that it gives you the additional two parts, *initialization* and *step*. Here's an example of a *for* statement that displays the printable ASCII characters:

```
using System;

class ForTestApp
{
    const int StartChar = 33;
    const int EndChar = 125;

    static public void Main()
    {
        for (int i = StartChar; i <= EndChar; i++)
        {
            Console.WriteLine("{0}={1}", i, (char)i);
        }
    }
}
```

The output of this program is shown in Figure 9-9.

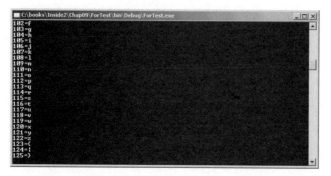

Figure 9-9 The *for* statement enables you to easily iterate through a collection—such as an array—of elements.

The order of events for this *for* loop is as follows:

1. A value-type variable (*i*) is allocated on the stack and initialized to 33. Note that this variable will be out of scope once the *for* loop concludes.

2. The embedded statement will execute while the variable *i* has a value less than 126. In this example, I used a compound statement. However, because this *for* loop consists of a single line statement, you could also write this code without the braces and get the same results.

3. After each iteration through the loop, the *i* variable will be incremented by 1.

Nested Loops

In the *embedded-statement* of a *for* loop, you can also have other *for* loops, which are generally referred to as *nested loops*. Using the previous example, I've added a nested loop that causes the application to print three characters per line, instead of one per line:

```
using System;

class NestedFor
{
    const int StartChar = 33;
    const int EndChar = 125;
    const int CharactersPerLine = 5;

    static public void Main()
    {
        Console.WriteLine("This simple app displays " +
```

```
            "the printable ASCII characters");
        Console.WriteLine("while illustrating the use " +
            "of nested for loops.\n");

        for (int i = StartChar; i <= EndChar;
            i+=CharactersPerLine)
        {
            for (int j = 0; j < CharactersPerLine;  j++)
            {
                Console.Write("{0}={1} ", i+j, (char)(i+j));
            }
            Console.WriteLine("");
        }
    }
}
```

Note that the variable *i* that was defined in the outer loop is still in scope for the internal loop. However, the variable *j* isn't available to the outer loop. Figure 9-10 shows the output that results from building and running the NestedFor application.

Figure 9-10   You can easily nest *for* statements in C#.

Using the Comma Operator

Not only can a comma can serve as a separator in method argument lists, but it can serve as an operator in a *for* statement. In both the *initialization* and *step* portions of a *for* statement, the comma operator can be used to delimit multiple statements that are processed sequentially. In the following example, I've taken the nested loop example you saw a moment ago and converted it to a single *for* loop by using the comma operator:

```
using System;

class CommaOp1
{
```

```
const int StartChar = 33;
const int EndChar = 125;
const int CharactersPerLine = 5;

static public void Main()
{
    Console.WriteLine("Output of printable " +
        "ASCII characters...\n");
    for (int i = StartChar, j = 1; i <= EndChar; i++, j++)
    {
        Console.Write("{0}={1} ", i, (char)i);
        if (0 == (j % CharactersPerLine))
        {
            // New line if j is divisible
            // by CharactersByLine var
            Console.WriteLine("");
        }
    }
}
}
```

If you build and run the CommaOpp1 application shown in Figure 9-11, you'll see a more visually appealing result than that produced by the ForTest application in which the ASCII characters were simply dumped to the standard output device without regard to formatting.

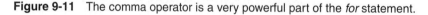

Figure 9-11 The comma operator is a very powerful part of the *for* statement.

Using the comma operator in the *for* statement can be powerful, but it can also lead to code that's ugly and difficult to maintain. Although the following code features the addition of constants, it's an example of using the comma operator in a technically correct but inappropriate manner:

```
using System;

class CommaOp2
```

```
{
    const int StartChar = 33;
    const int EndChar = 125;

    const int CharsPerLine = 5;
    const int NewLine = 10; // Carriage return character
    const int Space = 32;

    static public void Main()
    {
        Console.WriteLine("This output should be the same " +
            "as produced by CommaOp1");
        Console.WriteLine("However, the obtuse usage of " +
            "the for loop below");
        Console.WriteLine("makes this code much more " +
            "difficult to read and maintain.\n");

        for (int i = StartChar, extra = Space;
            i <= EndChar;
            i++, extra = ((0 == (i - (StartChar-1))
            % CharsPerLine)
            ? NewLine : Space))
        {
            Console.Write("{0}={1} {2}", i, (char)i,
                (char)extra);
        }
    }
}
```

You can see the output from the CommaOpp1 and CommaOpp2 applications in Figure 9-12. But looking at the code, which would you want to be responsible for maintaining?

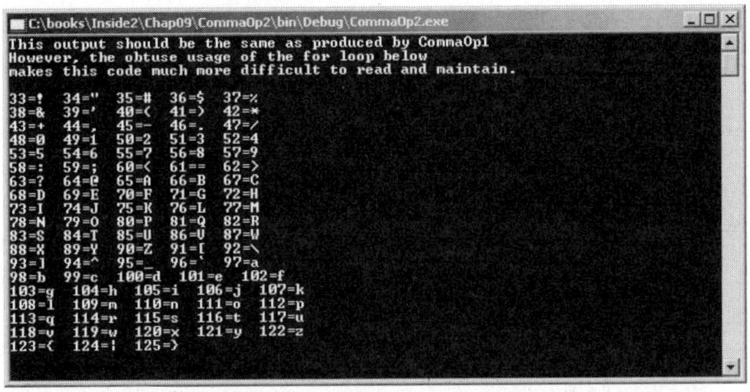

Figure 9-12   While the comma operator might seem fun to play with, take care not to become so obtuse with your code that it's unreadable to everyone else.

The *foreach* Statement

For years, languages such as Microsoft Visual Basic have had a special statement specifically designed for the iteration of arrays and collections. C# also has such a construct—the *foreach* statement, which takes the following form:

foreach (*type* in *expression*)

   embedded-statement

Take a look at the following array class:

```
class MyArray
{
    public ArrayList words;

    public MyArray()
    {
        words = new ArrayList();
        words.Add("foo");
        words.Add("bar");
        words.Add("baz");
    }
}
```

From the various iteration statements you've already seen, you know that this array can be traversed using any of several statements. However, to most Java and C++ programmers, the most logical way to write this application would be like this:

```
using System;
using System.Collections;

class MyArray
{
    public ArrayList words;

    public MyArray()
    {
        words = new ArrayList();
        words.Add("foo");
        words.Add("bar");
        words.Add("baz");
    }
}

class ForEach1
{
    public static void Main()
```

```
    {
        MyArray myArray = new MyArray();

        Console.WriteLine("Simply iterating through a " +
            "small array and printing");
        Console.WriteLine("out each element in order to " +
            "show the use of a for  loop.");
        Console.WriteLine("In this case, a foreach " +
            "statement would work better.\n");

        Console.WriteLine("{0} elements:\n",
            myArray.ToString());
        for (int i = 0; i < myArray.words.Count; i++)
        {
            Console.WriteLine("[{0}] = {1}", i,
                myArray.words[i]);
        }
    }
}
```

Figure 9-13 illustrates the results of using the *for* loop to iterate through and display the elements of our array.

Figure 9-13   The *for* loop can be used to easily iterate through an array of objects, but in C#, there are better, safer ways to perform this task.

Although this code certainly works, the approach is fraught with potential problems:

- If the *for* statement's initialization variable (*i*) isn't initialized properly, the entire list won't be iterated.

- If the *for* statement's Boolean expression isn't correct, the entire list won't be iterated.

- If the *for* statement's *step* isn't correct, the entire list won't be iterated.

- Collections and arrays have different methods and properties for accessing their count.

- Collections and arrays have different semantics for extracting a specific element.

- The *for* loop's embedded statement needs to extract the element into a variable of the correct type.

This code can go wrong many ways. Using the *foreach* statement, you can avoid these problems and iterate through any collection or array in a uniform manner. With the *foreach* statement, the previous code would be rewritten as follows:

```
using System;
using System.Collections;

class MyArray
{
    public ArrayList words;

    public MyArray()
    {
        words = new ArrayList();
        words.Add("foo");
        words.Add("bar");
        words.Add("baz");
    }
}

class ForEach2
{
    public static void Main()
    {
        Console.WriteLine("The foreach statement eliminates " +
            "many potential bugs when iterating through an " +
            "array or collection of objects.\n");

        MyArray myArray = new MyArray();

        Console.WriteLine("{0} elements:\n",
            myArray.ToString());
        foreach (string word in myArray.words)
        {
            Console.WriteLine("{0}", word);
        }
    }
}
```

As you can see in Figure 9-14, the ForEach2 application runs identically to the ForEach1 application. However, notice how much more intuitive using the *foreach* statement is. You're guaranteed to get every element because you don't have to manually set up the loop and request the count, and the statement automatically places the current element in a variable that you name. Furthermore, you need only refer to your variable in the embedded statement.

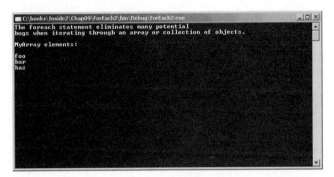

Figure 9-14   The *foreach* statement makes it easy to iterate through a collection of objects.

Branching with Jump Statements

Inside the embedded statements of any iteration statement we've covered in the previous sections, you can control the flow of execution with one of several statements collectively known as jump statements: *break*, *continue*, *goto*, and *return*.

The *break* Statement

You use the *break* statement to terminate the current enclosing loop or conditional statement in which it appears. Control is then passed to the line of code following the embedded statement of that loop or conditional statement. The *break* statement, which has the simplest syntax of any statement, has no parentheses or arguments and takes the following form at the point where you want to transfer out of a loop or conditional statement:

```
break
```

In the following example, the application will attempt print every number from 1 to 50, noting each number that's equally divisible by 5. However, when the count reaches 20, the *break* statement will cause the *for* loop to discontinue.

```
using System;

class BreakTest
{
    Console.WriteLine("This is a demo of the break " +
        "statement.\n");

    const int magicNumber = 5;
    const int limit = 50;
    const int breakPoint = 20;

    public static void Main()
    {
        for (int i = 1; i <= limit; i++)
        {
            if (0 == i % magicNumber)
            {
                Console.WriteLine("{0} is divisible by {1}",
                    i, magicNumber);
            }
            else
            {
                Console.WriteLine("{0} is NOT divisible by {1}",
                    i, magicNumber);
            }

            if (i == breakPoint)
            {
                break;
            }
        }
    }
}
```

Figure 9-15 illustrates the output generated from this application. Note that a *for* statement was used to loop from 1 to 50, but an *if* statement was used to determine whether the value was equally divisible by 5. Once the breakpoint (20) was reached, a *break* statement was used to discontinue the execution of the *for* loop.

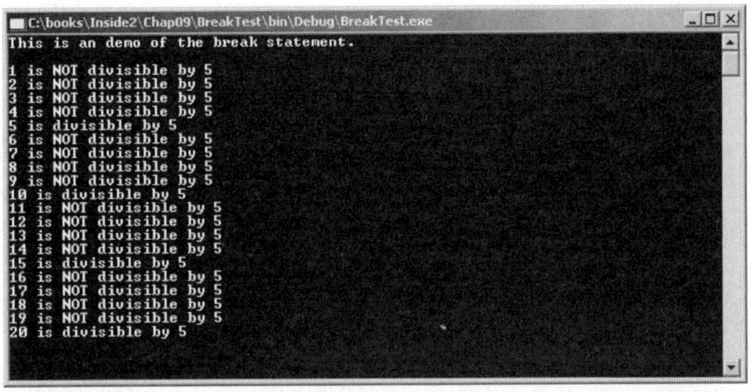

Figure 9-15   The *break* statement enables you to terminate the closest enclosing loop or expression so that control is immediately passed out of that context.

Breaking Out of Infinite Loops

Another use for the *break* statement is to create an infinite loop in which control is transferred out of the loop only by a *break* statement being reached. The following example illustrates a method of writing the number-guessing game (presented earlier in the chapter in the "The *if* Statement" section) with a *break* statement that's used to quit the loop once the user enters the letter *Q*. Notice that I changed the *while* statement to *while(true)* so that it won't end until a *break* statement is encountered.

```
using System;

class InfiniteLoop
{
    const int MIN = 1;
    const int MAX = 10;
    const string QUIT_CHAR = "Q";

    public static void Main()
    {
        Random rnd = new Random();
        double correctNumber;

        string inputString;
        int userGuess;

        bool correctGuess = false;
        bool userQuit = false;

        while(true)
        {
        correctNumber = rnd.NextDouble() * MAX;
        correctNumber = Math.Round(correctNumber);
```

```
Console.Write("Guess a number between {0} and " +
    "{1}...({2} to quit)",
    MIN, MAX, QUIT_CHAR);
inputString = Console.ReadLine();

if (0 == string.Compare(inputString, QUIT_CHAR, true))
{
    userQuit = true;
    break;
}
else
{
    userGuess = Convert.ToInt32(inputString);
    correctGuess = (userGuess == correctNumber);

    Console.WriteLine("The correct number was {0}\n",
        correctNumber);

    if ((correctGuess = (userGuess == correctNumber)))
    {
        break;
    }
}
}

if (correctGuess && !userQuit)
{
    Console.WriteLine("Congratulations!");
}
else
{
    Console.WriteLine("Maybe next time!");
}
}
```

Running this application should yield results similar to those shown in Figure 9-16.

Figure 9-16   *Break* statements are often used to control execution flow within an infinite loop.

One last point to make about infinite loops: although I used a *while(true)* statement and a *break* statement to control execution flow, I also could've used a *for* loop in the form of *for (;;)* with the *break* statement to achieve the same results. Both syntaxes work the same, so it comes down to a matter of taste.

The *continue* Statement

Like the *break* statement, the *continue* statement enables you to alter the execution of a loop. However, instead of ending the current loop's embedded statement, the *continue* statement stops the current iteration and returns control to the top of the loop for the next iteration. In the following example, I have an array of strings that I want to check for duplicates. One way to accomplish that is to iterate through the array with a nested loop, comparing one element against the other. However, I certainly don't want to compare an element to itself because doing so will register an invalid number of duplicates. Therefore, if the index into the array (*i*) is the same as the index into the array (*j*), it means that I have the same element—in which case, I don't want to compare the two. Thus, I use the *continue* statement to discontinue the current iteration and pass control back to the top of the loop.

```
using System;
using System.Collections;

class MyArray
{
    public ArrayList words;

    public MyArray()
    {
        words = new ArrayList();
```

```
            words.Add("foo");
            words.Add("bar");
            words.Add("baz");
            words.Add("bar");
            words.Add("ba");
            words.Add("foo");
        }
    }


    class Continue
    {
        public static void Main()
        {
            MyArray myArray = new MyArray();
            Console.WriteLine("Array contents:");
            for (int i = 0; i < myArray.words.Count; i++)
            {
                Console.WriteLine("Line {0} : {1}", i+1,
                    myArray.words[i]);
            }
            Console.WriteLine();

            Console.WriteLine("Processing array...");
            ArrayList dupes = new ArrayList();
            for (int i = 0; i < myArray.words.Count; i++)
            {
                for (int j = 0; j < myArray.words.Count; j++)
                {
                    if (i == j) continue;

                    if (myArray.words[i] == myArray.words[j]
                        && !dupes.Contains(j))
                    {
                        dupes.Add(i);
                        Console.WriteLine("'{0}' appears on lines " +
                            "{1} and {2}",
                            myArray.words[i],
                            i + 1,
                            j + 1);
                    }
                }
            }
            Console.WriteLine("\nSUMMARY:");
            Console.WriteLine("There were {0} duplicates found",
                ((dupes.Count > 0) ? dupes.Count.ToString() : "no"));
        }
    }
```

Figure 9-17 shows the results of running this demo.

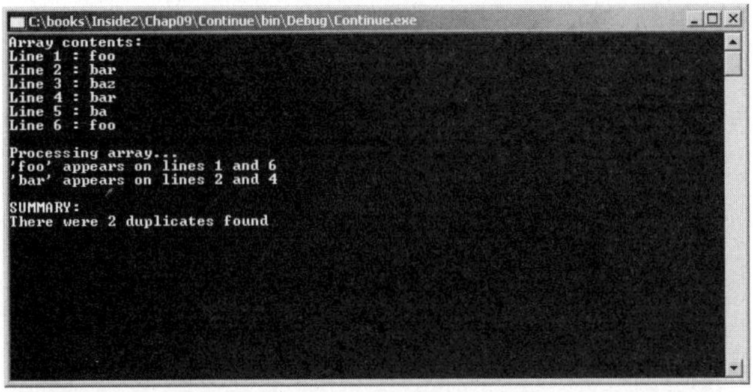

Figure 9-17   Although you probably won't use it often, the *continue* statement is quite handy in situations where control needs to be passed back to the top of the current enclosing loop or expression.

The Infamous *goto* Statement

Probably no other construct in programming history is as maligned as the *goto* statement. Therefore, before we get into the syntax for and some uses of the *goto* statement, let's look at why some people feel so strongly against using this statement and the types of problems that can be solved by using it.

A (Very) Brief History

The *goto* statement fell into disfavor upon the publication of a paper entitled "Go To Statement Considered Harmful," written by Edsger W. Dijkstra in 1968. At that time in programming history, a debate was raging over the issue of structured programming. Unfortunately, less attention was focused on the overall issues raised by structured programming than on a relatively small detail: whether particular statements, such as *go to* (now usually seen as the *goto* keyword), should be present in modern programming languages. As is too often the case, many people took Dijkstra's advice and ran to the extreme, concluding that all uses of *goto* were bad and that using *goto* should be avoided at all costs.

The problem with using *goto* isn't the keyword itself—rather, it's the use of *goto* in inappropriate places. The *goto* statement can be a useful tool in structuring program flow and can be used to write more expressive code than that resulting from other branching and iteration mechanisms. One example of using *goto* appropriately is the *loop-and-a-half problem*, as coined by Dijkstra. Here's the traditional flow of the loop-and-a-half problem in pseudocode:

```
loop
    read in a value
    if value == sentinel then exit
    process the value
end loop
```

The exit from the loop is accomplished only by the execution of the *exit* statement in the middle of the loop. This *loop/exit/end loop* cycle, however, can be quite disturbing to some people who, acting on the notion that all uses of *goto* are evil, would write this code as follows:

```
read in a value
while value != sentinel
    process the value
    read in a value
end while
```

Unfortunately, as Eric S. Roberts of Stanford University points out, this second approach has two major drawbacks. First, it requires the duplication of the statement or statements required to read in a value. Any time you duplicate code, it results in an obvious maintenance problem: any change to one statement must be made to the other. The second problem is more subtle and probably more damning. The key to writing solid code that's easy to understand—and therefore maintain—is to write code that reads in a natural manner. In any noncode description of what this code is attempting to do, you'd describe the solution as follows: First, I need to read in a value. If that value is *sentinel*, I stop. If not, I process that value and continue to the next value. Therefore, it's the code omitting the *exit* statement that's actually counterintuitive because that approach reverses the natural way of thinking about the problem.

More Info   For those of you who want to read more of Roberts's brilliant dissertation on the subject, it's available at *www.TheCodeChannel.com/docs/gotoRoberts.asp*.

Now let's look at some situations in which a *goto* statement can result in the best way to structure control flow.

Using the *goto* Statement

The *goto* statement can take any of the following forms:

goto *identifier*

goto case *constant-expression*

goto default

In the first usage of the *goto* statement, the target of the *identifier* is a label statement. The label statement takes this form:

identifier:

If that label doesn't exist in the current method, a compile-time error will result. Another important rule to remember is that the *goto* statement can be used to jump out of a nested loop. However, if the *goto* statement isn't within the scope of the label, a compile-time error will result. Therefore, you can't jump into a nested loop.

In the following example, the application is iterating through a simple array, reading each value until it reaches a sentinel value, whereupon it exits the loop. Notice that the *goto* statement acts like the *break* statement by causing the program flow to jump out of the *foreach* loop.

```
using System;
using System.Collections;

class MyArray
{
    public ArrayList words;
    public const string TerminatingWord = "stop";

    public MyArray()
    {
        words = new ArrayList();

        for (int i = 1; i <= 5; i++)
            words.Add(i.ToString());

        words.Add(TerminatingWord);

        for (int i = 6; i <= 10; i++)
            words.Add(i.ToString());
    }
}

class Goto
{
    public static void Main()
    {
        MyArray myArray = new MyArray();

        Console.WriteLine("{0} elements:\n",
            myArray.ToString());
        int i = 0;
        foreach (string word in myArray.words)
```

```
        {
            Console.WriteLine("[{0}] = {1}", i++, word);
        }

        Console.WriteLine("\nProcessing array searching " +
            "for '{0}'...\n",
            MyArray.TerminatingWord);

        i = 0;
        foreach (string word in myArray.words)
        {
            if (word == MyArray.TerminatingWord)
                goto finished;

            Console.Write("{0}...", word);
            i++;
        }

    finished:
        Console.WriteLine("Found {0} at array index {1}",
            MyArray.TerminatingWord, i);
    }
}
```

The output of this program is shown in Figure 9-18.

```
MyArray elements:

[0] = 1
[1] = 2
[2] = 3
[3] = 4
[4] = 5
[5] = stop
[6] = 6
[7] = 7
[8] = 8
[9] = 9
[10] = 10

Processing array searching for 'stop'...

1...2...3...4...5...Found stop at array index 5
```

Figure 9-18   Although the *goto* statement should definitely be used with caution, there are some valid situations in which its use is acceptable.

You could argue that a *break* statement could've been used just as effectively as the *goto* statement in this code and that a label wouldn't have been necessary. We'll now look at the other forms of the *goto* statement, and you'll see that the problems shown in each scenario can be resolved only with the *goto* statement.

In our discussion of the *switch* statement in the "Selection Statements" section of this chapter, I discussed the fact that fall-throughs aren't supported in C#. Even if fall-throughs were supported, it wouldn't solve the following problem. Let's say we have a *Payment* class (reused from the "Selection Statements" section) that accepts several forms of payment, or tenders: Visa, American Express, MasterCard, cash, and charge off (basically a credit). Because Visa, American Express, and MasterCard are all credit cards, we could combine them into a single case label and process them in the same manner. In the case of the charge off, we'd need to call methods specific to it, and in the case of the cash purchase, we'd only want to print a receipt. Also, we'd want to print a receipt in the other four cases. How could we have three distinct case labels but have the first two cases—the credit card and the charge back cases—branch to the cash label when done? As the following code illustrates, this problem is a good example of when to use the *goto* statement:

```
using System;

enum Tenders : int
{
    ChargeOff = 1,
    Cash,
    Visa,
    MasterCard,
    AmericanExpress
};

class Payment
{
    public Payment(Tenders tender)
    {
        this.Tender = tender;
    }

    protected Tenders tender;
    public Tenders Tender
    {
        get
        {
            return this.tender;
        }
        set
        {
            this.tender = value;
        }
    }
}
```

```
protected void ChargeOff()
{
    Console.WriteLine("Charge off completed.");
}

protected bool ValidateCreditCard()
{
    Console.WriteLine("Card approved.");
    return true;
}

protected void ChargeCreditCard()
{
    Console.WriteLine("Credit Card charged.");
}

protected void PrintReceipt()
{
    Console.WriteLine("Thank you and come again.");
}

public void ProcessPayment()
{
    switch ((int)(this.tender))
    {
        case (int)Tenders.ChargeOff:
            ChargeOff();
            goto case Tenders.Cash;

        case (int)Tenders.Visa:
        case (int)Tenders.MasterCard:
        case (int)Tenders.AmericanExpress:
            if (ValidateCreditCard())
                ChargeCreditCard();
            goto case Tenders.Cash;

        case (int)Tenders.Cash:
            PrintReceipt();
            break;

        default:
            Console.WriteLine("\nSorry - Invalid tender.");
            break;
    }
}
}

class GotoCase
```

```
{
    public static void DisplayMenu()
    {
        Console.WriteLine("Which type of transaction:");
        Console.WriteLine("\t1 = Charge Off");
        Console.WriteLine("\t2 = Cash");
        Console.WriteLine("\t3 = Visa");
        Console.WriteLine("\t4 = MasterCard");
        Console.WriteLine("\t5 = American Express");
        Console.Write("===>");
    }

    public static int GetTender()
    {
        int tenderChoice = -1;

        DisplayMenu();

        bool validTender = false;
        while (!validTender)
        {
            string str = Console.ReadLine();
            tenderChoice = Convert.ToInt32(str);

            if (tenderChoice >= 0
                && tenderChoice <= 5)
                validTender = true;
            else
                Console.WriteLine("Invalid choice - try again");
        }

        return tenderChoice;
    }

    public static void Main()
    {
        Tenders tenderChoice = (Tenders)GetTender();
        Payment payment = new Payment(tenderChoice);
        payment.ProcessPayment();
    }
}
```

Figure 9-19 shows the result of running this application. Note that instead of having to solve the problem counter intuitively, we simply tell the compiler that when a credit card or charge off case is finished, we want to branch to the cash label. Also note that if you branch out of a case label in C#, you shouldn't use a *break* statement, which would result in a compiler error for unreachable code.

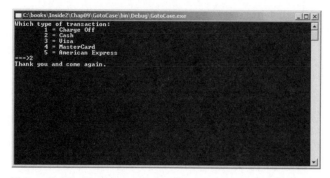

Figure 9-19   The *goto case* statement enables you to easily branch from one *case* statement to another.

The last form of the *goto* statement enables you to branch to the *default* label in a *switch* statement, thereby giving you another means of writing a single code block that can be executed as a result of multiple evaluations of the *switch* statement.

The *return* Statement

The *return* statement has two functions. It specifies a value to be returned to the caller of the currently executed code—when the current code isn't defined as returning *void*—and it causes an immediate return to the caller. The *return* statement is defined with the following syntax:

return [*return-expression*]

When the compiler encounters a method *return* statement that specifies a *return-expression*, it evaluates whether the *return-expression* can be implicitly converted into a form compatible with the current method's defined return value. The result of that conversion is passed back to the caller.

When using the *return* statement with exception handling, you have to understand some rules: If the *return* statement is a *try* block that contains an associated *finally* block, control is actually passed to the first line of the *finally* block, and when that block of code finishes, control is passed back to the caller. If the *try* block is nested in another *try* block, control will continue up the chain in this fashion until the final *finally* block has executed.

Summary

The C# conditional statements enable you to control program flow. The three categories of flow statements include the selection statements (such as *if* and *switch*), the iteration statements (*while*, *for*, and *foreach*), and the different jump statements (*break*, *continue*, *goto*, and *return*). Determining the best statements to use based on the material in this chapter will help you write better structured and more maintainable applications.

10

String Handling and Regular Expressions

This chapter breaks down into two main sections: strings and regular expressions, each represented by one primary class—*String* and *Regex*, respectively—and a set of ancillary classes. However, there's a great deal of overlap between the two: in most situations, you have the option to use all string methods, all regular expression operations, or some of each. Code based on the string functionality tends to be easier to understand and maintain, while code using regular expressions tends to be more flexible and powerful.

We'll start by looking at the *String* class, some of its simple methods, and its range of formatting specifiers. We'll then look at the relationship between strings and other .NET Framework classes—including *Console*, the basic numeric types, and *DateTime*—and how culture information and character encoding can affect string formatting. We'll also look at the *StringBuilder* support class and under the hood at string interning.

In the second part of this chapter, we'll look at the regular expression classes in the *System.Text* namespace—most notably *Regex* and its supporting classes, *Match*, *Group*, and *Capture*. We'll first examine how you can achieve the same results from either the *String* class or the *Regex* class and then move on to more sophisticated uses of regular expressions. We'll consider both pattern searching and string modifying through the set of *Regex* instance and static methods. We'll then see how *RegexOptions* modifies the behavior of the operation and finally peek under the hood to see how the system can compile regular expressions to assemblies.

Strings

The .NET Framework *System.String* class (or its alias, *string*) represents an immutable string of characters—immutable because its value can't be modified once it's been created. Methods that appear to modify a string actually return a new string containing the modification. Besides the *string* class, the .NET Framework classes offer *StringBuilder*, *StringFormat*, *StringCollection*, and so on. Together these offer comparison, appending, inserting, conversion, copying, formatting, indexing, joining, splitting, padding, trimming, removing, replacing, and searching methods.

Consider this example, which uses *Replace*, *Insert*, and *ToUpper*:

```
public class TestStringsApp
{
    public static void Main(string[] args)
    {
        string a = "strong";

        // Replace all 'o' with 'i'
        string b = a.Replace('o', 'i');
        Console.WriteLine(b);

        string c = b.Insert(3, "engthen");
        string d = c.ToUpper();
        Console.WriteLine(d);
    }
}
```

The output from this application will be:

```
string
STRENGTHENING
```

The *String* class has a range of comparison methods, including *Compare* and overloaded operators, as this continuation of the previous example shows:

```
if (d == c)        // Different
{
    Console.WriteLine("same");
}
else
{
    Console.WriteLine("different");
}
```

The output from this additional block of code is:

```
different
```

Note that the string variable *a* in the second to last example isn't changed by the *Replace* operation. However, you can always reassign a string variable if you choose. For example:

```
string q = "Foo";
q = q.Replace('o', 'i');
Console.WriteLine(q);
```

The output is:

```
Fii
```

You can combine string objects with conventional *char* arrays and even index into a string in the conventional manner:

```
string e = "dog" + "bee";
e += "cat";
string f = e.Substring(1,7);
Console.WriteLine(f);

for (int i = 0; i < f.Length; i++)
{
    Console.Write("{0,-3}", f[i]);
}
```

Here's the output:

```
ogbeeca
o  g  b  e  e  c  a
```

If you want a *null* string, declare one and assign *null* to it. Subsequently, you can reassign it with another string, as shown in the following example. Because the assignment to *g* from *f.Remove* is in a conditional block, the compiler will reject the *Console.WriteLine(g)* statement unless *g* has been assigned either *null* or some valid string value.

```
string g = null;
if (f.StartsWith("og"))
{
    g = f.Remove(2,3);
}
Console.WriteLine(g);
```

This is the output:

```
ogca
```

If you're familiar with the Microsoft Foundation Classes (MFC) *CString*, the Windows Template Library (WTL) *CString*, or the Standard Template Library

(STL) *string* class, the *String.Format* method will come as no surprise. Furthermore, *Console.WriteLine* uses the same format specifiers as the *String* class, as shown here:

```
int x = 16;
decimal y = 3.57m;
string h = String.Format(
    "item {0} sells at {1:C}", x, y);
Console.WriteLine(h);
```

Here's the output:

```
item 16 sells at £3.57
```

If you have experience with Microsoft Visual Basic, you won't be surprised to find that you can concatenate a string with any other data type using the plus sign (+). This is because all types have at least inherited *object.ToString*. Here's the syntax:

```
string t =
    "item " + 12 + " sells at " + '\xA3' + 3.45;
Console.WriteLine(t);
```

And here's the output:

```
item 12 sells at £3.45
```

String.Format has a lot in common with *Console.WriteLine*. Both methods include an overload that takes an open-ended (*params*) array of objects as the last argument. The following two statements will now produce the same output:

```
// This works because last param is a params object[].
Console.WriteLine(
    "Hello {0} {1} {2} {3} {4} {5} {6} {7} {8}",
    123, 45.67, true, 'Q', 4, 5, 6, 7, '8');

// This also works.
string u = String.Format(
    "Hello {0} {1} {2} {3} {4} {5} {6} {7} {8}",
    123, 45.67, true, 'Q', 4, 5, 6, 7, '8');
Console.WriteLine(u);
```

The output follows:

```
Hello 123 45.67 True Q 4 5 6 7 8
Hello 123 45.67 True Q 4 5 6 7 8
```

String Formatting

Both *String.Format* and *WriteLine* formatting are governed by the same formatting rules: the format parameter is embedded with zero or more format specifications of the form "{ *N* [, *M*][: *formatString*]}", *arg1, ... argN*, where:

- *N* is a zero-based integer indicating the argument to be formatted.

- *M* is an optional integer indicating the width of the region to contain the formatted value, padded with spaces. If *M* is negative, the formatted value is left-justified; if *M* is positive, the value is right-justified.

- *formatString* is an optional string of formatting codes.

- *argN* is the expression to use at the equivalent position inside the quotes in the string.

If *argN* is *null*, an empty string is used instead. If *formatString* is omitted, the *ToString* method of the argument specified by *N* provides formatting. For example, the following three statements produce the same output:

```
public class TestConsoleApp
{
    public static void Main(string[] args)
    {
        Console.WriteLine(123);
        Console.WriteLine("{0}", 123);
        Console.WriteLine("{0:D3}", 123);
    }
}
```

Here's the output:

```
123
123
123
```

We'd get exactly the same results using *String.Format* directly:

```
string s = string.Format("123");
string t = string.Format("{0}", 123);
string u = string.Format("{0:D3}", 123);
Console.WriteLine(s);
Console.WriteLine(t);
Console.WriteLine(u);
```

Therefore:

- The comma (*,M*) determines the field width and justification.

- The colon (*:formatString*) determines how to format the data—such as currency, scientific notation, or hexadecimal—as shown here:

```
Console.WriteLine(
    "{0,5} {1,5}", 123, 456);        // Right-aligned
Console.WriteLine(
    "{0,-5} {1,-5}", 123, 456);      // Left-aligned
Console.WriteLine(
    "{0,-10:D6} {1,-10:D6}", 123, 456);
```

The output is:

```
  123    456
123    456
```

Of course, you can combine them—putting the comma first, then the colon:

```
Console.WriteLine(
    "{0,-10:D6} {1,-10:D6}", 123, 456);
```

Here's the output:

```
000123     000456
```

We could use these formatting features to output data in columns with appropriate alignment—for example:

```
Console.WriteLine(
    "\n{0,-10}{1,-3}", "Name","Salary");
Console.WriteLine(
    "----------------");
Console.WriteLine(
    "{0,-10}{1,6}", "Bill", 123456);
Console.WriteLine(
    "{0,-10}{1,6}", "Polly", 7890);
```

This is the output:

```
Name      Salary
----------------
Bill      123456
Polly       7890
```

Format Specifiers

Standard numeric format strings are used to return strings in commonly used formats. They take the form *X0*, in which *X* is the *format specifier* and *0* is the *precision specifier.* The format specifier can be one of the nine built-in format characters that define the most commonly used numeric format types, as shown in Table 10-1.

Table 10-1
String and *WriteLine* Format Specifiers

Character	Interpretation
C or c	Currency
D or d	Decimal (decimal integer—don't confuse with the decimal data type)
E or e	Exponent
F or f	Fixed point
G or g	General
N or n	Number; similar to F with the addition of comma thousand separators
P or p	Percentage
R or r	Round-trip (for floating-point values only); guarantees that a numeric value converted to a string will be parsed back into the same numeric value
X or x	Hex

Let's see what happens if we have a string format for an integer value using each of the format specifiers in turn. The comments in the following code show the output.

```
public class FormatSpecApp
{
    public static void Main(string[] args)
    {
        int i = 123456;
        Console.WriteLine("{0:C}", i); // £123,456.00
        Console.WriteLine("{0:D}", i); // 123456
        Console.WriteLine("{0:E}", i); // 1.234560E+005
        Console.WriteLine("{0:F}", i); // 123456.00
        Console.WriteLine("{0:G}", i); // 123456
        Console.WriteLine("{0:N}", i); // 123,456.00
        Console.WriteLine("{0:P}", i); // 12,345,600.00 %
        Console.WriteLine("{0:X}", i); // 1E240
    }
}
```

The precision specifier controls the number of significant digits or zeros to the right of a decimal:

```
Console.WriteLine("{0:C5}", i); // £123,456.00000
Console.WriteLine("{0:D5}", i); // 123456
Console.WriteLine("{0:E5}", i); // 1.23456E+005
Console.WriteLine("{0:F5}", i); // 123456.00000
Console.WriteLine("{0:G5}", i); // 1.23456E5
Console.WriteLine("{0:N5}", i); // 123,456.00000
Console.WriteLine("{0:P5}", i); // 12,345,600.00000 %
Console.WriteLine("{0:X5}", i); // 1E240
```

The R (round-trip) format works only with floating-point values: the value is first tested using the general format, with 15 spaces of precision for a *Double* and seven spaces of precision for a *Single*. If the value is successfully parsed back to the same numeric value, it's formatted using the general format specifier. On the other hand, if the value isn't successfully parsed back to the same numeric value, the value is formatted using 17 digits of precision for a *Double* and nine digits of precision for a *Single*. Although a precision specifier can be appended to the round-trip format specifier, it's ignored.

```
double d = 1.2345678901234567890;
Console.WriteLine(
    "Floating-Point:\t{0:F16}", d);
    // 1.2345678901234600
Console.WriteLine(
    "Roundtrip:\t{0:R16}", d);
    // 1.2345678901234567
```

If the standard formatting specifiers aren't enough for you, you can use picture format strings to create custom string output. Picture format definitions are described using placeholder strings that identify the minimum and maximum number of digits used, the placement or appearance of the negative sign, and the appearance of any other text within the number, as shown in Table 10-2.

Table 10-2
Custom Format Specifiers

Format Character	Purpose	Description
0	Display zero placeholder	Results in a nonsignificant zero if a number has fewer digits than there are zeros in the format
#	Display digit placeholder	Replaces the pound symbol (#) with only significant digits

Table 10-2
Custom Format Specifiers

Format Character	Purpose	Description
.	Decimal point	Displays a period (.)
,	Group separator	Separates number groups, as in 1,000
%	Percent notation	Displays a percent sign (%)
E+0 E-0 e+0 e-0	Exponent notation	Formats the output of exponent notation
\	Literal character	Used with traditional formatting sequences such as "\n" (newline)
'ABC' "ABC"	Literal string	Displays any string within quotes or apostrophes literally
;	Section separator	Specifies different output if the numeric value to be formatted is positive, negative, or zero

Let's see the strings that result from a set of customized formats, using first a positive integer, then using the negative value of that same integer, and finally using zero:

```
int i = 123456;
Console.WriteLine();
Console.WriteLine("{0:#0}", i);                     // 123456
Console.WriteLine("{0:#0;(#0)}", i);                // 123456
Console.WriteLine("{0:#0;(#0);<zero>}", i);         // 123456
        Console.WriteLine("{0:#%}", i);             // 12345600%

i = -123456;
Console.WriteLine();
Console.WriteLine("{0:#0}", i);                     // -123456
Console.WriteLine("{0:#0;(#0)}", i);                // (123456)
Console.WriteLine("{0:#0;(#0);<zero>}", i);         // (123456)
Console.WriteLine("{0:#%}", i);                     // -12345600%
```

```
i = 0;
Console.WriteLine();
Console.WriteLine("{0:#0}", i);              // 0
Console.WriteLine("{0:#0;(#0)}", i);         // 0
Console.WriteLine("{0:#0;(#0);<zero>}", i); // <zero>
Console.WriteLine("{0:#%}", i);              // %
```

Objects and *ToString*

Recall that all data types—both predefined and user-defined—inherit from the *System.Object* class in the .NET Framework, which is aliased as *object*:

```
public class Thing
{
    public int i = 2;
    public int j = 3;
}


public class objectTypeApp
{
    public static void Main()
    {
        object a;
        a = 1;
        Console.WriteLine(a);
        Console.WriteLine(a.ToString());
        Console.WriteLine(a.GetType());
        Console.WriteLine();

        Thing b = new Thing();
        Console.WriteLine(b);
        Console.WriteLine(b.ToString());
        Console.WriteLine(b.GetType());
    }
}
```

Here's the output:

```
1
1
System.Int32

objectType.Thing
```

```
objectType.Thing
objectType.Thing
```

From the foregoing code, you can see that the statement

```
Console.WriteLine(a);
```

is the same as

```
Console.WriteLine(a.ToString());
```

The reason for this equivalence is that the *ToString* method has been over-ridden in the *Int32* type to produce a string representation of the numeric value. By default, however, *ToString* will return the name of the object's type—the same as *GetType*, a name composed of the enclosing namespace or namespaces and the class name. This equivalence is clear when we call *ToString* on our *Thing* reference. We can—and should—override the inherited *ToString* for any nontrivial user-defined type:

```
public class Thing
{
    public int i = 2;
    public int j = 3;

    override public string ToString()
    {
        return String.Format("i = {0}, j = {1}", i, j);
    }
}
```

The relevant output from this revised code is:

```
i = 2, j = 3
i = 2, j = 3
objectType.Thing
```

Numeric String Parsing

All the basic types have a *ToString* method, which is inherited from the *Object* type, and all the numeric types have a *Parse* method, which takes the string representation of a number and returns you its equivalent numeric value. For example:

```
public class NumParsingApp
{
    public static void Main(string[] args)
    {
        int i = int.Parse("12345");
        Console.WriteLine("i = {0}", i);
```

```
        int j = Int32.Parse("12345");
        Console.WriteLine("j = {0}", j);

        double d = Double.Parse("1.2345E+6");
        Console.WriteLine("d = {0:F}", d);

        string s = i.ToString();
        Console.WriteLine("s = {0}", s);
    }
}
```

The output from this application is shown here:

```
i = 12345
j = 12345
d = 1234500.00
s = 12345
```

Certain nondigit characters in an input string are allowed by default, including leading and trailing spaces, commas and decimal points, and plus and minus signs. Therefore, the following *Parse* statements are equivalent:

```
string t = "  -1,234,567.890  ";
//double g = double.Parse(t);       // Same thing
double g = double.Parse(t,
    NumberStyles.AllowLeadingSign |
    NumberStyles.AllowDecimalPoint |
    NumberStyles.AllowThousands |
    NumberStyles.AllowLeadingWhite |
    NumberStyles.AllowTrailingWhite);
Console.WriteLine("g = {0:F}", g);
```

The output from this additional code block is shown next:

```
g = -1234567.89
```

Note that to use *NumberStyles* you must add a *using* statement for *System.Globalization*. Then you either can use a combination of the various *NumberStyles* enum values or use *NumberStyles.Any* for all of them. If you also want to accommodate a currency symbol, you need the third *Parse* overload, which takes a *NumberFormatInfo* object as a parameter. You then set the *CurrencySymbol* field of the *NumberFormatInfo* object to the expected symbol before passing it as the third parameter to *Parse*, which modifies the *Parse* behavior:

```
string u = "£  -1,234,567.890  ";
NumberFormatInfo ni = new NumberFormatInfo();
ni.CurrencySymbol = "£";
double h = Double.Parse(u, NumberStyles.Any, ni);
Console.WriteLine("h = {0:F}", h);
```

The output from this additional code block is shown here:

```
h = -1234567.89
```

In addition to *NumberFormatInfo*, we can use the *CultureInfo* class. *CultureInfo* represents information about a specific culture, including the names of the culture, the writing system, and the calendar used, as well as access to culture-specific objects that provide methods for common operations, such as formatting dates and sorting strings. The culture names follow the RFC 1766 standard in the format "*<languagecode2>-<country/regioncode2>*", in which *<languagecode2>* is a lowercase two-letter code derived from ISO 639-1 and *<country/regioncode2>* is an uppercase two-letter code derived from ISO 3166. For example, U.S. English is "en-US", UK English is "en-GB", and Trinidad and Tobago English is "en-TT". For example, we could create a *CultureInfo* object for English in the United States and convert an integer value to a string based on this *CultureInfo*:

```
int k = 12345;
CultureInfo us = new CultureInfo("en-US");
string v = k.ToString("c", us);
Console.WriteLine(v);
```

This example would produce a string like this:

```
$12,345.00
```

Note that we're using a *ToString* overload that takes a format string as its first parameter and an *IFormatProvider* interface implementation—in this case, a *CultureInfo* reference—as its second parameter. Here's another example, this time for Danish in Denmark:

```
CultureInfo dk = new CultureInfo("da-DK");
string w = k.ToString("c", dk);
Console.WriteLine(w);
```

The output is:

```
kr 12.345,00
```

Strings and *DateTime*

A *DateTime* object has a property named *Ticks* that stores the date and time as the number of 100-nanosecond intervals since 12:00 AM January 1, 1 A.D. in the Gregorian calendar. For example, a ticks value of *312413760000000000L* has the string representation "*Friday, January 01, 0100 12:00:00 AM*". Each additional tick increases the time interval by 100 nanoseconds.

DateTime values are formatted using standard or custom patterns stored in the properties of a *DateTimeFormatInfo* instance. To modify how a value is displayed, the *DateTimeFormatInfo* instance must be writeable so that custom patterns can be saved in its properties.

```
using System.Globalization;

public class DatesApp
{
    public static void Main(string[] args)
    {
        DateTime dt = DateTime.Now;
        Console.WriteLine(dt);
        Console.WriteLine("date = {0}, time = {1}\n",
            dt.Date, dt.TimeOfDay);
    }
}
```

This code will produce the following output:

```
23/06/2001 17:55:10
date = 23/06/2001 00:00:00, time = 17:55:10.3839296
```

Table 10-3 lists the standard format characters for each standard pattern and the associated *DateTimeFormatInfo* property that can be set to modify the standard pattern.

Table 10-3
DateTime Formatting

Format Character	Format Pattern	Associated Property/ Description
D	*MM/dd/yyyy*	*ShortDatePattern*
D	*dddd, MMMM dd, yyyy*	*LongDatePattern*
F	*dddd, MMMM dd, yyyy HH:mm*	Full date and time (long date and short time)
F	*dddd, MMMM dd, yyyy HH:mm:ss*	*FullDateTimePattern* (long date and long time)
G	*MM/dd/yyyy HH:mm*	General (short date and short time)
G	*MM/dd/yyyy HH:mm:ss*	General (short date and long time)
M, M	*MMMM dd*	*MonthDayPattern*
r, R	*ddd, dd MMM yyyy HH':'mm':'ss 'GMT'*	*RFC1123Pattern*

Table 10-3
***DateTime* Formatting**

Format Character	Format Pattern	Associated Property/ Description
s	*yyyy-MM-dd HH:mm:ss*	*SortableDateTimePattern* (conforms to ISO 8601) using local time
t	*HH:mm*	*ShortTimePattern*
T	*HH:mm:ss*	*LongTimePattern*
u	*yyyy-MM-dd HH:mm:ss*	*UniversalSortable-DateTimePattern* (conforms to ISO 8601) using universal time
U	*dddd, MMMM dd, yyyy HH:mm:ss*	*UniversalSortable-DateTimePattern*
y, Y	*MMMM, yyyy*	*YearMonthPattern*

The *DateTimeFormatInfo.InvariantInfo* property gets the default read-only *DateTimeFormatInfo* instance that's culture independent (invariant). You can also create custom patterns. Note that the *InvariantInfo* isn't necessarily the same as the current locale info: *Invariant* equates to U.S. standard. Also, if you pass *null* as the second parameter to *DateTime.Format*, the *DateTimeFormat-Info* will default to *CurrentInfo,*as in:

```
Console.WriteLine(dt.ToString("d", dtfi));
Console.WriteLine(dt.ToString("d", null));
Console.WriteLine();
```

Here's the output:

```
06/23/2001
23/06/2001
```

Compare the results of choosing *InvariantInfo* with those of choosing *CurrentInfo*:

```
DateTimeFormatInfo dtfi;
Console.Write("[I]nvariant or [C]urrent Info?: ");
if (Console.Read() == 'I')
    dtfi = DateTimeFormatInfo.InvariantInfo;
else
    dtfi = DateTimeFormatInfo.CurrentInfo;
DateTimeFormatInfo dtfi =
    DateTimeFormatInfo.InvariantInfo;
```

```
Console.WriteLine(dt.ToString("D", dtfi));
Console.WriteLine(dt.ToString("f", dtfi));
Console.WriteLine(dt.ToString("F", dtfi));
Console.WriteLine(dt.ToString("g", dtfi));
Console.WriteLine(dt.ToString("G", dtfi));
Console.WriteLine(dt.ToString("m", dtfi));
Console.WriteLine(dt.ToString("r", dtfi));
Console.WriteLine(dt.ToString("s", dtfi));
Console.WriteLine(dt.ToString("t", dtfi));
Console.WriteLine(dt.ToString("T", dtfi));
Console.WriteLine(dt.ToString("u", dtfi));
Console.WriteLine(dt.ToString("U", dtfi));
Console.WriteLine(dt.ToString("d", dtfi));
Console.WriteLine(dt.ToString("y", dtfi));
Console.WriteLine(dt.ToString("dd-MMM-yy", dtfi));
```

Here's the output:

```
[I]nvariant or [C]urrent Info?: I
01/03/2002
03/01/2002

Thursday, 03 January 2002
Thursday, 03 January 2002 12:55
Thursday, 03 January 2002 12:55:03
01/03/2002 12:55
01/03/2002 12:55:03
January 03
Thu, 03 Jan 2002 12:55:03 GMT
2002-01-03T12:55:03
12:55
12:55:03
2002-01-03 12:55:03Z
Thursday, 03 January 2002 12:55:03
01/03/2002
2002 January
03-Jan-02


[I]nvariant or [C]urrent Info?: C
03/01/2002
03/01/2002

03 January 2002
03 January 2002 12:55
03 January 2002 12:55:47
03/01/2002 12:55
03/01/2002 12:55:47
03 January
Thu, 03 Jan 2002 12:55:47 GMT
```

```
2002-01-03T12:55:47
12:55
12:55:47
2002-01-03 12:55:47Z
03 January 2002 12:55:47
03/01/2002
January 2002
03-Jan-02
```

Encoding Strings

The *System.Text* namespace offers an *Encoding* class. *Encoding* is an abstract class, so you can't instantiate it directly. However, it does provide a range of methods and properties for converting arrays and strings of Unicode characters to and from arrays of bytes encoded for a target code page. These properties actually resolve to returning an implementation of the *Encoding* class. Table 10-4 shows some of these properties.

Table 10-4
String Encoding Classes

Property	Encoding
ASCII	Encodes Unicode characters as single, 7-bit ASCII characters. This encoding supports only character values between U+0000 and U+007F.
BigEndianUnicode	Encodes each Unicode character as two consecutive bytes, using big endian (code page 1201) byte ordering.
Unicode	Encodes each Unicode character as two consecutive bytes, using little endian (code page 1200) byte ordering.
UTF7	Encodes Unicode characters using the UTF-7 encoding. (UTF-7 stands for UCS Transformation Format, 7-bit form.) This encoding supports all Unicode character values and can be accessed as code page 65000.
UTF8	Encodes Unicode characters using the UTF-8 encoding. (UTF-8 stands for UCS Transformation Format, 8-bit form.) This encoding supports all Unicode character values and can be accessed as code page 65001.

For example, you can convert a simple sequence of bytes into a conventional ASCII string, as shown here:

```
class StringEncodingApp
{
    static void Main(string[] args)
    {
        byte[] ba = new byte[]
            {72, 101, 108, 108, 111};
```

```
            string s = Encoding.ASCII.GetString(ba);
            Console.WriteLine(s);
    }
}
```

This is the output:

```
Hello
```

If you want to convert to something other than ASCII, simply use one of the other *Encoding* properties. The following example has the same output as the previous example:

```
byte[] bb = new byte[]
    {0,72, 0,101, 0,108, 0,108, 0,111};
string t = Encoding.BigEndianUnicode.GetString(bb);
Console.WriteLine(t);
```

The *System.Text* namespace also includes several classes derived from—and therefore implementing—the abstract *Encoding* class. These classes offer similar behavior to the properties in the *Encoding* class itself:

- *ASCIIEncoding*

- *UnicodeEncoding*

- *UTF7Encoding*

- *UTF8Encoding*

You could achieve the same results as those from the previous example with the following code:

```
ASCIIEncoding ae = new ASCIIEncoding();
Console.WriteLine(ae.GetString(ba));
UnicodeEncoding bu =
    new UnicodeEncoding(true, false);
Console.WriteLine(bu.GetString(bb));
```

The *StringBuilder* Class

Recall that with the *String* class, methods that appear to modify a string actually return a new string containing the modification. This behavior is sometimes a nuisance because if you make several modifications to a string, you end up working with several generations of copies of the original. For this reason, the people at Redmond have provided the *StringBuilder* class in the *System.Text* namespace.

Consider this example, using the *StringBuilder* methods *Replace, Insert, Append, AppendFormat*, and *Remove*:

```
class UseSBApp
{
    static void Main(string[] args)
    {
        StringBuilder sb = new StringBuilder("Pineapple");
        sb.Replace('e', 'X');
        sb.Insert(4, "Banana");
        sb.Append("Kiwi");
        sb.AppendFormat(", {0}:{1}", 123, 45.6789);
        sb.Remove(sb.Length - 3, 3);
        Console.WriteLine(sb);
    }
}
```

This is the output:

```
PinXBananaapplXKiwi, 123:45.6
```

Note that—as with most other types—you can easily convert from a *StringBuilder* to a *String*:

```
string s = sb.ToString().ToUpper();
Console.WriteLine(s);
```

Here's the output:

```
PINXBANANAAPPLXKIWI, 123:45.6
```

Splitting Strings

The *String* class does offer a *Split* method for splitting a string into substrings, with the splits determined by arbitrary separator characters that you supply to the method. For example:

```
class SplitStringApp
{
    static void Main(string[] args)
    {
        string s = "Once Upon A Time In America";
        char[] seps = new char[]{' '};
        foreach (string ss in s.Split(seps))
            Console.WriteLine(ss);
    }
}
```

The output follows:

```
Once
Upon
```

```
A
Time
In
America
```

The separators parameter to *String.Split* is an array of *char*; therefore, we can split a string based on multiple delimiters. However, we have to be careful about special characters such as the backslash (\) and single quote ('). The following code produces the same output as the previous example did:

```
string t = "Once,Upon:A/Time\\In\'America";
char[] sep2 = new char[]{
    ' ', ',', ':', '/', '\\', '\''};
foreach (string ss in t.Split(sep2))
    Console.WriteLine(ss);
```

Note that the *Split* method is quite simple and not too useful if we want to split substrings that are separated by multiple instances of some character. For example, if we have more than one space between any of the words in our string, we'll get these results:

```
string u = "Once   Upon A Time In   America";
char[] sep3 = new char[]{' '};
foreach (string ss in u.Split(sep3))
    Console.WriteLine(ss);
```

Here's the output:

```
Once


Upon
A
Time
In


America
```

Later in this chapter, in the "Regular Expressions" section, we'll consider the regular expression classes in the .NET Framework, and we'll see how to solve this particular problem and many others.

Extending Strings

In libraries before the .NET era, it became common practice to extend the *String* class found in the library with enhanced features. Unfortunately, the *String* class in the .NET Framework is sealed; therefore, you can't derive from it. On the other hand, it's entirely possible to provide a series of encapsulated static methods that process strings. For example, the *String* class does offer the *ToUpper* and *ToLower* methods for converting to uppercase or lowercase, respectively, but this class doesn't offer a method to convert to proper case (initial capitals on each word). Providing such functionality is simple, as shown here:

```
public class StringEx
{
    public static string ProperCase(string s)
    {
        s = s.ToLower();
        string sProper = "";

        char[] seps = new char[]{' '};
        foreach (string ss in s.Split(seps))
        {
            sProper += char.ToUpper(ss[0]);
            sProper +=
            (ss.Substring(1, ss.Length - 1) + ' ');
        }
        return sProper;
    }
}

class StringExApp
{
    static void Main(string[] args)
    {
        string s  = "the qUEEn wAs in HER parLOr";
        Console.WriteLine("Initial String:\t{0}", s);

        string t = StringEx.ProperCase(s);
        Console.WriteLine("ProperCase:\t{0}", t);
    }
}
```

This will produce the output shown here. (Later in this chapter, we'll see how to achieve the same results with regular expressions.)

```
Initial String: the qUEEn wAs in HER parLOr
ProperCase:     The Queen Was In Her Parlor
```

Another classic operation that doubtless will appear again is a test for a palindromic string—a string that reads the same backwards and forwards:

```
public static bool IsPalindrome(string s)
{
```

```
    int iLength, iHalfLen;
    iLength = s.Length - 1;
    iHalfLen = iLength / 2;
    for (int i = 0; i <= iHalfLen; i++)
    {
        if (s.Substring(i, 1) !=
            s.Substring(iLength - i, 1))
        {
            return false;
        }
    }
    return true;
}

static void Main(string[] args)
{
    Console.WriteLine("\nPalindromes?");
    string[] sa = new string[]{
        "level", "minim", "radar",
        "foobar", "rotor", "banana"};

    foreach (string v in sa)
        Console.WriteLine("{0}\t{1}",
            v, StringEx.IsPalindrome(v));
}
```

Here's the output:

```
Palindromes?
level   True
minim   True
radar   True
foobar  False
rotor   True
banana  False
```

For more complex operations—such as conditional splitting or joining, extended parsing or tokenizing, and sophisticated trimming in which the *String* class doesn't offer the power you want—you can turn to the *Regex* class. That's what we'll look at next in the next section, "Regular Expressions."

String Interning

One of the reasons strings were designed to be immutable is that this arrangement allows the system to intern them. During the process of string interning, all the constant strings in an application are stored in a common place in memory, thus eliminating unnecessary duplicates. This practice clearly saves space at run time but can confuse the unwary. For example, recall that the equivalence operator (==) will test for value equivalence for value types and for address (or reference) equivalence for reference types. Therefore, in the following application, when we compare two reference type objects of the same class with the same contents, the result is *False*. However, when we compare two string objects with the same contents, the result is *True*:

```
class StringInterningApp
{
    public class Thing
    {
        private int i;
        public Thing(int i) { this.i = i; }
    }

    static void Main(string[] args)
    {
        Thing t1 = new Thing(123);
        Thing t2 = new Thing(123);
        Console.WriteLine(t1 == t2);    // False

        string a = "Hello";
        string b = "Hello";

        Console.WriteLine(a == b);    // True
    }
}
```

OK, but both strings are actually constants or literals. Suppose we have another string that's a variable? Again, given the same contents, the string equivalence operator will return *True*:

```
string c = String.Copy(a);
Console.WriteLine(a == c);        // True
```

Now suppose we force the run-time system to treat the two strings as objects, not strings, and therefore use the most basic reference type equivalence operator. This time we get *False*:

```
Console.WriteLine((object)a == (object)c);
```

Time to look at the underlying Microsoft intermediate language (MSIL), as shown in Figure 10-1.

```
StringInterningApp::Main : void(string[])                                    _|□|x|
IL_0000:   ldc.i4.s      123
IL_0002:   newobj        instance void StringInterning.StringInterningApp/Thing::.ctor(int32)
IL_0007:   stloc.0
IL_0008:   ldc.i4.s      123
IL_000a:   newobj        instance void StringInterning.StringInterningApp/Thing::.ctor(int32)
IL_000F:   stloc.1
IL_0010:   ldloc.0
IL_0011:   ldloc.1
IL_0012:   ceq
IL_0014:   call          void [mscorlib]System.Console::WriteLine(bool)
IL_0019:   ldstr         "Hello"
IL_001e:   stloc.2
IL_001F:   ldstr         "Hello"
IL_0024:   stloc.3
IL_0025:   ldloc.2
IL_0026:   ldloc.3
IL_0027:   call          bool [mscorlib]System.String::op_Equality(string,
                                                                   string)
IL_002c:   call          void [mscorlib]System.Console::WriteLine(bool)
IL_0031:   ldloc.2
IL_0032:   call          string [mscorlib]System.String::Copy(string)
IL_0037:   stloc.s       V_4
IL_0039:   ldloc.2
IL_003a:   ldloc.s       V_4
IL_003c:   call          bool [mscorlib]System.String::op_Equality(string,
                                                                   string)
IL_0041:   call          void [mscorlib]System.Console::WriteLine(bool)
IL_0046:   ldloc.2
IL_0047:   ldloc.s       V_4
IL_0049:   ceq
IL_004b:   call          void [mscorlib]System.Console::WriteLine(bool)
```

Figure 10-1 MSIL for string equivalence and object equivalence.

The crucial differences are as follows: For the first comparison (*t1==t2*), having loaded the two *Thing* object references onto the evaluation stack, the MSIL uses opcode *ceq* (compare equal), thus clearly comparing the references, or address values. However, when we load the two strings onto the stack for comparison with *ldstr*, the MSIL for the second comparison (*a==b*) is a *call* operation. We don't just compare the values on the stack; instead, we call the *String* class equivalence operator method, *op_Equality*. The same process happens for the third comparison (*a==c*). For the fourth comparison, *(object)a==(object)c*, we're back again to *ceq*. In other words, we compare the values on the stack—in this case, the addresses of the two strings.

More Info You'll see exactly how the *String* class can have its own equivalence operator method in Chapter 13, "Operator Overloading and User-Defined Conversions." For now, it's enough to know that the system will compare strings differently than other reference types.

What happens if we compare the two original string constants and force the use of the most primitive equivalence operator? Take a look:

```
Console.WriteLine((object)a == (object)b);
```

You'll find that the output from this is *True*. Proof, finally, that the system is interning strings—the MSIL opcode used is again *ceq*, but this time it results in equality because the two strings were assigned a constant literal value that was stored only once. In fact, the Common Language Infrastructure guarantees that the result of two *ldstr* instructions referring to two metadata tokens with the same sequence of characters return precisely the same string object.

Regular Expressions

The *System.Text* namespace provides a number of classes for regular expression processing. Regular expressions offer a powerful, flexible, and efficient strategy for processing text. The .NET Framework regular expressions have evolved from languages such as Perl and awk and are designed to be compatible with Perl 5 regular expressions. In addition, the .NET regular expressions include unique features such as right-to-left matching and on-the-fly compilation. Using regular expressions, you can quickly parse large amounts of text to find specific character patterns—to extract, edit, replace, or delete text substrings. These features are particularly useful for parsing HTML pages, http headers, XML files, system log files, and so on.

The regular expression language includes two basic character types: literal (normal) text characters and *metacharacters*. Regular expression metacharacters are an evolved extension of the ? and * metacharacters used with the MS-DOS file system to represent any single character or group of characters. The most commonly used metacharacters in the regular expression pattern syntax are listed in Table 10-5.

Table 10-5
Common Regular Expression Metacharacters

Expression	Meaning
.	Matches any character except \n
[*characters*]	Matches a single character in the list
[^*characters*]	Matches a single character not in the list
[*charX-charY*]	Matches a single character in the specified range
\w	Matches a word character; same as [a-zA-Z_0-9]
\W	Matches a nonword character
\s	Matches a whitespace character; same as [\n\r\t\f]
\S	Matches a nonwhitespace character
\d	Matches a decimal digit; same as [0-9]
\D	Matches a nondigit character

Table 10-5
Common Regular Expression Metacharacters

Expression	Meaning
^	Beginning of the line
$	End of the line
\b	On a word boundary
\B	Not on a word boundary
*	Zero or more matches
+	One or more matches
?	Zero or one matches
{*n*}	Exactly *n* matches
{*n*,}	At least *n* matches
{*n*,*m*}	At least *n* but no more than *m* matches
( )	Capture matched substring
(?<*name*>)	Capture matched substring into group name
|	Logical OR

For example, when applied to a body of text, the regular expression \sFoo matches all occurrences of the string "Foo" that are preceded by any whitespace character (such as space, tab, or carriage return/linefeed).

Note   Special escaped metacharacters such as \s must be preceded by an additional backslash (as in \\s) to prevent the regular expression engine from treating the \ and s as two separate characters.

As a simple introduction to regular expressions, let's revisit the *String.Split* method from the previous section, which splits a string into substrings according to specified separators. The *Regex* class in the *System.Text.RegularExpression* namespace can be used in the same way. Instead of setting up an array of characters containing the delimiters, we pass a parenthesized set of delimiter values to the *Regex* constructor:

```
class SplitRegExApp
{
    static void Main(string[] args)
    {
        string s = "Once Upon A Time In America";
//        char[] seps = new char[]{' '};
        Regex r = new Regex(" ");
//        foreach (string ss in s.Split(seps))
        foreach (string ss in r.Split(s))
        {
            Console.WriteLine(ss);
        }
    }
}
```

Here's the output:

```
Once
Upon
A
Time
In
America
```

Let's continue our comparison of the *String* and *Regex* features for splitting strings. We can also split strings on the basis of multiple different delimiters:

```
Console.WriteLine(
    "\nMultiple different delimiters:");
string t = "Once,Upon:A/Time\\In\'America";
//char[] sep2 = new char[]{
//    ' ', ',', ':', '/', '\\', '\''};
Regex q = new Regex(@" |,|:|/|\\|\'");
//foreach (string ss in t.Split(sep2))
foreach (string ss in q.Split(t))
{
    Console.WriteLine(ss);
}
```

Note the way we specify multiple delimiters to *Regex* by using the bitwise OR (|) operator. Now that our delimiters include such characters as the back-slash and single quote, we must ensure that the string is @-quoted to escape the special meaning of these delimiters. Let's see what happens when we try our version of the string with multiple spaces:

```
Console.WriteLine(
    "\nMultiple spaces, using \" \"");
string u = "Once   Upon A Time In   America";
//char[] sep3 = new char[]{' '};
```

```
Regex p = new Regex(" ");
//foreach (string ss in u.Split(sep3))
foreach (string ss in p.Split(u))
{
    Console.WriteLine(ss);
}
```

As you can see from the output, this result isn't quite right:

```
Multiple spaces, using " "
Once


Upon
A
Time
In


America
```

What's going on here? Our regular expression search pattern is a single space, so when the engine finds two spaces together, it splits between them. Furthermore, because the spaces are being discarded, we end up with an empty string. For instance, there are three spaces between "Once" and "Upon", so the sequence "Once Upon" is split four times: between "Once" and the following space, between that first space and the second (which results in an empty string), between the second and the third (another empty string), and between the third and "Upon". Therefore, we end up with four substrings: "Once", "", "", and "Upon". Can we fix this problem? Yes we can—the obvious solution is to test for empty strings upon output:

```
string u = "Once    Upon A Time In    America";
Regex p = new Regex(" ");
foreach (string ss in p.Split(u))
{
    if (ss.Length>0)
        Console.WriteLine(ss);
}
```

OK, it's working, but it seems a bit of a hodge, doesn't it? Isn't there a better way? The answer is yes. In the following example—which produces the same output—we specify \s as the pattern to match. *Regex* will interpret \s as any single whitespace character. We need to place the at sign (@) in front of the string, or the compiler will step in and complain about \s being an unrecognized escape sequence. Finally, we add a plus sign (+) to the end of the pattern to signify that we're happy to match multiple instances of the pattern—in this case, multiple instances of whitespace:

```
Console.WriteLine(
    "\nMultiple spaces, using \"[\\s]+\"");
string v = "Once   Upon A Time In   America";
Regex o = new Regex(@"[\s]+");
foreach (string ss in o.Split(v))
{
    Console.WriteLine(ss);
}
```

If we're concerned only with spaces and not other whitespace characters (such as tabs), we can reduce the expression to this:

```
Regex n = new Regex("[ ]+");
```

Finally, instead of using the square brackets to surround our search pattern, we can use parentheses—another of the metacharacters recognized by *Regex*. What difference do they make? Let's take our first (simplest) example:

```
Console.WriteLine(
    "\nSingle spaces, using ()");
string x = "Once Upon A Time In America";
Regex m = new Regex("( )");
foreach (string ss in m.Split(x))
{
    Console.WriteLine(ss);
}
```

Here's the output:

```
Single spaces, using ()
Once

Upon

A

Time

In

America
```

This time, we don't have empty strings between each substring. We now have now 11 substrings: the parentheses cause *Regex* to keep, or capture, the delimiters instead of discarding them. In a more sophisticated situation where we're not just splitting a string but performing some other modifications to it, we might want to keep the delimiters for other processing. The foregoing examples use regular expressions in a fairly simple manner, just to compare the *Regex* and *String* classes as closely as possible. We'll now see how to use regular expressions in a more powerful fashion.

Match and *MatchCollection*

The *System.Text* namespace also offers a *Match* class and a *MatchCollection* class. The *Match* class represents the results of a regular expression–matching operation. A *Match* object is immutable, and the *Match* class has no public constructor. Therefore, you can get a *Match* only from another class, such as *Regex*. In the following example, we use the *Match* method of the *Regex* class to return an object of type *Match* in order to find the first match in the input string. We also use the *Match.Success* property to indicate whether a match was indeed found.

```
class MatchingApp
{
    static void Main(string[] args)
    {
        Regex r = new Regex("in");
        Match m = r.Match("Matching");
        if (m.Success)
        {
            Console.WriteLine(
                "Found '{0}' at position {1}",
                m.Value, m.Index);
        }
    }
}
```

The output from this application is:

```
Found 'in' at position 5
```

Note that if we'd initialized the *Regex* object with "capturing" parentheses, the effect would be exactly the same:

```
Regex r = new Regex("(in)");
```

OK, but what if there are multiple occurrences of the pattern in the string? For this, we need to use the *MatchCollection* class. Like *Match*, this class is immutable and has no public constructor. In the following example, we use the same *Regex* object previously initialized to search for the pattern "in" and apply it to a longer string with multiple occurrences of the pattern. The results are returned in a *MatchCollection* object, which we can then iterate. We can also use the indexer to treat the collection as an array.

```
MatchCollection mc = r.Matches(
    "The King Was in His Counting House");
for (int i = 0; i < mc.Count; i++)
{
    Console.WriteLine(
        "Found '{0}' at position {1}",
        mc[i].Value, mc[i].Index);
}
```

The output from this new block of code is:

```
Found 'in' at position 5
Found 'in' at position 13
Found 'in' at position 25
```

The *Match* class stores and provides access to all the substrings extracted by the search. *Match* also remembers the string being searched and the regular expression being used, so it can use them to perform another search that starts where the last one ended. Therefore, we can also perform the previous search operation by using the following code—we find the first match, and as long as this succeeds, we continue searching with a call to *Match.NextMatch*:

```
string s2 = "The King Was in His Counting House";
Match m2;
for (m2 = r.Match(s2); m2.Success;
    m2 = m2.NextMatch())
{
    Console.WriteLine(
        "Found '{0}' at position {1}",
        m2.Value, m2.Index);
}
```

Suppose we only want to search for the pattern "in" as a word—when "in" occurs after and before a space. This situation is almost too trivial to mention; just bear in mind that the regular expression classes can search for any pattern you care to imagine:

```
Regex q = new Regex(" in ");
MatchCollection mm = q.Matches(
    "The King Was in His Counting House");
for (int i = 0; i < mm.Count; i++)
{
    Console.WriteLine(
        "Found '{0}' at position {1}",
        mm[i].Value, mm[i].Index);
}
```

The output from this new block of code is:

```
Found ' in ' at position 12
```

Finally, suppose we want to match multiple instances of multiple patterns:

```
Regex p = new Regex("((an)|(in)|(on))");
MatchCollection mn = p.Matches(
    "The King Kong Band Wins Again");
for (int i = 0; i < mn.Count; i++)
{
    Console.WriteLine(
        "Found '{0}' at position {1}",
        mn[i].Value, mn[i].Index);
}
```

The output from this new block of code is:

```
Found 'in' at position 5
Found 'on' at position 10
Found 'an' at position 15
Found 'in' at position 20
Found 'in' at position 27
```

Note that we can alternatively write the regular expression just shown like this:

```
Regex p = new Regex("(a|i|o)n");
```

This alternative pattern matching can be extended to a technique named *backtracking*. Backtracking occurs when the regular expression–matching engine needs to back up to re-examine part of the string that it's passed. For example, suppose we're looking for either spelling of the word "Gray": "Gray" or "Grey". Suppose that in a given string we have the substring "Grey". When the engine examines this string and finds the pattern "Gr", it must choose to compare the next character against the letter "a" or "e". Suppose it chooses to match "a". This comparison fails, so the engine must backtrack to try to match "e".

```
Regex n = new Regex("Gr(a|e)y");
MatchCollection mp = n.Matches(
    "Green, Grey, Granite, Gray");
for (int i = 0; i < mp.Count; i++)
{
    Console.WriteLine(
        "Found '{0}' at position {1}",
        mp[i].Value, mp[i].Index);
}
```

The output from this new block of code is:

```
Found 'Grey' at position 7
Found 'Gray' at position 22
```

Groups and Captures

The *System.Text* namespace also offers a *Group* class and a *GroupCollection* class. The *Group* class represents the results from a single regular expression–matching group. In the following example, we define three groups, "ing", "in", and "n", and then search the string "Matching" to find these patterns. As you can see, the *Match* class offers a *Groups* property that returns a *GroupCollection* object, and we can use an integer indexer into the *GroupCollection* to extract individual *Group* objects:

```
class GroupingApp
{
    static void Main(string[] args)
    {
        // Define groups 'ing', 'in', 'n'
        Regex r = new Regex("(i(n))g");
        Match m = r.Match("Matching");
        GroupCollection gc = m.Groups;

        Console.WriteLine(
            "Found {0} Groups", gc.Count);
        for (int i = 0; i < gc.Count; i++)
        {
            Group g = gc[i];
            Console.WriteLine(
                "Found '{0}' at position {1}",
                g.Value, g.Index);
        }
    }
}
```

The output from this application is:

```
Found 3 Groups
Found 'ing' at position 5
Found 'in' at position 5
Found 'n' at position 6
```

Note that the *for* loop just shown could've been written to use the *Capture* and *CaptureCollection* classes explicitly. The *Capture* class contains the results from a single subexpression capture, while the *CaptureCollection* class represents a sequence of substrings captured by a single capturing group:

```
for (int i = 0; i < gc.Count; i++)
{
    CaptureCollection cc = gc[i].Captures;
    for (int j = 0; j < cc.Count; j++)
```

```
        {
            Capture cap = cc[j];
            Console.WriteLine(
                "Found '{0}' at position {1}",
                cap.Value, cap.Index);
        }
    }
}
```

The relationship between matches, groups, and captures is indicated in Figure 10-2.

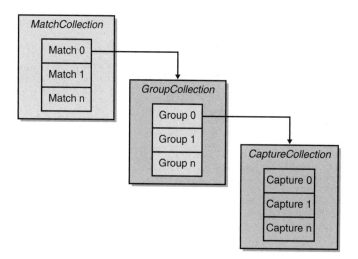

Figure 10-2   Matches, groups, and captures.

The *Group* class becomes much more powerful when used with named groups. You can make *Regex* put the captured substrings into *Group* objects with arbitrary names and then use these names via the *GroupCollection* string indexer:

```
Regex q = new Regex(
    "(?<something>\\w+):(?<another>\\w+)");
Match n = q.Match("Salary:123456");
Console.WriteLine(
    "{0} = {1}",
    n.Groups["something"].Value,
    n.Groups["another"].Value);
```

The output from this new block of code is:

```
Salary = 123456
```

Table 10-6 shows how the regular expression you just saw breaks down.

Table 10-6
Breakdown of a Typical Regular Expression

Element	Description
?<*something*>	Capture the matched substring into a group named "something".
\	Escape the following expression, which has a special meaning to *Regex*.
\w	A pattern that matches any "word" character (in other words, any alphabetic, numeric, or underscore character)—the same pattern as [a-zA-Z_0-9].
+	Allow for multiple instances of this pattern (in this case, any "word" characters).
:	Split the string at this delimiter.
?<*another*>\\w+	Capture the matched substring into a group named "another", matching any "word" characters.

String-Modifying Expressions

In addition to parsing strings to search for patterns by using methods such as *Split*, *Match*, and *Matches*, we can use methods in the *Regex* class for stripping out substrings, joining substrings, and generating modified strings. You can use *Regex.Replace* to perform common operations such as stripping leading and/or trailing whitespace, tokenizing or modifying pathnames, and splitting or joining lines of text. For example, to strip leading whitespace, we can initialize a *Regex* object with a regular expression that matches any number of whitespace characters at the beginning of a line (such as "^\s+") and then use *Regex.Replace* to replace all these characters with an empty string:

```
class RXmodifyingApp
{
    static void Main(string[] args)
    {
        string s = "    leading";
        string e = @"^\s+";
        Regex rx = new Regex(e);
        string r = rx.Replace(s,"");
        Console.WriteLine("Strip leading space: {0}", r);
    }
}
```

The output from this application is:

```
Strip leading space: leading
```

Table 10-7 breaks down the regular expression you just saw.

Table 10-7
Breakdown of Another Typical Regular Expression

Element	Description
@	"Escape" the \ in the pattern so that \s is treated as a single regular expression metacharacter.
^	At the beginning of the line...
\s	...match any whitespace character (space, tab, and so on)
+	...and any number of them.

The *Regex* class offers instance methods such as *Split*, *Replace*, and *Match* as well as static equivalents; therefore, you don't even have to instantiate a *Regex* object. This feature is particularly useful if you want to perform a series of regular expression operations. Because the *Regex* object is immutable, it might be more useful to use the static methods. The previous code can thus be rewritten like this:

```
//rx = new Regex(e);
//string r = rx.Replace(s,"");
string r = Regex.Replace(s, e, "");
```

By the same token—no pun intended—we can strip trailing spaces, modify pathnames, and convert date formats:

```
s = "trailing     ";
e = @"\s+$";
r = Regex.Replace(s, e, "");
Console.WriteLine("Strip trailing space: {0}", r);

Console.WriteLine();
s = @"C:\Documents and Settings\user1\Desktop\";
r = Regex.Replace(s, @"\\user1\\", @"\user2\");
Console.WriteLine(
    "Modify path:\n\t{0}\n\t{1}", s, r);

Console.WriteLine();
s = @"c:\foo\bar\file.txt";
e = @"^.*\\";
r = Regex.Replace(s, e, "");
Console.WriteLine(
    "Strip path from filename: {0}", r);

Console.WriteLine();
s = "03/16/57";
e =
```

```
    "(?<mm>\\d{1,2})/(?<dd>\\d{1,2})/(?<yy>\\d{2,4})";
string e2 = "${dd}-${mm}-${yy}";
r = Regex.Replace(s, e, e2);
Console.WriteLine(
    "Change date format from {0} to {1}", s, r);
```

The date-formatting regular expression just shown breaks down into three subpatterns, each with the same basic meaning, as shown in Table 10-8.

Table 10-8
Breakdown of a Date-Formatting Regular Expression

Element	Description
(?<*mm*>\\d{1,2})/	Capture the matched substring into a group named "mm", matching any decimal digit—of which there must be at least one and no more than two—followed by a forward slash.
${*mm*}-	Substitute the substring matched by (?<*mm*>) and follow it with a dash.

The output from these additional code blocks is:

```
Strip trailing space: trailing

Modify path:
        C:\Documents and Settings\user1\Desktop\
        C:\Documents and Settings\user2\Desktop\

Strip path from filename: file.txt

Change date format from 03/16/57 to 16-03-57
```

There's also a static version of *Regex.Match*, which can be used under similar circumstances. For example, to find the HREF link tags in some simple HTML:

```
Console.WriteLine();
s = @"<html>
    <a href=""first.htm"">first text</a>
    <br>loads of other stuff
    <a href=""second.htm"">second text</a>
    <p>more<a href=""third.htm"">third text</a>
    </html>";
e = @"<a[^>]*href\s*=\s*[""']?([^'"">]+)['""]?>";
MatchCollection mc = Regex.Matches(s, e);
foreach (Match mm in mc)
    Console.WriteLine("HTML links: {0}", mm);
```

Table 10-9 shows how the regular expression you just saw breaks down.

Table 10-9
Breakdown of a Typical HTML Regular Expression

Element	Description
<a[^>]*href	Match the character substring "<a" followed by zero or more instances of any characters except the ">" character, followed by the string "href",
\s*=\s*	followed by zero or more instances of whitespace, followed by the "=" character, followed by zero or more instances of whitespace,
['""]?	followed by zero or one instance of single or double quotes,
([^'"">]+)	followed by one or more instances of any characters except the single or double quotes or the closing ">",
['""]?>	followed by zero or one instance of either the single or double quotes.

The output from this additional code is:

```
HTML links: <a href="first.htm">
HTML links: <a href="second.htm">
HTML links: <a href="third.htm">
```

Finally, remember how in the "Strings" section of the chapter we used a custom method to convert a string to proper case (initial caps on each word in the string)? Here's another version that achieves the same result by using regular expressions instead of string processing:

```
public class RXProperCaseApp
{
    static void Main(string[] args)
    {
        string s  = "the qUEEn wAs in HER parLOr";
        Console.WriteLine("Initial String:\t{0}", s);

        s = s.ToLower();
        string e = @"\w+|\W+";
        string sProper = "";

        foreach (Match m in Regex.Matches(s, e))
        {
            sProper += char.ToUpper(m.Value[0])
                + m.Value.Substring(1, m.Length - 1);
        }
        Console.WriteLine("ProperCase:\t{0}", sProper);
```

```
        }
    }
```

This is the output:

```
Initial String: the qUEEn wAs in HER parLOr
ProperCase:     The Queen Was In Her Parlor
```

Regular Expression Options

Suppose that in a string we want to match some alternative patterns in which only the letter case differs. For instance, suppose we want to find any instance of the word "in"—or "In" or "IN" or "iN". We could use this pattern:

```
class RXOptionsApp
{
    public static void PrintMatches(Regex r)
    {
        Console.WriteLine();
        string s = "The KING Was In His Counting House";
        MatchCollection mc = r.Matches(s);
        for (int i = 0; i < mc.Count; i++)
        {
            Console.WriteLine(
                "Found '{0}' at position {1}",
                mc[i].Value, mc[i].Index);
        }
    }

    static void Main(string[] args)
    {
        Regex r = new Regex("in|In|IN|iN");    // Same
        PrintMatches(r);
    }
}
```

Here's the output:

```
Found 'IN' at position 5
Found 'In' at position 13
Found 'in' at position 25
```

Alternatively, we could use an overloaded *Regex* constructor that takes a *RegexOptions* enumeration value as its second parameter. For example, to get the same results as we just saw, we could use the *IgnoreCase* option:

```
r = new Regex("in", RegexOptions.IgnoreCase);
```

Another potentially useful *RegexOption* is *RightToLeft*:

```
r = new Regex("in",
    RegexOptions.IgnoreCase |
    RegexOptions.RightToLeft);
```

Given the previous behavior, the output from this version should be obvious:

```
Found 'in' at position 25
Found 'In' at position 13
Found 'IN' at position 5
```

Another feature—which is very useful if you're building complex expressions—is the ability to embed comments into a pattern by using the # delimiter. Of course, this wouldn't be much use if the *Regex* object then included the comments as part of the pattern to be searched. Therefore, you can construct a *Regex* with the *RegexOptions.IgnorePatternWhitespace* option—this ignores both embedded comments and any whitespace that isn't explicitly escaped:

```
r = new Regex(
    @"in         # this is the first pattern to match
    |[aeiou]s    # or any vowel followed by 's'
    ", RegexOptions.IgnorePatternWhitespace);
```

The output follows:

```
Found 'as' at position 10
Found 'is' at position 17
Found 'in' at position 25
Found 'us' at position 31
```

Compiling Regular Expressions

One of the *RegexOptions* enumeration values is *Compiled*:

```
r = new Regex("in", RegexOptions.Compiled);
```

The default behavior of the *regex* engine is to compile a regular expression to a sequence of internal instructions (not MSIL), which are interpreted upon execution. On the other hand, if you construct a *regex* object with the *regexoptions.compiled* option, the engine compiles the regular expression to explicit MSIL. This option allows the .NET framework's just-in-time compiler (JITter) to convert the expression to native machine code for higher performance.

For a complex expression that's used heavily, this conversion yields faster execution—of course, it also increases startup time. Also bear in mind that by using the *Compiled* option, you're effectively converting state data (which would be destroyed when the *Regex* object is garbage collected) into code (which is removed from memory only when the application terminates). So, choose when to use this option carefully.

A related feature is the ability to explicitly compile a regular expression to an assembly that's then persisted to disk by using the *Regex.CompileToAssembly* method. For example, suppose we have a lengthy regular expression such as one that parses an Internet Protocol (IP) address:

```
class RXassemblyApp
{
    static void Main(string[] args)
    {
        string s = "123.45.67.89";
        string e =
            @"([01]?\d\d?|2[0-4]\d|25[0-5])\." +
            @"([01]?\d\d?|2[0-4]\d|25[0-5])\." +
            @"([01]?\d\d?|2[0-4]\d|25[0-5])\." +
            @"([01]?\d\d?|2[0-4]\d|25[0-5])";
        Match m = Regex.Match(s, e);
        Console.WriteLine("IP Address: {0}", m);
        for (int i = 1; i < m.Groups.Count; i++)
            Console.WriteLine(
                "\tGroup{0}={1}", i, m.Groups[i]);
    }
}
```

This regular expression breaks down into four identical groups. Table 10-10 shows how each of these four groups breaks down.

Table 10-10
Breakdown of an IP Address Regular Expression

Element	Description
@"([01]?\d\d?	Either a 0 or 1 followed by any one or two digits,
|2[0-4]\d	or a 2 followed by any digit from 0 through 4, followed by any digit,
|25[0-5])	or the substring "25" followed by any digit from 0 through 5,
\.	followed by a "." character.

Here's the output:

```
IP Address: 123.45.67.89
        Group1=123
        Group2=45
        Group3=67
        Group4=89
```

We can explicitly compile this to a persistent assembly. First, set up an array of *RegexCompilationInfo* references—we need only one of these, but we have to have an array to pass to *Regex.CompileToAssembly*. Set up this one instance with the regular expression pattern, any *RegexOptions* flags, the name you want for your assembly, and any namespace you want to use for it. The final parameter is a Boolean value that indicates whether the regular expression should be public:

```
RegexCompilationInfo [] rci =
    new RegexCompilationInfo[1];
rci[0] = new RegexCompilationInfo(
    e, RegexOptions.Compiled,
    "MyRegexAssembly", "MyNamespace", true);
```

Then set up an *AssemblyName* object. The assembly cache manager uses the object for binding and retrieving information about an assembly. We need to set only one property of this object: the filename for the assembly itself. The extension .dll is assumed and will be appended automatically. Finally, pass both the *RegexCompilationInfo* array and the *AssemblyName* reference to *Regex.CompileToAssembly*:

```
AssemblyName an = new AssemblyName();
an.Name = "MyAss";
Regex.CompileToAssembly(rci, an);
```

When you run this code, you'll find that a new file named MyAss.dll has been created in the same location as the target for this current assembly, which is normally ..\bin\debug. If we examine the metadata for this assembly, shown in Figure 10-3, we'll see that it contains three classes: *MyRegexAssembly* (via the third parameter to the *RegexCompilationInfo* constructor) derived from *Regex*, *MyRegexAssemblyFactory* derived from *RegexRunnerFactory*, and *MyRegex-AssemblyRunner* derived from *RegexRunner*.

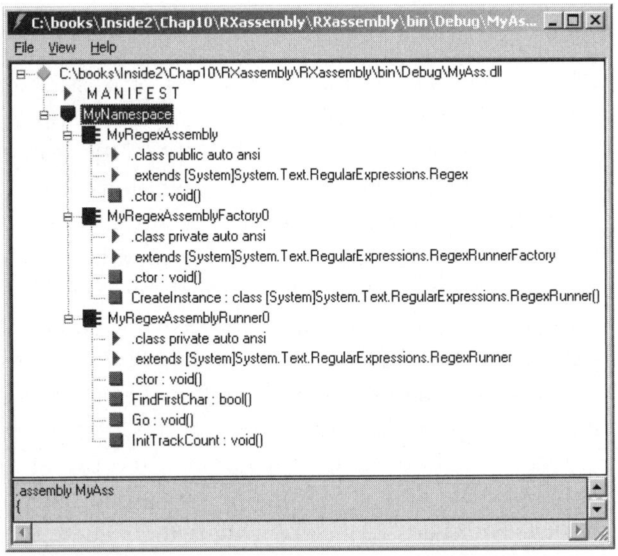

Figure 10-3   Metadata for compiled regular expression.

We could then use this customized derived *MyRegexAssembly* class in another project. In this example, I've added MyAss.dll as a reference to the new project:

```
using System;
using System.Text.RegularExpressions;
using MyNamespace;

    class TestAssemblyApp
    {
        static void Main(string[] args)
        {
            string s = "123.45.67.89";
            MyRegexAssembly r = new MyRegexAssembly();
            Match m = r.Match(s);
            Console.WriteLine("IP Address: {0}", m);
            for (int i = 1; i < m.Groups.Count; i++)
                Console.WriteLine(
                    "\tGroup{0}={1}", i, m.Groups[i]);
        }
    }
```

Summary

In this chapter, we examined two primary classes for processing strings, *String* and *Regex*, plus a range of ancillary classes that modify and support string operations. We explored the use of the *String* class methods for searching, sorting, splitting, joining, and otherwise returning modified strings. We also saw how many other classes in the .NET Framework support string processing—including *Console*, the basic numeric types, and *DateTime*—and how culture information and character encoding can affect string formatting. Finally, we saw how the system performs sneaky string interning to improve runtime efficiency.

In the second part of this chapter, we looked at *Regex* and its supporting classes—*Match*, *Group*, and *Capture*—for encapsulating regular expressions. We explored both pattern searching and string modifying through the set of *Regex* instance and static methods, and we examined the use of *RegexOptions* to modify the behavior of the operation. Finally, we saw how we can compile regular expressions to assemblies as a code management strategy.

Clearly, there's some overlap in functionality between strings and regular expressions. String-based code is probably simpler and easier to maintain, while *Regex*-based code will generally be much more flexible and powerful. In many situations, you'll find that a judicious mixture of both is the best approach.

11

File I/O with Streams

This chapter divides neatly into two main topics. First, we'll consider the .NET Framework classes, which meet the lower-level data transfer requirements of the streams-based I/O framework. These classes further divide into stream classes and file system classes—that is, classes that actually represent data streams, and classes that represent file system objects such as files and directories. The second topic we'll look at is how you can enhance any custom class to allow it to fit seamlessly into the standard I/O framework. This enhancement is based on a standard attribute that marks your class as capable of being serialized. The serialization process is used in conjunction with the stream classes to transfer your custom class objects from one place to another—in memory, to a remote location, or to persistent storage. As part of our exploration of the streams framework, we'll consider the different types of stream, types of file system objects, and potential application environments, including Microsoft Windows–based and Web-based environments.

Stream Classes

The .NET Framework classes offer a streams-based I/O framework, with the core classes in the *System.IO* namespace. All classes that represent streams inherit from the *Stream* class, and the key classes are listed in Table 11-1.

Table 11-1
Stream Classes in the .NET Framework

Class	Description
Stream	The abstract base class *Stream* supports reading and writing bytes.
FileStream	In addition to basic *Stream* behavior, this class supports random access to files through its *Seek* method and supports both synchronous and asynchronous operation.
MemoryStream	A nonbuffered stream whose encapsulated data is directly accessible in memory. This stream has no backing store and might be useful as a temporary buffer.
BufferedStream	A stream that adds buffering to another stream, such as a *NetworkStream*. (*FileStream* already has buffering internally, and a *MemoryStream* doesn't need buffering.) A *BufferedStream* object can be composed around some types of streams to improve read and write performance.
TextReader	The abstract base class for *StreamReader* and *StringReader* objects. While the implementations of the abstract *Stream* class are designed for byte input and output, the implementations of *TextReader* are designed for Unicode character output.
StreamReader	Reads characters from a *Stream*, using *Encoding* to convert characters to and from bytes.
StringReader	Reads characters from a *String*. *StringReader* allows you to treat a *String* with the same API; thus, your output can be either a *Stream* in any encoding or a *String*.
TextWriter	The abstract base class for *StreamWriter* and *StringWriter* objects. While the implementations of the abstract *Stream* class are designed for byte input and output, the implementations of *TextWriter* are designed for Unicode character input.
StreamWriter	Writes characters to a *Stream*, using *Encoding* to convert characters to bytes.
StringWriter	Writes characters to a *String*. *StringWriter* allows you to treat a *String* with the same API; thus, your output can be either a *Stream* in any encoding or a *String*.
BinaryReader	Reads binary data from a stream.
BinaryWriter	Writes binary data to a stream.

Two classes derived from *Stream* but not listed in Table 11-1 are offered in other namespaces. The *NetworkStream* class represents a *Stream* over a network connection and resides in the *System.Net.Sockets* namespace, and the *CryptoStream* class links data streams to cryptographic transformations and resides in the *System.Security.Cryptography* namespace.

The design of the *Stream* class and its derivatives is intended to provide a generic view of data sources and destinations so that the developer can interchangeably use any of these classes without redesigning the application. In general, *Stream* objects are capable of one or more of the following:

■ **Reading** The transfer of data from a stream into a data structure, such as an array of bytes

■ **Writing** The transfer of data from a data structure into a stream

■ **Seeking** The querying and modifying of the current position within a stream

Note that a given stream might not support all these features. For example, *NetworkStream* objects don't support seeking. You can use the *CanRead*, *CanWrite*, and *CanSeek* properties of *Stream* and its derived classes to determine precisely which operations a given stream does in fact support.

FileStream

Let's dive into some code. Consider this simple use of *FileStream*, which creates a file, writes out an array of bytes, and closes the file. The application then opens the file again, tests that the stream supports reading, and reads in the bytes one by one, converting each byte to a character and appending it to a string:

```
using System.IO;

    public class StreamsIOApp
    {
        public static void Main(string[] args)
        {
            byte[] buf1 = new Byte[]
                {76,101,116,32,116,104,101,114,101,
                32,98,101,32,108,105,103,104,116};
            Stream s = new FileStream(
                "Foo.txt", FileMode.Create);
            s.Write(buf1, 0, buf1.Length);
            s.Close();
```

```
        s = new FileStream(
            "Foo.txt", FileMode.Open);
        int i;
        string str = "";
        if (s.CanRead)
        {
            for (i = 0; (i = s.ReadByte()) != -1; i++)
            {
                str += (char)i;
            }
        }
        s.Close();
        Console.WriteLine(str);
    }
  }
}
```

Here's the output:

```
Let there be light
```

Note that we're using only the *Stream* (virtual) methods, so we can safely use a *Stream* reference to the derived *FileStream* object. Of course, we also could've written the code to use a *FileStream* reference:

```
//Stream s = new FileStream(
FileStream s = new FileStream(
```

It's no coincidence that the stream methods tend to use bytes and byte arrays—you can visualize a stream as a byte array that might be attached to some memory buffer or to some disk file or device. Streams use the concept of an internal stream pointer: when you open the stream, the stream pointer is normally positioned at the first byte of the stream. Most streams support *seeking*—the ability to move the internal stream pointer to an arbitrary position. Therefore, instead of the create-write-close-open-read-close pattern, we can avoid closing and opening when we want to switch between writing and reading by seeking in between.

For example, the following continuation code reopens the same file, reports on its length and the position of the internal stream pointer, and then tests to see whether the stream supports seeking. If the stream does, we seek 13 bytes from one of the three relative starting points: *SeekOrigin.Begin*, *SeekOrigin.Current*, or *SeekOrigin.End*. If we write to the stream at that point, we'll overwrite some of the data that was originally in the stream. We can then seek again—rather than closing and opening—before reading from the file:

```
byte[] buf2 = new Byte[]
    {97,112,112,108,101,115,97,117,99,101};
s = new FileStream(
    "Foo.txt", FileMode.Open);
Console.WriteLine(
    "Length: {0}, Position: {1}",
    s.Length, s.Position);
if (s.CanSeek)
{
    s.Seek(13, SeekOrigin.Begin);
    Console.WriteLine(
        "Position: {0}", s.Position);
    s.Write(buf2, 0, buf2.Length);
}

str = "";
s.Seek(0, SeekOrigin.Begin);
for (i = 0; (i = s.ReadByte()) != -1; i++)
{
    str += (char)i;
}
Console.WriteLine(str);
```

Here's the output:

```
Length: 18, Position: 0
Position: 13
Let there be applesauce
```

Note that if you want to seek from *SeekOrigin.End*, you should supply a negative value. However, if you want to seek from *SeekOrigin.Current*, you can supply either a positive or negative value depending on which direction you want to go. In addition to using the *Length* and *Position* properties, you could even arbitrarily set the length by using *Stream.SetLength*.

```
str = "";
s.SetLength(s.Length - 4);
s.Seek(0, SeekOrigin.Begin);
for (i = 0; (i = s.ReadByte()) != -1; i++)
{
    str += (char)i;
}
s.Close();
Console.WriteLine(str);
```

This is the output:

```
Let there be apples
```

> **Note**   A stream must support both writing and seeking for *SetLength*
> to work.

Instead of using *Seek*, we could achieve the same effect by using the *Position* property:

```
//s.Seek(0, SeekOrigin.Begin);
s.Position = 0;
```

Finally, we could append to the end of the file. If you open a stream for appending, the internal stream pointer will be positioned at the end of the stream, not the beginning, as is normally the case. *FileMode.Append* can be used only in conjunction with *FileAccess.Write*—any attempt to read from the file will fail and throw an *ArgumentException*. Hence, once we've opened the file for appending and have written out some more data, we must close it and reopen it before reading from it:

```
byte[] buf4 = new Byte[]
    {32,97,110,100,32,112,101,97,114,115};
s = new FileStream(
    "Foo.txt", FileMode.Append, FileAccess.Write);
s.Write(buf4, 0, buf4.Length);
s.Close();

s = new FileStream(
    "Foo.txt", FileMode.Open);
str = "";
for (i = 0; (i = s.ReadByte()) != -1; i++)
{
    str += (char)i;
}
Console.WriteLine(str);
s.Close();
```

This is the output:

```
Let there be apples and pears
```

> **Note**   If you construct a *FileStream* object with *FileMode.Append* and
> don't specify the access permissions, the object will be constructed with
> read permission. Therefore, the following statements are equivalent:

```
    s = new FileStream(
//      "Foo.txt", FileMode.Append, FileAccess.Write);
        "Foo.txt", FileMode.Append);
```

As a general rule, you should always protect your file-handling operations with the appropriate exception-handling code. In this chapter, we'll keep this code to a minimum because we'll address the subject properly in Chapter 12, "Error Handling with Exceptions."

StreamReader and *StreamWriter*

As you can see, *FileStream* is OK for reading and writing raw byte (binary) data. If you want to work with character data, classes such as *StreamReader* and *StreamWriter* are more suitable. These classes will use a *FileStream* object in the background, effectively interposing a character-interpolation layer on top of the raw byte processing. Closing the *StreamReader/StreamWriter* also closes the underlying *FileStream*:

```
public class ReadWriteApp
{
    public static void Main(string[] args)
    {
        FileStream s =
            new FileStream("Bar.txt", FileMode.Create);
        StreamWriter w = new StreamWriter(s);
        w.Write("Hello World");
        w.Close();

        s = new FileStream("Bar.txt", FileMode.Open);
        StreamReader r = new StreamReader(s);
        string t;
        while ((t = r.ReadLine()) != null)
        {
            Console.WriteLine(t);
        }
        w.Close();
    }
}
```

The output follows:

```
Hello World
```

Recall from Table 11-1 that the *StreamReader* and *StreamWriter* classes can use *Encoding* to convert characters to bytes and vice versa. To write our data to the file with some encoding other than the default, we need to construct the *StreamWriter* and *StreamReader* with an *Encoding* parameter, as shown here:

```
//StreamWriter w = new StreamWriter(s);
StreamWriter w = new StreamWriter(
s, System.Text.Encoding.BigEndianUnicode);
```

> **More Info**   Encoding is discussed in more detail in Chapter 10, "String Han-
> dling and Regular Expressions."

> **Note**   If you want to open a file that's been set to read-only, you need
> to pass an additional parameter to the *FileStream* constructor to spec-
> ify that you only want to read from the file:
>
> ```
> s = new FileStream(
>     "../../TextFile1.txt",
>     FileMode.Open, FileAccess.Read);
> ```

Paths in C#

Because C# treats the backslash the same way as C and C++ do, if you want to specify a path for a file, you have three choices. You can either use double backslashes, as in:

```
s = new FileStream(
    "C:\\temp\\Goo.txt", FileMode.Create);
```

or use forward (Unix-style) slashes:

```
s = new FileStream(
    "C:/temp/Goo.txt", FileMode.Create);
```

or use the at sign (@), which is a control-character suppressor:

```
s = new FileStream(
    @"C:\temp\Goo.txt", FileMode.Create);
```

Memory and Buffered Streams

The classes *MemoryStream* and *BufferedStream* are both derived from the abstract *Stream* class, just as *FileStream* is. Therefore, *MemoryStream* and *BufferedStream* share many of the same characteristics and functionality. Both are designed for streaming data into and out of memory rather than persistent storage. Both can be associated with a stream of another kind—such as a file—if required, and thus both can be used to act as a buffer between memory and persistent storage. The *MemoryStream* class offers methods such as *WriteTo*, which will write to another stream. Similarly, a *BufferedStream* object is normally associated with another stream upon construction, and when you close the *BufferedStream*, its contents are flushed to the associated stream. In the following example, we first create a *MemoryStream* object with an initial capacity of 64 bytes and print some arbitrary property values. Then we write out 64 bytes and report the same properties. We then use *MemoryStream.GetBuffer* to get a byte array of the entire contents of the stream and print the values, before finally closing the stream:

```
class MemStreamApp
{
    static void Main(string[] args)
    {
        MemoryStream m = new MemoryStream(64);
        Console.WriteLine(
            "Length: {0}\tPosition: {1}\tCapacity: {2}",
            m.Length, m.Position, m.Capacity);

        for (int i = 0; i < 64; i++)
        {
            m.WriteByte((byte)i);
        }
        Console.WriteLine(
            "Length: {0}\tPosition: {1}\tCapacity: {2}",
            m.Length, m.Position, m.Capacity);

        Console.WriteLine("\nContents:");
        byte[] ba = m.GetBuffer();
        foreach (byte b in ba)
        {
            Console.Write("{0,-3}", b);
        }

        m.Close();
    }
}
```

Here's the output:

```
Length: 0        Position: 0      Capacity: 64
Length: 64       Position: 64     Capacity: 64

Contents:
0  1  2  3  4  5  6  7  8  9  10 11 12 13 14 15 16 17 18 19
20 21 22 23 24 25 26 27 28 29 30 31 32 33 34 35 36 37 38 39
40 41 42 43 44 45 46 47 48 49 50 51 52 53 54 55 56 57 58 59
60 61 62 63
```

Given that the stream is already up to capacity, let's see what happens if we write some more data to it. Will it generate a run-time exception? Will it overrun into unallocated memory? Or will it just dynamically resize the buffer? The last scenario is, of course, the correct one—which you'll realize if you've examined the previous output closely. Although we set an initial capacity of 64, this wasn't the initial size of the memory buffer because the buffer was initialized to 0. So, clearly, the buffer is dynamically resized automatically.

```
string s = "Foo";
for (int i = 0; i < 3; i++)
{
    m.WriteByte((byte)s[i]);
}
Console.WriteLine(
    "\nLength: {0}\tPosition: {1}\tCapacity: {2}",
    m.Length, m.Position, m.Capacity);
```

Here's the output:

```
Length: 67       Position: 67     Capacity: 256
```

As you can see, the minimum block size is 256 bytes.

Finally, let's associate this *MemoryStream* with a *FileStream* before closing it:

```
FileStream fs = new FileStream("Goo.txt",
    FileMode.Create, FileAccess.Write);
m.WriteTo(fs);
m.Close();
```

If you examine the Goo.txt file, you should see the following contents:

```
_____  _____- !"#$%&'()*+,-./
0123456789:;<=>?Foo _____  _____- !"#$%&'()*+,-./
0123456789:;<=>?@ABCDEFGHIJKLMNOPQRSTUVWXYZ[\]^_`abcdefghijklmnopqrstu-
vwxyz{|}~-__,f,…†‡ˆ‰Š‹→___''""•---˜™š›¡__Ÿ ¡¢£'¥¦:¨©'«"-®¯"±²³´ ¶·¸¹º»¼½
```

Now let's do the same thing with a *BufferedStream* object. Although generally similar, there are some subtle differences between *MemoryStream* and *BufferedStream*. First, we can construct a *BufferedStream* only by initializing it to some other existing *Stream*—in this example, a file. The buffer in a *Buffered-Stream* is managed differently than that in the *MemoryStream*: if we don't specify an initial size when we construct the object, it defaults to 4096 bytes. Also, if we've written some data to the *BufferedStream* and want to read it back, we must use the *Read* method—because there is no *GetBuffer* method. Using the *Read* method means making sure the internal stream pointer is positioned correctly—in this case, at the beginning of the stream—before attempting the read:

```
class BufStreamApp
{
    static void Main(string[] args)
    {
        // Create a FileStream for the BufferedStream.
        FileStream fs = new FileStream("Hoo.txt",
            FileMode.Create, FileAccess.ReadWrite);
        BufferedStream bs = new BufferedStream(fs);
        Console.WriteLine(
            "Length: {0}\tPosition: {1}",
            bs.Length, bs.Position);

        for (int i = 0; i < 64; i++)
        {
            bs.WriteByte((byte)i);
        }
        Console.WriteLine(
            "Length: {0}\tPosition: {1}",
            bs.Length, bs.Position);

        // Reset to the beginning and read the data.
        Console.WriteLine("\nContents:");
        byte[] ba = new byte[bs.Length];
        bs.Position = 0;
        bs.Read(ba, 0, (int)bs.Length);
        foreach (byte b in ba)
        {
            Console.Write("{0,-3}", b);
        }

        // Write some more, exceeding capacity.
        string s = "Foo";
        for (int i = 0; i < 3; i++)
        {
            bs.WriteByte((byte)s[i]);
        }
        Console.WriteLine(
            "\nLength: {0}\tPosition: {1}\t",
            bs.Length, bs.Position);
```

```
        for (int i = 0; i < (256-67)+1; i++)
        {
            bs.WriteByte((byte)i);
        }
        Console.WriteLine(
            "\nLength: {0}\tPosition: {1}\t",
            bs.Length, bs.Position);

        bs.Close();
    }
}
```

The console output is listed here:

```
Length: 0       Position: 0
Length: 64      Position: 64

Contents:
0  1  2  3  4  5  6  7  8  9  10 11 12 13 14 15 16 17 18 19
20 21 22 23 24 25 26 27 28 29 30 31 32 33 34 35 36 37 38 39
40 41 42 43 44 45 46 47 48 49 50 51 52 53 54 55 56 57 58 59
60 61 62 63

Length: 67      Position: 67
```

Note that the Hoo.txt file will have the same contents as those in the *MemoryStream* example. We didn't have to explicitly write from the *BufferedStream* to the *FileStream* as we did for *MemoryStream* because the *BufferedStream* must be associated with another stream in the first place. All writes to the *BufferedStream* will be buffered for writing to the associated stream, and merely closing the *BufferedStream* object is enough to flush any pending writes to the file.

String Readers and Writers

Recall from Chapter 10 that objects of the *String* class are immutable but that you can process mutable objects of the *StringBuilder* class. The functionality offered by the *StringReader* and *StringWriter* classes overlaps somewhat with that of the *MemoryStream*, *BufferedStream*, *String*, and *StringBuilder* classes. You can use *StringWriter* to build a mutable string in memory and extract from it either a *String* or a *StringBuilder* class. *StringWriter* has a *Write* and a *WriteLine* method that function almost identically to those in the *Console* class, and you can build the internal string in a *StringWriter* by using any technique that works with a raw string. For example:

```
class StringReadWriteApp
{
    static void Main(string[] args)
```

```
    {
        StringWriter w = new StringWriter();
        w.WriteLine("Sing a song of {0} pence", 6);
        string s = "A pocket full of rye";
        w.Write(s);
        w.Write(w.NewLine);
        w.Write(
            String.Format(4 +" and " +20 +" blackbirds"));
        w.Write(new StringBuilder(" baked in a pie"));
        w.WriteLine();
        w.Close();
        Console.WriteLine(w);
    }
}
```

Here's the output:

```
Sing a song of 6 pence
A pocket full of rye
4 and 20 blackbirds baked in a pie
```

Clearly, when we pass the *StringWriter* reference to *Console.WriteLine*, the *ToString* method is being invoked. Note the call to *StringWriter.Close* in the preceding code. Although there's a *Flush* method in the *StringWriter* class, flushing the stream won't flush its underlying encoder unless you explicitly call *Close*. Closing the stream will automatically flush it and will ready it for destruction by calling *Dispose*. It's also instructive to step through this code in the debugger, where you'll clearly see that the *StringWriter* contains an internal *StringBuilder* field named *_sb*, which in turn contains a *String* field named *m_StringValue*. Figure 11-1 shows these fields.

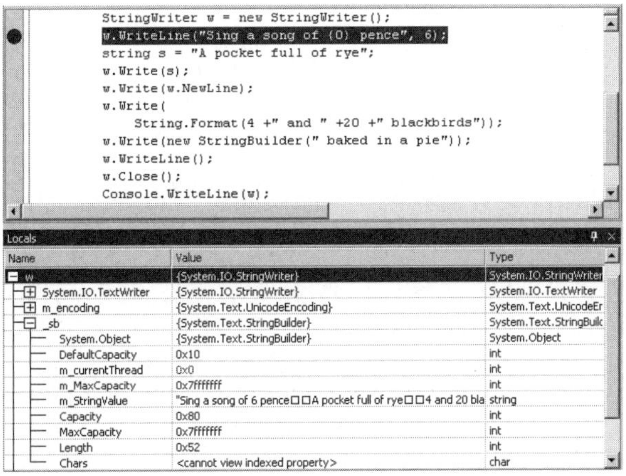

Figure 11-1   *StringWriter, StringBuilder*, and *String*.

Let's continue with this example to modify the string a little more: get a reference to the internal *StringBuilder* field, and make changes to the *String-Writer* via that reference, as shown next. Keep the call to the *Close* method at the bottom, after you've finished working with the stream.

```
StringBuilder sb = w.GetStringBuilder();
int i = sb.Length;
sb.Append("The birds began to sing");
sb.Insert(i, "When the pie was opened\n");
sb.AppendFormat(
    "\nWasn't that a {0} to set before the King",
    "dainty dish");
Console.WriteLine(w);
```

The additional output from this block of code is shown here:

```
Sing a song of 6 pence
A pocket full of rye
4 and 20 blackbirds baked in a pie
When the pie was opened
The birds began to sing
Wasn't that a dainty dish to set before the King
```

The *StringReader* class is very simple. We can construct a *StringReader* from the string in the *StringWriter* and then use the *Read*, *ReadLine*, *ReadBlock*, and *ReadToEnd* methods to read characters from the string. This additional code will produce the same output as the previous code block did:

```
Console.WriteLine();
StringReader r = new StringReader(w.ToString());
string t = r.ReadLine();
Console.WriteLine(t);
Console.Write((char)r.Read());
char[] ca = new char[37];
r.Read(ca, 0, 19);
Console.Write(ca);
r.ReadBlock(ca, 0, 37);
Console.Write(ca);
Console.WriteLine(r.ReadToEnd());
r.Close();
w.Close();
```

Note *Read* will read either one character or a block of characters. (If *Read* reads a block of characters, it behaves exactly as *ReadBlock* does.)

Binary Readers and Writers

Recall that the *StreamWriter* class provides a text-interpolation layer on top of another stream, such as a *FileStream*. The *StreamWriter.Write* method is heavily overloaded. Thus, not only can we pass it text, we also can pass it data of type *char, int, float,* or any other standard type—as well as an open-ended (*params*) number of objects and anything derived from objects. Of course, this works similarly to the way that *Console.Write* works: all data of all types is converted to text before being written to the stream. The *BinaryWriter* class allows you to write data to a stream without this text interpolation so that the data is written in binary form. For example, compare the two files that result from the following code—one written by using *StreamWriter*, the other with *BinaryWriter*:

```
class BinReadWriteApp
{
    static void Main(string[] args)
    {
        Stream s =
            new FileStream("Foo.txt", FileMode.Create);
        StreamWriter w = new StreamWriter(s);
        w.Write("Hello World ");
        w.Write(123);
        w.Write(' ');
        w.Write(45.67);
        w.Close();
        s.Close();

        Stream t =
            new FileStream("Bar.dat", FileMode.Create);
        BinaryWriter b = new BinaryWriter(t);
        b.Write("Hello World ");
        b.Write(123);
        b.Write(' ');
        b.Write(45.67);
        b.Close();
        t.Close();
    }
}
```

You can open the two output files in Notepad or from the Microsoft Visual Studio File | Open | File menu. The contents of Foo.txt are shown here:

```
Hello World 123 45.67
```

The contents of Bar.dat are shown here:

```
_Hello World {      ŏ(\_ÂÕF@
```

We'd probably accept that the unreadable stuff after "Hello, World " is the binary numeric data. A quick check of the ASCII table reveals that the decimal value 123 is the character "{", so the rest must be the floating-point value. But what's that unprintable character at the beginning of the file? If we open the file in Visual Studio instead of in Notepad, Visual Studio will use a binary/hex editor when it recognizes nonprintable characters in the file. Take a look at Figure 11-2.

```
Start Page | Class1.cs | Bar.dat |                                              ◁ ▷ ✕
00000000   0C 48 65 6C 6C 6F 20 57  6F 72 6C 64 20 7B 00 00   .Hello World {..
00000010   00 20 F6 28 5C 8F C2 D5  46 40                     . .(\...F@
```

Figure 11-2   A binary file in the binary/hex editor.

Now it becomes clearer. The string "Hello, World" is easy to see, followed by 0x20, which is the space; then the decimal 123, which is 0x7B (the character "{"); followed by another space; then 8 bytes of floating-point value. As you can see, the value of the very first byte in the stream is 0x0C, or decimal 12. Anyone with any experience using strings in Microsoft Visual Basic or using BSTRs in COM development will recognize this right away. It's the length of the following string—including the space at the end.

Naturally, if you plan to write binary data, you'll want to read back binary data by using the *BinaryReader* class, as illustrated in the following code. When you do so, remember to keep the *Close* calls at the end.

```
b.BaseStream.Position = 0;
BinaryReader r = new BinaryReader(t);
int i = 0;
while (true)
{
    i = b.BaseStream.ReadByte();
    if (-1 == i)
    {
        Console.WriteLine();
        break;
    }
    Console.Write("{0,-4}", i);
}

r.Close();
b.Close();
t.Close();
```

Here's the output from this revised application:

```
12  72  101 108 108 111 32  87  111 114 108 100 32
123 0   0   0   32  246 40  92  143 194 213 70  64
```

File System Classes

In addition to the *Stream* class and its various derivatives, the .NET Framework classes also offer a set of file system–related classes for encapsulating information and functionality that's suitable for processing files and directories. These classes reside in the *System.IO* namespace and are listed in Table 11-2.

Table 11-2
File System Classes in the .NET Framework

Class	Description
FileSystemInfo	The abstract base class for *FileInfo* and *DirectoryInfo* objects, this class contains methods that are common to both file and directory manipulation. Useful when processing a lot of files and directories.
DirectoryInfo	Supports creation, deletion, and manipulation of directories (only instance methods).
FileInfo	Supports creation, deletion, and manipulation of files (only instance methods).
Directory	Supports creation, deletion, and manipulation of directories. (All methods are static.)
File	Supports creation, deletion, and manipulation of files. (All methods are static.)
Path	Performs operations on a *String* that contains file or directory path information—the file or directory doesn't need to exist.

Directory and *DirectoryInfo*

The *FileInfo* and *DirectoryInfo* classes encapsulate information about files and directories as well as methods, such as *Create, Delete, Open, MoveTo,* and *CopyTo*. These classes two also offer behavior similar to that of *CFile* in the Microsoft Foundation Classes (MFC) and *fstream* in the Standard C++ library. The following example gets a *DirectoryInfo* object from the static *Directory.Get-CurrentDirectory* method and then calls the *DirectoryInfo.GetFiles* instance method to get a collection of *FileInfo* objects. Finally, we iterate this collection to report on some arbitrary properties of each file:

```
public class DirInfoApp
{
    public static void Main(string[] args)
    {
        DirectoryInfo dir = new DirectoryInfo(
            Directory.GetCurrentDirectory());
```

```
Console.WriteLine(
        "Current Dir: {0}", dir.FullName);

    foreach (FileInfo f in dir.GetFiles())
    {
        Console.WriteLine("{0,-14}{1,10}{2,20}",
            f.Name, f.Length, f.LastWriteTime);
    }
}
}
```

Here's the output:

```
Current Dir: C:\InsideCsharp\Chap11\DirInfo\DirInfo\bin\Debug
DirInfo.exe         6144 04/01/2002 21:06:30
DirInfo.pdb        13824 04/01/2002 21:06:30
```

In addition to using *GetCurrentDirectory*, we can construct *DirectoryInfo* objects by using a string for the desired path:

```
dir = new DirectoryInfo(".");
dir = new DirectoryInfo(@"C:\Winnt");
```

The first example, of course, will produce the same results as calling *Get-CurrentDirectory will*. Another useful method is *GetDirectories*, which will return as *DirectoryInfo* objects a collection of subdirectories of the current directory. The common parentage of *DirectoryInfo* and *FileInfo* is clear from the following code:

```
Console.WriteLine(
    "\n{0,-32}{1}", "Name", "LastWriteTime");
foreach (DirectoryInfo d in dir.GetDirectories())
{
    Console.WriteLine(
    "{0,-32}{1}", d.Name, d.LastWriteTime);
}
```

This is the output:

```
Name                            LastWriteTime
$NtUninstallQ301625$            24/12/2001 17:37:43
A5W_DATA                        11/02/2001 15:18:25
addins                          25/11/2001 12:16:25
AppPatch                        24/12/2001 15:14:34
Assembly                        24/12/2001 15:23:47
Config                          25/11/2001 12:17:06
Connection Wizard               07/01/2000 11:27:04
CSC                             25/11/2001 17:56:56
Cursors                         24/12/2001 15:15:07
Debug                           07/01/2002 09:00:23
Downloaded Program Files        16/12/2001 11:15:14
```

```
Driver Cache              07/01/2000 11:27:04
Fonts                     25/11/2001 15:17:08
Help                      24/12/2001 16:03:31
IIS Temporary Compressed Files  06/04/2001 10:46:27
⋮
```

The *DirectoryInfo* class offers a reasonable set of methods for creating, deleting, moving, and so on. For instance, we could create a new directory at some arbitrary location. (In the following example, the new directory is created within the current directory.) We could then create a subdirectory within the new directory, set and then get some attributes, and finally delete both the subdirectory and the newly created parent directory:

```
dir = new DirectoryInfo("Foo");
if (false == dir.Exists)
    dir.Create();

DirectoryInfo dis = dir.CreateSubdirectory("Bar");
dis.Attributes |=
    FileAttributes.Hidden | FileAttributes.Archive;

Console.WriteLine("{0,-10}{1,-10}{2}",
    dis.Name, dis.Parent, dis.Attributes);

dis.Delete(true);
dir.Delete(true);
```

The output follows:

```
Bar       Foo       Hidden, Directory, Archive
```

Recall that the library also offers the *Directory* class, which exposes only static methods. Thus, in the previous code, we could've used the static method *Directory.Delete* instead and achieved the same results:

```
//dir.Delete(true);
Directory.Delete(dir.Name, true);
```

The set of methods offered by the *Directory* class more or less parallels the instance methods in the *DirectoryInfo* class. The same parallelism is true for the *File* and *FileInfo* classes. In both cases, a couple of additional methods that aren't offered by the parallel class exist. For instance, the *Directory* class offers a *GetLogicalDrives* method:

```
string[] sa = Directory.GetLogicalDrives();
Console.WriteLine("Logical Drives:");
foreach (string s in sa)
{
    Console.Write("{0,-4}", s);
}
```

Here's the output:

```
Logical Drives:
A:\ C:\ D:\ E:\ F:\
```

File and *FileInfo*

In addition to offering a *Directory* class with only static methods and a *DirectoryInfo* class with only instance methods, the library offers a *File* class with only static methods and a *FileInfo* class with only instance methods. To explore these two classes, we'll rewrite our example from the "Stream Classes" section that used *FileStream*, *StreamReader*, and *StreamWriter*—first using *FileInfo*, then using *File*.

In the first example that follows, we use a *FileInfo* object and the *FileInfo.Create* method in place of the overloaded *FileStream* constructor. Similarly, we later open the same file by using *FileInfo.Open* in place of the *FileStream* constructor. When you open a file this way, you must supply the open mode (*Append*, *Create*, *CreateNew*, *Open*, *OpenOrCreate*, or *Truncate*), access permissions (*Read*, *ReadWrite*, or *Write*), and sharing permissions you want to grant to other objects using this file (*None*, *Read*, *ReadWrite*, or *Write*). As you can see, one advantage of using *FileInfo* instead of *FileStream* in this situation is that we can reuse the same *FileInfo* object—which contains property values such as the filename—and simply regenerate a *FileStream* object opened in the manner we require:

```
class FileFileInfoApp
{
    static void Main(string[] args)
    {
//        Stream s =
//            new FileStream("Bar.txt", FileMode.Create);
        FileInfo f = new FileInfo("Bar.txt");
        FileStream fs = f.Create();

        StreamWriter w = new StreamWriter(fs);
        w.Write("Hello World");
        w.Close();

//          s = new FileStream("Bar.txt", FileMode.Open);
        fs = f.Open(FileMode.Open,
                FileAccess.Read, FileShare.None);
        StreamReader r = new StreamReader(fs);
        string t;
        while ((t = r.ReadLine()) != null)
        {
```

```
            Console.WriteLine(t);
        }
        w.Close();
        fs.Close();
        f.Delete();
    }
}
```

The equivalent code using the *File* class static methods is this:

```
FileInfo f2 = new FileInfo("Bar.txt");
FileStream fs2 = File.Create("Bar.txt");

StreamWriter w2 = new StreamWriter(fs2);
w2.Write("Goodbye Mars");
w2.Close();

fs2 = File.Open("Bar.txt", FileMode.Open,
    FileAccess.Read, FileShare.None);
StreamReader r2 = new StreamReader(fs2);
while ((t = r2.ReadLine()) != null)
{
    Console.WriteLine(t);
}
w2.Close();
fs2.Close();
f2.Delete();
```

One advantage that the *FileInfo* and *File* classes have over the *FileStream* class in this situation is the *OpenText*, *CreateText*, and *AppendText* methods. These methods will return *StreamReader* or *StreamWriter* objects; therefore, we can use them as a kind of shortcut, bypassing the need for a *FileStream* object:

```
FileInfo f3 = new FileInfo("Bar.txt");
StreamWriter w3 = f3.CreateText();
w3.Write("Farewell Pluto");
w3.Close();

StreamReader r3 = f3.OpenText();
while ((t = r3.ReadLine()) != null)
{
    Console.WriteLine(t);
}
w3.Close();
```

Parsing Paths

The *Path* class is designed to enable you to easily perform common operations such as determining whether a filename extension is part of a path and combining two strings into one pathname. A *path* is a string that provides the location of a file or directory: it doesn't necessarily point to a location on disk. Most members of the *Path* class don't interact with the file system and don't verify the existence of the file specified by a path string. *Path* class members that modify a path string have no effect on the names of files in the file system. On the other hand, some of the members of the *Path* class do validate that a specified path string has the correct form, and they throw an exception if the string contains characters that aren't valid in path strings. All members of the *Path* class are static and can therefore be called without having an instance of a path. A path can contain *absolute* or *relative* location information. Absolute paths fully specify a location: the file or directory can be uniquely identified, regardless of the current location. Relative paths specify a partial location: the current location is used as the starting point when locating a file this way.

The following code illustrates how you might use the *Path* class to report on various parts of the string that represent the current directory and the name of the current executing module:

```
using System.Diagnostics;

class TestPathApp
{
    static void Main(string[] args)
    {
        Process p = Process.GetCurrentProcess();
        ProcessModule pm = p.MainModule;
        string s = pm.ModuleName;

        Console.WriteLine(
            Path.GetFullPath(s));
        Console.WriteLine(
            Path.GetFileName(s));
        Console.WriteLine(
            Path.GetFileNameWithoutExtension(s));
        Console.WriteLine(
            Path.GetDirectoryName(
            Directory.GetCurrentDirectory()));
        Console.WriteLine(
            Path.GetPathRoot(
            Directory.GetCurrentDirectory()));
        Console.WriteLine(
            Path.GetTempPath());
```

```
            Console.WriteLine(
                Path.GetTempFileName());
        }
    }
}
```

This is the output:

```
C:\Data\InsideCsharp\Chap11\TestPath\TestPath\bin\Debug\TestPath.exe
TestPath.exe
TestPath
C:\Data\InsideCsharp\Chap11\TestPath\TestPath\bin
C:\
C:\DOCUME~1\andrew\LOCALS~1\Temp\
C:\DOCUME~1\andrew\LOCALS~1\Temp\tmp115.tmp
```

Nonconsole Use of Streams

We've already seen how the design of the *Stream* class and its derivatives makes life easy for the developer. One particular advantage is that the developer can choose to write data to any kind of stream without worrying about the specifics of the stream class actually used. There is a high degree of interchangeability among file streams, memory streams, text and binary data, and so on. By the same token, you can use the streams and file system classes in a Windows GUI application or a Web application.

Windows *OpenFileDialog*

Another class from the library that's useful when manipulating files is the *OpenFileDialog* class. This class resides in the *System.Windows.Forms* namespace, implemented in the System.Windows.Forms.dll. This class encapsulates the behavior of the Open File common dialog box, where users can navigate the file system and select files. The class would normally be used in a Windows GUI application, and such an application would normally be developed using the graphical editors available in Visual Studio. However, it's entirely possible to use the class in a console application, which is what we'll do now to further illustrate the use of the streams classes:

```
using System.Windows.Forms;

    class FileDialogApp
    {
        private static OpenFileDialog ofd;

        static void Main(string[] args)
```

```
        {
            ofd = new OpenFileDialog();
            string s = Path.GetDirectoryName(
                Path.GetDirectoryName(
                Directory.GetCurrentDirectory()));

            ofd.InitialDirectory = s;
            ofd.FileOk +=
                new System.ComponentModel.CancelEventHandler(
                ofd_OK);
            ofd.ShowDialog();
        }
        public static void ofd_OK (object sender,
            System.ComponentModel.CancelEventArgs e)
        {
            StreamReader sr = new StreamReader(ofd.FileName);
            string s;
            while ((s = sr.ReadLine()) != null)
            {
                Console.WriteLine(s);
            }
            sr.Close();
        }
    }
```

We've declared a reference to an *OpenFileDialog* as a field in our class because we want to be able to use this reference across two methods and because the method signatures don't permit us to pass this reference as a parameter. We instantiate the *OpenFileDialog* object in *Main*, specifying an initial directory location two levels above the current directory. We use this arrangement because we want to read a text file. In a regular C# solution, the current directory would be .\bin\debug and would contain only binary files. Before displaying the dialog box, we also set an event handler for the OK button click. Event handlers will be discussed in Chapter 14, "Delegates and Event Handlers"—for now, all we need to know is that when the user clicks the OK button on the dialog box, our *ofd_OK* event-handling method is called. This method is where we extract the user's filename selection from the dialog box and read it with a *StreamReader*, printing the contents to the console. When you run this application, you'll see the OpenFileDialog shown in Figure 11-3.

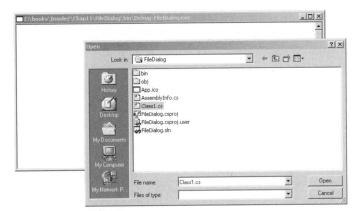

Figure 11-3   *OpenFileDialog.*

Reading Web Pages

The ability to easily stream data across the Internet is clearly a powerful feature of .NET. The possible uses of this technology are wide ranging. We'll consider just one example and write an application to use the streams classes to set up a simple Web scraper. We'll work with three new streams classes, listed in Table 11-3.

Table 11-3
Classes for Reading Web Pages

Class	Description
Uri	An object representation of a Uniform Resource Identifier (URI) that provides easy access to the parts of the URI.
WebRequest	This is an abstract class. Requests are sent to a particular *Uri*, such as a Web page from a server. The *Uri* is examined to determine the proper descendent class to create from a list of registered descendents (http or ftp). The specific class of the object returned is based on the *Uri* scheme passed to the static *Create* method.
WebResponse	An abstract base class that represents a response from a Web server, from which protocol-specific classes are derived.

To use the classes listed in Table 11-3, we'll have to add a *using* statement for the *System.Net* namespace. In this example, we'll just read an arbitrary Web page into a stream, then parse the resulting string to extract the header and print it. First, we set up a *Uri* object, pointing it to an arbitrary Web page. Then we create a *WebRequest* for the page. When the requested Web server responds with some HTML, we can get the response and read it into a *Stream*. From there on, it's all familiar territory:

```
using System.Net;

    public class WebPagesApp
    {
        [STAThread]
        public static void Main(string[] args)
        {
            string s = "http://www.microsoft.com";
            Uri uri = new Uri(s);
            WebRequest req = WebRequest.Create(uri);
            WebResponse resp = req.GetResponse();
            Stream str = resp.GetResponseStream();
            StreamReader sr = new StreamReader(str);

            string t = sr.ReadToEnd();
            int i = t.IndexOf("<HEAD>");
            int j = t.IndexOf("</HEAD>");
            string u = t.Substring(i, j);
            Console.WriteLine("{0}", u);
        }
    }
}
```

Here's the output:

```
<HEAD>
<META HTTP-EQUIV="Content-Type" CONTENT="text/html;
 charset=iso-8859-1" />
<TITLE>Welcome to the Microsoft Corporate Web Site</TITLE>
 ⋮
</HEAD>
```

Now that we've had a good look at the various library classes that support file and stream I/O for standard types, it's time to see how these classes are used to stream nonstandard types—that is, user-defined structs and classes.

Serialization

Serialization is the mechanism used by the .NET runtime to support streaming of user-defined types—that is, to persist custom objects in some form of storage or to transfer such objects from one place to another. The serialization design idiom is very similar to the one used in the MFC library. Serialization is open ended—you can make any custom type serializable.

You can use attributes to mark elements of your class as *Serializable* or *NonSerialized* to indicate that instances of the class can be serialized. In essence, the serialization mechanism converts the values of your class into a flat, or serial, byte stream, which can then be written to a file on disk or to any other streaming target. To actually write out this stream, you'd use the *Serialize* and *Deserialize* methods in classes that implement the *IFormatter* interface. The .NET Framework classes provide two such classes: *BinaryFormatter* and *Soap-Formatter*. The difference between these two classes lies in the way the data stream is formatted—that is, the nature of the additional information that's provided in the stream as well as the raw data values of the serialized class. It's fairly obvious that the *BinaryFormatter* provides a simple binary data stream with some additional type information, while the *SoapFormatter* formats the data stream as XML.

When your class is serialized to a stream, not only are the field member values saved, type information that describes the data stream is also saved. Sufficient type metadata is provided to enable the system to reconstruct an instance of the class from the stream—in other words, to reverse the serialization process. This process not only applies to a single serialized class object, it also applies to an entire graph of connected objects.

Serializing with *BinaryFormatter*

In the following example, we set up a collection of a custom type (*Insect*), write them to a binary file with a *BinaryFormatter*, and read them back. We're using a File class for the underlying stream, but the same serialization code would work with a memory stream—or anything else derived from *Stream*. To access the classes we need, we first must specify some additional namespaces:

```
using System;
using System.IO;
using System.Collections;
using System.Runtime.Serialization;
using System.Runtime.Serialization.Formatters.Binary;
```

Next we define our custom type. The *Insect* class as a whole is declared *Serializable* through the use of a standard attribute. However, because one of the *Insect* class fields is declared *NonSerialized*, this field doesn't get persisted:

```
[Serializable]
public class Insect
{
    private string name;

    [NonSerialized]
    private int id;

    public Insect(string name, int id)
    {
        this.name = name;
        this.id = id;
    }
    public override string ToString()
    {
        return String.Format("{0}: {1}", name, id);
    }
}
```

More Info   For a full discussion of attributes, see Chapter 6, "Attributes."

Before we worry about how this class would work in an application, let's have a quick look at Figure 11-4, which shows the metadata for the class. Notice that the *Insect* class is flagged *serializable*, and the *id* field is flagged *notserialized*.

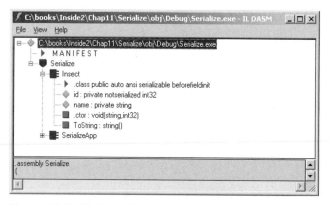

Figure 11-4   Metadata for a serializable type.

Now let's set up our application to make use of this serializable *Insect* class. For our first attempt, we'll instantiate just one *Insect*, create a file, and write out the *Insect* object using a *BinaryFormatter* and the *Serialize* method:

```
class SerializeApp
{
    public static void Main(string[] args)
    {
        Insect i = new Insect("Meadow Brown", 12);
        Stream sw = File.Create("Insects.bin");
        BinaryFormatter bf = new BinaryFormatter();
        bf.Serialize(sw, i);
        sw.Close();
    }
}
```

If you open the Insects.bin output file in Visual Studio, you should see the contents shown in Figure 11-5.

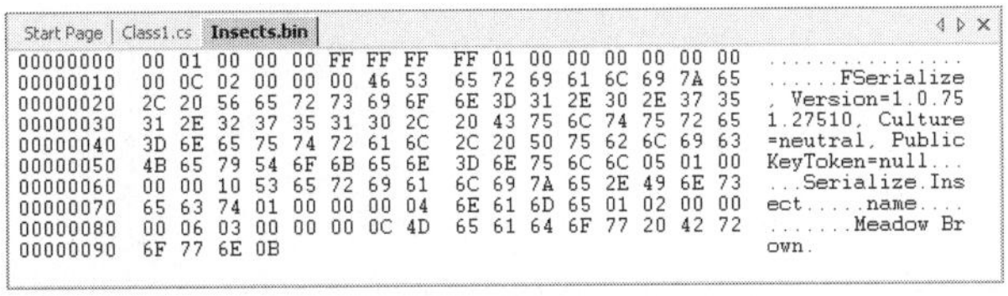

Figure 11-5   Custom type serialized to a file.

If you remember our discussion on assemblies in Chapter 1, "Building C# Applications and Libraries," some of this information should already be familiar to you: the name of the assembly, version number, culture, and public key token are all recognizable from the manifest. The name of the serializable class, *Serialize.Insect*, is then listed. The rest of the data is the serialization data—the field name *name*, and its value *Meadow Brown*. Of course, the *id* field wasn't serialized.

Now let's add several more *Insects* to our collection: we'll keep them in an *ArrayList* object and append them to the original data file. Then we'll close the file, reopen it for reading, and finally print all the *Insects* to the console. It should be clear from the following code that the *ArrayList* class supports serialization by ensuring that all elements in the collection are serialized in turn. This feature makes life very easy: we don't have to bother with the low-level routine of iterating through the collection to serialize individual objects.

```
ArrayList box = new ArrayList();
box.Add(new Insect("Marsh Fritillary", 34));
box.Add(new Insect("Speckled Wood", 56));
box.Add(new Insect("Milkweed", 78));
```

```
sw = File.Open("Insects.bin", FileMode.Append);
bf.Serialize(sw, box);
sw.Close();

Stream sr = File.OpenRead("Insects.bin");
Insect j = (Insect)bf.Deserialize(sr);
Console.WriteLine(j);

ArrayList bag = (ArrayList) bf.Deserialize(sr);
sr.Close();
foreach (Insect k in bag)
{
    Console.WriteLine(k);
}
```

The following is the output from this application. It should be clear why the *id* value is 0. (It was initialized to 0 during the construction of the *Insect* in the *foreach* loop.)

```
Meadow Brown: 0
Marsh Fritillary: 0
Speckled Wood: 0
Milkweed: 0
```

Notice that we were very careful to read back one *Insect* first—the first *Insect* that we'd serialized to the file—before reading back the collection. Also, when we use *Deserialize*, we must cast the return because this method always returns a generic object—a pattern you'll be very familiar with by now. This issue of reading back the data in two chunks should become clearer if we re-examine the file in the hex editor in Visual Studio, as shown in Figure 11-6.

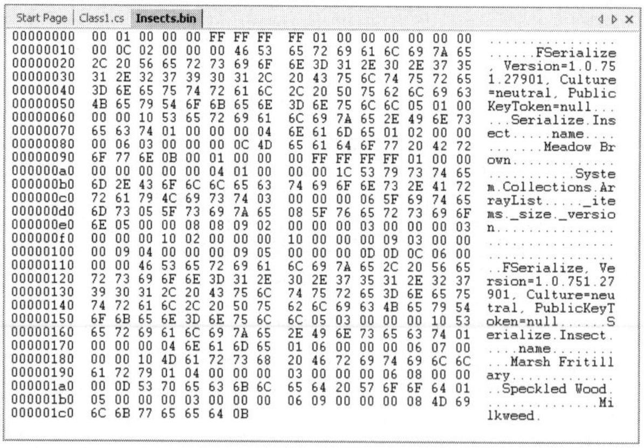

Figure 11-6 Multiple serialized objects.

As you can see, the format of serialized data closely models the class object graph: we first serialized a single *Insect*, then an *ArrayList*, which in turn contained a sequence of *Insect* objects. The data for the three *Insects* in the collection benefits from a little overhead savings because the *Insect* class type information needs to be recorded only for the beginning of the sequence, not for each and every object. This message should now be clear: serialization doesn't just store the data, it stores enough additional type information to reconstruct the correct objects dynamically from the serialized data stream. It's also interesting that the serialization mechanism clearly has no problem reading and writing private fields in a class.

Serializing with *SoapFormatter*

In the previous example, we explored the serialization of custom data types by using a *BinaryFormatter* to read and write binary data to a file. We can easily change our application to use a *SoapFormatter* to write XML-formatted data instead. To do so, we just need to make four changes:

- Add a reference for System.Runtime.Serialization.Formatters.Soap.dll to the solution.

- Change one of the *using* statements from *.Formatters.Binary* to *.Formatters.Soap*.

- Search and replace all *BinaryFormatter* instances to *SoapFormatter*.

- If you want Visual Studio to correctly interpret the resulting data file, make sure the data file has a .xml extension.

The run-time console output from this variation of the application will be the same as previously shown, but the resultant data file differs, as shown in Figure 11-7.

```
Start Page | Class1.cs | Insects.xml |                                    ◁ ▷ ×
<SOAP-ENV:Envelope xmlns:xsi="http://www.w3.org/2001/XMLSchema-instance"
<SOAP-ENV:Body>
<a1:Insect id="ref-1" xmlns:a1="http://schemas.microsoft.com/clr/nsassem/:
<name id="ref-3">Meadow Brown</name>
</a1:Insect>
</SOAP-ENV:Body>
</SOAP-ENV:Envelope>
<SOAP-ENV:Envelope xmlns:xsi="http://www.w3.org/2001/XMLSchema-instance"
<SOAP-ENV:Body>
<a1:ArrayList id="ref-1" xmlns:a1="http://schemas.microsoft.com/clr/ns/Sy:
<_items href="#ref-2"/>
<_size>3</_size>
<_version>3</_version>
</a1:ArrayList>
<SOAP-ENC:Array id="ref-2" SOAP-ENC:arrayType="xsd:anyType[16]">
<item href="#ref-3"/>
<item href="#ref-4"/>
<item href="#ref-5"/>
</SOAP-ENC:Array>
<a3:Insect id="ref-3" xmlns:a3="http://schemas.microsoft.com/clr/nsassem/:
<name id="ref-7">Marsh Fritillary</name>
</a3:Insect>
<a3:Insect id="ref-4" xmlns:a3="http://schemas.microsoft.com/clr/nsassem/:
<name id="ref-8">Speckled Wood</name>
</a3:Insect>
<a3:Insect id="ref-5" xmlns:a3="http://schemas.microsoft.com/clr/nsassem/:
<name id="ref-9">Milkweed</name>
</a3:Insect>
</SOAP-ENV:Body>
</SOAP-ENV:Envelope>
```

Figure 11-7   Insects serialized using *SoapFormatter*.

Serializing with *XmlSerializer*

Another thought on formatters: suppose we want XML, but we don't want the extra SOAP-specific stuff? A couple of options spring to mind: either write a class to implement *IFormatter* similarly to how you'd implement *SoapFormatter* but without the unwanted information, or use the library class *XmlSerializer*. This class doesn't use the *Serializable* attribute, but it does provide somewhat similar functionality, which we'll examine here for completeness. If we want to use our custom *Insect* class with *XmlSerializer* instead of using mainstream serialization, we need to make a few changes:

- Add a reference to System.Xml.dll, and add a *using* statement for the *System.Xml.Serialization* namespace.

- The *Serializable* and *NonSerialized* attributes will be ignored, so we can either leave or remove them. However, *XmlSerializer* does use the *XmlIgnore* attribute, which behaves like *NonSerialized*, so we should add *XmlIgnore* or use it in place of *NonSerialized*.

- *XmlSerializer* has no unsafe access to private members, so we need to either rewrite our private members as public or provide suitable public properties.

■ *XmlSerializer* requires that our class have a default constructor—which we'd probably have anyway.

```
using System;
using System.IO;
using System.Xml.Serialization;

//    [Serializable]
    public class Insect
    {
        public string name;
//        [NonSerialized]
        [XmlIgnore] public int id;
        public Insect(string name, int id)
        {
            this.name = name;
            this.id = id;
        }
        public override string ToString()
        {
            return String.Format("{0}: {1}", name, id);
        }
        public Insect() {}
    }
```

Given these changes, we can now use our revised *Insect* class with *XmlSerializer*. Note that because the constructor takes a *Type* parameter, the *XmlSerializer* object is specifically tied to this one class. As with the formatter classes previously discussed, we have a *Serialize* method and a *Deserialize* method that behave as you'd expect:

```
class SerializeRawXMLApp
{
    [STAThread]
    static void Main(string[] args)
    {
        Insect i = new Insect("Meadow Brown", 12);
        XmlSerializer x = new XmlSerializer(typeof(Insect));
        Stream s = File.Create("AnInsect.xml");

        x.Serialize(s,i);
        s.Seek(0, SeekOrigin.Begin);
        Insect j = (Insect)x.Deserialize(s);
        s.Close();
        Console.WriteLine(j);
    }
}
```

The resultant XML file containing the data for this one *Insect* is shown in Figure 11-8. If you compare this with Figure 11-7, you'll see that using *XmlSerializer* this way eliminates all the SOAP-specific extras that were provided by the *SoapFormatter*.

```
<?xml version="1.0"?>
<Insect xmlns:xsd="http://www.w3.org/2001/XMLSchema" xmlns:xsi="http://ww'
  <name>Meadow Brown</name>
</Insect>
```

Figure 11-8 *Insect* serialized by using *XmlSerializer*.

This simple example can be extended to make more use of the powerful features of *XmlSerializer*, which include attributes to control the XML tags, the use of XML schemas, and SOAP encoding.

More Info   XML will be discussed further in Chapter 15, "Documentation with XML."

Implementing *ISerializable*

If you want to user serialization for your classes but aren't completely happy with the way the data stream is organized, you can customize the behavior by implementing the *ISerializable* interface in your custom class. This interface offers just one method, *GetObjectData*. This method is designed to populate a *SerializationInfo* object with the data needed to serialize your class object. The formatter that you use (such as *BinaryFormatter*) will construct the *SerializationInfo* object and then call *GetObjectData* at serialization time. You therefore implement *GetObjectData* to add whatever values you choose from your class, mapped to whatever string names you choose. Note that if your class has a parent class that also implements *ISerializable*, you should call the parent class implementation of *GetObjectData* for your base class.

```
public virtual void GetObjectData(
    SerializationInfo s, StreamingContext c)
{
    s.AddValue("Something", myStringValue);
    s.AddValue("Another", myIntValue);
}
```

The *SerializationInfo* class contains three properties: *AssemblyName*, *FullTypeName*, and *MemberCount*. Recall from Figure 11-4 that this information is written to the serialized stream in addition to the object data. When implementing *GetObjectData*, the most common *SerializationInfo* method to call is *AddValue*, which has overloads for all the standard types (*int*, *char*, and so on). The *StreamingContext* parameter describes the source and destination of a given serialized stream so that we know whether we're serializing this object to persistent storage or across processes or machines.

If you implement *ISerializable*, you must also provide a constructor with a specific signature—significantly, this constructor has the same parameter list as *GetObjectData*:

```
private SomeClass(
    SerializationInfo s, StreamingContext c)
{
    name = s.GetString("Something");
    id = s.GetInt32("Another");
}
```

This constructor should be declared private or protected to prevent unwary developers from attempting to use it directly. This constructor will be used as part of the deserialization process: the formatter will deserialize the data from the stream and then instantiate the object via this constructor. *SerializationInfo* clearly offers a set of *Getxxx* methods that perform the complement of the various *AddValue* overloads for all the standard data types.

In the example that follows, we've modified the *Insect* class to implement *ISerializable* and provided the necessary *GetObjectData* and special constructor. On this occasion, we're serializing all the members:

```
[Serializable]
public class Insect : ISerializable
{
    private string name;
    private int id;
    public Insect(string name, int id)
    {
        this.name = name;
        this.id = id;
    }
    public override string ToString()
    {
        return String.Format("{0}: {1}", name, id);
    }
    public Insect() {}

    public virtual void GetObjectData(
        SerializationInfo s, StreamingContext c)
    {
        s.AddValue("CommonName", name);
```

```
        s.AddValue("ID#", id);
    }
    private Insect(
        SerializationInfo s, StreamingContext c)
    {
        name = s.GetString("CommonName");
        id = s.GetInt32("ID#");
    }
}
```

In addition to implementing the *ISerializable* interface, you must still declare the class *Serializable*; otherwise, the formatter will reject it before it gets a chance to check for the *ISerializable* implementation. As you'd expect, implementing *ISerializable* has no impact on the application that uses and serializes your class—the only difference is in the underlying behavior of the serialization process, which you've exerted a finer degree of control over.

```
class ImpISerialApp
{
    static void Main(string[] args)
    {
        Insect i = new Insect("Meadow Brown", 12);
        Stream s = File.Create("Insect.bin");
        BinaryFormatter b = new BinaryFormatter();
        b.Serialize(s, i);
        s.Seek(0, SeekOrigin.Begin);
        Insect j = (Insect)b.Deserialize(s);
        s.Close();
        Console.WriteLine(j);
    }
}
```

The binary data file produced from this code is shown in Figure 11-9, in which you can see the custom value names as well as the values themselves.

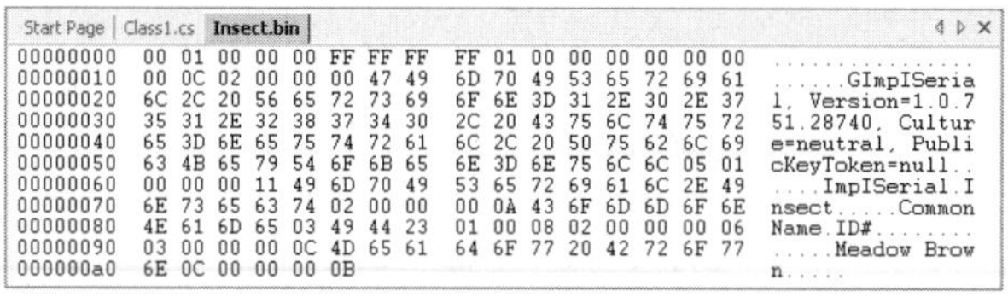

Figure 11-9   *Insect* custom serialized.

Summary

The .NET Framework includes a streams-based I/O subframework that's based on the *Stream* class and its specialized derivatives. Related classes that support file-based streaming include classes to represent files and directories, with an appropriate range of functionality. We've seen how an application can use the streams pattern to stream data between memory buffers or to persistent storage, with a comprehensive set of options for formatting and encoding the stream. The .NET Framework classes supply two primary stream formatting classes to support both binary and XML-formatted data, as well as a set of character encoding classes. Layered on top of the stream is the serialization pattern. This pattern has been very successfully implemented in other environments and provides an open-ended, easily customizable mechanism to stream any standard or user-defined data type by using any of the underlying stream-based classes. Finally, you saw how to choose the degree of control you want over the streaming process by using the *Serializable* attribute class and the *ISerializable* interface.

12

Error Handling with Exceptions

One of the main goals of the .NET common language runtime is for run-time errors to either be avoided by using features such as automatic memory and resource management when using managed code or at least caught at compile time by a strongly typed system. However, certain errors can be caught only at run time, and thus a consistent means of dealing with them must be used across all the languages that comply with the Common Language Specification (CLS). In light of that, this chapter focuses on the error-handling system implemented by the runtime—*exception handling*.

In this chapter, you'll first learn the general mechanics and basic syntax of exception handling. Once you have this baseline knowledge, you'll see how exception handling compares with today's more prevalent methods of error handling and discover the advantages that exception handling has over these other techniques. We'll then dive into some of the more specific .NET exception-handling issues, such as using the *Exception* class and deriving your own exception classes. Finally, the last part of this chapter will discuss how to properly design your system to use exception handling.

Overview of Exception Handling

Exceptions are error conditions that arise when the normal flow of a code path—that is, a series of method calls on the call stack—is impractical or imprudent. It's imperative to understand the difference between an exception and an expected event, such as reaching the end of a file. If you have a method that's sequentially reading through a file, you know that at some point it will reach the end of the file. Therefore, this event is hardly *exceptional* in nature and certainly doesn't prevent the application from continuing. However, if you're attempting to read through a file and the operating system alerts you that a disk error has been detected, this is an exceptional situation and definitely one that will affect the normal flow of your method's attempt to continue reading the file.

Most exceptions also have another problem: *context*. Let's look at an example. Assuming that you're writing tightly cohesive code—code in which one method is responsible for one action—your code might look something like this:

```
using System;

class Database
{
    public bool OpenDb()
    {
        // Attempt to lock and open physical file associated
        // with the data store.
        return true;
    }

    public bool LogIn(String userName, String password)
    {
        // Validate user login.
        return true;
    }

    // ... Other database-related members such as
    // LogOut, OpenTable, and so on.
}

class ExceptionExample1
{
    static void Main(string[] args)
    {
        Console.WriteLine("Instantiating Database object");
        Database db = new Database();

        Console.WriteLine("Opening database...");
        if (db.OpenDb())
        {
            Console.WriteLine("Successfully opened database");

            Console.WriteLine("Logging into database...");
            if (db.LogIn("Tom", "password"))
```

```
        {
            Console.WriteLine("Successfully logged " +
                "into database");
        }
    }

    Console.ReadLine();
    }
}
```

Note that if the *Database.OpenDb* method fails, it can't properly handle the error because it doesn't have the proper context. In other words, this method has no way of knowing whether the inability to open the database's underlying physical file constitutes a catastrophic error or an expected error condition.

This is what I mean by *context*. One method determines that an exceptional condition has been reached and because it's not in the proper context to handle the error, it signals to the common language runtime that an error has occurred. The runtime traverses back up the call stack until it finds a method that can properly deal with the error condition. Although our example was extremely simple, the issue of exception handling and context becomes even more critical when you're dealing with a more realistic code path that's several layers deep. However, before we dive into more complicated scenarios, let's look at the exception-handling syntax.

Basic Exception-Handling Syntax

Exception handling consists of only four keywords: *try*, *catch*, *throw*, and *finally*. The way these keywords work is simple and straightforward. When a method fails its objective and can't continue—that is, when it detects an exceptional situation—it throws an exception to the calling method by using the *throw* keyword. The calling method—assuming it has enough context to deal with the exception—then receives this exception via the *catch* keyword and decides what course of action to take. In the following sections, we'll look at the language semantics governing how to throw and catch exceptions as well as some code snippets that illustrate how this process works.

Throwing an Exception

When a method needs to notify the calling method that an error has occurred, it uses the *throw* keyword in the following manner:

throw [*expression*];

As you can see, the syntax for throwing an exception defines an optional expression. However, this expression can be omitted only if you are rethrowing an expression, which I'll cover in the "Rethrowing an Exception" section. When an expression is specified, it must resolve to an object of type *System.Exception* (or a derived class). The following is an example of a method that's determined that an unrecoverable error has occurred and that it needs to throw an exception to the calling method. Notice how the *System.Exception* object is instantiated and then thrown back up the call stack.

```
public void Foo()
{
    if (major_error)
        throw new Exception();
    else
        ContinueProcessing();
}
```

As you can see, the *Foo* method simply instantiates an object of type *Exception* directly in the call to throw that exception.

Catching an Exception

Because a method can throw an exception, there obviously needs to be a reciprocal part of this equation in which something catches the thrown exception. The *catch* keyword defines a block of code to be processed when an exception of a given type is caught. The code in this block is referred to as an *exception handler.*

Keep in mind that not every method needs to deal with every possible thrown exception, especially because a method might not have the context required to do anything with the error information. After all, the point of exception handling is that errors are handled by code that has enough context to do so correctly. For more information on this, see "Handling Errors in the Correct Context" later in this chapter. For now, let's deal with situations in which a method will catch any thrown exceptions from the method being called. We use two keywords to catch an exception: *try* and *catch.*

To catch an exception, you need to bracket the code you're attempting to execute in a *try* block and then specify in a *catch* block which types of exceptions thrown within that *try* block to handle. All the statements in the *try* block will be processed in order as usual, unless an exception is thrown by one of the methods being called. If that happens, control is passed to the first line of the appropriate *catch* block. By *appropriate catch block*, I mean the block that's defined as catching the type of exception that's thrown. Here's the previous database example from the previous section, in which a method (*Main*) employs the *try/catch* semantics to catch any exceptions that might be thrown by the *Database.OpenDb* method:

```
using System;

class Database
{
    public bool OpenDb()
    {
        // Attempt to lock and open physical file associated
        // with the data store.

        // Catastrophic error reached - throw exception!!
        throw new Exception("Physical file corrupted");

        return true;
    }

    public bool LogIn(String userName, String password)
    {
        // Validate user login.
        return true;
    }

    // ... Other database-related members such as
    // LogOut, OpenTable, and so on.
}

class ExceptionExample2
{
    static void Main(string[] args)
    {
        Console.WriteLine("Instantiating Database object");
        Database db = new Database();

        try
        {
            Console.WriteLine("Opening database...");
            if (db.OpenDb())
            {
                Console.WriteLine("Successfully opened " +
                    "database");

                Console.WriteLine("Logging into database...");
                if (db.LogIn("Tom", "password"))
                {
                    Console.WriteLine("Successfully logged " +
```

```
                    "into database");
                }
            }
        }
        catch(Exception e)
        {
            Console.WriteLine("Exception caught - '{0}'",
                e.Message);
        }

        Console.ReadLine();
    }
}
```

Because the *Database.OpenDb* method will always throw an exception, Figure 12-1 shows what will happen if you run this version of the example.

Figure 12-1   The syntax required to implement exception handling is simple and intuitive.

As you can see, there's absolutely nothing complex about the exception-handling syntax. In fact, the main learning curve for people new to exception handling certainly doesn't involve the syntax—rather, it involves learning concepts such as when and where to use exceptions, at what level of a code path to catch an exception (as opposed to letting it filter back up the call stack), and when and how to derive your own exception classes.

After looking at the previous code example, your next question might be, "What happens if *Database.OpenDb* throws the exception and *Main* doesn't catch it?" (This would be the case if the call to *OpenDb* weren't in a *try* block.) This situation almost sounds like the ancient riddle: "If a tree falls in the forest and no one's there to hear it, does it make a sound?" Although philosophers have argued about that riddle for centuries, there's no doubt as to what happens when an exception is thrown but not caught. The error message you receive depends on what environment you're running in, but the result is that the .NET runtime aborts any application that has unhandled exceptions. Figure 12-2 shows what would happen if you were running this application from the command line, and Figure 12-3 shows the error message you'd received if you were running within the Microsoft Visual Studio debugger.

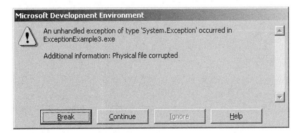

Figure 12-2   The just-in-time (JIT) debugger catches unhandled exceptions and gives you the opportunity to debug them using your configured debugger.

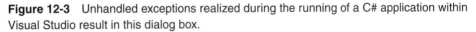

Figure 12-3   Unhandled exceptions realized during the running of a C# application within Visual Studio result in this dialog box.

If a method calls another method that does throw an exception, the design of the system must ensure that some method in the call stack handles the exception; otherwise, you'll have some rather unhappy end users. Later in this chapter, in the "Designing Your Code with Exception Handling" section, we'll get cover the topic of how to design your system so that the correct methods catch thrown exceptions.

Rethrowing an Exception

Sometimes, after a method catches an exception and does everything it can in its context, it will need to *rethrow* the exception back up the call stack so that further error processing can be done. You accomplish this with the same *throw* keyword that was used to initially raise the exception. As mentioned earlier, the only syntactical difference between throwing an exception and rethrowing one is that the latter is done via the *throw* keyword sans arguments. Once again, the database demo provides an excellent example.

In this version of the example, we'll include the *Stream* and *FileStream* classes that are used to read and write files.

More Info   The *Stream* and *FileStream* classes are covered in Chapter 11, "File I/O with Streams."

The *Database.OpenDb* method attempts to open a file that doesn't exist. Because the *FileStream* constructor can throw any of eight exceptions, the *OpenDb* method will catch the base class exception. In this example, the *Database* class is designed to log any encountered errors, which is certainly a realistic design for this class. However, after logging the error, the *OpenDb* method still needs to pass an exception back up the calling stack so that the caller knows that the database failed to open. Therefore, the *OpenDb* method rethrows the current exception:

```
using System;
using System.IO;

class Database
{
    Stream data;

    public bool OpenDb()
    {
        try
        {
            data = new FileStream("c:\\db.dat", FileMode.Open);
        }
        catch(Exception e)
        {
            Console.WriteLine("[Database.OpenDb] Caught " +
                "exception of type {0}", e.GetType());

            Console.WriteLine("[Database.OpenDb] Calling " +
                "LogError method...");
            LogError(e.Message);
```

```
            Console.WriteLine("[Database.OpenDb] Rethrowing " +
                "exception to caller...");
            throw;
        }

        return true;
    }

    protected void LogError(String error)
    {
        Console.WriteLine("[Database.LogError] Logging '{0}'",
            error);
    }

    public bool LogIn(String userName, String password)
    {
        // Validate user login.
        return true;
    }

    // ... Other database-related members such as
    // LogOut, OpenTable, and so on.
}

class RethrowExample
{
    static void Main(string[] args)
    {
        try
        {
            Console.WriteLine("[Main] Instantiating " +
                "Database object");
            Database db = new Database();

            Console.WriteLine("[Main] Opening database...");
            if (db.OpenDb())
            {
                Console.WriteLine("[Main] Successfully " +
                    "opened database");

                Console.WriteLine("[Main] Logging into " +
                    "database...");
                if (db.LogIn("Tom", "password"))
                {
                    Console.WriteLine("[Main] Successfully " +
                        "logged into database");
                }
            }
        }
```

```
        catch(Exception e)
        {
            Console.WriteLine("[Main] - Caught exception : " +
                "'{0}'", e.Message);
        }

        Console.ReadLine();
    }
}
```

If you build and run this application, you'll see the results shown in Figure 12-4.

Figure 12-4   Rethrowing exceptions is useful when various methods in the call stack need to do some error processing.

Cleaning Up with *finally*

One sticky issue of exception handling is ensuring that a piece of code is always run, regardless of whether an exception is caught. Continuing with our little database example, let's say that the *Database.OpenDb* method succeeded but a subsequent method call resulted in us prematurely aborting the application. Certainly we'd want to ensure that the database was closed. Using the following pseudocode obviously would be one way to solve this problem:

```
try
{
    Database db = new Database();
    if (db.OpenDb)
    {
        if (db.LogIn(user, password))
        {
            // Perform database work.
        }
        if (db.IsOpen())
        {
```

```
            db.CloseDb();
        }
    }
}
catch(Exception e)
{
    if (db.IsOpen())
    {
        db.CloseDb();
    }
}
```

There's an obvious problem with this snippet: because an exception causes a branch of control from the current instruction to the first instruction in the *catch* block, we need to have duplicate code to ensure that the required work is performed. We could, of course, move this code into another method and then call it from both places, but we're looking at a potential maintenance nightmare with what still amounts to duplicate code.

This situation is where the *finally* keyword comes into play. With this keyword, you can specify a block of code that's run whether or not an exception is ever raised in the *try* block. Let's modify our database example to open the database but to fail on the login procedure. This change will enable us to ensure that the database close code is called even when an exception is caught.

```
using System;
using System.IO;

class Database
{
    public Database()
    {
        isDbOpen = false;
    }

    protected Stream data;

    protected bool isDbOpen;
    public bool IsDbOpen
    {
        get { return isDbOpen; }
    }

    public bool OpenDb()
    {
        // Assume that we successfully opened the physical file.
        isDbOpen = true;
        return true;
    }
```

```csharp
public bool LogIn(String userName, String password)
{
    try
    {
        if (OpenTable("USERS"))
        {
            // Verify that user and password exist in table.
            // If not, this would not result in an exception
            // because it is not an exception situation. Rather,
            // the method would simply return false to
            // indicate failure to log in successfully.
        }
    }
    catch(Exception e)
    {
        Console.WriteLine("[Database.LogIn] Caught " +
            "exception of type {0}", e.GetType());

        Console.WriteLine("[Database.LogIn] Calling " +
            "LogError method...");
        LogError(e.Message);

        Console.WriteLine("[Database.LogIn] Rethrowing " +
            "exception to caller...");
        throw e;
    }

    return true;
}

public void CloseDb()
{
    // Close the data stream object.
    isDbOpen = false;
}

public bool OpenTable(String table)
{
    throw new Exception("Table not found!");
}

protected void LogError(String error)
{
    Console.WriteLine("[Database.LogError] Logging '{0}'",
        error);
}
}
```

```
class FinallyExample
{
    static void Main(string[] args)
    {
        Console.WriteLine("[Main] Instantiating Database " +
            "object");
        Database db = new Database();

        try
        {
            Console.WriteLine("[Main] Opening database...");
            if (db.OpenDb())
            {
                Console.WriteLine("[Main] Successfully " +
                    "opened database");

                Console.WriteLine("[Main] Logging into " +
                    "database...");
                if (db.LogIn("Tom", "password"))
                {
                    Console.WriteLine("[Main] Successfully " +
                        "logged into database");
                }
            }
        }
        catch(Exception e)
        {
            Console.WriteLine("[Main] Caught exception : '{0}'",
                e.Message);
        }
        finally
        {
            if (db.IsDbOpen)
            {
                Console.WriteLine("[Main] Closing database");
                db.CloseDb();
            }
        }

        Console.ReadLine();
    }
}
```

Building and executing this code will verify that the *Database.CloseDb* method is called, as shown in Figure 12-5.

Figure 12-5   The *finally* keyword helps to ensure that certain critical code always will be called, even if an exception is raised.

As you can see, the placement of the *finally* block ensured that the *Database.CloseDb* method would be called, without requiring us to place this code both in the *try* and the *catch* block.

Retrying Code

One question that I get a lot is, "Can I branch back to the *try* block from the *catch* block in order to retry an operation?" Although exceptions are usually unrecoverable by definition, there are situations in which this ability is useful. One example would occur if the user is running an especially long operation. Let's say that toward the end of that operation, one of the methods in the code path attempts to read from a file by using the *FileStream* class. If the file doesn't exist, the *FileStream* constructor throws a *FileNotFoundException*. In this case, it would be easy to display a message to the user indicating that the file couldn't be found and giving the user the opportunity to correct the error and retry the operation. Another example entails situations in which the author of a method knew that an operation could fail periodically—perhaps because of a networking timeout—and wanted to include code to retry the operation *n* times before giving up.

In both these cases, you could simply define a label just before the *try* block and then utilize the much-maligned *goto* statement (covered in more detail in Chapter 9, "Program Flow Control"). The following is an example of using a label before a *try* block that attempts to open a user-specified file. If I can't open the file, I give the user three opportunities to resolve the problem (including changing the filename) before giving up.

```
using System;
using System.IO;
```

```
class Retry
{

    static void Main()
    {
        StreamReader sr;

        int attempts = 0;
        int maxAttempts = 3;

        GetFile:
        Console.Write("\n[Attempt #{0}] Specify file " +
            "to open/read: ", attempts+1);
        string fileName = Console.ReadLine();

        try
        {
            sr = new StreamReader(fileName);

            Console.WriteLine();

            string s;
            while (null != (s = sr.ReadLine()))
            {
                Console.WriteLine(s);
            }
            sr.Close();
        }
        catch(FileNotFoundException e)
        {
            Console.WriteLine(e.Message);
            if (++attempts < maxAttempts)
            {
                Console.Write("Do you want to select " +
                    "another file: ");
                string response = Console.ReadLine();
                response = response.ToUpper();
                if (response == "Y") goto GetFile;
            }
            else
            {
                Console.Write("You have exceeded the maximum " +
                    "retry limit ({0})", maxAttempts);
            }


        }
        catch(Exception e)
        {
```

```
            Console.WriteLine(e.Message);
        }

        Console.ReadLine();
    }
}
```

Figure 12-6 shows an example of running this application.

Figure 12-6   Having the ability to retry operations that aborted because of an exception enables you to write more user-friendly applications.

Comparing Error-Handling Techniques

Now that you've seen the basics of throwing and catching exceptions, let's take a few minutes to compare the various approaches to error handling taken by programming languages.

The standard approach to error handling has typically been to return an error code to the calling method. The calling method is then left with the responsibility of deciphering the returned value and acting accordingly. The returned value can be as simple as a basic C or C++ type, or it can be a pointer to a more robust object containing all the information necessary to fully appreciate and understand the error. More elaborately designed error-handling techniques involve an entire error subsystem in which the called method indicates the error condition to the subsystem and then returns an error code to the caller. The caller then calls a global function exported from the error subsystem to determine the cause of the last error registered with the subsystem. You can find an example of this approach in the Microsoft Open Database Connectivity (ODBC) SDK. Semantics aside, the basic concept remains the same: the calling method calls a method in some way and inspects the returned value to verify the relative success or failure of the called method. Although this approach has been the standard for many years, it's severely flawed in a number of important ways. The following sections describe a few of the ways that exception handling provides tremendous benefits over using return codes.

Benefits of Exception Handling Over Return Codes

When using return codes, the called method returns an error code and the error condition is handled by the calling method. Because the error handling occurs outside the scope of the called method, there's no guarantee that the caller will check the returned error code. For example, let's say that you write a class named *CommaDelimitedFile* that wraps the functionality of reading and writing standard comma-delimited files. Part of what your class would have to expose includes methods to open and read data from the file. Using the older return code method of reporting errors, these methods would return some variable type that the caller would have to check to verify the success of the method call. If the user of your class called the *CommaDelimitedFile.Open* method and then attempted to call the *CommaDelimitedFile.Read* method without checking whether the *Open* call succeeded, this could—and, during a demo for your most important client, probably would—cause less than desirable results. However, if the class's *Open* method throws an exception, the caller would be forced to deal with the fact that the *Open* method failed. This is because each time a method throws an exception, control is passed back up the call stack until it's caught. Here's an example of what that code might look like:

```
using System;

class CommaDelimitedFile
{
    protected string fileName;

    public void Open(string fileName)
    {
        this.fileName = fileName;

        // Attempt to open file
        // and throw exception upon error condition.
        throw new Exception("[CommaDelimitedFile.Open] " +
            "Open failed");
    }

    public bool Read(string record)
    {
        // Code to read file.
        return false; // EOF
    }
}
```

```
class ThrowExceptionApp
{
    public static void Main()
    {
        try
        {
            Console.WriteLine("[Main] Attempting to open " +
                "a comma delimited file...");

            CommaDelimitedFile file = new CommaDelimitedFile();
            file.Open("c:\\test.csv");

            Console.WriteLine("[Main] Open successful");

            string record = "";
            Console.WriteLine("[Main] Reading from file...");

            while (file.Read(record) == true)
            {
                Console.WriteLine("[Main] record = {0}",
                    record);
            }

            Console.WriteLine("[Main] Finished reading file");
        }
        catch (Exception e)
        {
            Console.WriteLine(e.Message);
        }

        Console.ReadLine();
    }
}
```

In this example, if either the *CommaDelimitedFile.Open* method or the *CommaDelimitedFile.Read* method throws an exception, the calling method is forced to deal with it. If the calling method doesn't catch the exception and no other method in the current code path attempts to catch an exception of this type, the application will abort. Pay particular attention to the fact that because the *Open* method call is placed in a block, an invalid read—using our example, in which the *Open* method has thrown an exception—won't be attempted. This is because programmatic control would be passed from the *Open* call in the *try* block to the first line of the *catch* block. Therefore, one of the biggest benefits of exception handling over return codes is that exceptions are programmatically more difficult to ignore.

Handling Errors in the Correct Context

A general principle of good programming is the practice of *tight cohesion*, which refers to the objective or purpose of a given method. Methods that demonstrate tight cohesion are those that perform a single task. The main benefit of using tight cohesion in your programming is that a method is more likely to be portable and used in different scenarios when it performs only a single action. A method that performs a single action is certainly easier to debug and maintain. However, tightly cohesive code does cause one major problem with regards to error handling. Let's look at an example to see this problem and how exception handling solves it.

In this example, a class (*AccessDatabase*) is used to generate and manipulate Microsoft Access databases. Let's suppose this class has a static method named *GenerateDatabase*. Because the *GenerateDatabase* method would be used to create new Access databases, it would have to perform several tasks to create a database. For example, it would have to create the physical database file, create the specified tables (including any rows and columns your application needs), and define any necessary indexes and relations. The *Generate-Database* method might even have to create some default users and permissions.

The programmatic design problem I mentioned a moment ago is this: if an error were to occur in the *CreateIndexes* method, which method would handle it and how? Obviously, at some point, the method that originally called the *GenerateDatabase* method would have to handle the error, but how could it? The calling method would have no idea how to handle an error that occurred several method calls deep in the code path. As we've seen, the calling method isn't in the correct context to handle the error. In other words, the only method that could logically create any meaningful information about the error is the method that failed. Having said that, if return codes were used in our *Access-Database* class, each method in the code path would have to check for every single error code that every other method *might* return. One obvious problem with this is that the calling method might have to handle a ridiculously large number of error codes. In addition, maintenance would be difficult. Each time an error condition is added to any of the methods in the code path, every instance in the application where code calls that method would have to be updated to handle the new error code that can be returned. Needless to say, this is an expensive proposition in terms of software total cost of ownership (TCO).

Exception handling resolves all these issues by enabling the calling method to trap for a given type of exception. In our example, if a class named *AccessDatabaseException* were derived from *Exception*, it could be used for any types of errors that occur within any of the *AccessDatabase* methods. (I'll discuss the *Exception* class and deriving your own exception classes later in this chapter, in "Using the *System.Exception* Class.") Then if the *CreateIndexes* method failed, it would construct and throw an exception of type *AccessDatabaseException*. The calling method would catch that exception and be able to inspect the *Exception* object to decipher exactly what went wrong. Therefore, instead of handling every possible type of return code that *GenerateDatabase* and any of its called methods could return, the calling method would be assured that if *any* of the methods in that code path failed, the proper error information would be returned. Exception handling provides an additional bonus: because the error information is contained within a class, new error conditions can be added and the calling method will remain unchanged. And wasn't *extensibility*—the ability to build something and then add to it without changing or breaking existing code—one of the original promises of object-oriented programming to begin with? For these reasons, the concept of catching and dealing with errors in the correct context is the most significant advantage of using exception handling.

Improving Code Readability

When you use exception-handling code, your code readability improves enormously. This directly relates to reduced costs in terms of code maintenance. The difference between the way return codes are handled and the way exceptions are handled is the source of this improvement. If you used return codes with the *AccessDatabase.GenerateDatabase* method mentioned earlier, you'd need code similar to the following to handle error conditions:

```
public bool GenerateDatabase()
{
    if (CreatePhysicalDatabase())
    {
        if (CreateTables())
        {
            if (CreateIndexes())
            {
                return true;
            }
            else
            {
                // Handle error.
                return false;
            }
        }
```

```
        else
        {
            // Handle error.
            return false;
        }
    }
    else
    {
        // Handle error.
        return false;
    }
}
```

Add a few other validations to the preceding code and you wind up with a tremendous amount of error validation code mixed in with your business logic. If you indent your code four spaces per block, the first character of a line of code might not appear until column 20 or higher. None of this is disastrous for the code itself, but it does make the code more difficult to read and maintain—and the bottom line is that code that's difficult to maintain is a breeding ground for bugs. Let's look at this same example, only with exception handling applied:

```
// Calling code.
try
{
    AccessDatabase accessDb = new AccessDatabase();
    accessDb.GenerateDatabase();
}
catch(Exception e)
{
    // Inspect caught exception.
}

// Definition of AccessDatabase.GenerateDatabase method.
public void GenerateDatabase()
{
    CreatePhysicalDatabase();
    CreateTables();
    CreateIndexes();
}
```

Notice how much cleaner and more elegant the second solution is. This is because error detection and recovery code are no longer mixed with the logic of the calling code itself. Because exception handling has made this code more straightforward, maintaining the code becomes much easier.

Throwing Exceptions from Constructors

Another major advantage that exceptions have over other error-handling techniques is regarding object construction. Because a constructor can't return values, there's simply no easy, intuitive means of signaling to the constructor's calling method that an error occurred during object construction. Exceptions, however, can be used because the calling method need only wrap the construction of the object in a *try* block, as in the following code:

```
try
{
    // If the AccessDatabase object fails to construct
    // properly and throws an exception, it will now be caught.
    AccessDatabase accessDb = new AccessDatabase();
}
catch(Exception e)
{
    // Inspect the caught exception.
}
```

Using the *System.Exception* Class

As mentioned earlier, all exceptions that will be thrown must be of the type—or derived from—*System.Exception*. In fact, the *System.Exception* class is the base class of several exception classes that can be used in your C# code. Most of the classes that inherit from *System.Exception* don't add any functionality to the base class. So why does C# bother with derived classes if the derived classes won't significantly differ from their base class? The reason is that a single *try* block can have multiple *catch* blocks, with each *catch* block specifying a specific exception type. (You'll see this later in the section.) This enables the code to handle various exceptions in a manner applicable to each exception type.

Constructing an *Exception* Object

As of this writing, there are four constructors for the *System.Exception* class:

```
public Exception ();
public Exception(String);
protected Exception(SerializationInfo, StreamingContext);
public Exception(String, Exception);
```

The first of these constructors is the default constructor. It takes no arguments and simply defaults all member variables. This exception is typically thrown as follows:

```
// Error condition reached.
throw new Exception();
```

The second exception constructor takes as its only argument a *String* value that identifies an error message and takes the form that you've seen in most of the examples in this chapter. This message is retrieved by the code catching the exception via the *System.Exception.Message* property. Here's a simple example of both sides of this exception propagation:

```
using System;

class ThrowException3
{
    class FileOps
    {
        public void FileOpen(String fileName)
        {
            // ...
            throw new Exception("Oh bother");
        }

        public void FileRead()
        {
        }
    }

    public static void Main()
    {
        // Code catching exception.
        try
        {
            FileOps fileOps = new FileOps();

            fileOps.FileOpen("c:\\test.txt");
            fileOps.FileRead();
        }
        catch(System.Exception e)
        {
            Console.WriteLine(e.Message);
        }
    }
}
```

The third constructor initializes an instance of the *Exception* class with serialized data. And the last constructor not only enables you to specify an error message, it enables you to specify what's known as an *inner exception*. This is because when you handle exceptions, you'll sometimes want to *massage* the exception a bit at one level of the call stack before passing it further up the call stack. Let's look at an example of how you might use this feature.

Let's say that to ease the burden on your class's client, you decide to throw only one type of exception. That way, the client only has to catch one exception and reference the exception's *InnerException* property. This arrangement has an added benefit: if you decide to modify a given method to throw a new type of exception after the client code has been written, the client doesn't have to be updated unless it needs to do something specific with this exception.

In the following example, notice that the client code catches the top-level *System.Exception* and prints a message contained in that exception's inner exception object. If at later date the *DoWork* method throws other kinds of exceptions—provided it makes them inner exceptions of a *System.Exception* object—the client code will continue to work.

```
using System;
using System.Globalization;

class ValidateArgs
{
    protected bool IsValidParam(string value)
    {
        bool success = false;

        if (value.Length == 3)
        {
            char c1 = value[0];
            if (Char.IsNumber(c1))
            {
                char c2 = value[2];
                if (Char.IsNumber(c2))
                {
                    if (value[1] == '.')
                        success = true;
                }
            }
        }

        return success;
    }

    public void DoWork(string value)
    {
        if (!IsValidParam(value))
        {
            throw new Exception("", new FormatException(
                "Invalid parameter specified"));
```

```
        }
        Console.WriteLine("Work done with '{0}'", value);
    }
}

class InnerException
{
    public static void Main(string[] args)
    {
        ValidateArgs validateArgs = new ValidateArgs();
        try
        {
            validateArgs.DoWork(args[0]);
        }
        catch(Exception e)
        {
            if (null != e.InnerException)
            {
                Exception inner = e.InnerException;
                Console.WriteLine(inner.Message);

                Console.WriteLine("Syntax: InnerException x.y");
                Console.WriteLine("\tx = major version number");
                Console.WriteLine("\tx = minor version number");
            }
            Console.WriteLine(e.Message);
        }
    }
}
```

Figure 12-7 shows some examples of this application being run. Notice that the *Exception.InnerException* text is being output when the exception is caught.

Figure 12-7   *InnerException* objects are great for situations in which you want to wrap an exception in a generic exception while providing access to the original exception object.

Using the *StackTrace* Property

Another useful property of the *System.Exception* class is the *StackTrace* property. The *StackTrace* property enables you to determine—at any point where you have a valid *System.Exception* object—what the current call stack looks like. Take a look at the following code:

```
using System;

class StackTraceTestApp
{
    public void Open(String fileName)
    {
        Lock(fileName);
        // ...
    }
    public void Lock(String fileName)
    {
        // Error condition raised.
        Console.WriteLine("[StackTraceTestApp.Lock] " +
            "Throwing exception");
        throw new Exception("Failed to acquire lock on file");
    }

    public static void Main()
    {
        StackTraceTestApp test = new StackTraceTestApp();

        try
        {
            Console.WriteLine("[Main] Opening file...");
            test.Open("c:\\test.txt");
            Console.WriteLine("[Main] File successfully " +
                "opened.");
        }
        catch(Exception e)
          {
              Console.WriteLine("[Main] Caught exception '{0}'",
                  e.Message);
              Console.WriteLine("[Main] Dumping trace " +
                  "information for exception...");
              Console.WriteLine(e.StackTrace);
        }

        Console.ReadLine();
    }
}
```

If you build and run this demo, you'll see the results shown in Figure 12-8.

Figure 12-8   The *Exception.StackTrace* property enables you to print the stack (methods and line numbers) at the time of the exception.

As you can see, the *StackTrace* property returns the call stack at the point where the exception is caught, which can be useful for logging and debugging scenarios. Now let's look at another facet of exception handling—how to handle the catching of multiple exception types.

Catching Multiple Exception Types

In various situations, you might want a *try* block to catch different exception types. For example, a given method might be documented as throwing several exception types, or you might have several method calls in a single *try* block, where each method being called is documented as being able to throw a different exception type. This exception is handled by adding a *catch* block for each type of exception that your code needs to handle:

```
try
{
    Foo(); // Can throw FooException.
    Bar(); // Can throw BarException.
}
catch(FooException e)
{
    // Handle the error.
}
catch(BarException e)
{
    // Handle the error.
}

catch(Exception e)
{
}
```

Each exception type can now be handled with its distinct *catch* block—and error-handling code. However, one extremely important detail here is that the base class is handled last. Obviously, because all exceptions are derived from *System.Exception*, if you were to place that *catch* block first, the other *catch* blocks would be unreachable. Therefore, the compiler would reject the following code:

```
try
{
    Foo(); // Can throw FooException.
    Bar(); // Can throw BarException.
}
catch(Exception e)
{
    // ***ERROR - THIS WON'T COMPILE
}
catch(FooException e)
{
    // Handle the error.
}
catch(BarException e)
{
    // Handle the error.
}
```

Deriving Your Own *Exception* Classes

As I've said, sometimes you might want to provide extra information or formatting to an exception before you throw it to the client code. You might also want to provide a base class for that situation so that your class can publish the fact that it throws only one type of exception. That way, the client only need concern itself with catching this base class.

You also might want to derive your own *Exception* class if you want to perform some action—such as logging the event or sending an e-mail to someone at the help desk—every time an exception was thrown. In this case, you'd derive your own *Exception* class and put the needed code in the class constructor, like this:

```
using System;

public class MyExceptionClass : Exception
{
    // Base Exception class constructors.
    public MyExceptionClass()
        :base()
```

```
        {
            LogException();
        }

        public MyExceptionClass(String message)
            :base(message)
        {
            LogException();
        }

        public MyExceptionClass(String message,
            Exception innerException)
            :base(message, innerException)
        {
            LogException();
        }

        protected void LogException()
        {
            Console.WriteLine("[MyExceptionClass.LogException] " +
                "Logging '{0}'", this.Message);
        }
    }

public class DerivedExceptionApp
{
    public static void ThrowException()
    {
        Console.WriteLine(
            "[DerivedExceptionApp.ThrowException] Throwing " +
            "MyExceptionClass exception");
        throw new MyExceptionClass("ERROR encountered!!");
    }

    public static void Main()
    {
        try
        {
            Console.WriteLine("[Main] Calling " +
                "DerivedExceptionApp.ThrowException");
            ThrowException();
        }
        catch(Exception e)
        {
            Console.WriteLine("[Main] Caught exception " +
                "with catch(System.Exception)");
            Console.WriteLine("[Main] Examination is " +
                "actually of type {0}", e.GetType());
```

```
        }

        Console.ReadLine();
    }
}
```

If you run this application, you'll see that the *MyExceptionClass* exception was created and logged the intended error message, as Figure 12-9 shows. In addition, you can see that although the *Main* method's *catch* block specified the base class *Exception* class, you can still query the exception object about its real type—in this case, *MyExceptionClass*.

Figure 12-9 Deriving your own exception classes can be extremely beneficial to your overall system design when you want to add functionality to your exception classes beyond that provided by the .NET Framework exception classes.

Guidelines for Derived *Exception* Classes

Although it's not a hard-and-fast rule, it's good programming practice—and consistent with most C# code you'll see—to name your exception classes so that the name ends with the word *Exception*. For example, if you want to derive an *Exception* class for a class named *MyFancyGraphics*, you can name the class *MyFancyGraphicsException*.

Another rule of thumb when creating or deriving your own exception classes is to implement all three *System.Exception* constructors. Once again, this convention isn't absolutely necessary, but it does improve consistency with other C# code that your client will be using.

This code will generate the following output. Note that the *ToString* method results in a combination of properties being displayed: the textual representation of the exception class name, the message string passed to the exception's constructor, and the *StackTrace*.

```
TestException: error condition
   at DerivedExceptionTestApp.Main()
```

Designing Your Code with Exception Handling

So far, we've covered the basic concepts of using exception handling and the semantics related to throwing and catching exceptions. Now let's look at an equally important facet of exception handling: understanding how to design your system with exception handling in mind. Suppose you have three methods: *Foo*, *Bar*, and *Baz*. *Foo* calls *Bar*, which calls *Baz*. If *Baz* publishes the fact that it throws an exception, does *Bar* have to catch that exception even if it can't, or won't, do anything with it? How should code be split with regards to the *try* and *catch* blocks?

Design Issues with the *try* Block

You know how to catch an exception that a called method might throw, and you know that control passes up the call stack until an appropriate *catch* block is found. So now you might be asking yourself, "Should a *try* block catch every possible exception that a method within it can throw?" The answer is no, and the reason is that you want to maintain the biggest benefits of using exception handling in your applications: reduced coding and lower maintenance costs.

To illustrate this benefit, let's return to a demo that we looked at earlier in the chapter in the "Basic Exception-Handling Syntax" section: the FinallyExample application. You'll recall that in the demo, the *Database.LogIn* method called the *Database.OpenTable* method, which threw an exception. Although that demo worked fine for the point I was making at the time, it wasn't an ideal design for two reasons:

- The *Database.LogIn* method logged the exception that it caught. As we learned in the previous section, a much better design for logging all exceptions is to derive our own exception class and have that class's constructor do the logging. That way, we don't have to worry about an exception not being logged.

- The *Database.LogIn* method shouldn't have caught the exception thrown by *Database.OpenTable* to begin with. Even if we didn't want to derive our own *Exception* class, a better design would've been for the method raising the error (*Database.OpenTable*) to log the error. Once you remove the error-logging code from the *Database.LogIn* method, there's no longer a need for this method to catch the *Database.OpenTable* exception because it doesn't do anything with the exception other than rethrow it up the call stack. This is obviously inefficient and needless.

The following application is an example of a situation in which one method in the call stack simply ignores an exception being raised and assumes that a method higher up in the call stack is catching it:

```
using System;
using System.IO;

public class MyExceptionClass : Exception
{
    // Base Exception class constructors.
    public MyExceptionClass()
        :base()
    {
        LogException();
    }

    public MyExceptionClass(String message)
        :base(message)
    {
        LogException();
    }

    public MyExceptionClass(String message, Exception " +
        "innerException)
        :base(message, innerException)
    {
        LogException();
    }

    protected void LogException()
    {
        Console.WriteLine("[MyExceptionClass.LogException] " +
            "Logging '{0}'", this.Message);
    }
}

class Database
{
    public Database()
    {
        isDbOpen = false;
```

```
}

protected Stream data;

protected bool isDbOpen;
public bool IsDbOpen
{
    get { return isDbOpen; }
}

public bool OpenDb()
{
    // Assume that we successfully opened the physical file.
    isDbOpen = true;
    return true;
}

public bool LogIn(String userName, String password)
{
    // The OpenTable method might throw an exception,
    // but it's something that this method can't do anything
    // about. Therefore, there's no need for this method to
    // catch that particular exception.

    // However, the documentation for this method (LogIn)
    // should state that an exception can be thrown as
    // a result of calling this method. That way, the client
    // knows that a try/catch block needs to exist somewhere
    // in the call stack involving this method.
    if (OpenTable("USERS"))
    {
        // Verify that user and password exist in table.
        // If not, this would not result in an exception
        // because it is not an exception situation. Rather, the
        // method would simply return false to indicate
        // failure to log in successfully.
    }

    return true;
}

public void CloseDb()
{
    // Close the data stream object.
    isDbOpen = false;
}

public bool OpenTable(String table)
```

```
    {
        Console.WriteLine("[Database.OpenTable] Throwing " +
            "exception to caller...");
        throw new MyExceptionClass("Table not found!");
    }

    protected void LogError(String error)
    {
        Console.WriteLine("[Database.LogError] Logging '{0}'",
            error);
    }
}

class FinallyExample
{
    static void Main(string[] args)
    {
        Console.WriteLine("[Main] Instantiating Database " +
            "object");
        Database db = new Database();

        try
        {
            Console.WriteLine("[Main] Opening database...");
            if (db.OpenDb())
            {
                Console.WriteLine("[Main] Successfully " +
                    "opened database");

                Console.WriteLine("[Main] Logging into " +
                    "database...");
                if (db.LogIn("Tom", "password"))
                {
                    Console.WriteLine("[Main] Successfully " +
                        "logged into database");
                }
            }
        }
        catch(Exception e)
        {
            Console.WriteLine("[Main] Caught exception : '{0}'",
                e.Message);
        }
        finally
        {
            if (db.IsDbOpen)
            {
                Console.WriteLine("[Main] Closing database");
```

```
            db.CloseDb();
        }
    }

    Console.ReadLine();
}
}
```

Building and running this application will result in a better-designed and slightly more efficient version of the earlier FinallyExample application, as Figure 12-10 shows.

Figure 12-10   An often overlooked part of learning how to use exceptions effectively is understanding when and at what levels of the call stack to catch them.

Design Issues with the *catch* Block

The only code that should appear in a *catch* block is code that will at least partially process the caught exception. For example, at times, a method will catch an exception, do what it can to process that exception, and then rethrow that exception so that further error handling can occur. The following example illustrates this concept. Here we have a *Table* class that enables us to add a record to the table. The first task the *Table.AddRecord* method performs is to set a commitment (transaction) boundary. From there, the *AddRecord* method attempts to add a blank record to the table, update that record, and then commit the changes. Obviously, if an error occurs at any time during this process, we want the *Table* object to roll back any uncommitted changes. Otherwise, we run the risk of ending up with compromised data.

In this example, you'll see the *Table.AddRecord* wrap all these steps in a *try/catch* block. That way, if an error is raised, the *Table.Rollback* method can be called and the exception rethrown up the call stack for further processing by the class's client.

```csharp
using System;

class Table
{
    public void AddRecord(String record)
    {
        try
        {
            // Set a commitment boundary.
            Commit();

            // Create a blank row in the table.
            AddRow();

            // Update the row with the values passed.
            UpdateRow();

            // Commit the new data.
            Commit();
        }
        catch(Exception e)
        {
            // On error, roll back any uncommited
            // changes to ensure that an error has
            // not left our data compromised.
            Rollback();

            throw e; // Rethrow exception.
        }
    }

    public void Commit()
    {
        Console.WriteLine("[Table.Commit] Committing " +
            "changes to database");
    }

    public void Rollback()
    {
        Console.WriteLine("[Table.Rollback] Roll back " +
            "uncommitted changes to database");
    }

    protected void AddRow()
    {
        Console.WriteLine("[Table.AddRow] Adding blank " +
            "row to database...");
```

```
        // New row added successfully.
        Console.WriteLine("[Table.AddRow] Blank row added " +
            "to database.");
    }

    protected void UpdateRow()
    {
        Console.WriteLine("[Table.UpdateRow] Row " +
            "being updated...");
        // Error encountered updating row...

        Console.WriteLine("[Table.UpdateRow] Error " +
            "encountered. Throwing exception...");
        throw new Exception("Data values do not match " +
            "columns. Update failed.");
    }
}

class WhenToCatchApp
{
    public static void Main()
    {
        try
        {
            Table table = new Table();

            Console.WriteLine("[Main] Attempting to add " +
                "a new record to our fake table...");
            table.AddRecord("This would contain our data");
        }
        catch(Exception e)
        {
            Console.WriteLine("[Main] Exception caught '{0}'",
                e.Message);
        }

        Console.ReadLine();
    }
}
```

Figure 12-11 shows the results of running this application. The ability of each level of the call stack to do only the amount of error processing it's capable of, given its context, is an example of why exception handling is so important to the design of your system.

Figure 12-11   To fully take advantage of exception handling, care must be taken to understand design decisions such as when and at what level to handle thrown exceptions.

Summary

The C# exception-handling syntax is simple and straightforward, and implementing exception handling in your applications is as easy as designing your methods ahead of time. A primary goal of the .NET common language runtime is to help prevent run-time errors through a strong type system and to handle gracefully any run-time errors that do occur. The use of exception-handling code in your applications will make them more robust, dependable, and ultimately easier to maintain.

13

Operator Overloading and User-Defined Conversions

Throughout this book, you've learned that one of the principal goals of the C# design team has been to move the complexity of writing code to the class, away from the client. In Chapter 5, "Properties, Arrays, and Indexers," you learned how to use the [ ] operator with a class to programmatically index an object as though it were an array. In this chapter, we'll look at two closely related features of C# that provide the ability to create structure and class interfaces that are easier and more intuitive to use: *operator overloading* and *user-defined conversions*.

I'll start with a general overview of operator overloading in terms of the benefits it provides you. We'll then look at the actual syntax for redefining the default behaviors of operators as well as a realistic sample application that overloads the plus (+) operator to aggregate multiple *Invoice* objects. After that, you'll see a listing of which binary and unary operators are overloadable as well as some of the restrictions involved. The operator overloading discussion will end with some design guidelines to take into account when deciding whether to overload operators in your classes.

Once we've finished with operator overloading, you'll learn about a new concept, user-defined conversions. Once again, I'll start with broad strokes, explaining the basics of this feature, and then I'll dive into a class that illustrates how you can use conversions to enable the casting of a struct or class to a different struct, class, or basic C# type.

Operator Overloading

Operator overloading allows existing C# operators to be redefined so that one or both of the operators' operands are of a user-defined or *struct* type. Operator overloading has been referred to as *syntactic sugar* because the overloaded operator is simply another means of calling a method. It's also been said that the feature doesn't fundamentally add anything to the language. Although this is technically true, operator overloading does aid in one of the most important aspects of object-oriented programming: abstraction.

Suppose that you want to aggregate a collection of invoices for a particular customer. Using operator overloading, you can write code similar to the following, in which the += operator is overloaded:

```
Invoice summaryInvoice = new Invoice();
Foreach (Invoice invoice in customer.GetInvoices())
{
    summaryInvoice += invoice;
}
```

The benefits of such code include its natural syntax and the fact that the client is abstracted from having to understand the implementation details of how the invoices are being aggregated. Simply put, operator overloading aids in creating software that's less expensive to write and maintain.

Operator Overloading Syntax

As I've said, operator overloading is a means of calling a method. To redefine an operator for a class, you need only use the following pattern, in which *op* is the operator you're overloading:

public static *retval* operator*op* (*object1* [, *object2*])

Keep in mind the following facts when using operator overloading:

- All overloaded operator methods must be defined as *public* and *static*.

- Technically, the return value (*retval*) can be any type. However, it's common practice to return the type for which the method is being defined, with the exception of the *true* and *false* operators, which should always return a Boolean value.

- The number of arguments passed (*object1*, *object2*) depends on the type of operator being overloaded. If a *unary operator*—an operator with a single operand—is being overloaded, there will be one argument. If a *binary operator*—an operator taking two operands—is being overloaded, two arguments are passed.

- In the case of a unary operator, the argument to the method must be the same type as that of the enclosing class or struct. In other words, if you redefine the ! unary operator for a class named *Foo*, that method must take a variable of type *Foo* as its only argument.

- If the operator being overloaded is a binary operator, the first argument must be the same type as that of the enclosing class and the second argument can be any type.

In the pseudocode you saw a moment ago, I used the += operator with an *Invoice* class. For reasons you'll soon understand, you can't actually overload these compound operators. You can overload only the "base" operator—in this case, the + operator. Here's the syntax used to define the *Invoice* class's *operator+* method:

```
public static Invoice operator+ (Invoice invoice1,
    Invoice invoice2)
{
    // Create a new Invoice object.
    // Add the desired contents from
    // invoice1 to the new Invoice object.
    // Add the desired contents from
    // invoice2 to the new Invoice object.
    // Return the new Invoice object.
}
```

Operator Overloading Rules and Restrictions

Now that you've seen the syntax of overloading an operator in C#, let's take a look at the rules and restrictions regarding which operators can be overloaded and how. If your background is in C++, you'll find that you can't overload as many operators in C# as you can in C++. As I go through these restrictions, I'll try to cover why the C# design team decided to disallow the overloading of certain operators.

Note   The comma is used in this section to separate different operators. The comma operator, which is used in the *for* statement and in method calls, can't be overloaded.

The following are the restrictions of operator overloading in C#:

■ The operators that can be overloaded fall into two categories. The first category, unary operators, includes the +, −, !, ~, ++, −−, *true*, and *false* operators. The second set of operators that can be overloaded, binary operators, and includes the +, −, *, /, %, &, |, ^, <<, >>, ==, !=, >, <, >=, and <= operators.

■ The [] operators can't be overloaded. However, as you saw in Chapter 5, user-defined object indexing is supported through the definition of indexers.

■ The parenthesis operator isn't overloadable. A common use of overloading this operator in C++ is to provide an elegant means of subscripting a matrix with the syntax *matrix(x,y)* instead of using the more cumbersome *matrix[x][y]*. Although this type of overloading isn't possible in C#, you can overload the parenthesis operator as it pertains to casting. This type of overloading is known as a *conversion operator*, or a *user-defined conversion*, and is the subject of the second half of this chapter.

■ The conditional operators (&&, ||, and ?:) can't be overloaded. According to the C# design team, this decision was made because the benefit wouldn't have been worth the added complexity. After you read the "Design Guidelines" portion of this section, you'll see that I agree with this decision on the grounds that there are certain operators that have universal meaning. Changing that meaning does nothing but obfuscate the class's interface, which is contradictory to the intentions of using operator overloading to begin with.

■ Operators that currently aren't defined in the C# language can't be overloaded. You can't, for example, define ** as a means of defining exponentiation because C# doesn't define a ** operator. Also, an operator's syntax can't be modified. You can't change the binary * operator to take three arguments when, by definition, its syntax calls for two operands. Finally, an operator's precedence can't be altered; the rules of precedence are static.

More Info   See Chapter 8, "Expressions and Operators," for more on the rules of precedence.

- Operations that are defined by the runtime can't overloaded. These include member access (the . [dot] operator), member invocation, assignment (the = operator), and the *new* operator.

- The comparison operators (== and !=) can be overloaded. However, if you overload one operator, you must overload the other as well. Furthermore, if you overload these operators, you must also overload the *Equals* and *GetHashCode* methods.

- Although the assignment operator can't be overloaded, when you overload a binary operator, its compound assignment equivalent is implicitly overloaded. For example, if you overload the + operator, the += operator is implicitly overloaded in that the user-defined *operator+* method will be called.

- The < and > operators must be overloaded in pairs. In other words, if you overload one, you must overload the other.

As you can see, although the operator overloading syntax might look simple, there are quite a few rules and restrictions to keep in mind. Therefore, let's look at a few demo applications to clear up any questions you might have regarding how to implement certain operators with your own types.

Operator Overloading Examples

When it comes to understanding how to use a given language feature, nothing beats demo applications and sample code. In this section, we'll look at several practical applications of overloading operators.

Invoice Aggregation Example

In our first demo application, InvoiceAdd, we have two main classes: *Invoice* and *InvoiceDetailLine*. The *Invoice* class has a member variable of type *ArrayList* that represents a collection of all invoice detail lines. To allow for the aggregation of detail lines for multiple invoices, I've overloaded the + operator. (See the *operator+* method discussed later in this section for details.) The *Invoice.operator+* method creates a new *Invoice* object and iterates through both the first and the second operands' array of invoice detail lines, adding each detail line to the new *Invoice* object. This *Invoice* object is then returned to the caller. Obviously, in a real-world invoicing module, this process would be much more complex, but the point here is to somewhat realistically show how operator overloading could be used.

```
using System;
using System.Collections;

class InvoiceDetailLine
{
    double lineTotal;
    public double LineTotal
    {
        get
        {
            return this.lineTotal;
        }
    }

    public InvoiceDetailLine(double LineTotal)
    {
        this.lineTotal = LineTotal;
    }
}

class Invoice
{
    static private long nextInvoiceNumber;

    protected long invoiceNumber;
    public long InvoiceNumber
    {
        get
        {
            return invoiceNumber;
        }
    }

    public Invoice()
    {
        invoiceNumber = ++nextInvoiceNumber;
        DetailLines = new ArrayList();
    }

    public ArrayList DetailLines;

    public void PrintInvoice()
    {
        Console.WriteLine("Invoice Number : {0}", InvoiceNumber);
        Console.WriteLine("Line Nbr\tTotal");

        int i = 1;
        double total = 0;
```

```csharp
        foreach(InvoiceDetailLine detailLine in DetailLines)
        {
            Console.WriteLine("{0}\t\t{1}", i++, detailLine.LineTotal);
            total += detailLine.LineTotal;
        }

        Console.WriteLine("=====\t\t===");
        Console.WriteLine("Total\t\t{1}\n", i++, total);
    }

    public static Invoice operator+ (Invoice invoice1,
        Invoice invoice2)
    {
        Invoice returnInvoice = new Invoice();

        foreach (InvoiceDetailLine detailLine in
            invoice1.DetailLines)
        {
            returnInvoice.DetailLines.Add(detailLine);
        }

        foreach (InvoiceDetailLine detailLine in
            invoice2.DetailLines)
        {
            returnInvoice.DetailLines.Add(detailLine);
        }
        return returnInvoice;
    }
}

class InvoiceAddApp
{
    public static void Main()
    {
        Invoice i1 = new Invoice();
        for (int i = 0; i < 2; i++)
        {
            i1.DetailLines.Add(new InvoiceDetailLine(i + 1));
        }
        i1.PrintInvoice();

        Invoice i2 = new Invoice();
        for (int i = 0; i < 2; i++)
        {
            i2.DetailLines.Add(new InvoiceDetailLine(i + 1));
        }
        i2.PrintInvoice();
```

```
            Invoice summaryInvoice = i1 + i2;

            Console.WriteLine("*** Summary Invoice for " +
                "Invoices 1 & 2 ***");
            summaryInvoice.PrintInvoice();

            Console.ReadLine();
        }
    }
```

If you run this application now, you'll see the results shown in Figure 13-1, in which the first two invoices' detail lines are printed, followed by a summary invoice printout.

Figure 13-1   Operating overloading enables you to write extremely intuitive code on the client side.

Now that you've seen an example of how to overload an operator, let's look at a more involved example in which several operators are overloaded to produce a practical utility class.

RGB Color Incrementing Example

In this demo, we'll look at another practical application of operator overloading. This time, we'll build on the *RGB* class presented in Chapter 3, "Classes and Structs," and add the ability to increment (and decrement) the *RGB* color member's values via the overloaded ++ and -- operators. This ability is extremely useful in situations where you're determining the values to be used in painting a gradient fill.

The first thing I did was define an *RGBColor* struct. This class will hold a value (*0* through *255*) that defines a color. The *RGB* struct contains three *RGB-Color* members—one each for the colors red, green, and blue. I also defined the operator overloads at the *RGBColor* level. This operator overloading was done because it's much more common to want to increment one of the RGB values instead of the entire structure. In the next section, "Operator Overloading Design Guidelines," I'll get into some design guidelines to think about when deciding when and whether to overload operators.

Notice also that I define two static, read-only instances of the *RGBColor* struct (representing the values *0* and *255*) within the *RGBColor* struct itself. I did this because these values are used numerous times in the system. Therefore, this is a good C# technique to remember: whenever you have a struct (or class) that has a particular state that will be used over and over again, define an internal static instance representing that state. The result is that instead of having an instance in memory each time an object with that state is created, you'll have only one static instance per state.

Here's the entire code for the application:

```csharp
using System;

struct RGBColor
{
    public static readonly RGBColor EMPTY
        = new RGBColor(0x00);
    public static readonly RGBColor FULL
        = new RGBColor(0xFF);

    int colorValue;
    public int ColorValue
    {
        get { return colorValue; }
    }

    public RGBColor(int color)
    {
        colorValue = color;
    }

    public static RGBColor operator++(RGBColor color)
    {
        if (color.colorValue != 0xFF)
            color.colorValue++;
        return color;
    }

    public static RGBColor operator--(RGBColor color)
    {
        if (color.colorValue != 0x00)
            color.colorValue--;
        return color;
    }
```

```csharp
        public string ToString(string format)
        {
            return (colorValue.ToString(format));
        }
    }

    struct RGB
    {
        public static readonly RGB RED
            = new RGB(RGBColor.FULL, RGBColor.EMPTY,
            RGBColor.EMPTY);
        public static readonly RGB DARKRED
            = new RGB(new RGBColor(128), RGBColor.EMPTY,
            RGBColor.EMPTY);
        public static readonly RGB GREEN
            = new RGB(RGBColor.EMPTY, RGBColor.FULL,
            RGBColor.EMPTY);
        public static readonly RGB BLUE
            = new RGB(RGBColor.EMPTY, RGBColor.EMPTY,
            RGBColor.FULL);
        public static readonly RGB WHITE
            = new RGB(RGBColor.FULL, RGBColor.FULL,
            RGBColor.FULL);
        public static readonly RGB BLACK
            = new RGB(RGBColor.EMPTY, RGBColor.EMPTY,
            RGBColor.EMPTY);

        public RGB(RGBColor red, RGBColor green, RGBColor blue)
        {
            Red = red;
            Green = green;
            Blue = blue;
        }

        public RGBColor Red;
        public RGBColor Green;
        public RGBColor Blue;

        public override string ToString()
        {
            return
                (Red.ToString("X2")
                + Green.ToString("X2")
                + Blue.ToString("X2"));
        }
    }
```

```
class GradientFill
{
    static void PrintRGBValue(RGB rgb)
    {
        Console.Write("{0} ", rgb);
    }

    public static void Main()
    {
        Console.WriteLine("Getting RGB values for gradient " +
            "fill (dark red -> red)\n");
        for (RGB rgb = RGB.DARKRED;
            rgb.Red.ColorValue < 0xFF;
            rgb.Red++)
        {
            PrintRGBValue(rgb);
        }
    }
}
```

Notice the *operator++* method. You'll remember that in the InvoiceAdd example, I defined an *Invoice.operator+* method that returned an aggregate of the two passed *Invoice* objects. I returned a new *Invoice* object—as opposed to manipulating one of the passed *Invoice* objects—because a user would expect that the two passed invoices in the following example shouldn't be manipulated in any way:

```
Invoice summaryInvoice = invoice1 + invoice2;
```

However, in the case of an increment or decrement operator, it would be logical to assume that the object being incremented is being modified internally. Therefore, both the *operator++* and the *operator--* methods simply modify the passed *RGB* struct and return that same struct when finished.

In addition, notice that in the *Main* method, I can use a simple *for* loop and the increment operator to produce my gradient values:

```
for (RGB rgb = RGB.DARKRED;
    rgb.Red.ColorValue < 0xFF;
    rgb.Red++)
```

If you build and run this application, you should see the output shown in Figure 13-2.

Figure 13-2   The increment operator enables you to use user-defined types in constructs such as *for* loops.

The current version represents a good start, but there's one thing that's a bit clunky about it. Notice that in the *for* loop I needed to directly access the *RGBColor* struct's *ColorValue* property to control the loop. Instead, this code would be much cleaner if we also overloaded the > operator. You'll recall from the "Operator Overloading Rules and Restrictions" section that if you overload either the less-than or greater-than operator, you must overload the other. Therefore, the following code gives the *RGBColor* struct an implementation for making color comparisons between two *RGBColor* values:

```
public static bool operator<(RGBColor color1, RGBColor color2)
{
    return color1.colorValue < color2.colorValue;
}

public static bool operator>(RGBColor color1, RGBColor color2)
{
    return color1.colorValue > color2.colorValue;
}
```

As you can see, these methods simply take two *RGBColor* structs and compare their internal *colorValue* members. Now we can write code like the following:

```
if (rgb.Red < RGBColor.FULL).
```

The last thing we'll modify is the way that the increment is performed. Here we'll add an overload of the + operator so that when creating our gradient fill values, we can increment the *RGBColor* value by any value we want (instead of just 5). For completeness, I've also added an *operator–* overload.

```
public static RGBColor operator+(RGBColor color, int inc)
{
```

```
    if (0xFF >= (color.colorValue + inc))
        color.colorValue += inc;
    else
        color.colorValue = 0xFF;
    return color;
}

public static RGBColor operator-(RGBColor color, int dec)
{
    if (0 < (color.colorValue - dec))
        color.colorValue -= dec;
    else
        color.colorValue = 0x00;
    return color;
}
```

These two functions contain some very simple validation to ensure that the decrement or increment operations don't cause the code to exceed the lowest value (*0*) and highest value (*255*) possible, respectively. Now the *RGBColor* struct supports the +, −, ++, −−, <, and > operators, and we can update the *for* loop as follows:

```
for (RGB rgb = RGB.DARKRED;
    rgb.Red < RGBColor.FULL;
    rgb.Red+=5)
{
    PrintRGBValue(rgb);
}
```

Executing this version of the demo produces the results seen in Figure 13-3, where we're still creating our gradient values—but in higher increments.

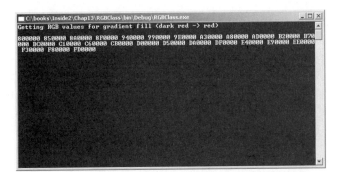

Figure 13-3   The more comfortable you get with the notion that operator overloading is a powerful yet easy-to-use feature, the more you'll see where it can help make you code easier to use and maintain.

Note   As you know, with the prefix versions of the increment operator and decrement operator—that is, *++a* and *−−a*, respectively—the operation is performed and then the value is produced. With the postfix versions of the increment operator and decrement operator—*a++* and *a−−*, respectively—the value is produced and then the operation is performed. In some languages, such as C++, you can overload the prefix and postfix operators independently. However, this isn't the case with C#. In C#, the implementation of these operators either can be for the postfix notation or for the prefix notation. It's not possible to have separate operator implementations for both notations.

As you've seen in these demos, operator overloading can provide a means of creating a slick and intuitive interface for your clients. However, there are certain design guidelines that you should keep in mind when deciding when and whether to incorporate operator overloading into your system. Let's look at some of those guidelines now.

Operator Overloading Design Guidelines

It's time to examine an often ignored aspect of operator overloading: design guidelines. First, I'll introduce you to some factors that should help you decide whether and when to employ operator overloading. Then we'll take a look at language operability and the impact of operator overloading not being defined in the Common Language Specification (CLS) on your system design.

Deciding When Operator Overloading Is Appropriate

You want to avoid the natural tendency to use a new feature just for the sake of using it—a phenomenon sometimes referred to as *a solution in search of a problem*. However, it's always a good design approach to remember the adage, "Code is read more than it's written." Keep the class's client in mind when determining whether and when to overload an operator or set of operators. Here's a rule of thumb: *overload an operator only if it makes the class's interface more intuitive to use*. For example, it makes perfect sense to be able to add invoices together. A few scenarios follow.

Let's say you're writing an *Invoice* class and you want the client to be able to discount the invoice. You and I might know that a credit line item will be added to the invoice, but the point of encapsulation is that your clients don't have to know the exact implementation details of the class. Therefore, one design would be to overload the * operator—so the operator can be used, as shown here—to discount the invoice. Not only is this a more elegant solution to simply providing a *DiscountInvoice* method, but this interface also serves to make the *Invoice* class's interface natural and intuitive:

```
// Overriding operators such as * and + for objects
// such as invoices makes sense and will probably
// be understood by the class's clients.
invoice *= .95; // 5% discount.

// Another common use of operator overloading is for
// simple arithmetic involving user-defined date
// and time objects. Not only is this useful, but
// the syntax makes it obvious what the result will be.
Date today = new Date();
today++; // Now it's tomorrow!
```

You shouldn't use operator overloading any time that the result changes a widely accepted definition of an operator's function or creates a counterintuitive interface. For example, if you saw the following code, chances are you'd have no idea what the result of using these operators would be:

```
// This is a bad design because the logical question
// would be, "What does adding two customers accomplish?"
Customer c1 = new Customer();
Customer c2 = new Customer();
Customer c3 = c1 + c2;

// Another bad design because the client is probably not
// going to understand the concept of incrementing an
// employee.
Employee e = new Employee();
e++;
```

The point here is to always be cognizant of the fact that although you can come up with some clever tricks with operator overloading, these tricks aren't nearly as clever for the person trying to debug your code at 3:00 AM! Therefore, for the benefit of all your fellow developers, please use equal parts imagination and common sense when incorporating this powerful concept into your system design.

Language Interoperability

As you know by now, one of the major benefits of the .NET Framework is the language interoperability. Therefore, if you're writing classes in C# to be consumed by clients written in other .NET languages, it's important to realize that operator overloading isn't defined by the CLS. Because .NET languages have

to implement only what's specified by the CLS, there's no guarantee that all
.NET languages will include operator overloading. Therefore, it would be prudent to ensure that you provide nonoverloaded alternatives for any overloaded operators.

As an example, look back at the invoice aggregation example shown earlier, in which I overloaded the + operator. In this case, the *Invoice* class should
also provide an *Add* method and have the *operator+* method call that method:

```
public class Invoice
{
    :

    public static Invoice operator+ (Invoice invoice1,
        Invoice invoice2)
    {
        return Add(invoice1, invoice2);
    }
    public static Add(Invoice invoice1, Invoice invoice2)
    {
        // Add the desired members of the two invoices together,
        // creating an aggregate invoice.
    }
    :
}
```

User-Defined Conversions

Earlier I mentioned that the parentheses used for casting can't be overloaded
and that user-defined conversions must be used instead. In short, user-defined
conversions enable you to declare conversions on structures or classes so that
the struct or class can be converted to other structures, classes, or basic C#
types. Why and when would you want to do this? Let's say you need to use the
standard Celsius and Fahrenheit temperature scales in your application so that
you can easily convert between the two. By creating user-defined conversions,
you could use the following syntax:

```
Fahrenheit f = 98.6F;    // Implicit conversion
Celsius c = (Celsius)f; // Explicit conversion
```

You'll no doubt note that you could also write the following syntax. However, I think you'll agree that the user-defined conversions once again enable
you to write code that's more elegant and more intuitive for your class's users.

```
Fahrenheit f = new Fahrenheit(98.6F);
Celsius c = f.ConvertToCelsius();
```

User-Defined Conversion Syntax

The syntax of the user-defined conversion uses the *operator* keyword to declare user-defined conversions:

public static implicit operator *conv-type-out* (*conv-type-in operand*)

public static explicit operator *conv-type-out* (*conv-type-in operand*)

Rules regarding the syntax of defining conversions are described next.

User-Defined Conversion Rules and Restrictions

- Any conversion method for a struct or class—you can define as many as you need—must be *static.*

- Conversions must be defined as either *implicit* or *explicit.* The *implicit* keyword means that the cast isn't required by the client and will occur automatically. Conversely, using the *explicit* keyword signifies that the client must explicitly cast the value to the desired type.

- All conversions either must take (as an argument) the type that the conversion is being defined on or must return that type.

- As with operator overloading, the *operator* keyword is used in the conversion method signature but without any appended operator.

I know the first time I read these rules, I didn't have the foggiest idea what to do, so let's look at a couple of practical examples to crystallize your understanding of how to use this feature of the C# language.

User-Defined Conversion Examples

In this example, we have two structures, *Celsius* and *Fahrenheit*, which enable the client to convert a value of type *float* to either temperature scale. I'll first present the *Celsius* structure and make some points about it, and then you'll see the complete working application.

```
struct Celsius
{
    public Celsius(float temp)
    {
        this.temp = temp;
    }

    public static implicit operator Celsius(float temp)
```

```
    {
        Celsius c;
        c = new Celsius(temp);
        return(c);
    }

    public static implicit operator float(Celsius c)
    {
        return((((c.temp - 32) / 9) * 5));
    }

    public float temp;
}
```

The first decision that you see is the one to use a structure instead of a class. I had no real reason for doing so other than the fact that using classes is more expensive than using structures—in terms of how the classes are allocated. In addition, a class isn't really necessary here because the *Celsius* structure doesn't need any C# class-specific features, such as inheritance.

Next, notice that I've declared a constructor that takes a *float* as its only argument. This value is stored in a member variable named *temp*. Now look at the conversion operator defined immediately after the structure's constructor. This is the method that will be called when the client attempts to cast a *float* to *Celsius* or use a *float* in a place where a *Celsius* structure is expected, such as with a method call. This conversion method doesn't have to do much, and in fact, it's fairly formulaic code that can be used in most basic conversions. Here I simply instantiate a *Celsius* structure and then return it. That return call will cause the last method defined in the structure to be called. As you can see, the method simply provides the mathematical formula for converting from a Fahrenheit value to a Celsius value.

Here's the entire application, including a *Fahrenheit* structure:

```
using System;

struct Celsius
{
    public Celsius(float temp)

    {
        this.temp = temp;
    }

    public static implicit operator Celsius(float temp)
    {
        Celsius c;
        c = new Celsius(temp);
```

```
            return(c);
    }

    public static implicit operator float(Celsius c)
    {
        return(((c.temp - 32) / 9) * 5));
    }

    public float temp;
}

struct Fahrenheit
{
    public Fahrenheit(float temp)
    {
        this.temp = temp;
    }

    public static implicit operator Fahrenheit(float temp)
    {
        Fahrenheit f;
        f = new Fahrenheit(temp);
        return(f);
    }

    public static implicit operator float(Fahrenheit f)
    {
        return(((f.temp * 9) / 5) + 32));
    }

    public float temp;
}

class Temp1App
{
    public static void Main()
    {
        float t;

        t=98.6F;
        Console.WriteLine("Setting {0} type to {1}",
            t.GetType(), t);
        Console.Write("Conversion of {0} ({1}) to Celsius = ",
            t.GetType(), t);
        Console.WriteLine((Celsius)t);

        Console.WriteLine();
```

```
        t=0F;
        Console.WriteLine("Setting {0} type to {1}",
            t.GetType(), t);
        Console.Write("Conversion of {0} ({1}) to " +
            "Fahrenheit = ", t.GetType(), t);
        Console.WriteLine((Fahrenheit)t);

        Console.ReadLine();
    }
}
```

If you compile and execute this application, you'll see the output shown in Figure 13-4.

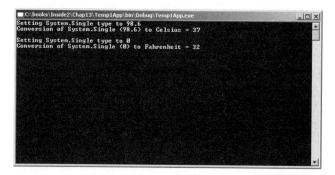

Figure 13-4 Classes and structs are often much easier to work with when user-defined conversions are implemented.

This works pretty well, and being able to write *(Celsius)98.6F* is certainly more intuitive than calling some static class method. But note that you can pass only values of type *float* to these conversion methods. For the previous application, the following won't compile:

```
// ERROR: This code will not compile in Temp1App because
// there is no explicit conversion method from Celsius
// to Fahrenheit defined.
Celsius c = new Celsius(55);
Console.WriteLine((Fahrenheit)c);
```

There's also a logical problem here. Because there's no Celsius conversion method that takes a *Fahrenheit* structure (or vice versa), the code has to assume that the value being passed in needs converting. In other words, if I call *(Celsius)98.6F*, I'll receive the value *37*. However, if that value is then passed to the conversion method again, the conversion method has no way of knowing that the value has already been converted and already represents a valid Celsius temperature—to the conversion method, it's just a *float*. As a result, the value gets converted again. Therefore, we need to modify the application so that each structure can take the other structure as a valid argument.

When I originally thought of doing this, I cringed because I was worried about how difficult this task would be. As it turns out, it's extremely easy. Here's the revised code with ensuing comments:

```
using System;

class Temperature
{
    public Temperature(float Temp)
    {
        this.temp = Temp;
    }

    protected float temp;
    public float Temp
    {
        get
        {
            return this.temp;
        }
    }
}

class Celsius : Temperature
{
    public Celsius(float Temp)
        : base(Temp) {}

    public static implicit operator Celsius(float Temp)
    {
        return new Celsius(Temp);
    }

    public static implicit operator Celsius(Fahrenheit F)
    {
        return new Celsius(F.Temp);
    }

    public static implicit operator float(Celsius C)
    {
        return((((C.temp - 32) / 9) * 5));
    }
}

class Fahrenheit : Temperature
```

```csharp
{
    public Fahrenheit(float Temp)
        : base(Temp) {}

    public static implicit operator Fahrenheit(float Temp)
    {
        return new Fahrenheit(Temp);
    }

    public static implicit operator Fahrenheit(Celsius C)
    {
        return new Fahrenheit(C.Temp);
    }

    public static implicit operator float(Fahrenheit F)
    {
        return((((F.temp * 9) / 5) + 32));
    }
}

class Temp2App
{
    public static void DisplayTemp(Celsius Temp)
    {
        Console.Write("Conversion of {0} {1} to Fahrenheit = ",
            Temp.ToString(), Temp.Temp);
        Console.WriteLine((Fahrenheit)Temp);
    }

    public static void DisplayTemp(Fahrenheit Temp)
    {
        Console.Write("Conversion of {0} {1} to Celsius = ",
            Temp.ToString(), Temp.Temp);
        Console.WriteLine((Celsius)Temp);
    }

    public static void Main()
    {
        Fahrenheit f = new Fahrenheit(98.6F);
        DisplayTemp(f);

        Celsius c = new Celsius(0F);
        DisplayTemp(c);

        Console.ReadLine();
    }
}
```

The first thing to note is that I changed the *Celsius* and *Fahrenheit* types from struct to class. I did this so that I'd have two examples—one using struct, and one using class. But a more practical reason for making this change is to share the *temp* member variable by having the *Celsius* and *Fahrenheit* classes derive from the same *Temperature* base class. Also, I now can use the inherited (from *System.Object*) *ToString* method in the application's output.

The only other notable difference is the addition of a conversion for each temperature scale that takes as an argument a value of the other temperature scale. Notice how similar the code is between the two *Celsius* conversion methods:

```
public static implicit operator Celsius(float temp)
{
    Celsius c;
    c = new Celsius(temp);
    return(c);
}

public static implicit operator Celsius(Fahrenheit f)
{
    Celsius c;
    c = new Celsius(f.temp);
    return(c);
}
```

The only tasks I had to do differently were to change the argument being passed and retrieve the temperature from the passed object instead of a hard-coded value of type *float*. This is why I noted earlier how easy and formulaic conversion methods are once you know the basics. Figure 13-5 shows the results of running the Temp2App demo application.

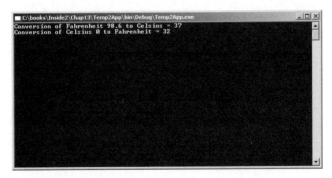

Figure 13-5   With user-defined conversions, you can easily convert between different user-defined types.

Building a TriState Component with User-Defined Conversions

Although the Celsius/Fahrenheit application served as a nice example of using user-defined conversions, you probably won't need this type of functionality in your code too often. Therefore, let's build on that example by creating another demo. This time, we'll build a slightly more elaborate example that will result in something that you just might want to plug into your own code and use—a tristate component.

Several years ago, while working for Equifax, I wrote a Pen computer–based medical insurance application. This application allowed medical professionals to go into the field and interview prospective customers using the same forms you'd fill out at a doctor's office before your initial visit with that doctor. The tricky part was that because this was a Pen system and the prospective customer was signing their name on the computer as though it were a legal document, legally we had to ensure that the actual windows looked and behaved exactly as those on a physical medical form. In addition, we weren't allowed to use standard check boxes because check boxes have a value of either off or on. We had to create a new type that had a third value—*null*, or not entered. This was also a legal requirement of the industry; it ensured that the patient had selected an option and that one hadn't been selected for them by default. In this example, we'll look at how to code a similar class using C# and user-defined conversions.

Because this application is a bit longer than most of the demos in this book, I'll first present and explain the main class (*TriState*) and then present the helper classes and client code that uses the *TriState* class.

TriState will hold three distinct values. The values are −1 (representing *null*, or no value), 0 (*false*, or no) and 1 (*true*, or yes). Before anyone asks, I realize that some people will naturally see 0 as the more logical value for *null*, but with my C/C++ background, I just can't see *false* as anything other than 0. Having said that, let's look at the first pieces of our *TriState* class.

Here you can see that I have a set of *enum* values that represent the only valid values that can be used in instantiating a *TriState* class:

```
public class TriState
{
    // A TriState object must be instantiated using
    // one of these values.
    public enum TriStateValue
    {
        Null = -1,
        False = 0,
        True = 1
    }
```

```
// This member holds the value of the TriState object.
protected TriStateValue value;

// The only thing the constructor does is to set
// the internal value member to the value passed.
public TriState(TriStateValue value)
{
    this.value = value;
}
```

Next I implement an implicit conversion method that works with *bool* types. The inclusion of this method means that a client can set the object to a *bool* value and the object will do the necessary conversion. For example, the client can state something such as *triState = false*, which is certainly more elegant than *triState.SetValue(false)*. As you can see, this method simply determines which *bool* value is being passed (*true* or *false*) and then instantiates—and returns—a *TriState* object initialized to that value:

```
// If the client has code such as triState = <bool value>,
// this method is called and returns a newly instantiated
// TriState object that is constructed using the
// TriStateValue equivalent of the passed bool value.
public static implicit operator TriState(bool value)
{
    if (true == value)
        return new TriState(TriStateValue.True);
    else
        return new TriState(TriStateValue.False);
}
```

Now I simply override the *ToString* method so that the client can have the object print out its current value:

```
public override String ToString()
{
    String value;

    switch(this.value)
    {
        case TriStateValue.Null :
            value = "[No Value]";
            break;

        case TriStateValue.False :
            value = "No";
            break;

        case TriStateValue.True :
```

```
            value = "Yes";
            break;

        default:
            throw new Exception("Invalid value");
    }
    return value;
}
```

The client creates a *FormQuestion* class that encapsulates a question-and-answer value that will be presented on the screen when we run the application:

```
class FormQuestion
{
    String question;
    public String Question
    {
        get
        {
            return question;
        }
    }

    TriState answer;
    public TriState Answer
    {
        get
        {
            return answer;
        }
        set
        {
            answer = value;
        }
    }

    public FormQuestion(String question)
    {
        this.question = question;
        this.answer =
            new TriState(TriState.TriStateValue.Null);
    }
}
```

The *Form* class contains a collection of *FormQuestion* objects, which are initialized in the constructor. However, it's the *AskQuestions* and *DisplayAnswers* methods that are interesting. The *Form.AskQuestions* method iterates through the *Form* object's *FormQuestion* objects. For each object,

Form.AskQuestions prints out the object's question—actually, *Form.AskQuestions* instructs the current *FormQuestion* to print out its own question. *Form.AskQuestions* then calls the *Form.GetResponse* method to retrieve the response to the question from the end user. Note that when the user's input is determined to be a **Y** or an **N**, the local response object is set to *true* or *false* accordingly. As you might have guessed, it's our implicit conversion method that makes that syntax work.

The *Form.DisplayAnswers* method then iterates through the *FormQuestion* collection, printing out the questions and the user's answers. Note that the *TriState.ToString* method is called as a result of the *FormQuestion.Answer* property being printed:

```
class Form
{
    private ArrayList formQuestions;

    public Form()
    {
        formQuestions = new ArrayList();
        formQuestions.Add(new FormQuestion("Are you sick?"));
        formQuestions.Add(new FormQuestion("How old are you?"));
        formQuestions.Add(new FormQuestion("Are you tired " +
            "of these questions?"));
    }

    public void AskQuestions()
    {
        Console.WriteLine("\n*** QUESTIONNAIRE ***");
        foreach (FormQuestion question in formQuestions)
        {
            Console.Write("{0} ", question.Question);
            question.Answer = GetResponse();
        }
    }

    static public TriState GetResponse()
    {
        TriState response =
            new TriState(TriState.TriStateValue.Null);

        String valueEntered = Console.ReadLine();
        if (1 == valueEntered.Length)
        {
            valueEntered = valueEntered.ToUpper();
            char ch = Convert.ToChar(valueEntered.Substring(0,
                1));
```

```
            if ('Y' == ch)
            {
                response = true;
            }
            else if ('N' == ch)
            {
                response = false;
            }
        }

        return response;
    }

    public void DisplayAnswers()
    {
        Console.WriteLine("\n*** ANSWERS ***");
        foreach (FormQuestion question in formQuestions)
        {
            Console.WriteLine("{0} {1}",
                question.Question, question.Answer);
        }
    }
}
```

The client's *Main* method need only instantiate a *Form* object and call its *AskQuestions* and *DisplayAnswers* methods:

```
class TriStateApp
{
    static public void Main()
    {
        Form form = new Form();
        form.AskQuestions();
        form.DisplayAnswers();

        Console.ReadLine();
    }
}
```

Figure 13-6 shows the result of running this application. Notice that because I failed to answer the second question, the *TriState* object properly reflects a *null* value. (For simplicity, the second question still expects a Yes, No, or null answer.)

Figure 13-6   Logical constructs such as our *TriState* class are much easier to write and more intuitive to use with user-defined conversions.

Adding Explicit Conversions to the TriState Component

So far, we've learned a good deal with our first two demos. However, if you try to add the following lines of code to the TriStateApp example, you'll receive a compile-time error:

```
TriState t1 = new TriState(TriState.TriStateValue.True);
bool b = (bool)t1;
```

The reason this code won't compile is that the system has no means of converting a *TriState* type to a *bool* value. Because this type of conversion could come in quite handy with our application, let's look at the code to add this functionality. Here I've added an explicit *bool* conversion method to solve our little problem. Note that I've intentionally removed all the code from the original *TriStateApp* that wasn't necessary for this application.

```
using System;
using System.Collections;

public class TriState
{
    // A TriState object must be instantiated using
    // one of these values.
    public enum TriStateValue
    {
        Null = -1,
        False = 0,
        True = 1
    }
```

```
    // This member holds the value of the TriState object.
    protected TriStateValue value;

    // The only thing the constructor does is to set
    // the internal value member to the value passed.
    public TriState(TriStateValue value)
    {
        this.value = value;
    }

    // Explicit conversion from TriState to bool.
    public static explicit operator bool(TriState triState)
    {
        return (triState.value == TriStateValue.True ?
            true : false);
    }
}

class TriState2App
{
    static public void Main()
    {
        Console.WriteLine("Instantiating a TriState object " +
            "as TriState.TriStateValue.True");
        TriState t1 = new TriState(TriState.TriStateValue.True);
        bool b1 = (bool)t1;
        Console.WriteLine("TriState object converted to {0}",
            b1);

        Console.WriteLine();

        Console.WriteLine("Instantiating a TriState object " +
            "as TriState.TriStateValue.False");
        TriState t2 =
            new TriState(TriState.TriStateValue.False);
        bool b2 = (bool)t2;
        Console.WriteLine("TriState object converted to {0}",
            b2);

        Console.ReadLine();
    }
}
```

If you build and run this application, you'll see the output as generated in Figure 13-7.

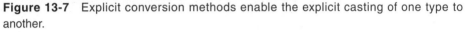

Figure 13-7   Explicit conversion methods enable the explicit casting of one type to another.

Summary

Operator overloading and user-defined conversions are useful for creating intuitive interfaces for your classes. While designing your classes, keep in mind the associated restrictions of using overloaded operators. For example, although you can't overload the = assignment operator, when a binary operator is overloaded, its compound assignment equivalent is implicitly overloaded. Follow the design guidelines for deciding when to use each feature. Keep the class's client in mind when determining whether to overload an operator or set of operators. With a little insight into how your clients will use your classes, you can utilize these powerful features to define your classes so that certain operations can be performed with a more natural syntax.

14

Delegates and Event Handlers

Another useful innovation of the common type system (CTS) is a type named *delegates*. From a consumer's perspective, delegates are reference types that encapsulate a method (either static or instance) with a specific signature. In the .NET world, delegates are used to provide *callback* functionality as well as *asynchronous event handling*. In this chapter, I'll define delegates—from a C# programmer's perspective as well as the Microsoft intermediate language (MSIL) implementation perspective. I'll also explain how delegates compare to interfaces, illustrate the C# syntax used to define them, and present several demo applications to show various problems that they were designed to address. Let's begin by defining the problems delegates solve.

Using Delegates as Callback Methods

Used extensively in programming for Microsoft Windows, callback methods enable you to pass a function pointer to another function that will then call you back (via the passed pointer). For example, the Win32 API *EnumWindows* function enumerates all the top-level windows on the screen, calling the supplied function for each window. Callbacks serve many purposes, but the following are the most common:

■ **Asynchronous processing** Callback methods are used in asynchronous processing when the code being called will take a good deal of time to process the request. Typically, the scenario works like this: Client code makes a call to a method, passing to it the callback method. The method being called starts a thread and returns immediately. The thread then does the majority of the work, calling the callback function as needed. This has the obvious benefit of allowing the client to continue processing without being blocked on a potentially lengthy synchronous call.

■ **Injecting custom code into a class's code path**   Callback methods are also commonly used when a class allows the client to specify a method that will be called to perform custom processing. Let's look at an example in Windows that illustrates this. Using the *ListBox* class in Windows, you can specify that the items be sorted in ascending or descending order. Besides some other basic sort options, the *ListBox* class can't really give you any latitude and remain a generic class. Therefore, the *ListBox* class also enables you to specify a callback function for sorting. That way, when *ListBox* sorts the items, it calls the callback function and your code can then do the necessary custom sorting.

Now let's look at an example of defining and using a delegate. In this example, we have a database manager class that keeps track of all active connections to the database and provides a method for enumerating those connections. Assuming that the database manager is on a remote server, it might be a good design decision to make the method asynchronous and allow the client to provide a callback method. Note that for a real-world application, you'd typically create this as a multithreaded application to make it truly asynchronous. However, to keep the example simple—and because we haven't covered multithreading yet—let's leave multithreading out.

To get started, let's see how you would define a delegate in the class that's publishing the callback:

```
class DBManager
{
    static DBConnection[] activeConnections;

    public delegate void EnumConnectionsCallback(
        DBConnection connection);
    public static void EnumConnections(
        EnumConnectionsCallback callback)
    {
        foreach (DBConnection connection in activeConnections)
        {
            callback(connection);
        }
    }
}
```

The class (server) must perform two steps to define a delegate as a callback. The first step is to define the actual delegate—*EnumConnectionsCallback*, in this case—that will be the signature of the callback method. The syntax for defining a delegate takes the following form:

```
<access modifier> delegate <returnType> MethodName ([parameters])
```

The second step is to define a method that takes as one of its parameters the delegate. In this case, the *EnumConnections* method takes as its only parameter an instance of the *EnumConnectionsCallback* delegate.

Now the user of this class (the client) simply needs to define a method that has the same signature as the delegate and—using the *new* operator—instantiate the delegate, passing it the name of the method. Here's an example of that:

```
public static void PrintConnections(DBConnection connection)
{
}

   ⋮

DBManager.EnumConnectionsCallback printConnections
    = new DBManager.EnumConnectionsCallback(PrintConnections);
```

Finally, the client simply calls the desired class's method, passing the instantiated delegate:

```
DBManager.EnumConnections(printConnections);
```

That's all there is to the basic syntax of delegates. Now let's look at the full example application:

```
using System;
using System.Collections;

class DBConnection
{
    protected static int NextConnectionNbr = 1;

    protected string connectionName;
    public string ConnectionName
    {
        get
        {
            return connectionName;
        }
    }

    public DBConnection()
```

```
        {
            connectionName = "Database Connection "
                + DBConnection.NextConnectionNbr++;
        }
    }

class DBManager
{
    protected ArrayList activeConnections;
    public DBManager()
    {
        activeConnections = new ArrayList();
        for (int i = 1; i < 6; i++)
        {
            activeConnections.Add(new DBConnection());
        }
    }

    public delegate void EnumConnectionsCallback(
        DBConnection connection);
    public void EnumConnections(EnumConnectionsCallback callback)
    {
        foreach (DBConnection connection in activeConnections)
        {
            callback(connection);
        }
    }
};

class InstanceDelegate
{
    public static void PrintConnections(DBConnection connection)
    {
        Console.WriteLine("[InstanceDelegate.PrintConnections] {0}",
            connection.ConnectionName);
    }

    public static void Main()
    {
        DBManager dbManager = new DBManager();

        Console.WriteLine("[Main] Instantiating the " +
            "delegate method");
        DBManager.EnumConnectionsCallback printConnections =
            new DBManager.EnumConnectionsCallback(
            PrintConnections);
```

```
        Console.WriteLine("[Main] Calling EnumConnections " +
            "- passing the delegate");
        dbManager.EnumConnections(printConnections);

        Console.ReadLine();
    }
};
```

If you compile and run this application, you'll see the output shown in Figure 14-1.

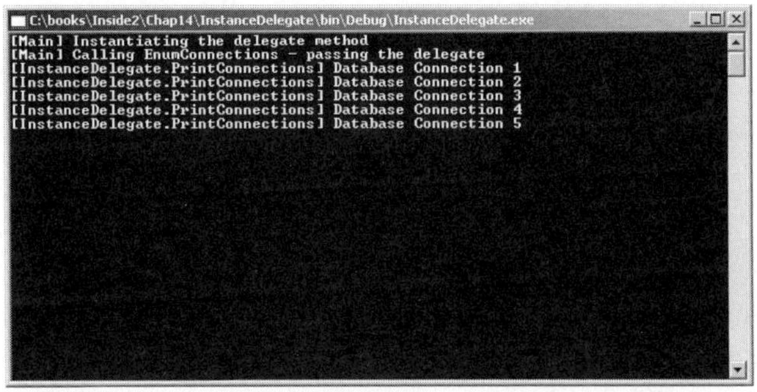

Figure 14-1   Callbacks are extremely easy to implement using delegates.

Inside Delegates

If you come from a C++ background, you probably noticed that delegates are very similar to C++ function pointers. In fact, many books describe them as *type-safe function pointers*. However, as you saw in the previous client code, once a delegate is defined, it's then instantiated like a C# class (via the *new* operator). I think that once we delve more deeply into the internals of how delegates are implemented by the MSIL, you'll agree with me that delegates are better defined as the .NET equivalent of a *functor*, or *function object*, concept. Functors are C++ classes that overload the parenthesis operators so that the result looks like a function but is actually a type-safe, polymorphic class.

So far, we've seen lots of MSIL and know what a class looks like. Figure 14-2 shows why delegates are more suitably referred to as functors rather than simple function pointers.

Figure 14-2   Under the hood, delegates are actually classes of type *System.MulticastDelegate.*

As you can see, the delegate defined in our example (*EnumConnections-Callback*) is a derived class of type *System.MulticastDelegate* and includes the following members:

■ *EnumConnectionCallback* constructor

■ *Invoke*

■ *BeginInvoke*

■ *EndInvoke*

We'll start with the delegate's constructor, which always has the same signature regardless of the definition of your delegate method. Look at the underlying MSIL of the delegate constructor in Figure 14-3, where I've highlighted the text of the actual constructor signature.

Figure 14-3   The delegate constructor yields some important information about how delegates are constructed internally.

The delegate constructor actually takes two parameters, but not the one it appears to take in our client code that instantiated the *EnumConnectionsCall-back* delegate. As you can see, the first parameter is of type *object*. The *object* parameter will either be the *this* value of the invocation object (if the instantiating method is an instance method) or a *null* value indicating that the method instantiating the delegate is a state method (as it is with our static *Main* method). The second parameter is then the method that has been assigned to the instance of this delegate.

Notice that attributes have been used to define the delegate constructor. Specifically, I'm referring to the *specialname* and the *rtspecialname* attributes. The *specialname* attribute indicates that the method (the delegate constructor, in this case) has special significance to tools other than the Common Language Infrastructure, and the *rtspecialname* attribute indicates that the method has special significance to the Common Language Infrastructure. Note that the Common Language Infrastructure's rules specify that any time an item is marked as *rtspecialname*, it must also be marked as *specialname*. Unlike most code that you'll see in MSIL, the implementation of this method—as well as the other delegate methods—is provided by the runtime. This is one reason the runtime can guarantee that the encapsulated function has the correct signature—the runtime verifies the signature within the hidden constructor code that you and I will never see.

Note   Delegates are classes that derive from *MulticastDelegate*. This behavior is a holdover from earlier incarnations of the type system in which the base class for a delegate (when used as a simple encapsulation of a method callback) was originally a class named *Delegate* and an extension to that class—the *MulticastDelegate* class—was used for asynchronous event handling. However, in the current version of the CTS, the extended (*MulticastDelegate*) class is used as the base class for both types of delegates.

Before we inspect the other delegate members, let's look at Figure 14-4, which shows the MSIL of delegate instantiation. I've highlighted the salient code in this figure.

```
InstanceDelegate::Main : void()                                          _|□|x|
.method public hidebysig static void  Main() cil managed
{
  .entrypoint
  // Code size        53 (0x35)
  .maxstack  3
  .locals init ([0] class DBManager dbManager,
           [1] class DBManager/EnumConnectionsCallback printConnections)
  IL_0000:  newobj     instance void DBManager::.ctor()
  IL_0005:  stloc.0
  IL_0006:  ldstr      "[Main] Instantiating the delegate method"
  IL_000b:  call       void [mscorlib]System.Console::WriteLine(string)
  IL_0010:  ldnull
  IL_0011:  ldftn      void InstanceDelegate::PrintConnections(class DBConnection)
  IL_0017:  newobj     instance void DBManager/EnumConnectionsCallback::.ctor(object,
                                                                         native int)
  IL_001c:  stloc.1
  IL_001d:  ldstr      "[Main] Calling EnumConnections - passing the deleg"
+ "ate"
  IL_0022:  call       void [mscorlib]System.Console::WriteLine(string)
  IL_0027:  ldloc.0
  IL_0028:  ldloc.1
  IL_0029:  callvirt   instance void DBManager::EnumConnections(class DBManager/EnumConnect
  IL_002e:  call       string [mscorlib]System.Console::ReadLine()
```

Figure 14-4 Although you can't tell from looking at C# code, delegate objects are actually instantiated with two parameters—the *this* pointer of the invoking method (if it's an instance method) and a method signature.

Remember that in our InstanceDelegate application, we instantiated the delegate in a static *Main* method. Therefore, the MSIL uses the *ldnull* opcode to load a *null* value onto the stack. This value indicates that a *static* method is instantiating this delegate. If the *Main* method had called an instance method that had then instantiated the delegate, you'd have seen the *ldarg.0* opcode used because it loads onto the stack the first argument to a given method— which is always the *this* pointer for instance methods.

The second opcode you see is the *ldftn* call. This opcode pushes onto the stack an unmanaged pointer to the implementation of the specified method. Therefore, in our situation, a pointer to the *InstanceDelegate.PrintConnections* method is what's being pushed onto the stack.

At this point, the stack is set up and the *newobj* opcode—the MSIL equivalent of the *new* operator—is used. As you already know, the two parameters specified are of type *object* and *int*, respectively. These parameters are popped off the stack in the delegate constructor.

The last bit of MSIL that we'll look at here is the actual code to invoke a delegate method. Remember that in our little demo application, it's the *DBManager.EnumConnections* method that performs this task, as shown in Figure 14-5.

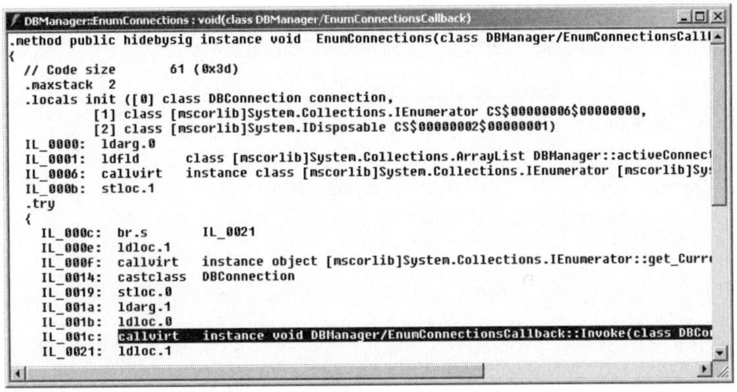

Figure 14-5 The *MulticastDelegate.Invoke* method is used to execute the delegate object's encapsulated method.

As you can see from the *callvirt* opcode, although the C# code implies that the server calls the specified delegate instance directly, the server actually calls the delegate method's *Invoke* method and the delegate calls the encapsulated method.

That's about it for the internals of how delegates work. Now let's look at another aspect of delegates—defining them as static class members.

Defining Delegates as Static Members

In addition to defining instances of delegates, C# allows you to define as a static class member the method that will be used in the creation of the delegate. Following is the example from the previous section, changed to use this format. Note that the delegate is now defined as a static member of the class named *printConnections* and that this member can be used in the *Main* method without the need for the client to instantiate the delegate.

```
using System;
using System.Collections;

class DBConnection
{
    protected static int NextConnectionNbr = 1;

    protected string connectionName;
    public string ConnectionName
    {
        get
        {
```

```
                return connectionName;
        }
    }

    public DBConnection()
    {
        connectionName = "Database Connection "
            + DBConnection.NextConnectionNbr++;
    }
}

class DBManager
{
    protected ArrayList activeConnections;
    public DBManager()
    {
        activeConnections = new ArrayList();
        for (int i = 1; i < 6; i++)
        {
            activeConnections.Add(new DBConnection());
        }
    }

    public delegate void EnumConnectionsCallback(
        DBConnection connection);
    public void EnumConnections(EnumConnectionsCallback callback)
    {
        foreach (DBConnection connection in activeConnections)
        {
            callback(connection);
        }
    }
};

class StaticDelegate
{
    static DBManager.EnumConnectionsCallback printConnections
        = new DBManager.EnumConnectionsCallback(
        PrintConnections);

    public static void PrintConnections(DBConnection connection)
    {
        Console.WriteLine("[StaticDelegate.PrintConnections] {0}",
            connection.ConnectionName);
    }

    public static void Main()
    {
```

```
        DBManager dbManager = new DBManager();

        Console.WriteLine("[Main] Calling EnumConnections - " +
            "passing the delegate");
        dbManager.EnumConnections(printConnections);

        Console.ReadLine();
    }
};
```

Running this application yields basically the same results you saw in Figure 14-1. However, what's interesting is the change that's occurring under the covers. Because our delegate object is now static, the code is no longer instantiating it, as Figure 14-6 shows.

Figure 14-6   When a delegate is declared as static, it has to be instantiated somewhere, but where?

Now the question becomes, "Where's the delegate being instantiated?" To answer that, I refer you back to the material on type initializers in Chapter 3, "Classes and Structs." As you learned in that chapter, a rule of the Common Language Infrastructure is that a static type can contain a special method known as a *type initializer* that the type uses to initialize itself. The rules of this method are that the method must be static, take no parameters, return no value, be decorated with the *rtspecialname* and *specialname* attributes, and be named *.cctor*. Now that we've had that refresher, we can dive into the *DelegateStatic.cctor* method, shown in Figure 14-7.

```
StaticDelegate::.cctor : void()
.method private hidebysig specialname rtspecialname static
        void  .cctor() cil managed
{
   // Code size      18 (0x12)
   .maxstack  3
   IL_0000:  ldnull
   IL_0001:  ldftn      void StaticDelegate::PrintConnections(class DBConnection)
   IL_0007:  newobj     instance void DBManager/EnumConnectionsCallback::.ctor(object,
                                                                              native int)
   IL_000c:  stsfld     class DBManager/EnumConnectionsCallback StaticDelegate::printConnections
   IL_0011:  ret
} // end of method StaticDelegate::.cctor
```

Figure 14-7   The *.cctor* method is a type initializer defined by the Common Language Infrastructure that static types use to initialize themselves.

Figure 14-7 shows how static delegates are supported. The first three lines of MSIL should look very familiar to you because they match how an instance delegate is instantiated (which you saw in Figure 14-4). The new opcode *stsfld* simply sets a static field value to that of a value on the stack. And there you have it—that's how C# delegates are interpreted at the underlying MSIL level.

Note   Because the standard naming convention for delegates is to append the word *Callback* to the method that takes the delegate as its argument, it's easy to mistakenly use the method name instead of the delegate name. If you do, you'll get a somewhat misleading compile-time error that states that you've denoted a method when a class was expected. If you get this error, remember that the actual problem is that you've specified a method instead of a delegate.

Creating Delegates Only When Needed

In the two examples you've seen so far, the delegate is created regardless of whether it's ever used. That was fine in those examples because I knew that the delegate would always be called. However, when defining your delegates, you should consider when to create them. Let's say, for example, that the creation of a particular delegate is time-consuming and not something you want to do gratuitously. In situations in which you know the client won't typically call a given callback method, you can put off the creation of the delegate until it's actually needed by wrapping its instantiation in a property. To illustrate how to do this, a modification of the demo application follows. This modified demo uses a read-only property to instantiate the delegate because only a getter method is present. The delegate won't be created until this property is referenced.

```
using System;
using System.Collections;

class DBConnection
{
    protected static int NextConnectionNbr = 1;

    protected string connectionName;
    public string ConnectionName
    {
        get
        {
```

```
                    return connectionName;
            }
        }


    public DBConnection()
    {
        connectionName = "Database Connection "
            + DBConnection.NextConnectionNbr++;
      }
}

class DBManager
{
    protected ArrayList activeConnections;
    public DBManager()
    {
        activeConnections = new ArrayList();
        for (int i = 1; i < 6; i++)
        {
            activeConnections.Add(new DBConnection());
        }
    }


    public delegate void EnumConnectionsCallback(
        DBConnection connection);
    public void EnumConnections(EnumConnectionsCallback callback)
    {
        foreach (DBConnection connection in activeConnections)
        {
            callback(connection);
        }
    }
};

class DelegateProperty
{
    void printConnections(DBConnection connection)
    {
        Console.WriteLine("[DelegateProperty.printConnections] " +
            "{0}", connection.ConnectionName);
    }
    public DBManager.EnumConnectionsCallback PrintConnections
    {
        get
        {
            return new DBManager.EnumConnectionsCallback(
                printConnections);
        }
    }
```

```
    public static void Main()
    {
        DelegateProperty app = new DelegateProperty();
        DBManager dbManager = new DBManager();

        Console.WriteLine("[Main] Calling EnumConnections - " +
            "passing the delegate");
        dbManager.EnumConnections(app.PrintConnections);

        Console.ReadLine();
    }
};
```

As you can see, all I needed to do was the following:

■ Define the method that will act as the delegate receiver with an access modifier that restricts external access to its usage.

■ Define a getter property that returns a delegate instance for that receiver method. When invoked, this property instantiates a delegate object using the receiver method.

■ Call the server's method that takes a delegate object as a parameter, invoking the delegate object–producing property in the parameter list.

Figure 14-8 shows the resulting MSIL. You should recognize the first three lines—they move the receiver object and receiver method to the stack and then instantiate the delegate object using those two values. If you look at the *.locals* section of this code, you'll see a local declaration of type *DBManager.EnumConnectionsCallback*. The code immediately following the creation of the delegate object simply pops the value off the stack into the local variable (*stloc*), branches accordingly (*br.s*), and pushes the local value back onto the stack (*ldloc*).

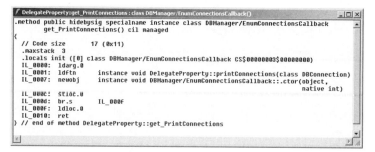

Figure 14-8   Properties can help to create a more elegant interface to instantiate your delegate objects.

Multicast Delegates

Combining multiple delegates into a single delegate creates what's referred to as a *multicast delegate* and is one of those subtle features of the .NET Framework that doesn't seem very handy at first. However, it's also a feature that you'll be happy the Common Language Infrastructure design team thought of if you ever do need it. Let's look at some examples in which delegate multicasting is useful. In the first example, we have a distribution system and a class that iterates through the parts for a given location, calling a callback method for each part that has an "on-hand" value of less than 50. In a more realistic distribution example, the formula not only would take into account "on-hand" values, it would also take into account "on order" and "in transit" values (which describe the items' lead times), it would subtract the safety stock level, and so on. But let's keep this simple: if a part's on-hand value is less than 50, an exception has occurred.

The twist is that we want two distinct methods to be called if a given part falls below stock: we want to log the event, and then we want to e-mail the purchasing manager. Let's take a look at how you programmatically create a single aggregate delegate from multiple delegates:

```
using System;
using System.Threading;

class Part
{
    public Part(string sku)
    {
        this.Sku = sku;

        Random r = new Random(DateTime.Now.Millisecond);
        double d = r.NextDouble() * 100;

        this.OnHand = (int)d;
    }

    protected string sku;
    public string Sku
    {
        get { return this.sku; }
        set { this.sku = value; }
    }

    protected int onHand;
    public int OnHand
    {
```

```
            get { return this.onHand; }
            set { this.onHand = value; }
        }
    };

    class InventoryManager
    {
        protected const int MIN_ONHAND = 50;

        public Part[] parts;
        public InventoryManager()
        {
            Console.WriteLine("[InventoryManager.InventoryManager]" +
                " Adding parts...");

            parts = new Part[5];
            for (int i = 0; i < 5; i++)
            {
                Part part = new Part("Part " + (i + 1));

                Thread.Sleep(10); // Randomizer is seeded by time.

                parts[i] = part;
                Console.WriteLine("\tPart '{0}' on-hand = {1}",
                    part.Sku, part.OnHand);
            }
        }

        public delegate void OutOfStockExceptionMethod(Part part);
        public void ProcessInventory(
            OutOfStockExceptionMethod exception)
        {
            Console.WriteLine("\n[InventoryManager.ProcessInventory]" +
                " Processing inventory...");
            foreach (Part part in parts)
            {
                if (part.OnHand < MIN_ONHAND)
                {
                    Console.WriteLine("\n\t{0} ({1} units) is " +
                        "below minimum on-hand {2}",
                        part.Sku,
                        part.OnHand,
                        MIN_ONHAND);

                    exception(part);
                }
            }
        }
    }
```

```
};

class CompositeDelegate
{
    public static void LogEvent(Part part)
    {
        Console.WriteLine("\t[CompositeDelegate.LogEvent] " +
            "logging event...");
    }

    public static void EmailPurchasingMgr(Part part)
    {
        Console.WriteLine("\t[CompositeDelegate" +
            ".EmailPurchasingMgr] emailing Purchasing " +
            "manager...");
    }

    public static void Main()
    {
        InventoryManager mgr = new InventoryManager();

        InventoryManager.OutOfStockExceptionMethod
            LogEventCallback = new
            InventoryManager.OutOfStockExceptionMethod(LogEvent);

        InventoryManager.OutOfStockExceptionMethod
            EmailPurchasingMgrCallback = new
            InventoryManager.OutOfStockExceptionMethod(
            EmailPurchasingMgr);

        InventoryManager.OutOfStockExceptionMethod
            OnHandExceptionEventsCallback =
            EmailPurchasingMgrCallback + LogEventCallback;

        mgr.ProcessInventory(OnHandExceptionEventsCallback);

        Console.ReadLine();
    }
};
```

Running this application will produce results similar to those shown in Figure 14-9. (Your results won't be identical because of the random number generation of the parts' on-hand value.) Therefore, using this feature of the language, we can dynamically discern which methods comprise a callback method, aggregate those methods into a single delegate by using the plus (+) operator, and pass the composite delegate as though it were a single delegate. The runtime will automatically see to it that all the methods are called in sequence. In addition, you can remove delegates from the composite by using the minus (-) operator.

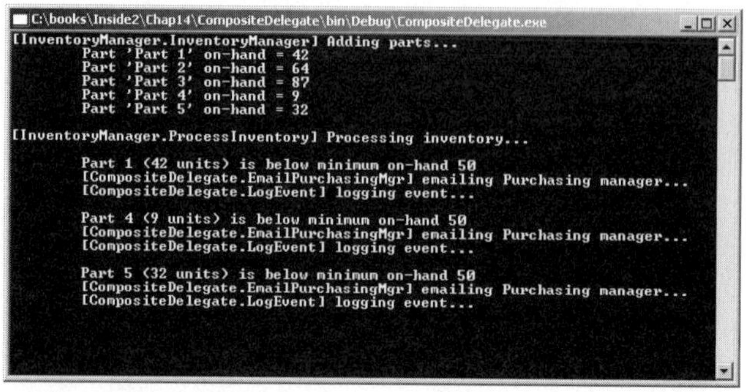

Figure 14-9   Multicast delegates enable you to combine multiple delegate objects into a single object.

Figure 14-10 shows how these delegates are actually chained together under the hood.

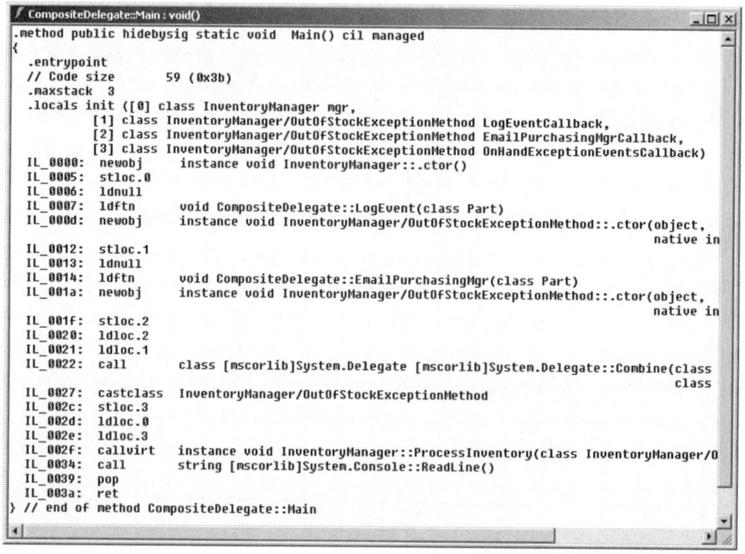

Figure 14-10   The *System.Delegate.Combine* method is internally called when delegate objects are aggregated by using the *Delegate* class's overloaded + operator.

The first thing you'll see is the *.locals* section, which contains the local declaration of the *InventoryManager* object and three delegate objects (*InventoryManager.LogEventCallback, InventoryManager.EmailPurchasingMgrCall-*

back, and *InventoryManager.OnHandExceptionEventsCallback*). After that, the *InventoryManager* object and the first two delegate objects are created using the same MSIL we've seen throughout this chapter—with the *stloc* opcode being used after each *newobj* operation to store the new object in its appropriate local variable.

The variation here begins at line IL_0020. The program loads two local delegate objects onto the stack (via *ldloc*) and then calls the *Delegate.Combine* method. I'll talk more about this method shortly, but for now, it's enough to know that *Delegate.Combine* is responsible for concatenating the supplied delegate objects into a single delegate object. After the delegates are combined, the result will be on the stack.

The instruction at IL_0027 is a *castclass* opcode. This instruction simply tests whether the value on the stack is of the type specified (*InventoryManager.OutOfStockExceptionMethod*, in this case). If value on the stack is not of the type specified, the program raises an *InvalidCastException* and—because we don't have a catch block for this exception—the .NET Framework would abort our application. However, the value on the stack *will* be the correct type, and thus the next statements push that value (which is now the multicast delegate) into the fourth local variable (*stloc.3*). Finally, the local *InventoryManager* object and the multicast delegate values are loaded onto the stack, and the *InventoryManager.ProcessInventory* method is called.

Now let's go back to the *Delegate.Combine* method. Although using the *Delegate* object's overloaded + operator does require less typing, you can call the *Delegate.Combine* method yourself. Let's look at how to do that.

This *Delegate.Combine* method has two overloaded versions. The first version takes two parameters, and—as you can see from the MSIL in Figure 14-10 — that's the version that's called when you combine delegates using the + operator.

```
public static Delegate Combine(Delegate, Delegate);
```

Here's an example of using the *Delegate.Combine* method in which I've simply modified the delegate creation and aggregation code from the *CompositeDelegate.Main* method:

```
⋮

// Create the first delegate instance (that logs the event).
InventoryManager.OutOfStockExceptionMethod LogEventCallback =
    new InventoryManager.OutOfStockExceptionMethod(LogEvent);

// Create the second delegate instance (that e-mails the manager).
InventoryManager.OutOfStockExceptionMethod
    EmailPurchasingMgrCallback =
    new InventoryManager.OutOfStockExceptionMethod(
```

```
EmailPurchasingMgr);

// Call the Delegate.Combine method to create
// a multicast delegate.
InventoryManager.OutOfStockExceptionMethod
    OnHandExceptionEventsCallback =
    (InventoryManager.OutOfStockExceptionMethod)
    Delegate.Combine(EmailPurchasingMgrCallback, LogEventCallback);

// Call the ProcessInventory method, passing it the multicast delegate.
mgr.ProcessInventory(OnHandExceptionEventsCallback);

    ⋮
```

The second overload takes an array of delegate objects as its only parameter:

```
public static Delegate Combine(Delegate[] delegates);
```

To use this version of the *Combine* method, simply define a delegate array, instantiate each delegate, place each delegate in the array, and call the *Combine* method, passing it the array of delegate objects. The *Combine* method will then return the multicast delegate that results from aggregating all the delegates in the array. Here's how that would look when implemented using our previous *CompositeDelegate.Main* method:

```
    ⋮

// Declare an array of two delegate objects.
InventoryManager.OutOfStockExceptionMethod[] delegates
= new InventoryManager.OutOfStockExceptionMethod[2];

// Instantiate each delegate and insert them into
// the delegates array.
delegates[0] = new
    InventoryManager.OutOfStockExceptionMethod(LogEvent);
delegates[1] = new
    InventoryManager.OutOfStockExceptionMethod(
    EmailPurchasingMgr);

// Call the Delegate.Combine method to create
// a multicast delegate.
InventoryManager.OutOfStockExceptionMethod
    OnHandExceptionEventsCallback
    = (InventoryManager.OutOfStockExceptionMethod)
    InventoryManager.OutOfStockExceptionMethod.Combine(delegates);

// Call the ProcessInventory method, passing it
```

```
// the multicast delegate.
mgr.ProcessInventory(OnHandExceptionEventsCallback);
```

⋮

As you've seen, there are three distinct ways to create a multicast delegate—using the + operator, calling the *Combine* method that takes two delegate parameters, or calling the *Combine* method that takes an array of delegates. All the methods yield the same output, and none surpasses the others in terms of performance benefits. Therefore, choosing which one to use is really just a matter of personal preference and depends on your particular situation. Now that we know how to work with multicast delegates and how they function internally, let's look at why they exist.

Multicast Delegate Justification

In the feedback for the several C# delegate articles I've seen on the Internet, the author always seems to get the question, "If all multicast delegates do is call a succession of methods, why can't I simply create a delegate and call all the necessary methods myself?" We could do that in the previous example (CompositeDelegate), where we have only two methods, which are always called as a pair. But let's make the example more complicated. Let's say we have several store locations, with each location dictating which methods are called. For example, Location1 might be the warehouse. Therefore, if a part falls below the minimum on-hand quantity, we'd want to log the event and e-mail the purchasing manager. If a part falls below the minimum on-hand quantity in a store, however, we want to log the event, e-mail the purchasing manager, *and* the e-mail the manager of that store.

Because we can create delegate objects at runtime—with their creation process governed by run-time criteria—they're a better solution for handling more complex scenarios. Without delegates, we'd have to write a method that not only would have to determine which methods to call, but would have to keep track of which methods had already been called and which ones were yet to be called during the call sequence. As you can see in the following code, delegates make this potentially complex operation very simple because we can now place our code that determines the ultimate code path in the context that we choose (when the delegate object is being created):

```
using System;
using System.Threading;

class Part
{
```

```
        public Part(string sku)
        {
            this.Sku = sku;

            Random r = new Random(DateTime.Now.Millisecond);
            double d = r.NextDouble() * 100;

            this.OnHand = (int)d;
        }

        protected string sku;
        public string Sku
        {
            get { return this.sku; }
            set { this.sku = value; }
        }

        protected int onHand;
        public int OnHand
        {
            get { return this.onHand; }
            set { this.onHand = value; }
        }
    };

class InventoryManager
{
    protected const int MIN_ONHAND = 50;

    public Part[] parts;
    public InventoryManager()
    {
        Console.WriteLine("[InventoryManager" +
            ".InventoryManager] Adding parts...");

        parts = new Part[5];
        for (int i = 0; i < 5; i++)
        {
            Part part = new Part("Part " + (i + 1));

            Thread.Sleep(10); // Randomizer is seeded by time.

            parts[i] = part;
            Console.WriteLine("\tPart '{0}' on-hand = {1}",
                part.Sku, part.OnHand);
        }
    }
```

```
    public delegate void OutOfStockExceptionMethod(Part part);
    public void ProcessInventory(
        OutOfStockExceptionMethod exception)
    {
        Console.WriteLine("\n[InventoryManager" +
            ".ProcessInventory] Processing inventory...");
        foreach (Part part in parts)
        {
            if (part.OnHand < MIN_ONHAND)
            {
                Console.WriteLine("\n\t{0} ({1} units) is " +
                    "below minimum on-hand {2}",
                    part.Sku,
                    part.OnHand,
                    MIN_ONHAND);

                exception(part);
            }
        }
    }
};

class CompositeDelegateJustification
{
    public static void LogEvent(Part part)
    {
        Console.WriteLine("\t[CompositeDelegate.LogEvent] " +
            "logging event...");
    }

    public static void EmailPurchasingMgr(Part part)
    {
        Console.WriteLine("\t[CompositeDelegate" +
            ".EmailPurchasingMgr] emailing Purchasing " +
            "manager...");
    }

    public static void EmailStoreMgr(Part part)
    {
        Console.WriteLine("\t[CompositeDelegate.EmailStoreMgr]" +
            " emailing Store manager...");
    }

    public static void Main()
    {
        InventoryManager mgr = new InventoryManager();

        InventoryManager.OutOfStockExceptionMethod[]
```

```
        exceptionMethods = new
            InventoryManager.OutOfStockExceptionMethod[3];

    exceptionMethods[0] = new
        InventoryManager.OutOfStockExceptionMethod(LogEvent);

    exceptionMethods[1] = new
        InventoryManager.OutOfStockExceptionMethod(
        EmailPurchasingMgr);

    exceptionMethods[2] = new
        InventoryManager.OutOfStockExceptionMethod(
        EmailStoreMgr);

    int location = 1;

    InventoryManager.OutOfStockExceptionMethod
        compositeDelegate;

    if (location == 2)
    {
        compositeDelegate = exceptionMethods[0]
            + exceptionMethods[1];
    }
    else
    {
        compositeDelegate = exceptionMethods[0]
            + exceptionMethods[2];
    }

    mgr.ProcessInventory(compositeDelegate);

    Console.ReadLine();
    }
};
```

Now the compilation and execution of this application yields different results based on the value you assign to the *location* variable.

Defining Events with Multicast Delegates

Almost all applications for Windows have some sort of asynchronous event-processing needs. Some of these events are generic, such as Windows sending messages to the application message queue when the user has interacted with the application in some fashion. Some are more problem domain–specific, such as an invoice being printed once all its picking tickets have been updated. No matter what the specific scenario, most practical, real-world applications have some asynchronous event-handling needs. In the world of .NET, these scenarios are implemented in code via multicast delegates and supported in C# with the *event* keyword.

The multicast delegate model closely follows the *Observer*, or *Publish/ Subscribe*, design pattern in which a class publishes an event that it can raise, and any number of classes can then subscribe to that event. Once the event is raised, the runtime takes care of notifying each subscriber that the event has occurred. The method called as a result of an event being raised is defined by a delegate. However, when using a delegate in this fashion, keep in mind these strict rules:

1. The delegate must be defined as taking two arguments.

2. These arguments always represent two objects: the object that raised the event (the publisher), and an event information object.

3. This second object must be derived from the .NET Framework's *EventArgs* class.

To see a situation in which implementing events would lead to a better system design, let's continue with our previous InventoryManager example. However, now we want to add the ability to monitor changes to inventory levels. One design would be to create a class named *InventoryManager* that would always be used to update inventory. This *InventoryManager* class would publish an event that would be raised any time inventory is changed via actions such as receiving inventory, sales, and physical inventory updates. Then any class needing to be kept updated would subscribe to the event. Here's how you'd code this in C# by using delegates and events:

```
using System;

class InventoryChangeEventArgs : EventArgs
{
    public InventoryChangeEventArgs(string sku, int change)
    {
        this.sku = sku;
        this.change = change;
    }

    string sku;
    public string Sku
    {
        get { return sku; }
    }
```

```
        int change;
        public int Change
        {
            get { return change; }
        }
    };

    class InventoryManager // Publisher
    {
        public delegate void InventoryChangeEventHandler(
            object source, InventoryChangeEventArgs e);
        public event InventoryChangeEventHandler
            OnInventoryChangeHandler;

        public void UpdateInventory(string sku, int change)
        {
            if (0 == change)
                return; // No update on null change.

            // Code to update database would go here.

            InventoryChangeEventArgs e =
                new InventoryChangeEventArgs(sku, change);

            if (OnInventoryChangeHandler != null)
            {
                Console.WriteLine("[InventoryManager" +
                    ".UpdateInventory] Raising event to " +
                    "all subscribers...\n");
                OnInventoryChangeHandler(this, e);
            }
        }
    };

    class InventoryWatcher // Subscriber
    {
        public InventoryWatcher(InventoryManager inventoryManager)
        {
            Console.WriteLine("[InventoryWatcher" +
                ".InventoryWatcher] Subscribing to " +
                "InventoryChange event\n");
            this.inventoryManager = inventoryManager;
            inventoryManager.OnInventoryChangeHandler += new
                InventoryManager.InventoryChangeEventHandler(
                OnInventoryChange);
        }
```

```
    void OnInventoryChange(object source,
        InventoryChangeEventArgs e)
    {
        int change = e.Change;
        Console.WriteLine("[InventoryManager.OnInventoryChange]" +
            "\n\tPart '{0}' was {1} by {2} units\n",
            e.Sku,
            change > 0 ? "increased" : "decreased",
            Math.Abs(e.Change));
    }
    InventoryManager inventoryManager;
}

class DelegateEvents
{
    public static void Main()
    {
        InventoryManager inventoryManager =
            new InventoryManager();

        Console.WriteLine("[DelegateEvents.Main] " +
            "Instantiating subscriber object\n");
        InventoryWatcher inventoryWatch =
            new InventoryWatcher(inventoryManager);

        inventoryManager.UpdateInventory("111 006 116", -2);
        inventoryManager.UpdateInventory("111 005 383", 5);

        Console.ReadLine();
    }
};
```

Let's look at the first two members of the *InventoryManager* class:

```
public delegate void InventoryChangeEventHandler
    (object source, InventoryChangeEventArgs e);
public event InventoryChangeEventHandler
    OnInventoryChangeHandler;
```

The first line of code is a delegate, which you by now know is a definition for a method signature. As mentioned earlier, all delegates that are used in events must be defined as taking two arguments: a publisher object (in this case, *source*), and an event information object (an object derived from *EventArgs*). The second line uses the *event* keyword, a member type with which you specify the delegate and the method or methods that will be called when the event is raised.

The last method in the *InventoryManager* class is the *UpdateInventory* method, which is called anytime inventory is changed. As you can see, this method creates an object of type *InventoryChangeEventArgs*. This object is passed to all subscribers and is used to describe the event that took place.

Now look at the next lines of code:

```
if (OnInventoryChangeHandler != null)
{
    Console.WriteLine("[InventoryManager" +
        ".UpdateInventory] Raising event to " +
        "all subscribers...\n");
    OnInventoryChangeHandler(this, e);
}
```

The conditional *if* statement checks to see whether the event has any subscribers associated with the *OnInventoryChangeHandler* method. If it does—in other words, if *OnInventoryChangeHandler* isn't *null*—the event is raised. That's really all there is to the publisher side. Now let's look at the subscriber code.

The subscriber in this case is the class named *InventoryWatcher*. All this class needs to do is perform two simple tasks. First, it adds itself as a subscriber by instantiating a new delegate of type *InventoryManager.InventoryChangeEventHandler* and adding that delegate to the *InventoryManager.OnInventoryChangeHandler* event. Pay special attention to the syntax used—it's using the += compound assignment operator to add itself to the list of subscribers to avoid erasing any previous subscribers.

```
inventoryManager.OnInventoryChangeHandler += new
    InventoryManager.InventoryChangeEventHandler(
    OnInventoryChange);
```

The only argument that needs to be supplied here is the name of the method that will be called if and when the event is raised.

The only other task the subscriber needs to perform is to implement its event handler. In this case, the event handler is *InventoryWatcher.OnInventoryChange*, which prints a message stating the part number and the change in inventory.

Finally, the code that runs this application instantiates *InventoryManager* and *InventoryWatcher* classes, and—every time the *InventoryManager.UpdateInventory* method is called—an event is automatically raised that causes the *InventoryWatcher.OnInventoryChanged* method to be called. The results of this are shown in Figure 14-11.

Figure 14-11   Delegates lie at the heart of implementing the *Observer* (*Publish/Subscribe*) pattern in .NET applications.

Summary

In this chapter, you learned that delegates are quite a bit more than type-safe equivalents to C++ function pointers. They're actually more akin to the concept of functors, or function objects, because they imbue the polymorphic attributes that we expect of classes (as opposed to simply pointers). In this chapter, not only did you learn how to work with delegates from a high-level C# perspective, you also delved into the underlying MSIL and learned how delegates work under the covers.

We started with the simple callback method scenario in which a method is called in an attempt to acquire information. This method then calls back the supplied delegate object in an asynchronous manner with the desired information. From there, we moved on to multicast delegates, which enable us to combine multiple delegates into a single composite delegate for a more sophisticated code tree creation. Finally, we ended the chapter by talking about the *Publish/Subscribe* pattern and how it's implemented via multicast delegates and the C# *event* keyword.

15

Documentation with XML

Documenting code has always been a difficult task. These days, developers are usually conscientious about commenting code, and their organizations' coding standards usually enforce a degree of consistency in terms of level of detail, key coverage, and format. However, moving from code comments to full-blown documentation is another matter. Over the years, a wide range of tools have helped to provide documentation, but in almost all cases, there's been a profound disconnection between the source code and the documentation. In this chapter, we'll see how to generate XML documentation from C# source code comments. This feature allows you to tie your code comments to the final documentation almost effortlessly. Because this feature is based on XML, it means that—like so many areas of the .NET Framework—it's completely open-ended and customizable.

Getting Started

In C#, you can document the code you write using XML. C# is currently the only programming language that supports this feature. When you create a new project with Microsoft Visual Studio, the wizard-generated starter code includes special comment lines (with three slashes) that are used by the compiler to generate XML. For example, if you create a default C# console application, you'll get three-slash (or "documentation") comments like this:

```
namespace SimpleXML
{
    /// <summary>
    /// Summary description for Class1.
    /// </summary>
    class Class1
```

```
    {
        /// <summary>
        /// The main entry point for the application.
        /// </summary>
        [STAThread]
        static void Main(string[] args) {}

        /// <summary>
        /// This method does something interesting.
        /// </summary>
        public static void Foo() {}
    }
}
```

The *<summary></summary>* tags are clearly intended for XML element tags. Indeed, if you remove the three-slash characters, the remainder is valid XML. To transition from these comments embedding XML to true XML, you could of course parse the source code file by using some kind of regular expression tool. Alternatively, you can compile the source code with the */doc* option, specifying the target file for the XML. You can either add this command-line switch if you're compiling at the command line:

```
csc /doc:SomeXMLFileName.xml SomeSourceFileName.cs
```

or set the project configuration properties by right-clicking the project in the Solution Explorer pane and selecting Properties, as shown in Figure 15-1. Set the Documentation File property to a filename of your choosing.

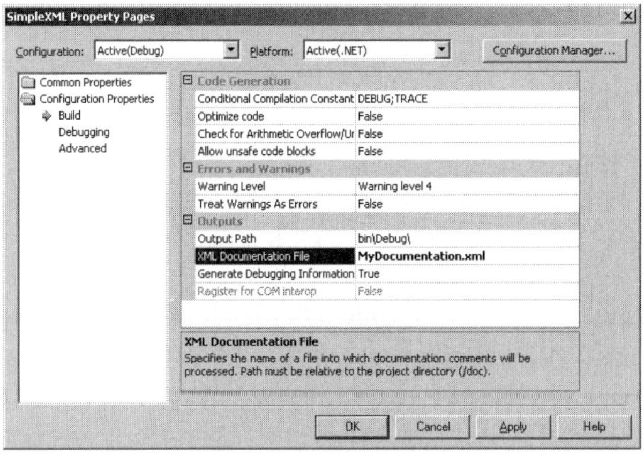

Figure 15-1   Setting the XML Documentation File property.

The C# compiler has been written to accommodate documentation comments; therefore, building the starter skeleton just shown will produce XML code like this:

```xml
<?xml version="1.0"?>
<doc>
    <assembly>
        <name>SimpleXML</name>
    </assembly>
    <members>
        <member name="T:SimpleXML.Class1">
            <summary>
            Summary description for Class1.
            </summary>
        </member>
        <member name="M:SimpleXML.Class1.Main(System.String[])">
            <summary>
            The main entry point for the application.
            </summary>
        </member>
    </members>
</doc>
```

Let's break this code down to see if we can make sense of the structure. First, the *<assembly>* element is pretty self-evident, although it doesn't correspond to any of the documentation comments in the source code. The compiler has obviously generated this code by using the name of the assembly. If you want to change the name of the assembly, you can do so in Visual Studio via the project properties, or you can do so at the command line with the *csc /out* switch. For example:

```
csc /out:Foo.exe /doc:SomeXMLFileName.xml SomeSourceFileName.cs
```

The */doc* compiler switch will be ignored in a compilation that uses */incremental*; therefore, you should use */incremental-* to ensure that the generated XML file is kept up to date. You can add this switch in Visual Studio by choosing Project | Properties, selecting Configuration Properties and then Advanced, and setting Increment Build to False. Note that if you compile with */target:module*, the target XML documentation file won't contain *<assembly>* tags—because, of course, you're not building an assembly. Also, if you have a multifile assembly, the *<assembly>* tags will specify the name of the file containing the assembly manifest for the output file of the compilation. Also, if your project contains multiple source code files, the source code file that contains *Main* is output first into the XML.

There follows a list of *<members>* in the assembly, and this list can include types as well as members of types. Thus, in our simple example, we have a type named *Class1*, indicated by the *T:SimpleXML.Class1* name attribute value, where "T" indicates a type, "SimpleXML" is the namespace, and "Class1" is the type name. By the same token, the *Main* method member name has an

"M:" prefix to indicate that it's a method. Although the compiler supplies the character prefix, all the remaining identifiers are within your control in the source code. So are the *<summary>* text entries. It should be clear from this simple example that the XML file isn't a hierarchical representation of your code because all the members of the assembly are presented as sibling elements. Rather, it's a flat list with a generated ID for each element.

Your XML *<summary>* comments can be used by Visual Studio IntelliSense, as long as the generated XML file has the same name as the assembly and resides in the same directory as the assembly.

Adding Elements

If you want to add new elements, you can simply type in three slashes and the Visual Studio C# editor will know that you want an XML comment tag. For example, if you add a new method that you want to document, as soon as you enter three slashes, Visual Studio will insert *<summary>* tags for you and leave space for you to enter your text description:

```
/// <summary>
///
/// </summary>
public static void Foo()
{
}
```

Once you've entered your description and built the project, the updated XML documentation will include the new element:

```
<member name="M:SimpleXML.Class1.Foo">
    <summary>
    This method does something interesting.
    </summary>
</member>
```

Acceptable Code Constructs

Clearly, the documentation comment is intended to be associated with a code construct, in order to form the basis of the documentation. There are restrictions on the code that you associate these comments with. A valid code construct is a class, struct, enum, method, property, field, indexer, delegate, or event. Indeed, if you don't associate the comment with any code construct, the compiler won't generate any XML for it. For example, suppose you arbitrarily type three slashes where there's no code construct that follows. You'll find that

Visual Studio won't supply *<summary>* element tags for you. If you go ahead and complete the tag yourself, like this:

```
/// <summary>
/// This will be ignored.
/// </summary>
```

but you don't add any corresponding code construct, when you build the project, this particular comment will simply be ignored. The same applies if you attempt to associate a comment block with an arbitrary block of code—the associated code must be a formal construct such as a class or method, not just a sequence of statements, not even delimited blocks such as loops and switches. Interestingly, a namespace isn't even considered an acceptable construct—if you think about this, it's actually consistent because a namespace isn't limited to any one assembly, so it can't be considered a member of an assembly.

Compiler-Generated Element IDs

For every comment in the source code correctly associated with a valid code construct, the compiler generates an ID string that includes predefined values. The ID string is intended to uniquely identify the code construct you've associated with the comment. The predefined values included in the string correspond to information that you could retrieve for the assembly via reflection. For example, as we saw from our simple wizard-generated console application project, "T" indicates a type, while "M" indicates a method. A full list of member type indicators is provided in Table 15-1.

Table 15-1
Compiler-Generated Type Indicators

Character	Description
N	Namespace
T	Type: class, interface, struct, enum, delegate
F	Field
P	Property (including indexers or other indexed properties)
M	Method (including special methods such as constructors and operators)
E	Event
!	Error: the compiler couldn't resolve this element, and the rest of the string provides information about the error

Fields, Properties, Events, and Indexers

The compiler doesn't distinguish among different access levels when it generates the XML. Therefore, a private field and a public field would be represented
the same way. Similarly, the modifiers *const*, *readonly*, and *static* have no effect
on the value of the resultant XML for fields. However, the compiler will modify
the order of the generated XML elements if you use *const*—and if you declare
nested types (including classes, structs, and delegate types). *Const* members
will be at the top of the list, while type members will be at the bottom. Note that
event properties are treated as events. To illustrate the type indicators, the following source code:

```
/// <summary>
/// A non-const field.
/// </summary>
public int a;

/// <summary>
/// A const field.
/// </summary>
public const long e = 0;

/// <summary>
/// A property.
/// </summary>
public string Name { get { return b; } }

/// <summary>
/// Nested delegate type.
/// </summary>
public delegate void MyEvent();

/// <summary>
/// Event field.
/// </summary>
public event MyEvent f;

/// <summary>
/// Event property field.
/// </summary>
public event MyEvent g
{
    add { f += value; }
    remove { f -= value; }
}
```

would produce the following XML:

```
<member name="F:SimpleXML.Class1.e">
    <summary>
    A const field.
    </summary>
</member>
<member name="F:SimpleXML.Class1.a">
    <summary>
    A non-const field.
    </summary>
</member>
<member name="P:SimpleXML.Class1.Name">
    <summary>
    A property.
    </summary>
</member>
<member name="E:SimpleXML.Class1.f">
    <summary>
    Event field.
    </summary>
</member>
<member name="E:SimpleXML.Class1.g">
    <summary>
    Property event field.
    </summary>
</member>
<member name="T:SimpleXML.Class1.MyEvent">
    <summary>
    Nested delegate type.
    </summary>
</member>
```

Note also that enum types are types, and enum fields are fields (as you'd expect):

```
/// <summary>
/// An enum type.
/// </summary>
public enum hType {hearts, clubs, spades, diamonds};

/// <summary>
/// An enum field.
/// </summary>
private hType h;
```

Here's the resultant XML:

```
<member name="F:SimpleXML.Class1.h">
    <summary>
    An enum field.
```

```
        </summary>
    </member>
    <member name="T:SimpleXML.Class1.hType">
        <summary>
        An enum type.
        </summary>
    </member>
```

Indexers are also considered properties:

```
/// <summary>
/// String indexer.
/// </summary>
public int this[string s] { get { return 0; } }
```

Here's the resultant XML:

```
<member name="P:SimpleXML.Class1.Item(System.String)">
    <summary>
    String indexer.
    </summary>
</member>
```

Methods

Following the type indicator, the compiler continues the generated value string with the fully qualified name of the item, starting at the root of the namespace. The name of the item, its enclosing type (or types), and the namespace are separated by periods. If the name of the item has periods, the compiler replaces them with the pound symbol (#). It's assumed that no item has a pound symbol directly in its name. For example, the fully qualified name of the *Class1* constructor would be *SimpleXML.Class1.#ctor*, while a static constructor's name would be *SimpleXML.Class1.#cctor*, and the name of a constructor that takes an *int* parameter would be *SimpleXML.Class1.#ctor(System.Int32)*. Continuing with the simple example, if you create these source code comments:

```
/// <summary>
/// My default constructor.
/// </summary>
public Class1() {}

/// <summary>
/// My static constructor.
/// </summary>
static Class1() {}

/// <summary>
/// My parameterized constructor.
```

```
/// </summary>
/// <param name="x">This param is for something.</param>
/// <param name="y">So is this one.</param>
public Class1(int x, float y) {}
```

the compiler would use them to generate the following XML:

```
<member name="M:SimpleXML.Class1.#ctor">
    <summary>
    My default constructor.
    </summary>
</member>
<member name="M:SimpleXML.Class1.#cctor">
    <summary>
    My static constructor.
    </summary>
</member>
<member name=
    "M:SimpleXML.Class1.#ctor(System.Int32,System.Single)">
    <summary>
    My parameterized constructor.
    </summary>
    <param name="x">This param is for something.</param>
    <param name="y">So is this one.</param>
</member>
```

When you associate a comment with a method (including properties and constructors) that takes parameters, Visual Studio automatically inserts a nested *<param>* element tag (which includes a *name=* attribute value) for each parameter. When the compiler generates the XML for such methods, the parameter list enclosed in parentheses follows. If there are no parameters, no parentheses are present. The parameters are separated by commas. Note that there's no differentiation between static and instance methods that aren't constructors. For example, the following source code comments:

```
/// <summary>
/// A static method with a parameter.
/// </summary>
/// <param name="z">Process this value.</param>
public static void Bar(int z) {}

/// <summary>
/// An instance method.
/// </summary>
/// <param name="q">Something.</param>
public void Goo(int q) {}
```

would generate the following XML:

```
<member name="M:SimpleXML.Class1.Bar(System.Int32)">
    <summary>
    A static method with a parameter.
    </summary>
    <param name="z">Process this value.</param>
</member>
<member name="M:SimpleXML.Class1.Goo(System.Int32)">
    <summary>
    An instance method.
    </summary>
    <param name="q">Something.</param>
</member>
```

The encoding of each parameter directly follows how it's encoded in a .NET Framework signature. This encoding is detailed in Table 15-2.

Table 15-2
Type Encoding Strings

Type	Description	Example
Base types	Regular types (*ELEMENT_TYPE_CLASS* or *ELEMENT_TYPE_VALUETYPE*) are represented as the fully qualified name of the type.	*SimpleXML.Class1*
Intrinsic types	*ELEMENT_TYPE_I4, ELEMENT_TYPE_OBJECT, ELEMENT_TYPE_STRING, ELEMENT_TYPE_TYPEDBYREF,* and *ELEMENT_TYPE_VOID* are represented as the fully qualified name of the corresponding full type.	*System.Int32* *System.Object*
Pointers	*ELEMENT_TYPE_PTR* is represented as a "*" following the modified type.	*System.Int32** *System.Single**
Ref Parameters	*ELEMENT_TYPE_BYREF* is represented as a "@" following the modified type.	*System.Int32@* *System.Single@*
Arrays	*ELEMENT_TYPE_ARRAY* is represented as [*lowerbound:size,lowerbound:size*], where the number of commas is the rank - 1, and the lower bounds and size of each dimension, if known, are represented in decimal. If a lower bound or size isn't specified, it's simply omitted. If the lower bound and size for a particular dimension are omitted, the ":" is omitted as well.	*System.String[]* *System.Int32[0:,0:]* *System.Int32[][]*

The foregoing indicators are illustrated in the following example. From this source code:

```
/// <summary>
/// Class-type parameter.
/// </summary>
/// <param name="c"></param>
public void Doo(Class1 c) {}

/// <summary>
/// A method with pointers.
/// </summary>
/// <param name="ip"></param>
/// <param name="fp"></param>
unsafe public void Hoo(int* ip, float* fp) {}

/// <summary>
/// A method with ref params.
/// </summary>
/// <param name="x"></param>
/// <param name="y"></param>
public void Joo(ref int x, ref float y) {}

/// <summary>
/// A method with a string array param.
/// </summary>
/// <param name="ss"></param>
public void Koo(string[] ss) {}

/// <summary>
/// Multidimensional array param.
/// </summary>
/// <param name="nums"></param>
public void Loo(int[,] nums) {}

/// <summary>
/// Jagged array param.
/// </summary>
/// <param name="nums"></param>
public void Moo(int[][] nums) {}
```

we would get this XML:

```
<member name="M:SimpleXML.Class1.Doo(SimpleXML.Class1)">
    <summary>
    Class-type parameter.
    </summary>
    <param name="c"></param>
</member>
<member name=
    "M:SimpleXML.Class1.Hoo(System.Int32*,System.Single*)">
    <summary>
```

```
    A method with pointers.
    </summary>
    <param name="ip"></param>
    <param name="fp"></param>
</member>
<member name=
    "M:SimpleXML.Class1.Joo(System.Int32@,System.Single@)">
    <summary>
    A method with ref params.
    </summary>
    <param name="x"></param>
    <param name="y"></param>
</member>
<member name="M:SimpleXML.Class1.Koo(System.String[])">
    <summary>
    A method with a string array param.
    </summary>
    <param name="ss"></param>
</member>
<member name="M:SimpleXML.Class1.Loo(System.Int32[0:,0:])">
    <summary>
    Multidimensional array param.
    </summary>
    <param name="nums"></param>
</member>
<member name="M:SimpleXML.Class1.Moo(System.Int32[][])">
    <summary>
    Jagged array param.
    </summary>
    <param name="nums"></param>
</member>
```

The calling convention and return type of a method aren't represented because they're never used for differentiating overloaded methods. However, the compiler does recognize a *<returns>* tag, and Visual Studio will generate a *<returns>* tag as part of its *<summary>* tag if you start to associate a comment with a method that has any nonvoid return. For example, this source code:

```
/// <summary>
/// A nonvoid method.
/// </summary>
/// <returns>The result of the operation.</returns>
public int Noo() { return 0; }
```

produces this XML:

```
<member name="M:SimpleXML.Class1.Noo">
    <summary>
    A nonvoid method.
```

```
    </summary>
    <returns>The result of the operation.</returns>
</member>
```

For conversion operators only (*op_Implicit* and *op_Explicit*), the return value of the method is encoded as a "~" followed by the return type indicated in Table 15-2. There's no distinction between implicit and explicit conversion operators. Visual Studio recognizes conversion operators as nonvoid parameterized methods and will supply both *<param>* and *<returns>* tags when you start typing a comment above such an operator. For example:

```
/// <summary>
/// Implicit conversion operator.
/// </summary>
/// <param name="c">source value</param>
/// <returns>target value</returns>
public static implicit operator int (Class1 c)
    { return 0; }
```

Here's the resultant XML:

```
<member name=
    "M:SimpleXML.Class1.op_Implicit(SimpleXML.Class1)~System.Int32">
    <summary>
    Implicit conversion operator.
    </summary>
    <param name="c">source value</param>
    <returns>target value</returns>
</member>
```

Well-Formed XML

To generate correct XML, the compiler must be given correct documentation comments. Specifically, the XML within the comments must be well-formed. If the XML isn't well-formed, the compiler generates a warning and the output documentation file will contain a comment saying that an error was encountered. By *well-formed XML*, we mean XML that follows the XML tag rules listed in the W3C Recommendation for XML 1.0. A well-formed XML document contains one or more elements: it has a single document element, with any other elements properly nested under it, and each of the parsed entities referenced directly or indirectly within the document is well-formed.

For example, given the following incorrectly formed comment:

```
/// <summary>
public void Foo() {}
```

the compiler would produce this error message in the resultant XML file:

```
<!-- Badly formed XML comment ignored for member
 "M:SimpleXML.Class1.Foo" -->
```

Although the following comment results in well-formed XML, it's clearly not of much use:

```
/// <summary/>
public void Bar() {}
```

Here's the resultant XML:

```
<member name="M:SimpleXML.Class1.Bar">
    <summary/>
</member>
```

But you could make it useful by simply appending some text:

```
/// <summary/>Some description.
public void Doo() {}
```

Here's the resultant XML:

```
<member name="M:SimpleXML.Class1.Doo">
    <summary/>Some description.
</member>
```

Clearly, an error in overlapping nesting also fails the well-formed test and will produce an error in the output XML:

```
/// <summary>
/// Some description.
/// <param name="x">Is this right?
/// </summary>
/// </param>
/// <param name="y"></param>
public void Goo(int x, float y) {}
```

However, you don't have to stick to the nesting scheme suggested by the Visual Studio wizard, as long as you end up with well-formed XML. For example, the following comments will produce correct XML, even though the ordering is different than what was originally suggested by Visual Studio:

```
/// <summary>
/// Some description
/// <param name="x">Do something with this.</param>
/// continued down here.
/// </summary>
public void Hoo(int x) {}
```

Here's the resultant XML:

```
<member name="M:SimpleXML.Class1.Hoo(System.Int32)">
    <summary>
    Some description
    <param name="x">Do something with this.</param>
    continued down here.
    </summary>
</member>
```

This becomes a coding standards issue. If the compiler is happy with any well-formed XML, to what degree should you adhere to the suggested structure generated by the Visual Studio wizard? The suggested structure is entirely reasonable and serves well as a guideline, but individual software vendors might have their own ideas about documentation structure. Also bear in mind that while the XML might be correct, the compiler is using the three-slash characters as part of its source code parsing operation to find the embedded XML. Thus, the following will also be rejected by the compiler:

```
/// <summary>
///
// </summary>
public void Joo() {}
```

Comment Web Pages

Once you've got the compiler to generate the XML file for you, you're free to do what you want with it. Typically, you'd format it into presentation-ready documentation. One way you can do this is to use another feature of Visual Studio: the Build Comment Web Pages command on the Tools menu, which will take your documentation-commented source code and build a Web page, complete with HTML and JPG objects. A start page is generated with hyperlinks for each project in the solution, and within each project, there will be links to the classes. For example, given the original wizard-generated starter code with comments for *Class1* and *Main*, if you select Tools and then Build Comment Web Pages, you'll be given the option to specify the target location for your Web pages and then Visual Studio will generate Web pages, as shown in Figure 15-2. Note that you don't have to build an XML output file from your documentation comments to use this feature of Visual Studio because the wizard takes your original source code documentation comments as its source.

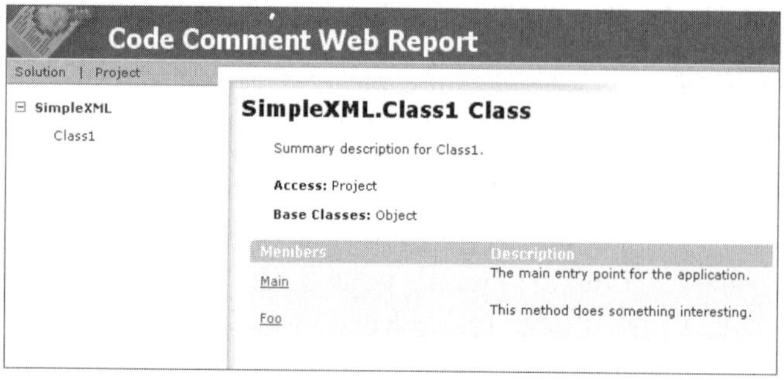

Figure 15-2   Visual Studio–generated comment Web pages.

It's the nature of XML to be entirely open-ended—your documentation comments can include any tags you like. Clearly, existing tools such as Visual Studio have been built to recognize and support a specific set of tags. Indeed, although the code-generating wizard in Visual Studio will happily generate one set of tags, the wizard that takes the output XML and formats it into code comment Web pages recognizes a slightly different set. For code comment Web pages, Visual Studio recognizes the following XML tags:

- *<newpara>*
- *<param>*
- *<remarks>*
- *<returns>*
- *<summary>*

Element Tags and Attributes

The compiler will process any tag that's valid XML. You are therefore free to create your own set of tags. However, as you've seen, there's a predefined set of tags that can be generated automatically by Visual Studio. Consider these a recommended set of core tags that you can adopt as part of your documentation scheme. Note that some of the recommended tags have special meanings—as Table 15-3 shows—either to the compiler or to Visual Studio when it uses the XML within the documentation comments to generate comment Web pages.

Table 15-3
Recommended Element Tags

Tag	Description
<c>	Indicates that text within a description should be marked as code.
<code>	Used to indicate that multiple lines should be marked as code.
<example>	Lets you specify an example of how to use some member. You'd probably use this in conjunction with the *<code>* tag.
<exception>	Lets you specify which exceptions a member can throw. Commonly used with the *cref* attribute.
<include>	Lets you refer to comments in another file that describe the types and members in your source code. This is an alternative to placing documentation comments directly in your source code file.
<list>	Used to define the heading row of either a table or definition list. Each item in the list is specified with an *<item>* block. A list or table can have as many *<item>* blocks as needed.
<newpara>	For use inside a tag, such as *<remarks>* or *<returns>*. Lets you add structure to the text.
<param>	Used to describe parameters. The compiler will verify that the parameter exists and that all parameters are described in the documentation. If the verification failed, the compiler issues a warning.
<paramref>	Generally the same as *<param>* (but there can be situations in which it's treated differently).
<permission>	Lets you document the code access security applied to a member.
<remarks>	Used to specify overview information about a class or other type, rather than specific details (for which you'd use *<summary>*).
<returns>	Used in the comment for a method declaration to describe the return value.
<see>	Lets you specify a link from within text.
<seealso>	Lets you specify the text that you might want to appear in a See Also section.
<summary>	Used to describe a member for a type. This element is also used by IntelliSense inside Visual Studio to display additional information about a type or member.
<value>	Lets you describe a property.

Several of these standard element tags also support predefined attributes, and two of these predefined attributes are used by more than one standard element tag. These are listed in Table 15-4.

Table 15-4
Standard Tag Attributes

Tag	Description
cref	Can be attached to any tag to provide a reference to a code element. The compiler will verify that this code element exists. If the verification failed, the compiler issues a warning. The compiler also respects any *using* statements when looking for a type described in the *cref* attribute.
name	The name of a parameter in a *<param>* or *<paramref>* element.

Further examples of using these standard tags and attributes are provided throughout the rest of this section.

The *<exception>* Tag and *cref* Attribute

This is intended to allow you to document either a derived *Exception* class or a method that can throw exceptions—similar to the exception specification construct in the C++ language. An example is given here:

```
/// <exception cref="System.Exception">
/// Throws a FileIOException when...
/// </exception>
public void Foo() {}
```

Note that the compiler won't generate any special XML for the exception tag and the Visual Studio comment Web pages won't offer any special treatment. You of course could nest the *<exception>* element within, say, a *<summary>* element:

```
/// <summary>
/// <exception cref="System.Exception">
/// Throws a FileIOException when...
/// </exception>
/// </summary>
public void Foo() {}
```

On the other hand, the compiler will check that the *cref* attribute points to a valid accessible entity. For example, if you misspell the value of the *cref* attribute, you'll get XML that includes an error message:

```
/// <exception cref="System.ExceptionQQQ">
/// Throws a FileIOException when...
```

```
/// </exception>
public void Goo() {}
```

Here's the resultant XML:

```
<member name="M:SimpleXML.Class1.Goo">
    <exception cref="!:System.ExceptionQQQ">
    Throws a FileIOException when...
    </exception>
</member>
```

The *<c>*, *<code>*, and *<example>* Tags

Both *<c>* and *<code>* are used to delimit some text that you want the formatter to interpret as code, thus formatting the text differently from the rest of the element text. The difference is that *<c>* is intended for inline text (similar to the / * */ comment delimiters), while *<code>* is intended for multiple lines of text. Again, no special XML is generated. Examples showing the use of these tags are given here. First, *<c>*:

```
/// <summary>
/// <c>Hoo</c> is a method in the <c>Class1</c> class.
/// </summary>
public void Hoo() {}
```

Here's the resultant XML:

```
<member name="M:SimpleXML.Class1.Hoo">
    <summary>
    <c>Hoo</c> is a method in the <c>Class1</c> class.
    </summary>
</member>
```

And now, *<code>*:

```
/// <summary>
/// The Joo method.
/// <example>This example shows how to use Joo:
/// <code>
/// <newpara/>
/// public static void Main()
/// {
///     Console.WriteLine(Class1.Joo());
/// }
/// <newpara/>
/// </code>
/// </example>
/// </summary>
public static int Joo() { return 0; }
```

Here's the resultant XML:

```
<member name="M:SimpleXML.Class1.Joo">
    <summary>
    The Joo method.
    <example>This example shows how to use Joo:
    <code>
    <newpara/>
    public static void Main()
    {
        Console.WriteLine(Class1.Joo());
    }
    <newpara/>
    </code>
    </example>
    </summary>
</member>
```

In this example, we've been careful to include extra *<newpara>* tags—meaning that when the *<code>*-delimited block is formatted, we're given some extra CRLFs. We could achieve the same result with traditional *
* tags. The Visual Studio comment Web pages feature pays no attention to *<c>* elements, but it does apply distinctive formatting to *<code>* elements, as Figure 15-3 shows.

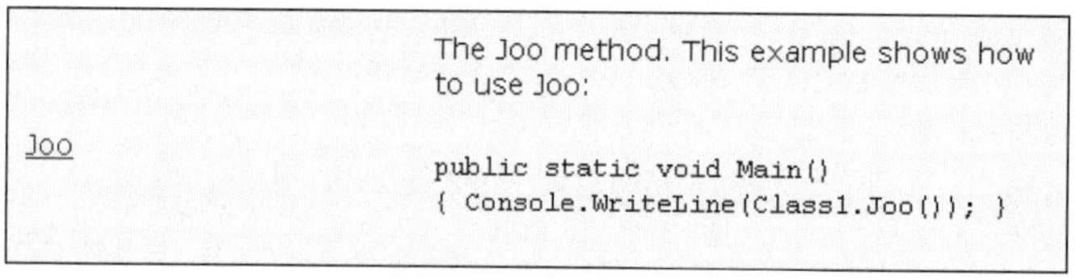

Figure 15-3   Comment Web pages for *<code>* elements.

The *<include>* Tag

The *<include>* tag lets you refer to comments in another file that describe the types and members in your source code, instead of putting documentation comments directly in your source code file. This strategy is conceptually similar to using *#include* files in C++ or stringtables in a separate resources file. The *<include>* element syntax is:

```
<include file='filename' path='tagpath[@name="id"]' />
```

where:

- ***filename***   The name of the file containing the documentation. The filename can be qualified with a path. Enclose *filename* in single quotation marks (' ').

- ***tagpath***   The path of the tags in *filename* that leads to the tag *name*. Enclose the path in single quotation marks (' ').

- ***name***   The name specifier in the tag that precedes the comments; *name* will have an *id*.

- ***id***   The identifier for the tag that precedes the comments. Enclose the identifier in double quotation marks (" ").

The *<include>* tag uses the XML *XPath* syntax. A basic *XPath* pattern describes a path through the XML hierarchy with a slash-separated list of child element names. The *XPath* pattern identifies all elements that match the path. In addition to describing a path down a known hierarchy, *XPath* can include wildcards for describing unknown elements. An element of any name is represented by "*".

For example, you could set up your project with one file containing the *<include>* tag, like this:

```
namespace SimpleXML
{
    /// <include file='supporting.xml'
    /// path='MyDocs/MyMembers[@name="Class1"]/*' />
    class Class1
    {
        public static void Main() {}
    }

    /// <include file='supporting.xml'
    /// path='MyDocs/MyMembers[@name="Class2"]/*' />
    class Class2
    {
        public void Foo() {}
    }
}
```

and a separate text file containing the referenced documentation comments. You could put these comments in any text file, but if you save it as an XML file, Visual Studio will perform color-highlighting in the editor:

```
<MyDocs>
    <MyMembers name="Class1">
        <summary>
        The summary for this type.
        </summary>
    </MyMembers>
    <MyMembers name="Class2">
        <summary>
        Another type description.
        </summary>
    </MyMembers>
</MyDocs>
```

When this project is built, the resultant XML will look like this:

```
<doc>
    <assembly>
        <name>SimpleXML</name>
    </assembly>
    <members>
        <member name="T:SimpleXML.Class1">
            <summary>
            The summary for this type.
            </summary>
        </member>
        <member name="T:SimpleXML.Class2">
            <summary>
            Another type description.
            </summary>
        </member>
    </members>
</doc>
```

You might think this hasn't achieved much—that we've created an XML file that's run through the C# compiler to produce another XML file that isn't very different. Of course, there are several differences: the compiler has checked for well-formed XML, performed any necessary validity checks (for example, *cref* values), and resolved the assembly members by using reflection-consistent identifiers. A more difficult issue to resolve is that we've separated the comments from the code. Putting the comments in a separate file makes them more susceptible to management—for instance, document parsing, indexing, and database storage. It also frees the code from noncode distractions. On the other hand, we could easily use the Visual Studio region collapse feature to hide documentation comments. Moreover, the ease with which you can generate presentable documentation via inline code comments should encourage you to comment as you go, which surely is a good thing.

The *<list>* Tag

This tag is used to define the heading row of either a table or definition list. Each item in the list is specified with an *<item>* block. When defining a table, you need only supply an entry for the term you're defining in the heading. When creating a definition list, you'll need to specify both the term you're defining and the description of the definition. However, for a table, bulleted list, or numbered list, you need only supply an entry for the description. A list or table can have as many *<item>* blocks as needed. The syntax of the *<list>* tag is as follows:

```
<list type="bullet" | "number" | "table">
    <listheader>
        <term>term</term>
        <description>description</description>
    </listheader>
    <item>
        <term>term</term>
        <description>description</description>
    </item>
</list>
```

where:

- **term**   A term to define, which will be defined in *description*.

- **description**   Either an item in a bulleted list or a numbered list, or the definition of a *term*.

An example follows:

```
/// <remarks>Here is an example of a bulleted list:
/// <list type="bullet">
/// <item>
/// <description>Item 1.</description>
/// </item>
/// <item>
/// <description>Item 2.</description>
/// </item>
/// </list>
/// </remarks>
static void Main(string[] args) {}
```

Neither the compiler nor Visual Studio will generate anything special for the list—you must apply your own custom formatting if that's what you want. That's a topic we'll move on to next.

Custom Formatting

If your primary aim in using documentation comments is to generate presentation-ready code documentation, the Visual Studio code comment Web pages facility is a good way to go. On the other hand, you might want the output XML for other reasons, and this output certainly contains all the significant information from your documentation comments without any user-interface features such as JPGs and table formatting. Therefore, the raw XML output is likely to be more useful to an organization for purposes other than creating pretty Web pages.

If you want to use the Visual Studio feature to generate Web pages but want to customize the appearance of these pages, you can simply use any standard HTML tags within your original documentation comments. For example, suppose we just want to insert some CRLFs into the final Web page text. To do so, we could use traditional *
* tags:

```
/// <summary>
/// This method does<br/>something<br/>interesting.
/// </summary>
public void Foo() {}
```

When you generate the code comment Web pages, the text will be formatted accordingly, as Figure 15-4 shows.

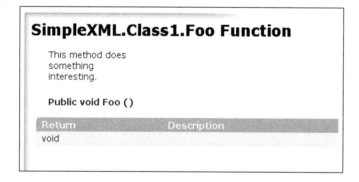

Figure 15-4   Customizing the Web page format.

You could extend this to suit your own requirements, by using *<font>*, *<p style>*, *<b>*, and other standard tags. For example, the following comments control the font face, font size, and font color of the *<summary>* and assign arbitrary character formatting to each *<param>*:

```
/// <summary>
/// <font face="courier" size="6" color="#FF0000">
```

```
/// A method with 3 params.
/// </font>
/// </summary>
/// <param name="a"><h3>This is a.</h3></param>
/// <param name="b"><h4><i>and b.</i></h4></param>
/// <param name="c"><h5><u>finally c.</u></h5></param>
public void Bar(int a, int b, int c) {}
```

The resultant Web page is shown in Figure 15-5.

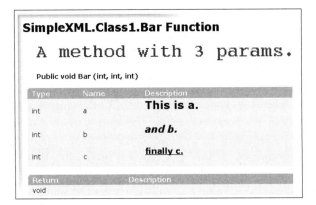

Figure 15-5   Customizing Web page colors and fonts.

One advantage of this approach to custom formatting is that you apply the formatting within your source code documentation comments. An alternative approach is to manually edit the XML output file after it's been generated. This approach clearly suffers from the problem that a later build will overwrite the file—although this problem isn't insurmountable. If you do choose this approach, you can apply XSL transformations to your XML.

You can use the generated XML with a browser that supports XSL to format the text according to the tags. There's currently no built-in support in Visual Studio for this process, but you can easily create your own XSL. For example:

```
<xsl:stylesheet xmlns:xsl="http://www.w3.org/TR/WD-xsl">
<xsl:template match="/">
  <html><body>
    <h1>Using XSL to Format XML</h1>
    <hr/>
    <h3>
      Assembly name: <xsl:value-of select="doc/assembly/name"/>
    </h3>
    <table border="1">
      <thead><h3>Members</h3></thead>
      <tbody>
        <tr>
```

```
        <td><b>Member</b></td>
        <td><b>Summary</b></td>
      </tr>
      <xsl:for-each select="doc/members/member">
        <tr>
          <td><xsl:value-of select="@name"/></td>
          <td><xsl:value-of select="summary/text()"/></td>
        </tr>
      </xsl:for-each>
    </tbody>
  </table>
 </body></html>
</xsl:template>
</xsl:stylesheet>
```

Having saved this XSL file and having built the project to generate an up-to-date XML file, you'd then manually add the following line to the top of the generated XML, where TestDoc.xsl is the name of the saved XSL file: <?xml-stylesheet type="text/xsl" href="TestDoc.xsl"?>.

Then when you open the XML file (for example, in Microsoft Internet Explorer—which you can do by right-clicking Test.xml in the Solution Explorer pane and selecting View In Browser), it will be formatted with the XSL, as Figure 15-6 shows.

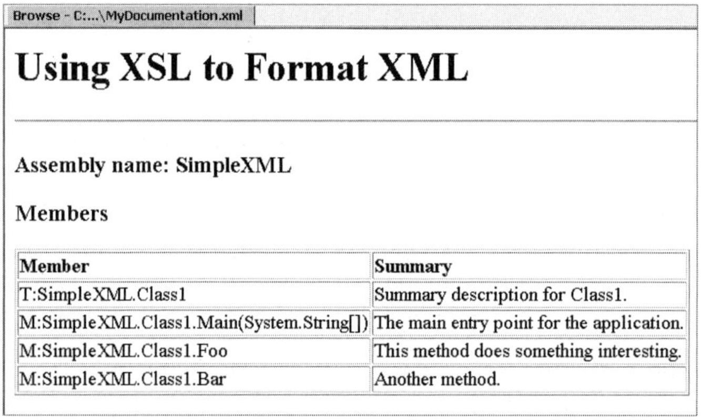

Figure 15-6   Custom XSL–formatted XML documentation.

Of course, this XSL is simple, but you're free to make it as sophisticated as you want—after all, this open-endedness is the point of using XML and XSL.

Thus, Visual Studio supports two complementary mechanisms for generating code documentation: raw XML output, and automatic HTML pages. Between the two features, Visual Studio covers the bases quite nicely. Most organizations will probably use some judicious mixture of both approaches, using the automatic HTML for presenting documentation and the raw XML for source code control and auditing.

XML and Data

A significant factor in the design of the entire .NET Framework is the relationship between XML and data. Many of the data-oriented classes in the .NET Framework support manipulation of the encapsulated data in XML format. For example, the *DataSet* class offers a *GetXml* method to extract the data represented by the *DataSet* into an XML string. When you open your XML documentation file (or any other XML file) in Visual Studio, the editor will present it as color-highlighted XML, but you'll notice a button at the bottom of the window to allow you to switch to a data view instead, as Figure 15-7 shows.

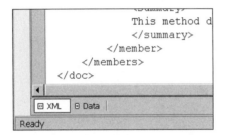

Figure 15-7   Visual Studio XML/Data editor toggle.

If you click the Data button, Visual Studio will present a tabular view of the XML data. You can then select the tables of interest—for example, *members* or *param*—and expand the grid to focus on the data of interest, as shown in Figure 15-8.

MyDocumentation.xml		
Data Tables:	**Data:**	
assembly	**Data for members**	
members	**members:**	
member	summary	name
		T:ReadXMLdoc.Class1
		M:ReadXMLdoc.Class1.Main(System.String[])
		M:ReadXMLdoc.Class1.Foo
		M:ReadXMLdoc.Class1.Bar

Figure 15-8   Visual Studio XML Data view.

It would be a simple matter to complete the circle and write C# code to open the XML file for processing. The following application takes in an XML filename as its command-line argument, opens the file, and reads the data into a *DataSet*. The application then extracts the *members* table from the *DataSet* and prints the values to the console:

```
static void Main(string[] args)
{
    if (args.Length != 1)
        return;

    // Open the XML file and read into a DataSet.
    FileStream fs =
        new FileStream (args[0], FileMode.Open);
    DataSet ds = new DataSet();
    ds.ReadXml(fs);

    // Use a DataTable to display the members.
    DataTable mt = ds.Tables["member"];
    for (int row = 0; row < mt.Rows.Count; row++)
    {
        for (int col = 0; col < mt.Columns.Count-1; col++)
        {
            Console.WriteLine("{0,-10}{1}",
                mt.Columns[col].Caption,
                mt.Rows[row][col].ToString().Trim());
        }
        Console.WriteLine();
    }
    fs.Close();
}
```

The output from this application, tested with an arbitrary XML documentation file, is shown here:

```
summary    An arbitrary class to encapsulate Main.
name       T:ReadXMLdoc.Class1

summary    Entry point to the assembly.
name       M:ReadXMLdoc.Class1.Main(System.String[])

summary    This method does something.
name       M:ReadXMLdoc.Class1.Foo

summary    This method doesn't do anything.
name       M:ReadXMLdoc.Class1.Bar
```

Summary

In this chapter, we saw another of the .NET Framework architectural primitives break the surface of our day-to-day programming. XML is a data structure technique that underlies much of what goes on in the .NET Framework classes and therefore in your own code. We saw how easy it is to generate XML documentation from source code comments, how we can use Visual Studio to generate HTML Web pages from these same XML comments, and how open-ended and customizable the system is. You can invent your own arbitrary XML tags, and you can format the XML in your preferred manner, either by using XSL style sheets or by directly manipulating the XML in code. By extension, it's an easy matter to store the XML documentation in a database and later retrieve it for further processing—again, via the underlying XML.

Part III
Advanced C#

16

Numerical Processing and the *Math* Class

There can be no more basic a task for computers than number crunching. After all, these magnificent machines owe their very existence to the most critical of all operations—numerical computation. Lest we forget, it was mathematicians who built the first mechanical computers almost 300 years ago principally for one reason—to perform arithmetic faster and with a higher degree of accuracy than possible by a mere mortal. Although it's easy to get lost in the excitement of language features such as properties, indexers, delegates, and interfaces, it's important to keep in mind that the true measuring stick of any language is its support for numbers and the operations that can be performed with them.

In this chapter, we'll cover the numeric types that are supported by the C# language. You'll see how these types differ from one another, how they're initialized, what the compiler generates when a numeric literal is used, and how numeric literals can be treated as any other object. After that, we'll look at the issues of integral overflow and see how to define whether to check for overflow and at what level (application level or statement level). Finally, we'll talk a bit about the new 128-bit *Decimal* class and the *System.Math* class.

Numeric Support in C# and .NET

The natural place to begin any chapter on math is in enumerating the numeric types supported by the language. In the case of C#, the numeric types are included in the set of predefined types and are divided into three distinct categories: *integral*, *floating-point*, and *decimal*. Table 16-1 lists these types by category and gives examples of how to assign literal values to each.

Table 16-1
Integral Types

Type	Category	Description
sbyte	integral	8-bit signed integer (Example assignment: sbyte val = 42;)
short	integral	16-bit signed integer (Example assignment: short val = 42;)
int	integral	32-bit signed integer (Example assignment: int val = 42;)
long	integral	64-bit signed integer (Example assignments: long val = 42; long val2 = 42L;)
byte	integral	8-bit unsigned integer (Example assignment: byte val = 42;)
ushort	integral	16-bit unsigned integer (Example assignment: ushort val = 42;)
uint	integral	32-bit unsigned integer (Example assignments: uint val = 42; uint val2 = 42U;);

ulong	integral	64-bit unsigned integer
		(Example assignments: ulong val = 42;
		ulong val2 = 42U;
		ulong val3 = 42L;
		ulong val4 = 42UL;)

float	floating-point	32-bit single-precision floating-point type (Example assignments: float val = 42; float val2 = 42.0F;)
double	floating-point	64-bit double-precision floating-point type (Example assignments: double val = 42.0; double val2 = 42.0D;)
Decimal	decimal	128-bit decimal type with 28 significant digits (Example assignments: decimal val = 42; decimal val2 = 42.0M;)

Is the *Decimal* Type a Primitive?

There's sometimes contradictory documentation about which types are defined as primitives (or built-in types) in C# and which are implemented by the .NET Framework classes. For example, some developers would say that the integral and floating-point types are both primitives, as is the *Decimal* type. However, other developers are quick to point out that the runtime documentation omits the *Decimal* type in its list of supported primitives. This contradiction really comes down to how you define the word *primitive*.

Some would say that any type for which a literal can be used in an assignment is a primitive, or built-in type. The *Decimal* type does fall into this category. However, let's look at the Microsoft intermediate language (MSIL) generated from some simple literal assignments with the various types. Here I've assigned literals to variables representing each of the 10 integral and floating-point types:

```
sbyte val = 1;
short val1 = 2;
int val2 = 3;
long val3 = 4;
byte val4 = 6;
ushort val5 = 7;
uint val6 = 9U;
ulong val7 = 12L;
float val8 = 1.14F;
double val9 = 1.16D;
```

Upon compiling this code, the C# compiler generates the following MSIL instructions to perform the stated assignment operations:

```
.method public hidebysig static void  Main() cil managed
{
  .entrypoint
  // Code size       43 (0x2b)
  .maxstack  1
  .locals init (int8 V_0,
           int16 V_1,
           int32 V_2,
           int64 V_3,
           unsigned int8 V_4,
           unsigned int16 V_5,
           unsigned int32 V_6,
           unsigned int64 V_7,
           float32 V_8,
           float64 V_9)  IL_0000:  ldc.i4.1
  IL_0001:  stloc.0
  IL_0002:  ldc.i4.2
```

```
IL_0003:   stloc.1
IL_0004:   ldc.i4.3
IL_0005:   stloc.2
IL_0006:   ldc.i4.4
IL_0007:   conv.i8
IL_0008:   stloc.3
IL_0009:   ldc.i4.6
IL_000a:   stloc.s    V_4
IL_000c:   ldc.i4.7
IL_000d:   stloc.s    V_5
IL_000f:   ldc.i4.s   9
IL_0011:   stloc.s    V_6
IL_0013:   ldc.i4.s   12
IL_0015:   conv.i8
IL_0016:   stloc.s    V_7
IL_0018:   ldc.r4     (85 EB 91 3F)
IL_001d:   stloc.s    V_8
IL_001f:   ldc.r8     1.1599999999999999
IL_0028:   stloc.s    V_9
IL_002a:   ret
} // end of method AssignmentTest::Main
```

In contrast to what you've just seen, let's now look at a variable of type
decimal that's being assigned a value:

```
decimal vala = 1.42M;
```

In this case, the C# compiler does not generate MSIL instructions to carry out
the assignments. Rather, the emitted code refers to a method of the .NET class
that actually implements the decimal type:

```
ldc.i4.s    142
ldc.i4.0
ldc.i4.0
ldc.i4.0
ldc.i4.2
newobj      instance void [mscorlib]System.Decimal::.ctor(int32,
                                                           int32,
                                                           int32,
                                                           bool,
                                              unsigned int8)
```

In conclusion, as you've seen from the MSIL (the ultimate arbiter), technically speaking, the *Decimal* type isn't a primitive type. However, this question
is largely an issue of semantics because the precise implementation of the
numeric types has no impact on your day-to-day programming reality. For this
reason, I—like most C# programmers—tend to refer to all the numeric types as
built-in.

Numeric Suffixes

As you no doubt noticed, there are times when the assignment of a literal to a variable of a numeric type requires a suffix. Table 16-2 lists these suffixes and the rules for when they must be specified.

Table 16-2
Suffixes for Numeric Literals

Type	Suffix	Description
long	l	Optional; case-insensitive
uint	u	Optional; case-insensitive
ulong	ul or lu	Optional; case-insensitive; case can be mixed—uL, Ul, and so on
float	f	Must be used if literal contains a decimal point; case-insensitive
double	d	Optional; case-insensitive
Decimal	m	Must be used if literal contains a decimal point; case-insensitive

A Numeric Type by Any Other Name...

Most new .NET developers are confused by the different layers of type definitions. When you define a variable in C#, you can specify either a .NET type or an *alias* that ultimately resolves to a .NET type. For example, the C# *int* type is an alias for the .NET *System.Int32* type. However, if you look at the compiler-generated MSIL, you'll see that the *int* resolves to something named *int32*. Hopefully, this will clear things up a bit:

■   As you learned back in Chapter 2, "The .NET Type System," the common type system (CTS) defines the types available to the .NET programmer as well as rules regarding how these types are declared, used, and managed in the runtime.

■   The Common Language Specification (CLS) then specifies a subset of these types that can be used for language interoperability. As a result, if you're writing code in C# to be consumed by other languages, you'll want to ensure that you use only types defined in the CLS.

■ The Common Language Infrastructure allows applications written in multiple high-level languages to be executed in different system environments without the rewriting of the application to take into consideration the unique characteristics of those environments. Part of this specification is the definition of a set of simpler types (compared to the CLS), collectively known as the *basic common language infrastructure types*.

■ Part of the Common Language Infrastructure specification is the definition of an instruction set, called the *common infrastructure language* (CIL), where the basic common language infrastructure types are represented by names unique to the CIL.

In Table 16-3, for each numeric type that can be used in C#, I've listed the C# alias, its CIL name—that is, the name you'll see when spelunking into the compiler's generated MSIL—and the name by which the type is known to .NET and the CTS. Also note that of these types, all are defined in the CLS except for the following: *System.SByte, System.UInt16, System.UInt32,* and *System.UInt64.*

Table 16-3
Numeric Type Names

C# Alias	CIL Name	.NET Class Library Name
sbyte	*int8*	*System.SByte*
short	*int16*	*System.Int16*
int	*int32*	*System.Int32*
long	*int64*	*System.Int64*
byte	*unsigned int8*	*System.Byte*
ushort	*unsigned int16*	*System.UInt16*
uint	*unsigned int32*	*System.UInt32*
ulong	*unsigned int64*	*System.UInt64*
float	*float32*	*System.Single*
double	*float64*	*System.Double*

Although you can use either the C# alias or the .NET class name when defining variables, you can use the CIL name only if you're directly writing in MSIL. Also, the significance of whether a type is defined by the CLS is that if you want your code to be accessible from all other .NET languages, you need to use only those types. This restriction means refraining from using the types *SByte*

(*sbyte*), *UInt16* (*ushort*), *UInt32* (*uint*), and *UInt64* (*ulong*). One last point before we move forward: notice the omission of the *Decimal* type in Table 16-2. This omission is intentional on my part because technically the *Decimal* type isn't defined in the CIL. However, I did state earlier that the *Decimal* type is a built-in type of the C# language. I explained this apparent contradiction earlier in "Is the *Decimal* Type a Primitive?"

More on Numeric Literals

The last issue I'll cover regarding numeric literals is how they're treated when compiled. If a literal doesn't contain a decimal or a suffix, the compiler will always try to generate assembler code for a 32-bit integer. Therefore, the following code:

```
Console.WriteLine(0);
Console.WriteLine(5);
Console.WriteLine(42);
```

will result in the following MSIL:

```
ldc.i4.0
call        void [mscorlib]System.Console::WriteLine(int32)
ldc.i4.5
call        void [mscorlib]System.Console::WriteLine(int32)
ldc.i4.s    42
call        void [mscorlib]System.Console::WriteLine(int32)
```

Notice that although the exact form of the *ldc* opcode varies, the *i4* portion specifically tells the runtime to load a 32-bit integer on the stack (*i4* = 4 bytes = 32 bits). Regarding that last portion of the *ldc* opcode, *ldc.i4.0* is the opcode for loading a zero, *ldc.i4.5* loads the value 5, and *ldc.i4.s* loads the specified value. The only time the compiler will generate code to use anything other than a 32-bit integer when dealing with literals without decimals is when the value is too large to be represented by 32 bits.

For example, the following code:

```
Console.WriteLine(5000000000);
```

would generate the MSIL

```
ldc.i8      0x12a05f200
call        void [mscorlib]System.Console::WriteLine(int64)
```

where the *ldc.i8* opcode refers to loading a constant value of type *int64* onto the stack.

If a literal contains a decimal (or uses exponential notation), a *double* is used. The only limitation here is that you'll receive a compile-time error if the literal you specify exceeds the high or low ranges of a double. Therefore:

```
Console.WriteLine(50.0);
```

results in:

```
ldc.r8    50.
call      void [mscorlib]System.Console::WriteLine(float64)
```

As you might guess, the *ldc.r8* opcode signifies that a float of 8 bytes (64 bits) will be pushed onto the stack. Also, recall from Table 16-3 that a *double* defined in C# is the equivalent of a *float64* in CIL—hence the use of that particular overloaded version of *Console.WriteLine.*

Finally, realize that rules come into play regardless of how the literal is being used. For example, if you're calling a method that takes a parameter of type *long* and you pass a literal that doesn't contain a decimal or a suffix, the compiler will still generate the *ldc.4* code for the *int32* type. However, the compiler will also generate the code to convert the value on the stack to the needed type.

In the following code, I have a *Test* method that takes a *long*. I then call that method from *Main*, passing a literal:

```
static void Test(long l)
{
    Console.WriteLine(l.GetType());
}

static void Main(string[] args)
{
    Test(42);
}
```

This code generates the following MSIL, in which the *ldc.4* proves that a 32-bit integer was pushed onto the stack (our literal *42*). However, the *conv.i8* opcode is then used to convert the value on the stack to an 8-byte (64 bit) value.

```
ldc.i4.s    42
conv.i8
call        void LiteralTest::Test(int64)
```

Because of this conversion, the code will correctly output the following:

```
l is of type System.Int64
```

Notice that the CIL assembler generated an *int64* for the C# *long* and that the runtime reported the type as *System.Int64.* You can test all the numeric types in the system for the various column values listed in Table 16-3.

I'll make one last point before we move into the specifics of some of these numeric types. You've all heard the mantra, "In C#, everything is an object."

Believe it or not, this treatment includes literals. The following code actually compiles:

```
Console.WriteLine("42 is of type {0} and has a value of {1}",
                  42.GetType(),
                  42.ToString());
```

If you compile and run this code snippet, you should see the following results:

```
42 is of type System.Int32 and has a value of 42
```

However, the really interesting bit is the MSIL generated for this rather odd-looking bit of code:

```
.method private hidebysig static void  Main(string[] args)
 cil managed
{
  .entrypoint
  // Code size       39 (0x27)
  .maxstack  3
  .locals init ([0] int32 CS$00000002$00000000)
  IL_0000:  ldstr      "42 is of type {0} and has a value of {1}"
  IL_0005:  ldc.i4.s   42
  IL_0007:  box        [mscorlib]System.Int32
  IL_000c:  call       instance class [mscorlib]System.Type
[mscorlib]System.Object::GetType()
  IL_0011:  ldc.i4.s   42
  IL_0013:  stloc.0
  IL_0014:  ldloca.s   CS$00000002$00000000
  IL_0016:  call       instance string
[mscorlib]System.Int32::ToString()
  IL_001b:  call
void [mscorlib]System.Console::WriteLine(string,
                                          object,
                                          object)
  IL_0020:  call       string [mscorlib]System.Console::ReadLine()
  IL_0025:  pop
  IL_0026:  ret
} // end of method IntTest::Main
```

Let's look first at the MSIL generated from calling *GetType* as a member of a numeric literal. Take a look at instruction IL_0005. Here the constant 42 is loaded onto the stack (via *ldc.i4.s*). Next the *box* opcode is executed to convert the value on the stack to a *System.Int32* object. Now the *Int32.GetType* instance method can be called because an instance of an *Int32* is on the stack. Note that the *System.Type* object (returned from the *GetType* method) is left on the stack for the *Console.WriteLine* that will be called shortly thereafter.

Now look at the local variable defined in the *.locals* section as *CS$00000002$00000000*. This compiler-generated variable will be used to contain an object reference to the literal 42. The rules governing how literals are translated into types (and the fact that the value 42 contains no decimal places and is within the range of a 32-bit integer) explain why the literal is defined as an Int32. Now direct your attention to instructions IL_0011 through IL_0014. Once again, the *ldc.i4.s* instruction is used to load the literal 42 onto the stack. The second instruction (*stloc.0*) then stores that value into the *CS$00000002$00000000* variable. Finally, the third instruction (*ldloca.s*) loads the address of the variable onto the stack. We now have a *this* pointer for an instantiated *Int32*. With that, we can call the *ToString* instance method, which will remove the object pointer from the stack and replace it with the string representation of its value. (This is the default behavior of *Int32.ToString*.)

At this point, we have a type object on the stack as well as the address of string representation of the literal 42. Now the overloaded version of the *Console*.WriteLine that takes a string and two objects (the two that are currently on the stack) can be called. You can see this call at instruction IL_001B. Note that the return value from the *ToString* method did not need to be boxed because a *string* object implicitly converts to object.

The compiler did all this, and all you wrote was a *WriteLine* statement! By the way, it's because of all this work required by the compiler to make this code function that Microsoft Visual Studio's IntelliSense won't show the available member when you type a dot after a numeric literal.

The last thing I'll mention is the rather odd variable name (*CS$00000002$00000000*) that served as a temporary variable for our literal. Actually, the only reason you're seeing that name in the ILDASM tool is because this name is located in the debug information for this code snippet. It's therefore worth mentioning here that local variables are never actually named in MSIL. Instead, variables and parameters are referred to by their indices. What's happening here is that the ILDASM tool is combining the debug information with the generated assembly to make for a more complete assembler listing. If you were to compile this code with the */debug-* switch (or by setting the project's Generate Debugging Information value to *False* in Visual Studio), you'd notice that the variable name becomes *V_x* where *x* represents the index of the declared variable. Once again, ILDASM makes it easier to read the IL.

Integral Ranges and Overflow Rules

In Table 16-1, I listed eight integral types. Actually, C# supports nine integral types, including the *char* type, which I won't discuss much here because it has little to do with numerical processing. The main difference between the various integral types is the amount of memory they take up and the range of values that they can hold:

- The *sbyte* type represents a signed 8-bit integer with a range of values from −128 through 127.

- The *byte* type represents an unsigned 8-bit integer with a range of values from 0 through 255.

- The *short* type represents a signed 16-bit integer with a range of values from −32,768 through 32,767.

- The *ushort* type represents an unsigned 16-bit integer with a range of values from 0 through 65,535.

- The *int* type represents a signed 32-bit integer with a range of values from −2,147,483,648 through 2,147,483,647.

- The *uint* type represents an unsigned 32-bit integer with a range of values from 0 through 4,294,967,295.

- The *long* type represents a signed 64-bit integer with a range of values that stretches from −9,223,372,036,854,775,808 through 9,223,372,036,854,775,807.

- The *ulong* type represents an unsigned 64-bit integer with a range of values from 0 through 184,467,440,737,095,551,615.

- The *char* type represents an unsigned 16-bit integer with a range of values from 0 through 65,535. This range is so broad because it encompasses all values corresponding to the Unicode character set.

Now that you know the ranges, you're probably wondering what happens when a value exceeds a range at run time. Let's look at the following example:

```
using System;

class IntegerOverFlow
{
    static void Main(string[] args)
    {
        short s = 32767;
        s++;
        Console.WriteLine(s);

        ushort us = 0;
        us--;
        Console.WriteLine(us);
    }
}
```

It's obvious that because a *short* has a maximum value of 32,767, incrementing *s* by 1 will cause it to overflow. Likewise, decrementing a value of type *unsigned short* such that the result is a negative number results in an underflow. The first thing you might wonder is why the compiler doesn't catch this problem. Well, actually it would if you wrote the following:

```
short s = 32767 + 1;
ushort us = 0 - 1;
```

> **Note**   Because overflow and underflow are handled in a consistent manner in C#, I'll just use the term *overflow* to represent both.

This code would fail to compile because you're using literals to initialize the types. Therefore, the compiler can easily determine that, in each case, the specified literal isn't compatible with the variable type to which it's being assigned. However, the compiler doesn't catch overflow when a variable is initialized on one line and then modified it on another such as to cause its overflow.

Is this a problem? It depends on the type of application you're writing. I worked on a team that had a system to compress and index incredibly large data files (bank documents and statements). The true programming gurus on the team wrote incredibly complex algorithms that would have made Thomas Cormen, author of *Introduction to Algorithms*, proud. Some of these algorithms included scenarios in which values were intentionally overflowed, so these programmers didn't want any type of overflow detection. However, mere mortals like myself usually want to know whether a variable is assigned a number outside its valid range. Therefore, I want range checking...most of the time.

These contradictory needs are the reason the C# compiler enables you to specify whether you want overflows to be checked at run time by means of the */checked+* switch. Therefore, if we were to compile (specifying overflow checking) and run the IntegerOverflow example from the command line, it would raise a *System.OverflowException* exception, as shown in Figure 16-1.

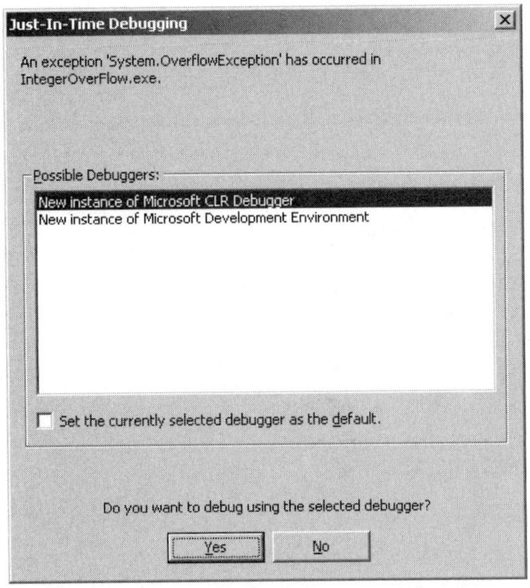

Figure 16-1   If a C# application is built with the */checked+* switch, any overflows will result in a run-time exception (*System.OverflowException*) being raised.

Obviously, the reverse of this procedure is to compile with the */checked-* switch, which means that all overflows will be ignored by the runtime. Compiling and running the IntegerOverflow application with this switch would result in the application executing without error. (By default, overflow checking is turned off.)

Note   To set the C# compiler's */checked* switch within Visual Studio, open the project's Properties dialog box and click Configuration Properties. Under the Code Generation heading, you'll see an entry entitled Check For Arithmetic Overflow/Underflow. Set this value to true or false, depending on your needs.

This switch works great if you want all your code either checked or unchecked. However, remember that I said that I wanted overflow checking *most of the time*. To address this need, C# includes two keywords—*checked* and *unchecked*—that allow you to override the application level overflow setting.

In the following code snippet, an exception will be thrown in the first block of code but not in the second block:

```
unchecked
{
    short s = 32767;
    s++;
    Console.WriteLine(s);
}

checked
{
    ushort us = 0;
    us--;
    Console.WriteLine(us);
}
```

Obviously, the *checked* and *unchecked* keywords turn overflow checking on and off within a block of code. Note also that the *checked* and *unchecked* keywords can be nested.

Note If you look at the MSIL generated for checked code, you'll see that the various CIL arithmetic opcodes have overflow checking versions that end in a *.ovf* suffix. For example, multiplication is done via either the unchecked *mul* opcode or the checked *mul.ovf* opcode.

Finally, let's look at the rules of overflows with constants. In the following code example, I'm attempting to use two constants (*MAXUSHORT* and *ONE*) to trick the compiler into letting my code compile. However, this code won't compile regardless of my compiler *checked* setting:

```
using System;

class IntegerOverFlowConst
{
    static void Main()
    {
        const ushort MAXUSHORT = 65535;
        const ushort ONE = 1;

        unchecked
        {
            ushort total = MAXUSHORT + ONE;
```

```
        }

        Console.ReadLine();
    }
}
```

Attempting to compile this code will result in the following error:

```
Constant value '65536' cannot be converted to a 'ushort'
```

The reason this won't compile has to do with the way the compiler adds constant values (as integers) and not whether it was in a checked context. To correct this, we simply perform a cast of the constants to the desired type:

```
using System;

class IntegerOverFlowConst
{
    static void Main()
    {
        const ushort MAXUSHORT = 65535;
        const ushort ONE = 1;

        unchecked
        {
            ushort total = (short)MAXUSHORT + ONE;
        }

        Console.ReadLine();
    }
}
```

The last remark I'll leave you with is that if your code is capable of overflowing and you want to catch that event, you should bracket the specific code with a *try..catch* exception block. If you don't care about overflow or are explicitly allowing it, specify overflow checking.

The *Decimal* Type

When writing monetary applications—such as accounting systems—one of the biggest challenges is dealing with extremely large and small numbers with many decimal places without losing any precision. Typically this task involves locating a third-party math library because most languages don't provide primitive data types that are appropriate for this type of application development.

For tasks like these, .NET provides the *Decimal* class. As mentioned earlier, this class, represented in C# by the *decimal* type, uses 128 bits (16 bytes) to store a value that can range from 1.0×10^{-28} to approximately 7.9×10^{28}, including 28 digits of precision.

The secret to how this type works is in how it stores values. The *Decimal* type is represented by a 96-bit integer scaled by a power of 10. For absolute values less than 1.0, the *Decimal* type represents the value exactly to the twenty-eighth decimal place. For absolute values greater than or equal to 1.0, the value is exact to 28 or 29 digits. The key here is that, contrary to the *float* and *double* types, decimal fractional numbers such as 0.1 are represented exactly. In the *float* and *double* representations, such numbers are often infinite fractions, making those representations more prone to round-off errors—an obvious problem in monetary applications.

The *System.Math* Class

The *System.Math* class consists of only constant values and static members used for logarithmic and trigonometric functions.

System.Math Constants

The two fields that *Math* does define are *E* and *PI*:

```
public const double E = 2.7182818284590452354;
public const double Math.PI = 3.14159265358979323846;
```

In the case of pi, we all know its significance as the ratio of the circumference of a circle to its diameter. *E* represents the natural logarithmic base, as shown here:

$$\lim_{x \to 0} (1 + x)^{\frac{1}{x}} = e = 2.7182818285\ldots$$

Working with a Number's Sign

The *Math* class has two methods that enable you to either determine a number's sign (positive or negative) or determine the absolute value of the number (regardless of its sign).

We'll start with the *Math.Sign* method. This overloaded method takes a single numeric type and returns 1 if the parameter value is positive, −1 if the value is negative, and 0 if the value is zero. Therefore, the following code:

```
Console.WriteLine("Math.Sign(1) = {0}", Math.Sign(1));
Console.WriteLine("Math.Sign(-1) = {0}", Math.Sign(-1));
Console.WriteLine("Math.Sign(0) = {0}", Math.Sign(0));
```

results in:

```
Math.Sign(1) = 1
Math.Sign(-1) = -1
Math.Sign(0) = 0
```

The *Abs* function—also overloaded to accept many different numeric types—returns the absolute value of the passed value. The following code:

```
Console.WriteLine("Math.Abs(5) = {0}", Math.Abs(5));
Console.WriteLine("Math.Abs(-5) = {0}", Math.Abs(-5));
Console.WriteLine("Math.Abs(0) = {0}", Math.Abs(0));
```

results in this output:

```
Math.Abs(5) = 5
Math.Abs(-5) = 5
Math.Abs(0) = 0
```

Minimum and Maximum Values

Almost all programmers at one time or another have had to determine the minimum or maximum value of something. In .NET, this task is accomplished via the *Math.Min* and *Math.Max* methods. Both of these methods simply take two numeric values and return either the minimum or maximum of the numbers passed.

Note that the following method is overloaded but the two parameters must match in type. As an example, let's say that you have the following:

```
int i = 5;
Console.WriteLine("Math.Min(1,2) = {0}", Math.Min(i,2.5F));
```

Although we know that *i* will be created in the *.locals* section as an *int32*, it will be implicitly converted to a *double* in this code. Therefore, the following MSIL would be produced:

```
.locals init ([0] int32 i)

<;$VE>

ldloc.0
conv.r4
ldc.r4    2.5
call      float32 [mscorlib]System.Math::Min(float32,
                                              float32)
```

Methods for Rounding and Truncating

The *System.Math* class includes several methods that allow you to control how numbers are rounded. We'll start with the most obvious, *System.Round*. This method has two forms. The first form enables you to round a value to the nearest whole number. Actually, this rounding gets a bit tricky if you're not careful: if the least significant digit is a 5, the number rounds to the even number. Therefore, 4.5 rounds down to 4, and 5.5 rounds up to 6! This behavior is defined by the IEEE as Standard 754, section 4 and is sometimes referred to as *banker's rounding*. Having said that, the following is true:

```
Math.Round(4.4) = 4
Math.Round(4.5) = 4
Math.Round(4.6) = 5
Math.Round(5.5) = 6
```

The second form of the *Round* method takes two parameters—the first is the value to be rounded, and the second is the precision (the number of significant fractional digits) that the returned value will have. Once again, banker's rounding is in play here. Therefore, the following code would be produced. Note that I'm requesting that each number be rounded to the first decimal place.

```
Math.Round(4.54,1)=4.5
Math.Round(4.55,1)=4.6 <- rounds up to even 4.6
Math.Round(4.65,1)=4.6 <- rounds down to even 4.6
Math.Round(4.56,1)=4.6
```

The last two methods we'll look at here are *Floor* and *Ceiling*. As their names indicate, these methods are opposites—the *Floor* method returns the largest whole number less than or equal to the specified value, and *Ceiling* returns the lowest whole number greater than or equal to the specified value. Therefore:

```
Floor(6.5) = 6
Floor(-6.5) = -7
Ceiling(6.5) = 7
Ceiling(-6.5) = -6
```

Summary

Numeric processing lies at the heart of almost any application. In this chapter, you learned the various numeric types that are supported by C#, how these types differ, how they're initialized, what the compiler generates when a numeric literal is used, and how numeric literals can be treated like any other object. From there, you learned how overflow is checked via the compiler */checked* switch and the *checked* keyword. Finally, we briefly covered both the *Decimal* class and the *System.Math* class.

17

Collections and Object Enumeration

One of the most powerful aspects of .NET development is the extensibility of the class library. Although the *System.Collections* namespace contains many basic collection types—such as the *Stack, Queue,* and *ArrayList* classes—the most impressive design element to the *System.Collections* namespace isn't the provided classes, but the underlying interfaces. These interfaces enable you to define more robust and problem domain–specific collection types. This chapter will focus on the *IEnumerable* type because it's the base interface of all types defined in the *System.Collections* namespace.

We'll begin by focusing on the syntax regarding the definition and implementation of the *IEnumerable* and *IEnumerator* interfaces and how to enumerate objects from the client's perspective. Several sections with demo applications will follow—each section presenting a different design issue regarding the definition, initialization, and implementation of enumerated types and describing how to address that issue. Finally, the chapter wraps up by examining some common problems associated with the storing of value types in a collection.

Implementing the Enumeration Interface

Almost any system you write will need to semantically group related items into a collection. Even many of the command-line applications in this book have used collection types such as *ArrayList* to create practical, real-world demonstrations of the various topics we've covered. In fact, the need for collections and the ability to enumerate those collections is so common that the interfaces upon which the .NET collections are built was made public for our use as well. The first of these interfaces—*IEnumerable*—is used to specify that the implementing class contains data that can be enumerated. This interface—which is implemented by every .NET collection type—is defined as follows:

```
public interface IEnumerable
{
    IEnumerator GetEnumerator();
}
```

As you can see, the *IEnumerable* interface has just one member—a method named *GetEnumerator*. This method returns the actual enumerator object that grants access to the collection's data. (From this point forward, I'll use the term *enumerator* to refer to this object.) The enumerator must then implement the *System.Collections.IEnumerator* interface:

```
public interface IEnumerator
{
    Boolean MoveNext();
    Object  Current { get; }
    void    Reset();
}
```

Now let's look at a standard way of defining the enumerator interfaces. As an example, we'll use a situation in which we have a database manager class (*DBManager*) that defines a collection of users who are currently logged in (*DBManager.onlineUsers*):

```
// Define class as implementing IEnumerable,
// indicating to clients that its data can be
// enumerated.
class DBManager : IEnumerable
{
    // Data to be enumerated
    ArrayList onlineUsers;

    // Mandatory method used by clients to retrieve
    // enumerator objects
    public IEnumerator GetEnumerator()
    {
        return new DBEnumerator(...);
    }

    // Enumerator object - needs to implement Current,
    // MoveNext, and Reset.
    class DBEnumerator : IEnumerator
    {
    }
};
```

As you can see, the *DBManager* class simply specifies that it implements the *IEnumerable* interface and defines a public *GetEnumerator* method. The *GetEnumerator* method then instantiates an *IEnumerator*-derived class and returns it. Note that although I've defined my enumerator within the main class, there's no rule that mandates this type of definition. However, this is a common way of defining enumerators because they're specific to the enclosing class.

Once you've defined the enumerator class, you need to implement the *IEnumerator* methods. The first design issue you have to consider is whether the enumerator will reflect a static snapshot of the data at a given point in time or a reference to the main class's data so that the data is always up –to date. I'll hold off on that subject for now in order to focus on the syntax of object enumeration; instead, I'll cover this issue in the "Constructing Enumerator Objects" section of this chapter. For now, we'll assume that the enumerator will contain a snapshot of the data and that any changes to the data after a call to the *GetEnumerator* will result in enumerators with different data sets.

When implementing the *IEnumerator* members, it's important to keep in mind that one of the main benefits of using this interface is that clients have a consistent means of enumerating your data. Having said that, you should implement the *IEnumerator* members as follows:

- **MoveNext**   Most enumerators define an internal index value (cursor) to keep track of where the client is while traversing the data. The *MoveNext* method should increment this index and return a value of *true* if there are more records to be read and *false* if the last record has been reached. This index should always be initialized to −1 when the enumerator object is instantiated. You'll see why momentarily, in the section "Using an Enumerator Object."

- **Current**   The *Current* property returns to the caller the object represented by the current index value. It''s customary to throw an exception of type *InvalidOperationException* if the client calls *Current* when the index value is −1.

- **Reset**   The *Reset* method is used to reinitialize the enumerator's state—not regarding its data—but by setting the index back to -1.

Using our *DBManager* example, let's see how these members might be implemented:

```
using System;
using System.Collections;

// Simple test class
class User
{
```

```
        public User(string name) { this.name = name; }
        string name;
        public string Name { get { return name; } }
};

// Define class as implementing Ienumerable,
// indicating to clients that its data can be
// enumerated.
class DBManager : IEnumerable
{
    // Data to be enumerated
    public DBManager()
    {
        // Add some dummy data to our collection.
        onlineUsers.Add(new User("Tom Archer"));
        onlineUsers.Add(new User("Krista Crawley"));
        onlineUsers.Add(new User("Emma Murdoch"));
    }

    // Data to be enumerated
    ArrayList onlineUsers = new ArrayList();

    // Mandatory method used by clients to retrieve
    // enumerator objects
    public IEnumerator GetEnumerator()
    {
        return new Enumerator(onlineUsers);
    }

    // Enumerator object
    class Enumerator : IEnumerator
    {
        const string INVALID_RECORD =
            "Use MoveNext before calling Current";

        public Enumerator(ArrayList onlineUsers)
        {
            foreach(User user in onlineUsers)
            {
                this.onlineUsers.Add(user);
            }
            Reset();
        }
        ArrayList onlineUsers = new ArrayList();

        // IEnumerator members
        int index;
        public bool MoveNext()
```

```
{
    // Increment index and compare to total number
    // of records. Return true if more records,
    // false if on last record.
    return (++index < onlineUsers.Count);
}

public object Current
{
    get
    {
        // If enumerator is in initialized state, throw
        // exception telling client to call MoveNext
        // before using Current.
        if (-1 == index)
            throw new InvalidOperationException(
                INVALID_RECORD);

        // We should never get here with index equal to
        // or greater than data set count, but you can
        // never be too sure.
        if (index < onlineUsers.Count)
            return onlineUsers[index]; // Return
                                       // current object
        else
            return null;
    }
}

// Initialized state of an enumerator should always be -1.
public void Reset() { index = -1; }
}
};
```

When the client calls the *DBManager.GetEnumerator* method, the code instantiates an *Enumerator* object, passing it the array of online users. The *Enumerator* constructor then copies the incoming array into a member array and calls the *Reset* method (which sets the *index* to −1). The *Current* property simply checks to see whether *index* is equal to −1 (in which case, it throws an exception). Otherwise, the object located at the specified index is returned. That's all there is to implementing the enumeration interface in your own classes. Now let's look at the client side.

Using an Enumerator Object

Now that we've seen how to implement the *IEnumerable* interface, let's look at how acquire and use an enumerator object:

```
class IEnumeratorApp
{
    static void Main(string[] args)
    {
        DBManager db = new DBManager();

        Console.WriteLine("[Main] Enumerating currently " +
            "logged in users...");

        IEnumerator e = db.GetEnumerator();

        while (e.MoveNext())
        {
            User user = (User)e.Current;
            Console.WriteLine("User={0}",user.Name);
        }
    }
}
```

As you can see, the client side is very easy to implement and is almost self-documenting. Once *Main* instantiates the *DBManager* object, it calls the *GetEnumerator* method. We've already seen that *GetEnumerator* creates a new enumerator and returns it to the client. From there, we need only use a simple *while* loop to enumerate the objects. Note that the returned value from the *Current* property is a *System.Object* type. Therefore, a cast is needed because we can't implicitly downcast from *System.Object* to *User*.

Building and executing this application results in the expected data being printed to the console, as shown in Figure 17-1.

Figure 17-1   The benefits derived from using the *IEnumerable* and *IEnumerator* interfaces more than outweigh the small amount of work involved.

Using the *foreach* Statement with Collections

Although this code is definitely easy to write, it's even easier to write if you use the *foreach* statement you learned about in Chapter 9, "Program Flow Control." Using *foreach*, the *Main* method can be rewritten as follows:

```
static void Main(string[] args)
{
    DBManager db = new DBManager();

    Console.WriteLine("[Main] Enumerating currently " +
        "logged in users...");
    foreach(User user in db)
    {
        Console.WriteLine("User={0}",user.Name);
    }
}
```

In case you're wondering why there isn't a call to *GetEnumerator* and how *foreach* can work with your type, let's look at the syntax and a few rules regarding the use of the *foreach* statement:

```
foreach (type-identifier in expression)
    embedded-statement
```

The *foreach* statement will work on *expression* as long as *expression* is a *collection type*. This rule means that *expression* must either implement *IEnumerable* (as we did here) or implement the *collection pattern*, which is defined as follows:

- The *expression* variable must contain a public instance method named *GetEnumerator* that takes no parameters and returns a struct, class, or interface.

- The type returned from the *GetEnumerator* method must contain a public instance method named *MoveNext* that takes no parameters and returns a *bool*.

- The type returned from the *GetEnumerator* method must contain a public instance method named *Current* that takes no parameters and returns a reference type.

If you look at the Microsoft intermediate language (MSIL) generated for the IEnumeratorApp application (shown in Figure 17-2), you'll see why the *foreach* statement specifies all these syntax rules.

```
IEnumeratorApp::Main : void(string[])                                    _ |□| x|
IL_0010:  ldloc.0
IL_0011:  callvirt   instance class [mscorlib]System.Collections.IEnumerator DBManager::GetEnu
IL_0016:  stloc.2
.try
{
  IL_0017:  br.s       IL_0035
  IL_0019:  ldloc.2
  IL_001a:  callvirt   instance object [mscorlib]System.Collections.IEnumerator::get_Current()
  IL_001f:  castclass  User
  IL_0024:  stloc.1
  IL_0025:  ldstr      "User={0}"
  IL_002a:  ldloc.1
  IL_002b:  callvirt   instance string User::get_Name()
  IL_0030:  call       void [mscorlib]System.Console::WriteLine(string,
                                                                object)

  IL_0035:  ldloc.2
  IL_0036:  callvirt   instance bool [mscorlib]System.Collections.IEnumerator::MoveNext()
  IL_003b:  brtrue.s   IL_0019
  IL_003d:  leave.s    IL_0050
} // end .try
```

Figure 17-2 The benefits derived from using the *IEnumerable* and *IEnumerator* classes more than outweigh the small amount of work involved.

Normally I like to highlight code in a figure that's salient to the topic at hand. However, the compiler generated almost every line of this code to support the *foreach* statement! Let's begin by looking at line IL_0011, where the *foreach* statement has determined that the *db* object (local variable *0*) implements the *GetEnumerator* call. After that call returns, the enumerator object is a local variable generated by the compiler.

Next a *.try* block catches any exceptions thrown as the result of improper casting. What's interesting here is that the code immediately jumps (*br.s*) to instruction IL_0035, which sets up a call to the enumerator's *MoveNext* method (IL_0036). Once the call to *MoveNext* returns, the returned value (now on the stack) is evaluated and control branches to instruction IL_0019 if the value is *true*. If the value is *false*, control continues and the next line branches out of the *.try* block (via the *leave.s* instruction).

At instruction IL_0019, we can see that the enumerator is pushed back onto the stack and the *Current* getter (which resolves to the *get_Current* method) is called. At instruction IL_001F, the code attempts to cast what *Current* placed on the stack to *User*—hence the need for a *.try* block. If the cast is successful, the object is pushed into the local variable *user* (IL_0024) and instructions IL_0025 through IL_0030 print the username to the output window.

Now that we know the syntactical rules of *foreach* and can see the generated MSIL, we know that we can remove *IEnumerable* from the *DBManager* class declaration and the code would continue to work because the *DBManager* and *DBEnumerator* classes implement the collection pattern. However, I'd strongly advise against this practice because many clients use the *is* or the *as* to test that a type implements a given interface before attempting to use the type.

You can easily test how removing *IEnumerable* from the *db* class affects the *is* operator. First, remove the *IEnumerable* implementation, and then modify the *Main* method as follows:

```
static void Main(string[] args)
{
    DBManager db = new DBManager();

    if (db is IEnumerable)
    {
        Console.WriteLine("[Main] Enumerating currently " +
            "logged in users...");
        foreach(User user in db)
        {
            Console.WriteLine("User={0}",user.Name);
        }
    }
    else
    {
        Console.WriteLine("I guess this type can't be " +
            "enumerated. Bummer...");
    }
}
```

If you run this application, the *is* operator will return *false* and the client will assume that the type isn't enumerable.

Two Interfaces for the Price of One

The first thing that most programmers ask when they discover the *IEnumerable* interface is why an extra level of indirection is needed. In other words, why doesn't *IEnumerable* define the *Current*, *MoveNext*, and *Reset* members, thereby eliminating the need for the *IEnumerator* interface? One reason for this indirection is flexibility. Let's say that instead of defining an enumerator object, the class containing the data simply provided public access to its internal data collection or implemented public accessor methods for that data. On the surface, this arrangement sounds reasonable, but it has drawbacks in certain scenarios.

What if the data changes often and you want to return to the client a snapshot of the data at the point of requisition? One way to solve this problem is to create an internal *data object* for each client. But then you'd need a way to associate each client with its data object—which is typically done through an attach and detach method pair. Now the user needs to pass in some sort of ID—

returned from the attach method—to retrieve his or her data. As you can see, we're setting ourselves up for a tremendous amount of work and certainly wandering far from a generic solution. With the *IEnumerable* and *IEnumerator* interface pair, that second data object is defined for you and its interface is well documented so that any client capable of using an enumerated object (such as the *foreach* statement) can use yours.

Constructing Enumerator Objects

The concept of static snapshots of data does bring up the interesting issue of how to initialize the enumerator object in terms of its data. The two basic means of initializing depend on how current you want the enumerator's data to be:

- **Snapshot method**   This technique involves defining the appropriate data members in the enumerator and copying data into those members when *GetEnumerator* is called. I used this technique in the IEnumeratorApp application, and it works well if the data changes often and the enumerator needs to reflect the data as it existed at a specific point in time. Obviously, this approach isn't recommended if the data set is extremely large and copying the data would be resource intensive (in terms of memory or time needed).

- **Reference method**   Using this technique, you'd define references in the enumerator that point to the actual data in the main class. This approach works great in situations where the data is static—hence, no need for a snapshot.

From these options, the choice does look simple. The second technique is much easier to implement and certainly less resource intensive. However, the second technique risks corrupting the enumerator's integrity if the data is dynamic. For example, let's say that a client requests an enumerator. The class passes back an enumerator containing references to *live data*—data that might change without the client being informed. You can run into trouble if during the client's processing of a given element in the class's data collection, the class deletes or modifies the item in question.

So what's a programmer to do if the data changes often but making snapshot copies of the data is too resource expensive? One solution is to use *versioned enumerators*.

Creating Versioned Enumerators

According to one member of the common language runtime team, the Framework's collection classes addressed the problems associated with creating enumerators for large amounts of dynamic data by implementing a simple versioning scheme. In the following code, I've modified the earlier example to show my version (no pun intended) of this technique. Note that I've removed the original comments and added comments that point out changes from the previous demo.

```
using System;
using System.Collections;

class User
{
    public User(string name) { this.name = name; }
    string name;
    public string Name { get { return name; } }
};

class DBManager : IEnumerable
{
    public DBManager()
    {
        onlineUsers.Add(new User("Tom Archer"));
        onlineUsers.Add(new User("Krista Crawley"));
        onlineUsers.Add(new User("Emma Murdoch"));
    }

    ArrayList onlineUsers = new ArrayList();

    // Add a version number. Make it static so that it
    // applies to all instances. Initialize to 0.
    static int version = 0;
    public static int Version { get { return version; } }


    public void AddItem(string userName)
    {
        // If data is changed, update version so that any
        // outstanding enumerators are now out of data!
        version++;
        onlineUsers.Add(new User(userName));
    }
```

```csharp
public IEnumerator GetEnumerator()
{
    // Pass current version number to any newly
    // created enumerators.
    return new DBEnumerator(version, onlineUsers);
}

class DBEnumerator : IEnumerator
{
    const string INVALID_RECORD =
        "Use MoveNext before calling Current";

    // Data-out-of-sync error message (for exception)
    const string DATA_OUT_OF_SYNC =
        "Data out of synch. Need to reacquire enumerator";

    // No need to initialize anymore as this will
    // simply be a reference to the enumerable class's
    // data.
    ArrayList onlineUsers;

    // Data version
    int version = 0;

    // Ctor now takes a version number as a param.
    public DBEnumerator(int version, ArrayList onlineUsers)
    {
        // Set version number.
        this.version = version;

        // Data is now referenced from enumerable class.
        this.onlineUsers = onlineUsers;

        Reset();
    }

    int index;
    public bool MoveNext()
    {
        CheckVersion(); // Check version number
                        // before doing anything!
        return (++index < onlineUsers.Count);
    }

    public object Current
    {
        get
        {
```

```
            CheckVersion(); // Check version number
                            // before doing anything!

            if (-1 == index)
                throw new InvalidOperationException(
                    INVALID_RECORD);

            if (index < onlineUsers.Count)
                return onlineUsers[index];
            else
                return null;
        }
    }

    public void Reset()
    {
        CheckVersion(); // Check version number
                        // before doing anything!
        index = -1;
    }

    // Simply compares version that was passed to this
    // enumerator with the current version number. If
    // they are different, throw an exception.
    void CheckVersion()
    {
        if (version != DBManager.Version)
            throw new InvalidOperationException(
                DATA_OUT_OF_SYNC);
    }
  }
};
```

As you can see, adding versioning support is a very simple modification. I simply define a static version number in the enumerable class, initialize the number to 0, and update it anytime the class's data changes. When a client requests an enumerator, the code creates a new enumerator and passes the current version to the enumerator's constructor. The enumerator then stores this version number and compares this value against the current enumerable class's version when one of its collection pattern methods is called. If the version numbers are different, the enumerator knows that the data has changed and it throws an *InvalidOperatorException* exception. Now, not only can we create enumerators in a less resource-intensive manner (because the members are references rather than copied data), we're also assured that a client will never have corrupt data as a result of changes occurring after enumerator creation.

Now the client code simply implements a *try..catch* block because any of the enumerator's methods might throw this new exception:

```
class VersionedEnumerator
{
    static void Main(string[] args)
    {
        DBManager db = new DBManager();

        Console.WriteLine("[Main] Enumerating currently " +
            "logged in users...");

        try
        {
            foreach(User user in db)
            {
                db.AddItem("This will cause an exception!!!");
                Console.WriteLine("User={0}",user.Name);
            }
        }
        catch(Exception e)
        {
            Console.WriteLine("Caught an exception - {0}",
                e.Message);
        }
    }
}
```

Note that I've inserted a line in the *foreach* statement that intentionally invalidates the data while the *Main* method is attempting to enumerate the collection. If you build and execute the application, you should see the raised exception shown in Figure 17-3.

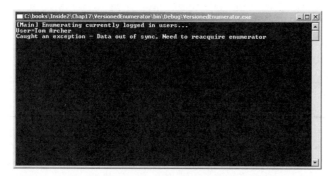

Figure 17-3   With versioned enumerators, you get the benefit of referencing dynamic data without the inherent dangers of enumerator corruption.

Combining *IEnumerable* and *IEnumerator*

In the section "Two Interfaces for the Price of One" earlier in this chapter, I mentioned that the benefit of having two interfaces (*IEnumerable* and *IEnumerator*) was that they ease the burden of keeping track of enumerators that represent snapshots of dynamic data. However, what if the data is static? In other words, why create a class that does nothing but implement methods that could've been implemented in the main class and define members that point to the main class's data? When these classes are implemented separately an enumerator object is instantiated each time an enumerator is requested, chewing up both CPU cycles and memory. Furthermore, when the requested enumerator's data is accessed, the enumerator simply references the main class's data, which also causes a small performance hit. In these situations, you might want to combine the two interfaces. In this version of the demo, I've commented the salient code to highlight the changes:

```
using System;
using System.Collections;

class User
{
    public User(string name) { this.name = name; }
    string name;
    public string Name { get { return name; } }
};

// Define class as implementing IEnumerable,
// indicating to clients that its data can be
// enumerated.
class DBManager : IEnumerable, IEnumerator
{
    const string INVALID_RECORD =
        "Use MoveNext before calling Current";

    public DBManager()
    {
        onlineUsers.Add(new User("Tom Archer"));
        onlineUsers.Add(new User("Krista Crawley"));
        onlineUsers.Add(new User("Emma Murdoch"));
    }

    ArrayList onlineUsers = new ArrayList();

    // Now that this class implements both the IEnumerable
    // and IEnumerator interfaces, I can simply return
    // an instance of this class.
```

```csharp
        public IEnumerator GetEnumerator()
        {
            Reset();
            return this;
        }

        // Implementation of the IEnumerator members
        int index;
        public bool MoveNext()
        {
            return (++index < onlineUsers.Count);
        }

        public object Current
        {
            get
            {
                if (-1 == index)
                    throw new InvalidOperationException(
                        INVALID_RECORD);

                if (index < onlineUsers.Count)
                    return onlineUsers[index]; // Return current
                                               // object
                else
                    return null;
            }
        }

        public void Reset() { index = -1; }
    };

    class CombinedEnumerator
    {
        static void Main(string[] args)
        {
            DBManager db = new DBManager();

            foreach(User user in db)
            {
                Console.WriteLine("User={0}",user.Name);
            }
        }
    }
```

Now our *DBManager* class allows for the enumeration of the *onlineUsers* collection without the performance overhead of creating an enumerator object for each client.

As a final note, the CombinedEnumerator application stores its data in an *ArrayList*, and its implemented *IEnumerator* methods don't do anything special. I'd only suggest using a class implementing both the *IEnumerable* and *IEnumerator* interfaces in cases where the data isn't stored in a collection (which is already enumerable) or if your enumerator methods will be doing something other than moving the cursor and returning data.

Conversely, if your class's data is stored in a collection, the quickest way to allow for enumeration of that data is to implement only the *IEnumerable* interface and to return the collection's enumerator object from the *GetEnumerator* method:

```
// Excerpt from the CombinedEnumerator2 application
// on the book's CD-ROM
class DBManager : IEnumerable
{
    ⋮
    ArrayList onlineUsers = new ArrayList();
    ⋮
    // Because ArrayList implements IEnumerable, I
    // can simply call its GetEnumerator method if
    // I don't want any processing beyond what it does.
    public IEnumerator GetEnumerator()
    {
        return onlineUsers.GetEnumerator();
    }
    ⋮
};
```

The benefit of this arrangement is that I don't have to needlessly implement the *IEnumerator* methods because they're already implemented by the *ArrayList* class's enumerator class.

Protecting Data While Allowing Enumeration

Pursuant to my remark in the previous section about simply returning the enumerator object of an embedded collection, let's imagine a scenario in which a class has several collections of data that can each be enumerated. For example, in addition to the *DBManager.onlineUsers* collection that we've used throughout this chapter, our *DBManager* class might have collections for open tables and locked records. In this case, a single *GetEnumerator* method wouldn't do. However, we could simply create properties for each collection, as in the following example, where we return the collection cast to *IEnumerable* (because all collections implement *IEnumerable*).

```
class DBManager
{
    ⋮
    ArrayList onlineUsers = new ArrayList();
    public IEnumerable OnlineUsers
    {
        get
        {
            return (IEnumerable)onlineUsers;
        }
    }
    ⋮
}
```

The client would then be modified as shown here:

```
DBManager db = new DBManager();
foreach(object user in db.OnlineUsers)
{
    Console.WriteLine(((User)user).Name);
}
```

So far, the code looks pretty good. Unfortunately, looks are very deceiving in this case because of one small detail. Because we're returning the actual collection (cast to *IEnumerable*), the client has full access to the collection's publicly accessible data and, as you can see from the following line of code, can severely compromise our data's integrity:

```
((ArrayList)db.OnlineUsers).RemoveAt(0);
```

So how can we allow a client to enumerate our private collection without giving up access to that collection's data? There are two ways to do this, depending on your needs for the client. The first way is to return the collection's enumerator object (instead of the collection object cast to *IEnumerable*).

```
ArrayList onlineUsers = new ArrayList();
public IEnumerator OnlineUsers
{
    get
    {
        return onlineUsers.GetEnumerator();
    }
}
```

Now if a client attempts to cast the returned enumerator object to *ArrayList*, an *InvalidCastException* will be raised. This reason for this exception is that the *ArrayList* itself doesn't implement the *IEnumerator* interface (it's actually implemented by *ArrayListEnumeratorSimple*).

```
DBManager db = new DBManager();

IEnumerator ie = db.OnlineUsers;
Console.WriteLine(ie); // <-- Shows that another class
                       // implements IEnumerator
((ArrayList)ie).RemoveAt(0); // <-- This line will throw
                             // an exception!
```

At this point, it looks like we've solved our problem of allowing clients to enumerate our collections without allowing access to the data. However, there's one drawback to this approach. As you learned earlier in the chapter, in the section "Using the *foreach* Statement with Collections," the *foreach* statement must be used with a type that implements the *IEnumerable* interface or the collection pattern. Because the *ArrayList* enumerator object does neither, the client can't use the *foreach* statement with the *OnlineUsers* property defined as it is. If this limitation isn't a problem, however, the client can still enumerate the users with a simple *while* loop:

```
DBManager db = new DBManager();

IEnumerator ie = db.OnlineUsers;
while (ie.MoveNext())
{
    Console.WriteLine(((User)ie.Current).Name);
}
```

However, for the sake of completeness, let's say that you do want the client to be able to use the *foreach* statement. Where does that leave us? We don't want to return the collection cast to *IEnumerable* because the client then has access to the collection's data. Returning an *IEnumerator* object means the client can't use the *foreach* statement. Because we certainly don't want to create an *IEnumerable*-derived class for each collection, the only resolution left is to write a generic wrapper class that will serve our purpose.

The following *Enumerable* class does just that. Note that the class's constructor takes an *IEnumerable* interface as its only parameter. This arrangement guarantees that any collection can be used with this class. The constructor calls the object's *GetEnumerator* method and stores the returned value as a private member variable. This value is then returned to any caller of the *Enumerable.GetEnumerator* method. The result is a generic wrapper that, while satisfying the *foreach* statement, protects the underlying collection from being accessed:

```
class Enumerable : IEnumerable
{
    public Enumerable(IEnumerable enumerable)
```

```
    {
        enumerator = enumerable.GetEnumerator();
    }

    IEnumerator enumerator;
    public IEnumerator GetEnumerator()
    {
        return enumerator;
    }
};
```

Now each collection's getter property would be written to return a newly instantiated *Enumerable* object:

```
ArrayList onlineUsers = new ArrayList();
public IEnumerable OnlineUsers
{
    get
    {
        return new Enumerable(onlineUsers);
    }
}
```

Finally, the client code—completely ignorant of the wrapper class—would enumerate the collection as any other:

```
DBManager db = new DBManager();

foreach(User user in db.OnlineUsers)
{
    Console.WriteLine(((User)user).Name);
}
```

Value Types

So far, all the demo applications have dealt with enumerating reference types. In this section, we'll take a look at the unique issues that result from storing value types in collections. I'll begin by illustrating how enumerating collected value types can adversely affect performance and then show the various means of correcting this problem. After that, I'll illustrate a common problem associated with modifying data once it's stored in a collection in the form of a value type.

Performance Issues

In the *DBManager* example that we've used throughout this chapter, the *User* construct has always been defined as a class. However, what if the data you need to enumerate is a value type? You can test what would happen by simply changing the *User* definition to a struct, as follows. Note that I've reintroduced the *while* loop because it will enable me to make some points more clearly.

```
using System;
using System.Collections;

struct User
{
    public User(string name) { this.name = name; }
    string name;
    public string Name { get { return name; } }
};

class DBManager : IEnumerable
{
    public DBManager()
    {
        onlineUsers.Add(new User("Tom Archer"));
        onlineUsers.Add(new User("Krista Crawley"));
        onlineUsers.Add(new User("Emma Murdoch"));
    }

    ArrayList onlineUsers = new ArrayList();

    public IEnumerator GetEnumerator()
    {
        return new DBEnumerator(onlineUsers);
    }

    class DBEnumerator : IEnumerator
    {
        const string INVALID_RECORD =
            "Use MoveNext before calling Current";

        public DBEnumerator(ArrayList onlineUsers)
        {
            foreach(User user in onlineUsers)
            {
                this.onlineUsers.Add(user);
            }
            Reset();
        }
```

```
            ArrayList onlineUsers = new ArrayList();

            int index;
            public bool MoveNext()
            {
                return (++index < onlineUsers.Count);
            }

            public object Current
            {
                get
                {
                    if (-1 == index)
                        throw new InvalidOperationException(
                            INVALID_RECORD);

                    if (index < onlineUsers.Count)
                        return onlineUsers[index]; // Return current
                                                   // object
                    else
                        return null;
                }
            }

            public void Reset() { index = -1; }
        }
    };

    class ValueTypePerf1
    {
        static void Main(string[] args)
        {
            DBManager db = new DBManager();

            Console.WriteLine("[Main] Enumerating currently " +
                "logged in users...");
            IEnumerator e = db.GetEnumerator();
            while (e.MoveNext())
            {
                User user = (User)e.Current;
                Console.WriteLine("User={0}",user.Name);
            }
        }
    }
```

Although this demo will output the same results as the other demos, the MSIL reveals the underlying problem. First off, take a look at the *DBManager* constructor, shown in Figure 17-4.

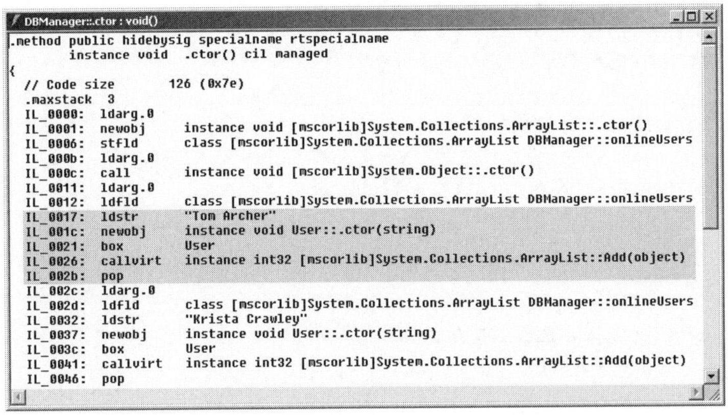

Figure 17-4   Placing a value type into an *ArrayList* results in a boxing operation.

As you can see (in lines IL_0017 through IL_002B), now that *User* is a struct, instantiating a *User* object and passing it to the *ArrayList.Add* method results in a boxing operation for every single user! This boxing isn't necessarily a problem if you're working with a very simple application (such as those presented in books). However, in real-world applications with large amounts of data, boxing every single piece of data in your collection could have a significant negative impact on your application's performance.

The first thing we can do to help prevent this performance penalty is to change the way the data is stored in the enumerator:

```
using System;
using System.Collections;

struct User
{
    public User(string name) { this.name = name; }
    string name;
    public string Name { get { return name; } }
};

class DBManager : IEnumerable
{
    public DBManager()
    {
        // Initialize array
        onlineUsers[0] = new User("Tom Archer");
        onlineUsers[1] = new User("Krista Crawley");
        onlineUsers[2] = new User("Emma Murdoch");
    }
```

```csharp
// Now create an array of value types
// instead of an ArrayList
User[] onlineUsers = new User[4];

public IEnumerator GetEnumerator()
{
    return new DBEnumerator(onlineUsers);
}

class DBEnumerator : IEnumerator
{
    const string INVALID_RECORD =
        "Use MoveNext before calling Current";

    // Change ctor to take an array of User value types.
    public DBEnumerator(User[] onlineUsers)
    {

        // Need to use Array.Length property.
        for (int i = 0; i < onlineUsers.Length; i++)
            this.onlineUsers[i] = onlineUsers[i];
        Reset();
    }

    // Initialize User array object.
    User[] onlineUsers = new User[4];

    int index;
    public bool MoveNext()
    {
        // Return EOF based on Array.Length.
        return (++index < onlineUsers.Length);
    }

    public object Current
    {
        get
        {
            if (-1 == index)
                throw new InvalidOperationException(
                    INVALID_RECORD);

            if (index < onlineUsers.Length) // If not at EOF
                return onlineUsers[index];
            else
                return null;
        }
    }
```

```
        public void Reset() { index = -1; }
    }
};

class ValueTypePerf2
{
    static void Main(string[] args)
    {
        DBManager db = new DBManager();

        Console.WriteLine("[Main] Enumerating currently " +
            "logged in users...");
        IEnumerator e = db.GetEnumerator();
        while (e.MoveNext())
        {
            User user = (User)e.Current;
            Console.WriteLine("User={0}",user.Name);
        }
    }
}
```

A peek at Figure 17-5 confirms that we have a few more MSIL instructions to deal with an array element, but they're far less costly than boxing operations.

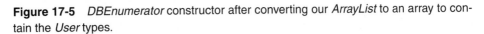

```
 DBManager::.ctor : void()                                      _|□|×|
.method public hidebysig specialname rtspecialname
        instance void  .ctor() cil managed
{
  // Code size       107 (0x6b)
  .maxstack  2
  IL_0000:  ldarg.0
  IL_0001:  ldc.i4.4
  IL_0002:  newarr      User
  IL_0007:  stfld       valuetype User[] DBManager::onlineUsers
  IL_000c:  ldarg.0
  IL_000d:  call        instance void [mscorlib]System.Object::.ctor()
  IL_0012:  ldarg.0
  IL_0013:  ldfld       valuetype User[] DBManager::onlineUsers
  IL_0018:  ldc.i4.0
  IL_0019:  ldelema     User
  IL_001e:  ldstr       "Tom Archer"
  IL_0023:  call        instance void User::.ctor(string)
  IL_0028:  ldarg.0
  IL_0029:  ldfld       valuetype User[] DBManager::onlineUsers
  IL_002e:  ldc.i4.1
  IL_002f:  ldelema     User
  IL_0034:  ldstr       "Krista Crawley"
  IL_0039:  call        instance void User::.ctor(string)
  IL_003e:  ldarg.0
```

Figure 17-5 *DBEnumerator* constructor after converting our *ArrayList* to an array to contain the *User* types.

At this point, we're feeling pretty good about ourselves. However, now look at the MSIL for the enumerator's *Current* property (getter method) in Figure 17-6.

ValueTypePerf1

```
DBEnumerator::get_Current : object()                                          _|□|×|
  IL_002e:  ldfld     int32 DBManager/DBEnumerator::index
  IL_0033:  callvirt  instance object [mscorlib]System.Collections.ArrayList::get_Item(int32)
  IL_0038:  stloc.0
  IL_0039:  br.s      IL_003F
  IL_003b:  ldnull
  IL_003c:  stloc.0
  IL_003d:  br.s      IL_003F
  IL_003f:  ldloc.0
  IL_0040:  ret
} // end of method DBEnumerator::get_Current
```

ValueTypePerf2

```
DBEnumerator::get_Current : object()                                          _|□|×|
  IL_002b:  ldfld     int32 DBManager/DBEnumerator::index
  IL_0030:  ldelema   User
  IL_0035:  ldobj     User
  IL_003a:  box       User
  IL_003f:  stloc.0
  IL_0040:  br.s      IL_0046
  IL_0042:  ldnull
  IL_0043:  stloc.0
  IL_0044:  br.s      IL_0046
  IL_0046:  ldloc.0
  IL_0047:  ret
} // end of method DBEnumerator::get_Current
```

Figure 17-6 The *DBEnumerator.get_Current* method now has to box each user because the method is defined as returning a reference type and the users are stored internally as value types.

To see the problem, look at lines IL_0033 through IL_0040 of the ValueTypePerf1 version. Here you can see that the *Current* property simply calls the *ArrayList::get_Item* method—showing that *ArrayList* implements the indexers you learned about in Chapter 5, "Properties, Arrays, and Indexers." Because the *Current* property is defined as returning a reference type, the reference type retrieved from the *ArrayList* can be returned without any boxing.

Now look at lines (IL_002B through IL_003A) of the ValueTypePerf2 version. Because the element is stored as a value type and the *Count* property needs to return a reference type, the code must perform a boxing operation before returning the data.

As you can see, all we did by changing the way the data was stored—from a reference-based collection to a value-based array—was move our performance problems to another area!

However, our problems don't end there. In both the ValueTypePerf1 and ValueTypePerf2 applications, we still have a problem in the *Main* method. Look at Figure 17-7 to see what I mean.

ValueTypePerf1

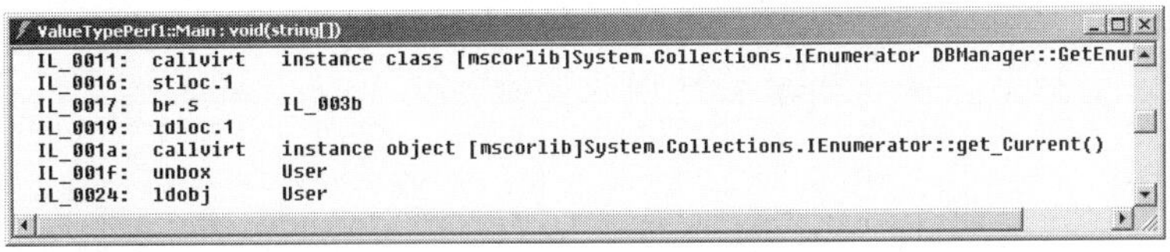

ValueTypePerf2

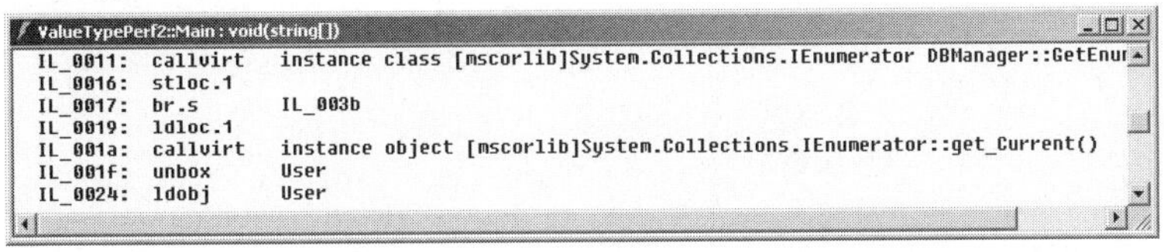

Figure 17-7   The *Main* method in both ValueTypePerf1 and ValueTypePerf2 unbox the type returned by *DBEnumerator.Current*.

As you can see, the MSIL for both applications' *Main* method needs to unbox the value returned from *Current*. This unboxing is a bit ironic because we don't want *Current* to box the value to begin with. However, the signature of the *Current* getter method specifically shows that it has to return a reference type. Therefore, if we really want to get the best performance from this application, we'll need to change that aspect. Our next version of the code looks like this:

```
using System;
using System.Collections;

struct User
{
    public User(string name) { this.name = name; }
    string name;
    public string Name { get { return name; } }
};

class DBManager : IEnumerable
{
    public DBManager()
    {
        onlineUsers[0] = new User("Tom Archer");
        onlineUsers[1] = new User("Krista Crawley");
        onlineUsers[2] = new User("Emma Murdoch");
    }

    User[] onlineUsers = new User[4];
```

```csharp
// New method!
public IEnumerator GetEnumerator()
{
    return new DBEnumerator(onlineUsers);
}

// Method changed to explicit interface implementation
IEnumerator IEnumerable.GetEnumerator()
{
    return GetEnumerator(); // Calls new method
}

public class DBEnumerator : IEnumerator
{
    const string INVALID_RECORD =
        "Use MoveNext before calling Current";

    public DBEnumerator(User[] onlineUsers)
    {
        for (int i = 0; i < onlineUsers.Length; i++)
            this.onlineUsers[i] = onlineUsers[i];
        Reset();
    }
    User[] onlineUsers = new User[4];

    int index;
    public bool MoveNext()
    {
        return (++index < onlineUsers.Length);
    }

    // Method changed to explicit interface implementation
    object IEnumerator.Current
    { get {   return Current; }   }

    // Only change here is that Current
    // returns a value type (User)
    public User Current
    {
        get
        {
            if (-1 == index || index >= onlineUsers.Length)
                throw new InvalidOperationException(
                    INVALID_RECORD);

            return onlineUsers[index];
        }
    }
}
```

```
            public void Reset() { index = -1; }
        }
    };

class ValueTypePerf3
{
    static void Main(string[] args)
    {
        DBManager db = new DBManager();


        Console.WriteLine("[Main] Enumerating currently " +
            "logged in users...");
        DBManager.DBEnumerator e =
            (DBManager.DBEnumerator)db.GetEnumerator();
        while (e.MoveNext())
        {
            User user = (User)e.Current;
            Console.WriteLine("User={0}",user.Name);
        }
    }
}
```

Before we look at the MSIL, let's look at the changes to the code. As you might recall from the section "Explicit Interface Member Name Qualification" in Chapter 7, "Interfaces," there are times when you'll want to explicitly qualify the name of the interface member you're implementing. I'm doing just that with the *DBManager.GetEnumerator* method. The reason I explicitly qualify the name is so that I can have my own version of the *GetEnumerator* method. This second version of *GetEnumerator*—which isn't bound by the rules that require an implementation of *IEnumerable.GetEnumerator* to return an *IEnumerable* type—returns *DBEnumerable*. Now I provide two versions of the *Current* property as well. Once again, I have a fully qualified *IEnumerator.Current* version and a non-qualified version. The former returns an object, and the latter returns a value type (*User*).

Finally, the *Main* method is modified to retrieve a *DBEnumerator* object so that when it calls *Current*, a *User* value type is returned and no unboxing operation is needed:

```
class ValueTypePerf3
{
    static void Main(string[] args)
    {
        DBManager db = new DBManager();

        Console.WriteLine("[Main] Enumerating currently " +
            "logged in users...");
```

```
        DBManager.DBEnumerator e =
            (DBManager.DBEnumerator)db.GetEnumerator();
        while (e.MoveNext())
        {
            User user = (User)e.Current;
            Console.WriteLine("User={0}",user.Name);
        }
    }
}
```

Now if you build and execute the ValueTypePerf3 application, you'll see that we finally achieved our goal of removing the gratuitous boxing and unboxing operations. Figure 17-8 shows the result.

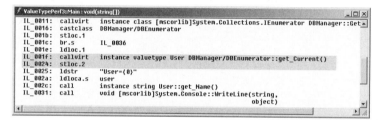

Figure 17-8   With a second *Current* method defined that returns a value type, our *Main* method no longer needs to unbox the value after calling *Current*.

Modified Collected Value Types

The last issue I want to discuss isn't tied to object enumeration but is a problem with value types and collections for many people new to .NET. In the following example, I once again have the *DBManager* class. I've removed all the enumeration code in order to focus on the problem:

```
using System;
using System.Collections;

struct User
{
    public User(string name) { this.name = name; }
    string name;
    public string Name
    {
        get { return name; }
        set { name = value; }
    }
};


class DBManager
{
```

```
    public DBManager()
    {
        onlineUsers.Add(new User("Tom Archer"));
    }

    public ArrayList onlineUsers = new ArrayList();

};

class MutatorInterfaces
{
    static void Main(string[] args)
    {
        DBManager db = new DBManager();
        Console.WriteLine( ((User)db.onlineUsers[0]).Name );
        ((User)db.onlineUsers[0]).Name =
            "NEW NAME"; // <-- Will not compile!!
    }
}
```

Here the *Main* method instantiates a *DBManager* object and then directly accesses the *DBManager.onlineUsers* array in a call to *Console.WriteLine*. However, the next line won't compile—even though the code syntax is identical to the previous line. This is the compile-time error you'll see if you attempt to build this application:

```
CS0131 - The left-hand side of an assignment must be a variable,
 property or indexer
```

To understand what's going on here (and why this code won't compile), comment out the attempt to set the user's *Name* field and then build the application. Once you've done that, you should see the MSIL shown in Figure 17-9.

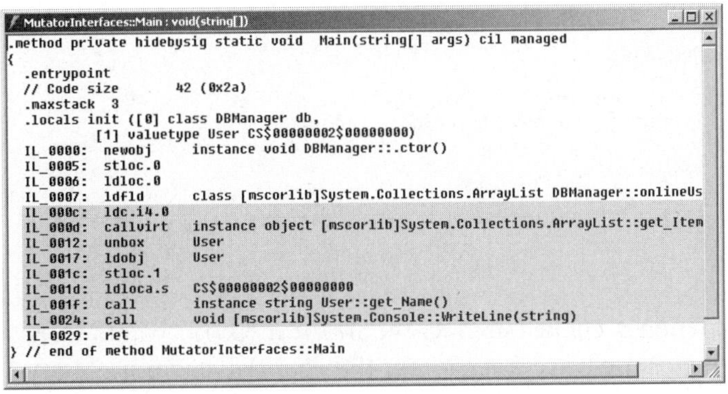

Figure 17-9   This MSIL reveals why the compiler rejects the line that attempts to set the user's *Name* field.

The bit that's important in this MSIL is the definition of a local variable (noted here as *CS$00000002$00000000*). In the C# code, it appears that we're *directly* referencing an element in the *ArrayList*. However, that's not the case. What's happening is that the compiler has generated MSIL that loads the item from the *ArrayList* and unboxes the item into the local variable noted earlier. The point is that you can't directly access a value type that's stored in an *Array-List* because it"s not stored as a value type. Having said that, the compiler then sees an attempt to modify a value type in the *ArrayList* and reports the error.

The solution here is to use what's known as a *mutator interface*. This interface will define the data that the *User* struct will implement:

```
using System;
using System.Collections;

interface IUserData
{
    string Name { get; set; }
}



struct User : IUserData
{
    public User(string name) { this.name = name; }
    string name;
    public string Name
    {
        get { return name; }
        set { name = value; }
    }
};

class DBManager
{
    public DBManager()
    {
        onlineUsers.Add(new User("Tom Archer"));
    }

    public ArrayList onlineUsers = new ArrayList();

};
```

Now when a client (such as the *Main* method) wants to access the *User* data, it retrieves the boxed version of the *User* data from the *ArrayList* and casts it to the mutator interface (*IUserData*):

```
class MutatorInterfaces
{
    static void Main(string[] args)
    {
        DBManager db = new DBManager();

        IUserData u = (IUserData)db.onlineUsers[0];

        Console.WriteLine( u.Name );
        u.Name = "NEW NAME";
        Console.WriteLine( u.Name );
    }
}
```

Running this application generates the following output, proving that the element in the *ArrayList* was modified:

```
Tom Archer
NEW NAME
```

Now if you look at the MSIL shown in Figure 17-10, you'll see another benefit of using mutator interfaces when accessing value types stored in a collection—no unboxing is required.

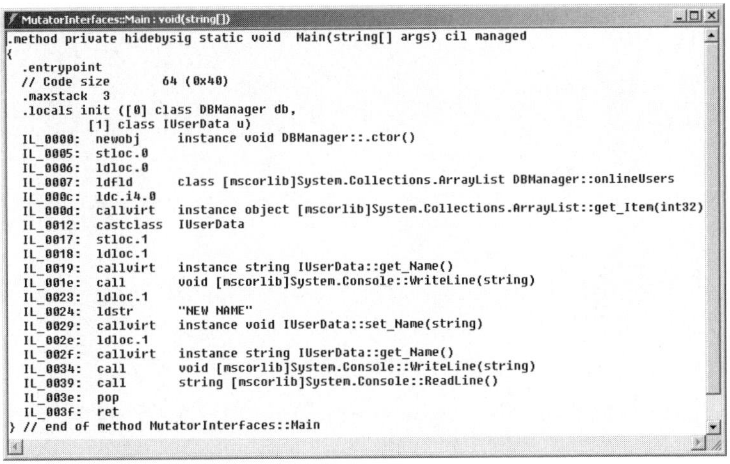

Figure 17-10   Mutator interfaces solve the problem of directly modifying value types stored as reference types.

Summary

Almost all applications require you to group logically related data into sets. For this reason, the .NET Framework provides a *System.Collections* namespace that defines many of the basic collection types. However, the most interesting feature of the *System.Collections* namespace isn't the high-level collection types but the underlying interfaces that give these types structure.

In this chapter, you learned a tremendous amount about the base interface of all types defined in the *System.Collections* namespace—*IEnumerable*—and its close cousin—*IEnumerator*. We began by focusing on the syntax regarding the definition and implementation of these two interfaces and, from a client's perspective, how to use an enumerated type. Once you learned the basics of defining object enumeration for your own types, several sections and demo applications followed—each one presenting a different design issue regarding the definition, initialization, and implementation of enumerated types and how to address that issue. Finally, the chapter wrapped up by examining some common problems associated with the storing of value types in a collection.

18

Multithreading and Asynchronous Programming

A multithreaded application is one that divides its workload into disparate threads—or units of execution. One reason for doing this is simplicity of design. Multiple threads allow for tight cohesion between tasks, meaning that each thread class should capture a single abstraction or idea. This design produces a divide-and-conquer strategy in which large, complex systems are split into more manageable units, resulting in systems that are less expensive to both build and maintain. The introduction of multiple threads also yields benefits such as increased concurrency, improved user interaction, and more efficient use of the CPU.

In this chapter, you'll first see how to create and start a worker thread. From there, you'll learn how to control the lifetimes of a thread—tasks that include suspending, resuming, and aborting threads. After that, we'll look at scheduling threads and synchronizing access to critical code. Finally, the chapter wraps up with a section that describes when it's a good idea to use threads and when it's not.

Getting Started with Threads

Before examining some of the different ways you can use threads in C#, let's see how easy it is to create a secondary thread in C#. After discussing the example, I'll look more closely at the *System.Threading* namespace and, specifically, the *Thread* class. In this example, I'm creating a second thread from the *Main* method. The method associated with the second thread then outputs a string that shows that the thread's been called. (I'm obviously keeping this example as simple as possible to focus on the mechanics of creating and starting a thread.)

```csharp
using System;
using System.Threading;

class SimpleThreadApp
{
    public static void WorkerThreadMethod()
    {
        Console.WriteLine("[WorkerThreadMethod] Worker " +
            "thread started");
    }

    public static void Main()
    {
        ThreadStart worker =
            new ThreadStart(WorkerThreadMethod);

        Console.WriteLine("[Main] Creating worker thread");

        Thread t = new Thread(worker);
        t.Start();

        Console.WriteLine(
            "[Main] Have requested the start of worker thread");

        Console.ReadLine();
    }
}
```

If you compile and execute this application, you'll see that the message from the *Main* method prints before the message from the worker thread, proving that the worker thread is indeed working asynchronously. Let's dissect what's going on here.

The first new item to note is the inclusion of the *using* statement for the *System.Threading* namespace. We'll delve into this particular namespace in more detail in the next section. For now, it's enough to understand that the *Threading* namespace contains the different classes necessary for creation and management of worker threads in the .NET environment. Now take a look at the first line of the *Main* method:

```csharp
ThreadStart WorkerThreadMethod =
    new ThreadStart(WorkerThreadMethod);
```

As you can discern from the fact that I've passed a method name to a class constructor, *ThreadStart* is a delegate. Specifically, it's the delegate that must be used when you create a new thread, and it's used to indicate the method that you want called as your *thread method*. From there, I instantiate a *Thread* object; the object's constructor takes a *ThreadStart* delegate as its only argument, like this:

```
Thread t = new Thread(worker);
```

Once the *Thread* object is created, all I have to do is call the *Thread.Start* method. That's it! Three lines of code to set up and run the thread and the thread method, and you're set. Now that we've see how easy it is to spawn a worker thread, let's look deeper into the *System.Threading* namespace and the classes that make all this happen.

Basic Thread-Handling Chores

Most everything you do with threads requires the *Thread* class. This section looks at using the *Thread* class to carry out basic threading tasks.

Creating Threads and *Thread* Objects

You can instantiate a *Thread* object in two ways. You've already seen one way: creating a new thread and, in the process, creating a *Thread* object with which to manipulate the new thread. The other way to obtain a *Thread* object is by calling the static *Thread.CurrentThread* method for the currently executing thread. Here I'm simply obtaining a thread object associated with the current thread, setting its *Name* property, and then outputting that name to the screen:

```
Thread current = Thread.CurrentThread;
current.Name = "My main thread";
Console.WriteLine("Thread name = {0}", current.Name);
```

Managing Thread Lifetimes

There are many tasks you might need to perform to manage the activity or life of a thread. You can manage all these tasks by using various *Thread* methods. For example, it's quite common to need to pause a thread for a given period of time. To do this, you can call the *Thread.Sleep* method. This method takes a single argument that represents the amount of time, in milliseconds, that you want the thread to pause. Note that the *Thread.Sleep* method is a static method and can't be called with an instance of a *Thread* object. There's a very good reason for this. You're not allowed to call *Thread.Sleep* on any other thread except the currently executing one. The static *Thread.Sleep* method calls the static *CurrentThread* method, which then pauses that thread for the specified amount of time. Here's an example of how the *Sleep* method is used:

```
using System;
using System.Threading;

class ThreadSleepApp
{
    public static void WorkerThreadMethod()
    {
        Console.WriteLine(
            "[WorkerThreadMethod] Thread started");

        int sleepTime = 5000;

        Console.WriteLine("\tsleeping for {0} seconds",
            sleepTime / 1000);
        Thread.Sleep(sleepTime); // Sleep for five seconds.
        Console.WriteLine("\twaking up");
    }

    public static void Main()
    {
        ThreadStart worker =
            new ThreadStart(WorkerThreadMethod);

        Console.WriteLine("[Main] Creating worker thread");

        Thread t = new Thread(worker);
        t.Start();

        Console.WriteLine(
            "[Main] Have requested the start of worker thread");

        t.Join();
        Console.WriteLine("[Main] Worker thread " +
            "finally woke up!");

        Console.ReadLine();
    }
}
```

Note that after starting the thread, the *Main* method calls the *Thread.Join* method. This method is used to determine when a given thread has terminated. Figure 18-1 shows the results of running this application.

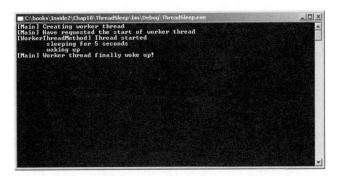

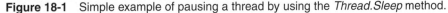

Figure 18-1   Simple example of pausing a thread by using the *Thread.Sleep* method.

In addition to passing the number of milliseconds to pause the thread to the *Sleep* method, there are two additional ways to call this method. The first involves passing a value of *0*. This call doesn't actually suspend the thread, but it causes the thread to relinquish the unused balance of its *time slice*. The second way to call *Thread.Sleep* is to pass a value of *Timeout.Infinite*. This call pauses the thread indefinitely until the suspension is interrupted by another thread calling the suspended thread's *Thread.Interrupt* method.

As with the *Sleep* method, the *Thread* class defines a method named *Suspend* that provides much of the same functionality. Keep in mind these important distinctions between these two methods:

■   The *Suspend* method takes no parameters and can be resumed only by another thread—via the *Thread.Resume* method.

■   The *Thread.Suspend* method can be called on the currently executing thread or on another thread, while the *Thread.Sleep* method can be called only on the current thread.

■   Once a thread suspends another thread, the first thread isn't blocked. The call returns immediately.

Also, regardless of how many times the *Thread.Suspend* method is called for a given thread, a single call to *Thread.Resume* will cause the thread to resume execution.

Destroying Threads

You can destroy a thread with a call to the *Thread.Abort* method. The runtime forces a thread to abort by throwing a *ThreadAbortException*. You'll recall that in Chapter 12, "Error Handling with Exceptions," I illustrated a means of employing the *goto* statement and labels to jump out of a *catch* block and retry the code that caused the exception. However, this technique won't work with this particular exception. In other words, once the system starts to abort your thread, you can catch the exception to log the event or perform cleanup, but you can't prevent the thread from terminating. The following two examples illustrate this arrangement.

In the first example, the *Main* method simply spins off a worker thread specifying the *WorkerThreadFunc* method. When the thread is started, the *WorkerThreadFunc* sets a label (*Work*) and calls *DoCounting* in a *try* block. The *DoCounting* method outputs a couple of numbers to the screen and then throws an exception. The code jumps out of the *catch* block with a *goto* statement and jumps to the *Work* label.

```csharp
using System;
using System.Threading;

class ThreadAbortApp
{
    public static void DoCounting()
    {
        Console.WriteLine("\n[DoCounting] Counting slowly " +
            "to 10");

        for (int i = 0; i < 10; i++)
        {
            if (3 == i)
                throw new Exception(
                    "[DoCounting] Error counting");

            Thread.Sleep(500);
            Console.Write("{0}...", i);
        }
    }

    public static void WorkerThreadMethod()
    {
        Console.WriteLine(
            "\n[WorkerThreadMethod] Thread started");

        int attempts = 1;

        Work:

        try
```

```
        {
            Console.WriteLine("[WorkerThreadMethod] " +
                "Attempt #{0} to call DoCounting",
                attempts);
            DoCounting();

            Console.WriteLine(
                "\n[WorkerThreadMethod] Finished counting");
        }
        catch(Exception e)
        {
            Console.WriteLine("\n\n[WorkerThreadMethod] " +
                "Caught exception {0}", e.GetType());
            if (attempts++ < 3)
            {
                Console.WriteLine("[WorkerThreadMethod] " +
                    "Retrying work");
                goto Work;
            }
        }
        finally
        {
            Console.WriteLine("[WorkerThreadMethod] " +
                "Cleaning up after exception");
        }
    }

    public static void Main()
    {
        ThreadStart worker =
            new ThreadStart(WorkerThreadMethod);

        Console.WriteLine("[Main] Creating worker thread");

        Thread t = new Thread(worker);
        t.Start();
    }
}
```

When you compile and execute this application, you'll see the output shown in Figure 18-2.

Figure 18-2   Normally you can use the *goto* statement and labels to jump out of exception *catch* blocks.

Now modify the *Main* method as follows:

```
public static void Main()
{
    ThreadStart worker =
        new ThreadStart(WorkerThreadMethod);

    Console.WriteLine("[Main] Creating worker thread");

    Thread t = new Thread(worker);
    t.Start();

    // Give the worker thread time to start.
    Console.WriteLine("[Main] Sleeping for 2 seconds");
    Thread.Sleep(2000);

    Console.WriteLine("\n[Main] Tired of waiting - " +
        "aborting thread");
    t.Abort();
}
```

In this modified code, I put the main thread to sleep for 2 seconds and then attempt to abort the worker thread. However, unlike the first version of this application, this version won't be able to jump out of the *catch* statement. In fact, if you look at Figure 18-3, you'll see that I was able to recover from a plain old *Exception* but couldn't escape the grips of the *ThreadAbortException*.

Figure 18-3   Although you can catch a *ThreadAbortException* exception, you can't prevent the termination of the thread on your own terms.

One last point about the *Thread.Abort* method is that there's no guarantee of exactly when the thread will cease execution. The runtime waits until the thread has reached what the documentation describes as a *safe point*. Therefore, if your code is dependent on something happening after the abort and you must be sure the thread has stopped, you can use the *Thread.Join* method. This synchronous call won't return until the thread's been stopped. Finally, note that once you abort a thread, it can't be restarted. In such a case, although you have a valid *Thread* object, you can't do anything useful with it in terms of executing code.

Scheduling Threads

When the processor switches between threads once a given thread's time slice has ended, the process of choosing which thread executes next is far from arbitrary. Each thread has an associated priority level that tells the processor how the thread should be scheduled in relation to the other threads in the system. This priority level is defaulted to *Normal* (more on this shortly) for threads that are created within the runtime. Threads that are created outside the runtime retain their original priority. You use the *Thread.Priority* property to view and set this value. The *Thread.Priority* property's setter takes a value of type *Thread.ThreadPriority*, an enum that defines these values: *Highest*, *AboveNormal*, *Normal*, *BelowNormal*, and *Lowest*.

To illustrate how priorities can affect even the simplest code, take a look at the following example, in which one worker thread counts from 1 to 10 and the other worker thread counts from 11 to 20. Note the nested loop within each *WorkerThread* method. Each loop represents work the thread would perform in a real application. Because these methods don't really do anything, not having these loops would result in each thread finishing its work in its first time slice!

```csharp
using System;
using System.Threading;

class ThreadSchedule1App
{
    public static void WorkerThreadMethod1()
    {
        Console.WriteLine("Worker thread started");

        Console.WriteLine("Worker thread - counting "
            "slowly from 1 to 10");
        for (int i = 1; i < 11; i++)
        {
            for (int j = 0; j < 100; j++)
            {
                Console.Write(".");
                // Code to imitate work being done.
                int a;
                a = 15;
            }
            Console.Write("{0}", i);
        }

        Console.WriteLine("Worker thread finished");
    }

    public static void WorkerThreadMethod2()
    {
        Console.WriteLine("Worker thread started");

        Console.WriteLine("Worker thread - counting " +
            "slowly from 11 to 20");
        for (int i = 11; i < 20; i++)
        {
            for (int j = 0; j < 100; j++)
            {
                Console.Write(".");
                // Code to imitate work being done.
                int a;
                a = 15;
            }
            Console.Write("{0}", i);
        }

        Console.WriteLine("Worker thread finished");
    }

    public static void Main()
```

```
    {
        ThreadStart worker1 =
            new ThreadStart(WorkerThreadMethod1);
        ThreadStart worker2 =
            new ThreadStart(WorkerThreadMethod2);

        Console.WriteLine("Main - Creating worker threads");

        Thread t1 = new Thread(worker1);
        Thread t2 = new Thread(worker2);

        t1.Start();
        t2.Start();
    }
}
```

If you build and run this application, you'll see that once the second thread is started, both threads get equal playing time with the processor, as Figure 18-4 shows.

Figure 18-4   When threads all run at the same priority, they receive the same amount of processor time, a scheme known as *round-robin scheduling*.

Now alter the *Priority* property for each thread as in the following code, and you'll see a much different result. Note that I've given the first thread the highest priority allowed and the second thread the lowest.

```
using System;
using System.Threading;

class ThreadSchedule2App
{
    public static void WorkerThreadMethod1()
```

```
{
    Console.WriteLine("Worker thread started");

    Console.WriteLine("Worker thread - counting " +
        "slowly from 1 to 10");
    for (int i = 1; i < 11; i++)
    {
        for (int j = 0; j < 100; j++)
        {
            Console.Write(".");
            // Code to imitate work being done.
            int a;
            a = 15;
        }

        Console.Write("{0}", i);
    }

    Console.WriteLine("Worker thread finished");
}

public static void WorkerThreadMethod2()
{
    Console.WriteLine("Worker thread started");

    Console.WriteLine("Worker thread - counting " +
        "slowly from 11 to 20");
    for (int i = 11; i < 20; i++)
    {
        for (int j = 0; j < 100; j++)
        {
            Console.Write(".");
            // Code to imitate work being done.
            int a;
            a = 15;
        }
        Console.Write("{0}", i);
    }

    Console.WriteLine("Worker thread finished");
}

public static void Main()
{
    ThreadStart worker1 =
        new ThreadStart(WorkerThreadMethod1);
    ThreadStart worker2 =
        new ThreadStart(WorkerThreadMethod2);
```

```
        Console.WriteLine("Main - Creating worker threads");

        Thread t1 = new Thread(worker1);
        Thread t2 = new Thread(worker2);

        t1.Priority = ThreadPriority.Highest;
        t2.Priority = ThreadPriority.Lowest;

        t1.Start();
        t2.Start();

        Console.ReadLine();
    }
}
```

You can see the results of this little test in Figure 18-5. Note specifically that the second thread has been set to such a low priority that it doesn't receive *any* cycles until after the first thread has completed its work.

Figure 18-5   Specifying the *Priority* property can dramatically alter how your threads execute in relation to one another.

One thing to keep in mind regarding thread priority is that you're contributing to—but not setting—when the thread will execute relative to other threads. The operating system eventually uses the value you indicate as part of its scheduling algorithm. In .NET, this algorithm is based on the priority level you specify (via the *Thread.Priority* property) as well as the process's *priority class* and *dynamic boost* values. All these values are then combined to create a numeric value (0–31 on an Intel processor) that represents the thread's priority. The thread with the highest value is the thread with the highest priority.

One last note on the subject of thread scheduling: use it with caution. Let's say you have a GUI application and a couple of worker threads that are doing some sort of asynchronous work. If you set the worker thread priorities too high, the user interface might become sluggish because the main thread in which the GUI application is running is receiving fewer CPU cycles. Unless you have a specific reason to schedule a thread with a high priority, it's best to let the thread's priority default to *Normal*.

Communicating Data to a Thread

At this point, you might be wondering how to pass data to a thread. After all, the *ThreadStart* delegate is defined as being parameterless, and if you attempt to pass to its constructor a method that defines parameters, the compiler will definitely bark at you. As it turns out, there are a few ways to accomplish this goal. One way is to use delegates. I'll cover that topic later in this chapter in "Using Delegates to Call Asynchronous Methods." For now, we'll look at the slightly simpler way—encapsulating both the thread delegate and the data in a single class. Here's an example of using this simpler technique, in which I have a class (*Sum*) that will be used to asynchronously add two numbers:

```
using System;
using System.Threading;

class Sum
{
    public Sum(int op1, int op2)
    {
        Console.WriteLine("[Sum.Sum] Instantiated with " +
            "values of {0} and {1}", op1, op2);
        this.op1 = op1;
        this.op2 = op2;
    }
    int op1;
    int op2;
    int result;
    public int Result{ get { return result; } }

    public void Add()
    {
        // Simulate work
        Thread.Sleep(5000);
        result = op1 + op2;
    }
};
```

```
class ThreadData
{
    static void Main()
    {
        Console.WriteLine("[Main] Instantiating the Sum " +
            "object and passing it the values to add");
        Sum sum = new Sum(6, 42);

        Console.WriteLine("[Main] Starting a thread using " +
            "a Sum delegate");
        Thread thread = new Thread(new ThreadStart(sum.Add));
        thread.Start();

        // Here we're simulating doing some work before
        // blocking on the Add method's completion.
        Console.Write("[Main] Doing other work");
        for (int i = 0; i < 10; i++)
        {
            Thread.Sleep(200);
            Console.Write(".");
        }

        Console.WriteLine("\n[Main] Waiting for Add to finish");
        thread.Join();

        Console.WriteLine("[Main] The result is {0}",
            sum.Result);
        Console.ReadLine();
    }
};
```

As you can see, the *Sum* class has a constructor that takes as parameters the two operands to be summed. These values are stored in member fields. The *Sum* class also defines a method named *Add* that will be used to construct a *StartThread* delegate.

Moving onto the *Main* method, we see that I'm simply instantiating a *Sum* object, passing it my favorite test values of *6* and *42*. Next I construct the *Start-Thread* delegate as mentioned and use it to create a new *Thread* object. Now when I call the *Thread.Start* method, the *Sum.Add* method will be called. The *Sum.Add* method has access to the two operands I want to add.

Once I've started the thread, I call the *Thread.Join* method to block the current thread until our *Sum.Add* method's thread has terminated. Finally, I simply reference the *Sum.Result* property. Figure 18-6 shows the results of running this application.

Figure 18-6   You can pass data to—and retrieve data from—threads by encapsulating both the thread delegate and the data in a single class.

Now that you've seen how to create threads, control their lifetimes, as well as pass and retrieve data, let's look at another important aspect of writing multithreaded applications—synchronizing access to critical code.

Thread Safety and Synchronization

When you're programming for a single-threaded environment, it's common to write methods in such a way that the object is in a temporarily invalid state at several points in the code. Obviously, if only one thread is accessing the object at a time, you're guaranteed that each method will complete before another method is called—meaning that the object is always in a valid state to any of the object's clients. However, when multiple threads are thrown into the mix, you can easily have situations in which the processor switches to another thread while your object is in an invalid state. If that thread also attempts to use this same object, the results can be quite unpredictable. Therefore, the term *thread safety* means that the members of an object always maintain a valid state when used concurrently by multiple threads.

So how do we prevent this unpredictable state? Actually, as is common in programming, there are several ways to address this well-known issue. In this section, I'll cover the most common means: synchronization. Through synchronization, you specify *critical sections* of code that can be entered by only one thread at a time, thereby guaranteeing that any temporary invalid states of your object aren't seen by the object's clients. We'll be looking at several means of defining critical sections, including the .NET *Monitor* and *Mutex* classes as well as the C# *lock* statement.

Protecting Code by Using the *Monitor* Class

The *System.Monitor* class enables you to serialize the access to blocks of code by means of locks and signals. For example, let's say that you have a method that updates a database and that this method can't be executed by two or more threads at the same time. If the work being performed by this method is especially time-consuming and you have multiple threads, any of which might call this method, you could have a serious problem on your hands. This situation is where the *Monitor* class comes in. Take a look at the following synchronization example. Here we have two threads, both of which will call the *Database.SaveData* method:

```
using System;
using System.Threading;

class Database
{
    public void SaveData(string text)
    {
        Console.WriteLine("[SaveData] Started");

        Console.WriteLine("[SaveData] Working");
        for (int i = 0; i < 50; i++)
        {
            Thread.Sleep(100);
            Console.Write(text);
        }

        Console.WriteLine("\n[SaveData] Ended");
    }
}

class ThreadMonitor1App
{
    public static Database db = new Database();

    public static void WorkerThreadMethod1()
    {
        Console.WriteLine("[WorkerThreadMethod1] Started");

        Console.WriteLine("[WorkerThreadMethod1] " +
            "Calling Database.SaveData");
        db.SaveData("x");

        Console.WriteLine("[WorkerThreadMethod1] Finished");
    }
```

```
public static void WorkerThreadMethod2()
{
    Console.WriteLine("[WorkerThreadMethod2] Started");

    Console.WriteLine("[WorkerThreadMethod2] " +
        "Calling Database.SaveData");
    db.SaveData("x");

    Console.WriteLine("[WorkerThreadMethod2] Finished");
}

public static void Main()
{
    ThreadStart worker1 =
        new ThreadStart(WorkerThreadMethod1);
    ThreadStart worker2 =
        new ThreadStart(WorkerThreadMethod2);

    Console.WriteLine("[Main] Creating and starting " +
        "worker threads");

    Thread t1 = new Thread(worker1);
    Thread t2 = new Thread(worker2);

    t1.Start();
    t2.Start();
}
}
```

If you look at Figure 18-7, you'll see that running this application confirms the worst: our application has both threads entering the *Database.SaveData* concurrently.

Figure 18-7   If code isn't thread-safe, you'll need to take extra precaution in ensuring that multiple threads can't call it concurrently.

The problem here is that if the *Database.SaveData* method needed to finish updating multiple tables before being called by another thread, we'd have a serious problem. Therefore, let's incorporate a *Monitor* object into the example to prevent a second thread from executing our *SaveData* method before the first thread exits the method.

To accomplish this task, simply insert a call to the static *Monitor.Enter* method where you want to begin code protection. When executed, this method attempts to obtain a monitor lock on the object. If another thread already has the lock, the method will block until that lock has been released. Note that there's no implicit box operation performed here, so you can supply only a reference type to this method. A call to the static *Monitor.Exit* method is then made to release the lock. Here's the example rewritten to force the serialization of access to the *Database.SaveData* method:

```
using System;
using System.Threading;

class Database
{
    public void SaveData(string text)
    {
        Console.WriteLine("[SaveData] Started");

        Monitor.Enter(this);
        Console.WriteLine("[SaveData] Working");
        for (int i = 0; i < 50; i++)
        {
            Thread.Sleep(100);
            Console.Write(text);
        }
        Monitor.Exit(this);

        Console.WriteLine("\n[SaveData] Ended");
    }
}

class ThreadMonitor2App
{
    public static Database db = new Database();

    public static void WorkerThreadMethod1()
    {
        Console.WriteLine("[WorkerThreadMethod1] Started");

        Console.WriteLine("[WorkerThreadMethod1] " +
            "Calling Database.SaveData");
```

```
        db.SaveData("x");

        Console.WriteLine("[WorkerThreadMethod1] Finished");
    }

    public static void WorkerThreadMethod2()
    {
        Console.WriteLine("[WorkerThreadMethod2] Started");

        Console.WriteLine("[WorkerThreadMethod2] " +
            "Calling Database.SaveData");
        db.SaveData("o");

        Console.WriteLine("[WorkerThreadMethod2] Finished");
    }

    public static void Main()
    {
        ThreadStart worker1 =
            new ThreadStart(WorkerThreadMethod1);
        ThreadStart worker2 =
            new ThreadStart(WorkerThreadMethod2);

        Console.WriteLine(
            "[Main] Creating and starting worker threads");

        Thread t1 = new Thread(worker1);
        Thread t2 = new Thread(worker2);

        t1.Start();
        t2.Start();

        Console.ReadLine();
    }
}
```

Now when you run the application, notice that even though the second thread called the *Database.SaveData* method, the *Monitor.Enter* method caused the second thread to block until the first thread had released its lock, as Figure 18-8 shows.

Figure 18-8   The *Monitor.Enter* method caused the second thread to block until the first thread released its lock.

Although our code does appear to work, there's one subtle but major error here. To see this error, modify the code as follows to throw an exception from *SaveData* and wrap both calls to *SaveData* in *try..catch* blocks:

```
using System;
using System.Threading;

class Database
{
    public void SaveData(string text)
    {
        Console.WriteLine("[SaveData] Started");

        Monitor.Enter(this);
        Console.WriteLine("[SaveData] Working");

        throw new Exception("ERROR!");

        for (int i = 0; i < 50; i++)
        {
            Thread.Sleep(100);
            Console.Write(text);
        }
        Monitor.Exit(this);

        Console.WriteLine("\n[SaveData] Ended");
    }
}

class ThreadMonitor3App
{
    public static Database db = new Database();
```

```
public static void WorkerThreadMethod1()
{
    Console.WriteLine("[WorkerThreadMethod1] Started");

    Console.WriteLine("[WorkerThreadMethod1] " +
        "Calling Database.SaveData");

    try
    {
        db.SaveData("x");
    }
    catch{}

    Console.WriteLine("[WorkerThreadMethod1] Finished");
}

public static void WorkerThreadMethod2()
{
    Console.WriteLine("[WorkerThreadMethod2] Started");

    Console.WriteLine("[WorkerThreadMethod2] " +
        "Calling Database.SaveData");
    try
    {
        db.SaveData("o");
    }
    catch{}

    Console.WriteLine("[WorkerThreadMethod2] Finished");
}

public static void Main()
{
    ThreadStart worker1 =
        new ThreadStart(WorkerThreadMethod1);
    ThreadStart worker2 =
        new ThreadStart(WorkerThreadMethod2);

    Console.WriteLine("[Main] Creating and starting " +
        "worker threads");

    Thread t1 = new Thread(worker1);
    Thread t2 = new Thread(worker2);

    t1.Start();
    t2.Start();

    Console.ReadLine();
}
}
```

Now if you run the application, you'll see results resembling those shown in Figure 18-9. Can you spot the problem? The first thread entered the *SaveData* method, whereupon access to the code was blocked (via the *Monitor.Enter* method). *SaveData* then threw an exception back to the caller (*WorkerThreadMethod1*). The problem is that *SaveData* never released the monitor! Now the second thread is blocked forever on the call to *Monitor.Enter*, and the application has hung.

Figure 18-9   If you're going to use the *Monitor* class, you must be sure to place the *Monitor.Exit* call in a *finally* block. Otherwise, you might hang up other threads upon an exception being caught.

To remedy this situation, simply place the code that you want protected in a *try* block and then call *Monitor.Exit* in the *finally* block. Here's the final version of the *SaveData* method:

```
public void SaveData(string text)
{
    Console.WriteLine("[SaveData] Started");

    try
    {
        Monitor.Enter(this);
        Console.WriteLine("[SaveData] Working");

        throw new Exception("ERROR!");

        for (int i = 0; i < 50; i++)
        {
            Thread.Sleep(100);
            Console.Write(text);
        }
    }
    finally
    {
```

```
        Monitor.Exit(this);
    }

    Console.WriteLine("\n[SaveData] Ended");
}
```

If you run the code with these modifications, you'll see that although the *SaveData* throws an exception for both threads, the application handles this situation and terminates normally. Simply remove the *throw* statement to get the same output as you saw in the ThreadMonitor2 application. Now let's take a look at the C# form of the *Monitor* class, the *lock* statement.

Using Monitor Locks with the C# *lock* Statement

Although the C# *lock* statement doesn't support the full array of features found in the *Monitor* class, it does enable you to obtain and release a monitor lock. To use the *lock* statement, simply specify the statement with the code being serialized in braces. The braces indicate the starting point and the stopping point of the code being protected, so there's no need for an *unlock* statement. The following code will produce the same synchronized output as the ThreadMonitor2 example:

```
using System;
using System.Threading;

class Database
{
    public void SaveData(string text)
    {
        lock(this)
        {
            Console.WriteLine("Database.SaveData - Started");

            Console.WriteLine("Database.SaveData - Working");
            for (int i = 0; i < 100; i++)
            {
                Console.Write(text);
            }

            Console.WriteLine("\nDatabase.SaveData - Ended");
        }
    }
}

class ThreadLockApp
{
```

```
public static Database db = new Database();

public static void WorkerThreadMethod1()
{
    Console.WriteLine("Worker thread #1 - Started");

    Console.WriteLine("Worker thread #1 - Calling " +
        "Database.SaveData");
    db.SaveData("x");

    Console.WriteLine("Worker thread #1 - Returned " +
        "from Output");
}

public static void WorkerThreadMethod2()
{
    Console.WriteLine("Worker thread #2 - Started");

    Console.WriteLine("Worker thread #2 - Calling " +
        "Database.SaveData");
    db.SaveData("o");

    Console.WriteLine("Worker thread #2 - Returned " +
        "from Output");
}

public static void Main()
{
    ThreadStart worker1 =
        new ThreadStart(WorkerThreadMethod1);
    ThreadStart worker2 =
        new ThreadStart(WorkerThreadMethod2);

    Console.WriteLine("Main - Creating worker threads");

    Thread t1 = new Thread(worker1);
    Thread t2 = new Thread(worker2);

    t1.Start();
    t2.Start();

    Console.ReadLine();
}
}
```

The generated Microsoft intermediate language (MSIL), shown in Figure 18-10, is what's interesting here. The first thing to look at is the fact that the *lock* statement actually does generate code to use the *Monitor* class. The second item of note is that the *lock* statement resulted in a *try..finally* block being inserted into our code, preventing us from hanging the system when a *Monitor* object is left locked.

```
 Database::SaveData : void(string)                                    _ □ ×
IL_000d:  call       void [mscorlib]System.Threading.Monitor::Enter(object)
.try
{
  IL_0012:  ldstr      "Database.SaveData - Working"
  IL_0017:  call       void [mscorlib]System.Console::WriteLine(string)
  IL_001c:  ldc.i4.0
  IL_001d:  stloc.0
  IL_001e:  br.s       IL_002a
  IL_0020:  ldarg.1
  IL_0021:  call       void [mscorlib]System.Console::Write(string)
  IL_0026:  ldloc.0
  IL_0027:  ldc.i4.1
  IL_0028:  add
  IL_0029:  stloc.0
  IL_002a:  ldloc.0
  IL_002b:  ldc.i4.s   100
  IL_002d:  blt.s      IL_0020
  IL_002f:  leave.s    IL_0038
} // end .try
finally
{
  IL_0031:  ldloc.1
  IL_0032:  call       void [mscorlib]System.Threading.Monitor::Exit(object)
  IL_0037:  endfinally
} // end handler
```

Figure 18-10   The *lock* statement prevents us from hanging the system when a *Monitor* object is left locked.

Synchronizing Code by Using the *Mutex* Class

The *Mutex* class—defined in the *System.Threading* namespace—is a run-time representation of the Win32 system primitive of the same name. You can use a mutex to serialize access to code just as you'd use a monitor lock, but mutexes are much slower because of their increased flexibility. The term *mutex* comes from *mutually exclusive*; just as only one thread at a time can obtain a monitor lock for a given object, only one thread at a time can obtain a given mutex.

You can create a mutex in C# with the following three constructors:

```
Mutex( )
Mutex(bool initiallyOwned)
Mutex(bool initiallyOwned, string mutexName)
```

The first constructor creates a mutex with no name and makes the current thread the owner of that mutex. Therefore, the current thread locks the mutex. The second constructor takes only a Boolean flag that designates whether the thread creating the mutex wants to own it (lock it). And the third constructor allows you to specify whether the current thread owns the mutex as well as allowing you to specify the name of the mutex. Let's now incorporate a mutex to serialize access to the *Database.SaveData* method:

```
using System;
using System.Threading;
```

```csharp
class Database
{
    static Mutex mutex = new Mutex(false);

    public static void SaveData(string text)
    {
        mutex.WaitOne();

        Console.WriteLine("Database.SaveData - Started");

        Console.WriteLine("Database.SaveData - Working");
        for (int i = 0; i < 100; i++)
        {
            Console.Write(text);
        }

        Console.WriteLine("\nDatabase.SaveData - Ended");

        mutex.Close();
    }
}

class ThreadMutexApp
{
    public static void WorkerThreadMethod1()
    {
        Console.WriteLine("Worker thread #1 - Started");
        Console.WriteLine("Worker thread #1 - Calling " +
            "Database.SaveData");
        Database.SaveData("x");

        Console.WriteLine("Worker thread #1 - Returned " +
            "from Output");
    }

    public static void WorkerThreadMethod2()
    {
      Console.WriteLine("Worker thread #2 - Started");
      Console.WriteLine("Worker thread #2 - Calling " +
          "Database.SaveData");
      Database.SaveData("o");

      Console.WriteLine("Worker thread #2 - Returned " +
          "from Output");
    }

    public static void Main()
```

```
    {
        ThreadStart worker1 =
            new ThreadStart(WorkerThreadMethod1);
        ThreadStart worker2 =
            new ThreadStart(WorkerThreadMethod2);

        Console.WriteLine("Main - Creating worker threads");

        Thread t1 = new Thread(worker1);
        Thread t2 = new Thread(worker2);

        t1.Start();
        t2.Start();

        Console.ReadLine();
    }
}
```

Now the *Database* class defines a *Mutex* field. We don't want the thread to own the mutex just yet because we'd have no way of getting into the *SaveData* method. The first line of the *SaveData* method shows you how you must attempt to acquire the mutex—with the *Mutex.WaitOne* method. At the end of the method is a call to the *Close* method, which releases the mutex.

The *WaitOne* method is also overloaded to provide more flexibility in terms of allowing you to define how much time the thread will wait for the mutex to become available. Here are the overloads:

```
WaitOne( )
WaitOne(TimeSpan time, bool exitContext)
WaitOne(int milliseconds, bool exitContext)
```

The basic difference between these overloads is that the first version—used in the example—will wait indefinitely, while the second and third versions will wait for the specified amount of time, expressed with either a *TimeSpan* value or an *int* value.

Using Delegates to Call Asynchronous Methods

One powerful and flexible way of starting a worker thread and passing it data is through asynchronous delegates. Recall from Chapter 14, "Delegates and Event Handlers," that when you define a delegate in C#, a *System.Multicast-Delegate*-derived class is actually created by the compiler and that, in addition to a constructor, this class contains the following three methods: *Invoke*, *Begin-Invoke*, and *EndInvoke*.

In Chapter 14, you learned all about the *Invoke* method, but I didn't talk much about the *BeginInvoke* and *EndInvoke* methods. This omission was made because these methods specifically address the issue of asynchronous method invocation, which I cover in this chapter. Therefore, let's see how to use these methods and the *IAsyncResult* interface that's used to synchronize on the asynchronous call.

In this example, I have a simple method that I'll call asynchronously and that will take three parameters—adding the first two and placing the result in the third:

```
using System;
using System.Threading;

class AsyncDelegatesBlocked
{
    public static int Add(int op1, int op2, out int result)
    {
        Thread.Sleep(3000); // Simulating work
        return (result = op1 + op2);
    }
    public delegate int AddDelegate(int op1, int op2,
        out int result);

    static void Main()
    {
        int result;
        AddDelegate add = new AddDelegate(Add);

        Console.WriteLine("[Main] Invoking the asynchronous " +
            "Add method");
        IAsyncResult iAR = add.BeginInvoke(6, 42, out result,
            null, null);

        // Here we're simulating doing some work before
        // blocking on the Add method's completion.
        Console.Write("[Main] Doing other work");
        for (int i = 0; i < 10; i++)
        {
            Thread.Sleep(200);
            Console.Write(".");
        }

        Console.WriteLine("\n[Main] Waiting for Add to finish");
        iAR.AsyncWaitHandle.WaitOne(); // Blocks until thread
                                       // is completed

        Console.WriteLine("[Main] Add finished, cleaning up");
        add.EndInvoke(out result, iAR);
```

```
        Console.WriteLine("[Main] The result is {0}", result);
        Console.ReadLine();
    }
};
```

The first thing to notice is that we have a method named *Add* and a delegate named *AddDelegate*. Now let's look at the MSIL, shown in Figure 18-11, for the *BeginInvoke* method.

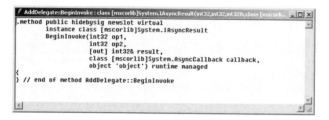

```
AddDelegate::BeginInvoke : class [mscorlib]System.IAsyncResult(int32,int32,int32&,class [mscorli..
.method public hidebysig newslot virtual
        instance class [mscorlib]System.IAsyncResult
        BeginInvoke(int32 op1,
                int32 op2,
                [out] int32& result,
                class [mscorlib]System.AsyncCallback callback,
                object 'object') runtime managed
{
} // end of method AddDelegate::BeginInvoke
```

Figure 18-11 The *BeginInvoke* method signature contains the parameters specified in the delegate's signature in addition to the parameters for a *System.AsyncCallback* object and a state object.

As you can see from the *BeginInvoke* method signature, this method takes the parameters that were defined for the delegate as well as taking a *System.AsyncCallback* delegate and two more parameters. The first of those parameters is a *System.AsyncCallback* delegate. Although this value can be *null*, it's also used to specify the method that you want the system to call when then asynchronous method has completed its work. The last parameter for the *BeginInvoke* method is a *state object*. This object can take any value you want and will be passed to the *AsyncCallback* delegate when the method finishes. Finally, the *BeginInvoke* method returns an *IAsynResult* interface pointer. This interface is used to retrieve the state object passed to the *BeginInvoke* method, block on the completion of the method, or query as to whether the method has completed.

Now let's look at the *Main* method to see how all this works. The first thing I do is create a local *AddDelegate* method named *add*. At this point, we could call this delegate synchronously as follows, thereby causing the delegate's *Invoke* method to be called:

```
int total;
Console.WriteLine(add(2, 2, out total));
```

However, we want to see how to use delegates for asynchronous processing. Therefore, I next call the delegate's *BeginInvoke* method, passing it two literal values to be added together and an out parameter that will contain the sum of those two numbers. This call has the effect of creating a worker thread on

which my *Add* method will be invoked. As mentioned earlier, the return value
from the *BeginInvoke* method is an *IAsyncResult* interface object.

Next I simulate some work by spinning through a simple *for* loop, and
then I tell the *IAsyncResult* object that I want the thread in which *Main* exists to
block until the *Add* method completes. This task is done by calling the *IAsyncResult.AsyncWaitHandle.WaitOne* method.

Once the *WaitOne* method returns, a call is placed to the delegate's *EndInvoke* method. If you take a look at Figure 18-12, you can see that the *EndInvoke* method can be used to return values in one of two ways.

```
AddDelegate::EndInvoke : int32(int32&,class [mscorlib]System.IAsyncResult)
.method public hidebysig newslot virtual
        instance int32  EndInvoke([out] int32& result,
                                class [mscorlib]System.IAsyncResult result) runtime managed
{
} // end of method AddDelegate::EndInvoke
```

Figure 18-12   The *EndInvoke* method signature defines a return value consistent with
the delegate's return value as well as a parameter for each out parameter defined for the
delegate.

As you can see from the *EndInvoke* signature, each out parameter that you
define on the delegate is automatically placed in the *EndInvoke* method's signature. This arrangement gives you the ability to have a thread return as many
values as you need without requiring the method to create a struct or class to
contain those values. In addition, if the delegate is defined as returning a single
value, the *EndInvoke* method is also defined as returning that value. Having
said that, in my example, the result being placed and returned in an out parameter was done to show you the two ways of returning values from an asynchronous method. In a practical application, you probably wouldn't return the same
value both ways. Figure 18-13 shows the results of running this application.

Figure 18-13   The AsyncDelegatesBlocked program in action.

Now let's look at how to use a callback method so that the asynchronous method can simply notify us upon its completion. As mentioned previously, the *BeginInvoke* method takes a callback method as its penultimate parameter and a state object as its last parameter. You'll also recall that I stated that the state object is used to pass information that will later be accessed by the callback method. Therefore, because we know that we can retrieve the asynchronous method's returned values by calling its *EndInvoke* method, all we need to do is pass the delegate as the state object! Take a look at the following demo to see an example of this:

```
using System;
using System.Threading;

class AsyncDelegatesCallback
{
    public static int Add(int op1, int op2, out int result)
    {
        Thread.Sleep(3000); // Simulating work
        return (result = op1 + op2);
    }
    public delegate int AddDelegate(int op1, int op2,
        out int result);

    public static void AnnounceSum(IAsyncResult iar)
    {
        AddDelegate add = (AddDelegate)iar.AsyncState;

        int result;
        add.EndInvoke(out result, iar);

        Console.WriteLine("[AnnounceSum] The result is {0}",
            result);
    }

    static void Main()
    {
        int result;
        AddDelegate add = new AddDelegate(Add);

        Console.WriteLine("[Main] Invoking the asynchronous " +
            "Add method");
        add.BeginInvoke(6, 42, out result,
            new AsyncCallback(AnnounceSum), add);

        Thread.Sleep(1000); // Give async method enough time
                            // to finish.
        Console.ReadLine();
    }
};
```

As you can see, the first thing I did was to define a callback method named *AnnounceSum*. Note that this method takes as its only argument the *IAsynResult* interface. In the *add.BeginInvoke* method call, I simply pass the parameters that *AddDelegate* requires as well as an *AsyncCallback* delegate (constructed with the *AnnounceSum* method) and a reference to the *add* delegate. Now when the system calls the callback method, all I need do is retrieve the state object (via the *IAsyncResult.AsyncState* member), cast that object to the *Add* delegate, and call *EndInvoke* to retrieve the completed method's returned values. Note that I've placed a call to *Thread.Sleep* at the end of the *Main* method; otherwise, the application would end before the asynchronous method finishes. The results of this application is as follows:

```
[Main] Invoking the asynchronous Add method (passing callback
 method)
[AnnounceSum] Callback invoked indicating that the async method
 is completed
[AnnounceSum] Casting state object to the Add delegate
[AnnounceSum] Calling EndInvoke method to retrieve async
 method's returned data
[AnnounceSum] The result is 48
```

Note   Although passing the delegate as a state object obviously works, it means either not passing state data or writing a wrapper class to include the state data and a delegate reference. Another way of being able to call the delegate's *EndInvoke* method from the callback method is to cast the *IAsyncResult* interface to the *AsyncResult* class (found in the *System.Runtime.Remoting.Messaging* namespace). You can then directly access its public *AsyncDelegate* property as follows:

```
using System.Runtime.Remoting.Messaging;

⋮

static void Main()
{
⋮
    // Client code can now pass null or a "true" state object
    add.BeginInvoke(6, 42, out result,
        new AsyncCallback(AnnounceSum), null);
⋮
}

public static void AnnounceSum(IAsyncResult iar)
{
⋮
```

```
        // Callback method can now use the IAsynResult
        // interface (cast to AsyncResult)
        // and not have to use a state object to
        // access the delegate
        AsyncResult ar = (AsyncResult)iar;
        AddDelegate add = (AddDelegate)ar.AsyncDelegate;

        int result;
        add.EndInvoke(out result, iar);
    ⋮
    }
```

So, what this all boils down to is that asynchronous delegates enable you to invoke methods (with parameters) on a separate thread, monitor that method for completion, and then determine the return value or values—without having to do anything with the *Threading* namespace! Now let's look at the issues of thread safety and some guidelines on when to incorporate multithreading into an application.

Thread Safety and the .NET Classes

One question I see quite often in the newsgroups and mailing lists is whether all the .NET *System.** classes are thread-safe. The answer is, "No, and they shouldn't be." You could severely cripple a system's performance if all classes serialized access to their functionality. For example, imagine attempting to use one of the collection classes if it obtained a monitor lock each time you called its *Add* method. Now let's say you instantiate a collection object and add about a thousand objects to it. Performance would be dismal—to the point of making the system unusable.

Threading Guidelines

When do you need to use threads and when, if ever, is it best to avoid them like the plague? In this section, I'll describe some common scenarios in which threads can be extremely valuable to your application and some situations in which it would be best to avoid using multiple threads.

When to Use Threads

You should use threads when you're striving for increased concurrency, simplified design, and better utilization of CPU time.

Increased Concurrency

Very often, applications need to accomplish more than one task at a time. For example, I once wrote a document retrieval system for banks that accessed data from optical disks that were stored in optical disk jukeboxes. Imagine the massive amounts of data we're talking about here: picture a jukebox with one drive and 50 platters serving up gigabytes of data. It could sometimes take as long as 5 to 10 seconds to load a disk and find the requested document. Needless to say, it wouldn't exactly be the definition of productivity if my application blocked user input while doing all this. Therefore, to deal with the user input case, I spun off another thread to do the physical work of retrieving the data, allowing the user to continue working. This thread would notify the main thread when the document was loaded. This is a great example of having independent activities—loading a document and handling the user interface—that can be handled with two separate threads.

Simplified Design

A popular way to simplify the design of complex systems is to use queues and asynchronous processing. Using such a design, you'd have queues set up to handle the various events that transpire in your system. Instead of methods being called directly, objects are created and placed in queues where they'll be handled. At the other end of these queues are server programs with multiple threads that are set up to "listen" for messages coming in to the queues. The advantage of this type of simplified design is that it provides for reliable, robust, and extendable systems.

Better Utilization of CPU Time

Many times, your application isn't really doing any work while it's enjoying its time slice. In my document retrieval example, one thread was waiting on the jukebox to load the platter. Obviously, this wait was a hardware issue and required no use of the CPU. Other examples of wait times include instances where you're printing a document or waiting on the hard disk or CD-ROM drive. In each case, the CPU isn't being utilized. Such cases are candidates for being moved to background threads.

When Not to Use Threads

Developers new to using threads make the common mistake of attempting to deploy them in every application. This overuse can be much worse than not using threads at all! As with any other tool in your programming arsenal, you should use threads only when appropriate. You should avoid using multiple threads in your application in at least three cases: when the costs outweigh the benefits, when you haven't benchmarked both cases, and when you can't come up with a reason to use threads.

Costs Outweigh Benefits

As you saw in the "Thread Safety and Synchronization" section earlier in this chapter, writing multithreaded applications takes a bit of time and effort in the design of the code. There will be times when the slight gains enjoyed by having multiple threads just isn't worth the extra time required to make your code thread-safe.

You Haven't Benchmarked Both Cases

If you're new to multithreaded programming, it might surprise you to find that often the overhead required by CPU thread creation and scheduling to achieve modest gains in CPU utilization can actually result in single-threaded applications running faster! It all depends on what you're doing and if you're truly splitting independent tasks into threads. For example, if you have to read three files from disk, spawning three threads won't do you any good because each thread has to use the same hard disk. Therefore, always be sure to benchmark a prototype of both a single-threaded version and a multithreaded version of your system before taking the extra time and incurring the extra cost of designing around a solution that might actually backfire in terms of performance.

No Good Reason Why You Should

Using multiple threads *shouldn't* be the default. Because of the inherent complexities of writing multithreaded applications, you should always default to single-threaded code unless you have a good reason to do otherwise.

Summary

Multithreading allows applications to divide a program into independent tasks to make the most efficient use of the processor's time. However, adding multiple threads to an application isn't the right choice in all situations and can sometimes slow the application down. Thread management and creation in C# is done through the *System.Threading.Thread* class. An important concept related to the creation and use of threads is thread safety. Thread safety means that the members of an object always maintain a valid state when used concurrently by multiple threads. Along with learning the syntax of multithreading, it's important that you understand when to use it—to increase concurrency, to simplify design, and to better utilize CPU time.

19

Querying Metadata with Reflection

One very powerful feature of .NET is that it allows you to write code to access an application's metadata through a process known as *reflection*. Put simply, reflection is the ability to discover type information at run time. This chapter will describe the Reflection API and explain how you can use it to iterate through an assembly's modules and types as well as to retrieve the different design-time characteristics of a type. You'll also see several advanced uses for reflection, such as dynamically invoking methods and use type information (through late binding) and even creating and executing Microsoft intermediate language (MSIL) code at run time!

More Info   The subject of reflection with regard to attributes is covered in Chapter 6, "Attributes."

The Reflection API Hierarchy

The .NET Reflection API is actually a lattice of classes—part of which is shown in Figure 19-1—that's defined in the *System.Reflection* namespace. These classes enable you to logically traverse assembly and type information. You can start at any place in this hierarchy, depending on your application's specific design needs.

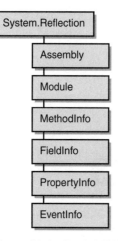

Figure 19-1   Partial .NET *System.Reflection* class hierarchy.

Note that these classes encompass a great deal of functionality. Rather than listing every method and field for each class, I'll present an overview of the key classes and then show a demo that illustrates the functionality you'd most likely need to incorporate in your applications.

The *Type* Class

At the center of reflection is the abstract *System.Type* class. This class is the root of all reflection operations and represents every type inside the system. This class is the primary way to access metadata, and it acts as a gateway to the Reflection API. As you'll soon see, the members of the *Type* class are used to retrieve information about a type declaration. This information includes any constructors, methods, fields, properties, and events defined for the type, as well as the module and the assembly in which the class is deployed. Let's now look at how to acquire a *Type* reference.

Retrieving a Type Reference

The first thing to note is that the *Type* class is a singleton in that two *Type* objects for a given type always refer to the same object. This arrangement is for the synchronization of multiple static method invocations and for comparison of *Type* objects using reference equality (*Object.ReferenceEquals*). Second, a *Type* object can represent any of the following types:

- Classes

- Value types

- Arrays

- Interfaces

- Pointers

- Enumerations (enum structures)

As you'll see throughout the next several demo applications, there are quite a few ways to acquire a *Type* reference.

Retrieving the Type of an Instance

You'll recall from Chapter 2, "The .NET Type System," that all classes ultimately derive from the *System.Object* class. One of the methods of that class is the *Get-Type* method, and it represents the easiest and most basic means of retrieving an object's type information. In the following example, the *Type* object associated with an instantiated *int* is retrieved and its name is displayed:

```
using System;
using System.Reflection;

class TypeObjectFromInstanceApp
{
    public static void Main(string[] args)
    {
        int i = 6;
        Type type = i.GetType();
        Console.WriteLine(type.Name);
    }
}
```

Retrieving the Type from a Name

In addition to being able to query any object instance for its associated *Type* object, you can call the *Type* class's *GetType* method, which takes the name of the desired type as one of its parameters. Excluding the inherited *GetType* method from *Object*, the *Type* class has three static overloaded versions of this method:

```
public static Type GetType(string name);
public static Type GetType(string name, bool throw);
public static Type GetType(string name, bool throw,
    bool ignoreCase);
```

In each case, *name* represents the fully qualified name (*namespace.type-name*) of the desired type. The parameter *throw* indicates that you want the runtime to throw an exception (*System.TypeLoadException*) if the specified type can't be found. Finally, the Boolean parameter *ignoreCase* indicates whether you want a case-sensitive search for the value indicated in the *name* parameter. Here's a simple example in which the application attempts to retrieve a *Type* object for the type name specified on the command line:

```
using System;
using System.Reflection;

class TypeObjectFromNameApp
{
    public static void DisplaySyntax()
    {
        Console.WriteLine("\nSyntax: TypeObjectFromName " +
            "<typename>\n");
    }

    public static void DisplayTypeInfo(string typename)
    {
        try
        {
            Type type = Type.GetType(typename, true);
            Console.WriteLine("\n'{0}' is located in the " +
                "module {1}", typename, type.Module);
        }
        catch(TypeLoadException e)
        {
            Console.WriteLine("\n'{0}' could not be " +
                "located. Did you qualify with a namespace?",
                typename);
        }
    }

    public static void Main(string[] args)
    {
        if (1 != args.Length) DisplaySyntax();
        else DisplayTypeInfo(args[0]);
    }
}
```

Passing a value of *System.ValueType* results in the following output:

```
'System.ValueType' is located in the module
CommonLanguageRuntimeLibrary
```

As you can see, the *Type* class defines a property named *Module* that indicates the module in which the type exists. In the next section, we'll look at the various data that can be retrieved about a type from the *Type* class. Also note that you can't use the C# aliases when calling the *Type.GetType* method because this class and method are part of the .NET Framework and not specific to C#.

Interrogating Types

As mentioned, once you've instantiated a *Type* object for a given type, you can query that type as to whether the type is abstract, an array, a class, and so on. The following code illustrates this by displaying several of these properties for the type name passed on the command line:

```
using System;
using System.Reflection;

class QueryTypesApp
{
    public static void DisplaySyntax()
    {
        Console.WriteLine("\nSyntax: QueryTypes <typename>\n");
    }

    public static void QueryType(string typename)
    {
        try
        {
            Type type = Type.GetType(typename, true, true);

            Console.WriteLine("Type name: {0}",
                type.FullName);
            Console.WriteLine("\tHasElementType = {0}",
                type.HasElementType);
            Console.WriteLine("\tIsAbstract = {0}",
                type.IsAbstract);
            Console.WriteLine("\tIsAnsiClass = {0}",
                type.IsAnsiClass);
            Console.WriteLine("\tIsArray = {0}",
                type.IsArray);
            Console.WriteLine("\tIsAutoClass = {0}",
                type.IsAutoClass);
            Console.WriteLine("\tIsAutoLayout = {0}",
                type.IsAutoLayout);
            Console.WriteLine("\tIsByRef = {0}",
                type.IsByRef);
            Console.WriteLine("\tIsClass = {0}",
                type.IsClass);
```

```csharp
        Console.WriteLine("\tIsCOMObject = {0}",
            type.IsCOMObject);
        Console.WriteLine("\tIsContextful = {0}",
            type.IsContextful);
        Console.WriteLine("\tIsEnum = {0}",
            type.IsEnum);
        Console.WriteLine("\tIsExplicitLayout = {0}",
            type.IsExplicitLayout);
        Console.WriteLine("\tIsImport = {0}",
            type.IsImport);
        Console.WriteLine("\tIsInterface = {0}",
            type.IsInterface);
        Console.WriteLine("\tIsLayoutSequential = {0}",
            type.IsLayoutSequential);
        Console.WriteLine("\tIsMarshalByRef = {0}",
            type.IsMarshalByRef);
        Console.WriteLine("\tIsNestedAssembly = {0}",
            type.IsNestedAssembly);
        Console.WriteLine("\tIsNestedFamANDAssem = {0}",
            type.IsNestedFamANDAssem);
        Console.WriteLine("\tIsNestedFamily = {0}",
            type.IsNestedFamily);
        Console.WriteLine("\tIsNestedFamORAssem = {0}",
            type.IsNestedFamORAssem);
        Console.WriteLine("\tIsNestedPrivate = {0}",
            type.IsNestedPrivate);
        Console.WriteLine("\tIsNestedPublic = {0}",
            type.IsNestedPublic);
        Console.WriteLine("\tIsNotPublic = {0}",
            type.IsNotPublic);
        Console.WriteLine("\tIsPointer = {0}",
            type.IsPointer);
        Console.WriteLine("\tIsPrimitive = {0}",
            type.IsPrimitive);
        Console.WriteLine("\tIsPublic = {0}",
            type.IsPublic);
        Console.WriteLine("\tIsSealed = {0}",
            type.IsSealed);
        Console.WriteLine("\tIsSerializable = {0}",
            type.IsSerializable);
        Console.WriteLine("\tIsSpecialName = {0}",
            type.IsSpecialName);
        Console.WriteLine("\tIsUnicodeClass = {0}",
            type.IsUnicodeClass);
        Console.WriteLine("\tIsValueType = {0}",
            type.IsValueType);
    }
    catch(System.TypeLoadException e)
    {
        Console.WriteLine("{0} is not a valid type",
```

```
                typename);
        }
    }

    public static void Main(string[] args)
    {
        if (1 != args.Length) DisplaySyntax();
        else QueryType(args[0]);

        Console.ReadLine();
    }
}
```

Calling this application and passing a value of *System.ValueType* on the command line results in the following output:

```
Type name: System.ValueType
        HasElementType = False
        IsAbstract = True
        IsAnsiClass = True
        IsArray = False
        IsAutoClass = False
        IsAutoLayout = True
        IsByRef = False

        IsCOMObject = False
        IsContextful = False
        IsEnum = False
        IsExplicitLayout = False
        IsImport = False
        IsInterface = False
        IsLayoutSequential = False
        IsMarshalByRef = False
        IsNestedAssembly = False
        IsNestedFamANDAssem = False
        IsNestedFamily = False
        IsNestedFamORAssem = False
        IsNestedPrivate = False
        IsNestedPublic = False
        IsNotPublic = False
        IsPointer = False
        IsPrimitive = False
        IsPublic = True
        IsSealed = False
        IsSerializable = True
        IsSpecialName = False
        IsUnicodeClass = False
        IsValueType = False
```

Working with Assemblies and Modules

As you learned in Chapter 1, "Building C# Applications and Libraries," an assembly is a physical file that consists of one or more .NET portable executable (PE) files and enables you to semantically group functionality for easier deployment and versioning. The .NET runtime's representation of an assembly—and the apex of the reflection object hierarchy—is the *Assembly* class.

You can do many things with the *Assembly* class. Here are some of the more common tasks that we'll look at:

■ Iterating through an assembly's types

■ Listing an assembly's modules

■ Determining identification information, such as the assembly's physical filename and location

■ Inspecting versioning and security information

■ Retrieving the assembly's entry point

Iterating Through the Types of an Assembly

A common use of reflection is to enumerate and reflect all the types in a given assembly. In fact, you can find many utilities online that show off the true power of reflection by enabling you to search through the entire Framework for a given type. When such a utility finds one of these given types, the utility displays all kinds of neat information about the type. One such utility is Microsoft FxCop, available at *www.gotdotnet.com/team/libraries/default.aspx*. Although writing a full-blown application of that magnitude is certainly beyond the scope of a single chapter, the following demo illustrates how to enumerate all the types of the specified assembly:

```
using System;
using System.Diagnostics;
using System.Reflection;

class Attr : System.Attribute
{
};

enum RGB
{
    red = 0xFF000,
    green = 0x00FF00,
    blue = 0x0000FF
```

```csharp
};

class BaseClass
{
    static readonly string Infinity;
    static BaseClass()
    {
        Infinity = "0/1";
    }
    protected BaseClass(string s) { }
};

class DerivedClass : BaseClass
{
    DerivedClass() : base("test") { }
};

struct Point
{
    int x;
    int y;
};

class GetAssemblyInfoApp
{
    protected static Assembly GetAssembly(string[] args)
    {
        Assembly assembly;

        if (0 == args.Length)
        {
            assembly = Assembly.GetExecutingAssembly();
        }
        else
        {
            assembly = Assembly.LoadFrom(args[0]);
        }

        return assembly;
    }

    public static void Main(string[] args)
    {
        Assembly assembly = GetAssembly(args);
        if (null != assembly)
        {
            Console.WriteLine("Loading type info for {0}",
                assembly);
```

```
        Type[] types = assembly.GetTypes();
        foreach(Type type in types)
        {
            Console.WriteLine("\nType: {0}", type);
            foreach(MemberInfo member in type.GetMembers())
            {
                Console.WriteLine("\tMember: {0}", member);
            }
        }
    }

    Console.ReadLine();
    }
};
```

Note   If you're attempting to run code that needs security clearance—such as code that uses the Reflection API—over an intranet, you'll need to modify your .NET security policy settings by using the Code Access Security Policy tool (CASpol.exe). This utility is covered in Chapter 23, "Security."

Main first calls *GetAssembly*, passing the command-line arguments. The *GetAssembly* method then determines whether an assembly name was specified. If an assembly name was specified, that assembly is loaded by using the static *Assembly.LoadFrom* method, which has the following two overloads:

```
public static Assembly LoadFrom(string filename);
public static Assembly LoadFrom(string filename, Evidence ev);
```

The *filename* parameter is used to specify the filename or path, while the *Evidence* parameter of the second overload is used to specify the security evidence used in loading the assembly.

More Info   Security evidence is covered in Chapter 23.

If an assembly name wasn't specified, *GetAssembly* calls the static *Assembly.GetExecutingAssembly* method. As the name suggests, this method simply determines the assembly containing the method that made the call and returns a reference to that assembly object.

Once you have an *Assembly* object, getting its defined array of *Type* objects is done via a call to the *GetTypes* instance method. I'm not doing anything fancy here—I'm simply using a *foreach* statement to iterate through the *Type* array and printing out the name of each type that was found in the assembly. In addition, the code calls the *Type* object's *GetMembers* method. This method returns an array of *System.Reflection.MemberInfo* objects. This namespace exists mainly to reflect on the members of a given type. Running this application results in this (somewhat) expected output:

```
Loading type info for GetAssemblyInfo, Version=1.0.794.21892,
 Culture=neutral, PublicKeyToken=null

Type: Attr
        Member: Boolean IsDefaultAttribute()
        Member: Boolean Match(System.Object)
        Member: System.Object get_TypeId()
        Member: Int32 GetHashCode()
        Member: Boolean Equals(System.Object)
        Member: System.String ToString()
        Member: System.Type GetType()
        Member: Void .ctor()
        Member: System.Object TypeId

Type: RGB
        Member: Int32 value__
        Member: RGB red
        Member: RGB green
        Member: RGB blue
        Member: System.String ToString(System.IFormatProvider)
        Member: System.TypeCode GetTypeCode()
        Member: System.String ToString(System.String, System.IFormatProvider)
        Member: Int32 CompareTo(System.Object)
        Member: Int32 GetHashCode()
        Member: Boolean Equals(System.Object)
        Member: System.String ToString()
        Member: System.String ToString(System.String)
        Member: System.Type GetType()

Type: BaseClass
        Member: Int32 GetHashCode()
        Member: Boolean Equals(System.Object)
        Member: System.String ToString()
        Member: System.Type GetType()

Type: DerivedClass
        Member: Int32 GetHashCode()
```

```
        Member: Boolean Equals(System.Object)
        Member: System.String ToString()
        Member: System.Type GetType()

Type: Point
        Member: Int32 GetHashCode()
        Member: Boolean Equals(System.Object)
        Member: System.String ToString()
        Member: System.Type GetType()

Type: GetAssemblyInfoApp
        Member: Int32 GetHashCode()
        Member: Boolean Equals(System.Object)
        Member: System.String ToString()
        Member: Void Main(System.String[])
        Member: System.Type GetType()
        Member: Void .ctor()
```

Note that I referred to *somewhat* expected results. If you look at some of the types and members that were displayed as a result of running this application, you'll notice that each type's inherited (from *Object*) members were displayed. If you look at the enum *RGB*, you'll see the red, green, and blue members print out as expected. However, look at the *BaseClass* printout. You'll notice that we seem to be missing quite a bit here. We don't have the static field, the type initializer for the static field, or the constructor. This omission occurs because of the particular overload of the *GetMembers* method that I used.

The *GetMembers* method has two overloaded versions, as shown here:

```
public MemberInfo Type.GetMembers();
public MemberInfo Type.GetMembers(BindingFlags flags);
```

As you can surmise, it's the *BindingFlags* type we're after. *BindingFlags* is actually a group of flags represented by an enumeration in the *Reflection* namespace. These flags control binding and the way in which the search for members and types is conducted by using reflection. In the case of the GetAssemblyInfo application just shown, the default is to return only the publicly declared members of the type because we didn't specify the *BindingFlags*.

There are actually three categories of *BindingFlags*—access control, change type, and operation type. The only flags that are relevant here are the access control flags listed in Table 19-1.

Table 19-1
Access Control *BindingFlags* Values

Binding Flag	Description
DeclaredOnly	This flag enables you to specify that you care only about members that were declared for this type, excluding any inherited members.
FlattenHierarchy	As the name implies, this flag has the logical effect of flattening out the hierarchy in that it returns the static members defined by the base types.
IgnoreCase	Used when searching for individual types, this flag enables case-insensitive searching.
IgnoreReturn	Used in COM interop, this flag indicates that the return value of the member can be ignored.
Instance	Specifies that instance members of the type should be returned.
NonPublic	Specifies that nonpublic members (protected, private, and internal) of the type should be returned.
Public	Used to indicate that public members should be searched.

So how do we update our little example application to retrieve the members that we defined? The following code change will do just that because we're interested in declared types (no inherited members), all public and nonpublic members, and all instance and static members:

```
BindingFlags bf = BindingFlags.DeclaredOnly
| BindingFlags.NonPublic
| BindingFlags.Public
| BindingFlags.Instance
| BindingFlags.Static;
foreach(MemberInfo member in type.GetMembers(bf))
{
    Console.WriteLine("\tMember: {0}", member);
}
```

Running the GetAssemblyInfo application with these flags returns the following results:

```
Loading type info for GetAssemblyInfo, Version=1.0.794.23511, Culture=neutral,
PublicKeyToken=null

Type: Attr
        Member: Void .ctor()
```

```
Type: RGB
        Member: Int32 value__
        Member: RGB red
        Member: RGB green
        Member: RGB blue

Type: BaseClass
        Member: System.String Infinity
        Member: Void .cctor()
        Member: Void .ctor(System.String)

Type: DerivedClass
        Member: Void .ctor()

Type: Point
        Member: Int32 x
        Member: Int32 y

Type: GetAssemblyInfoApp
        Member: System.Reflection.Assembly GetAssembly(System.String[])
        Member: Void Main(System.String[])
        Member: Void .ctor()
```

Note   To reflect on all the types of the core .NET library, use the following call to load the MSCORLIB.DLL assembly:

```
Assembly assembly = Assembly.Load("Reflectdotnet.exe");
```

Just be prepared for a long listing because this assembly defines more than 1500 types!

Listing an Assembly's Modules

As you saw in Chapter 1, you can combine modules into a single assembly. These modules can be retrieved from an *Assembly* object by using reflection in two ways. The first method is to request an array of all modules. This method allows you to iterate through all the modules and retrieve any needed information. The second method is to specify the desired module. Let's look at each of these approaches.

To illustrate how to iterate through an assembly's modules, we'll first need to create a multifile assembly. We'll do that by placing the *GetAssemblyName* method into a module named *AssemblyUtils*:

```
using System.Diagnostics;

namespace MyUtilities
{
    public class AssemblyUtils
    {
        public static string GetAssemblyName(string[] args)
        {
            string assemblyName;

            if (0 == args.Length)
            {
                Process p = Process.GetCurrentProcess();
                assemblyName = p.ProcessName + ".exe";
            }
            else
                assemblyName = args[0];

            return assemblyName;
        }
    }
}
```

Once you've entered this code, you can compile the module from the command line as follows:

```
csc /target:module AssemblyUtils.cs
```

Note Unfortunately, version 1 of Microsoft Visual Studio .NET doesn't allow you to create multifile assemblies. Therefore, you'll need to create these modules from the command line.

Once the module has been created, create a secondary module that will contain the application's entry point and will reference the *AssemblyUtils* class. Also notice the *using* statement in which the *MyUtilities* namespace is specified.

```
using System;
using System.Reflection;
using MyUtilities;

class GetModulesApp
{
    public static void Main(string[] args)
    {
```

```
    string assemblyName = AssemblyUtils.GetAssemblyName(args);

    Console.WriteLine("Loading info for " + assemblyName);
    Assembly a = Assembly.LoadFrom(assemblyName);

    Module[] modules = a.GetModules();
    foreach(Module m in modules)
    {
        Console.WriteLine("Module: " + m.Name);
    }
  }
}
```

To compile this application and have the AssemblyUtils.netmodule added to its assembly, you'll need to use the following command-line switches:

```
csc /addmodule:AssemblyUtils.netmodule GetModules.cs
```

At this point, you have an assembly with two different modules. Now, if you run the GetModulesApp application, the results should be as follows:

```
Loading info for GetModulesApp.exe
Module: GetModulesApp.exe
Module: AssemblyUtils.netmodule
```

As you can see from the code, I simply instantiated an *Assembly* object and called its *GetModules* method. From there, I iterated through the returned array and printed the name of each module.

Late Binding with Reflection

A few years back, I worked for the IBM Multimedia division on the IBM/World Book Multimedia Encyclopedia product. One challenge we had was coming up with an application that would allow the user to configure various communications protocols for use with the World Book servers. This had to be a dynamic solution because the user could continually add and remove different protocols—for example, TCP/IP, IGN, CompuServe, and so on—from their system. However, the application had to recognize which protocols were present so that the user could select a specific protocol for configuration and use.

The solution we came up with was to create DLLs with a special extension and install them in the application folder. Then when the user wanted to see a list of installed protocols, the application would call the Win32 *LoadLibrary* function to load each DLL and then call the *GetProcAddress* function to acquire a function pointer to the desired function. This is a perfect example of late binding in standard Win32 programming in that the compiler knows nothing about these calls at build time. As you'll see in the following example, this same task could be carried out in .NET by using the *Assembly* class, type reflection, and the *Activator* class.

To get things rolling, let's create an abstract class named *CommProtocol*. I'll define this class in its own DLL so that it can be shared across multiple DLLs that want to derive from it. Note that the command-line parameters are embedded in the code's comments.

```csharp
// CommProtocol.cs
// Build with the following command-line switches.
//          csc /t:library commprotocol.cs
public abstract class CommProtocol
{
    public const string DLLMask = "CommProtocol*.dll";
    public abstract void DisplayName();
}
```

Now I'll create two separate DLLs, each representing a communications protocol and containing a class derived from the abstract class *CommProtocol*. Note that both DLLs need to reference the CommProtocol.dll when compiled. Here's the IGN DLL:

```csharp
// CommProtocolIGN.cs
// Build with the following command-line switches.
//          csc /t:library CommProtocolIGN.cs /r:CommProtocol.dll
using System;

public class CommProtocolIGN : CommProtocol
{
    public override void DisplayName()
    {
        Console.WriteLine("This is the IBM Global Network");
    }
}
```

And here's the TCP/IP DLL:

```csharp
// CommProtocolTcpIp.cs
// Build with the following command-line switches.
//      csc /t:library CommProtocolTcpIp.cs /r:CommProtocol.dll
using System;

public class CommProtocolTcpIp : CommProtocol
{
    public override void DisplayName()
    {
        Console.WriteLine("This is the TCP/IP protocol");
    }
}
```

Let's look at how easy it is to dynamically load an assembly, search for a type, instantiate that type, and call one of its methods. (By the way, there's a command file named BuildLateBinding.cmd on this book's companion CD that will also build all these files.) Here's the main LateBinding.cs file:

```
using System;
using System.Reflection;
using System.IO;

class LateBindingApp
{
    public static void Main()
    {

        string[] fileNames = Directory.GetFiles
            (Environment.CurrentDirectory,
            CommProtocol.DLLMask);
        foreach(string fileName in fileNames)
        {
            Console.WriteLine("Loading DLL '{0}'", fileName);

            Assembly a = Assembly.LoadFrom(fileName);

            Type[] types = a.GetTypes();
            foreach(Type t in types)
            {
                if (t.IsSubclassOf(typeof(CommProtocol)))
                {
                    object o = Activator.CreateInstance(t);

                    MethodInfo mi = t.GetMethod("DisplayName");

                    Console.Write("\t");
                    mi.Invoke(o, null);
                }
                else
                {
                    Console.WriteLine("\tThis DLL does not " +
                        "have CommProtocol-derived class " +
                        "defined");
                }
            }
        }
    }
}
```

First I use the *System.IO.Directory* class to find all the DLLs in the current folder with a mask of CommProtocol*.dll. The *Directory.GetFiles* method will return an array of objects of type *string* that represents the names of files that match the search criteria. I can then use a *foreach* loop to iterate through the array, calling the *Assembly.LoadFrom* method that you learned about earlier in this chapter. Once an assembly is created for a given DLL, I iterate through all the assembly's types, calling the *Type.SubClassOf* method to determine whether the assembly has a type that's derived from *CommProtocol*. I'm assuming that if I find one of these, I'll have a valid DLL to work with. When I do find an assembly that has a type derived from *CommProtocol*, I instantiate an *Activator* object and pass to its constructor the type object. As you can probably guess from its name, the *Activator* class is used to dynamically create, or activate, a type.

I then use the *Type.GetMethod* method to create a *MethodInfo* object, specifying the method name *DisplayName*. Once I've done that, I can use the *MethodInfo* object's *Invoke* method, passing to it the activated type, and—voila!—the DLL's *DisplayName* method is called.

Implementing an Abstract Factory with Reflection

Because the *Activate* class allows us to instantiate types and call code, this class can help us implement a pattern that's extremely valuable to any object-oriented developer—an *Abstract Factory*.

There are times when a client needs to construct an instance of one class of a semantically related group of classes, without deciding which class to use at build time. To avoid duplicating the conditional logic required to make this decision everywhere an instance is created, we need a mechanism for creating instances of related classes without necessarily knowing which will be instantiated. The Abstract Factory solves this problem.

The process for defining an Abstract Factory is to first define an abstract class (or interface) that contains common members. These members are then implemented by *concrete classes*. The client can then call an object creation method of the Abstract Factory with the name of the class it wants to instantiate, and the Abstract Factory will instantiate the class and return the desired object to the client. This relationship between the Abstract Factory, concrete classes, and the client can be seen in Figure 19-2. Note that the client never actually creates an object but instead directs the Abstract Factory to do its bidding.

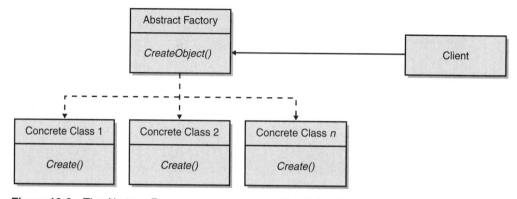

Figure 19-2 The Abstract Factory ensures a layer of insulation between the client and the concrete class. (Dotted lines show a possible method call.)

The biggest advantage of using reflection in the Abstract Factory is that any number of implementing concrete classes can be plugged in without breaking existing code. Here's a simple example of using reflection and the *Activate* class to implement the Abstract Factory pattern:

```
using System;
using System.Reflection;

class AbstractFactory
{
    public IReflect CreateObject(string classname)
    {
        IReflect objreflect;
        try
        {
            // Create the type, throwing an exception
            // if it can't be created.
            System.Type oType = System.Type.GetType(classname,
                true);

            // Create an instance and type-cast it
            // to our interface.
            objreflect =
                (IReflect)System.Activator.CreateInstance(
                oType);
        }
        catch(TypeLoadException e)
        {
            throw new InvalidOperationException("Type could " +
                "not be created. Check innerException " +
                "for details", e);
```

```
            }

            return objreflect;
        }
};

public interface IReflect
{
    string Name { get; }
};

class Reflect1 : IReflect
{
    public string Name
    {
        get { return "Reflect 1"; }
    }
};

class Reflect2 : IReflect
{
    public string Name
    {
        get { return "Reflect 2"; }
    }
}

class AbstractFactoryApp
{
    static void Main(string[] args)
    {
        callReflection(args[0]);
    }

    static void callReflection(string strClassName)
    {
        IReflect objReflect;

        AbstractFactory objFactory = new AbstractFactory();

        try
        {
            objReflect = objFactory.CreateObject(strClassName);
            Console.WriteLine("You constructed a {0} object",
                objReflect.Name);
        }
        catch(Exception e)
        {
```

```
                        Console.WriteLine("ERROR: {0}\n{1}",
                            e.Message,
                            (null == e.InnerException ?
                            "" : e.InnerException.Message));
                    }

            Console.ReadLine();
        }
    };
```

Now if you run this application, passing it either the *Reflect1* or *Reflect2* type names, you'll see that the appropriate *Name* property will be invoked.

Dynamic Code Generation

Now that you've seen how to reflect types at run time, late bind to code, and dynamically execute code, let's take the next logical step and create code on the fly. Creating types at run time involves using the *System.Reflection.Emit* namespace. Using the classes in this namespace, you can define an assembly in memory, create a module for an assembly, define new types for a module (including its members), and even emit the MSIL opcodes for the application's logic.

Although the code in this example is extremely simple, I've separated the server code—a DLL that contains a class creates a method named *Hel-loWorld*—from the client code, an application that instantiates the code-generating class and calls its *HelloWorld* method. (Note that the compiler switches are in the code comments.) An explanation follows for the DLL code, which is shown here:

```
// ILGenServer.cs - compile as follows:
// csc /t:library ILGenServer.cs
using System;
using System.Reflection;
using System.Reflection.Emit;

namespace ILGenServer
{
    public class CodeGenerator
    {
        public CodeGenerator()
        {
            // Get current currentDomain.
            currentDomain = AppDomain.CurrentDomain;

            // Create assembly in current currentDomain.
            assemblyName = new AssemblyName();
            assemblyName.Name = "TempAssembly";
```

```
        assemblyBuilder =
            currentDomain.DefineDynamicAssembly(
            assemblyName,
            AssemblyBuilderAccess.Run);

        // Create a module in the assembly.
        moduleBuilder =
            assemblyBuilder.DefineDynamicModule(
            "TempModule");

        // Create a type in the module.
        typeBuilder =
            moduleBuilder.DefineType("TempClass",
            TypeAttributes.Public);

        // Add a member (a method) to the type.
        methodBuilder = typeBuilder.DefineMethod(
            "HelloWorld", MethodAttributes.Public,
            null, null);

        // Generate MSIL.
        msil = methodBuilder.GetILGenerator();
        msil.EmitWriteLine("Hello World");
        msil.Emit(OpCodes.Ret);

        // Last "build" step : create type.
        type = typeBuilder.CreateType();
    }

    AppDomain currentDomain;
    AssemblyName assemblyName;
    AssemblyBuilder assemblyBuilder;
    ModuleBuilder moduleBuilder;
    TypeBuilder typeBuilder;
    MethodBuilder methodBuilder;
    ILGenerator msil;
    object obj;

    Type type;
    public Type T
    {
        get { return this.type; }
    }
}; // End of CodeGenerator class
}; // End of ILGenServer namespace
```

Let's walk through the code. First, we instantiate an *AppDomain* object from the current domain. After that, we instantiate an *AssemblyName* object.

The assembly cache manager uses the *AssemblyName* object to retrieve information about an assembly. Once we have the current application domain and an initialized assembly name, we call the *AppDomain.DefineDynamicAssembly* method to create a new assembly. Note that the two arguments that we're passing are an assembly name and the mode in which the assembly will be accessed. *AssemblyBuilderAccess.Run* designates that the assembly can be executed from memory but can't be saved. The *AppDomain.DefineDynamicAssembly* method returns an *AssemblyBuilder* object that we then cast to an *Assembly* object. At this point, we have a fully functional assembly in memory. Now we need to create its temporary module and that module's type.

We begin by calling the *Assembly.DefineDynamicModule* method to retrieve a *ModuleBuilder* object. Once we have the *ModuleBuilder* object, we call its *DefineType* method to create a *TypeBuilder* object, passing to it the name of the type "TempClass" and the attributes used to define it (*TypeAttributes.Public*). Now that we have a *TypeBuilder* object in hand, we can create any type of member that we want. In this case, we create a method by using the *TypeBuilder.DefineMethod* method.

Finally, we have a brand new type named *TempClass* with an embedded method named *HelloWorld*. Now all we do is decide what code to place in this method. To do this, the code instantiates an *ILGenerator* object by using the *MethodBuilder.GetILGenerator* method and calls the different *ILGenerator* methods to write MSIL code into the method.

Note that here we can use standard code such as *Console.WriteLine* by using different *ILGenerator* methods or we can emit MSIL opcodes by using the *ILGenerator.Emit* method. The *ILGenerator.Emit* method takes as its only argument an *OpCodes* class member field that directly relates to an MSIL opcode.

Finally, we call the *TypeBuilder.CreateType* method. This should always be the last step performed after you've defined the members for a new type. Then we retrieve the *Type* object for the new type by using the *Type.GetType* method. This object is stored in a member variable for later retrieval by the client application.

Now all the client has to do is retrieve the *CodeGenerator* class's *Type* member, create an *Activator* instance, instantiate a *MethodInfo* object from the type, and then invoke the method. Here's the code to do that, with a little error checking added to make sure things work as they should:

```
// ILGenClient.cs - compile as follows:
// csc ILGenClient.cs /r:ILGenServer.dll
using System;
using System.Reflection;
using ILGenServer;
```

```
public class ILGenClientApp
{
    public static void Main()
    {
        Console.WriteLine("Calling DLL function to generate " +
            "a new type and method in memory...");
        CodeGenerator gen = new CodeGenerator();

        Console.WriteLine("Retrieving dynamically " +
            "generated type...");
        Type t = gen.T;
        if (null != t)
        {
            Console.WriteLine("Instantiating the new type...");
            object o = Activator.CreateInstance(t);

            Console.WriteLine("Retrieving the type's " +
                "HelloWorld method...");
            MethodInfo helloWorld = t.GetMethod("HelloWorld");
            if (null != helloWorld)
            {
                Console.WriteLine("Invoking our dynamically " +
                    "created HelloWorld method...");
                helloWorld.Invoke(o, null);
            }
            else
            {
                Console.WriteLine("Could not locate " +
                    "HelloWorld method");
            }
        }
        else
        {
            Console.WriteLine("Could not access Type " +
                "from server");
        }
    }
}
```

Now if you build and execute this application, you'll see the following output:

```
Calling DLL function to generate a new type and method in memory...
Retrieving dynamically generated type...
Instantiating the new type...
Retrieving the type's HelloWorld method...
Invoking our dynamically created HelloWorld method...
Hello World
```

Summary

Reflection is the ability to discover type information at run time. The Reflection API lets you perform such tasks as iterating an assembly's modules, iterating an assembly's types, and retrieving the various design-time characteristics of a type. Advanced reflection tasks include using reflection to dynamically invoke methods and use types (via late binding) as well as to create and execute MSIL code at run time.

20

Pinning and Memory Management

Pinning is one aspect of memory management, and memory management in C# code can be divided into two broad categories: managing object lifetime in cooperation with the common language runtime and accessing memory directly through pointers. In the first part of this chapter, we'll see how the runtime offers a background garbage collection mechanism to clean up unreferenced heap memory. Garbage collection has been a problematic issue for some time in languages such as C and C++, and the proper management of object destruction is often nontrivial. We'll also see how the C# language supports the concept of object destruction through the *Object.Finalize* method. You can override this method to perform any cleanup you need to do when your object is destroyed. However, there are disadvantages to this process—most notably in terms of performance—and we'll look at a particular design pattern that helps alleviate these problems. We'll show how the judicious use of finalizers and the *Dispose* pattern can help you solve the object management problem without incurring excessive overhead. We'll also consider the *GC* class offered by the .NET Framework classes to provide the developer with a degree of control over the behavior of the garbage collector (GC).

The second part of this chapter focuses on the various ways in which you can work with raw memory addresses via pointers. To work with memory in this way, you have to indicate that the code is unsafe. The use of pointers is also restricted in terms of the types of variable that you're allowed to take the address of. We'll work with each of the pointer operators as well as the *unsafe* and *fixed* keywords and analyze situations in which it's appropriate to use pointers.

Garbage Collection

Although there's a *new* operator in C#, there's no equivalent to the *delete* operator as there is in C++. This means that in C# you can explicitly allocate heap memory with *new*, but you can't explicitly deallocate it. Instead, an automatic background garbage collector cleans up heap memory on your behalf when it's no longer needed. This begs the question, "How does the GC know when an object's no longer needed?" Unlike COM, the common language runtime doesn't use reference counting to govern object lifetime. Instead, the GC traces object references and identifies objects that can no longer be reached by running code. For example, in the following code, the *Thing* reference is declared and assigned an object on the heap, all within the *DoSomething* method. Once the *DoSomething* method returns, the *Thing* reference is no longer in scope and in fact no longer exists. Because there's no other reference to the *Thing* object on the heap, the GC can safely deallocate the object's memory any time after the last statement in the *DoSomething* method.

```
public class Thing
{
    private string name;
    public Thing(string name) { this.name = name; }
    override public string ToString() { return name; }
}

class TestGCApp
{
    static void Main(string[] args)
    {
        DoSomething();
    }

    static void DoSomething()
    {
        Thing t = new Thing("Foo");
        Console.WriteLine(t);
    }
}
```

There are a number of advantages of using the .NET Framework's traced garbage collection system, including these:

- Allocation of new objects in memory is extremely fast, in comparison to any COM-like reference-counting mechanism.

- Without an automatic garbage collector, writing robust code to cleanly track all memory allocations and ensure that the corresponding deallocations take place would be very time-consuming and potentially nontrivial, especially once you add exception handling and conditional branching to the mix.

- The GC doesn't take up processor resources by running constantly, but it kicks in periodically. If your application has lots of free heap memory available to it, there's clearly no need to recover any potentially collectable memory. One situation in which the GC will run occurs when you attempt to allocate some memory with *new* and fail because there isn't enough available.

A consequence of this last point is that heap memory garbage collection—and, by extension, object destruction—is nondeterministic. That is, under normal circumstances, you can't be absolutely sure *when* the GC will run and therefore when your object will finally be destroyed. This behavior leads to the one disadvantage of the GC: if your object is holding some unmanaged resources (window handles, database connections, and so on), you must be very careful to release these resources before your last reference to the object is lost. In C++, this type of behavior was traditionally the job of the class destructor, and you triggered this behavior in a deterministic manner by using the *delete* operator on the object reference. But in C# we don't have a *delete* operator, and even if we did, we don't have destructors. Or do we?

Overriding *Finalize*

Recall that all types in C# are based on the *Object* type, and all types inherit the *Object* methods. If you glance at the Microsoft Visual Studio help for the *Object* class members, you'll see the *Finalize* method, as shown in Figure 20-1. The accompanying description matches the description of a C++ destructor.

.NET Framework Class Library

Object Members

Object overview

Public Constructors

Object Constructor	Initializes a new instance of the **Object** class.

Public Methods

Equals	Overloaded. Determines whether two **Object** instances are equal.
GetHashCode	Serves as a hash function for a particular type, suitable for use in hashing algorithms and data structures like a hash table.
GetType	Gets the Type of the current instance.
ReferenceEquals	Determines whether the specified **Object** instances are the same instance.
ToString	Returns a String that represents the current **Object**.

Protected Methods

Finalize	Overridden. Allows an **Object** to attempt to free resources and perform other cleanup operations before the **Object** is reclaimed by garbage collection. In C# and C++, finalizers are expressed using destructor syntax.
MemberwiseClone	Creates a shallow copy of the current **Object**.

Figure 20-1 Documentation on the *Finalize* method.

The *Finalize* method is called automatically after an object becomes inaccessible, unless you've protected the object against finalization—we'll see how to do that later in this chapter, in the section "Overriding *Finalize*." During the shutdown of an application domain, *Finalize* is called automatically on all objects that you haven't protected against finalization, even those that are still accessible. *Finalize* is called automatically only once on a given instance—unless you reregister the object for finalization. So, we can't have a destructor in our class, but we've inherited a *Finalize* method, and presumably we can override this—even though it might not look like we can. In fact, to override *Finalize*, you must write a destructor. Let's be clear on this. The C# language doesn't strictly support destructors. On the other hand, it does support overriding the *Object.Finalize* method. The only twist in the tale is that to override *Finalize*, you must write a method that's syntactically identical to a destructor.

Let's enhance our previous *Thing* class with an override of *Finalize*. Realistically, of course, we'd write the *Finalize* method to do something useful (such as freeing some resources), but here we'll just make the class print out a suitable message so that we can see when it's being called. To override *Finalize* for our *Thing* class, we must write a method with the same name as the class (in this case, *Thing*), but with a tilde (~) in front. This syntax is the same as C++ destructor syntax. Note that the declaration for a destructor in C# can't include access modifiers (*public*, *private*, and so on) and that destructors can't take parameters (and therefore can't be overloaded):

```
public class Thing
{
    private string name;
    public Thing(string name) { this.name = name; }
    override public string ToString() { return name; }
    ~Thing() { Console.WriteLine("~Thing()"); }
}
```

So that we're clear on when the *Finalize* is called, let's add another line to the end of *Main*:

```
static void Main(string[] args)
{
    DoSomething();
    Console.WriteLine("end of Main");
}
```

This time, when the application runs, we get the following output:

```
Foo
end of Main
~Thing()
```

Therefore, in this application, our *Finalize* method is called as the very last operation before the application terminates. That means, of course, that we can't assume in our *Finalize* method that we have access to anything that was alive during the run of the application. This includes variables of all kinds as well as the console—thus, printing a message to the console window is a little risky. Normally, most of your *Finalize* methods will run at some other point during the run of the application and not at the very end. For a console application, it's usually safe to assume that we have access to the console as long as the application is running. Nonetheless, the point stands: make sure your *Finalize* method doesn't attempt to access anything that might not be available any longer because of the nondeterministic nature of the garbage collection mechanism.

We've been insisting that the *~Thing* method isn't a destructor but an override of *Finalize*, even though it looks like a destructor. To clear this up, let's look at the metadata for this application—see Figure 20-2.

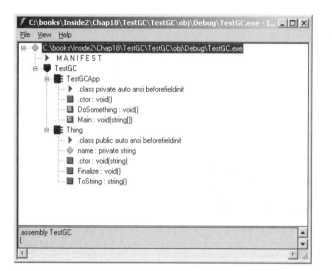

Figure 20-2   Metadata for an override of *Finalize*.

As you can see, the ~*Thing* method isn't listed in the type metadata, but *Finalize* is. If we also examine the Microsoft intermediate language (MSIL) for this *Finalize* method, we'll see that it's in fact the MSIL for our ~*Thing* method, as Figure 20-3 shows.

```
.method family hidebysig virtual instance void
        Finalize() cil managed
{
  // Code size       20 (0x14)
  .maxstack  1
  .try
  {
    IL_0000:  ldstr      "~Thing()"
    IL_0005:  call       void [mscorlib]System.Console::WriteLine(string)
    IL_000a:  leave.s    IL_0013
  } // end .try
  finally
  {
    IL_000c:  ldarg.0
    IL_000d:  call       instance void [mscorlib]System.Object::Finalize()
    IL_0012:  endfinally
  } // end handler
  IL_0013:  ret
} // end of method Thing::Finalize
```

Figure 20-3   MSIL for an override of *Finalize*.

It's also interesting to note that the compiler has wrapped the call to *Console.WriteLine*—that is, all the code in our *Finalize* override—in a *try* block and that the corresponding *finally* block is calling the base class *Object.Finalize*.

Overriding *Finalize* in Derived Classes

If the MSIL for our *Finalize* override includes a call to the base *Object.Finalize*, does this imply that if we override *Finalize* in a further derived class we should also call our base class *Finalize*? The answer is no. In fact, it's illegal to explicitly call *Finalize* (both via the *Finalize* name and via the *~XXXclass* name). Let's see what the MSIL looks like if we do further derive a class and override *Finalize* in the further derived class. Figure 20-4 shows the result.

```
public class SonOfThing : Thing
{
    public SonOfThing(string name) : base(name) {}
    override public string ToString() { return name; }
    ~SonOfThing()
    {
        Console.WriteLine("~SonOfThing()");
    }
}
```

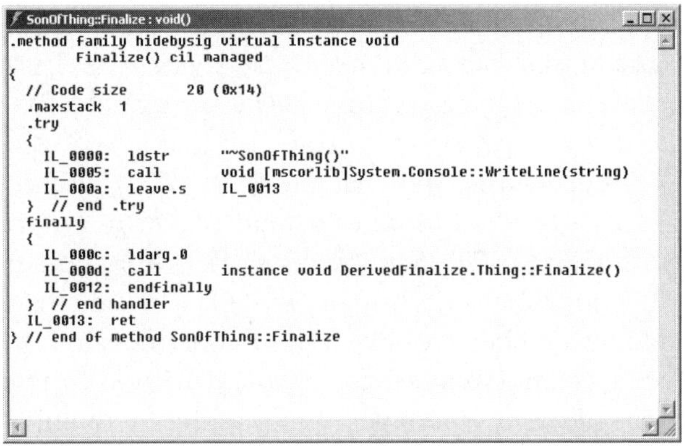

Figure 20-4   MSIL for a further derived override of *Finalize*.

If we modify our *DoSomething* method to use this further derived class, the output listed next should be entirely predictable. So that we can track the full sequence of construction and destruction, let's also add some printing code to the constructors:

```
public Thing(string name)
{
    this.name = name;
    Console.WriteLine("Thing()");
}
⋮
```

```
public SonOfThing(string name) : base(name)
{
    Console.WriteLine("SonOfThing()");
}
    :

static void DoSomething()
{
    SonOfThing s = new SonOfThing("Bar");
    Console.WriteLine(s);
}
```

Here's the output:

```
Thing()
SonOfThing()
Bar
end of Main
~SonOfThing()
~Thing()
```

Note the order of destruction: this is in the reverse order of construction—in other words, a last in, first out (LIFO) stack behavior. The first object to be constructed (*Thing*) is the last to be destroyed. The last object to be constructed (*SonOfThing*) is the first to be destroyed. Note also that if you were to remove *Finalize* in the *Thing* class, the MSIL for the *SonOfThing.Finalize* method would include a call to *Object.Finalize* instead of *Thing.Finalize*. OK, so through the ability to override *Finalize*, C# does offer—for all intents and purposes—the same functionality as destructors in C++. The only coding quirk is that we write what looks and behaves like a destructor but is in fact an override for *Finalize*. Indeed, it's common to call the *Finalize* method either a destructor or a finalizer. The mechanism works very well, and the compiler supports it with some behind-the-scenes cleverness.

This is what actually happens at run time: when you use the *new* operator to allocate heap memory for some object, the common language runtime determines whether this object is of a type that supports the *Finalize* method. If it does support *Finalize*, the runtime tracks the reference to this object by putting a copy of it in an internal *finalization* queue. Later, when a garbage collection has been triggered for unreferenced objects, the runtime calls the *Finalize* method for each object on the finalization queue before deallocating the objects' memory.

Clearly, having a finalizer in a class increases the overhead of object creation. The GC will run only when all managed threads in an application reach a safe state (for example, suspended). The reason for this behavior is that during the garbage collection process, the runtime will defragment memory on the application's managed heap, which therefore invalidates the references to objects that have been moved as part of this defragmentation. The runtime updates these references so that they are once again valid after defragmentation.

Each application has a logical collection of *root* references—namely, the managed object references for global and static objects and local variables that are currently on the stack and in registers. When the GC sweeps memory, it builds a graph of reachable objects, starting with all objects referenced by a root reference and recursively adding objects that are referenced by any added object. Before an object is added to the graph, the runtime checks that the object isn't already in the graph, thus avoiding an infinite loop caused by circular references.

At the end of this process, any object that isn't in the reachable object graph is considered unreachable and therefore garbage. Note that reference cycles between unreachable objects won't prevent the object's memory from being collected by the GC. For example, if object *A* references object *B* and object *B* references object *A*, both objects will be collected when they're no longer reachable from a root reference. If, when a GC sweep is triggered, an object is identified as unreachable and has a reference in the finalization queue, the GC will move the reference from the finalization queue to another queue known as the *freachable queue* (pronounced *F-reachable*). The freachable queue is a root reference; therefore, any object referenced by an entry in the freachable queue is no longer garbage.

The runtime has a special thread that services the freachable queue. The thread removes the freachable queue's references and invokes their object's finalizer. At this point, there typically aren't any more root references to these objects. However, the objects' memory won't be released until the next time that garbage collection is invoked. You can see that having a finalizer in a class can significantly delay the release of memory for instances of that class as well as for any instances that the class refers to, either directly or indirectly. Note also that the GC isn't required to use a specific thread to finalize objects, nor does it guarantee the order in which finalizers are called for objects that reference each other but are otherwise available for garbage collection.

The system is carefully designed and automatic, although there's some overhead involved. Despite the efficiency of the garbage collection mechanism, one issue remains: the mechanism is still nondeterministic. It's very nice that we don't have to track our object references and make sure we call *delete* in all the right places. However, being able to determine the exact point at which an object is destroyed can be useful. If C# provides a destructor-like mechanism, does C# offer us anything that behaves as operator *delete* does? We'll answer this question in two stages: first, we'll consider how we can force garbage collection, and then we'll look at a design pattern that supports the semantics of deterministic object destruction.

Forcing Garbage Collection

The .NET Framework offers a class that exposes some of the functionality of the garbage collector: the *GC* class. You can force a garbage collection operation at any time with the *GC.Collect* method. However, bear in mind that the garbage collector runs finalizers on a separate thread of execution, so even if *GC.Collect* has returned, it doesn't mean that a particular finalizer has been called yet. This is really a standard thread-synchronization issue and can be resolved if you call *WaitForPendingFinalizers* to suspend the current thread until the queue of finalizers waiting to run on that thread is empty. In the following example, we'll enhance our simple *Thing*-based application to force a garbage collection:

```
public class Thing
{
    private string name;
    public Thing(string name) { this.name = name; }
    override public string ToString() { return name; }
    ~Thing() { Console.WriteLine("~Thing()"); }
}

public class ForceCollectApp
{
    public static void Main(string[] args)
    {
        DoSomething();
        Console.WriteLine("some stuff");

        GC.Collect();
        GC.WaitForPendingFinalizers();
        Console.WriteLine("end of Main");
    }
    public static void DoSomething()
    {
        Thing t = new Thing("Foo");
        Console.WriteLine(t);
    }
}
```

If you follow the sequence of execution and tie it to the runtime output listed next, you'll see that although our *Thing* object is available for garbage collection immediately upon return of *DoSomething*, it doesn't actually get collected until we force a collection with *GC.Collect*:

```
Foo
some stuff
~Thing()
end of Main
```

If we wanted things to happen in a different order, we could simply move the forced collection to an earlier point in the code sequence—for instance, we could place it inside the *DoSomething* method. Of course, forcing a collection won't force the GC to collect something that's not available for collection. The *Thing* reference doesn't go out of scope until the end of the method, so if we want it to be available for collection before the reference goes out of scope, we'd have to reassign the reference or set it to *null*:

```
public class ForceCollectApp
{
    public static void Main(string[] args)
    {
        DoSomething();
        Console.WriteLine("some stuff");

//        GC.Collect();
//        GC.WaitForPendingFinalizers();
        Console.WriteLine("end of Main");
    }
    public static void DoSomething()
    {
        Thing t = new Thing("Foo");
        Console.WriteLine(t);
        t = null;
        GC.Collect();
        GC.WaitForPendingFinalizers();
    }
}
```

Here's the output from this revised code:

```
Foo
~Thing()
some stuff
end of Main
```

The result is that if we force a collection and wait for the finalizers to be called, we can introduce a degree of determinism to our code. However, this arrangement seems a little cumbersome to be useful on a broad scale. Also, the processing involved in actually sweeping heap memory for garbage collection does involve a certain amount of overhead—a performance penalty that you can't always justify. The normal trigger for a garbage collection sweep is heap exhaustion, and we don't normally want to force a garbage collection unless we really have to. In addition, if you do override *Finalize* in your class, you set up some extra work for the runtime to do at an indeterminate point in the future. So is there any other way to control object destruction? The final piece of this particular puzzle is the *Dispose* pattern.

The *Dispose* Pattern

Class instances often encapsulate control over resources not managed by the runtime. The .NET Framework supports both an implicit and an explicit way to free those resources. The implicit control is provided by implementing a finalizer. The GC calls this finalizer at some point after no valid references to the object remain—but as you'll recall, although you can force a garbage collection, you have no control over exactly when the finalizer call is made.

To achieve the necessary explicit control and precise determinism in the destructor-like cleanup of unmanaged resources, you're encouraged to implement an arbitrary *Dispose* method. The consumer of the object should call this method when the object is no longer required. This call can be made even if other references to the object are alive. Unlike the finalizer, the *Dispose* method is arbitrary—in terms of its name, signature, access modifiers, and attributes. In other words, you can invent any method you want that internally will clean up unmanaged resources the way that a C++ destructor traditionally would. You then can let everyone know what this method does and encourage developers using your class to call this method when they've finished with an instance of your class. Clearly, if every author of a class were to invent a different method to do this job, we'd be little further along in the development of reusable classes. For this reason, you're encouraged to use a public nonstatic method named *Dispose*, with a *void* return and no parameters. This is only a convention, but it's a sensible convention that most people are happy to adopt. More-over—and interestingly—the C# language has explicit support for this arbitrary method.

Let's enhance our previous *Thing* example with a *Dispose* method—again, to simulate some cleanup operation, we'll simply print out an arbitrary message. Clearly, if we plan to dispose of the object, we must do so before we set its reference to *null* (or before the reference goes out of scope and is lost):

```
public class Thing
{
    private string name;
    public Thing(string name) { this.name = name; }
    override public string ToString() { return name; }
```

```
    ~Thing() { Console.WriteLine("~Thing()"); }
    public void Dispose()
    {
        Console.WriteLine("Dispose()");
    }
}

public class GarbageDisposalApp
{
    public static void Main(string[] args)
    {
        DoSomething();
        Console.WriteLine("end of Main");
    }
    public static void DoSomething()
    {
        Thing t = new Thing("Foo");
        Console.WriteLine(t);
        t.Dispose();
        t = null;
        GC.Collect();
        GC.WaitForPendingFinalizers();
    }
}
```

The output from this code is shown here:

```
Foo
Dispose()
~Thing()
end of Main
```

Two issues arise from this code. First, if we've moved the cleanup operations to the *Dispose* method, there's no longer anything meaningful for the finalizer to do, but—as you can see from the output just shown—the finalizer is
called anyway. Second, if we now perform our cleanup in the *Dispose* method,
what happens if the object is finalized through some branch of code that
bypasses the call to *Dispose*?

The standard strategy used to resolve the first issue is to add a statement
to the *Dispose* method that will suppress the GC's call to the *Finalize* method:

```
public void Dispose()
{
    Console.WriteLine("Dispose()");
    GC.SuppressFinalize(this);
}
```

GC.SuppressFinalize will remove the object from the finalization queue, so although the memory for the object will get collected, the *Finalize* method won't be called. Note that the parameter passed to this method should be this current object, but the compiler *doesn't* enforce this. Therefore, although the following code will compile, it's wrong:

```
public class Thing
{
    private string name;
    public Thing(string name) { this.name = name; }
    override public string ToString() { return name; }
    ~Thing() { Console.WriteLine("~Thing()"); }
    public void Dispose()
    {
        Console.WriteLine("Dispose()");
        Another a = new Another();
//        GC.SuppressFinalize(this);
        GC.SuppressFinalize(a);
    }
}


public class Another
{
    ~Another() { Console.WriteLine("~Another()"); }
}
```

The result at run time is that the *~Another* finalizer is suppressed (possibly leaking resources), while the *~Thing* finalizer is called (possibly double-releasing some resource, and at best, wasting time).

Now let's now address the second issue I mentioned earlier: what happens if the object is finalized—for example, as a result of a conditional branch in our code, or as an exception that gets thrown—and bypasses the call to *Dispose*? Fixing this little snag is a simple matter: just call the *Dispose* in the finalizer. Therefore, if the developer has remembered to call *Dispose* and that branch of the code is executed, all's well. Equally, if the developer's explicit call to *Dispose* is bypassed in some way, the finalizer will be called (because it of course hasn't been suppressed by the *Dispose*) and will call the *Dispose*:

```
~Thing()
{
    Dispose();
    Console.WriteLine("~Thing()");
}
```

Other GC Features

It's possible that after you've suppressed finalization of an object, a condition will arise in your application that makes you want to reinstate the garbage collector's call to *Finalize*. The *GC* class supports this (admittedly somewhat remote) possibility through the *ReRegisterForFinalize* method. For example, in the following code, we've disposed of our object—including suppressing finalization—but then something untoward happens, prompting us to decide that we want the object finalized after all:

```
public class Thing
{
⋮

    public void Dispose()
    {
        Console.WriteLine("Dispose()");
        GC.SuppressFinalize(this);
    }
}

public class ReRegFinalApp
{
⋮

    public static void DoSomething()
    {
        Thing t = new Thing("Foo");
        Console.WriteLine(t);
        t.Dispose();

        // Some condition arises.
        GC.ReRegisterForFinalize(t);
        ⋮
    }
}
```

It's clear that this doesn't completely undo all the work of the *Dispose* method—which would realistically be cleaning up resource handles and so on—so the value of this technique is questionable. Still, it's nice to have the option. The *GC* class also offers the *GetTotalMemory* method, which retrieves the number of bytes currently thought to be allocated. This method takes a Boolean parameter to indicate whether the method should wait a short interval before returning while the runtime collects garbage and finalizes objects.

```
public static void Main(string[] args)
{
    long n = GC.GetTotalMemory(true);
    Console.WriteLine(
```

```
    "start of Main: {0} bytes allocated", n);
DoSomething();
n = GC.GetTotalMemory(true);
Console.WriteLine(
    "end of Main: {0} bytes allocated", n);
}
```

Note, however, that you can't control the exact extent of the wait interval—it's an internally specified limit determined by the current status of the garbage collection operation. Also, the GC doesn't guarantee that all inaccessible memory will be collected, so the values returned by this method aren't necessarily accurate. The output from the code just shown will therefore depend on circumstances but is likely to resemble this listing:

```
start of Main: 8368 bytes allocated
Foo
Dispose()
~Thing()
end of Main: 19736 bytes allocated
```

The *IDisposable* Interface

The *Dispose* pattern discussed in the previous section suffers from being arbitrary. To strengthen the support for this strategy, Microsoft introduced the *IDisposable* interface. This interface offers only one method: *Dispose*. You implement this interface in any class where you need to perform cleanup in order to expose a standard *Dispose* method for potential clients to use. Many of the .NET Framework classes implement this interface—most notably those involved in GDI, controls, containers, components, stream-readers and stream-writers, and so on, where there's a strong likelihood that resources (such as window handles, file handles, and so forth) will need to be released when the object dies. Besides standardizing the *Dispose* method and formalizing the strategy, implementing *IDisposable* has the added benefit of an application being able to test an object for this interface using the *is* or *as* operator. This practice in turn will tend to make your class more generically reusable.

Consider a variation on our *Thing* class. This time, we implement the *IDisposable* interface so that our *Dispose* method is an interface implementation. Because we already had the method with the correct signature, the only significant change is that we now specify the *IDisposable* implementation:

```
public class Thing : IDisposable
{
    private string name;
    public Thing(string name) { this.name = name; }
```

```
override public string ToString() { return name; }

~Thing()
{
    Dispose();
    Console.WriteLine("~Thing(): " +name);
}

public void Dispose()
{
    Console.WriteLine("Dispose(): " +name);
    GC.SuppressFinalize(this);
}
}
```

In the test application, we'll create an array of *Thing* objects, manually *Dispose* them, and rely on the GC to finalize them and clean them up. At each iteration, we'll report on the amount of heap memory in use in this application.

```
public class DisposableApp
{
    public static void Main(string[] args)
    {
        Console.WriteLine(
            "start of Main, heap used: {0}",
            GC.GetTotalMemory(true));
        DoSomething();
        Console.WriteLine(
            "end of Main, heap used: {0}",
            GC.GetTotalMemory(true));
    }

    public static void DoSomething()
    {
        Thing[] ta = new Thing[3];

        for (int i = 0; i < 3; i++)
        {
            ta[i] = new Thing(
                String.Format("object #" +i));
            Console.WriteLine(
                "Allocated {0} objects, heap used: {1}",
                i+1, GC.GetTotalMemory(true));
        }

        for (int i = 0; i < 3; i++)
        {
            ta[i].Dispose();
```

```
                ta[i] = null;
                GC.Collect();
                GC.WaitForPendingFinalizers();
                Console.WriteLine(
                    "Disposed {0} objects, heap used: {1}",
                    i+1, GC.GetTotalMemory(true));
            }
        }
}
```

If you tie up the source code with the following output, it should be clear that each *Thing* object involves 48 bytes of heap memory (including the reference in the array):

```
start of Main, heap used: 8368
Allocated 1 objects, heap used: 19912
Allocated 2 objects, heap used: 19960
Allocated 3 objects, heap used: 20008
Dispose(): object #0
Disposed 1 objects, heap used: 20036
Dispose(): object #1
Disposed 2 objects, heap used: 19976
Dispose(): object #2
Disposed 3 objects, heap used: 19928
end of Main, heap used: 19888
```

Derived Disposable Classes

Recall that that when you derive a finalizable class from a finalizable base class, the compiler will generate MSIL to call the base class *Finalize*. Of course, the compiler doesn't do any such thing in the case of the *Dispose* method. So, if you adopt the *Dispose* pattern and put your cleanup code in the *Dispose* method, you might end up in a situation where both your base class and derived class are independently holding some unmanaged resources that need cleaning up. In this case, you'd have to be careful to call the *Dispose* base class at an appropriate point during the execution of the *Dispose* derived class. The following code illustrates this scenario:

```
public class Thing : IDisposable
{
    protected string name;
    public Thing(string name) { this.name = name; }
    override public string ToString() { return name; }
    ~Thing() { Dispose(); Console.WriteLine("~Thing()"); }
    public void Dispose()
    {
        Console.WriteLine("Thing.Dispose()");
```

```
        GC.SuppressFinalize(this);
    }
}
public class SonOfThing : Thing, IDisposable
{
    public SonOfThing(string name) : base(name) { }
    override public string ToString() { return name; }
    ~SonOfThing()
    { Dispose(); Console.WriteLine("~SonOfThing()"); }
    new public void Dispose()
    {
        Console.WriteLine("SonOfThing.Dispose()");
        base.Dispose();
        GC.SuppressFinalize(this);
    }
}


class DerivedDisposeApp
{
    static void Main(string[] args)
    {
        DoSomething();
    }
    static void DoSomething()
    {
        SonOfThing s = new SonOfThing("Bar");
        Console.WriteLine(s);
        s.Dispose();
    }
}
```

If you want the derived class to implement the *IDisposable* interface, you must declare it to do so and implement the *Dispose* method of that interface—merely relying on the inherited base class implementation isn't enough. However, this leads to the situation where we have an identically signatured *Dispose* method in both the base class and the derived class, and the compiler will warn us about this situation unless we add the *new* keyword to the derived class declaration. You'll also notice from the output that both the derived class finalizer and base class finalizer are suppressed:

```
Bar
SonOfThing.Dispose()
Thing.Dispose()
```

Protecting Against Double Disposal

We've seen that in an inheritance situation it might be necessary to call the *Dispose* base class from a *Dispose* derived class. This arrangement imposes a small burden on the developer: in a sense, although C# protects the developer from having to track memory allocation and deallocation through the use of *delete*, it shifts the emphasis so that the developer must track *Dispose* calls. A related concern is what happens if you double-dispose—that is, call the *Dispose* method for a specific object more than once. This situation is really the same old C++ double-delete (or C double-free) problem resurfacing with different syntax. Because the developer is responsible for calling *Dispose*, suppressing finalization if he or she has called *Dispose*, calling *Dispose* from the class finalizer, and perhaps calling the base class *Dispose*, he or she is also responsible for ensuring that *Dispose* doesn't get called more than once per object. If *Dispose* is called more than once, the developer must ensure that there are no consequences.

The following enhancement to our *Thing* system illustrates one way to satisfy these requirements. We simply set a Boolean field in our *Dispose* and test it at the beginning of the method:

```
public class Thing : IDisposable
{
    private string name;
    public Thing(string name) { this.name = name; }
    override public string ToString() { return name; }

    ~Thing()
    {
        Dispose();
        Console.WriteLine("~Thing()");
    }

    private bool AlreadyDisposed = false;

    public void Dispose()
    {
        if (!AlreadyDisposed)
        {
            AlreadyDisposed = true;
            Console.WriteLine("Dispose()");
            GC.SuppressFinalize(this);
        }
    }
}
```

Now, unwary developers can call *Dispose* as many times as they like, without any unfortunate consequences:

```
public class DoubleDisposeApp
{
    public static void Main(string[] args)
    {
        Thing t = new Thing("Foo");
        Console.WriteLine(t);

        t.Dispose();
        t.Dispose();

        GC.Collect();
        GC.WaitForPendingFinalizers();
    }
}
```

Here's the output:

```
Foo
Dispose()
```

Note that, by extension, the Boolean *AlreadyDisposed* flag could be tested inside any of the nonprivate methods of the class. This would protect against a developer calling other methods on the object after it's been disposed. A reasonable strategy if a method is called after disposal is to throw an appropriate exception, as indicated here:

```
public class Thing : IDisposable
{
    ⋮
    public void Bar()
    {
        if (AlreadyDisposed)
        {
            throw new ObjectDisposedException("Thing");
        }
    }
}

public class DoubleDisposeApp
{
    public static void Main(string[] args)
    {
        Thing t = new Thing("Foo");
        t.Dispose();
```

```
    try
    {
        t.Bar();
    }
    catch (Exception e)
    {
        Console.WriteLine(e.Message);
    }
    }
}
```

Language Support for *Dispose*

Using conventional coding constructs, the best way to ensure that an object's lifetime is controlled and that resources are cleaned up deterministically is by enclosing the object in a *try* and *finally* block:

```
static void Main(string[] args)
{
    Thing t1 = new Thing("Ethel");
    try
    {
        Console.WriteLine(t1);
    }
    finally
    {
        if (t1 != null)
            ((IDisposable)t1).Dispose();
    }
}
```

This pattern is so standard that the C# language supports it through the use of the *using* statement. The previous code with a *try..finally* block can be rewritten as follows:

```
using (Thing t2 = new Thing("JimBob"))
{
    Console.WriteLine(t2);
}
```

The *using* statement requires that the class implement *IDisposable*. If you look at the MSIL for this statement, you'll see that it does in fact expand to the equivalent *try..finally* block, as Figure 20-5 shows.

```
TestUsingApp::Main : void(string[])                              _□×
  IL_001d:  ldstr      "JimBob"
  IL_0022:  newobj     instance void TestUsing.Thing::.ctor(string)
  IL_0027:  stloc.1
  .try
  {
    IL_0028:  ldloc.1
    IL_0029:  call       void [mscorlib]System.Console::WriteLine(object)
    IL_002e:  leave.s    IL_003a
  } // end .try
  finally
  {
    IL_0030:  ldloc.1
    IL_0031:  brfalse.s  IL_0039
    IL_0033:  ldloc.1
    IL_0034:  callvirt   instance void [mscorlib]System.IDisposable::Dispose(
    IL_0039:  endfinally
  } // end handler
```

Figure 20-5   MSIL for *using* statement.

Garbage Collector Generations

As a performance optimization measure, the GC is written to use the concept of object generations. Every object on the heap is assigned to a generation, arbitrarily starting at zero and increasing to a maximum of three on current versions of the .NET Framework. If a given object survives a garbage collection sweep, it's promoted to the next generation. This way, the newest objects are collected first—in other words, an object more local in scope will have a shorter lifetime than an object in a less local scope.

Remember that the primary reason for garbage collection is to ensure that sufficient memory is always available for a process's needs. When garbage collection is performed, the GC sweeps all generation 0 objects first. If this sweep results in sufficient memory, all remaining objects are promoted to the next available generation (0 to 1, 1 to 2, and so on). If, however, there's still not sufficient memory, all generation 1 objects will be swept and collected, followed by all generation 2 objects, and so forth.

In the following example, we first find out the maximum number of generations supported on this system. Then we create an array of *Thing* objects on the heap and report on the generation assigned to each object as it's created. Later we force a collection and then iterate the array disposing each object—again, reporting on its GC generation as we go.

```
public class GCgensApp
{
    public static void Main(string[] args)
    {
        Console.WriteLine(
            "Highest Generation Supported: "
            +GC.MaxGeneration);
        DoSomething();
```

```
        }

    public static void DoSomething()
    {
        Thing[] ta = new Thing[3];

        Console.WriteLine("\nAllocating objects...");
        for (int i = 0; i < 3; i++)
        {
            ta[i] = new Thing(
                String.Format("object #" +i));
            Console.WriteLine("object {0}, GC Generation = {1}",
                i+1, GC.GetGeneration(ta[i]));
        }

        GC.Collect();
        GC.WaitForPendingFinalizers();

        Console.WriteLine("\nDisposing objects...");
        for (int i = 0; i < 3; i++)
        {
            Console.WriteLine("object {0}, GC Generation = {1}",
                i+1, GC.GetGeneration(ta[i]));
            ta[i].Dispose();
            ta[i] = null;
            GC.Collect();
            GC.WaitForPendingFinalizers();
        }
    }
}
```

As you can see from the following output, when the three objects are created, they're assigned GC generation 0. When we force a collection, we still have live references to all three objects, so they all survive the first sweep and are therefore promoted to the next generation, which is generation 1. The first console output from the second (disposing) loop indicates this situation—we clearly have to report on the object before we destroy it. Of course, after the first iteration of the second loop, the two remaining objects will have been promoted to generation 2. Finally, on the third iteration, the one remaining object is still on generation 2—because that's the highest generation number supported on this system.

```
Highest Generation Supported: 2

Allocating objects...
object 1, GC Generation = 0
object 2, GC Generation = 0
object 3, GC Generation = 0
```

```
Disposing objects...
object 1, GC Generation = 1
object 2, GC Generation = 2
object 3, GC Generation = 2
```

In our example, we had only a small number of simple objects and no significant use of heap memory. In a more realistic application, memory consumption will be much higher and more complex. We should emphasize that in realistic applications, an object might well survive a garbage collection sweep even though it's available for collection—simply because sufficient heap memory was recovered without the need to collect that particular object. The key to the efficiency of the garbage collection mechanism is the generation-based sweeping algorithm. This scheme allows the GC to free up memory quickly at any given point in the application, without necessarily sweeping the whole heap. Note also that the *GC.Collect* method is overloaded—you can supply a generation number as the parameter if you want. This parameter forces garbage collection from generation 0 through the generation you specify (0, 1 or 2). Calling *GC.Collect* without passing a parameter forces a sweep of all generations.

Weak References

Recall that when you write a statement such as this

```
Thing t = new Thing("Foo");
```

you're declaring an instance of the *Thing* class, for which the runtime will allocate memory on the heap. The *t* variable isn't the object itself, but rather a reference to the object. This is what's known as a *strong reference*.

The *WeakReference* class is a wrapper for establishing a *weak reference* to an object. Objects referenced through the *WeakReference* class are kept alive only as long as there's at least one strong (that is, normal) reference to the object. For example, you can have a collection of weak references to objects, each of which stays alive only as long as something else has a strong reference to those objects.

The common language runtime supports two styles of weak reference: *short weak references* and *long weak references*. The distinction between the two styles is whether the reference is zeroed before or after finalization of the target object. The constructor for *WeakReference* takes a Boolean named *trackResurrection* and determines which of the two styles to use. By default, *trackResurrection* is set to *false* so that the object is tracked only until finalization—that is, the object was zeroed before finalization.

In the following example, we create a strong reference, *t1*, to a *Thing* and then get a weak reference to it while it's still alive. From the weak reference, we can create a second strong reference, *t2*, and print it out. We then destroy both strong references, force a garbage collection, and then test to see whether the weak reference is still alive (which, of course, it isn't).

```
public class WeakRefsApp
{
    public static void Main(string[] args)
    {
        Thing t1 = new Thing("Foo");

        WeakReference wr = new WeakReference(t1, false);
        if (wr.IsAlive)
        {
            Thing t2 = (Thing) wr.Target;
            Console.WriteLine("new WeakReference: {0}", t2);
            t2.Dispose();
            t2 = null;
        }

        t1.Dispose();
        t1 = null;
        GC.Collect();
        GC.WaitForPendingFinalizers();

        if (wr.IsAlive)
        {
            Thing t3 = (Thing) wr.Target;
            Console.WriteLine("using old WR: {0}", t3);
        }
        else
            Console.WriteLine("WeakReference is dead");
    }
}
```

Here's the output:

```
new WeakReference: Foo
Dispose
Dispose
WeakReference is dead
```

Note   As we've seen in Chapter 10, "String Handling and Regular Expressions," constant strings can be pooled by the runtime. Therefore, weak references to constant strings might live for the duration of the runtime.

When would you need to use a weak reference? One obvious use is for objects that are costly to set up and consume lots of memory. Say you've set up a large object and then the user switches to a different part of the application where the object isn't needed. We might want to release the memory, so we destroy all strong references. But what if the user switches back to the original part of the application he or she was using and needs the object again? Remember, it's costly to set up. So let's destroy all strong references as we did earlier, but let's get a weak reference first. Then the GC will collect the memory if we're low on memory (and won't collect the memory if we're not low on memory). And if the user switches back, we can use the weak reference to get back a strong reference, thereby avoiding the cost of setup. Now isn't that neat?

Unsafe Code

Programmers who come to C# from C or C++ are sometimes concerned about the degree of control—or the lack of it—that they might have over memory. If you're used to dealing with raw pointers, you'll know how powerful—and potentially dangerous—they can be. The C# language addresses this concern by providing the option to use pointers. The one caveat is that you can use only pointers in code marked *unsafe*. Despite its ominous name, unsafe code isn't inherently unsafe or untrustworthy—rather, it's C# code that bypasses the compiler's type checking and allows the use of raw pointers. A related concept is *unmanaged code*: code for which the .NET runtime doesn't control the allocation and deallocation of memory. Unmanaged code includes code written in earlier versions of Microsoft Visual Basic or in C++ without the managed extensions.

More Info In Chapter 21, "Using COM from C# Applications," and Chapter 22, "Using .NET Components in Unmanaged Code," you'll learn how to interoperate between managed and unmanaged code.

Unsafe code doesn't imply unmanaged code: you can mark any block of code as unsafe, even though objects within that block will be managed by the runtime and—where appropriate—by the GC. However, in most situations where you mark code as unsafe, it's because you want to work on memory addresses, and you usually don't want the runtime to manage this memory while you're working on it. In the "Pinning" section later in this chapter, you'll see how to make memory involved in your unsafe code unmanaged while you're working on it.

The ability to write unsafe code is most advantageous when you're using pointers to communicate with legacy code (such as C APIs) or when your application demands the direct manipulation of memory (typically for performance reasons).

You write unsafe code by using the keyword *unsafe*: this keyword denotes an *unsafe context*. An unsafe context is required for any operation involving pointers. You can apply *unsafe* as a modifier in the declaration of callable members such as methods, properties, and constructors. The scope of the unsafe context extends from the parameter list to the end of the method; therefore, pointers can also be used in the parameter list. Furthermore, *unsafe* can be used to specify an unsafe statement—a statement or block of multiple statements that's an unsafe context.

Using Pointers in C#

Let's look at some rules regarding the use of pointers and unsafe code in C# before diving into some examples. A pointer is a variable whose value is the address of another variable. You can make a pointer can point to anything—both value types and reference types. However, you can take only the address of a value type, not a reference type. If you're paying attention, you'll spot a lack of symmetry here. Indeed, it looks like a paradox: how can you have a pointer (which is the address of some variable) to a reference variable when you can't take the address of a reference variable? All this will be explained shortly. Table 20-1 illustrates how the standard C/C++ pointer semantics are upheld in C#.

Table 20-1
C# Pointer Operators

Operator	Description
&	The address-of operator returns a pointer that represents the memory address of the variable.
*	The primary pointer operator is used in two situations: to declare a variable to be a pointer of some type, and to dereference the pointer value to get to the value of the variable pointed to by the pointer.
->	The dereferencing and member access operator is used for member access and pointer dereferencing. It's a combination of the dereference (*) and member selection (.) operators—in other words, -> is the same as *.

The following example will look familiar to any C or C++ developer. Here we're calling a method that takes two pointers to variables of type *int* and modifies them by swapping their values before returning to the caller. Not very exciting, but it does illustrate how to use pointers in C#. The *Swap* method takes in two *int* pointers—that is, two pointers that point to *int* values. In other words, it takes in the addresses of two *int* variables. Inside the *Swap* method, we extract the value of the first *int* by dereferencing the pointer and store this value in a local variable named *tmp*. Next we dereference the second *int* pointer to get to the underlying variable value and use that value to overwrite the first variable (accessed via the dereferenced pointer again).

In the call to the *Swap* method, we pass the addresses of our two local variables by using the address-of operator. This way, the *Swap* method, through the indirection of the pointer/address operators, has access to the values in variables that are local to *Main* but are actually outside the scope of *Swap* itself. This is why pointers are so powerful—basically you can reach almost any location you want in memory, at any point in your application, and do anything you want with the values in that memory location. Clearly, this is situation in which pointers can be dangerous if you're not careful with them.

```
public class TestUnsafeApp
{
    unsafe public static void Swap(int* pi, int* pj)
    {
        int tmp = *pi;
        *pi = *pj;
        *pj = tmp;
    }

    public static void Main(string[] args)
    {
        int i = 3;
        int j = 4;
        Console.WriteLine("BEFORE: i = {0}, j = {1}", i, j);

        unsafe { Swap(&i, &j); }

        Console.WriteLine("AFTER:  i = {0}, j = {1}", i, j);
    }
}
```

The output from this application should be the following:

```
BEFORE: i = 3, j = 4
AFTER:  i = 4, j = 3
```

Note that the *unsafe* keyword must be used in both the declaration of the unsafe method and the call to the unsafe method because both the & and * pointer operators can be used only in an unsafe context. Because the call is an otherwise undelimited statement (or block of statements), you must delimit it with a pair of curly braces. All code within these curly braces is considered unsafe. This code needs to be compiled with the */unsafe* compiler option. The simplest way to set this option is to right-click the project in the Solution Explorer and select Properties. From the Properties dialog box, navigate to the Build properties and set the Allow Unsafe Code Blocks option to True, as Figure 20-6 shows.

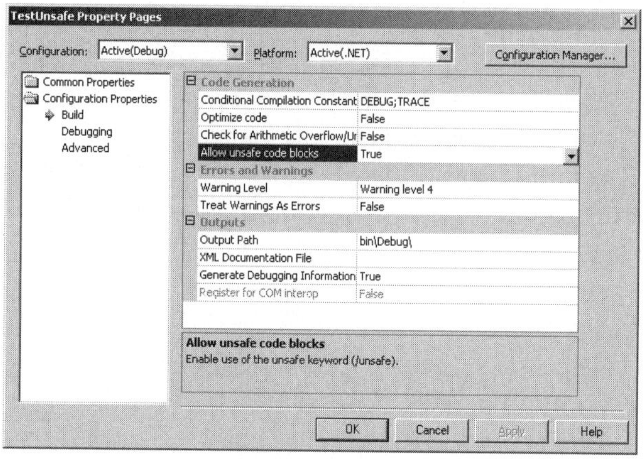

Figure 20-6 Allow unsafe code blocks.

If you look at the MSIL for this application and focus on the call to the unsafe *Swap* method, you'll see how the addresses of our local *int* variables are passed—by using the opcode *ldloca*, as Figure 20-7 shows. This opcode loads the address of the specified local variable onto the evaluation stack.

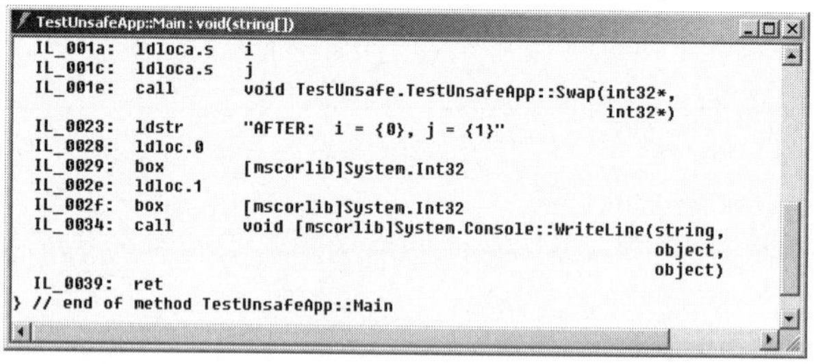

```
TestUnsafeApp::Main : void(string[])
  IL_001a:  ldloca.s   i
  IL_001c:  ldloca.s   j
  IL_001e:  call       void TestUnsafe.TestUnsafeApp::Swap(int32*,
                                                            int32*)
  IL_0023:  ldstr      "AFTER:  i = {0}, j = {1}"
  IL_0028:  ldloc.0
  IL_0029:  box        [mscorlib]System.Int32
  IL_002e:  ldloc.1
  IL_002f:  box        [mscorlib]System.Int32
  IL_0034:  call       void [mscorlib]System.Console::WriteLine(string,
                                                                 object,
                                                                 object)
  IL_0039:  ret
} // end of method TestUnsafeApp::Main
```

Figure 20-7 MSIL for method call passing addresses.

Figure 20-8 shows the MSIL for the *Swap* method itself, where you can see the use of the opcode *ldind.i4*: this opcode indirectly loads a value of type *int32* as an *int32* onto the evaluation stack. The detailed sequence of this opcode is to push the address of the variable onto the stack, pop the address from the stack and fetch the value located at that address, and push the fetched value onto the stack. This is clearly done twice in our *Swap* method because we have two *int* pointer parameters. Similarly, the opcode *stdind.i4* is used twice:

this pushes the address of the variable onto the stack, pushes a value onto the stack, pops the value and the address from the stack, and stores the value at the address.

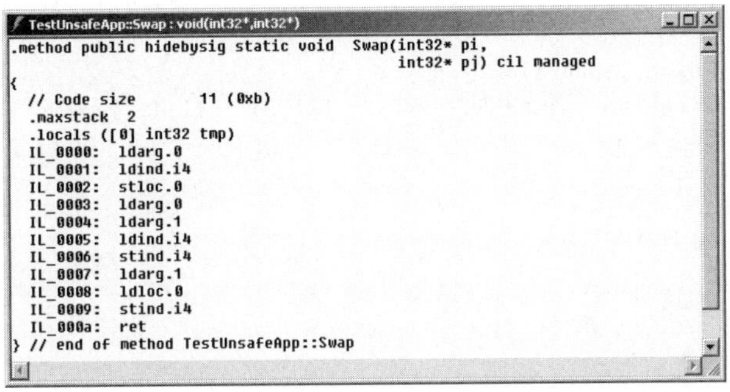

```
TestUnsafeApp::Swap : void(int32*,int32*)                                _|□|x|
.method public hidebysig static void  Swap(int32* pi,
                                           int32* pj) cil managed
{
  // Code size       11 (0xb)
  .maxstack  2
  .locals ([0] int32 tmp)
  IL_0000:  ldarg.0
  IL_0001:  ldind.i4
  IL_0002:  stloc.0
  IL_0003:  ldarg.0
  IL_0004:  ldarg.1
  IL_0005:  ldind.i4
  IL_0006:  stind.i4
  IL_0007:  ldarg.1
  IL_0008:  ldloc.0
  IL_0009:  stind.i4
  IL_000a:  ret
} // end of method TestUnsafeApp::Swap
```

Figure 20-8   MSIL for method modifying variables through their addresses.

In the following variation, we've written a struct that encapsulates the *Swap* method. We've also changed the signature of the *Swap* method so that it operates on *Insect* struct pointers, not just *int* pointers. Recall that you can take the address of any value type, including structs.

```
public struct Insect
{
    private int id;
    private decimal price;
    public Insect(int id, decimal price)
    {
        this.id = id;
        this.price = price;
    }
    override public string ToString()
    {
        return String.Format("{0}: {1}", id, price);
    }

    unsafe public static void Swap(Insect* pi, Insect* pj)
    {
        Insect tmp = *pi;
        *pi = *pj;
        *pj = tmp;
    }
}

class UnsafeStructApp
{
```

```
static void Main(string[] args)
{
    Insect i = new Insect(123, 45.67m);
    Insect j = new Insect(890, 98.76m);
    Console.WriteLine("Before Swap:\ti = {0}, j = {1}", i, j);

    unsafe { Insect.Swap(&i, &j); }
    Console.WriteLine("After Swap:\ti = {0}, j = {1}", i, j);
}
}
```

Here's the output:

```
Before Swap:    i = 123: 45.67, j = 890: 98.76
After Swap:     i = 890: 98.76, j = 123: 45.67
```

Pinning

Another technique used in unsafe code is *pinning*, for which you use the keyword *fixed*. This technique is permitted only in an *unsafe* context. The *fixed* keyword is responsible for the pinning of managed objects. Pinning is the act of specifying to the GC that the object in question can't be moved.

If you picture what happens during the execution of an application, you'll realize that objects are allocated and deallocated and that unused "spaces" in memory open up. To reduce the degree to which memory becomes fragmented, the .NET runtime moves objects around during garbage collection to try to consolidate used blocks of memory, thereby freeing up larger contiguous blocks. This system is clearly beneficial in making the most efficient use of the memory available. On the other hand, it's less useful when you have a pointer to a specific memory address and then—unbeknownst to you—the .NET runtime moves the object from that address, leaving you with an invalid pointer. This situation is why you have the option to pin a variable in memory if you want—but bear in mind that the reason the GC moves things around in memory is to increase application efficiency. Thus, you should pin variables only if you can't avoid doing so.

Note that you need only pin variables that might otherwise be moved by the runtime—therefore, this applies only to reference variables on the heap. The GC doesn't move value-type variables. Conceptually, our previous call to the *Swap* method behaves as indicated in the following code, where we pin the addresses of our variables before passing these addresses in the method call:

```
//unsafe { Swap(&i, &j); }
unsafe
{
```

```
fixed (int* pi = &i, pj = &j)
{
    Swap(pi, pj);
}
}
```

Although this is the conceptual behavior, the use of the *fixed* keyword isn't necessary here because value-type variables are always fixed in memory. Indeed, the compiler will reject this code as an error. If you don't need to pin value-type variables and you can't take the address of a reference-type variable, where does that leave you? Don't forget that all types ultimately will be made up of basic types—that is, at the lowest source code level, your custom class will consist of *ints, chars, decimals*, and so on. Therefore, you can use *fixed* to take the address of a value-type component of a reference-type variable. In the following example, we've done just that, with a simplified version of our *Insect* type—which, crucially, is now a class rather than a struct:

```
public class Insect
{
    public int id;
    public Insect(int id) { this.id = id; }
}


class UnsafeClassApp
{
    unsafe public static void Swap(int* pi, int* pj)
    {
        int tmp = *pi;
        *pi = *pj;
        *pj = tmp;
    }

    static void Main(string[] args)
    {
        Insect i = new Insect(123);
        Insect j = new Insect(456);
        Console.WriteLine(
            "Before Swap:\ti = {0}, j = {1}", i.id, j.id);

        unsafe
        {
            fixed (int* pi = &i.id, pj = &j.id)
            {
                Swap(pi, pj);
            }
        }
```

```
        Console.WriteLine(
            "After Swap:\ti = {0}, j = {1}", i.id, j.id);
    }
}
```

Here's the output:

```
Before Swap:    i = 123, j = 456
After Swap:     i = 456, j = 123
```

As you can see from the foregoing code, we can't take the address of an entire *Insect* because it's a managed reference-type object. On the other hand, if we want to process the fields in this object through their addresses, we must pin them in memory because the entire object might get moved by the GC. Note that the location of the pinned variable is fixed only during the execution of the *fixed* block of code. So, in our previous example, when we get to the final *Console.WriteLine*, none of our variables are pinned.

Pinning Array Elements

We can point to any object as long as we've pinned it—whether it's implicitly pinned because it's a value-type variable or explicitly pinned because it forms part of a reference-type variable. The situation with arrays is interesting. When you declare an array-type variable, you're declaring a reference to an array, which must later be assigned some contiguous memory on the heap. Consider this statement:

```
int[] ia = new int[5]{12,34,56,78,90};
```

The variable *ia* is a reference to the heap memory, but what does this mean? If you're familiar with pointers in C and C++, the answer is obvious: the value of *ia* is actually the address of the first value in the array—that is, the address of the *int* variable whose value is *12*. So, if the value of *ia* is an address, can we assign it to a pointer? The answer, of course, is yes:

```
unsafe
{
    fixed (int* pa = ia)
    {
        // Do something with pa.
    }
}
```

Notice that we don't take the address of *ia*, just its value, because its value is really the address of the *int* at the beginning of the array. Recall that although *ints* are value types, arrays (including arrays of *ints*) are reference types and are allocated on the heap. Just as we had to fix the address of a value-type member of a reference-type object, we also have to fix the address of a value-type element in a (reference-type) array. Let's put this together in a test application:

```
class FixedArrayApp
{
    unsafe public static void Foo(int* pa)
    {
        for (int* ip = pa; ip < (pa+5); ip++)
        {
            Console.Write("{0,-3}", *ip);
        }
        Console.WriteLine();
    }

    static void Main(string[] args)
    {
        int[] ia = new int[5]{12,34,56,78,90};

        unsafe
        {
            fixed (int* pa = ia)
            {
                Foo(pa);
            }
        }
    }
}
```

Here's the output:

```
12 34 56 78 90
```

Another interesting point arises. If you look closely at the *Foo* method, you'll see that we're doing some pointer arithmetic. Let's examine the *for* loop in detail:

```
for (int* ip = pa; ip < (pa+5); ip++)
{
    Console.Write("{0,-3}", *ip);
}
```

The *Foo* method has an *int* pointer (that is, the address of an integer) coming in as a parameter. We copy this into another *int* pointer, *ip*. Then we test to see whether the value of *ip* is still less than its original value plus 5, and we increment it each time around the loop. The expressions *pa+5* and *ip++* both use pointer arithmetic. Let's suppose for the sake of argument that the original value of *pa* is *12196684*: you'd expect *pa+5* to be *12196689*, wouldn't you?

But in fact it would be *12196700*. To explain this behavior, let's modify the output to print out the value of the pointer each time around the loop:

```
for (int* ip = pa; ip < (pa+5); ip++)
{
    Console.WriteLine(
        value {0} at address: {1}", *ip, (int)ip);
}
```

The output from this revised version is listed here:

```
value 12 at address: 12196684
value 34 at address: 12196688
value 56 at address: 12196692
value 78 at address: 12196696
value 90 at address: 12196700
```

Pointer arithmetic is performed based on the type of the pointer—that is, the type of the value that the pointer is pointing to. Because an *int* (that is, an *Int32*) is 4 bytes, the expression *ip++* evaluates to 12196684+4 and the expression *pa+5* evaluates to 12196684+(5*4).

Note that although you're permitted to perform arithmetic on pointers in this way, including incrementing and decrementing, it's your responsibility to make sure that the operation is safe. Suppose, for example, we were careless about using the loop counter and attempted to access element 6 in our five-element array:

```
unsafe public static void Foo(int* pa)
{
    for (int* ip = pa; ip < (pa+6); ip++)
    {
        Console.WriteLine(
            "value {0} at address: {1}", *ip, (int)ip);
    }
}
```

This would result in output that resembles the following, where clearly we've fallen off the end of the array and are accessing unknown values in memory:

```
value 12 at address: 12196664
value 34 at address: 12196668
value 56 at address: 12196672
value 78 at address: 12196676
value 90 at address: 12196680
value -2147483648 at address: 12196684
```

Now suppose that we did this:

```
int* jp = (int*)12345;
Console.WriteLine(
    "value {0} at address: {1}", *jp, (int)jp);
```

The outcome of this code at run time would almost certainly be a *NullReferenceException*: during the call to *WriteLine*, the runtime would attempt to access an object that it could use for the version of *WriteLine* being called and instead would find some memory that can't be interpreted as any object.

OK, so aside from the pointer arithmetic and assignment issues, we've seen that we can take the address of an *int* without using the & address-of operator because an array variable is really the address of the first element in the array. As we've seen, this works fine for value types such as *int*, but does it work for reference types? The answer, interestingly, is yes. In the following example, we have a method that clones an array of objects. We manage to take the address of a reference-type *Insect* object without using the address-of operator. Indeed, we couldn't use the address-of operator even if we wanted to because the compiler would complain that it's illegal to take the address of a managed reference-type object.

```
public struct Insect
{
    public int id;
    public Insect(int id) { this.id = id; }
}
class ClassAddressApp
{
    unsafe public static Insect[] CloneInsects(Insect[] box)
    {
        Insect[] ret = new Insect[box.Length];
        fixed (Insect* src = box, dest = ret)
        {
            Insect* pSrc = src;
            Insect* pDest = dest;
            for (int index = 0; index < box.Length; index++)
            {
                *pDest = *pSrc;
                pSrc++;
                pDest++;
            }
        }
        return ret;
    }

    static void Main(string[] args)
    {
        Insect[] box = new Insect[2];
```

```
    box[0] =  new Insect(123);
    box[1] = new Insect(456);

    Insect[] bag = CloneInsects(box);
    foreach (Insect i in bag)
    {
        Console.WriteLine(i.id);
    }
  }
}
```

Here's the output:

```
123
456
```

The crucial statement is the fixed expression

```
fixed (Insect* src = box, dest = ret)
```

where we're declaring a pointer to a reference type and assigning it the address of a reference-type object—without using the address-of operator—by assigning it the value of the array. The second subexpression also declares a pointer to an *Insect* and assigns it the address of an *Insect* by assigning it the new local array, which is the first element of the array, which is the address of an *Insect*.

As far as the copying operation is concerned, the significant expression is in the *for* loop

```
*pDest = *pSrc;
```

where we're dereferencing a pointer to an *Insect* to reach the actual *Insect* value and using that value to overwrite the value of another *Insect* pointed to by another pointer. Notice also that we're again relying on pointer arithmetic: the expression *pDest++* increments the pointer by the number of bytes taken up by an *Insect* reference—in other words, an *Insect* address, which is 4 bytes. We can prove this if we add an extra line to our code:

```
for (int index = 0; index < box.Length; index++)
{
    *pDest = *pSrc;
    Console.WriteLine(
        "{0} is at {1}", pDest->id, (int)pDest);
    pSrc++;
    pDest++;
}
```

Here's the output from this block of code:

```
123 is at 12196772
456 is at 12196776
```

The Dereference Member Operator

Recall from Table 20-1 that C# offers the *. and -> operators, which represent a combination of pointer dereference and member selection. Both forms of the syntax equate to the same operator. The operator performs a dereference on the left-hand operand—which is a pointer to a composite (such as a struct or class) type—and then accesses the member within that type specified by the right-hand operand. Therefore, this expression

```
(*pi).x;
```

is the same as this expression

```
pi->x;
```

and in both cases, the system dereferences the pointer *pi* to get to the composite object that the pointer points to and then accesses the *x* member of that object. Note that we need to protect the expression **pi* with parentheses because the member selection operator (.) has a higher level of precedence than the pointer dereference operator. In the following example, we revert to our struct type *Insect* for simplicity to illustrate the use of the dereference-member access operator:

```
public struct Insect
{
    public int id;
    private decimal price;
    public Insect(int id, decimal price)
    {
        this.id = id;
        this.price = price;
    }
    public void Foo() { Console.WriteLine("Foo"); }
}

class DerefMemberApp
{
    static void Main(string[] args)
    {
        Insect i = new Insect(123, 45.67m);

        unsafe
        {
            Insect* pi = &i;
            (*pi).Foo();
            pi->Foo();
```

```
            Console.WriteLine("id = {0}", pi->id);
        }
    }
}
```

Note that the integrity of the object is maintained; you can't use the deref-erence-member operator to access members that are protected because of their access levels—thus, we can't get to the private price field by using the pointer operators. The output from this code is shown here:

```
Foo
Foo
id = 123
```

***

> **Note**   Although the -> and *. operators are available in both C# and C++, they aren't the same as the pointer-to-member operators in C++ (.* and ->*), and these pointer-to-member operators aren't supported in C#.

***

Using *stackalloc*

As an alternative strategy to pinning, we can allocate data on the stack instead of on the heap by using the keyword *stackalloc*. This keyword will allocate a block of memory of sufficient size to contain the specified number of elements of the specified type; the address of the block is returned by the expression. Because this memory is on the stack, it isn't subject to garbage collection and therefore doesn't have to be pinned. For example, we could modify our earlier application that worked on an array of integers to put this array on the stack by using *stackalloc*:

```
class TestStackallocApp
{
    unsafe public static void Foo(int* pa)
    {
        for (int* ip = pa; ip < (pa+5); ip++)
        {
            Console.WriteLine(
                "value {0} at address: {1}", *ip, (int)ip);
        }
    }
```

```
        static void Main(string[] args)
        {
/*          int[] ia = new int[5]{12,34,56,78,90};

            unsafe
            {
                fixed (int* pa = ia)
                {
                    Foo(pa);
                }
            }
*/
            unsafe
            {
                int* pa = stackalloc int[5];
                pa[0] = 12;
                pa[1] = 34;
                pa[2] = 56;
                pa[3] = 78;
                pa[4] = 90;
                Foo(pa);
            }
        }
    }
```

Note that when using *stackalloc*, we can't initialize the array members—these must be assigned separately because *stackalloc* merely allocates the block of stack memory and doesn't perform any processing on the contents of that memory. The output from this revised code is the same as that of the earlier version (except, of course, that the address range is different):

```
value 12 at address: 1243296
value 34 at address: 1243300
value 56 at address: 1243304
value 78 at address: 1243308
value 90 at address: 1243312
```

A quick look at the MSIL for this expression—shown in Figure 20-9—will reveal the use of the *localloc* opcode. This opcode allocates a certain number of bytes from the local memory pool and pushes the address (a pointer) of the first allocated byte onto the evaluation stack. The runtime first loads the values 4 and 5 onto the stack—we want a block of memory big enough for five elements, each of which is 4 bytes in size—and then it performs a *mul* operation to calculate how much memory to allocate.

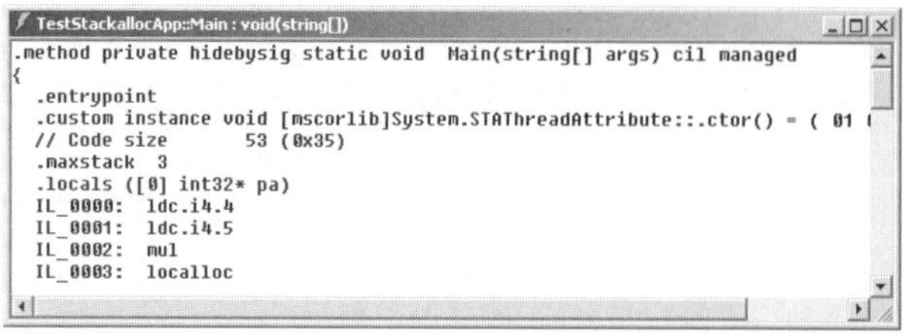

Figure 20-9   MSIL for *stackalloc*.

Summary

We've seen how to implement the functionality of destructors by overriding *Object.Finalize*. However, it should be clear to you that you should try to avoid overriding the *Finalize* method for your classes because this entails some runtime overhead, both upon creation and at some indeterminate time in the future.

   If you do need to ensure that some cleanup is done during the destruction of your object, you should adopt the *Dispose* pattern instead—the *Dispose* method can then be called at a precisely determined point, according to the requirements of the application. If you adopt this pattern and override *Finalize*, your finalizer will be delegated to a fail-safe tactic that merely calls *Dispose*, thus acting as a safety net if developer fails to call *Dispose* explicitly. If you do override *Finalize*, you should make it run fast—remember that the primary trigger for garbage collection is low-memory status, and you don't want to be doing a lot of work if you're low on memory. Furthermore, your *Finalize* should avoid synchronizing on other threads, it shouldn't block, and it shouldn't raise any exceptions. Also, be wary of calling methods on other objects during the *Finalize*—other objects might have already been finalized because the .NET Framework doesn't guarantee that finalizers will be called in any particular order.

   The second part of this chapter focused on ways in which you can work with raw memory addresses via pointers. To work with memory in this way, you have to indicate that the code is unsafe. Recall that the Common Language Specification requires that you don't expose any unsafe code at the public interface; therefore, the use of pointers is restricted to nonexposed parts of your code. This leaves the use of pointers firmly where it belongs: you use pointers in situations where you can improve performance by directly accessing memory.

21

Using COM from C# Applications

Throughout this book, one of the key concepts that I've focused on is *componentization* and how .NET—and specifically C#—enable you to break your applications into smaller, reusable, modular components. It's Microsoft's belief that C# represents the first truly object-oriented, componentized language. However, the fact that we now have a language that inherently supports component-based programming does leave us with a rather intriguing question: *Is COM—Microsoft's binary standard for writing component-based software for the past eight years—dead?*

This is a very good question—and understandable. After all, if the C# language supports componentization, why do we need COM? Additionally, several early articles written about C# stated that Microsoft had basically abandoned COM. Fortunately for those of you with an affinity for COM, I have some very good news. COM remains very much alive and well. In fact, I'll borrow a quote directly from Don Box, the man many feel is one of the most knowledgeable people on the subject of COM and interface programming in general: *"Virtually all aspects of the COM programming model have survived (interfaces, classes, attributes, context, and so on). Some may consider COM dead simply because common language runtime objects don't rely on IUnknown-compliant vptrs/vtbls. I look at the runtime as breathing new life into the programming model that I've spent the last seven years of my life working with, and I know there are other programmers out there who share this sentiment"* (MSDN Magazine, December 2000).

Although the news of COM's death was certainly a bit exaggerated, many questions remain regarding the role COM will play in the new .NET world. In this chapter, I'll attempt to answer many of these questions by exploring how .NET enables the use of COM components from managed code.

Along the way, I'll also use a very realistic demo application to illustrate how a COM component written using Active Template Library (ATL) 3 can be consumed, or used, from a .NET application written in C#. That way, you can see firsthand that COM continues to play a major role in the future of software development. Included in these examples are code illustrating how to early bind and late bind to COM components from C# as well as how to write event handlers for sourced COM events.

Where COM Fits in Today's .NET World

Back when the software development world was a much simpler place (circa 1993), Microsoft announced version 2 of OLE. At the same time, Microsoft explained that COM was the underpinning of OLE and represented the manner in which component-based systems were to be written. The features of this new and exciting framework were promising, to say the least:

- The ability to create reusable components, which reduced software development costs

- A binary standard, which meant that components could be used by any client regardless of the language used to write the component

- Dynamic interface discovery, which gave developers the ability to programmatically query components about their abilities before using them

- Reference counting, which made for better resource utilization

- Versioning, which gave developers a means of avoiding DLL hell

- A new error reporting system, which allowed error messages to propagate through the call chain regardless of the languages involved

COM did seem to promise it all, and as a result, many companies invested large sums of their software development budgets in writing their products around this object model. However, despite the hype and the fact that some high-profile applications have adopted COM as a standard, COM never attained the level of success that many had hoped, for one simple reason—*it's not nearly as easy as it first appears.*

You see, once you got past the hype, you quickly realized that reference counting didn't work the way most programmers thought it would, multithreading was a nightmare, and most people were so confused with the concept of marshaling that they just decided to use variants for everything—which, in most cases, was the worst thing to do.

With the introduction of the .NET Framework, component development has become a much more simplified process. Like COM, the .NET Framework affords you the ability to write components in virtually any language. The main difference is this: Much of what you did to make COM work in an efficient manner was manual—coding IDL files, spending countless hours testing and debugging problems related to threading, and so on. However, the .NET Framework provides much simpler and more powerful services.

By this point, you might be wondering, "If .NET is so great and COM is so hard, why do we even need COM anymore?" The answer is the age-old issue of legacy code. While I'd never recommend building COM components for use in an exclusively .NET environment, there's been too much money invested in COM for Microsoft to simply state, "We've got something better today, so throw out everything you did yesterday." Therefore, the .NET Framework does support a feature that allows for complete interoperation between COM components and code written using .NET compilers. This feature—named, appropriately enough, *COM interop*—is the focus of this chapter.

Using COM Components from C#

We'll begin our expose on using COM in the .NET world by doing the obvious—creating a classic COM component and using it from a C# client application. Our example will be an *Airline* component written in ATL 3 that contains an interface (*IAirlineInfo*), a method for determining airline flight information (*IAirlineInfo.GetAirlineTiming*), and a property for retrieving the current airport time (*IAirlineInfo.GetLocalTime*). Once we create this component, we'll consume (use) it from a C# console application. Let's get started!

Creating an ATL Component

Our first order of business is to use ATL to write a simple COM component that gives us the arrival details for a specific airline. For simplicity, we return details only for the 'Air Scooby IC 5678' airline and return an error for any other airline. That way, you can also see how the error raised by the COM component can be propagated back and caught by the calling .NET client application.

To get started, use the ATL Project Wizard to create a new project named AirlineInformation. On the Application Settings page of the wizard's dialog box, be sure that you select dynamic-link library (DLL) as the server type.

Once you've successfully created the project, select the Project->Add Class menu option. When the Add Class dialog box is displayed, select the ATL Simple Object option and click Open. This will cause the ATL Simple Object Wizard to start. From there, enter the short name **AirlineInfo**—the rest of the fields will fill in automatically—and click Finish. Now add a method named *GetAirlineTiming* and a property named *LocalTimeAtOrlando* so that when finished, the *IAirlineInfo* interface's IDL—located in the AirlineInformation.IDL file—looks like this:

⋮

```
interface IAirlineInfo : IDispatch
{

    [id(1), helpstring("method GetAirlineTiming")]
    HRESULT GetAirlineTiming([in] BSTR bstrAirline,
        [out,retval] BSTR* pBstrDetails);

    [propget, id(2), helpstring("property LocalTimeAtOrlando")]
    HRESULT LocalTimeAtOrlando([out, retval] BSTR *pVal);

};
```
⋮

Here's the implementation of the *GetAirlineTiming* method:

```
⋮
CAirlineInfo::GetAirlineTiming(BSTR bstrAirline, BSTR *pBstrDetails)
{
  _bstr_t bstrQueryAirline(bstrAirline);
  if(NULL == pBstrDetails) return E_POINTER;

  if(_bstr_t("Air Scooby IC 5678") == bstrQueryAirline)
  {
    // Return the timing for this Airline.
    *pBstrDetails =
      _bstr_t(_T("16:45:00 - Will arrive at Terminal 3")).copy();

  }
  else
  {
    // Return an error message if the Airline wasn't found.
    return Error(LPCTSTR(
      _T("Airline Timings not available for this Airline" )),
      __uuidof(AirlineInfo), AIRLINE_NOT_FOUND);
  }
  return S_OK;

}
⋮
```

Because our component is ready, let's take a look at generating some metadata from the component's type library so that the .NET client can use this metadata to talk to our component and invoke its methods.

Consuming a COM Component from a .NET Application

A .NET application that needs to talk to our COM component can't directly consume the functionality that the component exposes. Therefore, we need to generate some metadata. As you've learned throughout this book, metadata is used by the common language runtime to glean type information. In this case, the metadata is being used to dynamically generate something named a *Runtime Callable Wrapper* (RCW). The RCW handles the actual activation of the COM object and handles the marshaling requirements when the .NET application interacts with the object. The RCW also performs many other chores such as managing object identity, managing object lifetime, and managing interface caching. Object lifetime management is a very critical issue here because the .NET runtime moves objects around and garbage collects them. The RCW gives the .NET application the notion that it's interacting with a managed .NET component. The RCW also gives the COM component in the unmanaged space the impression that it's being called by a standard COM client. The RCW's creation and behavior varies depending on whether you're early binding or late binding to the COM object. Under the hood, the RCW does all the heavy lifting required to thunk the method invocations down to corresponding v-table calls into the COM component that lives in the unmanaged world. It's an ambassador of goodwill between the managed world and the unmanaged *IUnknown* world. Figure 21-1 graphically illustrates this process.

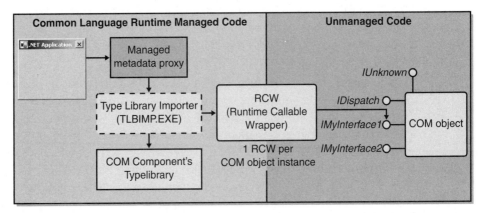

Figure 21-1   The Runtime Callable Wrapper (RCW) enables the consumption of a COM component from a .NET application.

Let's generate the metadata wrapper for our *Airline* COM component. To do that, we'll use a tool named the Type Library Importer (TLBIMP.EXE). This application ships with the .NET Framework SDK and can be located in the Bin subfolder of your SDK installation. Because I installed my SDK on drive D:, my particular path to TLBIMP is this:

```
D:\Program Files\Microsoft Visual Studio .NET\FrameworkSDK\Bin
```

If this folder isn't in your computer's search path, you should probably add the folder now because you'll be using this tool quite a bit for any COM interop work.

Now open a command window and change to the directory that contains the *AirlineInfo* component. Then type in the following command. (Remember that you'll need to fully qualify the call to TLBIMP if that folder isn't in your path.)

```
TLBIMP AirlineInformation.tlb /out:AirlineMetadata.dll
```

This command tells the type library importer to read your *AirlineInfo* COM type library and generate a corresponding metadata wrapper named AirlineMetadata.dll.

If everything went through fine, you should see a message indicating that the metadata proxy has been generated from the type library:

```
Type library imported to E:\COMInteropWithDOTNET\AirlineMetadata.dll
```

In keeping with the title *Inside C#*, we have to ask ourselves a question: "What exactly did that call to TLBIMP just generate?" To answer that question, we'll rely on our friend, the IL Disassembler (ILDASM). Start an ILDASM session, and open the AirlineMetadata.dll file, as shown in Figure 21-2. Take a look at the metadata generated, and you'll see the *GetAirlineTiming* method listed as a public method of the *IAirlineInfo* interface that's implemented by the *AirlineInfo* class. There's also a constructor that gets generated for the *AirlineInfo* class. The data types for the method parameters and return values have also been substituted to take their equivalent .NET counterparts. In our example, the *GetAirlineTiming* method's parameter with the BSTR data type has been replaced by the string—an alias for *System.String*—data type. Also notice that the parameter that was marked *[out,retval]* in the *GetAirlineTiming* method has been converted to the actual return value of the method, which was returned as a string. Finally, anytime a COM interface returns an *HRESULT* value indicating failure, the value is automatically converted to a .NET exception.

Figure 21-2   Once again, the ILDASM reveals all!

Binding to and Using the COM Component

Now that we've generated the metadata that's required by a .NET client, let's try invoking the *GetAirlineTiming* method in our COM object from the .NET client. Here's a simple C# client application that creates the COM object using the metadata that we generated earlier and invokes the *GetAirlineTiming* method. The first method call invocation should go through fine and yield the details of the airline "Air Scooby IC 5678". Then we'll pass in an unknown airline, "Air Jughead TX 1234", so that the COM object throws us the AIRLINE_NOT_FOUND error that we defined.

```
    ⋮
String strAirline = "Air Scooby IC 5678";
String strFoodJunkieAirline = "Air Jughead TX  1234";
try
{
    AirlineInfo objAirlineInfo;
    objAirlineInfo = new AirlineInfo();

    // Call the GetAirlineTiming method.
    System.Console.WriteLine("Details for Airline {0} --> {1}",
        strAirline,
        objAirlineInfo.GetAirlineTiming(strAirline));

    // This should make the COM object throw us the
```

```
    // AIRLINE_NOT_FOUND error as a COMException.
    System.Console.WriteLine("Details for Airline {0} --> {1}",
        strFoodJunkieAirline,
        objAirlineInfo.GetAirlineTiming(strFoodJunkieAirline));
}
catch(COMException e)
{
    System.Console.WriteLine("Oops, an error occured! " +
        "Error Code is : {0}. Error message is : {1}",
        e.ErrorCode,e.Message);
}
```

Here's how the output looks:

```
Details for Airline Air Scooby IC 5678 --> 16:45:00 - Will arrive at
 Terminal 3
Oops, an error occured! Error Code is : -2147221502.
 Error message is : Airline Timings not available for this Airline
```

Under the hood, the runtime fabricates an RCW, which maps the metadata proxy's class methods and fields to methods and properties exposed by the interface that the COM object implements. One RCW instance is created for each instance of the COM object. With regards to its interaction with the RCW, the .NET runtime cares only about managing its lifetime and handling garbage collection duties. The RCW takes care of maintaining reference counts on the COM object that the object is mapped to, thereby shielding the .NET runtime from managing the reference counts on the actual COM object.

As shown in the ILDASM view, the *AirlineInfo* metadata class is defined under a namespace named *AirlineMetadata*. This *AirlineInfo* class implements the *IAirlineInfo* interface. All you need to do is create an instance of the *AirlineInfo* class using the *new* operator and call the public class methods of the created object. When a given method is invoked, the RCW thunks down the call to the corresponding COM method. The RCW also handles all the marshaling and object lifetime issues. From the .NET client's viewpoint, the client appears to create a managed object and calls one of the object's public class members.

Anytime the COM method raises an error, the COM error is trapped by the RCW and the error is converted into an equivalent *COMException* class—found in the *System.Runtime.InteropServices* namespace. Of course, the COM object still needs to implement the *ISupportErrorInfo* and *IErrorInfo* interfaces for this error propagation to work so that the RCW knows that the object provides extended error information. The .NET client catches the error with the usual *try-catch* exception handling mechanism, and the client has access to the actual error number, description, source of the exception, and other details that would have been available to any COM-aware client.

If you return standard *HRESULT* values, the RCW will map them to the corresponding .NET exceptions that are thrown back to the client. For example, if you return an *HRESULT* of *E_NOTIMPL* from your COM method, the RCW will map this value to the .NET *NotImplementedException* exception and throw an exception of that type.

More Info   If you're new to exception handling, please refer to Chapter 12, "Error Handling with Exceptions," for an introduction to the subject. If you're already knowledgeable in exception handling, you might want to refer to the "Exception Handling: .NET vs. COM" section of Chapter 22, "Using .NET Components in Unmanaged Code," to learn more about how .NET exceptions are mapped to COM *HRESULT* values.

Dynamic Type Discovery with COM Components

How does the *QueryInterface* scenario work from the perspective of the .NET client when *QueryInterface* needs to check whether a COM object implements a specific interface? To call *QueryInterface* for another interface, you simply cast the object to the interface that you're querying for, and if the cast succeeds—voilà—your *QueryInterface* succeeds as well. In case you attempt to cast the object to some arbitrary interface that the object doesn't support, a *System.InvalidCastException* exception is thrown, indicating that the *QueryInterface* call has failed. The process is that simple. Again, the RCW does all the hard work under the covers. It's similar to the way the Microsoft Visual Basic runtime shields us from having to write any explicit *QueryInterface*-related code by simply calling *QueryInterface* for you when you set one object type to an object of another associated type.

An alternate way to check whether the object instance that you're currently holding supports or implements a specific interface type is to use C#'s *is* operator. As you learned in Chapter 7, "Interfaces," the *is* operator does runtime type checking to see whether the object can be cast safely to a specific type. If the operator returns a value of *true*, you can safely perform a cast to get the *QueryInterface* performed on your behalf. This way, the RCW ensures that you're casting to interfaces that are implemented by the COM object and not just any arbitrary interface type. As with .NET interfaces (also covered in Chapter 7), you can use C#'s *as* operator to cast from one type to another type that's compatible, as shown in the following example. These simple constructs are all that you need to switch between the different interfaces that a given COM object supports in a type-safe manner.

```
          ⋮
try
{
    AirlineInfo objAirlineInfo = null;
    IAirportFacilitiesInfo objFacilitiesInfo = null;

    // Create a new AirlineInfo object.
    objAirlineInfo = new AirlineInfo();

    // Invoke the GetAirlineTiming method.
    String strDetails = objAirlineInfo.GetAirlineTiming(strAirline);

    // Check to see whether the AirlineInfo object supports the
    // IAirportFacilitiesInfo interface using C#'s is operator.
    if(objAirlineInfo is IAirportFacilitiesInfo)
    {
        // Perform a cast to get the QueryInterface done.
        objFacilitiesInfo = (IAirportFacilitiesInfo)objAirlineInfo;

        // There's always more than one way to skin a cat.
        // You could even perform the cast using C#'s as operator.
        objFacilitiesInfo = objAirlineInfo as IAirportFacilitiesInfo;

        // Invoke a method on the IAirportFacilitiesInfo interface.
        System.Console.WriteLine("{0}",
            objFacilitiesInfo.GetInternetCafeLocations());

    }

    // Let's check against an arbitrary interface type.
    if(objAirlineInfo is IJunkInterface)
    {
        System.Console.WriteLine("We should never get here ");
    }
    else
    {
        System.Console.WriteLine("I'm sorry I don't implement " +
            "the IJunkInterface interface ");
    }

    // And now let's ask for some trouble and have the
    // COM interop throw us an invalid cast exception.
    IJunkInterface objJunk = null;
    objJunk = (IJunkInterface)objAirlineInfo;

}
catch(InvalidCastException eCast)
{
```

```
System.Console.WriteLine("Here comes trouble ... " +
   "Error Message : {0}",eCast.Message);

}
⋮
```

Here's how the output would look:

```
Your nearest Internet Cafe is at Pavilion 3 in Terminal 2
 - John Doe's Sip 'N' Browse Cafe
I'm sorry I don't implement the IJunkInterface interface
Here comes trouble ... Error Message : An exception of
 type System.InvalidCastException was thrown.
```

Late Binding to COM Objects

The examples that you just saw used the metadata proxy to early bind the .NET client to the COM object. Though early binding provides a smorgasbord of benefits—such as strong type checking at compile time, autocompletion capabilities from type information for development tools, and of course, better performance—there might be instances in which you really need to late bind to a COM object but don't have the compile-time metadata for that COM object. You can late bind to a COM object through a mechanism known as *reflection*. This process doesn't apply to COM objects alone. Even .NET managed objects can be late bound and loaded using reflection. Also, if your object implements a pure *dispinterface* only, you're pretty much limited to using reflection to activate your object and invoke methods on its interface.

When late binding to a COM object, you need to know the object's *ProgID* or *CLSID*. The *CreateInstance* static method of the *System.Activator* class allows you to specify the *Type* information for a specific class and will automatically create an object of that specific type. Instead of true .NET *Type* information, what we really have is a COM *ProgID* and COM *CLSID* for our COM object. Therefore, we need to get the *Type* information from the *ProgID* or *CLSID* using the *GetTypeFromProgID* or *GetTypeFromCLSID* static methods of the *System.Type* class. The *System.Type* class is one of the core enablers of reflection.

After creating an instance of the object using *Activator.CreateInstance*, you can invoke any of the methods and properties supported by the object using the *System.Type.InvokeMember* method of the *Type* object that you got back from *Type.GetTypeFromProgID* or *Type.GetTypeFromCLSID*. All you need to know is the name of the method or property and the kind of parameters that the method call accepts. The parameters are bundled into a generic *System.Object* array and passed to the method. You'd also need to set the appropriate binding flags depending on whether you're invoking a method or getting or setting the value of a property. That's all there is to late binding to a COM object. Here's how the code looks:

```
  ⋮
try
{

    object objAirlineLateBound;
    Type objTypeAirline;

    // Create an object array containing the input
    // parameters for the method.
    object[] arrayInputParams= { "Air Scooby IC 5678" };

    // Get the type information from the ProgID.
    objTypeAirline = Type.GetTypeFromProgID(
        "AirlineInformation.AirlineInfo");

    // Here's how you use the COM CLSID to get
    // the associated .NET System.Type:
    // objTypeAirline = Type.GetTypeFromCLSID(new Guid(
    //   "{F29EAEEE-D445-403B-B89E-C8C502B115D8}"));


    // Create an instance of the object.
    objAirlineLateBound = Activator.CreateInstance(
        objTypeAirline);

    // Invoke the GetAirlineTiming method.
    String str =  (String)objTypeAirline.InvokeMember(
        "GetAirlineTiming",
        BindingFlags.Default | BindingFlags.InvokeMethod,
        null,
        objAirlineLateBound,
        arrayInputParams);

    System.Console.WriteLine("Late Bound Call - Air Scooby " +
        "Arrives at : {0}",str);

    // Get the value of the LocalTimeAtOrlando property.
    String strTime = (String)objTypeAirline.InvokeMember(
        "LocalTimeAtOrlando",
        BindingFlags.Default | BindingFlags.GetProperty,
        null,
        objAirlineLateBound,
        new object[]{});
```

```
    Console.WriteLine ("Late Bound Call - Local Time at " +
        "Orlando, Florida is: {0}", strTime);

}/* end try */
catch(COMException e)
{
    System.Console.WriteLine("Error code : {0},
        Error message : {1}",
        e.ErrorCode, e.Message);
}/* end catch */
⋮
```

Take a look at the output this code produces:

```
Late Bound Call - Air Scooby Arrives at 16:45:00 - Will arrive
 at Terminal 3
Late Bound Call - Local Time at Orlando, Florida is: Sun Jul 15
 16:50:01 2001
```

Event Handling

One of the most important facets of COM is connection points and how they provide event-handling capabilities to COM components and clients. In Chapter 14, "Delegates and Event Handlers," you learned how *delegates* are used to provide event handling for .NET managed code. Therefore, in this section, I'll assume that you already know how .NET delegates work and will skip directly to a refresher on COM connection points. I'll then explain how the COM connection point model is mapped to the delegate event model via the RCW.

How COM Connection Points Work

As you probably know, the *Connection Points* event-handling mechanism is the primary facility for bidirectional communication between your COM components and their clients. As a refresher, let's see how this COM event-handling mechanism functions.

Generally, when a COM component supports event notifications, it has an *outgoing interface*. This interface is used by the component to call into the client when a specific event of interest to the client has occurred. These outgoing interfaces are marked with the *[source]* attribute in the *coclass* section of the component's IDL file. The *[source]* attribute exists to indicate to any development tools that the object supports an outgoing interface.

From there, consumers of the component usually set up a *sink object* that implements the outgoing interface. The client is then responsible for sending to the component an interface pointer to the sink object. By doing this, the client basically subscribes to an event that the component will publish. The component stores this pointer in a map of outgoing interface pointers to sink objects. Now, whenever the component needs to raise an event, it can simply iterate through this map, searching for all sink object pointers mapped to a given outgoing interface pointer. If this process sounds a little too abstract, allow me to try clarifying with a more concrete example.

Let's say you have a *WebSite* component that can alert clients when a new article is posted. The outgoing interface might be named something such as *INewArticleEvent*. Now suppose that you have a client application that needs to be alerted when a new article is posted. This consumer would have a sink object that implements the *INewArticleEvent* interface. The consumer would pass the sink object's pointer to the *WebSite* component. (You'll see how shortly.) The *WebSite* component now has an entry in its event map that maps the *INewArticleEvent* interface to the sink object. Now when the *WebSite* component wants to raise the *INewArticleEvent* event, the component simply iterates through that map and calls into the sink object, alerting the object of the event's occurrence.

That's the 50,000-foot view. Now let's drop down a level and look at the actual components and method names that are used to make this process work.

When a COM object supports outgoing interfaces, it implements an interface named *IConnectionPointContainer*. Any client that wants to receive event notifications calls *QueryInterface* on the COM object for the *IConnectionPointContainer* interface to determine whether the object supports outgoing interfaces. If the *QueryInterface* call fails, the object doesn't support events. However, if the *QueryInterface* call succeeds, the client calls the *FindConnectionPoint* method, passing it the IID of the outgoing interface. Alternatively, the client can choose to iterate through all the component's connection points by using the *EnumConnectionPoints* method.

If the *FindConnectionPoint* method is successful, the component returns to the client an *IConnectionPoint* interface pointer corresponding to the outgoing interface. Now the client has something tangible that it can use. The client uses the *IConnectionPoint* interface to call the component's *Advise* method—passing to this method the sink object's *IUnknown* pointer. Remember that this *IConnectionPoint* represents the desired event that the client needs to be notified of.

The component adds the passed sink object's *IUnknown* pointer to its map in order to maintain a list of all sink objects that have subscribed for notifications to this particular event. The *IConnectionPoint.Advise* method returns a token from the component to the client. This token represents the subscription to the event and can be used to unsubscribe to the event by calling the *IConnectionPoint.Unadvise* method, thus passing this token.

Now all the pieces are in place. When the COM object needs to raise a given event, the object simply iterates through the map, gets a list of all the sink object interface pointers, and calls the corresponding event methods on the outgoing interface, which is implemented by the sink object. Figure 21-3 shows this process.

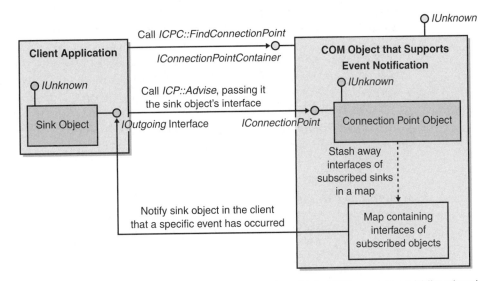

Figure 21-3 Connection points are the means by which COM provides a bidirectional event model between components and consumers (clients).

Creating an ATL COM Component That Sources Events

Let's take a look at how the Connection Points event-handling mechanism in COM translates to the delegate event-handling mechanism in the .NET world. We'll take a look at how you can use .NET managed event sinks to catch event notifications sent from COM objects. To get started, let's look at the COM object that will source events to your .NET application. Let's create a simple COM object that will page your .NET application whenever an airline flight arrives at a fictitious airport named John Doe International Airport. Figure 21-4 shows an ILDASM display of the metadata information created by TLBIMP from the *AirlineNotify* component.

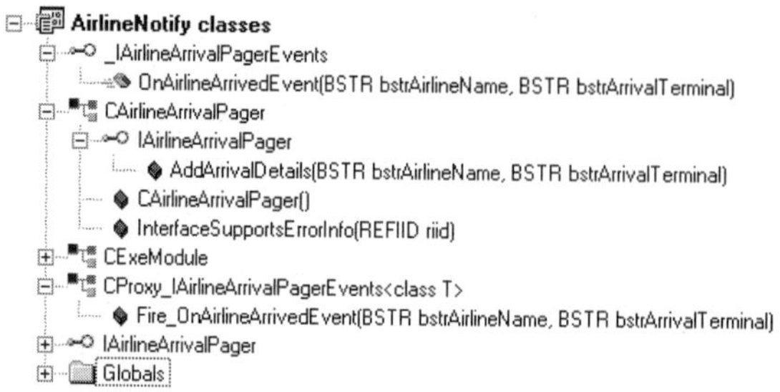

Figure 21-4   The *AirlineNotify* component illustrates how to source events in COM. A C# client application will receive notification when these events are raised.

We'll create an ATL .exe project that hosts an object named *AirlineArrival-Pager*. The *AirlineArrivalPager* object supports an incoming interface named *IAirlineArrivalPager* in addition to an outgoing interface named *_IAirlineArrivalPagerEvents*. Here's the interface definition of the *_IAirlineArrivalPagerEvents* outgoing interface. This interface is marked with the *[source]* attribute in the *coclass* definition:

```
⋮

interface IAirlineArrivalPager : IDispatch
{
    [id(1), helpstring("method AddArrivalDetails")]
        HRESULT AddArrivalDetails([in] BSTR bstrAirlineName,
        [in] BSTR bstrArrivalTerminal);
};

⋮

dispinterface _IAirlineArrivalPagerEvents
{
    properties:
    methods:
        [id(1), helpstring("method OnAirlineArrivedEvent")]
            HRESULT OnAirlineArrivedEvent(
            [in] BSTR bstrAirlineName,
            [in] BSTR bstrArrivalTerminal);
};

⋮

coclass AirlineArrivalPager
{
    [default] interface IAirlineArrivalPager;
    [default, source] dispinterface _IAirlineArrivalPagerEvents;
};

⋮
```

Take a look at the implementation of the incoming *IAirlineArrivalPager* interface's *AddArrivalDetails* method:

```
⋮
STDMETHODIMP CAirlineArrivalPager::AddArrivalDetails(
    BSTR bstrAirlineName,BSTR bstrArrivalTerminal)
{
    // Notify all subscribers that an airline arrived.
    Fire_OnAirlineArrivedEvent(bstrAirlineName,
        bstrArrivalTerminal);

    // Return the status to the caller.
    return S_OK;
}
⋮
```

The implementation of this method uses the *Fire_OnAirlineArrivedEvent* helper method to notify all those sink objects implementing *_IAirlineArrivalPagerEvents* that have subscribed for event notifications. *Fire_OnAirlineArrivedEvent* is a method of the helper proxy class derived from *IConnectionPointImpl* that's generated automatically by the ATL Implement Connection Point Wizard. Essentially, *Fire_OnAirlineArrivedEvent* iterates through the map where it stored the interface pointers to the sink objects when *IConnectionPoint::Advise* was called. The method uses these interface pointers to call the event notification method (*OnAirlineArrivedEvent*) implemented by the client's sink object.

If you were a C++ programmer coding a COM-aware client application to receive notifications, you'd set up a sink object in the client application that implements the *_IAirlineArrivalPagerEvents* interface. You'd then create the *AirlineArrivalPager* object and either pass it the *IUnknown* interface pointer of the sink object through a call to *IConnectionPoint::Advise* or use a helper method such as *AtlAdvise* to wire your sink to the object that raises events so that you can receive event notifications. With Visual Basic 6, it's as simple as using the *WithEvents* keyword in your declaration and defining a handler function for receiving notifications. Visual Basic does all the hard work under the covers to connect the notifications made on the outgoing interface to the appropriate handler function.

Event Handling Using Delegates

If you're already familiar with how delegates are used in .NET, you might want to skip this section. Event handling in .NET is primarily based on a delegate-based event model. A delegate is akin to the function pointers that we use in C and C++.

More Info   See Chapter 14 for more information on how delegates are used to provide event handling for .NET managed code.

The delegate-based event model was popularized by the simplicity of its use, right from the Windows Foundation Classes (WFC) in Microsoft Visual J++. Delegates allow an event raised by any component to be connected to a handler function or method of any other component, as long as the function signatures of the handler function or method match the signatures of the delegate. This simple example shows you how you can put delegates to use:

```
// Here's the SayGoodMorning delegate.
delegate string SayGoodMorning();

public class HelloWorld
{
    public string SpeakEnglish() {
        return "Good Morning";
    }

    public string SpeakFrench() {
        return "Bonjour";
    }

    public static void Main(String[] args) {

        HelloWorld obj = new HelloWorld();

        // Associate the delegate with a method reference.
        SayGoodMorning english =
            new SayGoodMorning(obj.SpeakEnglish);
        SayGoodMorning french =
            new SayGoodMorning(obj.SpeakFrench);

        // Invoke the delegate.
        System.Console.WriteLine(english());
        System.Console.WriteLine(french());

    }

}/* end class */
```

Here's the output from this example:

```
Good Morning
Bonjour
```

In this example, we declare a delegate named *SayGoodMorning*. Then we wire the delegate to reference the *SpeakEnglish* and *SpeakFrench* methods of the *HelloWorld* object. The *SpeakEnglish* and *SpeakFrench* methods must have the same signature as the *SayGoodMorning* delegate. The delegate is typically instantiated as though it were an object, passing in the referenced method as its parameter. The referenced method could be either an instance method or a static method of a class. The delegate maintains the reference to call the correct event handler. This arrangement makes delegates first-class object-oriented citizens. Delegates are also type-safe and secure to work with.

The .NET event-handling model is based primarily on the delegate-based event model. Take a look at the following example:

⋮

```
// Create a button.
private System.Windows.Forms.Button AngryButton = new Button();
```

⋮

```
// Add a delegate to the button's Click event list.
AngryButton.Click += new System.EventHandler(AngryButton_Click);
```

⋮

```
// Here's the handler function that the delegate references.
protected void AngryButton_Click(object sender,EventArgs e)
{
    MessageBox.Show("Please stop clicking me!!");
}
```

⋮

When your application deals with controls and wants to receive specific notifications, it creates a new instance of an *EventHandler* delegate that contains a reference to the actual handler function that will handle the events raised by the control. In the previous example, the *EventHandler* delegate contains a reference to the *AngryButton_Click* method. The *AngryButton_Click* method needs to have the same method signature as the *EventHandler* delegate. Here's the signature of the *System.EventHandler* delegate:

```
public delegate void EventHandler(object sender, EventArgs e);
```

The *EventHandler* delegate instance will then have to be added to the *Click* event's list of delegate instances. Delegates that extend *System.Multicast-Delegate* allow you to add multiple handler functions to the delegate's invocation list by using C# operators such as += and −=, which are wrappers for the *Delegate.Combine* and *Delegate.Remove* methods. Using an event provides a foolproof scheme for programmers to add or remove delegate instances to the event using the += and −= operators without accidentally overwriting the invocation list. When the control raises an event, each of the delegates that have been added to the button's *Click* event will be invoked and the delegate will route the event to the correct handler function that the delegate references.

In our example, whenever the user clicks the button, its *Click* event will be routed to the *AngryButton_Click* method. This should give you a fairly good idea of the role delegates and events play in the event-handling mechanism in the .NET Framework. Delegates are one of the primary enablers of the .NET event-handling model, and you need to understand this to appreciate how .NET applications use delegates to subscribe to event notifications from COM components.

Sinking Unmanaged COM Events in a .NET Application

Figure 21-5 shows a simple Visual Basic client application that assumes the role of the control tower at John Doe International Airport and calls the *AddArrival-Details* method in the incoming interface.

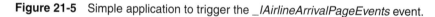

Figure 21-5   Simple application to trigger the _*IAirlineArrivalPageEvents* event.

The implementation of this method triggers the event notifications that are subsequently caught by the handler functions in the .NET application that have subscribed for *OnAirlineArrivedEvent* event notifications. The *AirlineArrival-Pager* COM object is itself a singleton object hosted in an out-of-proc COM server. Thus, the same instance of the object services both the Visual Basic–based control tower application that triggers events and the .NET pager applications that have subscribed for *OnAirlineArrivedEvent* event notifications. Here's how the code looks:

```
Dim AirlinePager As New AIRLINENOTIFYLib.AirlineArrivalPager

Private Sub AirlineArrived_Click()
    AirlinePager.AddArrivalDetails Me.AirlineName,
        Me.ArrivalTerminal
End Sub
```

Now let's see how a .NET managed application receives event notifications generated by the *AirlineArrivalPager* COM object. First, you need to generate a .NET metadata proxy from the COM object's typelib so that it can be consumed by a .NET application. Let's use TLBIMP to generate the metadata proxy assembly for us:

```
tlbimp AirlineNotify.tlb /out:AirlineNotifyMetadata.dll
```

This metadata proxy will be referenced in your .NET application. Figure 21-6 shows a simple .NET Windows Forms application that uses delegates to subscribe to event notifications from the *AirlineArrivalPager* COM component.

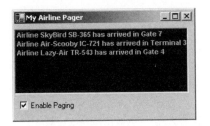

Figure 21-6   This simple Windows Forms application allows you to easily see the effect of subscribing to and unsubscribing from an event.

The relevant code is listed here:

```
⋮

using AirlineNotifyMetadata;

public class AirlineNotifyForm : System.WinForms.Form
{
  private System.Windows.Forms.CheckBox checkBoxPaging;
  private System.Windows.Forms.ListBox listPager;
  private AirlineArrivalPager m_pager = null;

  ⋮

  public AirlineNotifyForm() {

    ⋮

    // Subscribe to event notifications from
    // the AirlineArrivalPager component.
    subscribePaging();

  }
```

```
  ⋮
void subscribePaging() {

  // Create an AirlineArrivalPager object.
  m_pager = new AirlineArrivalPager();

  // Add the delegate instance that references the
  // OnMyPagerNotify method to the OnAirlineArrivedEvent
  // event list (ICP::Advise).
  m_pager.OnAirlineArrivedEvent += new
  _IAirlineArrivalPagerEvents_OnAirlineArrivedEventEventHandler(
  OnMyPagerNotify);

}/* end subscribePaging */

protected void checkBoxPaging_CheckedChanged (object sender,
  System.EventArgs e) {

  if(checkBoxPaging.Checked) {

    // If checked, add the delegate instance that references
    // OnMyPagerNotify to the OnAirlineArrivedEvent
    // event list (ICP::Advise).
    m_pager.OnAirlineArrivedEvent += new
  _IAirlineArrivalPagerEvents_OnAirlineArrivedEventEventHandler(
    OnMyPagerNotify);

  }
  else {

    // If unchecked, remove the delegate instance that
    // References OnMyPagerNotify from the OnAirlineArrivedEvent
    // event list (ICP::Unadvise).
    m_pager.OnAirlineArrivedEvent -= new
  _IAirlineArrivalPagerEvents_OnAirlineArrivedEventEventHandler(
    OnMyPagerNotify);

  }

}/* end checkBoxPaging_CheckedChanged */


public int OnMyPagerNotify(String strAirline,
  String strTerminal) {

  StringBuilder strDetails = new StringBuilder("Airline ");
  strDetails.Append(strAirline);
```

```
    strDetails.Append(" has arrived in ");
    strDetails.Append(strTerminal);
    listPager.Items.Insert(0,strDetails);
    return 0;

  }/* end OnMyPagerNotify */

}/* end class */
```

This is the statement that's most important here:

```
m_pager.OnAirlineArrivedEvent += new
  _IAirlineArrivalPagerEvents_OnAirlineArrivedEventEventHandler(
  OnMyPagerNotify);
```

Once you understand the semantics of how delegates work, you should have no problem comprehending what's happening here. What you're doing is adding to the *OnAirlineArrivedEvent* event list the *_IAirlineArrival-PagerEvents_OnAirlineArrivedEventEventHandler* delegate instance that references the *OnMyPagerNotify* method. Usually the name of the event (*OnAirlineArrivedEvent*) is the same as the method name in the outgoing interface. The delegate name (*_IAirlineArrivalPagerEvents_OnAirlineArrived-EventEventHandler*) usually follows the pattern *<InterfaceName_EventName-EventHandler>*.

That's all there is to receiving event notifications from COM components. You simply create an instance of the component and then add to the event list a delegate that references your handler function. Effectively, what you're doing is analogous to how you use *IConnectionPoint::Advise* in the COM world. Whenever the *OnAirlineArrivedEvent* event is raised by the COM component, the delegate calls the *OnMyPagerNotify* method to handle the event notification. .NET makes it that simple to wire a handler sink to receive event notifications from a COM object that sources events. The delegate-based event-handling mechanism is depicted in Figure 21-7.

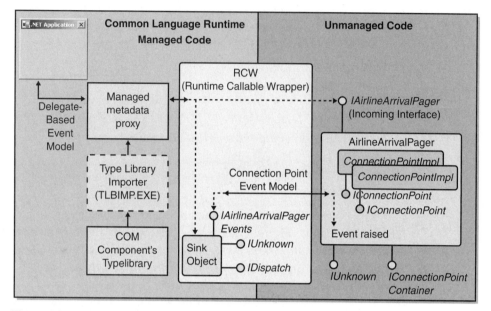

Figure 21-7 How the Connection Points event-handling mechanism in COM maps to the delegate-based event-handling mechanism in .NET.

When you no longer want to receive notifications, you can remove the delegate from the event list by calling the following:

```
m_pager.OnAirlineArrivedEvent -= new
    _IAirlineArrivalPagerEvents_OnAirlineArrivedEventEventHandler(
    OnMyPagerNotify);
```

This call is analogous to the *IConnectionPoint::Unadvise* method call that revokes further notifications by removing your sink object's interface pointer from the map by using the cookie that you received in the *Advise* call. But what handles the mapping between the Connection Points event-handling model in COM and the delegate-based event model in .NET? The metadata proxy generated by TLBIMP contains classes that act as adaptors to wire the Connection Points event model in the unmanaged world to the delegate-based event model in the .NET world via the RCW stub that's created at run time. If you're interested in examining what happens under the hood, I encourage you to open up the metadata proxy—AirlineNotifyMetadata.dll—using the ILDASM and examine the Microsoft intermediate language (MSIL) code for the various methods in the helper classes.

Using COM Collections

Using COM-based collections allows you to categorize objects together as a group that exhibits similar behavior. For example, a *BookCollection* collection could model all the books in a library. Each *Book* object stored in this collection could represent the details of a specific book, such as the author, ISBN, and so on. Iterating through the collection is extremely simple and allows you to get—on demand—objects that have been added to the collection. You can also model collections in other ways, such as by using a *SAFEARRAY*. However, the problem with a *SAFEARRAY* is that if the collection is large, getting data from the *SAFEARRAY* involves moving to the client entire data chunks that the *SAFEARRAY* represents.

Using collections allows you to get data on demand. Also, it's much more elegant to iterate through a collection from clients such as Visual Basic by using the *For Each..Next* syntax. If you have existing COM objects that represent COM-based collections, they will continue to work well with .NET applications. You can enumerate these collections just as easily from .NET clients. You'll soon see how. (If you're already familiar with how collections work in COM, you might want to skip this section.)

Creating a COM Collection Component Using ATL

For those of you who feel more at home churning out COM components with Visual Basic, you might want to skip this section and go to the "Creating a COM Collection Component Using Visual Basic" sidebar in this section. First, let's use ATL to put together a simple COM component that models an ice cream collection. The collection class we create represents a menu at an ice cream parlor that contains a variety of ice cream flavors. Take a look at the IDL file for this component:

```
[
    ⋮
]
interface IIceCreamMenu : IDispatch
{
    [propget, id(1), helpstring("property Count")]
            HRESULT Count([out, retval] long *pVal);

    [propget, id(DISPID_NEWENUM),
        helpstring("property _NewEnum"),
        restricted]
            HRESULT _NewEnum([out, retval] LPUNKNOWN *pVal);
```

```
    [propget, id(DISPID_VALUE), helpstring("property Item")]
            HRESULT Item([in] long lIndex,
            [out, retval] VARIANT *pVal);

    [id(2), helpstring("method AddFlavortoMenu")]
            HRESULT AddFlavortoMenu([in] BSTR bstrNewFlavor);
};
```

The *Count*, *_NewEnum*, and *Item* properties are standard properties that every COM collection supports. The *_NewEnum* property allows you to enumerate through the collection using constructs such as Visual Basic's *For Each..Next* and is always assigned a *DISPID* of *DISPID_NEWENUM(-4)* to indicate that it's the enumerator for the collection. This property usually returns an *IUnknown* interface pointer to an object that implements the *IEnumVariant* interface. The *IEnumVariant* interface provides all the methods that you need—such as *Next*, *Skip*, *Reset*, and *Clone*—for enumerating a collection containing *VARIANT* values.

The *Item* property is assigned a *DISPID* of *DISPID_VALUE(0)* to indicate that *Item* is the default property to be used if you omit the property name. The *Item* property allows you to locate an item in the collection by using an index. The actual index can be any type based on your business model. For example, a *BookCollection* collection could provide an ISBN number as a string for its *Item* index; the ISBN number could also act as a key value in a Standard Template Library (STL) map to locate the corresponding book. In the ice cream menu example, we use an index of type *long* to locate an ice cream flavor at a specified index. Because we've based our collection on an STL vector, an index of type *long* is convenient for accessing a specific element in the vector. The *ICollectionOnSTLImpl<>* base class that our *IceCreamMenu* collection component derives from provides us with a default implementation of *Item* based on an index of type *long*.

The *Count* property returns the number of elements in the collection. All three of our properties are read-only. You can add any number of helper methods that allow you to add, remove, and update elements in your collection. Take a look at this ATL code for the *IceCreamMenu* collection component:

```
// Forward definition
class _CopyPolicyIceCream;

// Define an STL vector to hold all the ice cream flavors.
typedef vector<_bstr_t> ICECREAM_MENU_VECTOR;

// Define a COM enumerator based on our ICECREAM_MENU_VECTOR.
typedef CComEnumOnSTL< IEnumVARIANT, &IID_IEnumVARIANT, VARIANT,
    _CopyPolicyIceCream, ICECREAM_MENU_VECTOR > VarEnum;
```

```cpp
// Collection class helper for STL-based containers.
typedef ICollectionOnSTLImpl< IIceCreamMenu,
    ICECREAM_MENU_VECTOR, VARIANT,
    _CopyPolicyIceCream, VarEnum > IceCreamCollectionImpl;

// Simulate deep copy semantics for the
// elements in our collection.
class _CopyPolicyIceCream
{
public:

    static HRESULT copy(VARIANT* pVarDest,
        _bstr_t* bstrIceCreamFlavor)
    {
        // Assign to a CComVariant.
        CComVariant varFlavor((TCHAR *)(*bstrIceCreamFlavor));

        // Perform a deep copy.
        return ::VariantCopy(pVarDest,&varFlavor);
    }

    static void init(VARIANT* pVar)
    {
        pVar->vt = VT_EMPTY;
    }

    static void destroy(VARIANT* pVar)
    {
        VariantClear(pVar);
    }

};

// Begin IceCreamMenu class.

class ATL_NO_VTABLE CIceCreamMenu :
    public CComObjectRootEx< CComSingleThreadModel >,
    public CComCoClass< CIceCreamMenu, &CLSID_IceCreamMenu >,
    public ISupportErrorInfo,
    public IDispatchImpl< IceCreamCollectionImpl,
        &IID_IIceCreamMenu,
        &LIBID_ICECREAMPARLORLib, 1, 0 >
{
public:

    ⋮
```

```
// IIceCreamMenu
public:
    STDMETHOD(AddFlavortoMenu)(/*[in]*/ BSTR bstrNewFlavor);

    // These three methods are not required because the
    // base class ICollectionOnSTLImpl<> provides us with
    // a default implementation.

    // STDMETHOD(get_Item)(/*[in]*/ VARIANT Index,
        /*[out, retval]*/ VARIANT *pVal);
    // STDMETHOD(get__NewEnum)(/*[out, retval]*/ LPUNKNOWN *pVal);
    // STDMETHOD(get_Count)(/*[out, retval]*/ long *pVal);

};
```

The *ICollectionOnSTLImpl<>* class that the *CIceCreamMenu* class extends provides the default implementation for the *Item, Count,* and *_NewEnum* collection properties. The underlying collection type that the class represents—in our case, a vector containing *_bstr_t* strings—is denoted by the *m_coll* instance. To add items to the collection, you just need to populate *m_coll* with the elements in your collection. *FinalConstruct* attempts to populate the underlying collection by adding some ice cream flavors into the *vector< _bstr_t >* represented by *m_coll*.

```
:
HRESULT CIceCreamMenu::FinalConstruct()
{
    // Fill up the menu with some flavors.
    m_coll.push_back(_bstr_t(_T("Chocolate Almond Fudge")));
    m_coll.push_back(_bstr_t(_T("Peach Melba")));
    m_coll.push_back(_bstr_t(_T("Black Currant")));
    m_coll.push_back(_bstr_t(_T("Strawberry")));
    m_coll.push_back(_bstr_t(_T("Butterscotch")));
    m_coll.push_back(_bstr_t(_T("Mint Chocolate Chip")));
    return S_OK;
}

STDMETHODIMP CIceCreamMenu::AddFlavortoMenu(BSTR bstrNewFlavor)
{
    m_coll.push_back(_bstr_t(bstrNewFlavor));
    return S_OK;
}
```

Creating a COM Collection Component Using Visual Basic

For the Visual Basic folks in the crowd, here's an equivalent Visual Basic implementation of the *IceCreamMenu* COM collection class. Be sure to tag the *NewEnum* function with a *DISPID* of −4 (*DISPID_NEWENUM*). You can tag the function by using the Tools->Procedure Attributes dialog box in the Visual Basic .NET IDE. You need to set the procedure ID for *NewEnum* to −4 and also ensure that you turn on the Hide This Member attribute.

```
Option Explicit
Private mIceCreamFlavors As Collection

Private Sub Class_Initialize()
    Set mIceCreamFlavors = New Collection
    mIceCreamFlavors.Add "Chocolate Almond Fudge"
    mIceCreamFlavors.Add "Peach Melba"
    mIceCreamFlavors.Add "Black Currant"
    mIceCreamFlavors.Add "Strawberry"
    mIceCreamFlavors.Add "Butterscotch"
    mIceCreamFlavors.Add "Mint Chocolate Chip"
End Sub

Public Function Count() As Integer
    Count = mIceCreamFlavors.Count
End Function

Public Function Item(varIndex As Variant) As String
    Item = mIceCreamFlavors(varIndex)
End Function

Public Function NewEnum() As IEnumVARIANT
    Set NewEnum = mIceCreamFlavors.[_NewEnum]
End Function

Public Function AddFlavortoMenu(strNewFlavor As String)
    mIceCreamFlavors.Add strNewFlavor
End Function
```

Consuming COM Collections in a .NET Application

To get a .NET application to consume the collection COM component that we just coded, we'll need to generate the .NET metadata proxy from the component's typelib. You can generate the .NET metadata proxy by using the following command from the command line:

```
tlbimp IceCreamParlor.tlb /out:IceCreamMenuMetadata.dll
```

Now open the IceCreamMenuMetadata.dll by using the ILDASMand look at the methods generated for the *IceCreamMenu* class, as shown in Figure 21-8.

Figure 21-8   Metadata proxy generated by TLBIMP for the *IceCreamMenu* collection component.

The *IceCreamMenu* class implements two interfaces: the *IIceCreamMenu* interface and the *System.Collections.IEnumerable* interface. Implementing the *IEnumerable* interface tells consumers that the class allows them to enumerate through elements in its collection. The *IIceCreamMenu* interface in the metadata proxy object has the *Count* and *Item* property preserved from the COM component's *IIceCreamMenu* interface. But what has TLBIMP done to the *_NewEnum* property that represents our collection's enumerator? It's replaced this property with the *GetEnumerator* method that returns the *IEnumerator* interface of the object that handles the actual enumeration, as illustrated in Figure 21-9.

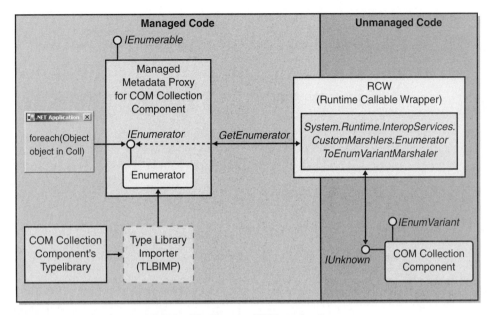

Figure 21-9   Consuming COM collections in .NET applications.

Because the *IceCreamMenu* class implements the *IEnumerable* interface, you can use extremely simple constructs such as C#'s *foreach* statement to enumerate through elements in such a collection. Here's how you could consume the *IceCreamMenu* collection COM component from your .NET application:

```
using System;
using IceCreamMenuMetadata;

public class IceCreamMenuClient
{
    public static void Main(String[] args)
    {
      // Create an instance of the collection class.
      IceCreamMenu menu = new IceCreamMenu();

      // Add a few more flavors to the menu.
      menu.AddFlavortoMenu("Blueberry");
      menu.AddFlavortoMenu("Chocolate Chip");


      // Use the foreach statement to iterate through
      // elements in the collection.
      foreach(Object objFlavor in menu)
      {
        System.Console.WriteLine("{0}",objFlavor);
```

```
        }

    }/* end Main */

}/* end class IceCreamMenuClient */
```

You can compile this code by using the following command line:

```
csc /target:exe /r:IceCreamMenuMetadata.dll
 /out:IceCreamMenuClient.exe IceCreamMenuClient.cs
```

Here's the output that you get:

```
Chocolate Almond Fudge
Peach Melba
Black Currant
Strawberry
Butterscotch
Mint Chocolate Chip
Blueberry
Chocolate Chip
```

Take a look at how easy it is to use C#'s *foreach* statement to iterate through the elements in the collection. Again, the RCW powers the enumeration under the covers by translating *IEnumVARIANT*-based COM collection semantics into a representation that can be serviced by *IEnumerator*-based methods and frees us from all the marshaling rigmarole.

Enumerating Elements in a .NET Collection

The *IEnumerable* and *IEnumerator* interfaces are the primary enablers for enumerating collections in the .NET world. As mentioned earlier, implementing the *IEnumerable* interface tells consumers that the object allows you to enumerate through elements in its collection. The *IEnumerator* interface consists of two methods, *MoveNext* and *Reset*, and one property, *Current*, that need to be implemented by the object that provides the enumerator for the collection.

If your class is based on a simple collection such as an array, your task is relatively easy. First, your *MoveNext* implementation needs to make an index move back and forth across the array. Your *Reset* implementation resets the index to point to the start of the array, and your *Current* implementation returns the array element at the current index position.

The code for enumerating a .NET collection isn't much more complex. The following example shows the two interfaces and one property required for a .NET collection class that allows enumeration:

```
using System;
using System.Collections;
```

```csharp
public class SevenDwarfs : IEnumerable , IEnumerator
{
    private int nCurrentPos = -1;
    private string[] strArrayDwarfs =
      new String[7] {"Doc", "Dopey", "Happy", "Grumpy",
      "Sleepy", "Sneezy", "Bashful"};
    SevenDwarfs() {}

    // Method : IEnumerable.GetEnumerator
    // Return an appropriate enumerator for the collection.
    public IEnumerator GetEnumerator()
    {
        return (IEnumerator)this;
    }

    // Method : IEnumerator.MoveNext
    // Move the enumerator to the next element in the collection
    // and return Boolean status regardless of whether we still
    // have elements to enumerate.
    public bool MoveNext()
    {
      if(nCurrentPos < strArrayDwarfs.Length - 1)
      {
          nCurrentPos++;
          return true;
      }
      else
      {
          return false;
      }
    }

    // Method : IEnumerator.Reset
    // Reset the enumerator to the beginning of the collection.
    public void Reset()
    {
      nCurrentPos = -1;
    }

    // Method : IEnumerator.Current
    // Return the element at the current enumerator position.
    public object Current
    {
        get
        {
          return strArrayDwarfs[nCurrentPos];
        }
    }
}
```

```
public static void Main(String[] args)
{
   // Create an instance of the SevenDwarfs object.
   SevenDwarfs SnowWhitesDwarfs = new SevenDwarfs();

   // Enumerate through the collection.
   foreach(string dwarf in SnowWhitesDwarfs)
   {
      System.Console.WriteLine("{0}",dwarf);
   }

}/* end Main */

}/* end class SevenDwarfs */
```

You can compile this code by using the following command line:

```
csc /target:exe /out:SevenDwarfs.exe SevenDwarfs.cs
```

Here's the output from the program:

```
Doc
Dopey
Happy
Grumpy
Sleepy
Sneezy
Bashful
```

Reusing COM Components in Managed Code

One of the nice features of the COM interop is that your managed .NET class can use the inheritance or containment models to reuse functionality provided by an existing COM component. The beauty of this system is that a .NET application consuming a managed .NET component never knows that the managed component is internally leveraging an unmanaged code implementation of a COM component.

COM has never subscribed to the idea of implementation inheritance, only to that of interface inheritance. The traditional reuse mechanisms in COM have been to use *containment* and *aggregation*. Let's examine each technique now.

Containment

Containment allows you to expose an outer component that totally subsumes the inner component, as shown in Figure 21-10. Only the outer component's interface is visible to clients. The methods exposed by the outer component's interface usually handle the implementation themselves and delegate the work to the inner component when needed. The outer component creates an instance of the inner component and, when it needs to leverage the functionality of the inner component, forwards method calls to the inner component. The client never knows that the outer component is shielding an inner one.

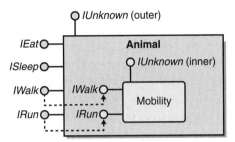
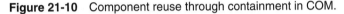

Figure 21-10   Component reuse through containment in COM.

Aggregation

With aggregation, the outer object no longer forwards method calls to the inner component. Instead, the outer object grants the client direct access to the inner component by exposing the inner component's interface pointer, as shown in Figure 21-11.

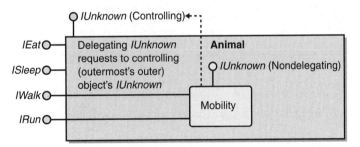
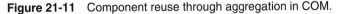

Figure 21-11   Component reuse through aggregation in COM.

The outer component no longer intercepts method calls on the inner component's interface because the client directly interacts with the inner component. The inner component uses a default *IUnknown* implementation—referred to as a *nondelegating unknown*—if the component isn't being aggregated. If the inner component is being aggregated, it uses the outer component's *IUnknown* implementation—referred to as a *controlling unknown* or *delegating unknown*. This arrangement ensures that the client always gets the *IUnknown* interface pointer of the outer component and never the nondelegating *IUnknown* interface pointer of the inner component. Again, the client doesn't know that there's an inner component. The client thinks that the inner component's interface is just another interface exposed by the outer component.

There are two methods by which a managed .NET component can reuse an existing COM component: *mixed-mode inheritance* and *mixed-mode containment*. Let's take a look at each of these techniques now.

Reuse Through Mixed-Mode Inheritance

In this reuse model, you can have your managed .NET class extend/inherit from an unmanaged COM *coclass*. In addition, the managed class has the option of overriding methods in the interface of the COM *coclass* or accepting the implementation of the base COM *coclass*. This model is very powerful; you get to mix both managed and unmanaged implementations within the same class, as Figure 21-12 shows.

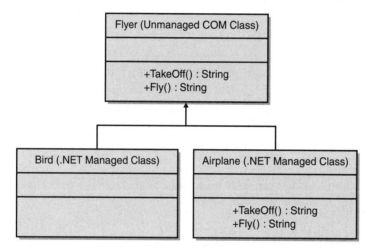

Figure 21-12 Inheriting unmanaged code from COM components in managed classes.

This code snippet can help you understand this concept a little better. We'll use ATL to create a COM object named *Flyer* that supports an interface named *IFlyer*. *IFlyer* has two methods, *TakeOff* and *Fly*. Here's the IDL declaration for the component:

```
[
    ⋮
]
interface IFlyer : IDispatch
{
    [id(1), helpstring("method TakeOff")]
```

```
        HRESULT TakeOff([out,retval] BSTR* bstrTakeOffStatus);
    [id(2), helpstring("method Fly")]
        HRESULT Fly([out,retval] BSTR* bstrFlightStatus);
};


[
    ⋮
]
coclass Flyer
{
    [default] interface IFlyer;
};
```

Here's the implementation of the two methods:

```
STDMETHODIMP CFlyer::TakeOff(BSTR *bstrTakeOffStatus)
{
    *bstrTakeOffStatus =
        _bstr_t(
        _T("CFlyer::TakeOff - This is COM taking off")).copy();
    return S_OK;
}

STDMETHODIMP CFlyer::Fly(BSTR *bstrFlyStatus)
{
    *bstrFlyStatus =
        _bstr_t(
        _T("CFlyer::Fly - This is COM in the skies")).copy();
    return S_OK;
}
```

Before this component can be consumed by managed code, you have to generate its metadata proxy from its typelib. To do that, you need to issue the following command from the command line:

```
tlbimp MyFlyer.tlb /out:MyFlyerMetadata.dll
```

We'll now create managed classes that inherit from this component by using the usual inheritance semantics so that the component's functionality can be reused. One of the managed classes, *Bird*, inherits from the metadata type corresponding to the *Flyer* COM object. This arrangement means that *Bird* inherits all the methods of the *Flyer* COM component.

The other managed class, *Airplane*, overrides the *Flyer* object's *TakeOff* and *Fly* methods with its own implementation. One caveat here: You can't selectively override specific methods from the COM *coclass* in your managed code. If you want to override a single method in the COM *coclass* in your managed code, you must override the other methods as well. For example, you can't provide an overridden implementation only for the *TakeOff* method and implicitly have the managed class use the *Fly* implementation from the COM object. You'd also need to override the *Fly* method the managed class and provide an implementation for it. If you need to reuse the implementation of the COM *coclass*, you can call *base.Fly* from the managed class's *Fly* implementation. You might get away with selectively overriding specific methods during compile time. But at run time, you'd end up running into a *System.TypeLoad-Exception* exception with an error message such as, "Types extending from COM objects should override all methods of an interface implemented by the base COM class."

Here's the implementation of the *Airplane* class:

```
using System;
using MyFlyerMetadata;

// Inherit from the metadata type representing
// the unmanaged COM component.
// Use the COM component's implementation
// of TakeOff and Fly. (Use the base class's implementation.)
public class Bird : Flyer
{

}/* end class Bird */

// Inherit from the metadata type representing
// the unmanaged COM component.
// Override the COM object's method implementations in our
// derived managed class.
//
 (Also call base class implementation when necessary using base.MethodName().)
public class Airplane : Flyer
{

    // Override the COM component's Flyer::TakeOff implementation
    // with our own implementation.
    public override String TakeOff() {

        return "Airplane::TakeOff - This is .NET taking off";

    }/* end TakeOff */

    // Override the COM component's Flyer::Fly implementation
    // with our own implementation.
    public override String Fly() {

        // Can call the base class's implementation too if you
```

```
        // want.
        System.Console.WriteLine(base.Fly());
        return "Airplane::Fly - This is .NET in the skies";

    }/* end Fly */

}/* end class Airplane */

public class FlightController
{
    public static void Main(String[] args)
    {
        Bird falcon = new Bird();
        System.Console.WriteLine("BIRD: CLEARED TO TAKE OFF");
        System.Console.WriteLine(falcon.TakeOff());
        System.Console.WriteLine(falcon.Fly());

        Airplane skyliner = new Airplane();
        System.Console.WriteLine("AIRPLANE: CLEARED TO TAKE OFF");
        System.Console.WriteLine(skyliner.TakeOff());
        System.Console.WriteLine(skyliner.Fly());

    }/* end Main */

}/* end FlightController */
```

You can compile this program by using the following command from the command line:

```
csc /target:exe /out:FlightClient.exe /r:MyFlyerMetadata.dll
 FlightClient.cs
```

The program produces the following output:

```
BIRD: CLEARED TO TAKE OFF
CFlyer::TakeOff - This is COM taking off
CFlyer::Fly - This is COM in the skies
AIRPLANE: CLEARED TO TAKE OFF
Airplane::TakeOff - This is .NET taking off
CFlyer::Fly - This is COM in the skies
Airplane::Fly - This is .NET in the skies
```

Consumers of the *Bird* and *Airplane* managed classes are shielded from having to know that these classes are actually reusing existing COM components via inheritance. Whenever necessary, the managed class overrides all the methods in the COM component with its own implementation.

Reuse Through Mixed-Mode Containment

In the mixed-mode containment model, the managed class stores as a member an instance of a metadata proxy class that represents the unmanaged COM component. Whenever the managed class requires the services of the COM component, it forwards a request to the component's methods, as shown in Figure 21-13.

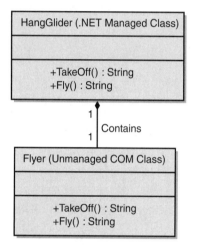

Figure 21-13   Reusing unmanaged COM code through containment.

The managed class has the ability to inject its own code before and after the call to the contained COM component. Here's an example:

```
using System;
using MyFlyerMetadata;

    ⋮

// Contains an instance of the metadata type representing
// the unmanaged COM component.
public class HangGlider
{
    private Flyer flyer = new Flyer();

    // Forward the call to the contained class's implementation.
    public String TakeOff()
    {
        return flyer.TakeOff();
    }
}
```

```
    // Forward the call to the contained class's implementation.
    public String Fly()
    {
        // Do what you need to do before or after fowarding the
        // call to flyer.
        System.Console.WriteLine("In HangGlider::Fly - Before " +
            "delegating to flyer.Fly");
        return flyer.Fly();
    }

}/* end class HangGlider */

public class FlightController
{
    public static void Main(String[] args)
    {
        ⋮

        HangGlider glider = new HangGlider();
        System.Console.WriteLine("HANGGLIDER: CLEARED TO TAKEOFF");
        System.Console.WriteLine(glider.TakeOff());
        System.Console.WriteLine(glider.Fly());

    }/* end Main */

}/* end FlightController */
```

Here's the output of the program:

```
HANGGLIDER: CLEARED TO TAKEOFF
CFlyer::TakeOff - This is COM taking off
In HangGlider::Fly - Before delegating to flyer.Fly
CFlyer::Fly - This is COM in the skies
```

In this example, the *HangGlider* class creates an instance of the *Flyer* COM component and stores it as a private member. Whenever a method call requiring the *Flyer* component's services arrives, *HangGlider* calls into the component using the stored private instance. Also, the *HangGlider* class has the ability to inject code before and after a call is delegated to the *Flyer* component's methods. This code injection isn't possible in the mixed-mode inheritance reuse model unless you override all the base class COM methods in your managed class.

A .NET View on COM Threading Models and Apartments

When I first started programming with COM, there were many concepts I didn't understand. I had only a vague notion of what threading models and apartments were. I thought it was cool that my object was free threaded and simply assumed that the free-threaded model would give the best performance.

I didn't realize what was happening under the covers. I never knew the performance penalties that were incurred when a single-threaded apartment (STA) client thread created my multithreaded apartment (MTA) object. Also, because my object was not thread-safe, I never knew that I'd be in trouble when concurrent threads accessed my object.

At that time, my ignorance of COM threading models truly was bliss. But that bliss was only ephemeral, and my server started crashing unexpectedly. It was then that I was forced to get my feet wet in the waters of COM threading models. I learned how each of those models behaved, how COM managed apartments, and the performance implications that arose when calling between two incompatible apartments.

As you know, a thread must declare its affiliation to an STA or MTA before it can call into a COM object. STA client threads call *CoInitialize(NULL)* or *CoInitializeEx(0, COINIT_APARTMENTTHREADED)* to enter an STA. MTA threads call *CoInitializeEx(0, COINIT_MULTITHREADED)* to enter an MTA. Similarly, in the .NET managed world, you have the option of allowing the calling thread in the managed space declare its apartment affinity.

By default, the calling thread in a managed application chooses to live in an MTA. It's as though the calling thread initialized itself by calling *CoInitializeEx(0, COINIT_MULTITHREADED)*. But think about the overhead and performance penalties you'd incur if the application were calling an STA COM component that was designed to be apartment threaded. The incompatible apartments would incur the overhead of an additional proxy/stub pair, which is certainly a performance penalty.

You can override the default choice of apartment for a managed thread in a .NET application by using the *ApartmentState* property of the *System.Threading.Thread* class. The *ApartmentState* property takes one of the following enumeration values: *MTA*, *STA*, or *Unknown*. The *ApartmentState.Unknown* value is equivalent to the default MTA behavior. You'll need to specify the *ApartmentState* for the calling thread before you make any calls to the COM object. It's not possible to change the *ApartmentState* after the COM object has been created. Therefore, it makes sense to set the thread's *ApartmentState* as early as possible in your code, as shown here:

```
// Set the client thread's ApartmentState to enter an STA.
Thread.CurrentThread.ApartmentState = ApartmentSTate.STA;

// Create our COM object through the COM interop.
MySTA objSTA = new MySTA();
objSTA.MyMethod()
```

You can also tag your managed client's *Main* entry point method with the *STAThread* attribute or the *MTAThread* attribute to start the client with the desired threading affiliation for consuming COM components. For example, take a look at this code snippet:

```
public class HelloThreadingModelApp {

    ⋮

    [STAThread]
    static public void Main(String[] args) {

        System.Console.WriteLine("The apartment state is: {0}",
            Thread.CurrentThread.ApartmentState.ToString());

    }/* end Main */

}/* end class */
```

Here's the output from this program:

```
The apartment state is: STA
```

If you set the *MTAThread* attribute, the client's *ApartmentState* property is set to MTA. If no thread state attribute is specified in the client's *Main* entry point or if the *ApartmentState* property isn't set for the thread from which the COM component is created, the *ApartmentState* property is set to *Unknown*, which defaults to MTA behavior.

Mapping Method Keywords to IDL Attributes

The COM interop uses certain rules when mapping C# method parameter keywords such as *out* and *ref* to and from their corresponding directional attributes, such as *[in]*, *[out]*, *[in,out]*, and *[out,retval]*. The following is a list of these rules:

- When the method parameter isn't qualified by a keyword in C#, it's usually mapped to the *[in]* attribute in IDL with pass-by-value semantics.

- The return value from the C# method is always mapped to the *[out, retval]* directional attribute in IDL.

- The *ref* method parameter keyword is mapped to the *[in,out]* directional attribute in IDL.

■ The *out* method parameter keyword is mapped to an *[out]* directional attribute in IDL.

In the .NET world, error-handling code throws an exception instead of returning an error value.

Table 21-1 shows a few examples of how C# parameter types map to the directional attributes in IDL.

Table 21-1
C# Parameter Types and Their IDL Equivalents

C# Method	IDL Equivalent	Calling Semantics in C#
public void Method(String strInput);	*HRESULT Method([in] BSTR strInput);*	*obj.Method("Hello There");*
public String Method();	*HRESULT Method([out, retval] BSTR* pRetVal);*	*String strOutput = obj.Method();*
public String Method(ref String strPassAndModify);	*HRESULT Method([in, out] BSTR* strPassAndModify, [out, retval] BSTR* pRetVal);*	*String strHello = "Hello There"; String strOutput = obj.Method(ref strHello);*
public String Method(out String strReturn);	*HRESULT Method([out] BSTR* strReturn, [out, retval] BSTR* pRetVal);*	*//Need not initialize strHello String strHello; String strOutput = obj.Method(out strHello);*
public String Method(String strFirst, out String strSecond, ref String strThird);	*HRESULT Method([in] BSTR bstrFirst, [out] BSTR* strSecond, [in, out] BSTR* strThird, [out, retval] BSTR* pRetVal);*	*String strFirst = "Hi There"; String strSecond; String strThird = "Hello World"; String strOutput = obj.Method(strFirst, out strSecond, ref strThird);*

Summary

Time to take a very deep breath. We went through a substantial amount of information in this chapter. We saw how COM components are exposed to .NET applications executing under the runtime. We discovered how the COM interop facility seamlessly allows us to reuse existing COM components from managed code. Then we explored several ways to invoke a COM component by using both early binding and late binding as well as ways to perform runtime type checking and dynamic type discovery.

We next examined how delegates work in .NET, the role they play in the .NET event-handling model, and how the COM interop acts as an adaptor to wire the Connection Point event-handling model in COM to the delegate-based event-handling model in .NET. We discussed how to expose COM collections to .NET applications and use C#'s *foreach* syntax to easily iterate through the elements of the collection. We also looked at how directional attributes in IDL files get mapped to the corresponding directional parameter types in C#.

Finally, we explained some of the reuse options available for COM components from .NET applications when using inheritance and containment, and we demonstrated how managed threads declare their apartment affiliations when invoking COM components. In the next chapter, we'll continue using COM in the .NET world, except we'll learn how to use .NET components in unmanaged code via COM.

22

Using .NET Components in Unmanaged Code

In this chapter, we'll see how to consume managed .NET components from unmanaged COM-aware clients. Limiting clients for .NET components to only managed clients would've been a tough pill to swallow for most developers who've spent a great deal of time over the years creating applications that can't be ported overnight to managed code. The .NET Framework allows disparate applications in different platforms to talk to managed applications by using wire protocols such as SOAP. Unmanaged COM-aware clients have even easier ways to talk to managed components. The .NET runtime allows unmanaged COM-aware clients to seamlessly access .NET components through the COM interop and through the tools provided by the Framework. This architecture ensures that COM-aware clients can talk to .NET components as though they were talking to plain-vanilla COM components.

Creating and Using .NET Components via COM

To begin with, let's put together a simple .NET component that allows you to look up the temperature in your city. Only public classes are added to the typelib and exposed to COM-aware clients. Also, if the class needs to be creatable from a COM-aware client, the class needs a public default constructor. A public class that doesn't have a public default constructor still appears in the typelib, although instances of the class can't be directly cocreatable from COM. The *Temperature* component has two methods, *DisplayCurrentTemperature* and *GetWeatherIndications*. The component has a public read-write property named *Temperature* that's defined with the corresponding *get* and *set* methods.

```csharp
using System;
using System.Windows.Forms;
using System.Runtime.InteropServices;

public enum WeatherIndications
{
    Sunny = 0,
    Cloudy,
    Rainy,
    Snowy
}

[ClassInterface(ClassInterfaceType.AutoDual)]
public class TemperatureComponent
{
    private float m_fTemperature = 0;

    // Public constructor
    public TemperatureComponent()
    {
        m_fTemperature = 30.0f;
    }

    //Public property accessors (define get/set methods)
    public float Temperature
    {
        get { return m_fTemperature; }

        set { m_fTemperature = value;}

    }/* end Temperature get/set property */

    // Public method that displays the current temperature
    public void DisplayCurrentTemperature()
    {
        String strTemp = String.Format("The current " +
            "temperature at Marlinspike is : " +
            "{0:####} degrees Fahrenheit", m_fTemperature);

        MessageBox.Show(strTemp,"Today's temperature");

    }/* end DisplayCurrentTemperature */

    // Another public method that returns an enumerated type
    public WeatherIndications GetWeatherIndications()
    {
        if(m_fTemperature > 70) {
```

```
        return WeatherIndications.Sunny;

    }
    else {

        // Let's keep this simple and just return Cloudy.
        return WeatherIndications.Cloudy;

    }

  }/* end GetWeatherIndications */

}/* end class Temperature */
```

You'll also notice that there's an attribute named *ClassInterface* that's tagged to the *Temperature* class with its value set to *ClassInterfaceType.Auto-Dual*. We'll see the significance of applying this attribute in the section "Snooping on the Generated Typelib" later in this chapter. For now, think of this attribute as a way to tell typelib generation tools such as REGASM.EXE and TLBEXP.EXE to export the public members of the .NET component's class into a default class interface in the generated typelib.

Remember that using a class interface to expose the public methods of a .NET class isn't generally recommended because it's creedless to COM versioning. Defining an interface explicitly, deriving your .NET component class from this interface, and then implementing the interface's methods in your .NET component is the recommended method to expose your .NET component to COM-aware clients. We'll compare these two approaches in detail. (The section "Snooping on the Generated Typelib" later in this chapter discusses why the former approach isn't recommended.)

If you're using Microsoft Visual Studio .NET, you can create a Microsoft Visual C# project and use the Class Library template to code the preceding component. If you're a command-line jockey, here's the command to build the component. The following command creates an assembly named Temperature.dll:

```
csc /target:library /r:System.Windows.Forms.dll
 /out:Temperature.dll TemperatureComponent.cs
```

Generating a Typelib from the Assembly and Registering the Assembly

You've just generated a .NET assembly that a COM-aware client such as Microsoft Visual Basic 6 is clueless about. You need to get some COM-friendly type information from the assembly so that your Visual Basic client will be happy to party around with it.

In Chapter 21, "Using COM from C# Applications," you used a tool named Type Library Importer (TLBIMP.EXE) to create a .NET metadata proxy from a

COM typelib. You need to reverse that process here. You need to take a .NET assembly and generate a typelib from it so that the assembly is usable from a COM-aware client. The .NET Framework provides a couple of tools for this process. You can use the Type Library Exporter utility (TLBEXP.EXE) or the Assembly Registration utility (REGASM.EXE), both of which you'll find in the Bin directory of your .NET SDK installation.

REGASM is a superset of the TLBEXP utility in that it does much more than generate a typelib. For example, REGASM is also used to register the assembly so that the appropriate Registry entries are made to facilitate the COM runtime and the .NET runtime to hook up the COM-aware client to the .NET component. We'll use REGASM.EXE in this project because we can get both the assembly registration and the typelib generation done in one step. But you also could use TLBEXP to generate the typelib and then use REGASM to register the assembly. Here's the appropriate REGASM command:

```
regasm Temperature.dll /tlb:Temperature.tlb
```

This call to REGASM.EXE makes the appropriate Registry entries and also generates a typelib (Temperature.tlb) from the .NET assembly so that the typelib can be referenced from our Visual Basic 6 client application.

Consuming the Component from a Visual Basic 6 Client

Let's put together a Visual Basic form–based application that creates and invokes our .NET component. You create the component the same way as you'd create a COM object. You can either reference the typelib and early bind to the component, or you can perform a *CreateObject* call by using the component's *ProgID* to late bind to the component. Usually, the *ProgID* generated is the fully qualified name of the class. In our case, the *ProgID* generated is *TemperatureComponent*. But you could use *ProgIDAttribute* to specify a user-defined *ProgID* to override the default *ProgID* that's generated.

```
Private Sub MyButton_Click()

    On Error GoTo ErrHandler

    ' Create an instance of the temperature component.
    Dim objTemperature As New TemperatureComponent

    ' Display the current temperature.
    objTemperature.DisplayCurrentTemperature

    ' Set the temperature property.
    objTemperature.Temperature = 52.7
```

```
' Display the current temperature after property mutation.
objTemperature.DisplayCurrentTemperature

' Check the weather indications.
If (objTemperature.GetWeatherIndications() = _
    WeatherIndications_Sunny) Then
    MsgBox "Off to the beach"
Else
    MsgBox "Stay at home and watch Godzilla on TV"
End If

    Exit Sub

ErrHandler:

    MsgBox "Error Message : " & Err.Description, _
        vbOKOnly, "Error Code " & CStr(Err.Number)
End Sub
```

To enable the .NET assembly resolver to find the assembly housing your component, you'll either need to place the component in the same directory as the application that's consuming it or deploy the assembly as a shared assembly in the global assembly cache (GAC). For now, just copy the Temperature.dll to the same directory as your Visual Basic client application executable. If Visual Basic can use the usual COM-based invocation mechanism and get away with invoking and consuming the .NET component, there must be a good Samaritan sitting between the Visual Basic 6 client and the .NET component and wiring the COM invocation requests to the actual .NET component. We'll soon see what happens under the covers.

Shedding More Light on the COM Interop Wizardry

Let's take a peek at the Registry entries that REGASM.EXE made when we registered our assembly, as shown in Figure 22-1.

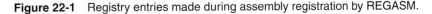

Figure 22-1   Registry entries made during assembly registration by REGASM.

You can check your component's *CLSID* in OLEVIEW.EXE by opening the typelib generated by REGASM. Check for the *uuid* attribute under the *coclass* section. If you navigate to your *HKCR\CLSID\{...component's CLSID...}* key in the Registry, you can see that REGASM has made the relevant Registry entries required by COM to activate an object hosted by an in-proc server. In addition, REGASM has created a few other Registry entries—such as *Class*, *Assembly*, and *RuntimeVersion*—that are used by the .NET runtime. The in-proc server handler (indicated by the *InProcServer32* key's default value) is set to MSCOREE.dll, which is the core common language runtime execution engine. The COM runtime calls the *DllGetClassObject* entry point in MSCOREE.dll. The runtime then uses the *CLSID* passed to *DllGetClassObject* to look up the *Assembly* and *Class* keys under the *InProcServer32* key to load and resolve the .NET assembly that will service this request.

The runtime also dynamically creates a COM Callable Wrapper (CCW) proxy—a mirror image of the Runtime Callable Wrapper (RCW)—to handle the interaction between unmanaged code and the managed components. This arrangement makes COM-aware clients think that they're interacting with COM components and makes .NET components think that they're receiving requests from a managed application. There's one CCW created per .NET component instance.

As the saying goes, "A picture is worth a thousand words," so let Figure 22-2 illustrate what's happening under the covers when a COM-aware client interacts with a .NET component. The interaction occurs as detailed here:

1. Generate typelib from .NET component, and make appropriate Registry entries.

2. Reference-generated typelib (for early binding).

3. COM object activation request (*CoCreateInstance*, *New*, *CreateObject*).

4. Look up the Registry for the in-proc server.

5. Load MSCOREE.DLL, and call *DLLGetClassObject* entry point.

6. Look up class and assembly details in the Registry.

7. Load and resolve assembly (if not already loaded).

8. Resolve assembly in the GAC or in the directory in which the application runs.

9. Load the assembly.

10. Return the class factory associated with the assembly that was loaded.

11. Call *CreateInstance* on the class factory that was returned.

12. Instantiate the .NET component, and fabricate a CCW based on the metadata.

How COM-Aware Clients Talk to .NET Components: Bridging the Gap

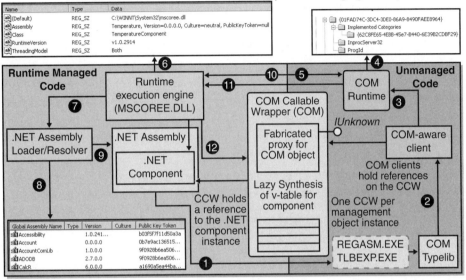

Figure 22-2   Under the hood: accessing .NET components from COM-aware clients.

The primary players here are the runtime and the CCW that gets fabricated by the .NET runtime. From that moment, the CCW takes over and handles most of the heavy lifting to get the client and the component to work together. The CCW handles the lifetime management issues here. COM clients in the unmanaged realm maintain reference counts on the CCW proxy rather than on the actual .NET component. The CCW holds only a reference to the .NET component.

The .NET component lives by the rules of the runtime garbage collector, as any other managed type would. The CCW lives in the unmanaged heap and is torn down when the COM-aware clients no longer have any outstanding references to the objects. As with the RCW, the CCW is responsible for marshaling the method call parameters that move between the unmanaged client and managed .NET components. The CCW is also responsible for synthesizing v-tables on demand. V-tables for specific interfaces are generated dynamically and are built lazily only when the COM-aware client actually requests a specific interface via a *QueryInterface* call. Calls on the CCW proxy are eventually routed to a stub that makes the call into the managed object.

Snooping on the Generated Typelib

Let's take a quick look at the kind of information that was put into the typelib generated by REGASM. Open the typelib through OLEVIEW's Type Library Viewer so that you can take a look at the IDL file that was reverse-engineered from the typelib:

```
// Generated IDL file (by the OLE/COM object viewer)
// typelib filename: Temperature.tlb

[
    uuid(A9F20157-FDFE-36D6-90C3-BFCD3C8C8442),
    version(1.0)
]
library Temperature
{
    // TLib : Common Language Runtime Library :
    // {BED7F4EA-1A96-11D2-8F08-00A0C9A6186D}
    importlib("mscorlib.tlb");
    // TLib : OLE Automation :
    // {00020430-0000-0000-C000-000000000046}
    importlib("STDOLE2.TLB");

    // Forward-declare all types defined in this typelib.
    interface _TemperatureComponent;

    typedef [uuid(0820402E-B8B6-330F-8D56-FF079E5B4659),
        version(1.0),
        custom({0F21F359-AB84-41E8-9A78-36D110E6D2F9},
        "WeatherIndications")]
    enum {
        WeatherIndications_Sunny = 0,
        WeatherIndications_Cloudy = 1,
        WeatherIndications_Rainy = 2,
        WeatherIndications_Snowy = 3
    } WeatherIndications;

    [
        uuid(01FAD74C-3DC4-3DE0-86A9-8490FAEE8964),
        version(1.0),
        custom({0F21F359-AB84-41E8-9A78-36D110E6D2F9},
        "TemperatureComponent")
    ]
    coclass TemperatureComponent {
        [default] interface _TemperatureComponent;
        interface _Object;
    };
```

```
[
    odl,
    uuid(C51D54FA-7C81-35A5-9998-3963EAB4AA12),
    hidden,
    dual,
    nonextensible,
    oleautomation,
    custom({0F21F359-AB84-41E8-9A78-36D110E6D2F9},
    "TemperatureComponent")
]
interface _TemperatureComponent : IDispatch {
    [id(00000000), propget]
    HRESULT ToString([out, retval] BSTR* pRetVal);
    [id(0x60020001)]
    HRESULT Equals([in] VARIANT obj,
        [out, retval] VARIANT_BOOL* pRetVal);
    [id(0x60020002)]
    HRESULT GetHashCode([out, retval] long* pRetVal);
    [id(0x60020003)]
    HRESULT GetType([out, retval] _Type** pRetVal);
    [id(0x60020004), propget]
    HRESULT Temperature([out, retval] single* pRetVal);
    [id(0x60020004), propput]
    HRESULT Temperature([in] single pRetVal);
    [id(0x60020006)]
    HRESULT DisplayCurrentTemperature();
    [id(0x60020007)]
    HRESULT GetWeatherIndications(
        [out, retval] WeatherIndications* pRetVal);
};
};
```

If you take a look at the *coclass* section, it specifies the default interface as the class name prefixed by an underscore character (_). This interface is known as the *class interface* and its methods comprise all the nonstatic public methods, fields, and properties of the class. The class interface is generated because you tagged your .NET class with the *ClassInterface* attribute. This attribute tells typelib-generation tools such as REGASM.EXE and TLBEXP.EXE to generate a default class interface and add all the public methods, fields, and properties of the class into the interface so that it can be exposed to COM-aware clients.

If you don't tag the *ClassInterface* attribute to a .NET component's class, a default class interface is still generated. But in this case, it's an *IDispatch*-based class interface that doesn't include any type information for the methods exposed and doesn't include their *DISPID*s. This type of class interface is available only to late-binding clients. This effect is the same as that of applying the *ClassInterfaceType.AutoDispatch* value to the *ClassInterface* attribute. The advantage of the *AutoDispatch* option is that because the *DISPID*s aren't cached and aren't available as a part of the type information, they don't break existing clients when a new version of the component is released. This is because the *DISPID*s are obtained at runtime by clients. (Calling *IDispatch::GetIDsOfNames* is one way to obtain the *DISPID*s.)

Only public methods are visible in the typelib and can be used by COM clients. The private members aren't in the typelib and are hidden from COM clients. The public properties and fields of the class are transformed into IDL *propget* and *propput* types. The *Temperature* property in our example has both *set* and *get* defined, so both *propset* and *propget* are emitted for this property. There's also an interface named *_Object* that's added to the *coclass*. In addition, the class interface contains four other methods. They are:

- *ToString*

- *Equals*

- *GetHashCode*

- *GetType*

These methods are added to the default class interface because it implicitly inherits from the *System.Object* class. Each of the methods and properties added to the interface gets a *DISPID* that's automatically generated. You can override this *DISPID* with a user-defined one by using the *DispId* attribute. You'll notice that the *ToString* method has been assigned a *DISPID* of 0 to indicate that it's the default method in the class interface. This means that if you leave out the method name, the *ToString* method will be invoked.

```
' Create an instance of the temperature component.
Dim objTemperature As New TemperatureComponent

' Invoke the ToString method (the default method).
MsgBox objTemperature
```

Let's examine the various ways in which we can facilitate the generation of the implicit class interface. We'll start by taking a look at the effect of applying the *ClassInterfaceType.AutoDual* value to the *ClassInterface* attribute:

```
[ClassInterface(ClassInterfaceType.AutoDual)]
public class TemperatureComponent
{
    ⋮
}
```

Notice that the (positional parameter) value assigned to the *ClassInterface* attribute is *ClassInterfaceType.AutoDual*. This option tells typelib generation tools to generate the class interface as a dual interface and export all the type information (for the methods, properties, and so on, as well as their corresponding dispatch IDs) into the typelib. Imagine what would happen if you decide to add another public method to the class. This addition mutates the class interface that gets generated and breaks the fundamental interface immutability law in COM because the v-table's structure changes. Late-bound clients also have their share of woes when they try to consume the component. The *DISPIDs* are regenerated because of the addition of the new method, and this breaks late-bound clients. As a general rule, using *ClassInterfaceType.AutoDual* is evil because it's totally agnostic about COM versioning.

Let's take a look at the next possible value that you can set for your *ClassInterface* attribute. Tagging your *ClassInterface* attribute with a value of *ClassInterfaceType.AutoDispatch* forces typelib generation tools to avoid generating type information in the typelib. Imagine you have your *TemperatureComponent* class tagged with the *ClassInterface* attribute, as shown here:

```
[ClassInterface(ClassInterfaceType.AutoDispatch)]
public class TemperatureComponent
{
    ⋮
}
```

Now the corresponding typelib generated by REGASM.EXE would have an IDL structure such as this:

```
// Generated IDL file (by the OLE/COM object viewer)
// typelib filename: Temperature.tlb

[
    uuid(A9F20157-FDFE-36D6-90C3-BFCD3C8C8442),
    version(1.0)
]
library Temperature
{
    ⋮

    [
        uuid(01FAD74C-3DC4-3DE0-86A9-8490FAEE8964),
            version(1.0),
            custom({0F21F359-AB84-41E8-9A78-36D110E6D2F9},
            "TemperatureComponent")
    ]
    coclass TemperatureComponent {
        [default] interface IDispatch;
        interface _Object;
    };
};
```

You'll notice that the default interface is an *IDispatch* interface and that neither the *DISPID*s nor the method type information is present in the typelib. This scheme leaves the COM-aware client to consume .NET components by using only late binding. Also, because the *DISPID* details aren't stored as a part of the type information in the typelib, the clients obtain these *DISPID*s on demand—for example, by using *IDispatch::GetIDsOfNames*. This arrangement allows clients to use newer versions of the components without breaking existing code. Using *ClassInterfaceType.AutoDispatch* is much safer than using *ClassInterfaceType.AutoDual* because classes tagged with *ClassInterfaceType.AutoDispatch* don't break existing client code when newer versions of the component are released—although the former allows late binding only.

The recommended way of modeling your .NET component to be exposed to COM-aware clients is to do away with the class interface itself and instead explicitly factor out the methods you're exposing into a separate interface and have the .NET component implement that interface. Let's try rewriting our *TemperatureComponent* by explicitly factoring out the methods into an interface and seeing how the typelib generation differs:

```
// Define the ITemperature interface.
public interface ITemperature {

    float Temperature { get; set; }
    void DisplayCurrentTemperature();
    WeatherIndications GetWeatherIndications();

}/* end interface ITemperature */

// (1) Implement the ITemperature interface in
//  the TemperatureComponent class.
// (2) Set the ClassInterfaceType for the ClassInterface
//  attribute to ClassInterfaceType.None.

[ClassInterface(ClassInterfaceType.None)]
public class TemperatureComponent : ITemperature
{
    ⋮

    //Implement the methods in your class.

    // Property accessors (define get/set methods)
    public float Temperature
    {
        get { return m_fTemperature; }
        set { m_fTemperature = value;}
```

```
}/* end Temperature get/set property */

// Displays the current temperature
public void DisplayCurrentTemperature() {
    ⋮
}/* end DisplayCurrentTemperature */

// Returns an enumerated type indicating weather condition
public WeatherIndications GetWeatherIndications() {
    ⋮
}/* end GetWeatherIndications */
```

```
}/* end class Temperature */
```

Here's how the corresponding IDL file looks for the generated typelib. Notice that the *TemperatureComponent* class's default interface is now the *ITemperature* interface that was implemented by the class:

```
// Generated IDL file (by the OLE/COM object viewer)
// typelib filename: Temperature.tlb

[
  uuid(A9F20157-FDFE-36D6-90C3-BFCD3C8C8442),
  version(1.0)
]
library Temperature
{
    ⋮

    [
        odl,
        uuid(72AA177B-C6B2-3694-B083-4FF535B40AD2),
        version(1.0),
        dual,
        oleautomation,
        custom({0F21F359-AB84-41E8-9A78-36D110E6D2F9},
            "ITemperature")
    ]
    interface ITemperature : IDispatch {
        [id(0x60020000), propget]
        HRESULT Temperature([out, retval] single* pRetVal);
        [id(0x60020000), propput]
        HRESULT Temperature([in] single pRetVal);
        [id(0x60020002)]
        HRESULT DisplayCurrentTemperature();
        [id(0x60020003)]
        HRESULT GetWeatherIndications(
            [out, retval] WeatherIndications* pRetVal);
```

```
    };

    [
        uuid(01FAD74C-3DC4-3DE0-86A9-8490FAEE8964),
        version(1.0),
          custom({0F21F359-AB84-41E8-9A78-36D110E6D2F9},
          "TemperatureComponent")
    ]
    coclass TemperatureComponent {
        interface _Object;
        [default] interface ITemperature;
    };
};
```

This approach—explicitly factoring out the methods of the .NET class into an interface and having the class derive from and implement the interface—is the recommended way to expose your .NET components to COM-aware clients. The *ClassInterfaceType.None* option tells the typelib generation tools that you don't require a class interface. This option ensures that *ITemperature* is the default interface. (If you didn't specify the *ClassInterfaceType.None* value for the class interface attribute, the class interface would've been made the default interface.)

Here's the gist of what we learned in this section:

■ Class interfaces with *ClassInterfaceType.AutoDual* are COM-version agnostic. Try to avoid using them.

■ Class interfaces with *ClassInterfaceType.AutoDispatch* don't export type information and *DISPID*s to the typelib. They are COM-versioning friendly. They can be accessed from COM-aware clients only through late binding.

■ Class interfaces are a hack. Try to avoid them whenever possible. Use explicit interfaces instead.

■ Use *ClassInterfaceType.None* to make your explicit interface the default interface.

Another interesting observation is the way that REGASM and TLBEXP generate a mangled method name in the IDL file by appending an underscore character (_) followed by a sequence number when you've overloaded methods in the .NET class or interface that you're exporting to a typelib. For example, imagine you'd exposed the following interface in your .NET component:

```
public interface MyInterface
{
    String HelloWorld();
    String HelloWorld(int nInput);
}
```

Now the IDL file corresponding to the typelib that REGASM and TLBEXP generated would look like this:

```
[
    ⋮
]
interface MyInterface : IDispatch {

    [id(0x60020000)]
    HRESULT HelloWorld([out, retval] BSTR* pRetVal);

    [id(0x60020001)]
    HRESULT HelloWorld_2([in] long nInput,
        [out,retval] BSTR* pRetVal);
};
```

Notice the _2 appended to the second *HelloWorld* method to distinguish it from the first method in the IDL file.

Using Attributes to Tweak the Generated Typelib Metadata

Knowing the rules that the REGASM and TLBEXP utilities use to generate the IDL—and subsequently, the typelib—by introspecting a .NET assembly allows you to mold the typelib generation to your requirements. You could inject into your assembly .NET attributes that give these utilities the hints they need to alter metadata in the IDL to affect the typelib that gets created. For example, you could change the interface type from dual to an *IUnknown*-based custom interface or to a pure *dispinterface* by using the *InterfaceTypeAttribute* attribute. This section presents some of the ways you can inject attributes to qualify the types in your .NET component and modify the generated typelib to suit your requirements.

Altering the Interface Type

By default, the interfaces used by a .NET class are transformed into dual interfaces in the IDL. This arrangement allows the client to get the best of both early binding and late binding. However, there might be occasions on which you want the interface to be a pure *dispinterface* or a custom *IUnknown*-based interface. In such instances, you can override the default type of the interface by using *InterfaceTypeAttribute*. Examine the following example:

```
[InterfaceType(ComInterfaceType.InterfaceIsDual)]
public interface ISnowStorm
{
```

```
    ⋮
}

[InterfaceType(ComInterfaceType.InterfaceIsIUnknown)]
public interface IHurricane
{
    ⋮
}

[InterfaceType(ComInterfaceType.InterfaceIsIDispatch)]
public interface ITyphoon
{
    ⋮
}

public interface IWeatherStatistics
{
    ⋮
}
```

As this example shows, the *InterfaceTypeAttribute* attribute is used to emit metadata information into the interface so that utilities such as REGASM and TLBEXP can use this information to generate the appropriate type of interface in the typelib. Here's the resulting IDL:

```
[
    odl,
    uuid(1423FBFA-BE13-3766-9729-9C1AAF5DB08A),
    version(1.0),
    dual,
    oleautomation,
    custom({0F21F359-AB84-41E8-9A78-36D110E6D2F9},
        "ISnowStorm")
]
interface ISnowStorm : IDispatch {
    ⋮
};

[
    odl,
    uuid(D95E54B8-FABC-3BDA-AA45-AC4EFF49AF92),
    version(1.0),
    oleautomation,
    custom({0F21F359-AB84-41E8-9A78-36D110E6D2F9},
        "IHurricane")
]
interface IHurricane : IUnknown {
    ⋮
```

```
};

[
    uuid(676B3B85-7DB8-306D-A1E9-B6AA1008EDF2),
    version(1.0),
    custom({0F21F359-AB84-41E8-9A78-36D110E6D2F9},
        "ITyphoon")
]
dispinterface ITyphoon {
    properties:
    methods:
};

[
    odl,
    uuid(A1A37136-341A-3631-9275-FC7B0F0DB695),
    version(1.0),
    dual,
    oleautomation,
    custom({0F21F359-AB84-41E8-9A78-36D110E6D2F9},
        "IWeatherStatistics")
]
interface IWeatherStatistics : IDispatch {
    ⋮
}
```

As you can see, setting the *InterfaceTypeAttribute* attribute to *ComInterfaceType.InterfaceIsIUnknown* results in the generation of an *IUnknown* only–based custom interface. Setting the *InterfaceTypeAttribute* attribute to *ComInterfaceType.InterfaceIsIDispatch* results in the generation of a pure dispatch–only *dispinterface*. Setting the *InterfaceType* attribute to *ComInterfaceType.InterfaceIsDual* or ignoring the *InterfaceTypeAttribute* attribute altogether (as we did in the *IWeatherStatistics* interface in the example) results in the emission of a dual interface.

Altering the GUID and the ProgID

GUIDs for types such as classes and interfaces are generated automatically by the REGASM and TLBEXP utilities when these types are exported into a typelib. But you still have your final say if you need to assign a specific GUID to the interface or class. You can use the *Guid* attribute to specify a user-defined GUID. You can also affect the way that a *ProgID* is generated for a specific class. By default, REGASM assigns the fully qualified type name of the class for the *ProgID*. You can use the *ProgID* attribute to assign a user-specified *ProgID* for your *coclass*:

```
[
    GuidAttribute("AD4760A9-6F5C-4435-8844-D0BA7C66AC50"),
    ProgId("WeatherStation.TornadoTracker")
]
public class TornadoTracker  {
    ⋮
}
```

Here's the IDL file after the *Guid* attribute has been used on the class:

```
[
    uuid(AD4760A9-6F5C-4435-8844-D0BA7C66AC50),
    version(1.0),
    custom({0F21F359-AB84-41E8-9A78-36D110E6D2F9},
        "TornadoTracker")
]
coclass TornadoTracker {
    ⋮
};
```

Notice that the *uuid* attribute (representing the *CLSID* of the COM class) in the *coclass* section contains the value of the GUID that we specified. If you check the *HCKR\CLSID\{AD4760A9-6F5C-4435-8844-D0BA7C66AC50}\ProgID* Registry key, you should see the value *WeatherStation.TornadoTracker* representing the class's *ProgID*.

Hiding Public Types from Exposure to COM

You saw earlier how all the public classes and interfaces of the class were automatically added to the typelib so that they can be referenced and used by COM-aware clients. But there might be circumstances under which you need to prevent certain public interfaces and public classes from being available to COM. You can do this by using the *ComVisible* attribute. Setting this attribute to *false* prevents the type to which it's applied from appearing in the typelib:

```
[ComVisible(false)]
public interface IWeatherStatistics
{
    float GetLowestTemperatureThisMonth();
    float GetHighestTemperatureThisMonth();
}
```

In this example, the *IWeatherStatistics* interface isn't exported as type information into the typelib. If the *IWeatherStatistics* type is used by any other type that's exposed to COM, the type is replaced by an *IUnknown* interface in the typelib. For example:

```
HRESULT SetWeatherStatistics(
    [in] IWeatherStatistics* pWeatherIndications);
```

becomes

```
HRESULT SetWeatherStatistics(
    [in] IUnknown* pUnkWeatherIndications);
```

There's a caveat here, though. It doesn't make sense to set *ComVisible* to *true* to turn on the visibility of private or protected members in the class because these members can never be exposed to COM.

Not only can the *ComVisible* attribute be applied to classes and interfaces, it can be applied to a slew of other types, such as assemblies, methods, fields, properties, delegates, and structs. Take a look at the following example, where we selectively hide specific methods in an interface so that they're not exposed to COM:

```
public interface IHurricaneWatch {
    void AlertWeatherStations(String strDetails);

    [ComVisible(false)]
    void PlotCoordinates();

    void IssueEvacuationOrders();
}
```

The previous snippet of code indicates to the typelib generator (REGASM and TLBEXP) that we intend to hide the *PlotCoordinates* method of the *IHurricaneWatch* interface so that it doesn't appear in the generated type library. Here's the IDL for the typelib that's generated:

```
[
    ⋮
]
interface IHurricaneWatch : IDispatch {
    [id(0x60020000)] HRESULT AlertWeatherStations(
        [in] BSTR strDetails);
    [id(0x60020002)] HRESULT IssueEvacuationOrders();
};
```

Altering the Marshaling Behavior for Types

When the runtime marshals managed types into the unmanaged world, it follows certain data type conversion rules. For example, a managed type such as a *String* is always converted to a *BSTR*. Types such as *String* could have more than one possible representation in the unmanaged world, such as an array of ANSI characters (*LPSTR*), an array of Unicode characters (*LPWSTR*), or a *BSTR*. Target data types in the unmanaged realm that have more than one possible representation of the underlying managed type are referred to as *nonisomorphic types*. The COM interop converts nonisomorphic types into a specific default target type. (For example, as noted earlier, a *String* always converts to a *BSTR*.) Consider the following method in a C# class:

```
public void SetProductName(String strProductName) { ... }
```

When this method is run through a typelib exporter such as TLBEXP or REGASM, the corresponding section of the IDL in the generated typelib looks like this:

```
HRESULT SetProductName([in] BSTR strProductName);
```

However, there might be occasions on which you need to provide alternate representations for the types. For example, you might want to convert a managed type such as a *String* to a null-terminated array of ANSI characters (*LPSTR*) instead of a *BSTR*. This conversion is where the *MarshalAs* attribute helps. You can use the *MarshalAs* attribute to control how the conversion happens between managed and unmanaged types. So if you want to have the managed *String* converted to a null-terminated ANSI character array, as opposed to a *BSTR*, you'd apply the *MarshalAs* attribute to the method parameter, as shown here:

```
public void SetProductName([MarshalAs(UnmanagedType.LPStr)]
                           String strProductName) { ... }
```

The resulting conversion would look something like this in the IDL representation:

```
HRESULT SetProductName([in] LPSTR strProductName);
```

Thus, the *MarshalAs* attribute can be very useful when you need to tweak data representation mappings between types in the managed and unmanaged worlds.

Exception Handling: .NET vs. COM

Let's take a look at how the exceptions raised by .NET components get mapped to COM-based *HRESULT* values. You'll notice that the return types from .NET component methods are converted into an *[out,retval]* IDL type when run through a typelib exporter. The actual return type for the method in the IDL is an *HRESULT* that indicates a success or failure of a method call.

A failed *HRESULT* is usually the result of a system exception or a user-defined exception raised because of failed business logic. If the method call goes through fine with no exception thrown from the .NET component, the CCW fills in the returned *HRESULT* with 0 (*S_OK*). If the method call fails or business logic validation fails, the .NET component is expected to raise an exception. This exception usually has a failure *HRESULT* assigned to it and an associated error description.

The CCW gleans details such as the error code, error message, and so on from the .NET exception and provides these details in a form that can be consumed by the COM client. The CCW does this conversion by implementing the *ISupportErrorInfo* interface (to indicate that it supports rich error information) and the *IErrorInfo* interface (through which it provides all the error information details), or through the *EXCEPTINFO* structure that's passed through an *IDispatch::Invoke* call (in case the COM-aware client was late binding through a *dispinterface*).

The error propagation happens seamlessly, meaning that .NET exceptions are mapped to their equivalent COM counterparts and delivered to the COM client by the CCW. Let's modify the *Temperature* property's *set* method to raise a user-defined error if the temperature specified isn't within acceptable limits. We'll soon see how the Visual Basic client traps this error by using the usual COM error-handling mechanisms.

```
public class TemperatureComponent
{
    private float m_fTemperature = 0;

    /* Temperature property (in Fahrenheit)*/
    public float Temperature
    {
        get
        {
            return m_fTemperature;
        }/* end get */

        set
        {
            if((value < -30) || (value > 150))
            {
                TemperatureException excep =
                    new TemperatureException(
                    "Marlinspike has never " +
                    "experienced such extreme temperatures. " +
                    "Please recalibrate your thermometer");
                throw excep;
            }

            m_fTemperature = value;

        }/* end set */

    }
```

```
}/* end class TemperatureComponent */

class TemperatureException : ApplicationException
{
    public TemperatureException(String message) : base(message)
    {
    }

}/* end class TemperatureException*/
```

Here's a Visual Basic client that tries to set the temperature in marlinspike to a value that's outside the temperature readings accepted by the method, which triggers an exception from the .NET component:

```
Private Sub MyButton_Click()

    On Error GoTo ErrHandler

    ' Create an instance of the temperature component.
    Dim objTemperature As New TemperatureComponent

    ' Set the temperature to the boiling point of water.
    objTemperature.Temperature = 212

    Exit Sub

ErrHandler:
    MsgBox "Error Message : " & Err.Description, _
        vbOKOnly, "Error Code: " & CStr(Err.Number)

End Sub
```

In this example, the Visual Basic 6 client's *ErrorHandler* block set through the *On Error Goto* statement uses Visual Basic's global intrinsic *Err* object to get all the error details that the CCW has mapped from the .NET exception into a COM-specific error object that implements the *IErrorInfo* interface. Figure 22-3 shows an error returned by the component that's been trapped by the Visual Basic client.

Figure 22-3 An error returned by the .NET component is trappable by the Visual Basic application.

The .NET component here raises a *TemperatureException*, which extends the *ApplicationException* class. An *ApplicationException* is usually thrown to indicate errors that relate to usual run-of-the-mill failures in application business logic. The *TemperatureException* calls the base class to initialize the error message. Because no explicit *HRESULT* was specified, a failure *HRESULT* is generated and returned by the *ApplicationException* class. If you want to take control of the *HRESULT* values instead of accepting the auto-generated *HRESULT* values by the base class, you can use the *HResult*-protected member of the *ApplicationException* class (that's accessible from the *TemperatureException* class) to specify a specific *HRESULT* value to be returned.

Another way to throw exceptions from your .NET component is to use the *ThrowExceptionForHR* method of the *System.Runtime.InteropServices.Marshal* class. This method takes an integer that represents a standard *HRESULT* parameter. Most of these standard *HRESULT* values map to .NET exception types, and the corresponding .NET exception is thrown. For example, the following statement throws an *OutOfMemoryException*:

```
System.Runtime.InteropServices.Marshal.ThrowExceptionForHR(
    COR_E_OUTOFMEMORY);
```

Handling Events from .NET Components in Unmanaged Event Sinks

We saw in Chapter 21 how COM objects in the unmanaged world raise events asynchronously using connection points and how these events could be consumed by .NET applications. We'll now take a look at doing this the other way around. We'll get a .NET component to raise events and then have an unmanaged sink consume these events.

A .NET component should declare events representing delegate instances for each of the methods in its outgoing event interface. When an event is raised, all the delegates in the event's list will be invoked. These delegates reference the notification target's handler and can therefore call into the correct handler function provided by the subscriber. The unmanaged sink goes about subscribing to events as though it were interacting with a COM object that supports outgoing interfaces by using connection points. The CCW takes care of mapping both these event-handling models so that a COM client's unmanaged handler could still receive notifications when a managed .NET event occurs.

Creating a .NET Component that Sources Events

Let's create a .NET component that notifies subscribers upon inclement weather conditions. The component allows the weather station master to set wind speeds that have been recorded. If the wind speeds exceed a certain limit (300 mph), the component senses an impending tornado and notifies subscribers by firing off the *OnTornadoWarning* event.

```csharp
using System;
using System.Runtime.InteropServices;
using System.Runtime.CompilerServices;
using System.Reflection;
using System.Diagnostics;

// Outgoing event interface that the sink implements. We'll
// use a dispinterface here so that it remains friendly to
// scripting clients.

[InterfaceType(ComInterfaceType.InterfaceIsIDispatch)]
public interface ITornadoWatchEvents
{
    void OnTornadoWarning(int nWindSpeed);

}/* end interface ITornadoWatchEvents */


// Incoming interface containing the methods
// being exposed to COM-aware clients
public interface IWeatherNotify {

    int WindSpeed { get; set; }

}/* end interface IWeatherNotify */
// Delegate representing the OnTornadoWarning method of the
// outgoing event interface
public delegate void TornadoWarningDelegate(int nWindSpeed);


[
    ComSourceInterfaces("ITornadoWatchEvents"),
    ClassInterface(ClassInterfaceType.None)
]
public class WeatherNotify : IWeatherNotify
{
    // Indicates wind speed in miles per hour
    private int m_nWindSpeed = 20;
```

```
// Define an event associated with the
// TornadoWarningDelegate.
public event TornadoWarningDelegate OnTornadoWarning;

// Constructor
public WeatherNotify() {
}

public int WindSpeed
{
    get {

        // Return the current wind speed.
        return m_nWindSpeed;
    }

    set {

        // Set the WindSpeed field to the new value.
        m_nWindSpeed = value;

        // Check whether the wind speed warrants
        // an event notification.
        if(value >= 300) {

            try {

                // Check whether the delegate instance
                // for the event exists.
                if(null != OnTornadoWarning) {

                    // Twister on the loose. Run for
                    // cover!!!.

                    // Fire the event to all the
                    // managed/unmanaged sink handlers that
                    // have registered for this event.

                    OnTornadoWarning(m_nWindSpeed);

                }/* end if */

            }/* end try */
            catch(Exception ex) {

                Trace.WriteLine(ex.Message);
            }/* end catch */

        }/* end if */
```

```
}/* end set */

  }/* End WindSpeed Property Accessors */
}/* end class WeatherNotify */
```

Let's dissect the code a bit and try to understand what's going on. The *ITornadoWatchEvents* interface is the outgoing interface that unmanaged sinks must implement to receive event notifications. This interface consists of a single method, *OnTornadoWarning*, which notifies clients of the possibility of an approaching tornado along with the current wind speed.

You'll notice that the outgoing interface, *ITornadoWatchEvents*, is tagged with an *InterfaceTypeAttribute* attribute with the positional parameter *Com-InterfaceType.InterfaceIsIDispatch*. This tagging is done because, by default, the interface would be exported into the IDL and subsequently into the typelib as a dual interface. Scripting clients generally fail when they try to sink in a dual interface and the interface is only pure *dispinterface* friendly. So we inject an *InterfaceTypeAttribute* attribute with a *ComInterfaceType.InterfaceIsIDispatch* value to force typelib generation tools to generate a pure *dispinterface* for the outgoing interface. You'd need to define a delegate (*TornadoWarningDelegate*) that matches the exact signature of the *OnTornadoWarning* method in the outgoing interface. If you had more than one method in the outgoing interface, you'd need to define matching delegates for each method.

We're now done with the definition of the outgoing interface and matching delegates for each of the methods in the outgoing interface. Now comes the most important part. You'd need to define events representing each of the delegates that you defined for the methods in the outgoing interface:

```
public event TornadoWarningDelegate OnTornadoWarning;
```

The delegate instance that the event represents must have the same name as the corresponding method in the outgoing interface. In other words, the event representing the *TornadoWarningDelegate* delegate instance must be named *OnTornadoWarning*. That's all there is to it.

You're now ready to send out event notifications. In our example, an event notification is sent out when the *WindSpeed* is set to a value greater than or equal to *300*. You first need to check whether the delegate instance for the event exists and then fire off the *OnTornadoWarning* event. Because the delegate represented by the event is a multicast delegate, all the COM sinks and subscribers in the delegate's invocation list will be notified that there's a twister looming on the horizon. You can build the .NET component just described by using the following command:

```
csc /target:library /r:System.dll
 /out:WeatherNotify.dll WeatherNotify.cs
```

You can now run the assembly through REGASM.EXE to register the assembly and generate a typelib from it. This typelib can then be referenced in the Visual Basic 6 client that will sink the events.

```
regasm WeatherNotify.dll /tlb:WeatherNotify.tlb
```

Handling Events in a Visual Basic Client Application

Here's a Visual Basic 6 client that subscribes to *OnTornadoWarning* event notifications from the *WeatherNotify* component. It's a simple form-based application that subscribes to event notifications by using the *WithEvents* keyword. The *objWeatherNotify_OnTornadoWarning* subroutine receives event notifications from the .NET component when the *WindSpeed* is set to a value greater than or equal to *300*, as Figure 22-4 shows.

Figure 22-4   Example of the Visual Basic Weather Station event sink object being notified of a weather event by our C# component through COM.

```
Dim WithEvents objWeatherNotify As WeatherNotify.WeatherNotify
Private Sub Form_Load()
    ' Create an instance of the WeatherNotify component
    Set objWeatherNotify = New WeatherNotify.WeatherNotify
End Sub

Private Sub SetWindSpeedButton_Click()

    ' Clear the warning label.
    Me.LabelWarning = ""

    ' Set the WindSpeed property in the WeatherNotify component.
    objWeatherNotify.WindSpeed = Me.WindSpeed

End Sub

Private Sub objWeatherNotify_OnTornadoWarning( _
    ByVal nWindSpeed As Long)

    ' We've received a notification from the WeatherNotify
    ' component that there could be a tornado on the prowl.
```

```
Me.LabelWarning = "Tornado Warning: Current Wind " & _
    "Speeds : " & nWindSpeed & " mph"

End Sub
```

Earlier you saw how the RCW and the metadata helper classes translated the connection point event handling to delegate-based event handling semantics so that a .NET application could sink events from COM components. Here the CCW does most of the plumbing to allow unmanaged code to subscribe to event notifications from .NET components and to deliver these events to the respective handlers in the unmanaged COM land.

Thread Affinity in .NET Components

In the Chapter 21, you saw how .NET applications could declare the calling thread's apartment affiliation before creating a COM component. Now let's take a look at the other side of the equation—in particular, the kind of threading behavior that .NET components exhibit when they're created from unmanaged COM-aware applications.

The thread affinity of a .NET component is defined by the context that the object lives in. As you learned in Chapter 18, "Multithreading and Asynchronous Programming," a context is essentially an environment hosted by the *AppDomain* (a lightweight process) in which the object gets created. Each context in turn hosts objects that share common usage requirements, such as thread affinity, object pooling, transaction, just-in-time (JIT) activation, and synchronization. These contexts are created either when required by the runtime, depending on the attributes, or when the interception services are required by the object. If there's an existing context that matches the usage rules that govern the object, the runtime offers the object accommodation in that context. If the runtime doesn't find a matching context, a new context is created for the object to live in.

With that said, every *AppDomain* hosts a *Default* context. The *Default* context in turn hosts *context-agnostic* (or *context-agile*) objects. These objects aren't bound to any context. Context-agile objects don't require any attributes, special usage policies, or interception services. Table 22-1 summarizes how .NET components behave in cross-context access scenarios based on their context agility. The first row contains cross-context calls within the same *AppDomain* (intra-*AppDomain* calls); the second row contains cross-context calls across *AppDomains* (inter-*AppDomain* calls).

Table 22-1
.NET Component Behavior in Cross-Context Access Scenarios

.NET Classes that Extend *MarshalByRefObject*	.NET Classes that Extend *ContextBoundObject*	.NET Classes that Don't Extend from *MarshalByRefObject* and *ContextBoundObject*
Context-agile. Direct access. (Emulates a COM object that aggregates the free-threaded marshaler.)	Context-bound. Object is accessed from any other context, only through a proxy.	Context-agile. Direct access. (Emulates a COM object that aggregates the free-threaded marshaler.)
Exhibit marshal-by-reference semantics. Object is accessed from any other context, only through a proxy.	Exhibit marshal-by-reference semantics. Object is accessed from any other context, only through a proxy.	Exhibit marshal-by-value semantics. When tagged with the *[serializable]* attribute, a copy of the object is re-created in the caller *AppDomain*'s context.

Thread-Neutral Behavior When Accessed by Unmanaged COM-Aware Clients

Figure 22-5 shows how a .NET component advertises its threading model to COM when an assembly is run through REGASM.EXE in order to make the appropriate Registry entries for COM-aware clients to examine.

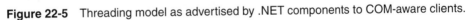

Name	Type	Data
(Default)	REG_SZ	C:\WINNT\System32\mscoree.dll
Assembly	REG_SZ	Temperature, Version=0.0.0.0, Culture=neutral, PublicKeyToken=null
Class	REG_SZ	TemperatureComponent
RuntimeVersion	REG_SZ	v1.0.2914
ThreadingModel	REG_SZ	Both

Figure 22-5   Threading model as advertised by .NET components to COM-aware clients.

The *ThreadingModel* key under *InprocServer32* has the value *Both*. In COM, objects that advertise their *ThreadingModel* as *Both* are willing to move into their caller's apartment, be it a single-threaded apartment (STA) or a multi-threaded apartment (MTA). In addition, threaded objects marked as *Both* that also aggregate the free-threaded marshaler give other apartments to which they're marshaled direct interface pointer references (as opposed to proxies). Context-agile .NET components (those that don't extend from *ContextBound-Object*) are analogous to thread-neutral COM objects that aggregate the free-threaded marshaler.

Let's see how the .NET component behaves as we pass interface references to the .NET component across COM apartments in the unmanaged client. Take a look at this simple C# class that we'll be exposing to the unmanaged COM client:

```
using System;
using System.Runtime.InteropServices;

public interface IHelloDotNet {

    String GetThreadID();

}/* end interface IHelloDotNet */

[ClassInterface(ClassInterfaceType.None)]
public class HelloDotNet : IHelloDotNet
{
    public HelloDotNet() {
    }

    public String GetThreadID() {

        return AppDomain.GetCurrentThreadId().ToString();
    }

}/* end class HelloDotNet */
```

This class implements the *GetThreadID* method from the *IHelloDotNet* interface. This method returns the ID of the current thread that's executing in the *AppDomain* into which this object is loaded. To build this class into an assembly and to make the appropriate Registry entries for COM, issue the following commands from the command line:

```
csc /target:library /out:HelloDotNet.dll HelloDotNet.cs
regasm HelloDotNet.dll /tlb:HelloDotNet.tlb
```

We'll now consume the .NET component from a COM-aware client. We'll use a C++ console application that will create the .NET component in its main thread (an STA) and then pass the component across to two other apartments (an STA and an MTA) by spawning two worker threads. We'll take a look at what happens when a raw interface pointer to the object is passed across apartments. Then we'll take a look at what happens when a marshaled reference is passed across apartments by using explicit inter-thread marshaling calls that use the *CoMarshalInterface* and *CoUnmarshalInterface* API family. Look at the following code (with error checking omitted for brevity):

⋮

```cpp
#import "mscorlib.tlb"
// Import the .NET component's typelib.
#import "HelloDotNet.tlb" no_namespace

// Worker thread functions
long WINAPI MySTAThreadFunction(long lParam);
long WINAPI MyMTAThreadFunction(long lParam);

// Use the compiler-generated smart pointer wrappers.
IHelloDotNetPtr spHelloNET = NULL;

// Stream pointer that will contain the marshaled interface
IStream* g_pStream1 = NULL;
IStream* g_pStream2 = NULL;

int main(int argc, char* argv[])
{
    ⋮

    // Make the primary thread enter an STA.
    ::CoInitialize(NULL);

    // Log the thread ID.
    cout << "The Thread ID of the primary STA thread is : "
        << ::GetCurrentThreadId() << endl;

    // Create the .NET object via the COM interop.
    hr = spHelloNET.CreateInstance(__uuidof(HelloDotNet));

    cout << "From .NET when called from the primary STA thread : "
        << spHelloNET->GetThreadID() << endl;

    ⋮

    // Marshal the interface pointer to a stream so that the
    // worker threads can get back an unmarshaled reference
    // from it.
    hr = CoMarshalInterThreadInterfaceInStream(
        _uuidof(IHelloDotNet),
        spHelloNET,
        &g_pStream1);

    hr = CoMarshalInterThreadInterfaceInStream(
        _uuidof(IHelloDotNet),
        spHelloNET,
        &g_pStream2);
```

```
    // Create a worker thread that enters an STA.
    hThreadSTA = CreateThread(NULL,0,
        (LPTHREAD_START_ROUTINE)MySTAThreadFunction,
        NULL, 0,&dwThreadIDSTA);

    // Log the thread ID.
    cout << "The thread ID of the STA-based worker thread is : "
        << dwThreadIDSTA << endl;

    // Create a worker thread that enters an MTA.
    hThreadMTA = CreateThread(NULL, 0,
        (LPTHREAD_START_ROUTINE)MyMTAThreadFunction,
        NULL, 0, &dwThreadIDMTA);

    // Log the thread ID.
    cout << "The thread ID of the MTA-based worker thread is : "
        << dwThreadIDMTA << endl;


    // Wait for both the worker threads to complete.
    ::WaitForSingleObject(hThreadSTA, INFINITE);
    ::WaitForSingleObject(hThreadMTA, INFINITE);

    // Return the status.
    return 0;

}/* end main */
/*
 * Worker thread function that enters an STA
 */
long WINAPI MySTAThreadFunction(long lParam)
{
    // Let the thread enter an STA.
    ::CoInitializeEx(NULL, COINIT_APARTMENTTHREADED);

    // Invoke the method using the raw interface pointer.
    cout << "From .NET when called from the STA worker "
        << "thread (direct access) : "
        << spHelloNET->GetThreadID() << endl;

    // Unmarshal the interface pointer from the stream.
    IHelloDotNetPtr spHello = NULL;
    HRESULT hr = CoGetInterfaceAndReleaseStream(g_pStream1,
        __uuidof(IHelloDotNet),
        (void **)&spHello);

    if(S_OK == hr)
```

```
    {
        cout << "From .NET when called from the STA worker "
            << "thread (marshaled) : "
            << spHello->GetThreadID() << endl;
    }

    // Exit from the thread.
    return 0;

}/* end MySTAThreadFunction */



/*
 * Worker thread function that enters an MTA
 */
long WINAPI MyMTAThreadFunction(long lParam)
{

    // Let the thread enter an MTA.
    ::CoInitializeEx(NULL, COINIT_MULTITHREADED);

    // Invoke the method using the raw interface pointer.
    cout << "From .NET when called from the MTA worker "
        << "thread (direct access) : "
        << spHelloNET->GetThreadID() << endl;

    // Unmarshal the interface pointer from the stream.
    IHelloDotNetPtr spHello = NULL;
    HRESULT hr = CoGetInterfaceAndReleaseStream(g_pStream2,
        __uuidof(IHelloDotNet),
        (void **)&spHello);

    if(S_OK == hr)
    {
        cout << "From .NET when called from the MTA Worker "
        "thread (marshaled) : "
            << spHello->GetThreadID() << endl;
    }

    // Exit from the thread.
    return 0;

}/* end MyMTAThreadFunction */
```

Here's the output that you get when the console application is run:

```
The thread ID of the primary STA thread is : 2220
From .NET when called from the primary STA Thread : 2220
The thread ID of the STA-based worker thread is : 2292
```

```
The thread ID of the MTA-based worker thread is : 2296
From .NET when called from the STA worker thread
(direct access) : 2292
From .NET when called from the STA worker thread (marshalled)
: 2292
From .NET when called from the MTA worker thread (direct access)
: 2296
From .NET when called from the MTA worker thread (marshalled)
: 2296
```

Notice that for all these calls, no thread switch occurs between the thread making the call in the client and the thread invoking the actual method in the .NET component. In other words, the .NET component is context-agile and always executes in the caller's thread. From the previous code snippet, observe that the effect of marshaling an object reference (using inter-thread marshaling APIs such as *CoMarshalInterThreadInterfaceInStream* and *CoGetInterface-AndReleaseStream*) is the same as that of passing a direct object reference across apartments. Eventually, the receiving apartment gets an apartment-neutral interface pointer that it can use to call into the .NET component. The .NET component exhibits all the behavior that's reminiscent of *Both*-threaded COM components that aggregate the free-threaded marshaler.

Summary

In this chapter, we explored how COM-aware clients from the pre-.NET era could consume .NET components as though they were COM components. We saw how the CCW and the runtime make this a seamless process from a programming perspective. We briefly explored the possibilities of using attributes to emit metadata into .NET types so that the typelib generated could be tailored and fine-tuned to your requirements. We looked at how the exception-handling mechanisms in the two worlds are correlative. We also discussed how to go about receiving asynchronous event notifications from .NET components in unmanaged event sinks. Then we turned our attention to the deployment options available and how to deploy .NET components as shared assemblies. Finally, we discussed the thread-neutral behavior of .NET components and saw how context-agile .NET components are analogous to COM *Both*-threaded components that aggregate the free-threaded marshaler.

23

Security

Because so many spheres of human enterprise increasingly rely on software systems, the threats to the security of such systems are constantly increasing. Wherever there's someone or some organization that wants to build something constructive and useful, there's someone who feels the need to damage and destroy it. Microsoft developers have paid very careful attention to all aspects of .NET security. All the various ways that software can be made insecure have been addressed, including providing defenses against malicious attacks from the outside as well as against careless coding or design from the inside.

In this chapter, we'll first set the groundwork for .NET security by considering the various types of security threat. Then we'll see how the totality of the .NET security model covers all the bases by offering a range of security strategies, including verifiable type safety, code access security, role-based security, and isolated storage.

.NET Security

Security in .NET isn't limited to a single strategy. Instead, a range of strategies has been developed to address various security issues. Some of these strategies involve the developer making design and coding decisions. Others are intended more for administrative use and are supported by a range of administrative tools. The range of .NET security strategies is summarized here:

- **Verifiable type safety** Assures that code is well-formed and accesses memory in well-defined ways.

- **Code signing** Defines an assembly's unique identity and assures consumers that the code hasn't been tampered with after being built.

- **Cryptographic services**   Provides many cryptographic mechanisms for protecting data, notably when the data's being streamed to or from persistent storage or remote locations.

- **Code access security**   Protects resources outside a piece of code—for example, the file system, the Registry, or the network—by restricting access to those resources based on security policy.

- **Role-based security**   Allows code to check the identity and role membership of a user and make resource access decisions based on this identity.

- **Isolated storage**   Provides safe client-data storage, isolated per assembly and per user, optionally with a quota applied.

Note that the .NET security support is in addition to whatever underlying operating system security is in place. You can't bypass or replace the native machine or network security—you can only enhance and extend it. The underlying Microsoft Windows security model is based on user authentication and object-based access control. A user's identity is authenticated and then mapped against the authorization settings for a securable object (such as a file, Registry key, or device). Authentication on Windows is provided by three different mechanisms: Kerberos, NTLM, and public key certificates. This system is reasonable but somewhat primitive or coarse in granularity. This is because once a user is authenticated, most code run by that user has access to all the resources that the user can access. The .NET Framework's security model imposes additional run-time checking of code and allows security control that's not only based on the identity of the user, but also on the identity of the code. The access to resources granted to a given assembly is governed by security policy, and this policy is established and maintained as an administrative task. This system makes it very difficult to write code that can circumvent .NET security.

Threats to Security

One way to categorize security threats to software systems is by dividing them into the innocent and the malicious. Innocent security threats include situations in which users—who are authorized but unwary—accidentally cause damage to some part of the system either through carelessness or by using code that contains security loopholes. The same innocent users could also get access to sensitive information they shouldn't have access to, simply because the granularity of the system security isn't flexible enough to fine-tune their permitted accesses. Malicious attacks are a superset of innocent attacks because one of the standard approaches of a malicious attack is to impersonate an authorized user. Another malicious approach is to modify an existing piece of code so that it no longer functions as intended. The exploitation of buffer overruns is a classic example of this technique. Issues that a robust security model must address include:

- **Breach of privacy**   In such a security threat, unauthorized users or code gains access to sensitive data—for example, personnel and payroll data, or customer data that could be exploited in commercial competition. The term *unauthorized user* includes both an innocent user who has simply been granted excess authorization and a malicious user.

- **Falsification of auditing**   Security and other administrative systems rely on the ability to trace and log operations on securable objects and attempts to breach security. A malicious attack could attempt to falsify these logs either after an attack or as a matter of course to establish false patterns to obscure a later attack.

- **Spoofing identity**   This is one of the oldest approaches to breaching security, in which an attacker attempts to assume the identity of an authorized user. This impersonation includes both traditional username/password identity and IP-address identity, in which rogue packets are sent, purporting to originate from a trusted address. Standard defenses include insisting on user passwords of a certain minimum length with a mixture of uppercase and lowercase characters and numbers and enforcing password changes at frequent intervals. A traditional attack would run a pattern-permutating routine to try all viable combinations of characters until an acceptable match is found.

- **Elevation of privilege**   Having gotten past the first security barrier—authentication—it's often easier to get past the second barrier and gain additional privileges (such as administrator privileges) as an authorized user.

- **Denial of service**   This security threat is an attack that attempts to disable a valid service—for example, by flooding a Web server with false requests to prevent it from handling genuine requests or by disabling a computer by deleting system files.

- **Mobile code**   This is an increasing security threat, represented by code that can be attached to e-mails or downloaded from Web pages, including ActiveX controls. Most e-mail servers allow administrative configuration to bar attachments of a certain kind (for example, binary files) or files larger than a certain size, but again, this control is very coarse-grained. Similarly, although a Web browser can detect HTML containing script, in general it can only reject it or accept it unconditionally—there's limited capacity for selective acceptance or rejection. An ActiveX control can be signed to assure clients that it comes from a trusted source, but this system doesn't address the problem of a control that's been tampered with after signing.

The .NET security model addresses all these security threats. Although some aspects of .NET security are entirely automatic, others can be fine-tuned programmatically and still others can be extensively configured through administrative tools.

Verifiable Type Safety

Developers familiar with C and C++ will know that C++ purports to be a more type-safe language than C because—to give an example—the C++ compiler insists on the correct data types being passed as parameters to a function. C++ also offers constructs such as *static_cast<>* and *dynamic_cast<>* to increase the level of type safety when converting data from one type to another. The C# *is* and *as* operators can be seen as evolving from *static_cast<>* and *dynamic_cast<>*. However, C and C++—including C++ with managed extensions running on .NET—still allow the use of raw pointers. And, of course, you can basically cast any type of pointer to any other type of pointer whenever you want. This casting works because all pointers are really the same type—they're all 32-bit values.

C and C++ also allow you to treat any 32-bit value as a pointer and vice versa. One of the reasons for this leniency is to gain flexibility. Traditional C has no concept of either polymorphism or delegates, so the C solution for the same requirement is to use callback functions. But callback functions need to be very open-ended, so they tend to take *void* pointers or *int* pointers as parameters, with the clear understanding that the developer is free to pass a pointer to anything he or she likes. Clearly, this system is very difficult—in fact, impossible—to police at run time. The C# language, therefore, will allow the use of raw pointers only in an unsafe context.

More Info   For details on unsafe code, see Chapter 20, "Pinning and Memory Management."

For example, suppose we write a piece of code that's demonstrably unsafe—that is, wrong. This task is actually quite difficult to do in C# because the compiler is so strict about what it considers safe and unsafe. For our first attempt, we'll create an application directly in Microsoft intermediate language (MSIL) and compile it with ILASM. The following is the MSIL source code:

```
.assembly Foo{}
.class Bar
{
    .method public static void Main() il managed
    {
        .entrypoint
        pop
        ret
    }
}
```

This MSIL code is acceptable for a .NET assembly: it specifies the assembly, which contains one class encapsulating a conventional *Main* entry point. The only thing wrong is that the application attempts to pop a value off the stack, although it hasn't yet placed a value on the stack. This operation is wrong and will result in a run-time error—a stack underflow error—if the program is allowed to run. We can build this source code with the following command line:

```
ilasm UnsafeILsource.il
```

where *UnsafeILsource.il* is the name of the file containing the MSIL source code. ILASM will be quite happy to build this code into an executable assembly despite the obvious error—when you write code down at this level, it's fairly easy to write rubbish statements that will get through the compiler. We could then run the resultant EXE target back through ILDASM, as shown in Figure 23-1.

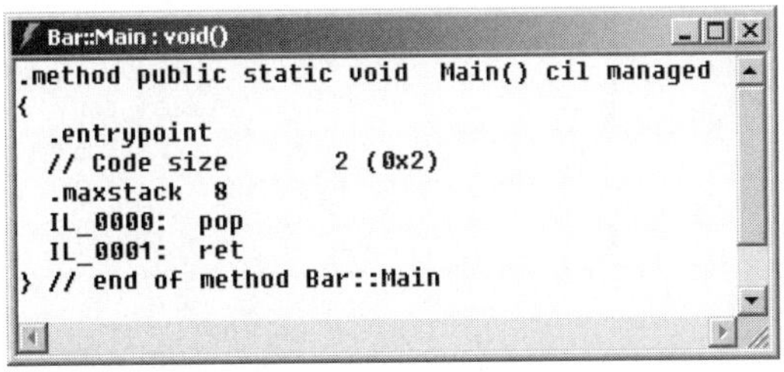

Figure 23-1   MSIL from a deliberately incorrect assembly.

When you attempt to run this application, the runtime will throw the following exception:

```
Unhandled Exception: System.InvalidProgramException:
Common Language Runtime detected an invalid program.
   at Bar.Main()
```

which is exactly what we'd hope for. By default, the common language runtime performs a type-safety verification step as part of the just-in-time (JIT) compile process. On this occasion, the runtime decided that the code was invalid and refused to run it. We can perform the same type-safety verification step on a built assembly by using the PEVerify.exe tool supplied with the .NET Framework SDK:

```
peverify UnsafeILsource.exe
```

This command will report the following errors:

```
Microsoft (R) .NET Framework PE Verifier  Version 1.0.3705.0
Copyright (C) Microsoft Corporation 1998-2001. All
 rights reserved.

[IL]: Error: [c:\data\insidecsharp\chap23\unsafeilsource\
unsafeilsource.exe : Bar::Main] [offset 0x00000000]
 [opcode pop] Stack underflow.
[IL]: Error: [c:\data\insidecsharp\chap23\unsafeilsource\
unsafeilsource.exe : Bar::Main]  [HRESULT 0x80004005]
 - Unspecified error

2 Errors Verifying unsafeilsource.exe
```

OK, the previous application was clearly wrong, and the runtime did a good job of detecting that. But suppose we want to write an application that uses raw pointers in a safe way. You could argue that this statement is a contradiction in terms—that any use of raw pointers is inherently unsafe—and we'll return to this argument later in the section. For example, the following application—which we examined in detail in Chapter 20—uses raw pointers in an unsafe context:

```
public class TestUnsafeApp
{
    unsafe public static void Swap(int* pi, int* pj)
    {
        int tmp = *pi;
        *pi = *pj;
        *pj = tmp;
    }

    public static void Main(string[] args)
    {
        int i = 3;
```

```
        int j = 4;
        Console.WriteLine("BEFORE: i = {0}, j = {1}", i, j);
        unsafe { Swap(&i, &j); }
        Console.WriteLine("AFTER:  i = {0}, j = {1}", i, j);
    }
}
```

This code builds and runs perfectly well. The output from this application
is as follows:

```
BEFORE: i = 3, j = 4
AFTER:  i = 4, j = 3
```

Note that the C# compiler forces us to use the *unsafe* keyword in both the
invocation of the method and the definition of the method. We're also forced to
compile with the */unsafe* compiler switch. Of course, the specifics of the code
are harmless. (Or are they? We'll discuss this later in the section.) We can see
that the code is performing a simple, innocuous operation that happens to use
raw pointers for efficiency. In a way, the use of the *unsafe* keyword is an indication to the runtime that the code is potentially unsafe. But how does the runtime know that we've used the *unsafe* keyword? As soon as you build a project
with */unsafe*, the compiler will add additional code to the manifest, notably
including a security permission request to skip run-time verification, as Figure
23-2 shows.

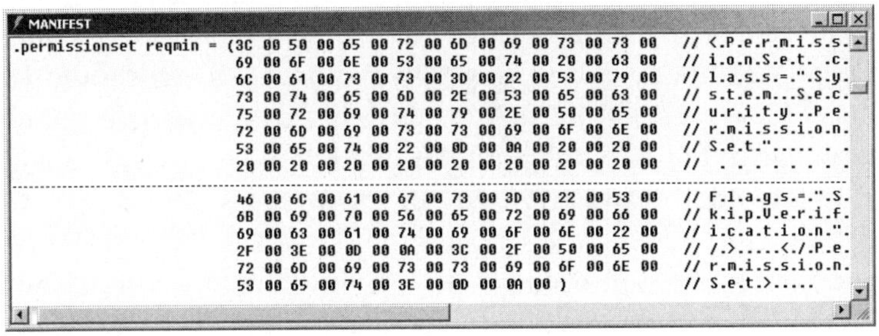

Figure 23-2 Manifest entry for unsafe code.

We'll look at this security permission request again later, in the section
entitled "Code Access Security," where we'll see how you can make similar
requests programmatically. For now, we'll focus on the meaning of the request
and the consequences for our assembly. It should be clear from these two
examples that compiling with */unsafe* tells the runtime not to perform the usual
type-safety verification step on this assembly, thereby allowing the code to run.
Indeed, if we explicitly perform a type-safety verification on the assembly by
using PEVerify, we'll get a report like this:

```
[IL]: Error: [c:\data\insidecsharp\chap23\testunsafe\testunsafe
\bin\debug\testunsafe.exe : TestUnsafe.TestUnsafeApp::Main]
 [offset 0x00000009] [opcode ldloc.0]
initlocals must be set for verifiable methods with one or more
 local variables.
[IL]: Error: [c:\data\insidecsharp\chap23\testunsafe\testunsafe
\bin\debug\testunsafe.exe : TestUnsafe.TestUnsafeApp::Main]
 [offset 0x0000000F] [opcode ldloc.1]
initlocals must be set for verifiable methods with one or more
 local variables.
[IL]: Error: [c:\data\insidecsharp\chap23\testunsafe\testunsafe
\bin\debug\testunsafe.exe : TestUnsafe.TestUnsafeApp::Main]
 [offset 0x0000001F] [opcode ldloc.0]
initlocals must be set for verifiable methods with one or more
 local variables.
[IL]: Error: [c:\data\insidecsharp\chap23\testunsafe\testunsafe
\bin\debug\testunsafe.exe : TestUnsafe.TestUnsafeApp::Main]
 [offset 0x00000025] [opcode ldloc.1]
initlocals must be set for verifiable methods with one or more
 local variables.
4 Errors Verifying testunsafe.exe
```

Through type-safety verification, the runtime ensures that you can't treat an object of one type as though it were an object of another type. You can't simply walk through memory from the beginning of an object to bypass the object's class member access definition, and you can't call a method through its address to bypass any security policy in force.

The C# compiler will (grudgingly) allow us to write and build unsafe code, as long as we indicate that we're doing so. If we give the compiler this indication, we're basically telling it that we know what we're doing and that it should let the code through. Although this process doesn't allow us to write absurdly incorrect code, there's always the possibility that we've misunderstood the operations we're performing with our raw pointers and that we could end up with code that's truly—not just potentially—unsafe. If you're developing in languages such as MSIL and C++, you don't have this compiler-level protection and must rely on the runtime's just-in-time compiler (JITter) to verify the type safety of the code. This verification is yet another reason (if you need one) to use C#.

I mentioned earlier that the specifics of this code might not always be as harmless as they seem. Because we think we know what we're doing, we've instructed both the compiler and the runtime to let the code through. However, recall that one of the basic requirements of compliance with the Common Language Specification (CLS) is that an assembly mustn't expose any unsafe code through a public interface. Unfortunately, that's exactly what we've done with our

Swap method. We've therefore introduced a loophole: although we might think we're using our own code in a responsible, safe manner, it's clearly dangerous to publicly expose potentially unsafe code to arbitrary consuming applications.

To make our assembly CLS-compliant, we could simply make the offending unsafe method private and wrap it in a safe public method. This restriction becomes more important if you consider that potential consumers of your assembly might include code written in languages that permit direct access to memory, such as C, C++, and MSIL. MSIL generated by these compilers usually fails the type-safety verification process. The .NET Framework can use an assembly's type safety to determine assembly isolation and security enforcement and to ensure that assemblies can't adversely affect each other. Note that under the default security policy, all code that isn't installed on the local computer will go through the JIT verification step. We'll see how to configure this security later in the chapter, in the section entitled "Code Access Security."

Code Signing

If you want—and most coding standards suggest that you should as a matter of course—you can sign your assembly with a strong name. This signing serves several purposes:

- It provides a unique identity for each assembly, which you can further use not only as a factor in your deployment strategy, but also in configurable security.

- Because the code-signing mechanism is based on public key cryptography, it assures your assembly's consumers of its provenance. A strong name is very difficult to falsify.

- The common language runtime will perform signature verification checks as part of its loading operation to ensure that the assembly hasn't been tampered with.

A major factor in any strategy for deploying .NET assemblies is whether the assembly is strong-named. An assembly that will be used only by one application and can be installed in the same file system directory as that application—or in a specific set of subdirectories—can be deployed without a strong name. This type of assembly is known as a *private assembly* because it's private to the consuming application, and it can easily be installed and uninstalled simply by copying or deleting the file. If you want to deploy an assembly to some other location (either on the local file system or remotely), make it shareable by multiple applications, or take full advantage of the runtime's security checking, your assembly must be signed with a strong name.

In addition to strong-named code signing, you can also use Authenticode. An Authenticode signature guarantees that a specific trusted publisher signed the assembly and hasn't since revoked the certificate associated with the signature. Although Authenticode and .NET code signing serve two different purposes, they are entirely complementary. Note that the Authenticode signature must be applied after the strong-named signature.

Private Assemblies

Let's take private assemblies first. The following code is built into a class library assembly named HelloLib.dll:

```
public class HelloClass
{
    public static void HelloMethod()
    {
        Console.WriteLine("Hello");
    }
}
```

We also specify the version of this assembly with the following code. The Microsoft Visual Studio project wizard will generate a separate assemblyinfo.cs file for this and other assemblywide attributes, but the code would work fine in the same C# source file.

```
[assembly: AssemblyVersion("1.0.0.0")]
```

Alternatively, if you build the assembly with the assembly linker tool (AL.exe), you can use the */v:* switch. Next we build a consuming client application named HelloClient.exe with the following code as well as a reference to the *HelloLib* class library assembly:

```
static void Main(string[] args)
{
    HelloClass.HelloMethod();
}
```

Note that in the manifest for this client application there's a reference to the *HelloLib* class library assembly, as shown in Figure 23-3. You can also see from this manifest that the only other referenced assembly—*mscorlib*—has a strong name, as indicated by the presence of a public key token, while *HelloLib* doesn't have a strong name.

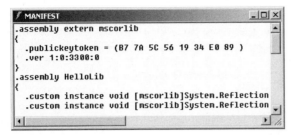

Figure 23-3   Manifest reference to a dependent assembly.

So our client assembly's manifest specifies that it's dependent on the *HelloLib* assembly, version 1.0.0.0. When you add a reference to a dependent assembly in Visual Studio, by default Visual Studio will take a local copy of the assembly into the target directory of the client application. If you build and run this suite so far, everything will work fine. However, what happens if we build another version of the *HelloLib* class library assembly—say version 2.0.0.0—and use it to overwrite the old version in the client's target directory? We'll change the console output but ensure that the code is still compatible with the old version:

```
public class HelloClass
{
    public static void HelloMethod()
    {
        Console.WriteLine("Hello v2");
    }
}
```

To test this library, you need to run the HelloClient.exe from a command window because if you run it from Visual Studio, you'll get another local copy of the original assembly, overwriting the new one. You should find that this suite still works, although the client is now using version 2.0.0.0. Thus, although the runtime checked for an assembly with a matching (simple) name, it didn't check the version information. Let's take this test one step further. Suppose we write a third version but deliberately make this version incompatible:

```
public class HelloClass
{
    public static void Incompatible()
    {
        Console.WriteLine("incompatible");
    }
}
```

This version isn't compatible because we no longer expose a public *HelloMethod* method. If we again use this version to overwrite the one the client's expecting to use, the runtime will throw an exception:

```
Unhandled Exception: System.MissingMethodException:
 Method not found: Void Hello
Lib.HelloClass.HelloMethod().
    at HelloClient.HelloClientApp.Main(String[] args)
```

Having loaded the incorrect assembly into memory, the runtime has found that there's no method matching the one the client's attempting to call—hence, the exception. The moral of this story is that the runtime doesn't care very much about versions when it's dealing with private assemblies—that is, those not strong-named. Therefore, you can infer that the behavior of the runtime differs when it's dealing with strong-named assemblies. We'll look at these assemblies next.

Strong-Named Assemblies

How do you create a strong-named assembly? The scheme adopted by .NET uses asymmetric public key cryptography. Here's how it works:

1. You generate a long sequence of binary data consisting of two logical parts: the public key and the private key. Exactly how this sequence of data is established depends on the specifics of the cryptographic algorithm you're using. Regardless of which method is used—and there are many—you can be reasonably certain that the result will be unique. (Consider that the data is significantly larger than a UUID.) The standard .NET tool for generating this key pair is SN.exe.

2. Next you apply this key pair to your assembly as part of the build by using either CSC.exe or AL.exe. When you apply a cryptographic key pair, the compiler (or assembly linker) hashes the contents of the assembly and then uses the private key from the key pair to encrypt the hash. Then the encrypted hash (or *strong-named signature*) and the public key are stored in the manifest of the assembly.

3. Later, when the runtime loads the assembly, it extracts the encrypted hash and public key from the manifest and decrypts the hash using the public key. Then it performs another hash of the assembly contents and compares this hash with the decrypted hash from the manifest. If the two hashes match, all is good and the assembly runs; otherwise, the assembly is rejected, and the runtime throws an exception.

4. When you build a client assembly that consumes the strong-named assembly, the strong-named assembly's public key is extracted from its manifest and hashed to create the public key token, which is then stored in the manifest of the consuming assembly as part of an *AssemblyRef* entry. The public key token is therefore a hash of the public key—and is therefore much smaller than the public key itself.

Thus, the developer of an assembly holds the private key—which is never released publicly. On the other hand, the signed assembly itself contains the public key, and consuming client assemblies will end up with a hash of the public key. Once the data is encrypted with the private key, it can be decrypted only with the public key. This also works in reverse: the code could be encrypted with the public key and decrypted only with the private key—hence, *asymmetric* cryptography. Furthermore, by using the private key to encrypt the original hash of the assembly, the signer is asserting that he or she has access to the genuine private key. If at runtime the hash values don't match, this means that either the signer didn't use the correct private key (and the assembly can therefore be considered rogue), or the assembly contents or its encrypted hash have been tampered with (and again, this is easily policed by the runtime).

Let's explore this process with a practical example. We can use the same code as we used before, but this time we'll apply it to a class library assembly named StrongNamedLib.dll:

```
public class SomeClass
{
    public static void SomeMethod()
    {
        Console.WriteLine("Hello from StrongNamed Lib");
    }
}
```

To generate the cryptographic key pair, use **SN –k <*keyfilename*>**. For example, from a command window, you could type this command:

```
sn -k StrongNamedLib.snk
```

Alternatively, from Visual Studio, you could add SN.exe as an external tool on the Tools menu. To do this, select Tools | External Tools | Add. In the External Tools dialog box, type **sn** for the title, and click the Browse button to navigate to where SN.exe resides (probably C:\Program Files\Microsoft Visual Studio .NET\FrameworkSDK\Bin\sn.exe). For arguments, specify the *–k* switch as well as the solution directory and target name variables with an extension of .snk. Also specify that the standard output from SN.exe should be redirected to the Visual Studio output window so that you can see any error reports that might be made, as shown in Figure 23-4.

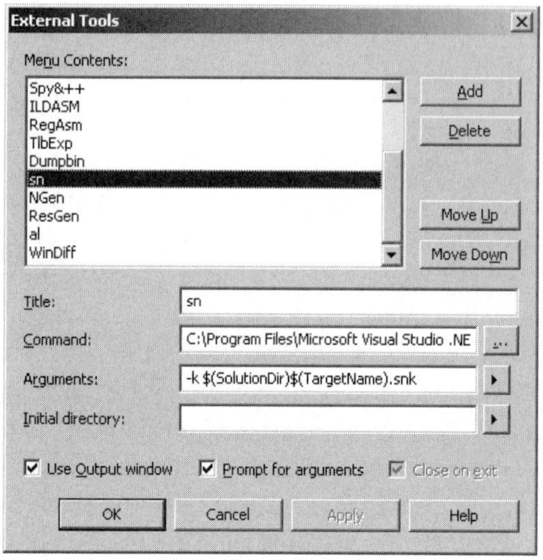

Figure 23-4   Adding SN.exe as an external tool.

When you run SN.exe, you should get a report like this:

```
Microsoft (R) .NET Framework Strong Name Utility
 Version 1.0.3705.0
Copyright (C) Microsoft Corporation 1998-2001. All rights
 reserved.

Key pair written to C:\Data\InsideCsharp\Chap23\StrongNamedLib\StrongNamedLib.s
nk
```

To incorporate the key pair into the assembly build, you must add this code just as you did with the version information, either in the assemblyinfo.cs or in the main source file:

```
[assembly: AssemblyKeyFile("StrongNamedLib.snk")]
```

Alternatively, if you build the assembly with the assembly linker tool (AL.exe), you can use the */keyfile:* switch. When you've built the assembly, examine it with ILDASM. The manifest will now include the public key shown in Figure 23-5.

```
/ MANIFEST                                                              _|□| x|
.publickey = (00 24 00 00 04 80 00 00 94 00 00 00 06 02 00 00   // .$..............
              00 24 00 00 52 53 41 31 00 04 00 00 01 00 01 00   // .$..RSA1........
              BF C6 63 A3 D6 FA A6 05 E7 EC 4C 09 55 AC 35 68   // ..c.......L.U.5h
              B9 61 6F 7B 28 C2 8C 65 34 FB B6 64 B7 2A 23 98   // .ao{(..e4..d.*#.
              24 44 00 9D 50 D0 1B E8 6F 3F 66 65 1D 3D 61 E5   // $D..P...o?fe.=a.
              D3 1E 9D 49 CE 19 91 58 D4 D5 D1 4E 04 F8 D5 57   // ...I...X...N...W
              92 C3 35 FF 85 18 54 9C EF 2B 96 EE FA 3E 76 EE   // ..5...T..+...>v.
              85 5C C1 6F 2C 0E E5 D9 59 DF 95 05 33 42 FF 2B   // .\.o,...Y...3B.+
              C5 92 86 CE 39 01 7A 6D 1E 06 C1 89 AE 8A F7 12   // ....9.zm........
              CB 9E E4 68 24 C5 E1 43 B3 68 0C 3F A3 1C A8 9B ) // ...h$..C.h.?....
.hash algorithm 0x00008004
.ver 2:0:0:0
}
```

Figure 23-5   The public key of a strong-named assembly.

Finally, if we have a client consumer of this strong-named assembly, we'll see from ILDASM that it embeds the public key token in its own manifest, as Figure 23-6 shows.

```
/ MANIFEST                                      _|□| x|
.assembly extern mscorlib
{
  .publickeytoken = (B7 7A 5C 56 19 34 E0 89 )
  .ver 1:0:3300:0
}
.assembly extern StrongNamedLib
{
  .publickeytoken = (10 96 39 37 37 7A 4F 11 )
  .ver 1:0:0:0
}
.assembly ClientOfSNLib
{
  .custom instance void [mscorlib]System.Reflection
  .custom instance void [mscorlib]System.Reflection
```

Figure 23-6   Client manifest with dependent assembly public key token.

So, how does the runtime behave if we try to force the client to use a different version of the dependent assembly? Let's create another version of StrongNamedLib. This new version is identical to the previous in all respects—including the cryptographic key pair used to sign the assembly hash—except that the version is changed to, say, 2.0.0.0. We'll also change the console output so that we know which version we're getting at runtime.

```
public static void SomeMethod()
{
    Console.WriteLine("Hello from v2");
}
```

If we overwrite the expected assembly with our new version, the runtime will throw an exception and report it using an extract from the Assembly Binding Log (or *Fusion Log*). This log is maintained by the runtime for assemblies that fail to load:

```
Unhandled Exception: System.IO.FileLoadException: The located
 assembly's manifest definition with name 'StrongNamedLib'
 does not match the assembly reference.
File name: "StrongNamedLib"
   at ClientOfSNLib.Class1.Main(String[] args)

Fusion log follows:
=== Pre-bind state information ===
LOG: DisplayName = StrongNamedLib, Version=1.0.0.0,
 Culture=neutral, PublicKeyToken=10963937377a4f11
 (Fully-specified)
LOG: Appbase = C:\Data\InsideCsharp\Chap23\ClientOfSNLib
\ClientOfSNLib\bin\Debug\
LOG: Initial PrivatePath = NULL
Calling assembly : ClientOfSNLib, Version=1.0.770.32643,
 Culture=neutral, PublicKeyToken=null.
===

LOG: Application configuration file does not exist.
LOG: Publisher policy file is not found.
LOG: Host configuration file not found.
LOG: Using machine configuration file from C:\WINNT\Microsoft.NET\Framework\v1.
0.3705\config\machine.config.
LOG: Post-policy reference: StrongNamedLib, Version=1.0.0.0,
 Culture=neutral, PublicKeyToken=10963937377a4f11
LOG: Attempting download of new URL file:///C:/Data/InsideCsharp/Chap23/Cli-
entOf
SNLib/ClientOfSNLib/bin/Debug/StrongNamedLib.DLL.
WRN: Comparing the assembly name resulted in the mismatch:
 Major Version
```

If you want a bit more detail, you can run the Fusion Log Viewer (Fus-LogVw.exe), shown in Figure 23-7. This offers a dialog box–based GUI: from the list of applications, select the one you're interested in and either double-click it or click the View Log button.

Figure 23-7   Fusion Log Viewer.

This automatic, enforced version checking seems like a pretty good reason to sign your assemblies with strong names. But is there a downside? Well, yes—a slight performance penalty is incurred at load time because the runtime loader is verifying the version information by using the public key and the assembly hash. This verification is surely a price worth paying in most situations—especially when you consider what you're getting for your trouble:

- You don't run the risk of using an incompatible version of the DLL because the version is checked.

- If the runtime on your machine uses your copy of the public key to decrypt the hash in the dependent assembly and everything matches, it means that the dependent assembly came from the trusted source you expected it to come from.

- This must also mean that the assembly couldn't have been tampered with on its way to you.

Let's examine that last point more closely. Reverting to our private assembly, suppose we open the built DLL with a binary editor and tamper with it. Will the runtime complain? Let's try that. In Visual Studio, you can select File | Open | File and specify the correct version of the HelloLib.dll file that the client is using (from the expected directory). In the Open File dialog box, drop down the Open With menu and select Binary Editor. Then change something harmless such as the text string to output, as illustrated in Figure 23-8. We don't want to cause an unrelated failure; we just want to see whether we can tamper with the built assembly.

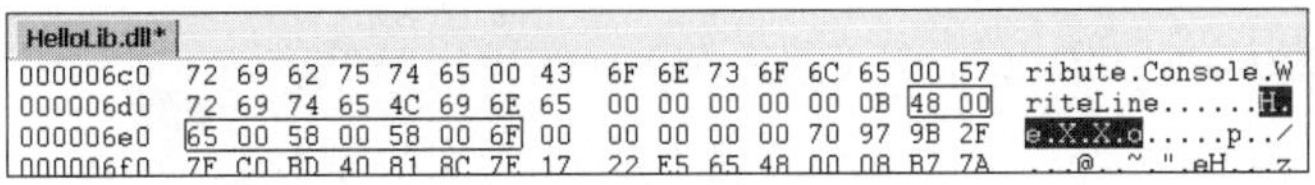

Figure 23-8   Tampering with a built assembly by using the Visual Studio Binary editor.

When you attempt to run the client, you should find that the runtime again doesn't check the contents—because this is a private assembly. However, if we do the same thing with a strong-named assembly, the runtime does check the contents, fails to load the assembly that's been tampered with, and throws an exception (followed by another extract from the Fusion Log). The exception is shown here:

```
Unhandled Exception: System.IO.FileLoadException:
 Strong name validation failed for assembly 'StrongNamedLib'.
File name: "StrongNamedLib"
   at ClientOfSNLib.Class1.Main(String[] args)
```

You'll get similar results if you tamper with a strong-named executable assembly. If you attempt to execute such an assembly directly, the runtime will display a message box before throwing an exception, as Figure 23-9 shows.

```
Unhandled Exception: System.IO.FileLoadException:
 Strong name validation failed for assembly 'HelloSN.exe'.
File name: "HelloSN.exe"
```

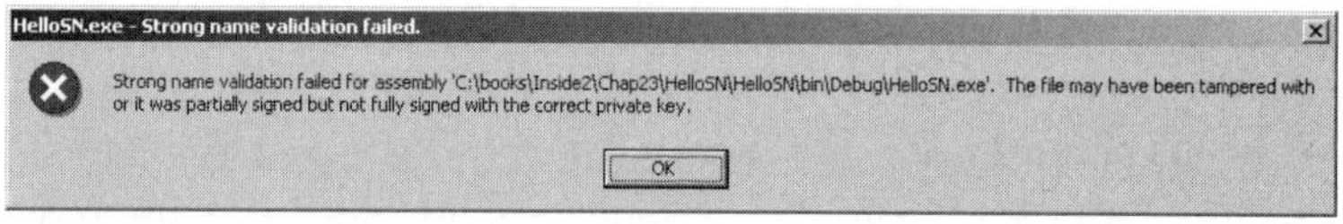

Figure 23-9   Attempt to execute a compromised primary assembly.

The Global Assembly Cache

If you sign your assembly with a strong name, you can take advantage of an alternative deployment strategy: you can put your assembly into the global assembly cache (GAC). The GAC is conceptually a merger of .\winnt\system32 and the Windows Registry—a place where you put assemblies that are shared by multiple (possibly unknown) client applications, that's widely known and accessible, and that imposes some form of structure and internal integrity checking. You can view the contents of the GAC using the ShFusion.DLL shell extension that's installed when the .NET Framework is installed. Simply open Windows Explorer and navigate to .\winnt\assembly, as shown in Figure 23-10. This view presents the contents of the GAC in an arbitrary manner that conceals the underlying structure.

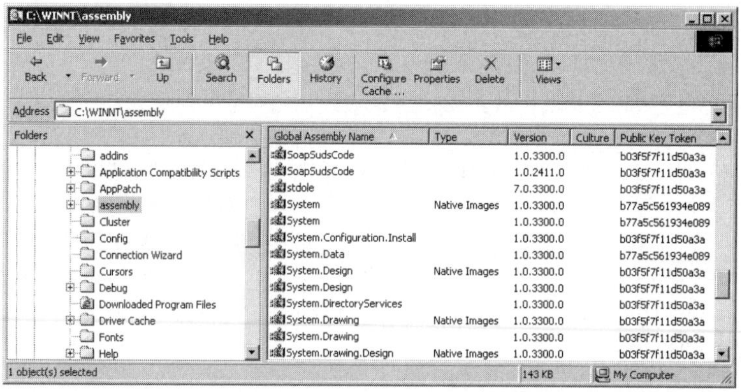

Figure 23-10   The global assembly cache viewed with Windows Explorer.

In reality, the GAC isn't a flat listing. You'll notice, for instance, that there are two versions of some of the system assemblies (such as System.dll): one regular, one preJITted. The PreJit versions reside in the native image cache—these have been JITted to native machine code on installation, to speed up their use at run time. You'll also notice in Figure 23-10 that there are two copies of SoapSudsCode.dll in the GAC, but neither is a native image. Their public key token is the same, but the version number is different. If you want to see the structure of the GAC as it really is instead of the virtual list that ShFusion offers us, you need to look at .\winnt\assembly in a command window:

```
Directory of C:\WINNT\Assembly

10/03/2001  18:24    <DIR>        downloaded
08/02/2002  23:43    <DIR>        GAC
06/05/2001  10:06    <DIR>        global
08/02/2002  22:23    <DIR>        NativeImages1_v1.0.3705
08/02/2002  22:23    <DIR>        temp
08/02/2002  22:23    <DIR>        tmp
```

Let's say you want to find System.dll. If you navigate down the directory structure in the command window, you'll eventually come to the real location, which will be something like:

```
Directory of C:\WINNT\Assembly\GAC\System\1.0.3300.0__b77a5c
561934e089

08/02/2002  23:43    <DIR>        .
08/02/2002  23:43    <DIR>        ..
08/02/2002  23:41         1,163,264 System.dll
08/02/2002  23:43               145 __AssemblyInfo__.ini
```

The naming of the subdirectories is clearly composed of the assembly version number and its public key token. It should now be clear how we can have more than one version of an assembly in the GAC—each version is simply placed in a different subdirectory. This arrangement is obviously a great improvement over winnt\system32—which suffered from DLL hell because only one version of a filename could exist in the system directory at any one time. The same problem under a different guise was true of the Registry: any given COM object was mapped to one and only one hosting server, and multiple versions were marginally supported through differentiated ProgIDs—a weak strategy at best.

To put an assembly into the GAC, you have two choices: use the ShFusion explorer shell extension, or use the GAC management utility (GACutil.exe). Using GACutil is very simple:

```
gacutil -i MyStrongNamedLib.dll
```

You can list the contents of the GAC with **gacutil –l** and uninstall an assembly from the GAC with **gacutil –u**. Using ShFusion is even simpler: simply drag and drop your assembly into the GAC (or delete it from Windows Explorer to uninstall it). Whichever method you use, the GAC will reject the assembly if it isn't strong-named. The GAC will also reject the assembly if it already contains an assembly with the same simple name and the same version number, unless the culture is different. Note, however, that the GAC will accept code marked unsafe.

Also note that although you can use a configuration file (application, publisher, or machine) to redirect assembly binding from one version of an assembly to another, you can't redirect to an assembly with a different public key than the original. If you attempt this redirection and make only the new version of the dependent assembly available (for example, in the same directory as the client executable), the assembly will fail to load and the runtime will emit a "public key mismatch" error.

Delay-Signed Assemblies

Another interesting feature of .NET code signing is the option to delay-sign an assembly. Recall that a cryptographic key pair consists of both a private and public key. The public key is made publicly available to consuming client applications, is visible in the assembly manifest, and so on. On the other hand, the private key is kept very secure. If the security of the private key is compromised, consumers holding the public key can no longer trust an assembly that's correctly verified by the runtime. Therefore, as an added security measure, it's reasonable to withhold the private key from developers until the last possible moment (or to withhold it altogether). During the development and testing phases of a project, the developers are given only the public key. Client assemblies will need this key, so it must be present for building and testing multiassembly systems. The delay-signing strategy works like this:

1.   Whoever in the organization has the appropriate authority generates the key pair as normal.

2.   Then that person runs SN again on the generated key pair file, to extract only the public key, by using the –p switch. For example:

```
sn -p MyKeyPair.snk MyPublicOnly.snk
```

3.   The public key is distributed to developers in the organization.

To use the public key in place of the full key pair, the code of an assembly not only must include the *AssemblyKeyFile* attribute as normal, but also the *AssemblyDelaySign* attribute. The *AssemblyKeyFile* attribute, of course, specifies the public key file, not the full key pair file. For example:

```
[assembly:AssemblyKeyFile("MyPublicOnly.snk")]
[assembly:AssemblyDelaySign(true)]
```

Alternatively, if you build the assembly with the assembly linker tool (AL.exe), you can use the */delaysign+* and *keyfile:* switches.

A delay-signed assembly doesn't, of course, have a valid strong-named signature—rather, the compiler reserves space in the assembly for the strong name. So the runtime's loader would reject the assembly during the signature verification stage. For this reason, you can instruct the runtime to skip this verification on the current machine, using the *–Vr* switch to SN. For example:

```
sn -Vr MyAssembly.dll
```

Later, when the appropriate product development stage has been reached, the assembly must be properly signed with the full key pair by using the *–R* switch to SN to re-sign a partially signed assembly. Note that this task might be for the designated security administrator rather than individual developers. The syntax of the command is illustrated here:

```
sn -R MyAssembly.dll MyKeyPair.snk
```

Signature verification should also be turned back on for the assembly:

```
sn -Vu MyAssembly.dll
```

Note that any clients of the assembly don't have to be rebuilt because they had access to the public key when they were built and therefore could create a valid *AssemblyRef* within their own assembly metadata.

Cryptographic Services

In a sense, the code-signing features of .NET assemblies can be seen as a particular use of cryptographic services. We've seen how the C# compiler and the assembly linker will apply cryptographic functionality to the signing of strong-named assemblies. You can also use the rich set of cryptographic support services offered by the .NET Framework class library for encrypting data (in the *System.Security.Cryptography* namespace). Cryptography protects data from being viewed or modified by unauthorized third parties and provides secure communication over otherwise insecure channels. For example, you can encrypt data (referred to as *plaintext*) at source by using a cryptographic algorithm and transmit the encrypted (*ciphertext*) data across any secure or insecure channel, and the intended recipient can later decrypt the data for final access. If a third party intercepts the encrypted data during this process, it will be difficult for them to decipher the data.

The mechanism must provide assurance that the data received hasn't been modified by anyone during transmission and that the data really has come from the trusted source and not someone impersonating the trusted source. The same mechanism applies whether you're transmitting the data to some remote location or persisting it to storage for later retrieval. The Framework class library provides a very comprehensive set of cryptographic services, and a sophisticated security system can be built by using a combination of cryptographic primitives. These primitives are listed with their corresponding Framework classes in Table 23-1.

Table 23-1
Cryptographic Primitives

Primitive	Description	Framework Classes
Private key encryption	Transforms data, preventing it from being read by unauthorized third parties. This type of encryption is also referred to as *symmetric encryption* because the same key is used for both encryption and decryption. Private key encryption algorithms are extremely fast (compared to public key algorithms) and are well suited for performing cryptographic transformations on large streams of data.	*DESCryptoServiceProvider* *RC2CryptoServiceProvider* *RijndaelManaged* *TripleDESCryptoServiceProvider*
Public key encryption	Transforms data, preventing it from being read by unauthorized third parties. This type of encryption uses two keys: a private key that must be kept secret from unauthorized users, and a public key that can be made public to anyone. The two keys are mathematically linked; data encrypted with the public key can be decrypted only with the private key and vice versa. Public key cryptographic algorithms are also known as *asymmetric algorithms* because one key is required to encrypt data while another is required to decrypt data.	*DSACryptoServiceProvider* *RSACryptoServiceProvider*

Table 23-1
Cryptographic Primitives

Primitive	Description	Framework Classes
Digital signatures	This approach also uses public key encryption and closely parallels the code-signing mechanism used by .NET assemblies: to use public key cryptography to digitally sign some data, you first apply a hash algorithm to the data to create a compact and unique representation of it. You then encrypt this hash with your private key to create your personal signature. Upon receiving the data and signature, the recipient decrypts the signature by using the public key to recover the hash and then hashes the data by using the same hash algorithm as the original. If the two hashes match, the data hasn't been tampered with and must have come from the expected trusted source.	*DSACryptoServiceProvider* *RSACryptoServiceProvider*
Hashes	Hash algorithms map binary values of any length to small binary values of a fixed length, known as *hash values*. A hash value is a unique and extremely compact numerical representation of the hashed data. It's computationally improbable to find two distinct inputs that hash to the same value.	*HMACSHA1* *MACTripleDES* *MD5CryptoServiceProvider* *SHA1Managed* *SHA256Managed* *SHA384Managed* *SHA512Managed*

The following example illustrates a simple use of the .NET cryptographic services for data encryption. This example uses private key (symmetric) encryption to encrypt data before writing it to a file. First, we create a *FileStream* object for the underlying persistent storage, and then we lay a *CryptoStream* object on top of that. This pattern is similar to the use of an interpolating *StreamWriter* object layered on top of an underlying *Stream* object, as we discussed in Chapter 11, "File I/O with Streams." We're using the *RijndaelManaged* class, which is a private key encryption class that encapsulates the Rijndael algorithm. When we create the encryptor with *CreateEncryptor*, we're allowing the class to default to a randomly generated private key and a randomly generated initialization vector for the encryption algorithm. We then layer a *StreamWriter* on top of the *CryptoStream* layer and perform the familiar write operations. In this way, the data we write will be encrypted before being written out to the underlying stream. Clearly, we could use, say, a *MemoryStream* or a *NetworkStream* here in place of a *FileStream* without impacting the rest of the design.

```
public static void Main(string[] args)
{
    string sFile = "foo.txt";

    FileStream fs = File.Create(sFile);
    RijndaelManaged rm = new RijndaelManaged();
    CryptoStream cs = new CryptoStream (
        fs, rm.CreateEncryptor(), CryptoStreamMode.Write);

    StreamWriter sw = new StreamWriter(cs);
    sw.WriteLine("Hello World");

    sw.Close();
    cs.Close();
    fs.Close();
}
```

If we examine the contents of the output file, we'd expect to see encrypted data similar to the data shown in Figure 23-11.

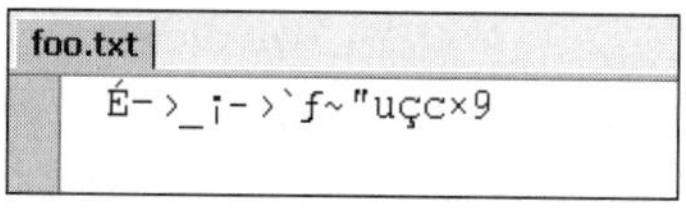

Figure 23-11   Rijndael-encrypted data.

Of course, we could perform very similar steps to decrypt the data, using *CreateDecryptor* to layer a decrypting *CryptoStream* on top of the underlying *FileStream*:

```
fs = File.Open(sFile, FileMode.Open);
cs = new CryptoStream(
fs, rm.CreateDecryptor(), CryptoStreamMode.Read);

StreamReader sr = new StreamReader(cs);
Console.Write("Decrypted original message: {0}",
    sr.ReadToEnd());
```

Private key algorithms—also known as *block ciphers*—are used to encrypt one block of data at a time. Thus, classes such as *RijndaelManaged* use a key and an initialization vector (IV) to perform cryptographic transformations on the data. For a given private key, a simple block cipher that doesn't use an initialization vector will encrypt the same input block of plaintext into the same output block of ciphertext. Therefore, if you have duplicate blocks within your plaintext stream, you'll have duplicate blocks within your ciphertext stream. This clearly makes it less difficult for someone to decipher the known ciphertext block and possibly recover your key. To combat this problem, information from the previous block is mixed into the process of encrypting the next block. Thus, the output of two identical plaintext blocks is different. Because this technique uses the previous block to encrypt the next block, an IV is used to encrypt the first block of data.

In our example application, if we wanted to take more control over the encryption, we could specify a private key—as an array of byte values—instead of accepting a randomly generated one. We could also specify an initialization vector. The minimum size for both of these is 16, and the Rijndael algorithm supports values up to 32. For example:

```
byte[] Key =
    {1, 2, 3, 4, 5, 6, 7, 8, 9, 10, 11, 12, 13, 14, 15, 16};
byte[] IV =
    {1, 2, 3, 4, 5, 6, 7, 8, 9, 10, 11, 12, 13, 14, 15, 16};

FileStream fs = File.Create(sFile);
RijndaelManaged rm = new RijndaelManaged();
CryptoStream cs = new CryptoStream (
//fs, rm.CreateEncryptor(), CryptoStreamMode.Write);
fs, rm.CreateEncryptor(Key, IV), CryptoStreamMode.Write);
```

If we choose this approach, we must be sure to use the same key and initialization vector for decrypting:

```
cs = new CryptoStream(
//fs, rm.CreateDecryptor(), CryptoStreamMode.Read);
fs, rm.CreateDecryptor(Key, IV), CryptoStreamMode.Read);
```

Code Access Security

Code access security (CAS) is a feature of the .NET Framework that allows you to establish and enforce security restrictions on assemblies and the code within them. As it loads an assembly, the .NET Framework grants that assembly a set of permissions to access system resources—such as the file system, the Registry, printers, the environment table, and so on. A group of permissions is known as a *permission set*, and these permissions are based on security policy. There's a standard set of permission sets, and an administrator can create new permission sets. There's also a standard set of code groups, and an administrator can create new code groups. A code group maps assemblies to permission sets. This mapping is done by gathering evidence about an assembly, including its strong-named identity. The result is that an assembly with a particular identity is mapped to a specific set of access permissions. The security policy system is entirely open-ended and configurable through administrative tools supplied with the .NET Framework SDK. Your code can also make programmatic checks and requests for permissions.

Evidence

At what point is evidence about an assembly gathered, and what constitutes this evidence? The .NET Framework includes three runtime hosts: the shell host, the ASP.NET host, and the Microsoft Internet Explorer host. When you run an application from a command window or by double-clicking it in Windows Explorer, you're using the shell host. It's the runtime host loading the assembly that gathers the initial evidence about the assembly and then presents that evidence to the .NET Framework security system. The security system uses this evidence to determine which permissions to grant to the assembly, based on the security policy in force at the time. This evidence will include the following for an assembly:

- Strong name—that is, the simple name, version number, and public key

- Publisher (if supplied), as evidenced by its Authenticode signature

- Originating zone—for example, Local Machine, Local Intranet, Internet

- Originating location—for example, the file system directory on the local machine, or a remote URL

Note that some forms of evidence are more difficult to falsify than others and are therefore considered stronger. Strong evidence includes the cryptographic strong name of an assembly. Weaker evidence includes the originating location because that's easier to falsify. When, as an administrator, you establish the security policy, you can make arbitrary decisions about how to map evidence to permissions, but you should clearly depend more heavily on strong forms of evidence than weak ones.

Security Policy

The .NET Framework security policy imposes four policy levels: enterprise policy level, machine policy level, user policy level, and an optional application domain policy level. Each of these levels consists of a collection of code groups, organized in hierarchies, and each code group has a set of permissions associated with it. It's likely that a code group at the root level will have very limited (or no) permissions associated with it. As you add child code groups, you'll likely assign more and more permissions, at the same time requiring stronger and more restricted evidence. In this way, a child code group at the bottom of the hierarchy is likely to offer an extensive set of permissions but also require a very narrow set of strong evidence of an assembly before that assembly is granted these permissions.

An assembly can match one or more code groups at each policy level. The .NET Framework security system will calculate the union of the permission sets associated with each matching code group within a given level and then move on to the next level. The evaluation order of levels is enterprise, machine, user. The permission set that's finally granted to an assembly is an intersection of the permission sets calculated at each policy level. Figure 23-12 shows the .NET Framework configuration tool, MSCorCfg.msc (which we'll examine more closely later in the section), to illustrate the relationship between policy levels and code groups.

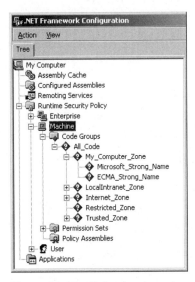

Figure 23-12   Policy levels and code groups.

There are three aspects of security policy to consider:

- Code access permissions, including named permission sets
- Code groups
- Policy levels

Code access permissions are used to protect specific resources and operations from unauthorized use. The Framework class library offers a set of classes to represent each defined permission. All these classes derive from the *CodeAccessPermission* class, which means that all code access permissions have methods in common, such as *Demand, Assert, Deny, PermitOnly, IsSubsetOf, Intersect,* and *Union.* A code access permission represents either the right to access a protected resource, such as the file system or the Registry; or the right to perform a protected operation, such as accessing unmanaged code. You can use these classes in your code to request or deny permissions, and the runtime will grant or reject such requests based on current security policy. Table 23-2 lists the Framework classes and their corresponding permissions represented.

Table 23-2
Framework Permission Classes

Framework Class	Permission Represented
DirectoryServicesPermission	Access to the *System.DirectoryServices* classes.
DnsPermission	Access to Domain Name System (DNS).
EnvironmentPermission	Read or write environment variables.
EventLogPermission	Read or write access to event log services.
FileDialogPermission	Access files that have been selected by the user in an Open dialog box.
FileIOPermission	Read, append, or write files or directories.
IsolatedStorageFilePermission	Access private virtual file systems.
IsolatedStoragePermission	Access isolated storage, which is storage that's associated with a specific user and with some aspect of the code's identity, such as its Web site, publisher, or signature.
MessageQueuePermission	Access message queues through the managed Microsoft Message Queuing (MSMQ) interfaces.

Table 23-2
Framework Permission Classes

Framework Class	Permission Represented
OleDbPermission	Access to databases using OLE DB.
PerformanceCounterPermission	Access performance counters.
PrintingPermission	Access printers.
ReflectionPermission	Discover information about a type at run time.
RegistryPermission	Read, write, create, or delete Registry keys and values.
SecurityPermission	Execute, assert permissions, call into unmanaged code, skip verification, and other rights.
ServiceControllerPermission	Access running or stopped services.
SocketPermission	Make or accept connections on a transport address.
SqlClientPermission	Access to Structured Query Language (SQL) databases.
UIPermission	Access user interface functionality.
WebPermission	Make or accept connections on a Web address.

A simple example to illustrate how you might use these classes is shown in the code listed next. Before the application attempts an operation on a specific file, it demands security permission to read the file. This demand doesn't alter the permission granted, it merely states that the code must have this permission to proceed with the operation. If the security policy in force doesn't grant this permission, the demand will result in a *SecurityException*.

```
class GetPermApp
{
    static void Main(string[] args)
    {
        FileIOPermission filePerm = new FileIOPermission(
            FileIOPermissionAccess.Read, "C:\\Foo.txt");
        try
        {
            filePerm.Demand();
            Console.WriteLine(
                "We have permission to read the file");
        }
```

```
        catch (SecurityException e)
        {
            Console.WriteLine(e.Message);
        }
    }
}
```

Note that the permission request in this example is actually redundant because any attempt to work on the file would likely use the *File*, *FileInfo*, or *FileStream* classes, and they in turn will make the necessary permission requests on our behalf during construction.

When you establish a set of permissions and configure the security policy to use this set, you must give the set a name and description (by using the configuration tool). This set then becomes a *named permission set*. You can then apply this permission set to any code group or groups you choose. The .NET Framework ships with six predefined permission sets:

- **Nothing**   That is, no permissions at all (code can't execute).

- **Execution**   Permits code to execute, but grants no other access to resources or protected operations.

- **Internet**   Allows code to execute in order to create safe top-level windows and file dialog boxes (but no other user interface elements), to make Web connections to the same site that the assembly originates from, and to use isolated storage with an imposed quota.

- **LocalIntranet**   Allows code to execute in order to create user interface elements without restrictions; to make Web connections to the same site the assembly originates from; to use isolated storage without a quota; to use DNS services; to read the USERNAME, TEMP, and TMP environment variables; and to read files in the same folder as the assembly.

- **Everything**   Grants all standard permissions except the permission to skip verification.

- **FullTrust**   Grants full access to all protected resources.

> **Note**   You can't modify the predefined permission sets. However, you can create custom permission sets with the same or similar permissions and then use these as a base for your security policy.

As mentioned earlier, code group is a mapping between a set of evidence and a set of permissions. These mappings are entirely arbitrary and must be determined as an administrative task when designing the overall security policy. When you create a code group, you decide on a set of conditions that an assembly must meet to become part of the group. Generally, these conditions will equate to assembly evidence. For example, you might decide that to gain membership of a particular code group, an assembly must have a specific public key or must originate from a particular URL. Any assembly that matches the set of conditions will then be granted the corresponding set of permissions. Code groups are arranged hierarchically, and the runtime will walk the hierarchy when it loads an assembly to match the assembly evidence with each group in turn. An example of a code group hierarchy at one policy level is shown in Figure 23-13.

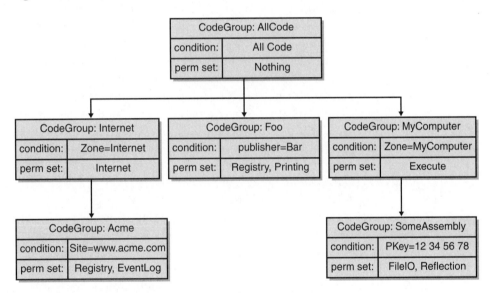

Figure 23-13 Example code group hierarchy.

Let's say an assembly has the following evidence:

Origin:	The local machine
Simple name:	*SomeAssembly*
Version:	1.0.0.0
Public key:	12 34 56 78 …
Publisher:	(none specified)
Site:	(not applicable)

To ascertain what permissions to grant this assembly, given the example code group hierarchy shown in Figure 23-13, the runtime would start at the root code group, *AllCode*, and match the condition against the assembly. In this case, the condition is *All Code*, so the assembly satisfies the condition and is granted the corresponding permission set—in this case, *Nothing*. Next the runtime navigates its way down through the hierarchy. The next code group is Internet, with a membership condition of *Internet*, which this assembly doesn't match. Therefore, the runtime doesn't grant the associated permissions, nor does it bother checking any child code groups of this code group. The assembly also doesn't match the membership conditions of the *Foo* code group. It does, however, become a member of the *MyComputer* code group and is granted permission to execute. The runtime navigates to the next level in the code group hierarchy and skips the *Acme* code group—only nodes whose parents had their conditions met will be evaluated. The runtime does match the assembly against the *SomeAssembly* code group and, having matched the public key, it grants *File IO* and *Reflection* permissions. The union of the permission sets for the matching code groups is computed: in this case: *Nothing* union *Execute* union *FileIO* + *Reflection* = *Execute*, *FileIO*, and *Reflection*.

This process is repeated for each policy level in turn (enterprise, machine, and user). The permission sets computed at each policy level are intersected to compute the final permission granted. Let's say that at the next level, the *AllCode* group offers the permission set *FullTrust*. In this case, the final intersection would be (*Execute*, *FileIO*, and *Reflection*) intersect *FullTrust* = *Execute*, *FileIO*, and *Reflection*.

Note that each code group can optionally be assigned two attributes: *Exclusive* and *LevelFinal*. Using either one attribute or both attributes at the same time is permissible. If you assign the *Exclusive* attribute to a code group, you're specifying that members of this code group are granted only this code group's permission set and no others. This means that no other code groups will be taken into consideration, even though a given assembly might otherwise match the membership conditions of another code group. If you assign *LevelFinal*, you're specifying that the runtime mustn't evaluate any additional policy levels.

Configuring Security

Two tools shipped with the .NET Framework SDK allow you to configure security: CASpol.exe and MSCorCfg.msc. The first is a command-line utility, the second a Microsoft Management Console (MMC) snap-in. The graphical user interface of the MSCorCfg MMC snap-in is easier to use and allows you to visualize the overall security configuration more readily. CASpol is quicker and can be used in scripts or batch files. To explore the use of these tools, we'll set up a new permission set and a new code group hierarchy and test this structure with a specific assembly. We'll do this test first with MSCorCfg and then tear the structure down and set it up again with CASpol.

The test assembly we'll use is a simple Windows Forms application with a button and a text box. When the user clicks the button, the application demands two arbitrary security permissions, one after the other: a *File IO* permission to read the C:\WINNT directory, and an *Environment* permission to read the USERNAME environment variable. If a demand succeeds, a simple message is added to the text box. If either demand fails—that is, if the assembly isn't granted the requested permission—the corresponding error string is added to the text box instead:

```
private void btnTestPerms_Click(
    object sender, System.EventArgs e)
{
    try
    {
        FileIOPermission p = new FileIOPermission(
            FileIOPermissionAccess.Read, "C:\\WINNT");
        p.Demand();
        textBox1.Text += "FileIOPermission OK\r\n";
    }
    catch (Exception ex)
    {
        textBox1.Text += ex.Message + "\r\n";
    }
    try
    {
        EnvironmentPermission p = new EnvironmentPermission(
            EnvironmentPermissionAccess.Read, "USERNAME");
        p.Demand();
        textBox1.Text += "EnvironmentPermission OK\r\n";
    }
    catch (Exception ex)
    {
        textBox1.Text += ex.Message + "\r\n";
    }
}
```

Build and test the application as is before making any coding or security configuration changes. At run time, the application presents a GUI, as indicated in Figure 23-14.

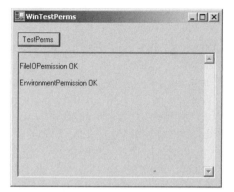

Figure 23-14   Windows Forms application to test security permissions.

Before we start the security configuration, create a new directory in some suitable location (for example, C:\InsideCsharp\Chap23\), and name it Win-TestPerms. The plan is to set up security so that assemblies running from the specified directory will be given some arbitrary permissions—which we can experiment with by using the MSCorCfg snap-in. To start the CAS configuration, we'll first create a new named permission set. From the Start menu, select Programs | Administrative Tools | Microsoft .NET Framework Configuration. Alternatively, select Run, and type **MSCORCFG.MSC**. This command will run the MMC snap-in, as shown in Figure 23-15.

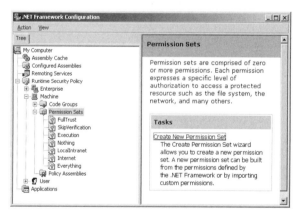

Figure 23-15   MSCorCfg MMC snap-in viewing Machine policy-level permissions.

Expand the Machine policy level and the Permission Sets node. Then either right-click the Permission Sets node and select New, or click the Create New Permission Set hyperlink in the description pane. For the name, type **Test**, and for the description, type some arbitrary description. We'll set up this permission set to provide some arbitrary minimum permissions suitable for a Windows Forms application, as Figure 23-16 shows.

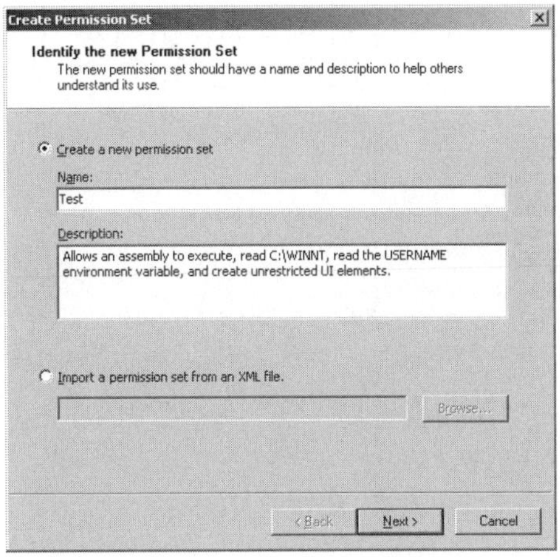

Figure 23-16   Create Permission Set dialog box.

When you click Next, you're offered a list of individual permissions: you can choose one or more of these to assign to the permission set. For our example, add *Security*, and in the Permission Settings dialog box, check the Enable Assembly Execution check box only (as shown in Figure 23-17) and then click OK. This selection will allow an assembly to execute.

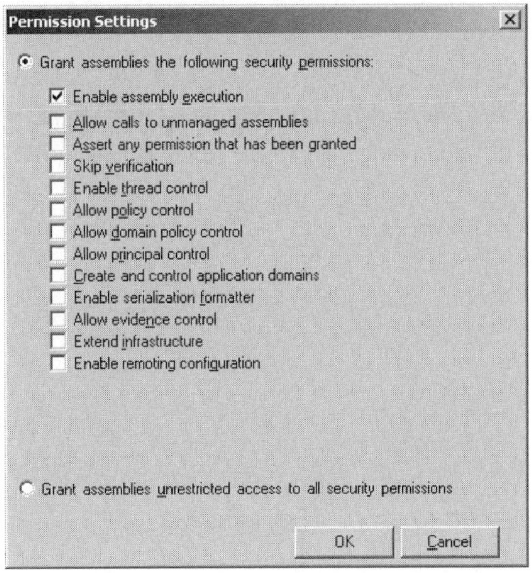

Figure 23-17   Permission Settings dialog box.

Now add some more permissions to the new named permission set: *File IO*, with the property set to read C:\WINNT (see Figure 23-18); *Environment Variables*, with the property set to read USERNAME; and *User Interface*, with unrestricted permissions. Click Finish at this point, and the new permission set will be added to the Permission Sets node in the snap-in tree list.

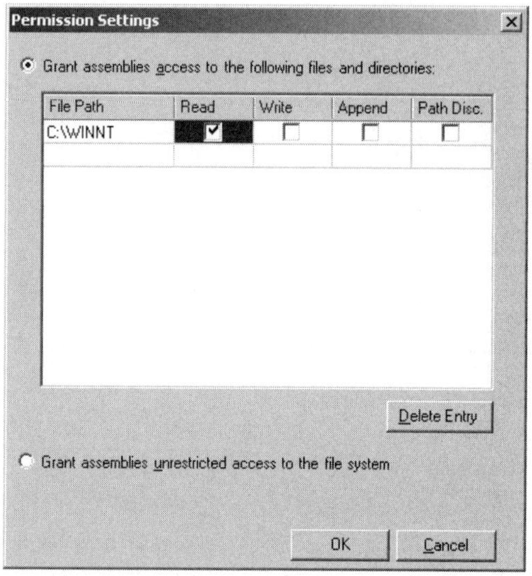

Figure 23-18   Restricted *File IO* permission settings.

Now expand the Code Groups node (still in the Machine policy level), and the All_Code node. We'll add a new code group. To do this, either right-click the All_Code node and select New, or click the Add A Child Code Group hyperlink in the description pane. For the name, specify **Test_Group**, and enter some arbitrary description for this code group, as shown in Figure 23-19.

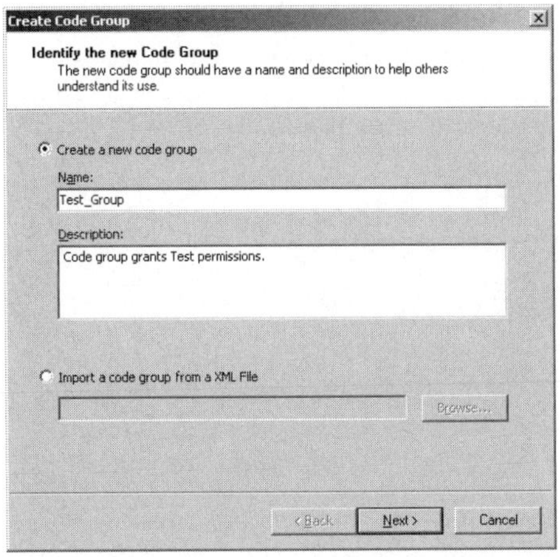

Figure 23-19   Create Code Group dialog box.

Click Next, and then for the condition type, select URL. In the URL text box, enter the location of the test directory you created—for example, **file:// C:/InsideCsharp/Chap23/WinTestPerms/***—and click Next, as shown in Figure 23-20.

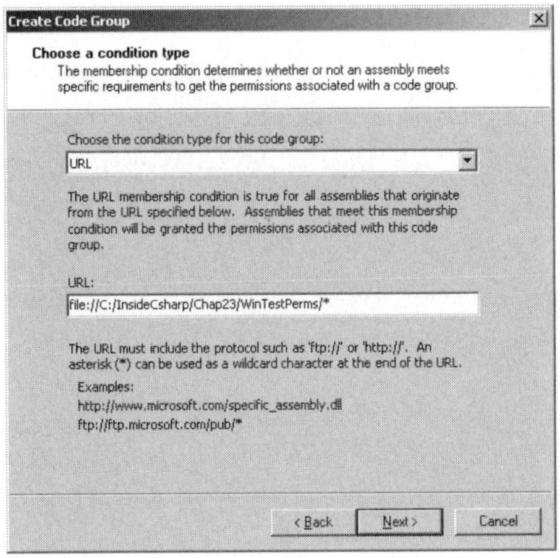

Figure 23-20   Choosing a code group condition type.

The next step allows us to assign a permission set to this code group, so now select your new *Execute* permission set. Click Next and then Finish to complete this new code group. The new code group should now be listed in the snap-in, alongside its description, condition, and permission set. The last property to set is the *Exclusive* attribute, which can be set only after you've created the code group. To set this attribute, click the Edit Code Group Proper-ties link and check the first check box, as shown in Figure 23-21.

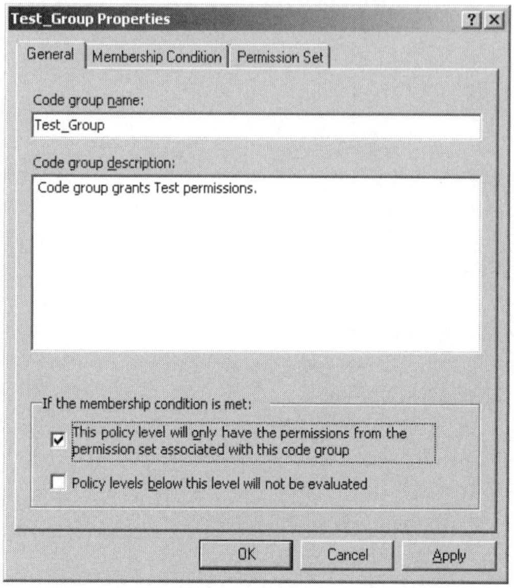

Figure 23-21   Setting the *Exclusive* code group attribute.

Now to test the application. From Windows Explorer, copy the WinTest-Perms.exe assembly into the newly configured WinTestPerms directory and double-click it to run it from there. At this stage, everything should run as before, with all permission requests granted. For the second test, in the MSCorCfg snap-in, select the Test_Group code group and click the Edit Code Group Properties link. From the dialog box, select the Permission Set tab and change the permission set for this code group to, say, LocalIntranet. Then click OK. Figure 23-22 illustrates this test.

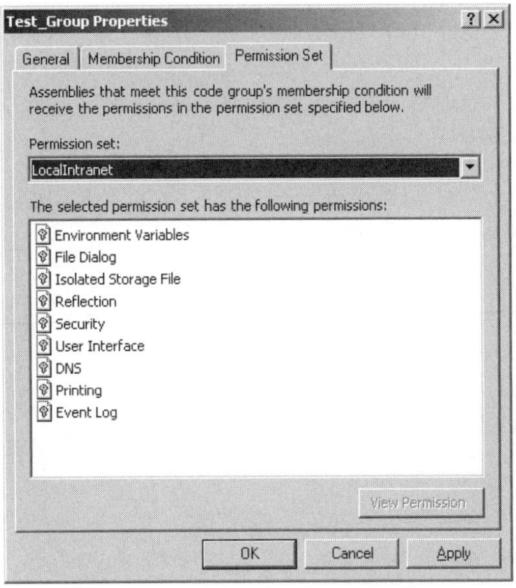

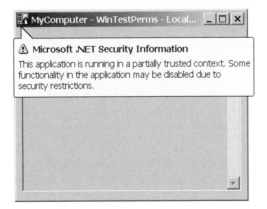

Figure 23-22   Changing a code group's permissions set.

Now try to run the application again: you should find that although the application still executes and the request for the specific *Environment* permission succeeds, the request for *File IO* permission fails. Change the permission set again, this time to *Internet*. This time, although the application executes, the runtime presents an alert message (shown in Figure 23-23) indicating that the assembly is running in a partially trusted security context and warning you that some functionality might not be available.

Figure 23-23   Runtime alert of partially trusted security context.

You can click the alert message to remove it. Indeed, when you click the Test button, you'll find that neither of the requested permissions has been granted, as Figure 23-24 shows.

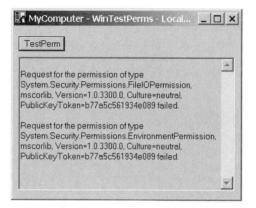

Figure 23-24   Exceptions thrown on failed security permission requests.

If you make one final test and change the permission set to *Nothing*, you'll find that the application won't even execute and the runtime will throw an exception. To round out your understanding of the various predefined permission sets (as well as any custom sets you've set up), you could experiment with replacing the permission requests as indicated in the following code, first to *AllAccess* for the root of C:\, and then to *PermissionState.Unrestricted*:

```
FileIOPermission p = new FileIOPermission(
//FileIOPermissionAccess.Read, "C:\\WINNT");
//FileIOPermissionAccess.AllAccess, "C:\\");
PermissionState.Unrestricted);
```

Similar options are available for all the library permission classes. For example:

```
EnvironmentPermission p = new EnvironmentPermission(
//EnvironmentPermissionAccess.Read, "USERNAME");
PermissionState.Unrestricted);
```

CASpol

Now that you've seen how to use MSCorCfg to configure code access security, let's do the same thing with the command-line tool, CASpol.exe. First, use MSCorCfg to undo all the custom work you did earlier—that is, delete the *Test* permission set and the Test_Group code group from the Machine policy level.

To create a permission set with CASpol, you first need to create an XML file detailing the individual permissions you want. For example:

```
<PermissionSet class="NamedPermissionSet"
    version="1"
    Name="Test"
    Description="Permission set containing my custom permission">
    <IPermission class=
        "System.Security.Permissions.EnvironmentPermission"
        Read="USERNAME"/>
    <IPermission class=
        "System.Security.Permissions.FileIOPermission"
        Read="C:\WINNT"/>
    <IPermission class=
        "System.Security.Permissions.SecurityPermission"
        Flags="Execution"/>
    <IPermission class=
        "System.Security.Permissions.UIPermission"
        Unrestricted="true"/>
</PermissionSet>
```

The *<PermissionSet>* root element must be present and has a class attribute with the value *NamedPermissionSet* or *System.Security.NamedPermissionSet*. For this version of the .NET Framework, the version attribute is *1*. The *Name* attribute is the name of the permission set as it appears in the MSCorCfg tree list, and the *Description* attribute is any arbitrary description of the permission set, which appears in the MSCorCfg right-hand pane. The *<PermissionSet>* element can contain any number of *<IPermission>* elements, which represent the permissions in the permission set—these can be Framework library classes or custom permission classes.

When you've created and saved this XML file, you can apply it to the security policy in one of two ways. The first approach uses MSCorCfg: select the Permission Sets node for the policy level you want (in this case Machine), and click the Create New Permission Set link. This process differs from what you did before in that instead of using the ensuing dialog boxes to create the permission set, you select the Import A Permission Set From An XML File option and specify the path to the XML file containing the permissions, as shown in Figure 23-25.

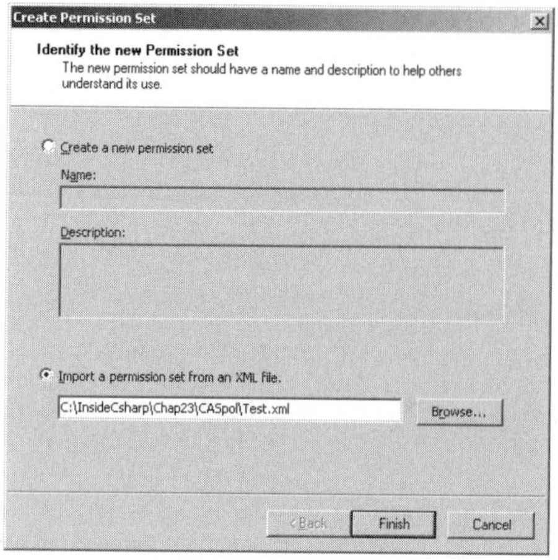

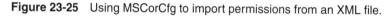

Figure 23-25   Using MSCorCfg to import permissions from an XML file.

Using CASpol instead, you use this command line:

```
caspol -machine -addpset Test.xml
```

where *–machine* indicates the policy level to add the permission set to, and Test.xml is the file containing the required permissions. CASpol will prompt to make sure you want to proceed—enter **Y** to confirm. Whichever way you've set up these permissions, you can now examine them in MSCorCfg. (You might need to close and reopen MSCorCfg before the changes are displayed.) You can also list the permissions with this CASpol command line:

```
caspol -machine -listpset
```

This command will produce a listing of all permission sets for the specified policy level. Somewhere in the middle of this list you should recognize your custom permission set. For example:

```
7. Test (Permission set containing my custom permission) =
<PermissionSet class="System.Security.NamedPermissionSet"
               version="1"
               Name="Test"
               Description="Permission set containing my custom
permission">
   <IPermission class="System.Security.Permissions.Environment
Permission, mscorlib, Version=1.0.3300.0, Culture=neutral,
PublicKeyToken=b77a5c561934e089"
               version="1"
               Read="USERNAME"/>
   <IPermission class="System.Security.Permissions.FileIO
Permission, mscorlib, Version=1.0.3300.0, Culture=neutral,
```

```
PublicKeyToken=b77a5c561934e089"
                version="1"
                Read="C:\WINNT"/>
  <IPermission class="System.Security.Permissions.Security
Permission, mscorlib, Version=1.0.3300.0, Culture=neutral,
PublicKeyToken=b77a5c561934e089"
                version="1"
                Flags="Execution"/>
  <IPermission class="System.Security.Permissions.UIPermission,
mscorlib, Version=1.0.3300.0, Culture=neutral,
PublicKeyToken=b77a5c561934e089"
                version="1"
                Unrestricted="true"/>
</PermissionSet>
```

The second operation is to add a new code group, including its membership condition and permission set. In the following command, All_Code is the parent code group to which we want to add a new child, the membership condition is a specified file URL, the permission set is *Test*, the new code group will be named Test_Group, and we want this to apply exclusively:

```
caspol -addgroup All_Code -url file://C:/InsideCsharp/Chap23
/WinTestPerms/* Test -n Test_Group -exclusive on
```

Imperative and Declarative CAS

The previous example application used *Demand* to ensure that a specific permission was available before attempting some operation that would require that permission. There are actually two ways you can programmatically state your need for a security permission. The technique used in the previous example is known as *imperative permission* requests. The second approach is to use *declarative permission* requests. With this second approach, you attach security attributes to your class or method to assert, demand, deny, or permit chosen permissions. For example, the button *Click* event-handling method in the previous example could be reworked—providing the same functionality—to call two attributed methods instead of using imperative *Demand* calls, like this:

```
private void btnTestPerms_Click(
          object sender, System.EventArgs e)
{
    try
    {
        GetFilePerm();
        textBox1.Text += "\r\nFileIOPermission OK\r\n";
    }
    catch (Exception ex)
```

```
    {
        textBox1.Text += "\r\n" + ex.Message + "\r\n";
    }
    try
    {
        GetEnvPerm();
        textBox1.Text += "\r\nEnvironmentPermission OK\r\n";
    }
    catch (Exception ex)
    {
        textBox1.Text += "\r\n" + ex.Message + "\r\n";
    }
}


[FileIOPermissionAttribute(
    SecurityAction.Demand, Read = "C:\\WINNT")]
private void GetFilePerm()
{
}

[EnvironmentPermissionAttribute(
    SecurityAction.Demand, Read = "USERNAME")]
private void GetEnvPerm()
{
}
```

Another point to note about this approach is that when the runtime gets such a demand, it walks the call stack to ensure that this assembly and all calling assemblies have the demanded permission. You can also use the *Assert* method to force this stack walk to stop at the current assembly, thereby allowing permissions to callees irrespective of a caller's permissions. However, this tactic clearly could present a potential security loophole and isn't recommended. This approach might be appropriate if you write code that requires some permission that the caller might not have and you ensure that the consequences of acquiring this permission don't propagate out of your code. If the called assembly's permission grants are opaque to the calling assembly, the calling assembly can't exploit this in an unauthorized manner.

Working in the other direction, you can also prevent code that you call—either directly or indirectly—from getting a specific permission. To do this, you call the *Deny* method. When your code calls *Deny* for a specific permission, all demands for that permission by any downstream callers are doomed to fail—even if they've been granted the permission. But bear in mind that if a downstream assembly calls *Assert* for the permission, calling *Deny* from your code will have no effect. Similarly, the *PermitOnly* method limits downstream assemblies to only the specific permission on which you call *PermitOnly*—although, again, this can be overridden by a call to *Assert*.

Conceptually, the *Assert*, *Deny*, and *PermitOnly* methods are considered *security permission overrides* because they override the default behavior of the security system. When different overrides are present in the same stack frame, the runtime evaluates these overrides in the following order: *PermitOnly*, then *Deny*, and finally *Assert*. Within the current stack frame, you can also undo the work of these calls by calling the *RevertAssert*, *RevertDeny*, or *RevertPermitOnly* methods. These will deactivate an active call to the *Assert*, *Deny*, or *PermitOnly* methods, respectively.

Identity Permissions

Another security feature that's susceptible to programmatic intervention is the use of identity permissions. These are similar to code access permissions but derive directly from the assembly evidence instead of from security policy. For instance, if you build a suite of assemblies, none of which is generically reusable (perhaps for security reasons), within the code of any of these assemblies, you could ensure that this assembly is called only by a specific known assembly—represented by the other assembly's strong name identity. The identity permission classes in the Framework class library are listed in Table 23-3.

Table 23-3
Framework Identity Permission Classes

Framework Class	Identity Represented
PublisherIdentityPermission	The assembly publisher's digital signature
SiteIdentityPermission	The Web site where the assembly came from.
StrongNameIdentityPermission	The strong name of the assembly—that is, the simple name, version, and public key.
URLIdentityPermission	The URL where the assembly came from, including the protocol (http, ftp, and so on).
ZoneIdentityPermission	The zone where the assembly came from.

An example of the use of identity permissions follows. This example appears in two parts. The restricted-use assembly is a class library with one class, *RestrictedLibClass*, that has one method, *SomeMethod*. Attached to this class is a *StrongNameIdentityPermission* attribute, ensuring that only a specific assembly is permitted to use this class. Note that the *PublicKey* property of the identity permission is the full public key as a hex string, not just the public key token, and must be extracted from the assembly manifest using ILDASM or SN:

```
[StrongNameIdentityPermissionAttribute(
    SecurityAction.LinkDemand,
    PublicKey = "00 24 00 00 04 80 00 00 94 00 00 00 06 02 00
00 00 24 00 00 52 53 41 31 00 04 00 00 01 00 01 00 0D 82 98 80
2F 41 CC 73 14 41 2D 37 F0 DE 6E C3 C5 01 BD 9C BE AB 46 B8 9C
5C D0 0C AE 36 03 46 14 DE C2 DC 6D 64 EB 3C DB 4A BD 50 2A 50
EB EB 13 DC AF 5C BC A7 61 B0 6E 02 26 CE 9B 05 2E 15 AB E8 22
7C 5F C0 41 E0 6C 4E 79 15 14 E7 81 29 2D 3C 81 81 9B 7F F4 5A
57 62 33 2F CA 50 54 AF 82 85 26 68 F0 20 8C B1 7A D7 CE A5 DB
4D 0F C4 A5 A6 7D 56 30 AE 41 12 6F E7 25 D1 FD 93 31 F2",
    Name = "UseRestrictedLib", Version = "1.2.3.4")]
public class RestrictedLibClass
{
    public static void SomeMethod()
    {
        Console.WriteLine("Hello from Restricted Lib");
    }
}
```

The significance of the *SecurityAction.LinkDemand* is to specify that the immediate caller has this identity—in this scenario, we don't want to have the runtime perform a full stack walk because callers further back in the call stack won't have the same identity. The *LinkDemand* flag is the only demand that's resolved at JIT-compile time. Other flags such as *Demand*, *Assert*, *Deny*, and *PermitOnly* are resolved at run time. The calling assembly is a simple console application with the specified strong name, as shown here:

```
class UseRestrictedLibApp
{
    static void Main(string[] args)
    {
        RestrictedLib.RestrictedLibClass.SomeMethod();
    }
}
```

Any change in the calling assembly—to a different assembly or a different version—will cause the use of the restricted called assembly to fail, throwing a security exception as follows:

```
Unhandled Exception: System.Security.SecurityException:
 Request for the permission of type System.Security.Permissions
.StrongNameIdentityPermission, mscorlib, Version=1.0.3300.0,
 Culture=neutral, PublicKeyToken=b77a5c561934e089 failed.
   at UseRestrictedLib.UseRestrictedLibApp.Main(String[] args)
```

```
The state of the failed permission was:
<IPermission class="System.Security.Permissions.StrongName
IdentityPermission, mscorlib, Version=1.0.3300.0,
 Culture=neutral, PublicKeyToken=b77a5c561934e089" version="1"
         PublicKeyBlob="00240000048000009400000006020000000
2400005253413100040000010001000D8298802F41CC7314412D37F0DE6EC3
C501BD9CBEAB46B89C5CD00CAE36034614DEC2DC6D64EB3CDB4ABD502A50EB
EB13DCAF5CBCA761B06E0226CE9B052E15ABE8227C5FC041E06C4E791514E7
81292D3C81819B7FF45A5762332FCA5054AF82852668F0208CB17AD7CEA5DB
4D0FC4A5A67D5630AE41126FE725D1FD9331F2"
         Name="UseRestrictedLib"
         AssemblyVersion="1.2.3.4"/>
```

Assembly Permission Requests

The final strategy for interacting with CAS programmatically is the use of assembly permission requests. These are specified in the code by attributes and are examined by the runtime when an assembly is loaded. There are three kinds of assembly permission requests:

- **RequestMinimum**   The minimum set of permissions this assembly needs to work (and therefore, to be loaded). If the runtime can't grant these permission requests when it loads the assembly, it will throw a *PolicyException* and not execute the code. If an assembly doesn't make a minimum permission request, this is equivalent to making a minimum permission request of *Nothing*.

- **RequestRefused**   Permissions this assembly must never be granted. If an assembly doesn't make a refused permission request, this is equivalent to making a refused permission request of *Nothing*.

- **RequestOptional**   Permissions this assembly code can use but can also run without. If the runtime can't grant these optional requests, the assembly will still be allowed to run. If an assembly doesn't make an optional permission request, this is equivalent to making an optional permission request of *FullTrust*. If you think about this for a minute, you should realize that making an optional permission request might well limit the permissions for an assembly to a subset of the permissions it might otherwise have been granted. Limiting your assembly permissions in this way is a reasonable plan to adopt because it maintains tight security without compromising the functionality of the assembly.

The syntax for permission requests is similar to other declarative security attributes, except that the attribute must be declared as an assembly-level attribute and the *SecurityAction* can be only *RequestMinimum, Request-Optional,* or *RequestRefused.* The following example requests to be denied the *FullTrust* named permission set but requests a minimum grant of *Execution* and *SkipVerification*:

```
[assembly: SecurityPermissionAttribute(
SecurityAction.RequestMinimum, Execution = true)]

[assembly: SecurityPermissionAttribute(
SecurityAction.RequestMinimum, SkipVerification = true)]

[assembly:PermissionSetAttribute(
SecurityAction.RequestRefuse, Name = "FullTrust")]

namespace PermReqs
{
    class PermReqsApp
    {
        static void Main(string[] args)
        {
            Console.WriteLine("Hello from PermReqs");
        }
    }
}
```

The manifest for this assembly will include two entries for the permission request information: one for the two *RequestMinimum* requests, and one for the *RequestRefuse* request. See Figure 23-26, and compare this with the manifest shown in Figure 23-2.

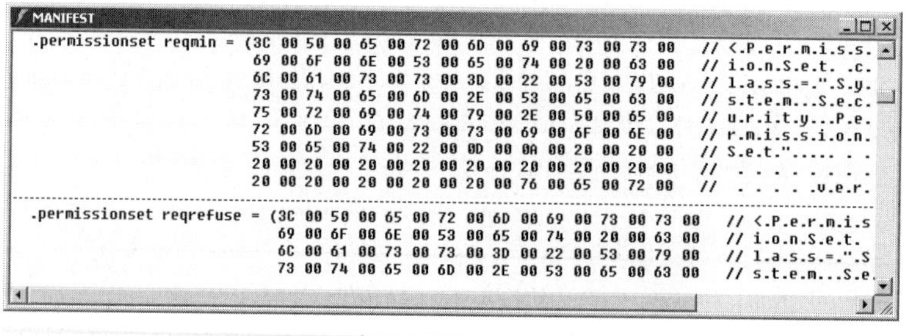

Figure 23-26   Permission request entries in the manifest.

As a final note for this section, consider the PermView.exe tool shipped with the .NET Framework SDK. This is intended to view permissions on an assembly. If you run PermView on the previous example assembly, you should get a report similar to the following, detailing the minimum, optional, and refused permissions:

```
Microsoft (R) .NET Framework Permission Request Viewer.
  Version 1.0.3705.0
Copyright (C) Microsoft Corporation 1998-2001. All rights
  reserved.

minimal permission set:
<PermissionSet class="System.Security.PermissionSet"
               version="1">
   <IPermission class="System.Security.Permissions
.SecurityPermission, mscorlib,
 Version=1.0.3300.0, Culture=neutral, PublicKeyToken=
b77a5c561934e089"
               version="1"
               Flags="SkipVerification, Execution"/>
</PermissionSet>

optional permission set:
  Not specified

refused permission set:
<PermissionSet class="System.Security.PermissionSet"
               version="1"
               Unrestricted="true"/>
```

Role-Based Security

A common approach to security is to provide access to data or resources based on the identity of a user. Once that identity has been authenticated, the system can map the identity against an arbitrary role that confers a set of permissions. This pattern is very similar to code access security, in which a code group maps between some condition of membership—which in turn equates to some evidence of identity—and a set of permissions. The difference with role-based security is that the evidence relates to a user, not an assembly.

Two terms are often used in the context of role-based security: *authentication* and *authorization*. Authentication is the process of finding and verifying the identity of a user. Authorization is the process of determining whether an authenticated user's request for some access should be granted. Role-based security in .NET also centers around two Framework library interfaces: *IIdentity* and *IPrincipal*. The library also offers classes that implement these interfaces, including *WindowsIdentity* and *WindowsPrincipal*. A *WindowsIdentity* object typically encapsulates the user's login name, while a *WindowsPrincipal* object encapsulates the user's role membership. All these interfaces and classes are defined in the *System.Security.Principal* namespace.

The following example shows how to use the *WindowsIdentity* and *WindowsPrincipal* classes. The application first gets the *WindowsIdentity* of the currently logged-in user and uses this to initialize a *WindowsPrincipal*. It then reports on the properties of this principal:

```
public class UseRBSApp
{
    public static void Main(string[] args)
    {
        WindowsIdentity wi = WindowsIdentity.GetCurrent();
        WindowsPrincipal wp = new WindowsPrincipal(wi);

        Console.WriteLine("Principal/Identity values:");
        Console.WriteLine("Name: " +wp.Identity.Name);

        Console.WriteLine("AuthenticationType: "
            +wi.AuthenticationType);
        Console.WriteLine("IsAuthenticated: "
            +wi.IsAuthenticated);
        Console.WriteLine("IsAnonymous: " +wi.IsAnonymous);
        Console.WriteLine("IsGuest: " +wi.IsGuest);
        Console.WriteLine("IsSystem: " +wi.IsSystem);
        Console.WriteLine("Token: " +wi.Token);
    }
}
```

The output from this application will be specific to the currently logged-in user and the local machine but will follow the pattern indicated here:

```
Principal/Identity values:
Name: VENUS\Andrew
AuthenticationType: NTLM
IsAuthenticated: True
IsAnonymous: False
IsGuest: False
IsSystem: False
Token: 312
```

The foregoing doesn't show how the identity that's part of the principal is then mapped to roles, but the following additional code illustrates this:

```
Console.WriteLine("IsInRole \"Administrators\": "
//      +wp.IsInRole("BUILTIN\\Administrators"));
    +wp.IsInRole(WindowsBuiltInRole.Administrator));

Console.WriteLine("Identity==VENUS\\\\Andrew: " +
```

```
(String.Compare(wp.Identity.Name,
    "VENUS\\Andrew")==0));
```

Note that we have two different ways to specify the role we're interested in: either as a simple string or by using the *WindowsBuiltInRole* enumeration. The output from this code follows:

```
IsInRole "Administrators": True
Identity==VENUS\\Andrew: True
```

PrincipalPermission Requests

The test just shown could also be performed by using the *PrincipalPermission* class, as shown next. If you want to use *PrincipalPermission*, you must additionally set the *CurrentPrincipal* property of the current thread, which is otherwise *null*. This assignment is also valuable in situations where the principal must be validated several times or where it must be validated by other code running in your application:

```
try
{
    Thread.CurrentPrincipal = wp;
    PrincipalPermission pp =
        new PrincipalPermission(
        "VENUS\\Andrew",
        "BUILTIN\\Administrators");
    pp.Demand();
    Console.WriteLine("PrincipalPermission OK");
}
catch (Exception e)
{
    Console.WriteLine(e.Message);
}
```

As with other security permission requests, we could demand *Principal-Permission* declaratively by using an attribute, as shown next. Of course, the call to such a method would need to be within the scope of a suitable *try* block so that if the demand were to fail, we'd have a *catch* block to handle the exception that would be thrown.

```
[PrincipalPermissionAttribute(SecurityAction.Demand,
    Name = "VENUS\\Andrew", Role = "BUILTIN\\Administrators")]
public static void TestDeclarative()
{
    Console.WriteLine("Declarative PrincipalPermission OK");
}
```

Unlike most other permission classes, *PrincipalPermission* isn't derived from *CodeAccessPermission*. This is because it's not a code access permission: instead of being granted based on the identity of the executing assembly, it's granted based on the identity of the user. It does, however, implement the *IPermission* interface and therefore offers the familiar *Demand*, *Union*, *Intersect*, and *IsSubsetOf* methods. If you think about this for a minute, you'll realize that these methods aren't all useful in this class. In particular, *Intersect* is unlikely to be useful because no two identities will have the same name and role. *Union*, on the other hand, does make sense because it can be used to request permissions in situations where more than one identity would be acceptable. For example, the following code requests *PrincipalPermission* on the basis of the user being either Andrew or Polly, with their respective roles:

```
try
{
    PrincipalPermission pp1 = new PrincipalPermission(
        "VENUS\\Andrew", "BUILTIN\\Administrators");
    PrincipalPermission pp2 = new PrincipalPermission(
        "VENUS\\Polly", "BUILTIN\\Backup Operators");
    (pp1.Union(pp2)).Demand();
    Console.WriteLine("Union Demand OK");
}
catch (Exception e)
{
    Console.WriteLine(e.Message);
}
```

Impersonation

The *WindowsIdentity* class also encapsulates the ability to impersonate another user. The following example demonstrates how to impersonate a user and then revert to the original identity. The example uses the *DllImport* attribute to import the *LogonUser* Win32 API function because this is one of the very few functions for which there's no equivalent in the .NET Framework library. For further details on the *DllImport* attribute, see Chapter 6, "Attributes." The bulk of the remaining code is the same as for the previous example of using role-based security. The significant difference is that the application uses the token returned from *LogonUser* to initialize a *WindowsIdentity* object. Just before the call to *Impersonate*, we cache the initial user information in a *WindowsImpersonationContext* object so that we can revert to this initial user after we're done impersonating—which we do with a call to *Undo*.

```
public class UseRBS_ImpersonateApp
{
```

```
[DllImport("advapi32.dll")]
public static extern bool LogonUser(
    string lpszUsername, string lpszDomain,
    string lpszPassword, int dwLogonType,
    int dwLogonProvider, out int phToken);

public static void Main(string[] args)
{
    try
    {
        int token1 = 0;
        bool loggedOn = LogonUser(
                "Bill", "VENUS", "banana", 3, 0, out token1);
        IntPtr token2 = new IntPtr(token1);
        WindowsIdentity wi = new WindowsIdentity(token2);
        WindowsImpersonationContext wic =
                wi.Impersonate();

        Console.WriteLine("Principal/Identity values:");
        Console.WriteLine("Name: " +wi.Name);
        Console.WriteLine("AuthenticationType: "
                +wi.AuthenticationType);
        Console.WriteLine("IsAuthenticated: "
                +wi.IsAuthenticated);
        Console.WriteLine("IsAnonymous: " +wi.IsAnonymous);
        Console.WriteLine("IsGuest: " +wi.IsGuest);
        Console.WriteLine("IsSystem: " +wi.IsSystem);
        Console.WriteLine("Token: " +wi.Token);

        wic.Undo();
    }
    catch (Exception e)
    {
        Console.WriteLine(e.Message);
    }
}
}
```

Isolated Storage

The idea behind isolated storage is that when an application stores data in a file, security measures must be in place to ensure that the file isn't vulnerable to corruption, misappropriation, or loss by any other application or unauthorized user. When using isolated storage, applications save data to a unique place that's associated with some aspect of the identity of the code as well as the executing user. In this way, such storage is isolated on a per-user and per-assembly basis. The "place" where the data is stored isn't actually a file or folder, rather it's an abstraction that's mapped by the system to a physical file system location. In the Framework class library, this "place" is represented by the *IsolatedStorageFile* class. The files to be created and saved within this storage are represented by the *IsolatedStorageFileStream* class.

Another benefit of isolated storage arises from the administrative perspective in that administrators can impose a quota on each isolated storage. You'll recall from our consideration of code access security that one of the differences between the predefined *Internet* and *LocalIntranet* permission sets is that although both can use isolated storage, the *Internet* permission imposes a quota while the *LocalIntranet* permission does not. Clearly, the ability to identify data on the file system and relate it to a particular user or assembly makes an administrator's life easier when it comes to cleaning up the file system.

The following example gets an isolated store for the currently executing assembly and then creates some arbitrary files in this storage:

```csharp
public class IsoApp
{
    public static void Main()
    {
        IsolatedStorageFile iso =
            IsolatedStorageFile.GetStore(
            IsolatedStorageScope.User |
            IsolatedStorageScope.Assembly,
            null, null);

        IsolatedStorageFileStream s1 =
            new IsolatedStorageFileStream(
                "Foo1.Txt", FileMode.Create, iso);
        IsolatedStorageFileStream s2 =
            new IsolatedStorageFileStream(
                "Foo2.Txt", FileMode.Create, iso);
        IsolatedStorageFileStream s3 =
            new IsolatedStorageFileStream(
                "Foo3.Txt", FileMode.Create, iso);

        s1.Close();
        s2.Close();
        s3.Close();
```

The application continues by enumerating through the files in the storage and reporting some information about these files (their total size in the storage):

```csharp
        iso.Close();
        iso = IsolatedStorageFile.GetStore(
            IsolatedStorageScope.User |
```

```
        IsolatedStorageScope.Assembly,
        null, null);

    IEnumerator e = IsolatedStorageFile.GetEnumerator(
        IsolatedStorageScope.User);

    long total = 0;
    while (e.MoveNext())
    {
        IsolatedStorageFile store =
            (IsolatedStorageFile)e.Current;
        total += (long)store.CurrentSize;
    }
    Console.WriteLine("Total size = " + total);
  }
}
```

Before running this application, it would be worth running the Sto-reAdm.exe isolated storage administration tool:

```
StoreAdm /list
```

This command should produce no output because this user doesn't currently have any isolated storage associated with him or her. If you then run the Iso example application, it should produce this output:

```
Total size = 3072
```

Note that this isn't the size of the data files because, of course, we only created them—we didn't write any data to them, so they're zero-length files. Instead, it's the size of the storage allocation, where the minimum block size is 1024 bytes. Having run the example application, if you then run StoreAdm again, you should get output similar to the following:

```
Microsoft (R) .NET Framework Store Admin 1.0.3705.0
Copyright (C) Microsoft Corporation 1998-2001. All rights
 reserved.

Record #1
[Assembly]
<System.Security.Policy.Url version="1">
   <Url>file://C:/InsideCsharp/Chap23/Iso/Iso/bin/Debug/
Iso.exe</Url>
</System.Security.Policy.Url>

        Size : 3072
```

Only one question remains: Where exactly is the isolated storage located in the file system? The answer is, somewhere like this:

```
C:\Documents and Settings\<username>\Local Settings\Application
Data\IsolatedStorage\g2se4o5ssf5sz1hjrpzi5ygc\Url.mnd1kemyzsnxn
3lvaxt5y0t2e51xpych\AssemFiles
```

When you're done experimenting with isolated storage, you can delete it with the following command line:

```
StoreAdm /remove
```

Summary

In this chapter, we considered the various ways that security is threatened on modern computer systems and the considerable strategies deployed by the .NET Framework to combat these threats. Not only is the wide-ranging security provision very comprehensive in its coverage, it's also extremely flexible and robust. We've seen how the ability to enforce verifiable type safety provides assurance that code can access memory only in well-defined and predictable ways, thus eliminating potential exploitation of the loose code that was so often attacked on earlier systems. We've seen how signing code with a strong name provides assurance that the code hasn't been tampered with after being built and that it comes from a trusted source.

In a similar fashion, data can also be signed by using the range of cryptographic services supported in .NET. Code access security protects machine resources by restricting access to those resources based on security policy, which is in turn based on the identity of an executing assembly as well as configurable administrative decisions about permissible access. Role-based security allows code to check the identity and role membership of a user and to make resource access decisions based on this identity. Finally, we looked at a technique for isolating file system storage on a per-assembly and per-user basis. The message should be clear: Microsoft developers have made a considerable effort in designing a very rich set of security mechanisms that can be used to implement custom security policy in a sophisticated and robust manner.

Appendix

MSIL Instruction Table

Throughout this text, I've often employed the ILDASM utility to illustrate the Microsoft intermediate language (MSIL) that the C# compiler generates. I used ILDASM to give you a more complete understanding of the lower-level workings of the C# compiler. Although I briefly explain what each MSIL instruction does in the context of the chapter in which the instruction is used, I thought it would be nice to have a central listing of all the instructions. In the following table, I list each MSIL instruction, its opcode, the parameters that are passed to the instruction, and the resulting stack transition.

Here are a few notes that should help you when reading the table:

■ Because *pushing* means to place something on the stack, I use the phrase *pushing a value* rather than the more verbose *pushing the value onto the stack.*

■ Because *popping* is widely understood to mean taking something off the stack, I use the phrase *popping the value* instead of the more verbose *popping the value off the stack.*

■ When I use the word *indirect*, I'm referring to retrieving a value through its address. Therefore, the phrase *pushes (indirect) value* should be understood to mean *pushes the value pointed at by an address onto the stack.*

■ The term *native int* represents a 32-bit integer on all 32-bit versions of Microsoft Windows.

■ The letter *F* represents the *native floating point.*

■ The state transition column is intended to illustrate a before-and-after picture of the stack. For example, the stack transition: "..., *value1, value2*-> ..., *result*" indicates that before the instruction is executed, the stack must contain two values (*value1,value2*), and that after the instruction is executed, these values will be replaced with one value (*result*). Note that the ellipsis character simply indicates unknown values on the stack that have nothing to do with this instruction.

Table A-1
MSIL Instructions

Instruction (Opcode)	Description	Stack Transition
add (0x58)	Adds two values, pushing result	...,*val1*,*val2*->...,*result*
add.ovf (0xD6)	Adds integer values, pushing result; throws exception on overflow	...,*val1*,*val2*->...,*result*
add.ovf.un (0xD7)	Adds unsigned integer values, pushing result; throws exception on overflow	...,*val1*,*val2*->...,*result*
and (0x5F)	Bitwise AND of two integral values, pushing an integral value	...*val1*,*val2*->...,*result*
arglist (0xFE 0x00)	Pushes argument list handle for current method	...->...,*argListHandle*
beq int32 (0x3B)	Branches to specified offset if two top stack values are equal	...,*value*,*value*->...
beq.s int8 (0x2E)	Branches to specified offset if two top stack values are equal	...,*value*,*value*->...
bge int32 (0x3C)	Branches to specified offset if *value1* is greater than or equal to *value2*	...,*value1*,*value2*->...
bge.s int8 (0x2F)	Branches to specified offset if *value1* is greater than or equal to *value2*	...,*value1*,*value2*->...
bge.un int32 (0x41)	Branches to specified offset if *value1* is greater than or equal to *value2* (unsigned or unordered)	...,*value1*,*value2*->...
bge.un.s int8 (0x34)	Branches to specified offset if *value1* is greater than or equal to *value2* (unsigned or unordered)	...,*value1*,*value2*->...
bgt int32 (0x3D)	Branches to specified offset if *value1* is greater than *value2*	...,*value1*,*value2*->...
bgt.s int8 (0x30)	Branches to specified offset if *value1* is greater than *value2*	...,*value1*,*value2*->...
bgt.un int32 (0x42)	Branches to specified offset if *value1* is greater than *value2* (unsigned or unordered)	...,*value1*,*value2*->...

Table A-1
MSIL Instructions

Instruction (Opcode)	Description	Stack Transition
bgt.un.s int8 (0x35)	Branches to specified offset if *value1* is greater than *value2* (unsigned or unordered)	...,*value1,value2*->...
ble int32 (0x3E)	Branches to specified offset if *value1* is less than or equal to *value2*	...,*value1,value2*->...
ble.s int8 (0x31)	Branches to specified offset if *value1* is less than or equal to *value2*	...,*value1,value2*->...
ble.un int32 (0x43)	Branches to specified offset if *value1* is less than or equal to *value2* (unsigned or unordered)	...,*value1,value2*->...
ble.un.s int8 (0x36)	Branches to specified offset if *value1* is less than or equal to *value2* (unsigned or unordered)	...,*value1,value2*->...
blt.un int32 (0x44)	Branches to specified offset if *value1* is less than *value2* (unsigned or unordered)	...,*value1,value2*->...
blt.un.s int8 (0x37)	Branches to specified offset if *value1* is less than *value2* (unsigned or unordered)	...,*value1,value2*->...
bne.un.s int8 (0x33)	Branches to specified offset if *value1* isn't equal to *value2* (unsigned or unordered)	...,*value1,value2*->...
blt int32 (0x3F)	Branches to specified offset if *value1* is less than *value2*	...,*value1,value2*->...
blt.s int8 (0x32)	Branches to specified offset if *value1* is less than *value2*	...,*value1,value2*->...
bne.un int32 (0x40)	Branches to specified offset if *value1* isn't equal to *value2* (unsigned or unordered)	...,*value1,value2*->...
box type (0x8C)	Converts value type to object reference	...,*valType*->...,*obj*
br int32 (0x38)	Unconditional branch to specified offset	...->...

Table A-1
MSIL Instructions

Instruction (Opcode)	Description	Stack Transition
br.s int8 (0x2B)	Branches to specified offset	...->...
Break (0x01)	Informs the debugger that a break-point has been reached	...->...
brfalse int32 (0x39)	Branches to specified offset if value on stack is *false*	...,*value*->...
brfalse.s int8 (0x2C)	Branches to specified offset if value on stack is *false*	...,*value*->...
brtrue int32 (0x3A)	Branches to specified offset if value on stack is *true*	...,*value*->...
brtrue.s int8 (0x2D)	Branches to specified offset if value on stack is *true*	...,*value*->...
call method (0x28)	Calls a method	...->...
calli signature (0x29)	Calls method indicated by address on stack; stack also contains 1...*n* arguments	...,*arg1,arg2,argN, method*->*retVal*[1]
callvirt method (0x6F)	Calls virtual method of *obj*	...,*obj,arg1... argn*->...,*retVal*[2]
castclass type (0x74)	Casts *obj* to *class*	...,*obj*->...,*obj2*
ceq (0xFE 0x01)	Compares equality of two values on stack; pushes *1* if equal; otherwise, pushes *0*	...,*val1,val2*->...,*result*
cgt (0xFE 0x02)	Compares to see whether *val1* is greater than *val2*; pushes *1* if *true* and *0* if *false*	...,*val1,val2*->...,*result*
cgt.un (0xFE 0x03)	Compares to see whether *val1* is greater than *val2* (unsigned or unordered); pushes *1* if *true* and *0* if *false*	...,*val1,val2*->...,*result*
ckfinite (0xC3)	Checks for a finite real number; exception thrown if not a number (NaN) or (+/-)infinity; otherwise, value is left on stack	...,*value*->...,*value*

Table A-1
MSIL Instructions

Instruction (Opcode)	Description	Stack Transition
clt (0xFE 0x04)	Compares to see whether *val1* is less than *val2*; pushes *1* if *true* and *0* if *false*	...,*val1*,*val2*->...,*result*
clt.un (0xFE 0x05)	Compares to see whether *val1* is less than *val2* (unsigned or unordered); pushes *1* if *true* and *0* if *false*	...,*val1*,*val2*->...,*result*
conv.i (0xD3)	Converts value to *native int*, pushing resulting *native int*	...,*value*->...,*result*
conv.i1 (0x67)	Converts value to *int8*, pushing *int32*	...,*value*->...,*result*
conv.i2 (0x68)	Converts value to *int16*, pushing *int32*	...,*value*->...,*result*
conv.i4 (0x69)	Converts value to *int32*, pushing *int32*	...,*value*->...,*result*
conv.i8 (0x6A)	Converts value to *int64*, pushing *int64*	...,*value*->...,*result*
conv.ovf.i (0xD4)	Converts value to *native int*, pushing resulting *native int*; throws exception on overflow	...,*value*->...,*result*
conv.ovf.i.un (0x8A)	Converts unsigned value to *native int*, pushing resulting *native int*; throws exception on overflow	...,*value*->...,*result*
conv.ovf.i1 (0xB3)	Converts value to *int8*, pushing resulting *int32*; throws exception on overflow	...,*value*->...,*result*
conv.ovf.i1.un (0x82)	Converts value to *uint8*, pushing resulting *int32*; throws exception on overflow	...,*value*->...,*result*
conv.ovf.i2 (0xB5)	Converts value to *int16*, pushing resulting *int32*; throws exception on overflow	...,*value*->...,*result*
conv.ovf.i2.un (0x83)	Converts value to *uint16*, pushing resulting *int32*; throws exception on overflow	...,*value*->...,*result*

Table A-1
MSIL Instructions

Instruction (Opcode)	Description	Stack Transition
conv.ovf.i4 (0xB7)	Converts value to *int32*, pushing resulting *int32*; throws exception on overflow	*...,value->...,result*
conv.ovf.i4.un (0x84)	Converts value to *uint32*, pushing resulting *int32*; throws exception on overflow	*...,value->...,result*
conv.ovf.i8 (0xB9)	Converts value to *int64*, pushing resulting *int64*; throws exception on overflow	*...,value->...,result*
conv.ovf.i8.un (0x85)	Converts value to *uint64*, pushing resulting *int64*; throws exception on overflow	*...,value->...,result*
conv.ovf.u (0xD5)	Converts value to *native unsigned int*, pushing resulting *native unsigned int*; throws exception on overflow	*...,value->...,result*
conv.ovf.u.un (0x8B)	Converts unsigned value to *native unsigned int*, pushing resulting *native int*; throws exception on overflow	*...,value->...,result*
conv.ovf.u2 (0xB6)	Converts value to *uint16*, pushing resulting *int32*; throws exception on overflow	*...,value->...,result*
conv.ovf.u2.un (0x87)	Converts unsigned value to *uint16*, pushing resulting *int32*; throws exception on overflow	*...,value->...,result*
conv.ovf.u4 (0xB8)	Converts value to uint32, pushing resulting int32; throws exception on overflow	*...,value->...,result*
conv.ovf.u4.un (0x88)	Converts unsigned value to *uint32*, pushing resulting *int32*; throws exception on overflow	*...,value->...,result*
conv.ovf.u8 (0xBA)	Converts value to *uint16*, pushing resulting *int64*; throws exception on overflow	*...,value->...,result*

Table A-1
MSIL Instructions

Instruction (Opcode)	Description	Stack Transition
conv.ovf.u8.un (0x89)	Converts unsigned value to *uint64*, pushing resulting *int64*; throws exception on overflow	*...,value->...,result*
conv.ovf.u1 (0xB4)	Converts value to *uint8*, pushing resulting *int32*; throws exception on overflow	*...,value->...,result*
conv.ovf.u1.un (0x86)	Converts unsigned value to *uint8*, pushing resulting *int32*; throws exception on overflow	*...,value->...,result*
conv.r.un (0x76)	Converts unsigned integer to floating point, pushing *F*	*...,value->...,result*
conv.r4 (0x6B)	Converts value to *float32*, pushing *F*	*...,value->...,result*
conv.r8 (0x6C)	Converts value to *float64*, pushing *F*	*...,value->...,result*
conv.u (0xE0)	Converts value to *native unsigned int*, pushing *native int*	*...,value->...,result*
conv.u1 (0xD2)	Converts value to *uint8*, pushing resulting *int32*	*...,value->...,result*
conv.u2 (0xD1)	Converts value to *uint16*, pushing resulting *int32*	*...,value->...,result*
conv.u4 (0x6D)	Converts value to *uint32*, pushing *int32*	*...,value->...,result*
conv.u8 (0x6E)	Converts value to *uint32*, pushing *int32*	*...,value->...,result*
cpblk (0xFE 0x17)	Copies *size* bytes from *srcAddr* to *destAddr* in memory	*...,destAddr,srcAddr, size->...*
cpobj type (0x70)	Copies a value type	*...,destAddr, srcAddr->...*
div (0x5B)	Divides *value1* by *value2*, pushing result	*...,val1,val2->...,result*
div.un (0x5C)	Divides (unsigned) integer values, pushing result	*...,val1,val2->...,result*

Table A-1
MSIL Instructions

Instruction (Opcode)	Description	Stack Transition
dup (0x25)	Duplicates the value at top of stack	...,*value*-> ...,*value,value*
endfilter (0xFE 0x11)	Returns from the *filter* clause of an SEH exception	...,*value*->...
endfinally (0xDC)	Returns from a *finally* clause	...->...
jmp method (0x27)	Transfers control to the specified method	...->...
initblk (0xFE 0x18)	Initializes a block of *size* memory starting at *addr* with *value*	...,*addr,value,size*->...
initobj classToken (0xFE 0x15)	Initializes a value type	...,*valueObjAddr*->...
isinst type (0x75)	Tests whether an object is an instance of a type or interface, pushing resulting cast if successful or *null* on failure[3].	...,*obj*->...,*result*
ldarg uint32 (0xFE 0x09)	Pushes argument at specified index	...->...,*value*
ldarg.0 (0x02)	Pushes the first argument of a method	...->...,*value*
ldarg.1 (0x03)	Pushes the second argument of a method	...->...,*value*
ldarg.2 (0x04)	Pushes the third argument of a method	...->...,*value*
ldarg.3 (0x05)	Pushes the fourth argument of a method	...->...,*value*
ldarg.s uint8 (0x0E)	Pushes specified argument	...->...,*value*
ldarga uint32 (0xFE 0x0A)	Pushes address of argument at specified index	...->...,*address*
ldarga.s uint8 (0x0F)	Pushes address of specified argument	...->...,*value*
ldc.i4.m1 (0x15)	Pushes the literal value, *−1*	...->...,*−1*

Table A-1
MSIL Instructions

Instruction (Opcode)	Description	Stack Transition
ldc.i4 int32 (0x20)	Pushes specified 32-bit value	...-> ...,*value*
ldc.i4.0 (0x16)	Pushes the literal value, *0*	...->...,*0*
ldc.i4.1 (0x17)	Pushes the literal value, *1*	...->...,*1*
ldc.i4.2 (0x18)	Pushes the literal value, *2*	...->...,*2*
ldc.i4.3 (0x19)	Pushes the literal value, *3*	...>...,*3*
ldc.i4.4 (0x1A)	Pushes the literal value, *4*	...->...,*4*
ldc.i4.5 (0x1B)	Pushes the literal value, *5*	...->...,*5*
ldc.i4.6 (0x1C)	Pushes the literal value, *6*	...->...,*6*
ldc.i4.7 (0x1D)	Pushes the literal value, *7*	...->...,*7*
ldc.i4.8 (0x1E)	Pushes the literal value, *8*	...->...,*8*
ldc.i4.s int8 (0x1F)	Pushes specified 8-bit value as 32-bit	...->...,*value*
ldc.i8 int64 (0x21)	Pushes specified 64-bit value	...->...,*value*
ldc.r4 float32 (0x22)	Pushes specified 32-bit floating point	...->...,*value*
ldc.r8 float64 (0x23)	Pushes specified 64-bit floating point	...->...,*value*
ldelem.i (0x97)	Pushes array element (*native int*) as *native int*	...*array,index*->..., *value*
ldelem.i1 (0x90)	Pushes array element (*int8*) as *int32*	...*array,index*->..., *value*
ldelem.i2 (0x92)	Pushes array element (*int16*) as *int32*	...*array,index*->..., *value*
ldelem.i4 (0x94)	Pushes array element (*int32*) as *int32*	...*array,index*->..., *value*
ldelem.i8 (0x96)	Pushes array element (*int64*) as *int64*	...*array,index*->..., *value*
ldelem.r4 (0x98)	Pushes array element (*float32*) as *F*	...*array,index*->..., *value*

Table A-1
MSIL Instructions

Instruction (Opcode)	Description	Stack Transition
ldelem.r8 (0x99)	Pushes array element (*float64*) as *F*	...*array,index*->..., *value*
ldelem.ref (0x9A)	Pushes array element (*object*) as *object*	...*array,index*->..., *value*
ldelem.u1 (0x91)	Pushes array element (*uint8*) as *int32*	...*array,index*-> ...,*value*
ldelem.u2 (0x93)	Pushes array element (*uint16*) as *int32*	...*array,index*-> ...,*value*
ldelem.u4 (0x95)	Pushes array element (*uint32*) as *int32*	...*array,index*-> ...,*value*
ldelema type (0x8F)	Pushes the address of an array element	...,*array,index*-> ...,*addr*
ldfld field (0x7B)	Pushes field of an object	...,*obj*->...,*value*
ldflda field (0x7C)	Pushes field address of an object	...,*obj*->...,*addr*
ldftn method (0xFE 0x06)	Pushes the method pointer referenced by *method*	...->...,*ftn*
ldind.i (0x4D)	Pushes (indirect) value of type *native int* as *native int*	...,*addr*->...,*value*
ldind.i1 (0x46)	Pushes (indirect) value of type *int8* as *int32*	...,*addr*->...,*value*
ldind.i2 (0x48)	Pushes (indirect) value of type *int16* as *int32*	...,*addr*->...,*value*
ldind.i4 (0x4A)	Pushes (indirect) value of type *int32* as *int32*	...,*addr*->...,*value*
ldind.i8 (0x4C)	Pushes (indirect) value of type *int64* as *int64*	...,*addr*->...,*value*
ldind.u1 (0x47)	Pushes (indirect) value of type *uint8* as *int32*	...,*addr*->...,*value*
ldind.u2 (0x49)	Pushes (indirect) value of type *uint16* as *int32*	...,*addr*->...,*value*

Table A-1
MSIL Instructions

Instruction (Opcode)	Description	Stack Transition
ldind.u4 (0x4B)	Pushes (indirect) value of type *uint32* as *int32*	*...,addr->...,value*
ldind.r4 (0x4E)	Pushes (indirect) value of type *float32* as F	*...,addr->...,value*
ldind.r8 (0x4F)	Pushes (indirect) value of type *float64* as *F*	*...,addr->...,value*
ldind.ref (0x50)	Pushes (indirect) *object ref* as *o*	*...,addr->...,value*
ldlen (0x8E)	Pushes the length of an array	*...,array->...,length*
ldloc uint32 (0xFE 0x0C)	Pushes local variable at specified index	*...->...,value*
ldloc.0 (0x06)	Pushes the first local variable	*...->...,value*
ldloc.1 (0x07)	Pushes the second local variable	*...->...,value*
ldloc.2 (0x08)	Pushes the third local variable	*...->...,value*
ldloc.3 (0x09)	Pushes the fourth local variable	*...->...,value*
ldloc.s uint8 (0x11)	Pushes the specified local variable	*...->...,value*
ldloca uint32 (0xFE 0x0D)	Pushes address of local variable at specified index	*...->...,address*
ldloca.s uint8 (0x12)	Pushes address of specified local variable	*...->...,value*
ldnull (0x14)	Pushes *null* reference	*...->...,null*
ldobj type (0x71)	Pushes value	*...,addrValueObj->...,valueObj*
ldsfld field (0x7E)	Pushes static field of an object	*...->...,value*
ldsflda field (0x7F)	Pushes static field address of an object	*...->...,value*
ldstr type (0x72)	Pushes a literal string	*...,->..,string*
ldtoken token (0xD0)	Loads the common language runtime representation of a metadata token	*...->...,runtimeHandle*

Table A-1
MSIL Instructions

Instruction (Opcode)	Description	Stack Transition
ldvirtftn method (0xFE 0x07)	Pushes the method pointer referenced by *method*	*...,obj->...,ftn*
leave int32 (0xDD)	Branches out of a protected block of code (*try, filter, catch*) to target (*int32* offset)	*...->...*
leave.s int8 (0xDE)	Branches out of a protected block of code (*try, filter, catch*) to target (*int8* offset)	*...->...*
localloc (0xFE 0x0F)	Allocates *size* (*native unsigned int*) bytes from the local dynamic memory pool and pushes *address*	*...,size->...,address*
mkrefany type (0xC6)	Pushes a typed reference on the stack	*...,ptr->...,typedRef*
mul (0x5A)	Multiplies two values, pushing result	*...,val1,val2->...,result*
mul.ovf (0xD8)	Multiplies signed integer values, pushing result; throws exception on overflow	*...,val1,val2->...,result*
mul.ovf.un (0xD9)	Multiplies unsigned signed integer values, pushing result; throws exception on overflow	*...,val1,val2->...,result*
neg (0x65)	Negates the value on the stack	*...,value->...,result*
newarr elementType (0x8D)	Creates a one-dimensional array of *elementType*	*...,numberOfElements->...,array*
newobj method (0x73)	Creates a new object (calling its ctor)	*...,arg1...argn->...,obj*
not (0x66)	Computes bitwise complement of value on stack, pushing result	*...,value->...,result*
nop (0x00)	*Null* operation used only to fill in space if bytecodes are patched	*...->...*
or (0x60)	Bitwise OR of two integral values, pushing an integral value	*...val1,val2->...,result*

Table A-1
MSIL Instructions

Instruction (Opcode)	Description	Stack Transition
pop (0x26)	Pops top element of stack	...,*value*->...
refanytype (0xFE 0x1D)	Pushes the type token out of typed reference	...,*typedRef*->...,*type*
refanyval type (0xC2)	Loads the address out of a typed reference	...,*typedRef*->...,*addr*
rem (0x5D)	Computes remainder of dividing *value1* by *value2*	...,*val1,val2*->...,*result*
rem.un (0x5E)	Computes remainder of dividing *value1* by *value2* (both unsigned)	...,*val1,val2*->...,*result*
ret (0x2A)	Returns control from current method to caller	...,*retVal*->[4]...,*retVal*[5]
rethrow (0xFE 0x1A)	Only valid within a *catch* block; this instruction rethrows the current exception back up the call stack	...->...
shl (0x62)	Shift-left operation in which signed integer value and number of decimal places to shift are on stack	...,*value,shiftAmount*->...,*result*
shr (0x63)	Shift-right operation in which signed integer value and number of decimal places to shift are on stack	...,*value,shiftAmount*->...,*result*
shr.un (0x64)	Shift-right operation in which unsigned integer value and number of decimal places to shift are on stack	...,*value,shiftAmount*->...,*result*
sizeof valueType (0xFE 0x1C)	Pushes the size (in bytes) of the specified *valueType*	...->...,*size*
starg uint32 (0xFE 0x0B)	Stores a value to argument at specified index	...,*value*->...
starg.s uint8 (0x10)	Pops value to specified method argument	...,*value* ->...
stelem.i (0x9B)	Overwrites array element at *index* with value on the stack	...,*array,index,value*->...

Table A-1
MSIL Instructions

Instruction (Opcode)	Description	Stack Transition
stelem.i1 (0x9C)	Overwrites array element at *index* with *int8* value on the stack	*...,array,index,value->* ...
stelem.i2 (0x9D)	Overwrites array element at *index* with *int16* value on the stack	*...,array,index,value->* ...
stelem.i4 (0x9E)	Overwrites array element at *index* with *int32* value on the stack	*...,array,index,value->* ...
stelem.i8 (0x9F)	Overwrites array element at *index* with *int64* value on the stack	*...,array,index,value->* ...
stelem.r4 (0xA0)	Overwrites array element at *index* with *float32* value on the stack	*...,array,index,value->* ...
stelem.r8 (0xA1)	Overwrites array element at *index* with *float64* value on the stack	*...,array,index,value->* ...
stelem.ref (0xA2)	Overwrites array element at *index* with *reference* value on the stack	*...array,index,value->* ...
stfld field (0x7D)	Stores into a field of an object	*...,obj,value->...*
stind.ref (0x51)	Stores *object reference* value into *addr*	*...,addr,value->...*
stind.i (0xDF)	Stores *native int* value into *addr*	*...,addr,value->...*
stind.i1 (0x52)	Stores *int8* value at *addr*	*...,addr,value->...*
stind.i2 (0x53)	Stores *int16* value at *addr*	*...,addr,value->...*
stind.i4 (0x54)	Stores *int32* value at *addr*	*...,addr,value->...*
stind.i8 (0x55)	Stores *int64* value at *addr*	*...,addr,value->...*
stind.r4 (0x56)	Stores *float32* value at *addr*	*...,addr,value->...*
stind.r8 (0x57)	Stores *float64* value at *addr*	*...,addr,value->...*
stloc uint32 (0xFE 0x0E)	Pops value to local variable at specified index	*...,value->...*
stloc.0 (0x0A)	Pops value to first local variable	*...,value ->...*
stloc.1 (0x0B)	Pops value to second local variable	*...,value ->...*
stloc.2 (0x0C)	Pops value to third local variable	*...,value ->...*
stloc.3 (0x0D)	Pops value to fourth local variable	*...,value ->...*

Table A-1
MSIL Instructions

Instruction (Opcode)	Description	Stack Transition
stloc.s uint8 (0x13)	Pops value to specified local variable	*..,value ->...*
stobj type (0x81)	Copies *valObj* into *addr*	*...,addr,valObj->...*
stsfld field (0x80)	Stores a static field	*...,value->...*
sub (0x59)	Subtracts *value2* from *value1*, pushing result	*...,val1,val2->...,result*
sub.ovf (0xDA)	Subtracts integer values, pushing result; throws exception on overflow	*...,val1,val2->...,result*
sub.ovf.un (0xDB)	Subtracts unsigned integer values, pushing result; throws exception on overflow	*...,val1,val2->...,result*
switch uint32 (N) + N(int32) (0x45)	Implements a jump table in which first argument (*uint32*) is number of targets (specified as offsets); remaining arguments (*int32*) are the target offsets	*...,value->...*
tail (0xFE 0x14)	This prefix indicates termination of current method via subsequent *call*, *calli*, or *callvirt* instructions	*...->...*
throw (0x7A)	Throws an exception of type *o*	*...,object->...*
unaligned uint8 (0xFE 0x12)	Specifies that *addr* shouldn't be aligned	*...,addr->...,addr*
unbox type (0x79)	Converts boxed value type to raw form	*...,obj->..., valueTypePtr*
volatile (0xFE 0x13)	This prefix specifies that the pointer reference (on the stack) is volatile	*...,addr->...,addr*
xor (0x61)	Bitwise exclusive OR of two integral values, pushing an integral value	*...val1,val2->...,result*

1. retVal is not always pushed onto the stack as a result of the *calli signature* instruction.

2. Not always pushed onto the stack for the *callvirt method* instruction.

3. A null is defined by the CLI as zero (having a bit pattern of all bits zero).

4. Not always pushed onto the stack for the *ret* instruction.

5. Not always pushed onto the stack for the *ret* instruction.

Index

Symbols

Tom Archer

Aside from his hobby of helping fellow developers through Web sites such as TheCodeChannel.com and CodeProject, Tom also does consulting for Visual C++/MFC and .NET/C# projects. His client lists includes IBM, AT&T, Equifax, EMC, and Peachtree Software, and among his proudest professional accomplishments is being the lead programmer on two award-winning applications (at IBM and Peachtree). Tom also enjoys traveling the world evangelizing the virtues of .NET development and is available for both corporate and university training sessions. If you have a product idea on which you'd like Tom's input or are interested in his training sessions, he can be reached through his Web site (*www.TheCodeChannel.com*).

On a personal note, Tom currently has homes in both Atlanta, GA, and Ibiza, Spain, and as an avid pool player (9-ball and one pocket) he's always looking for a challenging game. So, if you're in one of these areas and would like to play seriously or just have fun, be sure and drop him a line. In the meantime, remember Willie Mosconi's response when asked the secret to great pool: "Don't miss!"

Andrew Whitechapel

During his time in the software industry, Andrew Whitechapel has developed in C++, C, COBOL, Modula, Ada, SQL, dBase, Clipper, and Fortran, as well as sed, awk, UNIX shell scripting, and 8086 assembler. Having spent several years on UNIX platforms, he migrated to Windows when it first appeared and hasn't looked back since. His experience covers the banking and finance sector, transport and distribution, petro-chem, telecoms, defense, and other public sector areas. He also has many years experience as a trainer, delivering bespoke courses and standard MOC.

Like so many developers, Andrew worked through the years of the COM/DNA era in a kind of love-hate relationship with COM and ATL. He firmly believes that .NET, C#, and XML/SOAP will bring a sorely needed breath of fresh air to the industry and will revolutionize the way we build enterprise systems. This is the start of a new era, and a brave new world!

In his spare time, Andrew plays rugby (as a very slow winger) for Battersea Ironsides rugby club in London—the best club in the world.

Circular Saw Blade

Portable, hand-held circular saws, probably the most widely used power saw, have an electric motor that rotates a circular blade at high speed. By using a circular saw blade with the appropriate hardness and tooth design, portable circular saws can cut almost any material. The breakthrough C# development language can also handle any cutting-edge task.

At Microsoft Press, we use tools to illustrate our books for software developers and IT professionals. Tools are an elegant symbol of human inventiveness and a powerful metaphor for how people can extend their capabilities, precision, and reach. From basic calipers and pliers to digital micrometers and lasers, our stylized illustrations of tools give each book a visual identity and each book series a personality. With tools and knowledge, there are no limits to creativity and innovation. Our tag line says it all: *The tools you need to put technology to work.*

The manuscript for this book was prepared and galleyed using Microsoft Word. Pages were composed by Microsoft Press using Adobe FrameMaker+SGML for Windows, with text in Garamond and display type in Helvetica Condensed. Composed pages were delivered to the printer as electronic prepress files.

Cover Designer: Methodologie, Inc.
Interior Graphic Designer: James D. Kramer
Principal Compositor: Dan Latimer
Interior Artist: Michael Kloepfer
Copy Editor: Michelle Goodman
Indexer: Julie Kawabata

Get a **Free**
e-mail newsletter, updates,
special offers, links to related books,
and more when you

register on line!

Register your Microsoft Press® title on our Web site and you'll get a FREE subscription to our e-mail newsletter, *Microsoft Press Book Connections.* You'll find out about newly released and upcoming books and learning tools, online events, software downloads, special offers and coupons for Microsoft Press customers, and information about major Microsoft® product releases. You can also read useful additional information about all the titles we publish, such as detailed book descriptions, tables of contents and indexes, sample chapters, links to related books and book series, author biographies, and reviews by other customers.

Registration is easy. Just visit this Web page and fill in your information:

http://www.microsoft.com/mspress/register

Microsoft®

Proof of Purchase

Use this page as proof of purchase if participating in a promotion or rebate offer on this title. Proof of purchase must be used in conjunction with other proof(s) of payment such as your dated sales receipt—see offer details.

Inside C#, Second Edition
0-7356-1648-5

CUSTOMER NAME

Microsoft Press, PO Box 97017, Redmond, WA 98073-9830

MICROSOFT LICENSE AGREEMENT

Book Companion CD

IMPORTANT—READ CAREFULLY: This Microsoft End-User License Agreement ("EULA") is a legal agreement between you (either an individual or an entity) and Microsoft Corporation for the Microsoft product identified above, which includes computer software and may include associated media, printed materials, and "online" or electronic documentation ("SOFTWARE PRODUCT"). Any component included within the SOFTWARE PRODUCT that is accompanied by a separate End-User License Agreement shall be governed by such agreement and not the terms set forth below. By installing, copying, or otherwise using the SOFTWARE PRODUCT, you agree to be bound by the terms of this EULA. If you do not agree to the terms of this EULA, you are not authorized to install, copy, or otherwise use the SOFTWARE PRODUCT; you may, however, return the SOFTWARE PRODUCT, along with all printed materials and other items that form a part of the Microsoft product that includes the SOFTWARE PRODUCT, to the place you obtained them for a full refund.

SOFTWARE PRODUCT LICENSE

The SOFTWARE PRODUCT is protected by United States copyright laws and international copyright treaties, as well as other intellectual property laws and treaties. The SOFTWARE PRODUCT is licensed, not sold.

1. **GRANT OF LICENSE.** This EULA grants you the following rights:

   a. **Software Product.** You may install and use one copy of the SOFTWARE PRODUCT on a single computer. The primary user of the computer on which the SOFTWARE PRODUCT is installed may make a second copy for his or her exclusive use on a portable computer.

   b. **Storage/Network Use.** You may also store or install a copy of the SOFTWARE PRODUCT on a storage device, such as a network server, used only to install or run the SOFTWARE PRODUCT on your other computers over an internal network; however, you must acquire and dedicate a license for each separate computer on which the SOFTWARE PRODUCT is installed or run from the storage device. A license for the SOFTWARE PRODUCT may not be shared or used concurrently on different computers.

   c. **License Pak.** If you have acquired this EULA in a Microsoft License Pak, you may make the number of additional copies of the computer software portion of the SOFTWARE PRODUCT authorized on the printed copy of this EULA, and you may use each copy in the manner specified above. You are also entitled to make a corresponding number of secondary copies for portable computer use as specified above.

   d. **Sample Code.** Solely with respect to portions, if any, of the SOFTWARE PRODUCT that are identified within the SOFTWARE PRODUCT as sample code (the "SAMPLE CODE"):

      i. **Use and Modification.** Microsoft grants you the right to use and modify the source code version of the SAMPLE CODE, *provided* you comply with subsection (d)(iii) below. You may not distribute the SAMPLE CODE, or any modified version of the SAMPLE CODE, in source code form.

      ii. **Redistributable Files.** Provided you comply with subsection (d)(iii) below, Microsoft grants you a nonexclusive, royalty-free right to reproduce and distribute the object code version of the SAMPLE CODE and of any modified SAMPLE CODE, other than SAMPLE CODE, or any modified version thereof, designated as not redistributable in the Readme file that forms a part of the SOFTWARE PRODUCT (the "Non-Redistributable Sample Code"). All SAMPLE CODE other than the Non-Redistributable Sample Code is collectively referred to as the "REDISTRIBUTABLES."

      iii. **Redistribution Requirements.** If you redistribute the REDISTRIBUTABLES, you agree to: (i) distribute the REDISTRIBUTABLES in object code form only in conjunction with and as a part of your software application product; (ii) not use Microsoft's name, logo, or trademarks to market your software application product; (iii) include a valid copyright notice on your software application product; (iv) indemnify, hold harmless, and defend Microsoft from and against any claims or lawsuits, including attorney's fees, that arise or result from the use or distribution of your software application product; and (v) not permit further distribution of the REDISTRIBUTABLES by your end user. Contact Microsoft for the applicable royalties due and other licensing terms for all other uses and/or distribution of the REDISTRIBUTABLES.

2. **DESCRIPTION OF OTHER RIGHTS AND LIMITATIONS.**

   - **Limitations on Reverse Engineering, Decompilation, and Disassembly.** You may not reverse engineer, decompile, or disassemble the SOFTWARE PRODUCT, except and only to the extent that such activity is expressly permitted by applicable law notwithstanding this limitation.

   - **Separation of Components.** The SOFTWARE PRODUCT is licensed as a single product. Its component parts may not be separated for use on more than one computer.

   - **Rental.** You may not rent, lease, or lend the SOFTWARE PRODUCT.

- **Support Services.** Microsoft may, but is not obligated to, provide you with support services related to the SOFTWARE PRODUCT ("Support Services"). Use of Support Services is governed by the Microsoft policies and programs described in the user manual, in "online" documentation, and/or in other Microsoft-provided materials. Any supplemental software code provided to you as part of the Support Services shall be considered part of the SOFTWARE PRODUCT and subject to the terms and conditions of this EULA. With respect to technical information you provide to Microsoft as part of the Support Services, Microsoft may use such information for its business purposes, including for product support and development. Microsoft will not utilize such technical information in a form that personally identifies you.

- **Software Transfer.** You may permanently transfer all of your rights under this EULA, provided you retain no copies, you transfer all of the SOFTWARE PRODUCT (including all component parts, the media and printed materials, any upgrades, this EULA, and, if applicable, the Certificate of Authenticity), **and** the recipient agrees to the terms of this EULA.

- **Termination.** Without prejudice to any other rights, Microsoft may terminate this EULA if you fail to comply with the terms and conditions of this EULA. In such event, you must destroy all copies of the SOFTWARE PRODUCT and all of its component parts.

3. **COPYRIGHT.** All title and copyrights in and to the SOFTWARE PRODUCT (including but not limited to any images, photographs, animations, video, audio, music, text, SAMPLE CODE, REDISTRIBUTABLES, and "applets" incorporated into the SOFTWARE PRODUCT) and any copies of the SOFTWARE PRODUCT are owned by Microsoft or its suppliers. The SOFT-WARE PRODUCT is protected by copyright laws and international treaty provisions. Therefore, you must treat the SOFTWARE PRODUCT like any other copyrighted material **except** that you may install the SOFTWARE PRODUCT on a single computer provided you keep the original solely for backup or archival purposes. You may not copy the printed materials accompanying the SOFTWARE PRODUCT.

4. **U.S. GOVERNMENT RESTRICTED RIGHTS.** The SOFTWARE PRODUCT and documentation are provided with RESTRICTED RIGHTS. Use, duplication, or disclosure by the Government is subject to restrictions as set forth in subparagraph (c)(1)(ii) of the Rights in Technical Data and Computer Software clause at DFARS 252.227-7013 or subparagraphs (c)(1) and (2) of the Commercial Computer Software—Restricted Rights at 48 CFR 52.227-19, as applicable. Manufacturer is Microsoft Corporation/One Microsoft Way/Redmond, WA 98052-6399.

5. **EXPORT RESTRICTIONS.** You agree that you will not export or re-export the SOFTWARE PRODUCT, any part thereof, or any process or service that is the direct product of the SOFTWARE PRODUCT (the foregoing collectively referred to as the "Restricted Components"), to any country, person, entity, or end user subject to U.S. export restrictions. You specifically agree not to export or re-export any of the Restricted Components (i) to any country to which the U.S. has embargoed or restricted the export of goods or services, which currently include, but are not necessarily limited to, Cuba, Iran, Iraq, Libya, North Korea, Sudan, and Syria, or to any national of any such country, wherever located, who intends to transmit or transport the Restricted Components back to such country; (ii) to any end user who you know or have reason to know will utilize the Restricted Components in the design, development, or production of nuclear, chemical, or biological weapons; or (iii) to any end user who has been prohibited from participating in U.S. export transactions by any federal agency of the U.S. government. You warrant and represent that neither the BXA nor any other U.S. federal agency has suspended, revoked, or denied your export privileges.

DISCLAIMER OF WARRANTY

NO WARRANTIES OR CONDITIONS. MICROSOFT EXPRESSLY DISCLAIMS ANY WARRANTY OR CONDITION FOR THE SOFTWARE PRODUCT. THE SOFTWARE PRODUCT AND ANY RELATED DOCUMENTATION ARE PROVIDED "AS IS" WITHOUT WARRANTY OR CONDITION OF ANY KIND, EITHER EXPRESS OR IMPLIED, INCLUDING, WITHOUT LIMITA-TION, THE IMPLIED WARRANTIES OF MERCHANTABILITY, FITNESS FOR A PARTICULAR PURPOSE, OR NONINFRINGEMENT. THE ENTIRE RISK ARISING OUT OF USE OR PERFORMANCE OF THE SOFTWARE PRODUCT REMAINS WITH YOU.

LIMITATION OF LIABILITY. TO THE MAXIMUM EXTENT PERMITTED BY APPLICABLE LAW, IN NO EVENT SHALL MICROSOFT OR ITS SUPPLIERS BE LIABLE FOR ANY SPECIAL, INCIDENTAL, INDIRECT, OR CONSEQUENTIAL DAM-AGES WHATSOEVER (INCLUDING, WITHOUT LIMITATION, DAMAGES FOR LOSS OF BUSINESS PROFITS, BUSINESS INTERRUPTION, LOSS OF BUSINESS INFORMATION, OR ANY OTHER PECUNIARY LOSS) ARISING OUT OF THE USE OF OR INABILITY TO USE THE SOFTWARE PRODUCT OR THE PROVISION OF OR FAILURE TO PROVIDE SUPPORT SERVICES, EVEN IF MICROSOFT HAS BEEN ADVISED OF THE POSSIBILITY OF SUCH DAMAGES. IN ANY CASE, MICROSOFT'S ENTIRE LIABILITY UNDER ANY PROVISION OF THIS EULA SHALL BE LIMITED TO THE GREATER OF THE AMOUNT ACTUALLY PAID BY YOU FOR THE SOFTWARE PRODUCT OR US$5.00; PROVIDED, HOWEVER, IF YOU HAVE ENTERED INTO A MICROSOFT SUPPORT SERVICES AGREEMENT, MICROSOFT'S ENTIRE LIABILITY REGARDING SUPPORT SERVICES SHALL BE GOVERNED BY THE TERMS OF THAT AGREEMENT. BECAUSE SOME STATES AND JURISDICTIONS DO NOT ALLOW THE EXCLUSION OR LIMITATION OF LIABILITY, THE ABOVE LIMITATION MAY NOT APPLY TO YOU.

MISCELLANEOUS

This EULA is governed by the laws of the State of Washington USA, except and only to the extent that applicable law mandates governing law of a different jurisdiction.

Should you have any questions concerning this EULA, or if you desire to contact Microsoft for any reason, please contact the Microsoft subsidiary serving your country, or write: Microsoft Sales Information Center/One Microsoft Way/Redmond, WA 98052-6399.